MODERN LOGIC - A SURVEY

Historical, Philosophical, and Mathematical Aspects of Modern Logic and its Applications

Edited by

EVANDRO AGAZZI
Dept. of Philosophy, University of Genoa, Italy

D. REIDEL PUBLISHING COMPANY
DORDRECHT : HOLLAND / BOSTON : U.S.A.
LONDON : ENGLAND

Library of Congress Cataloging in Publication Data

Main entry under title:

Modern logic – a survey.

(Synthese library ; v. 149)
Includes bibliographies and index.
1. Logic, Modern–Addresses, essays, lectures. I. Agazzi, Evandro.
BC38.M54 160 80–22027
ISBN 90–277–1137–2

Published by D. Reidel Publishing Company,
P.O. Box 17, 3300 AA Dordrecht, Holland

Sold and distributed in the U.S.A. and Canada
by Kluwer Boston Inc.,
190 Old Derby Street, Hingham, MA 02043, U.S.A.

In all other countries, sold and distributed
by Kluwer Academic Publishers Group,
P.O. Box 322, 3300 AH Dordrecht, Holland

D. Reidel Publishing Company is a member of the Kluwer Group.

Italian Edition by
Istituto Della Enciclopedia Italiana

Printed in The Netherlands

MODERN LOGIC – A SURVEY

SYNTHESE LIBRARY

STUDIES IN EPISTEMOLOGY,

LOGIC, METHODOLOGY, AND PHILOSOPHY OF SCIENCE

VOLUME 149

TABLE OF CONTENTS

PREFACE

Logic has attained in our century a development incomparably greater than in any past age of its long history, and this has led to such an enrichment and proliferation of its aspects, that the problem of some kind of unified recomprehension of this discipline seems nowadays unavoidable. This splitting into several subdomains is the natural consequence of the fact that Logic has intended to adopt in our century the status of a science. This always implies that the general optics, under which a certain set of problems used to be considered, breaks into a lot of specialized sectors of inquiry, each of them being characterized by the introduction of specific viewpoints and of technical tools of its own. The first impression, that often accompanies the creation of one of such specialized branches in a discipline, is that one has succeeded in isolating the 'scientific core' of it, by restricting the somehow vague and redundant generality of its original 'philosophical' configuration. But, after a while, it appears that some of the discarded aspects are indeed important and a new specialized domain of investigation is created to explore them. By following this procedure, one finally finds himself confronted with such a variety of independent fields of research, that one wonders whether the fact of labelling them under a common denomination be nothing but the contingent effect of a pure historical tradition. At this stage a need of conceptual clarification is perceived, that is the need of understanding why we still accept to call the whole of these different fields, e.g., 'Logic', or 'Physics', or 'Biology', etc. and this question can be answered only through a work of philosophical understanding and historical reconstruction.

All this is true for every science and for Logic as well, which has accomplished not only its transition from the condition of being a branch of philosophy to the fully-fledged shape of an articulate science, but has also given rise (like several 'pure' sciences) to a great lot of applications. This is why an adequate understanding of what modern logic is requires an interdisciplinary approach, and at the same time an effort of philosophical appreciation, not in order to interpret it again as a part of Philosophy but in the sense of making it the object of a philosophical analysis and interpretation.

This was the aim of an international conference on *Modern Logic* organized in Rome by the Institute of the Italian Encyclopedia and by the Italian

E. Agazzi (ed.), Modern Logic – A Survey, vii–viii.

Society of Logic and Philosophy of Science in September 1976. The present volume contains the papers presented at that meeting, each of them being a general survey of one of the most relevant fields in which Logic is subdivided, or of one of the most important sets of problems which are connected with Logic in our days. A simple glance at the table of contents shows the width of the horizon that has been explored (thorough completeness could not be reached and was not an ambition of the organizers). The purpose of the conference was to provide a general appreciation of modern logic which could be accessible to cultivated people, without need of any specific technical competence. In other words, the cultural position and role of Logic was hoped to become apparent, rather than the exact patterns of its technical machinery. This, in particular, explains the subdivision of the topics according to a line which takes into account the different kinds of intellectual 'interest' under which Logic may be approached today, and which go from its historical development, to its impact on mathematics, to its internal subdivision, to its different applications, to its philosophical commitments.

Of course every contributor has conceived this task according to his own estimation and this has led to different levels of clarity, of technical complexity, of specialization or generality.

It is left therefore to the reader to chose the papers with which to start in reading this book, according to his personal taste and background, but one can be confident that a singificant image of modern logic as a whole may be obtained from this volume, which might hardly be shaped even by the careful study of several good textbooks.

EVANDRO AGAZZI

PART 1

INTRODUCTION

J. M. BOCHENSKI

THE GENERAL SENSE AND CHARACTER OF MODERN LOGIC

By 'Modern Logic' (abridged as 'ML') the class of studies is meant which were originated by Leibniz, developed, among others, by Boole, Peirce, Frege, Peano, Leśniewski and their followers; in other terms the class of studies listed in Alonzo Church's Bibliography and in *The Journal of Symbolic Logic*.

The expression 'ML' is sometimes used, it is true, in other ways, e.g. to denote studies in Hegelian dialectics. Those uses are irrelevant for the sake of the present paper which will be exclusively concerned with ML as described above. It may be only said, that no other known sort of contemporary logic can compare with the latter as far as standards of procedures and quality of results are concerned.

The aim of the paper is to describe – as the title selected by the organizers of the conference indicates – the general sense and character of ML thus understood. In other terms an attempt will be made to find the fundamental characteristics of ML-al studies.

The method used will be comparative. We are going to ask: How does ML compare with three fields with which it is usually linked: logic, mathematics and philosophy? Is ML Logic and, if so, how does it differ from other types of logic? Is it a mathematical discipline and, if that is the case, what is the difference between it and other mathematical sciences? Is it philosophy and, this being admitted, what is its place among the other philosophical disciplines?

The present paper will be mostly concerned with the first class of problems, the comparison between ML and the other types of logic; the other two classes of problems will be treated only marginally. As far as the main problems are concerned, the method will necessarily be historical: for, contrary to mathematics and philosophy, all other forms of logic with which ML may be compared belong to the past.

I

It will be convenient to begin with a summary classification of the main parts and systems of ML. They can be classified under two headings: either

E. Agazzi (ed.), Modern Logic – A Survey, 3–14.

from the point of view of the problems dealt with, or from that of the method, respectively of the primitives employed. Applying that distinction to Rescher's 'Map of Logic' we obtain the following scheme (which is not supposed to be exhaustive).

A. *Classification from the point of view of the problems*

1. *General Logic*
   - 1.1 *Pure Logic*
     - 1.11 Logic of propositions
     - 1.12 Logic of terms
       - 1.121 Logic of predicates
       - 1.122 Logic of classes
       - 1.123 Logic of identity
       - 1. 24 Logic of relations
   - 1.2 *General applied logic*
     - 1.21 Logical semiotics
       - 1.211 Logical syntax
       - 1.212 Logical semantics
       - 1.213 Logical pragmatics
     - 1.22 General methodology
       - 1.221 Methodology of deductive sciences
       - 1.222 Methodology of empirical sciences
2. *Special developments of logic*
   - 2.1 *Mathematical developments*
   - 2.2 *Developments for empirical sciences*
     - 2.21 Physical
     - 2.22 Biological
     - 2.23 Sociological, etc.
   - 2.3 *Developments for philosophical sciences*
     - 2.31 Epistemological
     - 2.32 Ontological
     - 2.33 Ethical
     - 2.34 Rhetorical, etc.

B. *Classification from the point of view of the method and of the primitives used*

1. *Classical Logic*
2. *Non-classical Logic*
   - 2.1 *Non-classical methods* 'natural' logic, etc.

2.2 *Non-classical primitives*
- 2.21 Minimal logic
- 2.22 Leśniewski's logic
- 2.23 Temporal logic
- 2.24 Modal logic
- 2.25 Many-valued logic
- 2.26 Intuitionistic logic
- 2.27 Combinatory logic

The following remarks may clarify the foregoing classification: By 'general logic' is meant a set of theories which have either a quite general application, or, as in the case of the methodology of deduction, an application in a very large group of sciences. On the contrary 'developments of logic' refers to doctrines which have only a limited application, like, e.g. deontic logic.

'Classical logic' means logical systems which are, basically, similar to that of the *Principia Mathematica*. All other systems are classified here under 'non-classical' logic.

The title 'philosophical logic' does not appear in tha above tabulation, for it is ambiguous: it may refer either to philosophy of logic, (which is not logic at all), or to the developments of logic for applications in philosophy (A2, 3).

II

Is ML logic? This has sometimes been denied both by philosophers and mathematicians. The problem at hand is not so much one concerning the meaning of 'ML' as rather that of 'logic', for the latter is a notoriously ambiguous term.

Before proceeding to an analysis of 'logic' a few misunderstandings must be discarded.

(1) The problem has nothing to do with the question whether mathematics can or cannot be reduced to logic. For, whatever the answer given to that question, it will concern not ML alone but every kind of formal logic. Our problem of the relations of ML to logic will, consequently, not be affected by such answers.

(2) Logic proper has to be sharply distinguished from the philosophy of logic. While the former is the study of certain objects, in order to establish theorems about them, to study their mutual connections and so forth, the latter is a set of reflections about logic so constituted: e.g. questions about

the subject-matter of logic, about its unity and relativity, about universals, etc. It is a known historical fact, that philosophers who held widely different philosophies of logic used and sometimes developed the same sort of logic, e.g. Buridan and Burleigh, Leśniewski and Łukasiewicz.

(3) ML should not be confused with *one system* of ML. As a matter of fact it has often been identified with the system of the *Principia Mathematica*. The truth is, that ML, like every other type of logic, contains many different systems.

Having said this, we may turn to our main task, namely to the analysis of 'logic'. In both past and contemporary literature the term has been used in many different ways. There are e.g. transcendental and dialectical logics, even 'logics of the heart'. It seems utterly impossible to find anything common in the referents of 'logic' in its different uses.

However, all these logics have always been opposed to formal logic, and there is a sufficiently general agreement as to the existence of a set of investigations called 'formal logic'. There is also little doubt that Aristotle, the old Stoics, the Schoolmen and the Hindou Nyāyayikas were formal logicians. And, as formal logic has always been the foundations for logical semiotics and general methodology of thought, there exists also a rather clearly demarcated larger class of investigations which may be easily distinguished from the aforementioned sorts of non-formal logic.

This class will here be called 'logic'. The problem at hand is to know whether ML is logic on *this* meaning of the term. It will be logic, if and only if it deals with the problems, uses the conceptual tools and establishes theorems found in the works of the above named logicians.

The answer to this question is affirmative: ML deals with all basic problems of logic, as defined; it uses all its basic conceptual tools and contains among its theorems practically all theorems established in it. Consequently, it obviously is logic.

For, first, ML is concerned with practically all the problems with which the older logicians dealt. Of course, many new problems did arise, but the basic ones are still those stated by Aristotle: What are the formal laws, valid independently of any 'matter'? What are the conditions of coherence? How can it be shown that a system is coherent? From what principles may the given set of theorems be deduced? What are the rules to be used? How can we deal with logical paradoxes?

Moreover, most *classes* of problems dealt with in general ML were investigated by the only old logic we know adequately, namely in Scholastic logic. Thus among the eight classes listed in our survey above of general

ML only one (the logic of relations) was certainly unknown, while another, pragmatics, was probably unknown during the Middle Ages. The main problems of all the other classes were not only known, but in most cases they were even highly elaborated. Moreover, at least two sets of problems listed under our second classification (B), namely those with which modal and temporal logic are concerned, were known and studied, sometimes in a high sophisticated way.

Second, the basic conceptual *tools* used in ML are those invented, so it seems, by Aristotle and extensively employed by him. Again, many new tools have been produced in the course of history, and especially in ML. But ML still uses the Aristotelian variables, his quantifiers, his concept of deduction, his idea of the axiomatic system and many others.

Third, as far as the *theorems* are concerned, ML contains, it is true, many more of them than any other type of logic. But it also contains everything valid which has ever been established by the older formal logicians. It has *all* the Stoic rules of inference, the whole of assertoric and modal syllogistics, the same solutions to the paradoxes which the Scholastics once proposed, following, it seems, certain Stoics, and so forth.

This is why every modern logician who turns to the old thinkers immediately sees, that they were his prodecessors, men who did work in his own field. That is what happened, e.g. to Peirce and Łukasiewicz when they came upon Stoic and Scholastic logic.

III

However, ML is not only logic, it is a *particular type* of logic: along with the characteristics present in every logic it also has properties by which it is clearly distinguished from all other types of logic. These properties are methodological, partly material, i.e. they are concerned with the content of the systems.

We shall deal first with the methodological aspect. It may be said that the different types of logic are mutually distinguished by the method used. Thus the difference between (later) Scholastic and Aristotelian formal logic consists mainly in the fact that the former uses metalanguage nealy exclusively, while Aristotelian logic is mostly object-linguistic. But the differences between ML and all other known forms of logic go deeper than that.

One simple way of stating the methodological properties of ML is to say that it is mathematical: ML took over from mathematics several methodological principles. Of these three seem to be the most relevant: the use of an artificial language, formalism and objectivism.

(1) ML is first of all *symbolic logic*. By this rather unfortunate expression (every word in any language is a symbol, and, as every logic has to use a language, it is always 'symbolic') is meant the use of an *artificial* language. This again refers to two different, if usually closely connected characteristics: ML employs artificial *expressions* and builds up its own languages with syntactical *rules* laid down by the logician for this purpose. That these two characteristics are distinct can be seen by considering a language which would have artificial expressions instead of words in English, and yet use the same syntactical rules as English. Such a language is certainly conceivable. But, as a matter of fact, symbolic languages practically always possessed both characteristics, and that is also the case with ML. Nevertheless, it will be useful to consider them separately.

As far as the use of artificial *expressions* is concerned, it is not new in logic. The first to employ such expressions here as in so many other fields was Aristotle. He introduced the variables, tokens which do not exist in Greek nor in any other known natural language. He has been followed in this by Scholastic and Conventional logicians, whereas it seems that the Hindous never attained his level in this respect.

But ML is by far more radical than Aristotle: not only variables are artificial but practically all logical constants are such. Thus ML is the first known type of logic which employs a nearly competely artificial vocabulary.

Although this may seem to be a rather superficial and irrelevant property, it is not at all in reality. There were several reasons for adopting an artificial vocabulary: the necessity to shorten the formulas, the needs of formalization and so on. None of them is a necessary condition for the work of the modern logician. The most that can be said is, that the use of the artificial symbols considerably facilitates his work. However, besides these classicial reasons there is one which does not seem to have been sufficiently stressed, but which appears to be of capital importance, viz. the need to operate with concepts so simple, that there are no convenient words for them in natural languages. One simple instance is provided by the concepts of disjunction, in the wide meaning of the term, all expressed in natural languages by the word 'or' and its equivalents. In a bivalent system of propositional logic there are three such different terms, defined respectively by the truth-tables 1110, 0111 and 0110. Hence, if logic had to operate with such very simple concepts – as indeed it must – it was imperative to employ artificial symbols.

There is a close analogy here between ML and the Galilean physics. Galileo's epochal relevance does not consist in the fact that he established a new physical theory, for many such theories are formulated from period to period. It consists rather in the establishment of a new *type* of theory. It is expressed namely in mathematical, artificial terms, and can deal therefore with very simple concepts.

Along with the artificial vocabulary ML has artificial *syntactical rules*. This again is perhaps not quite new. It may be argued, that many logicians of the past twisted the natural language they were using in such a way that to a certain degree it became artificial, i.e. that its rules were artificial. But, again, ML is the first known type of logic where the principle of constituting complete artificial languages with their own artificial rules was clearly laid down and thoroughly applied.

The result is, that ML, contrary to all older types of logic, not only deals with very simple concepts, but also with very simple syntactical rules. If one considers the ingenuity – genious, it might be said – exercised, e.g. in Scholastic and Hindou logic in order to master the very complex rules of natural languages, it must be said once again, that the introduction of artificial languages with their simple rules was an epoch-making advance. It is probably one of the main reasons for the great success of ML.

(2) ML is not only symbolic, it is also *formalistic*. It seems that there is a certain amount of confusion in this respect, at least in the way we are speaking. Sometimes the mere translation of a statement in an artificial language is called 'formalization' – which is obviously is not. At other times formal and formalistic are not distinguished, while they are two very different things: a system of logic may be formal, like that of Aristotle, without being formalized; and a system may be formalized without being a formal system, i.e. a system of formal logic, as, e.g. with some parts of physics.

By formalism' we understand a system built up by the use of the formalistic method. And the formalistic method is one the rules of which refer exclusively to the graphic shape of tokens, and not to be the meaning of the terms used. Thus 'formalism' and 'calculus' are synonymous.

As in the case of the symbolic character, the formalism of ML is perhaps not entirely new in logic. At least some Scholastic logicians, like Albert of Saxony, seem to have arrived at a clear understanding of its nature. But, as in the case of the artificial language, ML is the first type of logic in which formalism is applied thoroughly and universally even since Boole, following Leibniz, formulated its principle. Boole also expressed the hope, that the use of this method, up until then limited to mathematics in the narrow meaning of the term, would allow considerable progress in logic. One hundred and thirty years after he wrote this down we may say that he was right: the use of formalism along with that of an artificial language did fulfill his hope.

(3) Finally, a third methodological characteristic of ML may be mentioned: ML is *objective*. We mean by that that ML disregards completely the subjective factors, such as thinking, judging, subjective concept-building and so on, with which most other types of logic are replete. It has in this respect one great model from the past: the first book of the *Prior Analytics* where there is not a single mention of such subjective factors. However, it is not from Aristotle that ML took its objective attitude. It took it simply from mathematics which it wished to imitate in its early, Boolean period.

This must be well understood. A modern logician is no more dispensed from thinking and judging than is an astronomer or a botanist. But ML has as little to do with the private acts of the logician as astronomy has to do with the mental processes of the astronomer and botany with the feelings of the botanist.

On the other hand, it is also true, that ML can and must be applied to thinking. But so must the rules of astronomy be applied to the thinking of an astronomer and those of botany to the mental acts of the botanist. The only difference is, that since logic formulates the most general laws and rules, its results have to be applied everywhere and not just to restricted fields.

These then seem to be the most important methodological characteristics of ML: it is symbolic, formalistic and objective. By the application of these methods ML was able to make out of logic a science in the strongest meaning of the term.

IV

As far as the content of ML is concerned, an outline of its main chapters has been given above. In order to characterize it fully, it would be necessary to mention at least its main results. This, however, cannot be done here. We shall limit ourselves therefore to a summary comparison of the results of ML with those of the older types of logic.

The relation of ML to its predecessors is similar to that which exists between contemporary mathematics and its older stages: the basic problems are the same, practically all the acquired results have been taken over, and yet ML contains far more than any other logic in nearly all respects. There are more problems dealt with and more theorems established. The method is more rigorous, the degree of refinement attained in analysis is higher. In this respect there is only one point on which doubts are permitted: it is not impossible that both Scholastic and later (Navya) Hindou logic did contain more and better things in semantics than ML has to offer now.

Two other points may be mentioned marginally. First, ML contains not only more chapters than the older logic, it also contains more systems in each of them. Moreover, while in every period of logic there were several systems, each of them was seen by its adherents as the only valid system. In ML it is an established insight that there can be and in fact are many different equally valid systems in each field.

Second, there is another novelty. ML is the first known type of logic which has actually been applied. It is true that logicians always claimed that their discipline is supremely important in its applications. But for one exception (the application of the Aristotelian theory of deduction by Euclid) there is no known case of a successful application of older logics to any field. On the contrary, ML has been successfully applied to many fields, among which the group of sciences called 'cybernetics' is the most outstanding but by no means the only instance.

V

If we turn now to the relations of ML to mathematics and philosophy, the first problem which arises is whether ML is an autonomous science. We shall say that a discipline is autonomous when it has its own set of techniques, which are developed to such an extent that a high degree of training is necessary to master them. Alternatively, it may be said that a discipline is autonomous when it is cultivated exclusively or nearly exclusively by those persons who devote themselves exclusively or nearly exclusively to its study. Whichever of these two criteria is chosen ML must be said to be an autonomous science. As a matter of fact it possesses its own highly refined techniques and is being developed by members of a clearly determined class of scholars.

This however does not answer the question about the relations between ML and mathematics or philosophy. A high level of technicality has always been a property of logic during the periods of its full development. A 'general philosopher', without a full training in the logic of his time, be it late Stoic, Scholastic or Navya–Nyāya logic, would no doubt understand as little about it as contemporary existentialists and similar philosophers understand about ML. In this sense a highly developed logic in each period was an autonomous science. And yet it was often thought to be a part of philosophy.

On this point it may be objected, that the degree of sophistication reached in ML is so high, that today it is no longer possible for a specialist in any other science to master it. But this is doubtful. Several modern philosophers or specialists in other sciences came to master ML to the point of being creative thinkers in its field. It will suffice to mention Peirce, Whitehead and Russell in philosophy, Woodger among the biologists. With regard to ML such thinkers continued the tradition of, say, Crysippos, Vasubandhu or Albert the Great. It is very difficult to see any differences here.

We may conclude, therefore, that the mere fact that ML is an autonomous science does not answer the question concerning its relations to other disciplines, to mathematics and philosophy in particular.

VI

Logic and mathematics have been closely linked in the past by their mutual influence – at least during Greek Antiquity. However, the problems concerning their mutual relation were never set forth, as far as is known, before the rise of ML. Now, on the contrary, they seem to belong to the most debated problems of the philosophy of logic.

We may distinguish two classes of such problems. The first is concerned with the reducibility of mathematics to ML, being an aspect of the classical problem of the foundation of mathematics. The other contains above all two questions: is ML a mathematical science? If so, in what respect does it differ from other mathematical disciplines? We shall deal only with the latter questions.

Is ML a mathematical discipline? It seems that this cannot be denied. For the only convenient way to define a mathematical discipline is by its method; but ML uses exactly the same method as other mathematical sciences: it is symbolic, formalistic, deductive, objective and so on. It makes no sense to say that logic is a set of mental rules and becomes mathematics when written down and formalized. For ML (like all logic) is a set of theorems and rules which are written down. Before that, we had no science at all.

In what respect does ML differ from other mathematical sciences? If it is taken as a whole, it is rather difficult to give a satisfactory answer to that question. The boundaries between ML and other mathematical sciences are not clear. Quine went as far as to say that even the logic of classes is not logic but mathematics. There is also the notorious case of set theory which can just as readily be called a logical as a mathematical discipline. However, on the whole two characteristics of ML appear to distinguish it rather clearly from other parts of mathematics.

One is its utmost generality, or at least utmost generality of its basic chapters, such as the logic of propositions, the first-level logic of predicates and the logic of relations. ML is in fact first of all the study of theorems upon which rules are based which must be and are applied everywhere.

The other characteristic is its supreme rigor. It is true that ML started as an attempt to use mathematical rigor in logic, as an attempt to imitate algebra. Later on with Frege, however, it proposed to be able to formulate and teach the rules of true rigor to mathematics. As a matter of fact, anyone who is familiar with the Fregean practice of the *lückenloser Beweis* knows how superior this method is to the common way of proceeding in mathematics. Thus Łukasiewicz could say: 'because of lack of space, we cannot supply a rigorous proof; we shall therefore apply the method commonly used in mathematics'; and Menger's efforts to render mathematical symbolism somewhat less ambiguous are also known.

VII

The problem of the relations between ML and philosophy is, contrary to that concerning mathematics, not a new one. In Hellenistic philosophy there was ample discussion over the question whether logic is a part (*μέρος*) or merely a tool (*ὄργανον*) of philosophy. It is known that the latter name was given to the collection of logical works by Aristotle.

The actual difficulty here stems from the fact that there is no general agreement as to the definition of philosophy. If we assume, however, that philosophy is basically the study of foundations and/or of the most general, i.e. most abstract properties of objects, then ML, like every kind of logic, is quite obviously a part of philosophy. It is in fact concerned with the 'ultimate foundations' and consists of an axiomatic inquiry into the most abstract properties of any objects whatsoever. Heinrich Scholz therefore claimed, and correctly it would seem, that ML is ontology, which in turn is the basic part of philosophy understood in the above manner.

Moreover, surprisingly enough, there seem to exist stronger links between philosophy and ML than between it and the older forms of logic. This seems to be true both in so far as ML is considered a tool and a part of philosophy. As to the first, it is doubtful whether the older forms of logic were ever seriously applied in the analysis of philosophical problems. Just one example will suffice to show this. Acquinas never employs formal logic in his elaborate proofs for the existence of God, and of course he could not do so because the logic of his time did not contain the necessary theorems. But presently ML has become a favored tool of every serious philosophical inquiry. Only those philosophers who reject rational procedures do not use it.

On the other hand, the statement that ML is a part of philosophy is substantiated by the fact that it brought out a number of philosophical results, in fact solutions to a number of traditional philosophical problems, which, as far as is known, never happened with other types of logic. Here are three instances.

The first is Russell's treatment of the logical paradoxes, with his theory of systematic ambiguity. This is nothing less than a solution of the age-old problem of 'univocity of being' with a proof that the Scotistic solution is incoherent.

The second is Tarski's definition of truth. Here, for the first time in history it seems, the realistic definition has been adequately formulated. This is perhaps not a complete breakthrough, like the theory of types, but it is still a considerable contribution to the solution of an ancient philosophical problem.

The third is Gödel's first theorem. According to it, the impossibility of all all-embracing philosophical systems – like that of Hegel – has been shown once and for all, again a considerable philosophical advance.

ML has therefore to be seen not only as a tool, but also as a part of philosophy.

It may be asked how this is possible, since it is a part of mathematics? The answer is, that it is the most general and most basic part of mathematics. And if so, there is nothing peculiar about its ambivalent situation. For, it seems, the same is true for the basic parts of every science.

Fribourg, Switzerland

STANISLAW J. SURMA

THE GROWTH OF LOGIC OUT OF THE FOUNDATIONAL RESEARCH IN MATHEMATICS

I. INTRODUCTION

The present day logic takes its origin from too many sources to be justified univocally and exhaustively by referring merely to the particular ones. Mathematics and the foundational studies, singled out as the only major root of logic, prove to be inadequate for the purpose of the justification of our reasoning. Therefore it is quite natural that so much attention has been also paid to the motivation of logic through the philosophical analysis of our knowledge of the external world including the realm of mathematical entities. The third major root of logic lies in the sphere of our intuition. The basic problem here is how and to what extent the intuitive notions of reasoning and its linguistic forms are rendered into logic as a formal system.

Generally speaking, logic cannot be justified directly by our appealing to any single one of the above mentioned roots, for instance, to the foundational research in Mathematics only. Nevertheless, it might be of interest to try to approach the problem of the growth of logic out of the foundational research in Mathematics but provided that this problem was specified in a definite way. In what follows a conceivable though perhaps even arbitrary meaning of this problem is adopted.

The paper is set up as follows. First, a justification of the classification of logic into proof theory, model theory and decidability theory is given. We follow here the paper [9]. Then, the most known object-linguistic or, so to speak, inner definitions of logic are discussed. The discussion includes axiomatic approach (cf. [3]), natural deduction (cf. [2] and [5]), dyadic trees (cf. [7]) and Gentzen sequents (cf. [2]), the best known methods of introducing logic as a formal calculus. In the course of the discussion the methods are mutually compared in relation to their operational meaning, especially important for those using logic in mathematical practice or applying it into Computer Science.

Now we formulate our problem: given a formal mathematical theory find the conditions to be imposed upon the primitive notions of this theory in order to make logic, definable in terms of these notions, to be two-valued. The definitions of this sort are metalinguistic or, so to speak, outer defini-

E. Agazzi (ed.), Modern Logic – A Survey, 15–33.

tions of logic, as contrasted with the previously mentioned inner definitions. More specifically, we quote here three such definitions of the two-valued logic. First, we define logic in terms of the consequence operation (cf. [12]), recently treated as a particular case of the closure operation, a more general algebraic notion. Then, we define logic in terms of the notion of consistency which can be viewed as an example of the family of the proper filters in a distributive set lattice. At last, we define logic in terms of the notion of completeness, a counterpart of the family of the ultrafilters in a distributive set lattice. Here we make use of some results from the papers [8, 10, 14, and 15].

In the closing section it is shown how to modify the conditions imposed upon the primitive notions of a given mathematical theory in order to make logic, definable in terms of these notions, to be three-valued Łukasiewiczian.

To make our description simplest we restrict ourselves to the zero-order language with implication, in symbol, C, and negation, in symbol, N, although this description can be carried over to more complicated logical systems and, in particular, to logical systems that can be formulated in first order languages.

II. CLASSIFICATION OF LOGIC INTO PROOF THEORY, MODEL THEORY AND DECIDABILITY THEORY

The question what logic really is has not been answered yet in a way acceptable by the majority of logicians, mathematicians and philosophers as correct and exhaustive. Working logicians prefer to use logic rather than to define it. When using it they usually lay particular stress only on two aspects of logic, namely,

(i) the explicative aspect according to which logic is a tool of analysis, explication and eventually formalization of fragments of colloquial languages in Science and, especially, in Mathematics,

(ii) the calculative or algorithmic aspect according to which logic is considered as a tool of formalized calculi intended to replace intuitive and informal reasonings of working scientists and mathematicians.

By the first aspect logic becomes a rival to General Linguistics since it constitutes an efficient formalism for revealing deep structures of colloquial languages. The second aspect reduces logic to a general theory of reasoning or inference, especially, of deductive inference.

Logic considered from the calculative or algorithmic viewpoint is expected to answer the following three questions:

(i) how to describe the deducibility of a from X,
(ii) how to describe the non-deducibility of a from X, and
(iii) how to describe the undecidability of the problem of deducibility of a from X,

where X is an arbitrary set of sentences and a is a sentence, a and X being built over the same alphabet.

The part of logic answering question (i) is the earliest and the best worked out and it includes, among others, the axiomatic method (coming back to D. Hilbert or even to Euclide), the method of natural deduction (which derives from G. Gentzen, S. Jaśkowski, and others), the methods of Gentzen sequents, and various versions of the method of finitely generated trees (E. W. Beth's method of semantic diagrams, Hintikka's method of tableaux, R. Smullyan's method of dyadic trees). The best name for this part of logic is proof theory.

The part of logic answering question (ii) comprises the theory of models which was not, in fact, worked out until the forties and fifties yielding a natural and expected extension of proof theory. By means of the theory of models, as it is well-known, many important problems in logic and in algebra have been solved.

Now we proceed to question (iii). The first examples of formalized deductive systems with sentences neither provable nor refutable are due to K. Gödel. Such systems form now the subject to the theory of decidability, one of the most important, and difficult parts of modern logic. It is just the theory of decidability which answers question (iii).

Are logical systems constructed by means of different methods different logics, or are they only different approaches to one and the same intuitive logic? From the 'outside' standpoint, i.e., using the so called 'naive' set theory one can prove that logical systems constructed by means of different methods are equivalent. Contrary to this monistic point of view, the 'inside' standpoint is pluralistic since it forces the statement on the existence of a great number of logics. The mutual complementation of proof theory and model theory expressed through the well-known completeness theorem speaks in favour of the uniqueness of logic. Another argument supporting the uniqueness statement is connected with the fact that each particular method of construing logic has disadvantages as well as advantages. Frequently enough the disadvantages of one of these methods are compensated by the advantages of the others.

III. AXIOMATIC METHOD

The axiomatic method reduces the intuitively given logic to a formalized theory of the so called logical connectives such as implication, negation etc., and it replaces the intuitive metalinguistic notion of entailment by the formal and object-linguistic notion of implication.

The axiomatic method is historically the first method that satisfies the formalistic requirement: to objectify and to formalize the intuitive and informal reasonings. However, the proofs carried out by means of the axiomatic method are rather long and boring and this is the most serious disadvantage of this method. Consequently, any pedantic use of the axiomatic method is quite artificial and, in fact, practically ignored. In addition, this method provides no prescriptions or directives or hints on how to carry on particular proofs. This method does not also provide any instruction how to refute sentences that are not logical theorems.

Any axiomatic system is the smallest set of formulas of a language under consideration containing all its axioms and closed under all its rules of inference.

One of the simplest axiomatic definitions of the two-valued zero order logic states that this logic is the smallest set, say L, such that for any zero order formulas x, y, and z:

(Ax1) $CxCyx \in L$,
(Ax2) $CCxCyzCCxyCxz \in L$,
(Ax3) $CCNxyCCNxNyx \in L$,
(MP) if $x \in L$ and $Cxy \in L$, then $y \in L$.

It can be shown that the set of theorems provable by means of the axioms (Ax1)–(Ax3) and the rule (MP) of Modus Ponens coincides with the set of all two-valued tautologies. This means that the definition above is correct.

To evaluate the definition from an instrumental or operational point of view we prove the formula below:

(+) $CCxyCCyzCxz$

as a theorem of this axiomatic system. Here is the proof.

(1) $CCyzCCxCyzCCxyCxz \in L$
(Ax1) $[x/CCxCyzCCxyCxz, y/Cyz]$, (Ax2)

Explanation of the notation used. The step number (1) is obtained from the step (Ax2), i.e., from the formula: $CCxCyzCCxyCxz$ and from the step (Ax1) $[x/CCxCyzCCxyCxz, y/Cyz]$, i.e., from the formula:

$CCCxCyzCCxyCxzCCyzCCyzCCxCyzCCxyCxz$

resulting from the axiom (Ax1) by the substitution of the formula:

$CCxCyzCCxyCxz$

for the formula x and of the formula: Cyz for the formula y and by applying to the two steps the rule (MP) of Modus Ponens.

(2) $CCCyzCxCyzCCyzCCxyCxz \in L$
(Ax2)[x/Cyz, $y/CxCyz$, $z/CCxyCxz$], (1)
(3) $CCyzCCxyCxz \in L$
(Ax1)[x/Cyz, y/x], (2)
(4) $CCCyzCxyCCyzCxz \in L$
(Ax2)[x/Cyz, y/Cxy, z/Cxz], (3)
(5) $CCCxyzCyCxy \in L$
(Ax1)[x/y, y/x], (Ax1)[$x/CyCxy$, $y/CCxyz$]
(6) $CCCxyzCyz \in L$
(4)[y/Cxy, x/y], (5)
(7) $CCuCCxyzCuCyz \in L$
(3)[$y/CCxyz$, z/Cyz, x/u], (6)
(8) $CCxCyzCyCxz \in L$
(7)[$u/CxCyz$, z/Cxz], (Ax2)
(9) $CCxyCCyzCxz \in L$
(8)[x/Cyz, y/Cxy, z/Cxz], (3)

This proof is seen to be rather long and complicated although the formula (+) being proved is so simple.

IV. NATURAL DEDUCTION

The method of natural deduction reduces the intuitive notion of entailment to the formal notion of deducibility. This method and, in particular, the well-known deduction theorem, it is based upon, is to a greater extent natural and economical. As a rule, this method supplies more prescriptions and directives on how to construct particular proofs. The proofs made by means of the method of natural deduction are relatively shorter. The main disadvantage of this method is that it does not instruct how to refute formulas that can be refuted.

Let X and Y be finite sets of zero order formulas. The symbol: $X \vdash y$ reads "the formula y is deducible from the set of formulas X as the set of hypotheses". We write: $\vdash x$ instead writing: $\emptyset \vdash x$ where $\emptyset$ denotes the empty set, and we read the symbol: $\vdash x$ as "x is a logical theorem". We also use the symbol: $X, y \vdash z$ as an abbreviation of $X + \{y\} \vdash z$. One of the definitions of natural deduction states that the notion of deducibility satisfies all the conditions below:

(D1) $x \vdash x$,
(D2) if $X \vdash y$, then $X - \{z\} \vdash Czy$,
(D3) if $X \vdash x$ and $Y \vdash Cxy$, then $X + Y \vdash y$,
(D4) if $X, Nx \vdash y$ and $X, Nx \vdash Ny$, then $X \vdash x$.

Now we prove by means of natural deduction the same formula

(+) $CCxyCCyzCxz$
(1) $Cxy \vdash Cxy$
(D1)
(2) $x \vdash x$
(D1)
(3) $Cxy, x \vdash y$
(1), (2), (D3)
(4) $Cyz \vdash Cyz$
(D1)
(5) $Cxy, Cyz, x \vdash z$
(3), (4), (D3)
(6) $Cxy, Cyz \vdash Cxz$
(5), (D2)
(7) $Cxy \vdash CCyzCxz$
(6), (D2)
(8) $\vdash CCxyCCyzCxz$

This proof, certainly, is more simple and more intuitive than the axiomatic proof of the same formula.

It can be shown that the set of theorems provable by the method of natural deduction coincides with the set of theorems obtainable by the axiomatic definition above. This means that both definitions are mutally equivalent.

V. DYADIC TREES

The method of finitely generated trees consists in reducing the very logical problem of entailment to that of indirectly constructed inconsistencies. This method does not correspond to the intuitive and informal reasonings which can be found in practice. Considering that proofs made by means of this method consist in decomposing formulas in question into their subformulas it is rather nearer to the 'intuition' of the theorem-proving computers. Owing to the subformula property the method of finitely generated trees gives clear instructions on how to refute formulas which are refutable in finite models, and to prove provable formulas. This method is very efficient and most advantageous from the instrumental point of view.

The present formulation of this method has been first done in R. Smullyan's [5] in 1966 but the idea goes back to the method of E. W. Beth's semantic diagrams (cf. [1]) and to the J. Hintikka's tableaux (cf. [4]) and ultimately it derives from G. Gentzen's method of sequents.

In the language with two-valued implication and negation as the only connectives the finitely generated trees reduce to the dyadic trees. Recall that by an ordered dyadic tree we mean the sequence $\pi = \{P, h, R\}$ such that P is an arbitrary non-empty set whose elements are called points or vertices, h is a function from P to the set of integers which assigns to each $x \in P$ the number $h(x)$ called the level of x, and R is a binary relation of being successor defined on P such that the following conditions are fulfilled.

(i) there is a unique point $x_1 \in P$ called the origin of the tree π such that $h(x_1) = 1$,

(ii) every point other than the origin has a unique predecessor with respect to R,

(iii) for any points $x, y \in P$ if xRy, then $h(y) = h(x) + 1$,

(iv) for any point $x \in P$ the image $R(\{x\})$ of x is an ordered set such that either $R(\{x\})$ is two-element, or it is one-element, or at last it is empty. In the last case the point x is called an end of π.

By a dyadic tree for a zero order formula with implication and negation, denote it by x, we mean an ordered dyadic tree with x as its origin and such that for every point y of this tree the following conditions are fulfilled:

(T1) if there is a formula z such that $y = NNz$, then we adjoin z as the sole successor to the end point of every branch passing through the point y,

(T2) if there are formulas z and u such that $y = NCzu$, then we successively adjoin z as the sole successor to the end point of every branch passing through the point y, and then we adjoin Nu as the sole successor of z,

(T3) if there are formulas z and u such that $y = Czu$, then we simultaneously adjoin Nz as the left and u as the right successors to the end point of every branch passing through the point y.

A dyadic tree for a formula is said to be closed if on every branch of this tree there are two points of the form: x and Nx. By a proof of a formula x we mean any closed dyadic tree for the formula Nx.

For the logic constructed by means of dyadic trees one can prove the completeness theorem stating that every formula is provable in the sense defined above if and only if it is a two-valued zero order tautology.

According to the definition above the following tree gives a formal proof of the formula

(+) $CCxyCCyzCxz$

The number of the step | The rule used

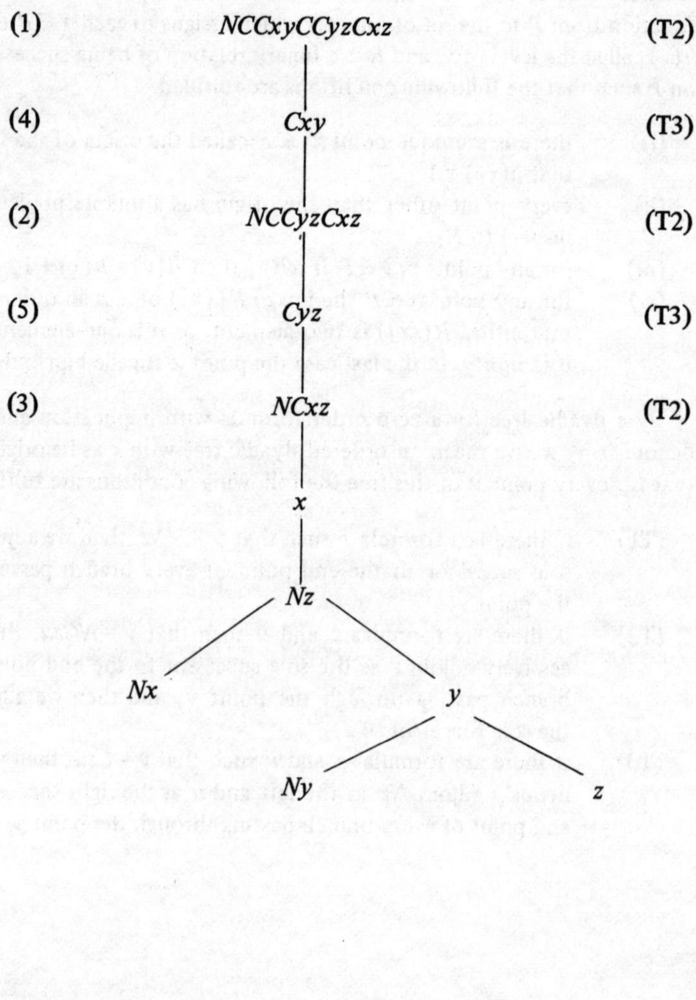

(1)
NCCxyCCyzCxz
(T2)
(4)
Cxy
(T3)
(2)
NCCyzCxz
(T2)
(5)
Cyz
(T3)
(3)
NCxz
(T2)
x
Nz
Nx
y
Ny
z

As it is seen all the branches of the tree are closed.

Another version of the method of finitely generated trees, to be described now, makes use of especially chosen metalinguistic operators. In the case of dyadic trees this version can be described as follows. We denote by $a_1[.]$ and $a_2[.]$ two metalinguistic operators and we assume that for any formula x:

$a_1[x]$ is true if and only if x is false

and

$a_2[x]$ is true if and only if x is true.

Instead of (T1)–(T3) we accept the following new rules of decomposition:

to replace $a_1[Nx]$ by $a_2[x]$
to replace $a_2[Nx]$ by $a_1[x]$
to replace $a_1[Cxy]$ by $a_2[x]$ and $a_1[y]$
to replace $a_2[Cxy]$ by $a_1[x]$ or $a_2[y]$.

We also accept the following new definitions. A dyadic tree for a formula is closed if on each branch of the tree there are two points of the form: $a_1[x]$ and $a_2[x]$. By a proof of a formula x we mean any closed dyadic tree for the formula $a_1[x]$.

VI. GENTZEN SEQUENTS

The method of Gentzen sequents resembles the method of dyadic trees since it replaces formal proofs by decompositions of formulas under proofs into special subformulas of the formulas. This time, however, the simplest irreducible subformulas are to be instances of a special axiom schema rather than instances of the contradiction. So the method of Gentzen sequents appears to be a formalization of the direct intuitive reasonings rather than indirect ones.

Let X and Y be finite, possibly empty sets of zero order formulas. The ordered pair $\{X, Y\}$, symbolized here as X/Y, is called a sequent where X is its antecedent and Y its consequent. To construct logic by means of Gentzen sequents we define one axiom and two rules of inference for each connective. The construction runs as follows. The set of all provable sequents is the smallest set satisfying the following conditions:

(Ax) $X, z/Y, z$ is an axiom,
(R1) from $X, x/Y, y$ infer $X/Y, Cxy$,
(R2) from $X/Y, x$ and $X, y/Y$ infer $X, Cxy/Y$,

(R3) from $X/Y, x$ infer $X, Nx/Y$,
(R4) from $X, x/Y$ infer $X/Y, Nx$.

Let $X = \{x_1, ..., x_n, Ny_1, ..., Ny_k\}$. Define a one-to-one mapping such that $X^* = x_1, ..., x_n/y_1, ..., y_k$. Using this definition it is easy to see that a formula x is provable by means of dyadic trees if and only if the sequent $-/x$ is provable in the above system of Gentzen sequents and hence the two definitions of logic are equivalent.

Here is a formal proof of the formula

(+) $CCxyCCyzCxz$

as a theorem of the system of Gentzen sequents.

$y, x/y$ $\qquad$ $y, z/z$ (Ax)

$Cyz, x/x, z$ $\qquad$ $y, Cyz, x/z$ (R2)

$Cxy, Cyz, x/z$ (R2)

$Cxy, Cyz/Cxz$ (R1)

$Cxy/CCyzCxz$ (R1)

$-/CCxyCCyzCxz$ (R1)

VII. LOGIC DEFINED BY THE CONSEQUENCE OPERATION

Now we proceed to the consequence operation and the logic defined by it. The notion of consequence operation is a formalization of the non-formal intuitive notion of inference.

Let S be the set of all zero order formulas built from the propositional variables by means of implication (C) and negation (N). Let $X \subset S$ and $x \in S$. The following definitions are most known definitions of the notion of the consequence operation.

$Cn_1(X)$ is the set of all $x \in S$ such that there are $x_1, ..., x_n \in S$ where

$x_n = x$ and for every $i \leqslant n$ either $x_i \in X$, or there are $j < i$ and $k < i$ such that $x_j = Cx_k x_i$.

$Cn_2(X)$ is the set $\cup \{Cn^{(n)}(X)$: n is an integer$\}$ where the function $Cn^{(n)}$ is defined inductively as follows: $Cn^{(1)}(X) = X$ and $Cn^{(k+1)}(X)$ is the union of the set $Cn^{(k)}(X)$ and of the set $\{x \in S$: there are $y, z \in Cn^{(k)}(X)$ such that $y = Czx\}$.

$Cn_3(X)$ is the least set containing X and closed under the rule of Modus Ponens, i.e., if $y \in Cn_3(X)$ and $Cyz \in Cn_3(X)$, then $z \in Cn_3(X)$ for any $y, z \in S$.

$Cn_4(X)$ is the set of all $x \in S$ such that for any homomorphism h sending the language $\{S, C, N\}$ into the two-element algebra $\{\{0, 1\}, C, N\}$ similar to it if $h(X) \subset \{0, 1\}$, then $h(x) = 1$.

One can prove that all the consequence operations above are identical, i.e., $Cn_i(X) = Cn_j(X)$ for any $X \subset S$ and for $i, j \leqslant 4$.

The definitions above concern the consequence operation based on the rule of Modus Ponens as the only rule of inference. But it is not difficult to base them on arbitrary sets of rules. For illustration we generalize the definition of Cn_1 to that of the consequence operation $Cn_1(R\ ...)$ based on a non-empty set R of rules of inference. $Cn_1(R, X)$ is the set of all $x \in S$ such that there are $x_1, ..., x_n \in S$ such that $x_n = x$ and for any $i \leqslant n$ either $x_i \in X$, or there is $r \in R$ and there are $i_1 < i, i_2 < i, ..., i_k < i$ such that x_i follows from $x_{i_1}, x_{i_2}, ..., x_{i_k}$ by the rule r.

The notion of consequence operation was axiomatized by A. Tarski in the thirties. Les S, C, N and Cn be all primitive symbols. We accept the following axioms:

(S1) S is a non-empty at most denumerable set,
(S2) if $x \in S$, then $Nx \in S$,
(S3) if $x, y \in S$, then $Cxy \in S$,
(Cn1) if $X \subset S$, then $Cn(X) \subset S$,
(Cn2) if $X \subset S$, then $X \subset Cn(X)$
(Cn3) if $X \subset S$, then $Cn[Cn(X)] \subset Cn(X)$,
(Cn4) if $X \subset Y \subset S$, then $Cn(X) \subset Cn(Y)$,
(Cn5) if $X \subset S$, then $Cn(X) \subset \cup \{Cn(Y)$: Y is finite and $Y \subset X\}$,
(Cn6) if $X \subset S$ and $x, y \in S$, then $Cxy \in Cn(X)$ if and only if $y \in Cn(X + \{x\})$,
(Cn7) if $x \in S$, then $Cn(\{x, Nx\}) = S$,
(Cn8) if $x \in S$, then $Cn(\{x\}) \cdot Cn(\{Nx\}) = Cn(\emptyset)$,

According to (S1)–(S3) the set S can be treated as an algebra. According to (Cn1)–(Cn5) Cn can be treated as a closure operator in S. One can prove that the operation Cn satisfies the condition (Cn6) if and only if the set $Cn(\emptyset)$ coincides with the set of all theorems of the implicational logic in the sense of Hilbert. One can also prove that the operation Cn satisfies the conditions (Cn6)–(Cn8) if and only if $Cn(\emptyset)$ coincides with the set of all theorems of the two-valed logic with implication and negation previously denoted by L. Thus, the Tarski's axiom system for Cn is adequate for the two-valued logic and L can be defined by the equality:

$$L = Cn(\emptyset)$$

The equality states that L is the smallest set of zero order formulas closed under the operation Cn satisfying the conditions (Cn1)–(Cn8).

Any of the consequence operations Cn_i with $i \leqslant 4$ as defined above can be shown to be the smallest operation satisfying all the conditions (Cn1)–(Cn8). The same is, of course, true about the operations $Cn_i(R\ ...)$ and the conditions (Cn1)–(Cn5).

The above axiom system for Cn can be considerably modified and even simplified. Namely, the axioms (Cn1)–(Cn8) are equivalent to the following four axioms:

(Cn9) $Cn(S) \subset S$,
(Cn10) if $X, Y \subset S$, then $X + Cn(X) + Cn[Cn(Y) \subset$
$\subset Cn(X+Y) \cdot \cup \{Cn(Z)\colon Z$ is a finite subset of $X+Y\}$,
(Cn11) if $X \subset S$ and $y \in S$, then $y \in Cn(X)$ if and only if
$Cn(X + \{Ny\}) = S$,
(Cn12) if $X \subset S$ and $x, y \in S$, then $Cxy \in Cn(X)$ if and only if
$Cn(X + \{x, Ny\}) = S$.

The axioms (Cn11) and (Cn12) can be, in turn, shown to be equivalent to the following axiom:

(Cn13) if $X \subset S$ and $x_1, x_2, ..., x_n, y \in S$, then
$Cx_1Cx_2 \ldots Cx_ny \in Cn(X)$ if and only if
$Cn(X + \{x_1, x_2, ..., x_n, Ny\}) = S$.

VIII. LOGIC DEFINED BY THE NOTION OF CONSISTENCY

Now we proceed to the logic defined in terms of the notion of consistency. The following is the list of the primitive terms: S, C, N, as before, and $Cons$, intended to denote the class of all consistent sets of formulas included in S. We adopt the following list of axioms:

(S1) S is a non-empty at most denumerable set,
(S2) if $x \in S$, then $Nx \in S$,
(S3) if $x, y \in S$, then $Cxy \in S$,
(Cons1) $Cons \subset 2^S$
(Cons2) if $X \subset Y \in Cons$, then $X \in Cons$,
(Cons3) if $X \subset S$ and $X \notin Cons$, then there is a finite subset Y in X such that $Y \notin Cons$,
(Cons4) if $x \in S$ and $X \in Cons$, then either $X + \{x\} \in Cons$, or $X + \{Nx\} \in Cons$,
(Cons5) if $x \in S$, then $\{x, Nx\} \notin Cons$,
(Cons6) if $x, y \in S$, then $X + \{x, Ny\} \in Cons$ if and only if $X + \{NCxy\} \in Cons$.

According to the axioms (Cons1)–(Cons3) *Cons* is a finite character property as it is used in set theory and in topology.

With the aid of the axioms above it can be shown that

$$L = \{x \in S\colon \{Nx\} \notin Cons\}$$

coincides with the set of all theorems of the two-valued zero order logic. Making use of the following definitions:

$$Cn(X) = \{x \in S\colon X + \{Nx\} \notin Cons\}$$

and

$$Cons = \{X \subset S\colon Cn(X) \neq S\}$$

it can also be proved that the axiom system (S1)–(S3), (Cn1–(Cn8) for the consequence operation is equivalent to the axiom system (S1)–(S3), (Cons1)–(Cons6) for the notion of consistency.

IX. LOGIC DEFINED BY THE NOTION OF COMPLETENESS

Logic can also be defined in another metamathematical way without any explicit appeal to the notion of consequence or to that of consistency. To show this consider the following list of primitive terms: S, C, N, as before, *Max*, intended to denote the class of all complete, i.e., maximal consistent, deductively closed sets of formulas, *Ext*, an extension operation sending 2^S to *Max*, and *Int*, an intersection operation sending *Max* to 2^S. We adopt the following axiom system:

(S1) S is a non-empty at most denumerable set,

(S2) if $x \in S$, then $Nx \in S$,
(Max1) $Max \subset 2^S$,
(Max2) if $X \subset S$, then $Int[Ext(X)] \subset S$,
(Max3) if $X, Y \subset S$, then $Ext(X+Y) = Ext(X) \cdot Ext(Y)$,
(Max4) if $X \subset S$ and $Ext(X) = \emptyset$, then there is a finite subset Y of X such that $Ext(Y) = \emptyset$,
(Max5) if $x \in S$, then $Ext(\{x\}) \cdot Ext(\{Nx\}) = \emptyset$,
(Max6) if $x \in S$, then $Ext(\{x\}) + Ext(\{Nx\}) = Max$,
(Max7) if $X \subset S$, then $Y \in Ext(X)$ if and only if $X \subset Y$ and $Y \in Max$,
(Max8) if $X \subset S$, then $Ext(X) \subset Ext(Int[Ext(X)])$,
(Max9) if $X \subset S$ and $x_1, x_2, ..., x_n, y \in S$, then $Cx_1 Cx_2 ... Cx_n y \in Int[Ext(X)]$ if and only if $Ext(X) \cdot Ext(\{x_1\}) \cdot Ext(\{x_2\}) \cdot ... \cdot Ext(\{x_n\}) \cdot Ext(\{Ny\}) = \emptyset$.

The condition (Max9) is equivalent to the following two conditions:

(Max10) if $X \subset S$ and $x \in S$, then $x \in Int[Ext(X)]$ if and only if $Ext(X) \cdot Ext(\{Nx\}) = \emptyset$,
(Max11) if $X \subset S$ and $x, y \in S$, then $Cxy \in Int[Ext(X)]$ if and only if $Ext(X) \cdot Ext(\{x\}) \cdot Ext(\{Ny\}) = \emptyset$.

Making use of the axioms (S1), (S2), and (Max1)–(Max9) it can be shown that

$$L = Int(Max)$$

coincides with the set of all theorems of the two-valued zero order logic with implication and negation. A rather stronger theorem can be proved according to which the axiom system (S1), (S2), and (Max1)–(Max9) is equivalent to the axiomatic consequence theory or, what means the same, to the axiomatic consistency theory as presented above. To show this it is enough to accept either the definitions:

$$Cn(X) = Int[Ext(X)]$$
$$Max = \{X \subset S\colon X = Cn(X) \text{ and } x \in X \text{ if and only if } Nx \notin X \text{ for every } X \in S\}$$

or the definitions:

$$Cons = \{X \subset S\colon X \subset Y \text{ and } Y \in Max \text{ for some } Y \subset S\}$$
$$Max = \{X \in Cons\colon \text{for any } Y \subset S \text{ if } Y \in Cons, \text{ then } Y \subset X\}.$$

As the two last approaches to logic are not widely known some consequences of the axiom system (S1), (S2), and (Max1)–(Max9) are quoted below:

(1) if $X \in Cons$, then $X \neq S$,
(2) $Max \subset Cons$,
(3) if $X \subset S$, then $X \in Cons$ if and only if $Ext(X) \neq \emptyset$,
(4) if $X \subset S$, then X is complete if and only if $Y = Z$ for any $Y, Z \in Ext(X)$,
(5) if $X \subset S$, then X is independent if and only if $Ext(X - \{x\} + \{Nx\}) \neq \emptyset$ for every $x \in X$,
(6) $Ext(S) = \emptyset$,
(7) $Ext(\emptyset) = Max$,
(8) if $x \in S$, then the following conditions are mutually equivalent:
 (i) $x \in Int(Max)$,
 (ii) $Ext(\{x\}) = Max$,
 (iii) $Ext(\{Nx\}) = \emptyset$,
(9) if $\emptyset \neq K \subset 2^S$, then $Ext(\cup \{X: X \in K\}) = \cap \{Ext(X): X \in K\}$,
(10) if $X \subset S$, then $Ext(X) \subset Max \cdot 2^S$,
(11) if $X \in Max$, then $X \neq \emptyset$ and $X \neq S$ and $X = Int[Ext(X)]$,
(12) if $X \in Max$ and $x, y \in X$, then $NCxNy \in X$,
(13) if $X \in Max$, $x \in X$ and $Cxy \in Int(Max)$, then $y \in X$,
(14) if $X \in Max$ and $x \in S$, then $x \in X$ if and only if $Nx \notin X$,
(15) if $x, y \in S$, then $Ext(\{x\}) \cdot Ext(\{y\}) = Ext(\{NCxNy\})$,
(16) $Max = \cup \{Ext(\{x\}): x \in S\}$,
(17) if $X, Y \in Max$ and $X \neq Y$, then there is $x \in S$ such that $X \in Ext(\{x\})$ and $Y \in Ext(\{Nx\})$,
(18) if $\emptyset \neq K \subset 2^S$ and $\cap \{Ext(X): X \in K\} = \emptyset$, then there is a finite subclass K' in K such that $\cap \{Ext(X): X \in K'\} = \emptyset$.

The theorems (6)–(10) show that the operation *Ext* is a dual homomorphism of the complete upper semi-lattice 2^S into the complete lower semi-lattice *Max*. The theorems (11)–(14) show that *Max* is a family of ultrafilters in 2^S while the theorems (15)–(18) show that *Max* can be considered as a totally disconnected compact toplogical space if one puts $B = \{Ext(\{x\}): x \in S\}$ as its basis and one defines the family of open sets in *Max* as $\{X \in Max: X = \cup \{Y: Y \in B_0\}$ for some $B_0 \subset B\}$.

X. AN EXTENSION OF THE APPROACH TO THE THREE-VALUED ŁUKASIEWICZ LOGIC

The above constructions refer to the two-valued zero order logic. Analogical constructions may be, in principle, repeated in relation to any multiple-valued logic although the direct definitions or the more or less indirect assumptions forcing these logics may seem to be less natural and more complex.

We illustrate these constructions by making use of the three-valued Łukasiewicz logic with implication and negation.

Axiomatic definition (cf. [13]). One of the axiomatic definitions of the three-valued Łukasiewicz zero order logic, denote it by $Ł$, states that it is the smallest set such that for any $x, y, z \in S$

(Ax′1) $CxCyx \in Ł$,
(Ax′2) $CCxyCCyzCxz \in Ł$,
(Ax′3) $CCNxNyCyx \in Ł$,
(Ax′4) $CCCxNxxx \in Ł$,
(MP) if $x \in Ł$ and $Cxy \in Ł$, then $y \in Ł$.

Natural deduction for the three-valued Łukasiewicz logic may be defined as follows:

(D′1) $X, x \vdash x$,
(D′2) $CCxNxx \vdash x$,
(D′3) if $X - \{x\} \vdash Cxy$, then $X, x \vdash y$,
(D′4) if $X, x \vdash y$, then $X \vdash Cxy$,
(D′5) if $X - \{Nx\}, Ny \vdash Nx$, then $X, x \vdash y$.

It can be proved that every formula is provable by means of the above mentioned rules if and only if it is a tautology of the three-valued zero order Łukasiewicz logic.

Finitely generated trees for $Ł$ are defined as follows (cf. [11]). We choose three metalinguistic operators: $a_1[\,.\,]$, $a_2[\,.\,]$ and $a_3[\,.\,]$ and we assume them to satisfy the conditions below:

$a_1[x]$ is true if x is false, otherwise $a_1[x]$ is false,
$a_2[x]$ is true if x is undetermined, otherwise $a_2[x]$ is false,
$a_3[x]$ is true if x is true, otherwise $a_3[x]$ is false.

Then we accept the following decomposition rules:

to replace $a_i[Nx]$ by $a_{3-i+1}[x]$ where $i = 1, 2, 3$,
to replace $a_1[Cxy]$ by $a_3[x]$ and $a_1[y]$,

to replace $a_2[Cxy]$ either by $a_3[x]$ and $a_2[y]$,
or by $a_2[x]$ and $a_1[y]$,
to replace $a_3[Cxy]$ either by $a_1[x]$,
or by $a_2[x]$ and $a_2[y]$,
or by $a_3[y]$.

The decomposition tree with $a_i[x]$ as the origin is said to be closed if on each branch of that tree there are vertices of the form: $a_j[y]$ and $a_k[y]$ where $j \neq k$ and y is a subformula of the formula x. The formula x is said to be provable if for every $i < 3$ the decomposition tree for $a_i[x]$ is closed.

It can be proved that every formula is provable in this sense if and only if it is a tautology in the three-valued zero order Łukasiewicz logic.

Gentzen sequents for Ł. Let X, Y, and Z be finite sets of zero order formulas, and let $a, b \in S$. The ordered triples of the form $\{X, Y, Z\}$ denoted here by $X/Y/Z$ are called sequents. To construct the three-valued Łukasiewicz logic as a calculus of sequents we accept the following three axioms:

$X/Y, a/Z, a,$
$X, a/Y/Z, a,$
$X, a/Y, a/Z$

and the following rules of inference:

to replace $X, a/Y/Z$ by $X/Y/Z, Na,$
to replace $X/Y, a/Z$ by $X/Y, Na/Z,$
to replace $X/Y/Z, a$ by $X, Na/Y/Z,$
to replace $X, a/Y/Z, b$ by $X/Y/Z, Cab,$
to replace $X, a/Y, b/Z$
and
$X/Y, a/Z, b$ by $X/Y, Cab/Z,$
to replace $X/Y/Z, a$
and
$X/Y, a, b/Z$
and
$X, b/Y/Z$ by $X, Cab/Y/Z.$

Let us define the following one-to-one mapping $A \to A^*$ where

$$A = \{a_3[x_1], ..., a_3[x_k], a_2[y_1], ..., a_2[y_m], a_1[z_1], ..., a_1[z_n]\}$$

putting

$$A^* = x_1, ..., x_k/y_1, ..., y_m/z_1, ..., z_n.$$

Using this definition it is easy to prove the completeness theorem for the system of Gentzen sequents just described.

Definition of Ł in terms of Cn. The following conditions force the operation Cn to define logic to be the three-valued zero order Łukasiewicz logic (cf. [6]): (S1)–(S3) and (Cn1)–(Cn5) as before and

(Cn′6) if $X \subset S$, $a, b \in S$, $a \notin X$ and $Cab \in Cn(X)$, then $b \in Cn(X + \{a\})$,
(Cn′7) if $X \subset S$, $a, b \in S$ and $b \in Cn(X + \{a\})$, then $Cab \in Cn(X)$,
(Cn′8) if $X \subset S$, $a, b \in S$, $Na \notin X$ and $Na \in Cn(X + \{Nb\})$, then $b \in Cn(X + \{a\})$,
(Cn′9) if $a \in S$, then $Cn(\{a\}) \cdot Cn(\{CaNa\}) = Cn(\emptyset)$.

The conditions imposed upon the class *Cons* or the class *Max* and the operations *Ext* and *Int* in order to make logic, definable in terms of them, to be three-valued Łukasiewicz can be described in an analogous way.

Jagiellonian University of Cracow

BIBLIOGRAPHY

[1] Beth, E. W., 'Semantic Entailment and Formal Derivability', *Mededelingen der Koninklijke Nederlandse Akademie van Wetenschappen, Afd. Letterkunde, n.s.* 18 (1955), 309–342.

[2] Gentzen, G., 'Untersuchungen über das logische Schliessen', *Mathematische Zeitschrift* 39 (1934–35), 176–210 and 405–443.

[3] Hilbert, D. and Bernays, P. *Grundlagen der Mathematik*, Vol. 1, Berlin 1934 and Vol. 2, Berlin 1939.

[4] Hintikka, K. J. J., 'Form and Content in Quantification Theory', *Acta Philosophica Fennica* 8 (1955), 7–55.

[5] Jaśkowski, S. 'On the Rules of Suppositions in Formal Logic', *Studia Logica*, Warszawa 1934, 32 pp.

[6] Pogorzelski, W. A. and Słupecki, J., 'Basic Properties of Deductive Systems Based on Non-Classical Logics, Part I', *Studia Logica* 9 (1960), 163–176. (In Polish with English summary).

[7] Smullyan, R., 'Trees and Nest Structures', *J. Symbolic Logic* 31 (1966), 303–321.

[8] Surma, S. J., 'On the Relation of Formal Inference and Some Related Concepts', (In Polish with English summary). *Universitas Iagellonica Acta Scientiarum Litterarumque, Schedae Logicae* 1 (1964), 37–55.

[9] Surma, S. J., 'Some Observations on Different Methods of Construing Logical Calculi', *Teoria a Metoda, Czechoslovak Academy of Sciences* 6 (1974), 37–52.

[10] Surma, S. J., 'On the Axiomatic Treatment of the Theory of Models. II: Syntactical Characterization of a Fragment of the Theory of Models', *Universitas Iagellonica Acta Scientiarum Litterarumque, Schedae Logicae* 5 (1970), 43–55.

[11] Surma, S. J., 'A Method of the Construction of Finite Lukasiewiczian Algebras and Its Application to a Gentzen-Style Characterization of Finite Logics', *Reports on Mathematical Logic* 2 (1974), 49–54.

[12] Tarski, A., Über einige fundamentale Begriffe der Metamathematik', *Comptes Rendus des Séances de la Société des Sciences et des Lettres de Varsovie* 23 (1930), 22–29.

[13] Wajsberg, M., 'Axiomatization of the Three-Valued Propositional Calculus', *Polish Logic*, S. McCall (ed.), Oxford 1967, pp. 264–284.

[14] Wybraniec-Skardowska, U., 'On Mutual Definability of the Notions of Entailment and Inconsistency', (In Polish with English summary). *Zeszyty Naukowe Wyższej Szkoly Pedagogicznej w Opolu, seria Matematyka* 15 (1975), 75–86.

[15] Żandarowska, W. 'On Certain Connections Between Consequence, Inconsistency and Completeness', (In Polish with English summary), *Studia Logica* 18 (1966), 165–174.

PART 2

PURE LOGIC

KURT SCHÜTTE

PROOF THEORY

Proof theory was established at first by David Hilbert to gain a foundation of classical mathematics by very elementary methods which he called finitary (*finit*). The idea was to formalize the particular parts of classical mathematics and to prove the consistency of the corresponding formal systems only in a syntactical way without reference to the intended meanings of the formal systems.

But Gödel's incompleteness theorems revealed 1931 the impossibility to prove consistency of arithmetic or stronger mathematical systems only by finitary methods. Therefore, it was necessary to extend the first strict standpoint of Hilbert by constructive methods in a more general sense to obtain consistency proofs for nontrivial parts of mathematics.

I will speak about some proof theoretical results which are obtained in the meantime and about the methods which were needed for these results.

The first important proof theoretical result was the *Hauptsatz* of first order predicate calculus by G. Gentzen (1934). According to this theorem, every deducible formula of first order predicate calculus is deducible only by inferences whose premises are combined only by parts of the conclusion. That means that one can eliminate the inferences which Gentzen called cuts (*Schnitte*) whose simplest special case is the inference from A and $A \to B$ to B. The Hauptsatz of first order predicate calculus is proved in a finitary way. It gives the possibility to make some conclusions from the structure of a formula to the deducibility of the formula.

It was useful for many further proof theoretical investigations to eliminate all cuts or at least some cuts in a proof-figure of a formal system. If it is possible to eliminate all cuts in a formal system, then it follows trivially that the system is consistent.

The next important result in proof theory was the consistency proof for pure number theory by Gentzen 1936. In the formal system of pure number theory containing the formalized mathematical induction on natural numbers, the cut rule cannot be eliminated. Gentzen proved the consistency of this system only by replacing some cuts by other cuts which are simpler in a certain way. The proof could not be perfouned in a finitary way, but it was

E. Agazzi (ed.), Modern Logic – A Survey, 37–43.

obtained by transfinite induction on a constructive system of ordinals up to the least ϵ-number ϵ_0. This proof is constructive in a strict sense.

Another consistency proof for pure number theory was given by Gödel 1958 by means of an interpretation using constructive functionals of arbitrary finite type. This proof is also constructive in a strict sense, but it is not finitary. Both methods, the transfinite induction as well as the interpretation by functionals were generalized for consistency proofs of stronger systems. Let me speak at first about consistency proofs by transfinite induction for some subsystems of classical analysis.

For these consistency proofs, one needs stronger constructive notation systems of ordinals than for pure number theory. There are some different notations systems of ordinals used in proof theory, and the relations between these systems are mainly well-known. I will explain a particular notation system which in my opinion is the best one to understand it from the point of view of the classical theory of ordinals, and which is sufficient for the hitherto obtained consistency proofs. It is based on normal functions θ_α defined by S. Feferman.

We consider ordinals and cardinals in a system of set theory, for instance in the system of Zermelo–Fraenkel with the axiom of choice. For any ordinal α let Ω_α be the least ordinal of cardinality $\aleph_\alpha$. We give a simultaneous *Inductive definition* of the ordinal classes $\mathrm{Cl}_\alpha(\beta)$, $\mathrm{In}(\alpha)$ and the normal functions θ_α for arbitrary ordinals α, β.

(1) $\xi = 0$ or $\xi < \beta \Rightarrow \xi \in \mathrm{Cl}_\alpha(\beta)$
(2) $\xi, \eta \in \mathrm{Cl}_\alpha(\beta) \Rightarrow \xi + \eta \in \mathrm{Cl}_\alpha(\beta)$
(3) $\xi, \eta \in \mathrm{Cl}_\alpha(\beta), \xi < \alpha \Rightarrow \theta_\xi(\eta) \in \mathrm{Cl}_\alpha(\beta)$
(4) $0 < \xi \in \mathrm{Cl}_\alpha(\beta), \beta < \Omega_\xi \Rightarrow \Omega_\xi \in \mathrm{Cl}_\alpha(\beta)$
(5) $\mathrm{In}(\alpha) := \{\beta \mid \beta \notin \mathrm{Cl}_\alpha(\beta)\}$
(6) $\theta_\alpha :=$ ordering function of the class $\mathrm{In}(\alpha)$.

$\mathrm{Cl}_\alpha(\beta)$ is the closure of the set of ordinals containing 0 and all ordinals $< \beta$ with respect to addition, θ_ξ for $\xi < \alpha$ and the Ω-function. Of course, $\mathrm{Cl}_\alpha(\beta)$ is a set of ordinals.

$\mathrm{In}(\alpha)$ is the class of those ordinals β which are inaccessible from 0 and ordinals $< \beta$ by applications of addition, θ_ξ for $\xi < \alpha$ and the Ω-function. We call this proper class $\mathrm{In}(\alpha)$ the class of α-inaccessible ordinals.

Since $\mathrm{In}(\alpha)$ is a closed class, θ_α is a normal function. That means that θ_α is strictly monotonous and continuous. $\theta_\alpha(\beta)$ is defined for all ordinals α and β. For simplicity, we write $\theta\alpha\beta$ for $\theta_\alpha(\beta)$.

$\mathrm{In}(0)$ is the class of principal numbers of addition, therefore $\theta 0 \beta = \omega^\beta$.

In (1) is the class of ϵ-numbers, therefore $\theta 1 \beta = \epsilon_\beta$.

In (2) is the class of critical ϵ-numbers. One has always In $(\beta) \subset$ In (α) for $\alpha < \beta$.

We define the *level* of an ordinal α as the least ordinal ν such that $\alpha < \Omega_{\nu+1}$. One can easily prove

$$\theta \alpha \Omega_\nu = \Omega_\nu \text{ for } \nu \neq 0.$$

Therefore, $\theta \alpha \beta$ and β have the same level.

The ordinals of level 0 are the ordinals of the first and second number class, that means of all finite and countable infinite ordinals.

There is a notation system for ordinals which denotes exactly those ordinals which can be expressed only by combining the symbols $0, +, \theta, \Omega$ in a correct way. We will call this notation system $\theta(\Omega)$.

A certain generalization of this notation system was at first investigated by J. Bridge (1972). Afterwards, W. Buchholz (1974) could prove that the ordering relation of this generalized system and therefore also of $\theta(\Omega)$ is decidable. (In fact it is primitive recursive according to the proof of Buchholz). Therefore, the notation system $\theta(\Omega)$ can be used for constructive investigations in proof theory, especially for consistency proofs.

Let $\theta_0(\Omega)$ be the set of ordinals of level 0 which are denoted in the system $\theta(\Omega)$. This set is exactly a segment of ordinals.

$$\theta_0(\Omega) = \{\xi \mid \xi < \theta \Lambda 0\},$$

where Λ is the least ordinal such that $\Omega_\Lambda = \Lambda$. Of course, Λ and $\theta \Lambda 0$ do not belong to the notation system. Λ is the least ordinal such that no ordinal $\geqslant \Lambda$ belongs to $\theta(\Omega)$, and $\theta \Lambda 0$ is the least ordinal which does not belong to $\theta(\Omega)$.

We are interested only in the ordinals of the segment $\theta_0(\Omega)$. Ordinals of higher levels are only used as auxiliary symbols in the notations of ordinals $< \theta \Lambda 0$.

For technical reasons, it is convenient to use a modification $\overline{\theta}(\Omega)$ of the notation system $\theta(\Omega)$ to obtain unique notations for the ordinals. But this system $\overline{\theta}(\Omega)$ denotes the same ordinals as $\theta(\Omega)$. It is not necessary here to explain the system $\overline{\theta}(\Omega)$.

I have now to speak about proof theoretical investigations of some subsystems of classical analysis.

We consider a formal system of classical second order arithmetic with two kinds of variables:

$a, b, ..., x, y, z$ for natural numbers,
$U, V, ..., X, Y, Z$ for sets of natural numbers

with quantification on both kinds of variables.

The formal language may contain also numerals denoting the natural numbers, symbols for primitive recursive functions and the usual logical symbols. If $A(x)$ is a formula of this language, then we obtain by *comprehension* the set-term $\{x \mid A(x)\}$ denoting the set of natural numbers x for which $A(x)$ holds. The axioms and inference rules are the usual logical axioms and inference rules and the Peano axioms for natural numbers including the formalized mathematical induction, furthermore the axioms for primitive recursive functions. If comprehension is allowed in general, then the formal system represents the whole classical theory of real numbers. One can define subsystems by certain restrictions of comprehension.

Instead of the formal system one can also consider a semi-formal system in which the mathematical induction is replaced by the stronger ω-rule

$$A(n) \text{ for each numeral } n \vdash \forall x A(x).$$

A proof-figure of such a semi-formal system is an infinite tree whose depth can be described by an ordinal.

There was a question of Kreisel about the predicative provability of well-orderings. This problem was solved 1961. It was proved that there is an ordinal

$$\Gamma_0 = \theta \Omega_1 0 \text{ (in the notation system } \theta(\Omega))$$

such that for any ordinal $\alpha < \Gamma_0$ there is a well-ordering of order type α which can be proved in a predicative way to be well-ordered. But there does not exist a well-ordering of order type $\geqslant \Gamma_0$ whose well-ordering is provable in a strict predicative way.

This leads to a characterization of those parts of classical analysis which can be interpreted in a predicative way. Kreisel (1960) suggested to characterize predicativity by the restriction of comprehension to Δ_1^1-formulas. That means that the only predicative comprehension besides the elementary arithmetical comprehension is of the kind

$$\{x \mid \forall Y A(x, Y)\}$$

if an equivalence

$$\forall Y A(x, Y) \leftrightarrow \exists Y B(x, Y)$$

is provable where $A(x, Y)$ and $B(x, Y)$ do not contain other bound set variables than Y.

This characterization of predicativity could be verified by S. Feferman (1962) in the following way. Feferman proved that a semi-formal system of second order arithmetic can be interpreted in a predicative system of ramified analysis if comprehension is restricted to Δ_1^1-formulas and the depths of the proof-figures are restricted to ordinals $<\Gamma_0$. In this way, one obtains the most general part of classical analysis which can be interpreted in a strict predicative way. Feferman gave also some other characterizations of predicativity which are very close to the mentioned characterization.

If we consider only the formal system of second order arithmetic with the usual mathematical induction instead of the ω-rule, where all proof-figures are finite, then we obtain by the restriction of comprehension to Δ_1^1-formulas the formal system of Δ_1^1-analysis. The consistency of this system is provable by transfinite induction up to

$$\theta\omega 0 = \theta(\theta 0(\theta 00))0$$

in the notation system $\theta(\Omega)$.

A much stronger formal system as this system of Δ_1^1-analysis is the formal system of Π_1^1-analysis. This is the formal system of second order arithmetic with only the following set-terms:

(1) $\{x \mid \forall Y A(x, Y)\}$ where $A(x, Y)$ does not contain another bound set variable than Y.

(2) Set-terms which are obtained from set-terms by substitutions of set-terms for free set variables and by first order operations.

The consistency of this formal system of Π_1^1-analysis was proved at first by G. Takeuti (1967). His paper gives also a consistency proof for the formal system of Π_1^1-analysis with bar-induction for arithmetical relations. The proofs were given by transfinite induction on well-orderings which Takeuti described by ordinal diagrams.

In the meantime, we know the limiting numbers for several formal systems. We will say that an ordinal λ is the *limiting number* of a formal system Σ if the following holds:

(1) The consistency of Σ is provable by transfinite induction up to λ.

(2) For any $\alpha < \lambda$ there is a well-ordering of order type α which can be proved in Σ to be well-ordered.

It follows by the theorems of Gödel that in this case λ is the least ordinal such that the consistency of Σ is provable by transfinite induction up to λ.

I will call *elementary analysis* the formal system of second order arithmetic where comprehension is restricted to arithmetical formulas that means to formulas which do not contain bound set variables.

Then, we have the following limiting numbers for the following formal systems:

formal system	limiting numbers	
Pure number theory	$\epsilon_0 = \theta 1 0$	(G. Gentzen)
Elementary analysis	$\theta 1 \epsilon_0$	(W. Tait)
Δ_1^1-analysis	$\theta \omega 0$	(W. Tait)
Π_1^1-analysis	$\theta(\Omega_\omega \cdot \epsilon_0)0$	(W. Buchholz)
Π_1^1-an + *BI*	$\theta \epsilon_{\Omega_\omega + 1} 0$	(W. Pohlers)
Δ_2^1-analysis	$\theta \Omega_{\epsilon_0} 0$	(H. M. Friedman, W. Pohlers)

There is a close connection between Π_1^1-analysis and systems of generalized inductive definitions. The well-orderings up to the limiting numbers of Π_1^1-analysis and stronger systems are not provable in a predicative way. But they are provable in some general systems of generalized inductive definitions.

The limiting numbers for Π_1^1-analysis without or with bar-induction are not to obtain from the original consistency proofs of Takeuti. They are obtained by investigations about the precise connections between Π_1^1-comprehension and generalized inductive definitions. In this way using results of Friedman also the limiting number for Δ_2^1-analysis could be obtained.

I spoke about consistency proofs by transfinite induction, and I want to add some remarks about the other method to prove consistency by interpretations.

Gödel's interpretation of pure number theory was generalized in a certain way by C. Spector (1962) to a formal system of the whole classical theory of real numbers. His interpretation gives a consistency proof which is by no means constructive, but it uses only methods of a natural extension of intuitionistic mathematics.

There are also, for instance by W. Howard, consistency proofs established for weaker systems of intuitionistic mathematics by interpretation as well as by the corresponding transfinite induction.

Of course, there are also many other important investigations and results in proof theory which I cannot mention here in short time.

Munich

BIBLIOGRAPHY

[1] Feferman, S., 'Systems of Predicative Analysis', *J. Symbolic Logic* 29 (1964), 1–30.

[2] Gödel, K., 'Über eine bisher noch nicht benützte Erweiterung des finiten Standpunktes', *Dialectica* 12 (1958), 280–287.

[3] Hilbert, D. and Bernays, P., *Grundlagen der Mathematik I, II*, Springer-Verlag, Heidelberg, New York 1968, 1970.

[4] Schütte, K., *Proof Theory*, Springer-Verlag, Berlin, Heidelberg, New York 1977.

[5] Spector, C., 'Provably Recursive Functionals of Analysis: A Consistency Proof of Analysis by an Extension of Principles Formulated in Current Intuitionistic Mathematics', *Proc. Symp. Pure Math. AMS* V (1962), 1–27.

[6] Takeuti, G., *Proof Theory*, North-Holland Publ. Co., Amsterdam 1975.

ANGUS MACINTYRE

MODEL THEORY

0. INTRODUCTION

I have been invited to talk in Section 1 (Pure Logic), and not in Section 2, (The Interplay between Logic and Mathematics). Since model theory is surely the scene of most interplay between logic and mathematics, and since I am uncertain as to what pure model theory is or should be, I have had problems in delineating an appropriate subject matter.

In my view, model theory is now a mathematical discipline, increasingly detached from foundational questions. It is evident that the subject began from the foundational activity of the period 1870–1930. The ideas emerging then were:

(a) Formal languages
(b) Interpretations of languages
(c) Truth
(d) Definability in formal languages.

Of course, the decisive theorem, Gödel's completeness theorem of 1930, involves in its very formulation the notion of formal derivability. From a naive point of view, the latter notion is not regarded as model-theoretic, but it has long been recognized that analysis of derivability is a powerful method in definability theory. In particular, much of infinitary model theory was first established by proof-theoretic methods. But later in the evolution of a model theory, the list of basic concepts has dwindled to:

Language L;
L-formulas;
L-structures;
satisfaction.

It is worthwhile at the beginning to seek a distinction between model theory and the older subject of universal algebra. It is not enough to say that universal algebra does not deal with satisfaction. Obviously it does. But it deals only with a restricted class of formulas (e.g. universal identities, formulas without relation symbols). So there is absolutely no problem in defining satisfaction. The real distinction comes in the use of existential quantifiers.

E. Agazzi (ed.), Modern Logic – A Survey, 45–65.

This seen, one can ask for disciplines beyond classical model theory. These may occur by varying the notions of structure, language, or satisfaction.

My intention is to locate the forces that acted on model theory in its escape from the foundations of mathematics. I will argue that the strongest forces have been from algebra and topology. In the light of this explanation, one can pose questions about future directions in model theory.

During the period of reflection prior to writing the paper, my prejudices have shifted very little. Loosely speaking, I belong to Robinson's school in model theory. I want to see model theory taking constructions from mathematics, generalizing them, and giving back applications.

I draw the reader's attention to interesting articles by Chang and Vaught in the Tarski birthday volume [Chapter VII]. I believe that the purpose of these articles is similar to that of mine, but the authors belong to a different school, and stress different aspects of the subject. The difference shows itself in our attitudes towards set theory, but it is not easy to make precise. Later I will hazard some remarks on this.

I thank Kreisel for some penetrating observations.

1. THE BEGINNING

I cannot improve on Vaught's discussion of model theory before 1945, but I want to supplement some of his remarks.

1.1. By the first decade of this century one had a presentation of higher order logic as a formalized deductive system. Though the distinction between first-order and higher-order logic could be made, there was no reason to stress it. The future would show that the model theory of first-order logic contains many important and difficult theorems. We still do not know if there is a mathematically interesting model theory of higher-order logic.

1.2. Several interesting categorical axiom systems were known, for example Peano's axioms for $\mathbb{N}$ and Cantor's axioms for $\mathbb{R}$. One of the first achievements of model theory would be to reveal the essential role of higher-order logic in this categoricity.

1.3. There was no need to have a precise mathematical definition of truth or satisfaction in order to prove the fundamental theorems of model theory (Löwenheim–Skolem Theorems, Completeness/Compactness Theorem). Tarski's definition of truth works for higher-order logic, but led to no real progress in the model theory of higher-order logic.

1.4. By virtue of Lindstrom's remarkable result, the Downward Löwenheim–Skolem Theorem and the Compactness Theorem characterize first-order logic in an informative way. So in some sense every theorem in first order model theory is a consequence of these early theorems. Kreisel stresses another aspect of Lindstrom's discovery, namely that when we try to go beyond first order logic we must seek new general ideas, since we know in advance that we cannot take the classical ideas with us.

1.5. The basic notions of model theory are:
(i) a (first-order) logic L;
(ii) formulas and sentences σ of L;
(iii) structures M for L;
(iv) the notion $M \models \sigma$ (σ holds in M).
The basic theorems are:

THEOREM 1 (Compactness: Gödel–Malcev). If Σ is a set of L-sentences, and every finite subset of Σ has a model, then Σ has a model.

THEOREM 2 (Löwenheim–Skolem). If Σ has a model M of cardinal $K \geqslant$ card (L), and X is a subset of M, then there is a substructure N of M with $X \subseteq N \subseteq M$, $N \models \Sigma$, and card $(N) = \max(\text{card}(X), \text{card}(L))$.

Remarks. (α) For L countable, Theorem 1 is a trivial consequence of Gödel's Completeness Theorem. The latter theorem is perhaps the culmination of the foundational effort of the Hilbert school (but see [26, pp. 104–108]), and (for me at least) though very satisfying is not surprising. Theorem 1 can still surprise me. Note also that from the standpoint of proof theory the transition to uncountable languages is unmotivated. But from the standpoint of the algebraist Malcev the utility of uncountable languages in embedding problems was clear.

(β) Theorem 2 is easier to prove than Theorem 1. It needs only Skolem functions, prenex normal form, and the notion of the closure of a set under a set of functions. Notice that Skolemization, whether of structures or of axioms, tends to make model theory look even more like universal algebra. Nevertheless, the theorem revealed a foundational point of basic importance, namely the existence of nonstandard ϵ-models of set theory. Later the upward Löwenheim–Skolem Theorem would yield the existence of nonstandard models of first-order number theory. So a simple theorem has substantial foundational consequences. And, in addition, the method of Skolemization, in various refinements, has been involved in some of the deepest work in mathematical logic (e.g. Gödel's work on the continuum hypothesis, the work of Ehrenfeucht-Mostowski on automorphisms, and Jensen's fine structure of the constructible universe).

(γ) The interpretation of Theorem 2 is that the notion *uncountable* is not first-order definable (although it is definable in higher-order logic). Similarly, the notion *finite* is not first-order definable. (This is a simple consequence of the Compactness Theorem). And, finally, the notion *countable* ist not first-order definable, because of

THEOREM 3 (Upward Löwenheim–Skolem Theorem. Due to Malcev), If Σ has a model of cardinal $\geqslant \aleph_0$ then Σ has a model in each cardinal $\geqslant$ card (L).

Theorem 3 follows easily from Theorems 1 and 2 using Malcev's method of constants. The latter comes naturally from the notion of the multiplication table of a group, and in the hands of Malcev and Robinson [44] gave an efficient uniform method for proving embedding theorems in algebra.

(δ) The topological significance of Theorem 1 was quickly apparent, no doubt because of Tarski. One had his foundational work on the methodology of deductive systems, in particular the isolation of *theories* as mathematical objects. In addition there was his work on the topological interpretation of propositional calculi, culminating in his version of Stone duality. From these insights one could interpret Theorem 1 as expressing the compactness of a space of theories. Already in 1937 Mostowski applied the Cantor–Bendixson Theorem to this space to obtain definitive results on the number of complete extensions of countable theories. This method still flourishes. The greatest success came in Morley's solution of the Łos Conjecture, and even more recently there have been important applications to the still unresolved Vaught Conjecture [57].

(ϵ) Part of Stone's theory concerns the equivalence between Boolean algebras and Boolean rings. This may at first sight seem a formal curiosity. But from Stone's paper there issued a long (and continuing) series of papers on representation of rings. The modern descendants of Stone's Theorem are theorems about sheaf representations of semisimple rings.

Theorem 1 is little more than Stone's Theorem. For example, Kreisel and Krivine [29] obtain Theorem 1 using just Skolemization and arguments relating to Stone's Theorem. And Halmos showed that Theorem 1 is essentially equivalent to the semisimplicity of polyadic algebras (where

$$\frac{\text{propositional calculus}}{\text{Boolean algebras}} = \frac{\text{predicate calculus}}{\text{polyadic algebras}}).$$

So the Compactness Theorem can be made to look very algebraic. And the space of complete theories relates readily to the prime spectrum of a ring.

(ϕ) I think it is worth noting that Theorems 1 and 3 lead to a very remarkable algebraic conclusion. Steinitz had proved that any two algebraically closed fields of the same characteristic and the same uncountable cardinality are isomorphic. (The proof uses transcendence bases, and the Steinitz Exchange Lemma). On the basis of this fact, and the model theory above one can prove: Any injective morphism of an algebraic variety to itself is surjective.

In the special case of $\mathbb{C}$, the field of complex numbers, the result can be proved by appeal to the theory of analytic functions of several complex variables. So the key ingredients are connectedness and local compactness.

For the general case, one can get pleasure by putting the question to an algebraic geometer and watching him squirm.

One should note that the application was not observed until 1968, by [2]. An algebraic proof may be found (or may not be found) in Gröthendieck [18].

2. DEFINABILITY

2.1. In (ϕ) above, the appeal to Steinitz can be avoided because of Tarski's famous quantifier-elimination for algebraically closed fields [54]. Tarski proved:

THEOREM 4. For each formula $\phi(v_1, ..., v_n)$ of the language of field theory one can effectively find a formula $\psi(v_1, ..., v_n)$ without quantifiers such that the equivalence $\phi \leftrightarrow \psi$ follows from the axioms for algebraically closed fields.

Is this model theory or algebra? If we regard it as a study of the first-order definable subsets of say $\mathbb{C}^n$, then it is model theory. But it is as well to remember that there is a famous theorem of algebraic geometry from the same period (due to Chevalley) which is obviously the *algebraic* version of Tarski's result.

Note too that in the above Tarski used neither compactness or Löwenheim–Skolem (so that the theorem has useful extensions to richer logics [24]). Later Robinson found a proof based on compactness, via that part of Steinitz's theory which gives existence and uniqueness of algebraic closure.

2.2. In Tarski we find systematic model-theoretic study of definability in arbitrary structures. In Gödel's wonderful 1931 paper [17] we have a very different study of definability, concerning the most basic of all mathematical structures, ℕ. For example, there is the ingenious proof that on ℕ exponentiation is first-order definable from addition and multiplication. (Notice that the situation is quite different on ℝ, by Tarski's work). More generally, Gödel studies the number-theoretic relations on ℕ invariantly defined in all models of a given axiom system, thereby giving the recursive relations a model-theoretic interpretation.

Gödel's 2nd Incompleteness Theorem has of course startling model-theoretic implications about first-order Peano arithmetic (e.g. the existence of models containing an infinitely long 'proof' of $0 = 1$). But it took many years before the theorem itself could be obtained via model theory. This was first done by Kreisel in [27]. Recently Paris and Kirby have developed model-theoretic techniques yielding the unprovability in Peano arithmetic of true variants of Ramsey's Theorem in finite combinations [41].

After Matejasevic [36] completed the negative solution of Hilbert's 10th Problem, one could obtain the existence of diophantine incorrect nonstandard models of P (first-order Peano arithmetic). We say a model is diophantine correct if every diophantine equation over ℕ, unsolvable in ℕ, remains unsolvable in the model. Long before Matejasevic, Rabin had applied elementary model theory to Gödel's work to show that every nonstandard model M of P has an extension M_1, also a model of P, so that some diophantine equation over M, unsolvable over M, has a solution in M_1. (Taking a concept from field theory, one might say that M is not algebraically closed among models of P.)

2.3. To my mind, the other great theorem up to 1945 is Tarski's quantifier-elimination for ℝ. (It seems that the idea for such a theorem originated with Herbrand). Tarski, in the 1948 version [54], was well aware that this analysis works for real closed fields, and consequently that any first-order theorem about ℝ, even if the only natural proof involves topology of ℝ, is true for any real closed field. As is well-known now [22], this has deep consequence, e.g. for nonassociative division algebras over real closed fields. In analytical situations (e.g. partial differential equations, or generalized functions [14, 21] Tarski's theorem for ℝ has been very useful.

2.4. Another early contribution of Tarski is a converse, in higher-order logic, to Padoa's method for establishing undefinability. This is not hard, needing only the Dedekind-Frege explicit version of inductive definition. (Gödel, in proving that primitive recursive sets are first-order definable, had crossed this method with the Chinese Remainder Theorem).

Still to come was Beth's beautiful theorem, the converse to Padoa for first-order logic. This can be proved from Theorem 1, or by proof-theoretic means. The theorem has rarely proved useful in practise, until now, despite its obvious position as an analogue of the Completeness Theorem. The only exception known to me is [60]. Various attractive reformulations, and topological interpretations, can be found in [42].

3. 1945–1955

In this period model theory fanned out in various directions. Apart from Beth's theorem, the main achievements are readily related to algebra and topology.

3.1. A convenient starting point is Henkin's new proof [19] of the completeness theorem. Both in this proof, and in much of Robinson's work of this time, the method of *constants* is basic. As mentioned, this goes back to Malcev.

3.2. In Henkin's work there is precise discussion of nonstandard models for higher-order logic. The idea is to construe a standard structure for say second-order logic as a two-sorted structure for an extended first-order logic. Basically we adjoin all the sets of our domain to our domain, and we now distinguish an additional relation, *membership*. If we have some axiom Σ in higher-order logic, let Σ^* be the obvious induced axioms in the many sorted logic. The key point is that some models of Σ^* do not arise from standard models of Σ. So, although there is no compactness theorem for higher-order logic with the standard semantics, one can get a 'fake' compactness theorem by allowing nonstandard models in which set quantification means not quantification over all subsets of a set, but quantification over some prescribed subcollection of subsets of a set.

One could be forgiven for doubting the value of these nonstandard models. However in Robinson's hands they later proved illuminating for many branches of mathematics.

3.3. In the 1930's Garrett Birkhoff proved his famous theorem which characterized varieties of algebras as classes closed under the natural operations of substructures, homomorphic images and direct products. This stimulated a search for corresponding theorems in first-order logic. Many such preservation theorems were found. A typical form is: If the class of models of σ is closed under ...., then σ is logically equivalent to something of the form ~~~~~~~~.

More general versions apply to formulas and properties, and are part of definability theory. The theorems are typically proved by elementary compactness arguments. Specimens are

(a) Łos–Tarski (sentences preserved under substructures are equivalent to universal sentences);

(b) Chang–Łos–Suszko (sentences preserved under direct limits are equivalent to universal-existential sentences).

Only Robinson systematically tried to apply these results to algebra.

3.4. Robinson worked mainly with the dual of the Łos–Tarski theorem, namely the theorem identifying existentially defined properties as those preserved under extension. There is an obvious relativized version (relative to an axiom system).

From the start he used this result as a main technique in his metamathematical project for generalizing notions related to *algebraic*.

Much of the remainder of my talk will deal with the unravelling of the tangle of notions around *algebraic*. I do not claim that a result in model theory is uninteresting if it does not come from this explication, but the results that most fascinate me all come thence.

3.5. Tarski's Limit Theorem was first published in 1957 (though from Vaught's article it appears that Tarski knew this much earlier). This is an absolutely fundamental result of mathematical model theory (whereas it seems without interest for the foundations of logic). It uses no compactness, and in fact applies to $L_{\infty,\omega}$ (see Barwise's talk). It gives us the always powerful method of 'passage to the limit'. From the standpoint of category theory, it reveals the advantage of elementary maps over arbitrary injections. (This advantage would be consolidated later, regarding the amalgamation property. See my later remarks on homogeneous-universal models).

3.6. In 1952 Mostowski proved the natural result that the theory of a product of two structures depends only on the respective theories of the two structures. His proof is elementary and constructive, so yielding decidability results. The main result allows one to define unambiguously the product of two complete theories, and from his proof one can see that with this product the space of complete theories (for a given L) is a topological semigroup. If one then applies the theorem of topological algebra that a compact totally disconnected semigroup is a projective limit of finite semigroups, one is led to the notion of autonomous system which Galvin used much later in an important paper [16].

Mostowski's theorem was the forerunner for similar theorems involving various operations on structures. The paper of Feferman–Vaught [13] remains the classic on this subject. Because of the generally constructive nature of their proofs, these theorems can be useful in proving decidability of important algebraic systems.

3.7. There is no doubt that in his early work Robinson was trying to generalize *relatively algebraically closed* from field theory. Tarski's theorems on quantifier elimination for fields were Robinson's inspiration. But Robinson quickly realized that Tarski's methods are special. (In the later history of the subject no hard theorem was ever proved first by quantifier-elimination. However, as Kreisel points out, the recent applications to algebra of rapid quantifier-elimination, e.g. by Brown and Monk [9, 39], give sharp estimates apparently unobtainable by any other method of model theory.) So Robinson had to generalize Tarski's concepts. He saw that Tarski's theorem for algebraically closed fields gives a (weak) version of that cornerstone of classical algebraic geometry, Hilbert's Nullstellensatz. (For this version, see Lang [30] and Robinson [44]). Then he saw the converse, which is now the famous Robinson's Test. I choose to formulate it nonstandardly (I have a lengthier discussion in [34, 35]. He essentially defined the notion of a theory having the Nullstellensatz, and proved (by compactness and Tarski's Limit Theorem) that if T has the Nullstellensatz then relative to T every formula is equivalent to an existential formula. (Notice that one cannot replace existential by quantifier-free, but one get Tarski's Theorem from Hilbert's Nullstellensatz by an auxiliary compactness argument [44].) In the above situation, T is called model-complete, and it is easily seen that T is model-complete precisely when any embedding between models of T is elementary.

Robinson gave an independent proof of Tarski's theorem for algebraically closed fields, without using the Nullstellensatz. The essential idea is to use a compactness argument and the Steinitz theory. From Steinitz one takes the basic observations about transcendense bases, and the existence and uniqueness of the algebraic closure of a field. See [44].

Now here are notions to generalize! Let us list some:

(i) algebraic extension;

(ii) relatively algebraically closed;
(iii) transcendence base;
(iv) algebraic closure.

None of these notions has been easy to generalize, but by now, due to the efforts of several model-theorists of different persuasions, we have quite a rich and useful mathematical analysis of them.

Robinson flopped on (i). (See [44]). I know of nothing he did on (iii). For (iv) he established a beautiful theory, although he left many essential problems untouched.

I have mentioned the operation of algebraic closure on fields. This carries fields to algebraically closed fields. There is an analogous closure operation on ordered fields, yielding real-closed fields. The operation has uniqueness properties formally identical to those for algebraic closure. From this Robinson could give a new proof of Tarski's theorem on real closed fields.

So one wants some notion of *closed* models for a given theory, and a uniqueness theorem for embeddings in closed models. Even now this has not been obtained in a general setting, though Shelah [52] has proved some very remarkable theorems in this direction. Robinson took a different track. He described a relation between *theories*: T^* is a model-completion of T. The original case was:

T = theory of fields,
T^* = theory of algebraically closed fields.

For expository purposes, it is easier to consider a much later notion [4]:

T^* is a model-companion of T.

This means that every model of T is embeddable in a model of T^*, and vice versa and T^* is model complete.

Robinson proved, by construction of a suitable limit model, that T^* is *unique*, if it exists. (Much later [4] he and his associates considered the existence problem). So we have here a metamathematical version of algebraic closure.

Robinson's methods gave absolutely no information about a closure operation on models of T, when T^* exists. We now know that there is in general no uniqueness statement.

This development gave back to algebra several nice applications. The first was Robinson's elegant treatment [44] of Hilbert's 17th Problem, dispensing with the difficult specialization arguments of Artin. The other was Robinson's invention, on the basis of Seidenberg's elimination theory [50], of the class of differentially closed fields (at first only in characteristic 0). This was a strange case. One could construct the model completion of the theory of differential fields of characteristic 0, but one knew nothing about uniqueness of differential closure for differential fields.

Finally, there is no dispute that Robinson's proof for R, and his clear exposure of the structure of the proof, gave one a model for analyzing other interesting fields, e.g. Q_p. For more detail, and a discussion of the achievement of Ax–Kochen–Ersov, see [35].

4. 1955–1968

4.1. One can conveniently summarize this period by saying that powerful methods became available for constructing a variety of models for a particular theory. Previously, the only difference one could impose on models of a theory was a difference in cardinality (Theorems 2 and 3). Research now focused on the problem of categoricity in power. A theory is κ-categorical if all its models of power κ are isomorphic. Stray examples were known. For $\kappa > \aleph_0$, one had the Steinitz theorem for algebraically closed fields of fixed characteristic. For $\kappa = \aleph_0$, one had Cantor's theorem for dense linear order (topological characterization of Q). An extension of Cantor's theorem had been obtained by Hausdorff, for the so-called η_α-sets. Quite amazingly, from the few clues in those examples, a rich metamathematical theory arose.

4.2. Perhaps the best known construction in model theory is the ultraproduct construction [51]. This was anticipated by Skolem in his 1934 construction of nonstandard models of arithmetic, and it has antecedents also in functional analysis. In 1954 Łos proved his theorem relating the theory of an ultraproduct to the theories of the factors (cf. Section 3.6). It was quickly realized (see for example [51]) that the theorem gives Theorem 1 and 3 'in a more algebraic way'. In addition, the construction is functorial, and enables one to eliminate gruesome syntactic arguments. (Kochen's [59] is a beautiful demonstration of the elegance of the method). Finally, the deep Keisler–Shelah Theorem [51] enables one to give an algebraic definition of elementary equivalence and elementary maps. So vast organizational simplifications are possible.

However, it seems that the above list exhausts the truly essential uses of ultraproducts in obtaining important new results. The mean research on ultraproducts is a part of topology or set theory, and is painfully involved with independence questions.

4.3. In [32] Łos formulated his very fertile conjecture, which inspired some of the best work in the subject. He conjectured that a countable theory categorical in one uncountable power is categorical in any other uncountable power. The intuition must have been that a theorem about uncountable categoricity must come from a transcendence base phenomenon, as in algebraically closed fields or vector spaces.

4.4. The first breakthrough came with the paper [12] of Ehrenfeucht and Mostowski. From their work came deep applications to algebra, set theory, and functional analysis [28, 52, 53]. One can interpret their achievement as coming through the following transmutation of an analogy from algebra. How do you make a group act on a field? Since any group is embeddable in symmetric group, it suffices to make a symmetric group act. Obviously a symmetric groups acts (by permutation of the generators) on a free field, i.e. a purely transcendental extension of a base field. So to get automorphism of general models of a theory T one should try to get a model freely generated by a set.

By Skolemization one reduces to the case where T has a universal set of axioms. Then one sees an obstruction for orders. For if $x < y$ then one cannot permute x and y to get an automorphism. The amazing thing is that this is the only obstruction. One arrives at a notion of order indiscernibility, and proves the existence of models with indiscernibles. So any group of automorphisms of an ordered set can act on some model of T. Two proofs are known, the original using Ramsey's Theorem, and Gaifman's functorial proof [15] using iterated ultrapowers.

The mere existence of models with automorphisms can easily be obtained using saturated models (see Section 4.8). It was the invention of indiscernibility which was critical for the future. One had arrived at the notion by isolating one feature of transcendence bases in Steinitz's theory, namely that the field generated by a transcendence base is acted on by automorphisms of the base.

An interesting point, not immediately observed, is the existence of Stretching Theorems [24] for indiscernibles, and consequently an approach to the analogue of Theorem 3 for infinitary logic.

4.5. *Types.* Next, Ehrenfeucht made the first advance on the Łos Conjecture, via a fundamental omitting types theorem.

The *type* of an n-tuple of elements over a set in a model generalizes notions like *minimum polynomial, ideal, variety* from commutative algebra.

See [51] for the definition. To attack the Łos Conjecture one must construct models omitting certain types.

For countable models it is not difficult to do this, by the fundamental Omitting Types Theorem (see Section 4.7 below). However for uncountable models no simple method works. Ehrenfeucht's achievement was the construction of uncountable models realizing few types, by choosing models generated by indiscernibles with special order types. These models are now called E–M models.

4.6. By 1960 it had become commonplace to talk of the space of complete theories. For a given T the set of n-types, $S_n(T)$, has a corresponding topology. Recalling the analogy above (types as ideals), one sees that one was dealing with the same sort of space as Stone and his successors (e.g. Jacobson) in representation theory of rings.

One striking feature from this point on was that advances in model theory could come from applying to space like $S_n(T)$ such classical theorems of general topology as Baire's Theorem and the Cantor–Bendixson Theorem. It is worth noticing that the above algebraists never applied this method, sometimes to their cost (recently Miraglia [37] used topological selection theorems to obtain sharp representation theorems for biregular rings, a subject stalled for many years).

The Łos Conjecture was solved by Morley in [38], in a paper widely regarded as the most beautiful of the subject. He used the Cantor–Bendixson Theorem, which originally analyzed closed sets in $\mathbb{R}$, to give a classification of types over a theory T. Ehrenfeucht's work yields that for T κ-categorical ($\kappa > \aleph_0$) the spaces $S_n(T)$ (and various natural extensions) are countable. This means that they get 'filtered to 0' by iteration of the Cantor–Bendixson derivative. The types filtered out at stage 0 are the isolated (or algebraic) types. At stage 1 one filters out the types isolated among the 'transcendental' types left. And so on. Here we have a very sophisticated metamathematical analysis of *algebraic* and *ideal*. Types have *ranks*, which are ordinals, and *degrees*, which are integers. Powerful inductive arguments are made possible. The theories to which Morley's analysis applies are now called ω-stable (they needn't be $\aleph_1$-categorical). Later it appeared [7, 52] that in concrete algebraic situations such theories have natural *artinian* and *noetherian* properties.

A fundamental technical point is that in ω-stable theories order indiscernibility implies full indiscernibility. Another useful point is that it is often easy to prove that a theory is ω-stable.

In the course of his analysis Morly made a major contribution to the study of closure operations on models. Suppose M is an L-structure embeddable in a model of T. A prime extension of M to a model of T is an embedding

$$M \longrightarrow M^*$$

of M into a model of T, so that for any other such $M \longrightarrow M^\#$ we have an elementary map $M^* \longrightarrow M^\#$ so that

$$\begin{array}{ccc} M & \longrightarrow & M^* \\ & \searrow & \downarrow \\ & & M^\# \end{array}$$

commutes. Morley proved that if T is ω-stable then an embedding $M \longrightarrow M^*$ always exists. Then a simple back and forth argument shows that if M is countable the embedding $M \longrightarrow M^*$ is unique up to isomorphism over M. For general M, no uniqueness statement was evident.

Notice of course that when T is the theory of algebraically closed fields, $M \longrightarrow M^*$ is the embedding of M in its algebraic closure. Morley's work does not immediately apply to ordered fields, since then T is not ω-stable, but it is simple to adapt his ideas to take account of this case [49].

Blum [8] exploited those ideas to prove the existence of a differential closure for differential fields of characteristic 0, thereby resolving a problem of Robinson (cf. Section 3.7).

4.7. *Countable models.* The fundamental theorem about countable models is the Omitting Types Theorem. This says (for countable L) that a non-isolated member of $S_n(T)$ can be omitted in some countable model. The relevance for the problem of $\aleph_0$-categoricity is immediate, and one obtains the striking and useful theorem that T is $\aleph_0$-categorical if and only if each $S_n(T)$ is finite [48]. For the easier half of the theorem, Cantor's back and forth argument is used (as it is in Morley, in an uncountable version). The Omitting Types Theorem is the main tool in Vaught's classic paper [58], where there are applications to the theory of prime models, further advancing our analysis of *algebraic*.

We now see that the Omitting Types Theorem is simply the Baire Category Theorem applied to the space of complete extensions of T in a logic got by adjoining infinitely many constants. We see it also as a forcing method, though much more primitive than Cohen's [11]. (The connection between forcing and Baire category was made by Ryll–Nardzewski and Takeuti. See [40]).

Much energy is now being expended in the search for a topological interpretation that will give the possible number of isomorphism types of countable models of a countable theory [57].

4.8. *Saturation.* Beginning with Jonsson's work of the mid 1950's, a systematic study was made of certain large structures which generalize Hausdorff's η_α-sets. For example, one may construct a group (necessarily of cardinal $\geqslant 2^{\aleph_0}$) in which all possible configurations of countable groups occur. The construction appeals to

(i) the closure of the class of groups under direct limits;

(ii) the amalgamation property for the class of groups,

as well as a transfinite enumeration. Jonsson isolated (i) and (ii) and then did an axiomatic construction of the so-called homogeneous-universal members of a class [23]. Now, as a matter of fact, this construction yields all *uncountable* algebraically closed fields. (No doubt not coincidentally, Jonsson worked through this period on a notion of *algebraic extension* of models).

Picturesquely, one may say that the homogeneous-universal members of a class **C** exhibit all possible configurations of members of **C**, subject to the obvious cardinality constraints.

Partial analogues were noted in the ultraproduct construction. For example, an ultrapower of Q is, except in trivial cases, an η_1-set. Using this sort of observation, Kochen [59] gave a new proof of Tarski's theorem on real-closed fields. Keisler realized that in suitable ultraproducts all possible types, subject to the obvious cardinality constraints, are realized [51]. From this came the notion of *saturated* models, which flourished through the 1960's, and is now being replaced by cardinality-insensitive analogues [6]. From a metamathematical standpoint, it makes sense to say that saturated models have the maximum compactness possible, although they are generally not compact in any natural topology.

A definitive account is in Morley–Vaught [33], where the existence of saturated models and homogeneous-universal models is derived from a category-theoretic generalization of Jonsson's method.

In his 1967 thesis [43] Reyes gave an approach to homogeneous-universal models via a κ-Baire space for relational systems. The connection to Cohen genericity is clearly revealed (generic objects are homogeneous-universal). Finally there is an application of the topological structure of the group of automorphisms of a generic structure to problems in definability theory.

4.9. *Nonstandard analysis.* In 1960 Robinson established nonstandard analysis [45]. All the machinery was ready, saturated models and the reduction of higher-order structures to one-sorted structures. Robinson had to overcome the prejudice that elementary extensions of standard models were not sufficiently nonstandard to be interesting. (This was the predominant sentiment among workers in models of arithmetic.)

There is available a good deal of expository work on nonstandard analysis. Here I choose to remark only that it gives us a general functorial method of completing models to richer models 'satisfying' the same axioms. One of the most exciting ideas is that of replacing classical iterated limiting arguments by nonstandard counting arguments. It seems now that nonstandard analysis yields major foundational improvements and powerful new techniques in measure theory, notably in potential theory [31] and stochastic processes [1]. Of course I am not forgetting the connection to Leibnitz, but that story doesn't need retelling.

In an unfinished program, Robinson applied the method to number theory [46]. The relevance for profinite groups and Haar measure arguments is clear. But it takes deep insight to think the method can interact with ideas from diophantine approximation. It does [47]. It is however too soon to say if model theory can lead to advances in diophantine geometry.

5. 1968–1977

This takes us into the period after Cohen's revolution in set theory.

5.1. *Forcing.* Everyone looked for uses of Cohen's method in model theory. These didn't come immediately. As mentioned above, Reyes made a reasonable application, in 1967. But these was no hint of the combinatorial suppleness of the uses of forcing in set theory. It is worth noting that one can use Cohen's method to get an exciting nonstandard analysis, but not Robinson nonstandard analysis (Takeuti [55]).

From 1969 onwards Robinson developed various notions of forcing relative to a first-order theory T. The forcing conditions were fragments of diagrams of models of T. If one uses finite fragments, one gets finite forcing. If one uses arbitrary fragments, one gets infinite forcing. The notion

p forces Φ

is defined, following Cohen, in the obvious way. One gets two notions to study:

(a) Generic structures, where forcing and satisfaction coincide;
(b) The forcing companion (theory of the generic structures).

Let us assume L is countable. Then both kinds of generic structures exist. Most remarkably:

THEOREM (Barwise–Robinson). If T has a model-companion T^*, then T^* is (either) forcing companion.

So, even though T^* does not exist in general, one has several metamathematical completion processes which give it when it does exist.

Although it could have been done twenty years earlier, only now did one get a definition of *algebraically closed* for models of an arbitrary theory. An L-structure M is T – e.c. (T existentially closed) if M is embeddable in a model of T and whenever $M \subseteq N \models T$ and $\Phi(\vec{m})$ is an existential sentence with parameters from M then $M \models \Phi(\vec{m}) \Leftrightarrow N \models \Phi(\vec{m})$. The generic structures are T – e.c. Also, a universal algebraic argument shows that every model of T is embeddable in a T – e.c. structure. When T = theory of fields, the T – e.c. structures are exactly the algebraically closed fields. When T = theory of skew fields, the T – e.c. structures form a chaotic class of skew fields [20]. Using indiscernibles in infinitary logic, one may show that they have no Steinitz structure theory.

So here is yet another case where a powerful method is linked to ideas around *algebraic*.

5.2. *The Baldwin–Lachlan Theorem.* A careful look at the analogy with algebraically closed fields leads one to the conjecture that the countable models of an $\aleph_1$-categorical theory T should be classified by some sort of transcendence degree, and so strung out linearly in type $\leqslant \omega$. One made the further conjecture that if T is not $\aleph_0$-categorical then there are exactly ω different countable models. This was proved in [3] by Baldwin–Lachlan, extending work of Marsh and Morley. This time, what was needed was an analysis of the notion of algebraic *dependence*, yet another facet of the Steinitz theory. For the details, see [3]. Let me just record that the ultimate version, *algebraic dependence* inside a minimal set, is no simple-minded generalization of Steinitz's ideas.

5.3. *Uniqueness of Prime Model Extension*. During most of the last decade Shelah has been a dominant influence on model theory. Early on he generalized ω-stability to κ-stability [52]. The notion of *stable theory* came to the center of investigations. Shelah proved that if a theory is stable then every infinite set of order indiscernibles in a model is a set of indiscernibles. The converse is not quite correct, but something very clcse to this holds. Another 'cardinal-free' characterization was given by Lachlan in [30].

Shelah has contributed many very deep theorems towards the problem that most interests him, namely finding the function that gives the number of isomorphism types of a theory T in a cardinal κ. Of course any solution is likely to uncover a structure theory, but in its present formulation I find the problem unappealing. In private conversation I call such a problem 'cardinal-sensitive', and I know no one outside of logic who cares how many models there are in general for arbitrary uncountable cardinals. I have the same squeamishness about two cardinal theorems, and above all about the generic generalized quantifier 'there exist unbearably many'.

Shelah's methods typically seem more like set theory than the model theory I have discussed till now. But sometimes they have consequences of fundamental algebraic interest. Let us recall the problem of uniqueness of prime model extension for differential fields in characteristic 0. For countable fields, this is easy. For uncountable fields, the only known proof comes from Shelah's uniqueness of prime model extension for ω-stable theories and involves a difficult argument using induction on ranks and degree [49]. His proof is a hard 'set-theoretic' argument using stationary sets. In characteristic p a similar result holds, but is even harder [52]. It is quite perplexing to obtain a (weak) structure theorem in differential algebra by heavy set-theoretic arguments. This beautiful example is what keeps me from trying to get a working definition of 'cardinal-sensitive' model theory. But I readily confess to my prejudice, and see it as explaining the difference between my account and Chang–Vaught.

The use of stationary sets to prove results in algebra is by now well established. Jensen's combinatorial principles suggest new enumerations and limit constructions impossible in conventional set theory. The best example is undoubtedly Shelah's construction of a free basis for a Whitehead group. I feel that for now no one interested in the construction of uncountable algebras should remain ignorant of model-theoretic techniques involving stationary sets, and I commend the study of generalized logics based on notions around stationary [5].

6. CONCLUDING REMARKS

I conclude with some speculations. I believe that the most significant happenings right now in model theory concern generalized models. Representation of rings, and the inspiring Grothendieck program in algebraic geometry *force* us to consider sheaves of classical structures. Reyes will no doubt explain in depth, but let me just record that we already see connections with forcing, intuitionistic logic, generalized products, and nonstandard analysis.

Coming from another direction are Keisler's starfinite models, equipped with Loeb measures [25]. Fenstad will perhaps discuss them. Keisler and associates plan to use them in applied mathematics. I plan to use them in number theory, to analyze Galois groups with Haar measure. Already there are interesting analogues of old results. Subfields of the algebraic closure of Q are classified by their Galois groups. Referring to the measure, one gets a notion of a 'generic' such field. By a result of Jarden, such fields model axioms from Ax's famous 1969 paper [2], and by later work of McKenna and me the generic fields is model-complete, but of course not algebraically closed.

Perhaps the main problem of all is to study patiently Gröthendieck's monumental work (which transformed classical algebraic geometry for the sake of formulating a cohomology theory needed for the Weil Conjectures) and to understand the metamathematical structure of this enterprise. In particular the functorial methods deserve the closest attention. Given that model theory till now has lived off ideas from commutative algebra, we can hope for future enrichment if we understand modern algebraic geometry.

Yale University

BIBLIOGRAPHY

[1] R. Anderson, 'A Nonstandard Representation for Brownian Motion and Itô Integration', *Israel Journal* 25 (1976), 9–14.

[2] J. Ax, 'The Elementary Theory of Finite Fields', *Ann. Math.* 88 (1968), 239–271.

[3] J. T. Baldwin and A. H. Lachlan, 'On Strongly Minimal Sets', *J. Symbolic Logic* 36 (1971), 79–96.

[4] J. Barwise and A. Robinson, 'Completing Theories by Forcing', *Ann. Math. Logic* 2 (1970), 119–142.

[5] J. Barwise, M. Kaufmann, and M. Makkai, 'Stationary Logic', to appear.

[6] J. Barwise and J. Schlipf, 'On Recursively Saturated Models of Arithmetic', in *Lecture Notes in Mathematics* 498, Springer-Verlag, 1975, pp. 42–55.

[7] W. Bauer, G. Cherlin, and A. Macintyre, 'Totally Categorical Groups and Rings', submitted to *J. Algebra.*

[8] L. Blum, Ph.D. Thesis, M.I.T., 1968.

[9] S. Brown, Ph.D. Thesis, Princeton, 1976.

[10] C. C. Chang, 'Model Theory 1945–1971', in *Proceedings of the Tarski Symposium*, L. Henkin *et al.* (eds.), A.M.S. Symposia Proceedings XXV, Providence, 1974, pp. 173–186.

[11] P. J. Cohen, *Set Theory and the Continuum Hypothesis*, Benjamin, New York, 1966.

[12] A. Ehrenfeucht and A. Mostowski, 'Models of Axiomatic Theories Admitting Automorphisms', *Fund. Math.* 43 (1956), 50–68.

[13] S. Feferman and R. L. Vaught, 'The First-Order Properties of Products of Algebraic Systems', *Fund. Math.* 47 (1959), 57–103.

[14] A. Friedman, *Generalized Functions and Partial Differential Equations*, Prentice Hall, Englewood, N.J., 1963.

[15] H. Gaifman, 'Uniform Extension Operators for Models', in *Sets, Models and Recursion Theory,* Crossley (ed.), North-Holland, Amsterdam, 1967, pp. 122–155.

[16] F. Galvin, 'Horn Sentences', *Ann. Math. Logic* 1 (1970), 389–422.

[17] K. Gödel, 'Über Formal unentscheidbare Sätze der Principia Mathematica und verwandter Systeme. I', *Monatsh. Phys.* 38 (1931), 173–198.

[18] A. Grothendieck, 'Eléments de Géometrie Algébrique', *Publ. Math. I.H.E.S.* 28 (1966), Chapter IV, Part III.

[19] L. Henkin, 'The Completeness of the First-Order Functional Calculus', *J. Symbolic Logic* 14 (1949), 159–166.

[20] J. Hirschfeld and W. H. Wheeler, *Forcing, Arithmetic, Division Rings, Lecture Notes in Mathematics*, Springer-Verlag, 1975, p. 454.

[21] L. Hörmander, *Linear Partial Differential Operators*, Academic Press, N.Y., 1963.

[22] N. Jacobson, *Lectures on Abstract Algebra*, Vol. III, Van Nostrand, p. 1.

[23] B. Jonsson, 'Homogeneous Universal Relational Systems', *Math. Scand.* 8 (1960), 137–142.

[24] H. J. Keisler, *Model Theory for Infinitary Logic*, North-Holland, Amsterdam, 1971.

[25] H. J. Keisler, *Starfinite Models*, preprint, Madison, 1977.

[26] G. Kreisel, 'What Have We Learnt from Hilbert's Second Problem?', in *Am. Math. Soc. Symposia Proceeding XVIII (Hilbert Problems),* Providence, 1976, pp. 93–130.

[27] G. Kreisel, 'A Survey of Proof Theory', *J. Symbolic Logic* 33 (1968), 321–388.

[28] J. L. Krivine, 'Sous-espaces de dimension finie des espaces de Banach réticulés', *Ann. Math.* 104 (1976), 1–29.

[29] G. Kreisel and J. L. Krivine, *Elements of Mathematical Logic, Model Theory*, North-Holland, Amsterdam, 1967.

[30] S. Lang, *Introduction to Algebraic Geometry*, Interscience, New York - London, 1958.

[31] P. Loeb, 'Applications of Nonstandard Analysis to Ideal Boundaries in Potential Theory', *Israel J.* 25 (1976), 154–188.

[32] J. Łos, 'On the Categoricity in Power of Elementary Deductive Systems and Some Related Problems', *Colloq. Math.* 3 (1954), 58–62.

[33] M. Morley and R. L. Vaught, 'Homogeneous Universal Models', *Math. Scand.* 11 (1962), 37–57.

[34] A. Macintyre, 'Abraham Robinson, 1918–1974', *Bull. Am. Math. Soc.* 83(1977), 646–665.

[35] A. Macintyre, 'Model Completeness', to appear in *A Handbook of Mathematical Logic*, J. Barwise (ed.), North-Holland, Amsterdam, 1977.

[36] Ju. V. Matejasevic, 'Recursively Enumerable Sets are Diophantine', *Dokl. Akad. Nauk SSSR* 191 (1970), 279–282 (Russian).
[37] F. Miraglia, Ph.D. Thesis, Yale, 1977.
[38] M. Morley, 'Categoricity in Power', *Trans. Am. Math. Soc.* 114 (1965), 514–538.
[39] L. Monk, Ph.D. Thesis, Berkeley, 1975.
[40] A. Mostowski, *Constructible Sets with Applications*, North-Holland, Amsterdam.
[41] J. Paris and L. Harrington, 'A Mathematical Incompleteness in Peano Arithmetic', to appear in *A Handbook of Mathematical Logic*, J. Barwise (ed.), North-Holland, Amsterdam, 1977.
[42] G. Reyes, 'Local Definability Theory', *Ann. Math. Logic* 1 (1970), 15–137.
[43] G. Reyes, Ph.D. Thesis, Berkeley, 1967.
[44] A. Robinson, *Introduction to Model Theory and to the Metamathematics of Algebra*, 2nd ed., North-Holland, Amsterdam, 1965.
[45] A. Robinson, *Nonstandard Analysis*, North-Holland, Amsterdam, 1966.
[46] A. Robinson, 'Topics in Nonstandard Algebraic Number Theory', in *Applications of Model Theory to Algebra, Analysis and Probability*, Luxemburg (ed.), New York, 1969, pp. 1–17.
[47] A. Robinson and P. Roquette, 'On the Finiteness Theorem of Siegel and Mahler Concerning Diophantine Equations', *J. Number Theory* 7 (1975), 121–176.
[48] C. Ryll-Nardzewski, 'On the Categoricity in Power $\leqslant \aleph_0$', *Bull. Acad. Polon. Sci. Sér. Sci. Math. Asst. Phys.* 7 (1959), 545–548.
[49] G. Sacks, *Saturated Model Theory*, Benjamin, 1972.
[50] A. Seidenberg, 'An Elimination Theory for Differential Algebra', *Univ. California Publications in Math.* 3 (1956), 31–66.
[51] C. C. Chang and H. H. Keisler, *Model Theory*, North-Holland, 1973.
[52] S. Shelah, 'The Lazy Model-Theoretician's Guide to Stability', *Logique et Analyse* 72–72 (1975), 241–308.
[53] J. Silver, 'Some Applications of Model Theory in Set Theory', *Ann. Math. Logic* 3 (1971), 45–110.
[54] A. Tarski and J. C. C. McKinsey, *A Decision Method for Elementary Algebra and Geometry*, 1st ed., The Rand Corp., Santa Monica, Calif., 1948; 2nd ed., Berkeley - Los Angeles, 1951.
[55] G. Takeuti, *Boolean Valued Analysis I, II, III*, Preprints, Urbana, 1975.
[56] R. L. Vaught, 'Model Theory Before 1945', pages 153–172 in *Proceedings of the Tarski Symposium*, L. Henkin *et al.* (eds.), *Am. Math. Soc. Symposia Proceedings XXV*, Providence, 1974.
[57] R. L. Vaught, 'Invariant Sets in Topology and Logic', *Fund. Math.* 82 (1974), 269–293.
[58] R. L. Vaught, 'Denumerable Models of Complete Theories', in *Infinitistic Methods*, Oxford - Warsaw, 1961, pp. 303–321.
[59] S. Kochen, 'Ultraproducts in the Theory of Models', *Am. Math.* 2,74 (1961), 221–261.
[60] L. van den Dries and P. Ribenborn, 'Lefschetz Principle in Galois Theory', Queen's Mathematics Preprint, 1976, No. 5.

G. KREISEL

CONSTRUCTIVIST APPROACHES TO LOGIC

ABSTRACT. The first part of this paper recalls contributions of *general philosophical interest* which have been made by foundational research, and lists some specific contributions of this sort made by constructivist foundations; in particular, to the history of ideas, and to the correction of wide-spread convictions. The second part goes into the *heuristic* value of developing constructivist foundations systematically, and into the conflict between the (naive) requirement of (i) solving a problem by means of constructive operations, and the additional (sophisticated) requirement of establishing (i) by a constructive proof. The third part contains some new results on constructive propositional logic (also of interest to specialists in the subject), which illustrate *pedagogic* uses of constructivist foundations; in particular, for understanding phenomena in advanced model-theoretic socalled classical logic, in connection with functional and deductive completeness, or with extending the domain of definition of familiar operations.

I. GENERAL FOUNDATIONAL LESSONS

Before going into details of constructivist foundations and, in particular, into the role played by (constructivist) logic, I propose to recall experience in non-constructive, especially set-theoretic foundations. This will serve for orientation, and thereby establish what seems to me the greatest general interest of foundational research: how experience in one part of foundations prepares us for developments in other parts.

(a) The general ups and downs of widely held opinions, *alias* convictions, and their analysis.

> *100 years ago:* the notion of set was barely mentioned in the mathematical literature, and Cantor considered himself a misunderstood martyr.

> *50 years ago:* set theory was described (i) as a paradise where all (mathematics) was smooth and easy, or as a kind of necessity without which (all) mathematics would be stunted, but also (ii) as illegitimate, and, in particular, the general power set operation, of forming the collection of subsets of any given set, was rejected.

E. Agazzi (ed.), Modern Logic – A Survey, 67–91.

> *To-day:* As to (i), with much imagination *some* areas of mathematics were discovered where set theoretic notions are demonstrably necessary or at least measurably profitable; cf. (b) below. As to (ii), the principal problems concerning the power set operation do not concern its legitimacy, but either the number of iterations or, more delicately, the choice of variants, for example, of taking only subsets defined by specified means (not: all subsets).

In constructive foundations the notion of *choice sequence* [12] developed in a similar way to the notion of set. To be precise, 100 years ago, 'choice sequence' had not yet been mentioned explicitly, but similar ideas were involved in the passage from set theoretic to algebraic topology. And today we are still looking for convincing uses (cf. end of note 9 on page 93 of the review of [1] or its elaboration in 6.12 on pp. 99–100 of [12]), the principal problem being the choice of variants such as lawless sequences or suitable projections.

Remark: Sets and choice sequences are used here for illustration because they both differ in a spectacular way from old-fashioned (finitist) school mathematics, the kind of mathematics to which Kant referred in the *Critique of Pure Reason* (though calculus was of greater interest already at his time). Instead one could simply use *logic* since old-fashioned mathematics is logic-free; non-constructive logic in place of sets, constructive logic in place of choice sequences. But then it would be harder to find even candidates for convincing uses.

The foundational analyses of the notions mentioned above provide memorable (counter) examples in connection with many grand philosophical issues, of which two are considered in (b) and (c) below.

(b) *Metaphysics and science.* There may be doubt about any exact demarcation between those two domains of knowledge. There is no doubt that the gap between higher set theory and (Kant's) old-fashioned school mathematics is so large that these two parts of mathematics can *serve as a model* of metaphysics and science resp. (Similarly, the theory of choice sequences can serve as a model of 'idealist' metaphysics).

The work in (a) shows that the question of 'principle':

> Is metaphysics *ever* relevant to science?

has a trivial (positive) answer. The matter becomes delicate if the domains involved are more closely specified, for example, if the theory of real numbers belongs to science then the case of Borel-determinacy illustrates the relevance of spectacular metaphysics [9], roughly speaking, of uncountably many iterations of the power set operation. If only simple combinatorial statements like finite versions of Ramsey's Theorem belong to science then (on present knowledge) only mild metaphysics, e.g. the (nonrecursive) sets involved in the infinite version of Ramsey's Theorem, is seen to be relevant, [5] and [10]. – Given this sensitivity, one may well have second thoughts on the usefulness of the distinction between science and metaphysics. And if it is not useful, it may be hard to make a (correct) precise formulation of the intended distinction convincing:

Choices are always difficult when they don't matter.

(c) *Reductionism (Ockham's razor) and reliability*. Unquestionably, the single most effective 'method' for improving the reliability of basic axiom systems is *analysis*, a description of the objects one is talking about – and not such reductions as eliminations or metamathematical consistency proofs. (Evidently, for a perceptible improvement, the doubts about the axioms involved have to be genuine, not 'theoretical' since in the latter case the doubts themselves are liable to be dubious). Familiar examples are (i) the description of (segments of) the cumulative hierarchy of those sets which are generated from the empty set by iterating the power set construction, and (ii) the description of particular, socalled lawless sequences (repeated, for example, in Troelstra's lecture).

As matters stand at present there is a striking asymmetry between analyses and reductions: the former are established by one-liners, observations without elaborations (= *Konstatierungen*), while there are quite general *techniques* for the latter. And reductions are indeed constantly used in advanced mathematics and logic; for example, (i) various model constructions reduce extensions of familiar axiomatic set theory ZFC (say, by adding the continuum hypothesis or its negation) to ZFC itself, and (ii) the socalled elimination of choice sequences reduces dubious axioms for choice sequences to established ones; cf. CS in Troelstra's lecture. These 'advanced' reductions genuinely improve the reliability of conclusions obtained from dubious axioms, for example, if an arithmetic theorem has been proved (i) from one of those dubious extensions of ZFC in the nonconstructive case or (ii) from the axioms CS in the constructive case.

In fact, as will be elaborated in the next section, both the reductions mentioned involve *constructivization* in the popular, familiar sense (going back to Euclid), which is nowadays more often called 'predicativity.' Here the stress is on an explicit list of operations for generating the objects considered; of course, choice sequences are not constructive in *this* sense. French mathematicians, who are ill at ease with traditional terminology, speak of *esprit de finesse* (as in algebra, with explicit lists of operations) and *esprit de géometrie* (where we think of arbitrary points, not only those constructed by use of Euclid's operations, a ruler and a pair of compasses).

I should draw the following foundational conclusion from the discussion above of the relative role of reductions and analyses. For the whole canvas of (mathematical) knowledge the distinction is of quite minor interest, particularly for the purpose in question, of improving reliability. At least on present evidence the distinction has some significance if we consider separately early stages of knowledge and its elaborations: as is to be expected, in the former case, analyses, in the latter, reductions are more rewarding. The existence of border-line cases between elementary and advanced knowledge corresponds quite well to border-line cases between analyses and reductions: after all, an analysis in terms of given (familiar) notions is *ipso facto* a reduction to those notions.

II. CONSTRUCTIVITY: OPERATIONS AND PROOFS

For background it is convenient to go back to the two reductions touched on a little earlier (of the geometric plane some 2000 years ago and of the cumulative hierarchy of sets). Realistically speaking, the *full* plane and the *full* power set operation are clearest in the sense that, for them, simple facts are evident; specifically, Dedekind's principle (of completeness) for the plane, and the comprehension principle for sets. In contrast, investigation is needed to determine which socalled first order instances of these principles are satisfied by the Euclidean points of the plane, resp. by the ramified hierarchy of sets (generated by the 'thin' variant of the power set operation which collects together only those subsets of a set S which are defined by applying the logical operations to S). This thin hierarchy was called *constructible* by Gödel in accordance with the popular sense of the word: as is well-known, it takes some work to verify that this hierarchy satisfies comprehension (when the quantifiers range over the whole 'thin' hierarchy).

The parallel in the case of choice sequences, which (like the elements of the full cumulative hierarchy of sets) are also not all generated or, as one says, 'named' by a specified list of operations, is less well-known: here too, simple facts are easy to prove, more easily than after elimination of choice sequences;

cf. the exposition in 2.16 on p. 28 of [12]. It is certainly not surprising that the use of choice sequences is *satisfaisant pour l'esprit de géométrie*, having been introduced by the topologist Brouwer. Naturally, it is alien to the *esprit de finesse* which, as already mentioned, confines itself to

objects 'constructed' by limited means.

(To be precise, that *esprit de finesse* has been modified by experience: one considers not only the – smallest class of – objects constructed by given operations, but all collections closed under those operations. Such closure conditions are formulated axiomatically.)

After these preliminaries about parallels in set theory it is time to turn to the (principal) current ideas of constructivity which embrace both *l'esprit de géométrie* and *l'esprit de finesse*.

(a) *Constructive logic:* a link between extremes. Except for finitist, logic-free reasoning familiar from elementary school mathematics, assertions involve 'hidden' operations besides the objects (in the ranges of the variables) and the operations explicitly mentioned; namely, the operations involved in the logical symbolism. Propositional operations act on (possibly, generalized) truth values or even, in the interpretation of Brouwer and Heyting, on proofs; existential quantifiers are operations on the objects in the ranges of all the variables not subordinate to those quantifiers, and so forth; for a precise discussion, see the specialized literature (though for the present purpose, the broad indications on pp. 87–88 of the review [1] are quite sufficient). Trivially, when the range of a variable is widened *dans l'esprit de géométrie*, say from points constructed by limited methods to all those determined by choice sequences, then the

operations on that widened range are liable to be restricted,

for example (as in Brouwer's topology) to those which are continuous in an appropriate sense. Certainly, as it stands, this restriction is definitely not *dans l'esprit de finesse*, since not all continuous operations are built up according to some (familiar) algebraic scheme. But, as is well-known, the restriction is strong enough to *make the law of the excluded middle invalid*, in the following precise sense where f ranges over numerical valued (choice) sequences:

$$\neg\forall f\exists x\{f(x)=0\vee\neg\exists y[f(y)\neq 0]\}.$$

COROLLARY. Though the 'fine' restrictions to *objects* constructed by limited means are at the opposite pole to the 'geometric' conception of a rich domain of objects, at the next level, of operations, *ces extrèmes se touchent*: the geometric conception implies restrictions tacitly (whereas the algebraic conception will list explicitly methods for generating the operations to be considered). This similarity is quite sufficient to ensure *some* formal similarities in – anything like current – systematic expositions of the two extremes, specifically, in the laws of logic valid for the two sorts of interpretations.

Examples. The most familiar systems in the intuitionistic literature are indeed valid for (a large number of) interpretations *et dans l'esprit de géométrie et de finesse*. In an obvious empirical sense, none of these interpretations has as privileged a role (among all of them) as the usual model-theoretic interpretation has among all those for which the classical laws are valid; for more specific examples, see Troelstra's lecture. The brutal fact, of an incomparably *greater* latitude in the interpretations of constructivist formal systems, is obscured by the – perfectly true, but trivial – generalities in the intuitionistic literature about the inherent ambiguities of (all) formal systems;[1] 'trivial' since, after all, some systems are complete, others not.

(b) *Constructive logic:* a basic conflict. As already mentioned in (a), constructive *logic* introduces a package deal, utterly different from the role of constructive operations in the mainstream of mathematics (from geometry to set theory). The package includes the restriction to constructive proofs.

The conflict between this package and the old tradition (of simply solving a problem by means of given constructions) does not depend on any detailed analysis of the concept of 'constructive proof', but only on the fact that *some* restriction (on proofs) is involved. To see this, use as a model any, necessarily incomplete formal system in which the formula $\forall n[f(n) = 0]$ cannot be proved though it is true. In other words, we have a (definition of a)

> number-theoretic function f, which is constant and equal to 0, but there is no constructive proof of $\forall n[f(n) = 0]$.

Consider now the problem of solving constructively $\forall n \exists m[f(n) = m]$ by means of an explicit $g : n \mapsto m$. Of course, f itself is a solution (which is trivially constructive, if f is defined constructively). But

$$g : n \mapsto 0$$

is a *simpler* solution, which by hypothesis cannot be established constructively.

This brutal conflict is *overlooked* in the foundational literature on constructivity; possibly because it is obscured by glamour issues of mathematical existence and the like. Whoever sees the conflict, is bound to ask the question (*Q*):

> Is constructive logic a mere oversight?

and hence – in Bourbaki's phrase – a historical curiosity. I still think that the *negative* answer to *Q*, specially stressed in the review of [1], is good:

> If random (or choice) sequences are to be objects of study – that is, if their properties are not to be merely paraphrased (in set-theoretic or measure-theoretic terms) – then the laws of classical logic are simply not valid, but those of constructive logic are.

Warnings. Naturally, this answer will appear perverse to the majority of constructivists who, on the basis of (dubious) views about 'existence' and 'certainty', see the main virtue of constructive logic in the illegitimacy of set-theoretic notions, and also see that the notion of choice sequence is problematic (tacitly, for those same dubious views). This is as it should be: if the foundational claims for constructive logic are ill-founded, a good answer to the question *Q* above had better *not* appeal to the assumptions behind those claims! Equally, the answer is alien to the pious tradition of 'tolerance', popular in marginal operations in all walks of life (and stressed in some lectures in this volume). Specifically, one discretely ignores the foundational source of constructive logic, and relies on the 'intrinsic' interest of the latter, though, as a matter of empirical fact, *constructive logic has no appeal without those foundational claims.* Be that as it may, in the present case there is a price to pay for 'tolerance': Even if *Q* has a negative answer, we shall not find it since, in the 'tolerant' tradition, we have no reason to ask the question.

(c) *Recursive number-theoretic functions*: a successful enterprise and its limitations. To put first things first: experience of the constructions studied in the mainstream of mathematics (from Euclid to Abel, on radicals in algebra) present little evidence for a *general theory of constructive operations*, in neither sense of the word 'general'. What is common to all such operations may well be trivial for *each* particular set. As for a *largest* class of constructions, this may either be hopelessly arbitrary or else an object which does not lend itself to a rewarding theory.

It may fairly be said that, when applied to number-theoretic (and of course 'related' kinds of) functions, the notion of *recursiveness* is rewarding. It is by no means trivial when applied to particular, for example, the *ring* operations (for describing significant properties of the class of diophantine relations). It is even of some, albeit limited use for its original purpose, that is, as an idealization of computers. Naturally, as with most uses of early 'abstract' idealizations, realistic problems about computers will combine a *little general recursion theory* with a *lot of analysis specific* to the case in hand.

Reminder (for readers of Macintyre's lecture on model theory). The notion of an *arbitrary axiom system*, when restricted to first order axioms, has a parallel place in model-theoretic foundations to *recursiveness* here, when restricted to number-theoretic functions. As a matter of empirical fact, until some 15 years ago, mathematical practice had not suggested (even to some generally very perceptive mathematicians) that the class of arbitrary *first order* axioms has a theory which is rewarding when applied to particular axioms. But also – as Macintyre stressed – on present evidence the restriction is significant. All socalled fundamental logical notions such as *satisfaction* can be defined for second order logic too (in fact, by use of exactly the same set-theoretic notions!); but in this case, there is – evidence that there is – no comparably rewarding theory. Incidentally, this reminder concerns yet another parallel between different areas of foundations, of the kind which, as mentioned at the outset, is probably the most *generally* interesting discovery of foundational research. Readers can easily elaborate the parallel by looking at the widely divergent conclusions which were drawn from the first results on recursiveness and first order logic; some regarded these notions as ultimate criteria of precision, others as devastating restrictions on expressive power.

Example (for specialists) of a neglected conflict between recursiveness and a common measure of *simplicity of operations*, namely,

the set of significant parameters;

a solution σ of a problem is called simpler than σ' if σ depends only on a *subset* of the parameters of σ'. Suppose we have proved

$$\forall n \forall m \exists p A(n, m, p),$$

and we want to know if p really depends on both parameters n and m. It does not if, say,

$$\forall n \exists p \forall m A(n, m, p)$$

is also true. There is a trivial example where this is the case, provided we admit that

p depends constructively on *n and m*, but
p does not depend constructively on *n* alone;

(modulo: constructive = recursive). For Kleene's *T*-predicate,

$$\forall n \forall m \exists p [T(n, n, p) \vee \neg T(n, n, m)]$$

holds with: $p = m$; also

$$\forall n \exists p \forall m [T(n, n, p) \vee \neg T(n, n, m)]$$

is true, but there is no recursive function $\pi : n \mapsto p$, for which

$$\forall n \forall m \{T[n, n, \pi(n)] \vee \neg T(n, n, m)\}.$$

COROLLARY. Quite often, a problem $\forall x \exists y R(x, y)$ which has no solution: $x \mapsto y$ by means of (given) constructions, *does* have such solutions if the *data x* are 'enriched'. This is familiar from real algebra if the coefficients of a polynomial, given by real numbers, are 'enriched' by adding suitable *representations* of those real numbers; in other words, if – in intuitionistic terminology – one uses real number generators.

Reminder. The fact that research on traditional foundational questions has been of very limited heuristic value for mathematics (either in the sense of making progress in mathematics or of increasing the certainty of its conclusions), certainly contradicts *some* expectations, for example, those of Leibniz. To *correct* such false expectations is itself of some heuristic value! Besides, the discovery that they are false is of interest; perhaps to a greater number of generally educated people than most mathematical progress. In this connection, the situation in foundations seems to be admirably suited to illustrate the well-known view of (all!) progress which was once expressed in terms of *theses, antitheses* and *syntheses*, and nowadays in terms of *refutations*; a view which contradicts the bulk of our every-day scientific experience where we use concepts which are obviously here to stay. But this view is by no means absurd if we separate *early* and *advanced* stages of knowledge, foundations being typical of an early stage, as already mentioned at the end of Part I. Of course, cosmology, evolution and, generally, any ambitious, undeveloped scientific theory can also be used to illustrate the view, but with this difference: nobody knows much, let alone any synthesis, and so we have a case of illustrating *obscurum per obscurius*. From this point of view the use of simple examples in this paper is quite natural (though, as a matter of empirical fact, mathematically more delicate illustrations are more memorable – to mathematicians; pedagogy is a statistical business, and one needs a few different styles of presentation).

III. ELEMENTARY LOGIC: INCOMPLETENESS PROPERTIES

As already mentioned in II (a), no one of several constructivist interpretations[2] of the usual logical symbolism has a particularly privileged role in present day constructive mathematics. In fact, constructive logic does not have an interest within constructive (mathematical) reasoning which is comparable to that of first order classical logical within non-constructive mathematics. This so to speak negative discovery has also a 'positive' *pedagogic* use, for a better understanding of elementary classical logic by *contrast*. (What do they know of England who only England know?) By comparison with constructive logic, it becomes clear which (special) properties make familiar classical logic useful. As a consequence one is prepared for the diminishing returns of work in advanced, for example, second order logic (which lacks those special properties). We consider here two specific issues concerning the choice of a logical language.

(a) Functional completeness, which concerns the question whether *all* logical operations are listed, and thus, primarily, the *notion* of 'logical operation' (not: the usefulness of that notion).

(b) Deductive completeness of rules (in the literal or some extended sense) or more simply, the complexity of the set of those formulae in some given language which are valid for the interpretation considered.

The *usefulness* of a language depends of course on its expressive power, on the class of sets which are (invariantly) definable in that language. This is in *conflict* with the deductive completeness of 'simple' rules since the validity predicate is not definable in the language. (The latter fact, though not the conflict, has been much stressed by Tarski.) At least for the interpretation intended by Brouwer and Heyting, first order constructive logic has greater expressive power than classical logic. Contrary to a widespread misunderstanding, here too

bigger is not always better,

namely, if the language with greater expressive power does not have a simple enough theory.

(a) *Functional completeness.* One of the first, and surely most satisfying contributions of ordinary logic is the familiar (positive) answer to the question:

> (*) Can all propositional operations (with a finite number of variables) be built up from $\neg, \wedge, \vee, \rightarrow$?

(In fact, $\wedge$ and $\neg$ are enough). The answer applies to socalled classical or Aristotelean logic where the only data used are the *truth values* of propositions; specifically, one considers those propositions which have one of the truth values T or $\bot$, and one ignores other (and perhaps more interesting) properties of those propositions. A moment's reflection shows that

(i) for a positive answer some analysis of the data used is needed, while

(ii) for a negative answer (naturally, for a different choice of data, that is, for propositions that simply do not have definite truth values, or just for different aspects of propositions), it is best to use specific examples.

Warning. Contrary to an almost universal misunderstanding there is no mystery about the *notion* of propositional operation. It is a map from the data used (to determine propositions) into such data. If a proposition is determined by its set of possible proofs (normed in some suitable way), a propositional operation is a map taking such sets as arguments and values. The problem is elsewhere: whether the class of *all* such maps is appropriate. More pedantically, if the class of maps (which respect equality of proofs) is taken to be the *intended* meaning of propositional operation, the question is whether the propositional aspects of the piece of reasoning under consideration are significant.

There are two obvious candidates for a negative answer to (*) in the constructivist case; one uses

> infinitary operations, say $\bigwedge$ or $\bigvee$, that is, infinite conjunctions and disjunctions,
> the other uses propositional quantification.

Of course, analogues to such 'candidates' exist also in the classical case; but, by functional completeness they do not define new operations.

The incompleteness results below, though valid for a wide variety of interpretations of the logical operators, are in sharp contrast to the current literature where the principal aim is to establish completeness of $\{\neg, \wedge, \vee, \rightarrow\}$ in some sense. For example, McCullough [15] considers Kripke's semantics, and makes (severe) restrictions on the metamathematical means used for defining the semantics. Zucker [16] considers a socalled inferential interpretation which involves (severe) restrictions on the rules of inference to be used. The operator o in Example 1 below provides a good illustration of the kind of finitary rules that are excluded (at least in the case of monadic operators when the set of theorems is recursive).

Example 1: the operator o, where

$$o(p) \underset{\text{def}}{=} \bigvee\!\!\!\bigvee_n A_n$$

and A_n ranges over all *monadic* operations which are defined in $\{\neg, \wedge, \vee, \rightarrow\}$ and not identically true. Then o is not equivalent to any (monadic) operator defined in $\{\neg, \wedge, \vee, \rightarrow\}$ itself; cf. Celluci's proof [2] for a certain formalist meaning of 'equivalence', and Goad's [4] for a proof valid for the wide variety of interpretations listed by him.

A few points are worth noting. Classically, $o(p) \leftrightarrow T$ since $\bigvee\!\!\!\bigvee_n A_n$ includes both p and $\neg p$ (even if A_n ranges only over those operators which are not classical tautologies). More interestingly,

$$\{\neg, \wedge, \vee, \rightarrow, o\} \text{ is complete with respect to } \{\neg, \wedge, \vee, \rightarrow, \bigwedge\!\!\!\bigwedge, \bigvee\!\!\!\bigvee\}$$

for *monadic* operators, and the *monadic* theory is decidable. So, although o is only the first new operator that comes to mind, it has an intrinsic significance, in the broad context of *arbitrary* infinite conjunctions and disjunctions, at least in the monadic case. The negative answer is made most convincing by taking a particular proposition, say, p', depending on a lawless parameter α, and proving

$$\neg\forall\alpha[o(p') \leftrightarrow A_n'], \quad \text{and} \quad \neg\forall\alpha[o(p')]$$

instead of merely showing that: $o(p) \leftrightarrow A_n$ and $o(p)$ itself are *not* derivable by given (possibly incomplete) rules.

Example 2: the operator $\boxtimes$ where

$$\boxtimes(p) \underset{\text{def}}{=} \exists q[p \leftrightarrow (\neg q \vee \neg\neg q)]$$

and q ranges over propositions. To see that $\boxtimes$ is also not definable in $\{\neg, \wedge, \vee, \rightarrow\}$, one uses (the very complete knowledge of monadic operators definable in $\{\neg, \wedge, \vee, \rightarrow\}$ provided by) the lattice of Rieger–Nishimura. Since

$$\neg\neg(\neg q \vee \neg\neg q) \text{ we have } \boxtimes(p) \rightarrow \neg\neg p.$$

(*Added Nov.* 79) In the original lecture obvious examples of propositions p were mentioned for which $\boxtimes p$, but not p nor $\neg p$ holds. The topological interpretation in the *connected space* S^1 was used to provide an open set p_0, the punctured disc, for which $\neg\neg p_0$ is, but $\boxtimes p_0$ is not valid (since p_0 cannot be split into two sets $\neg q, \neg\neg q$ at all). This took care of all candidates of operations in $(\neg, \wedge, \vee, \rightarrow)$ for defining $\boxtimes$, modulo the topological interpretation. – To make the result significant for the intended constructive meaning, some substitute had to be found for the standard passage from the topological interpretation to (propositions about) lawless sequences, since the latter do not form a connected space. I neglected this problem till spring 1979. In the meantime A. S. Troelstra and his student G. F. van der Hoeven had made significant progress with compounds, later called 'projections', of lawless sequences, and I expressed my hope (to A.S.T.) that a suitable kind of projection would provide the required substitute. This was done by Troelstra, who presented his results at Montecatini in October 1979; cf. also his Report 79-14, Department of Mathematics, University of Amsterdam and the PS (p. 91).

Additional remarks. (1) Evidently, $\boxtimes(p)$ reduces to p classically. This is a special case of the general formula for the elimination of quantifiers

$$(\dagger) \qquad \exists q A \rightarrow A[q/A[q/T]],$$

where A is an arbitrary predicate of propositions q. The formula defining $\boxtimes$ shows that ($\dagger$) does not hold generally in intuitionistic propositional logic.

For if

A is $[p \leftrightarrow (\neg q \vee \neg\neg q)[$, then $A[q/T]$ reduces to p and
$A[q/A[q/T]]$ reduces to $p \leftrightarrow (\neg p \vee \neg\neg p)$, that is, to p itself.

(2) The formula ($\dagger$) holds intuitionistically if $\exists qA$ is replaced by $\exists\, !qA$.
For then

$(A \wedge A') \rightarrow (q \rightarrow q')$, and so
$(A \wedge q) \rightarrow (A' \rightarrow q')$. So
$(A \wedge q) \rightarrow \exists q(A \wedge q)$ and $\exists q(A \wedge q) \rightarrow (A' \rightarrow q')$.
But $\exists q(A \wedge q)$ reduces to $A[q/T]$, and so
$[(\exists !qA) \wedge A'] \rightarrow (q' \leftrightarrow A[q/T])$.

In other words, we have a simple *definability theorem for all fragments of propositional logic in which T is definable*. Fragments are emphasized because $\{\neg, \wedge, \vee, \rightarrow\}$ is itself a fragment, being functionally incomplete. – Result (2) was first noted in Theorem 1 of my abstract on p. 389 of *J. Symbolic Logic* 25 (1960).

Exercise. Suppose B is $p \leftrightarrow (q \vee \neg q)$; this is superficially similar to A in Example 2. Show that $\exists qB \leftrightarrow B[q/B[q/T]]$, in fact, $\leftrightarrow \neg\neg p$ provided only the range of the variable q is closed under the operations $\{\neg, \wedge, \vee, \rightarrow\}$. (Hint: Clearly, $(\exists qB) \rightarrow \neg\neg p$; but $(\neg\neg p) \rightarrow B[q/p]$ since $(\neg\neg p) \rightarrow [p \leftrightarrow (p \vee \neg p)]$.

Discussion of the exercise. Any thoughtful reader will be ill at ease with the mind-boggling notion of an *arbitrary* proposition. This notion is, realistically speaking, incomparably more obscure than, say, the notion of an arbitrary set of natural numbers. The exercise is set out so as to be unaffected by uncertainties about the notion of arbitrary proposition; specifically, it is shown that $\exists qB$ is *invariant* for a wide variety of ranges of q. As usual, such insensitivity can be expressed by use of the notion of *basis* (for $\exists qB$), in particular, the basis formed by the operations $\{\neg, \wedge, \vee, \rightarrow\}$. – The time-honoured alternative to the use of bases or, for that matter, of simple (counter) examples is provided by *axiomatic formulations*; for example on p. 102 of [12] or in the presentation of Friedman's results in Troelstra's lecture. Such formulations are often more compact, but – as experience has shown – require familiarity with the axioms used. Otherwise one does not know what one is talking about, for example whether the objects (propositions) may or even have to involve such things as lawless sequences. In contrast such uncertainties about the precise extent of the objects to be considered, do not affect specific examples, in particular specific bases: here it is enough that we want to know about those things in front of our eyes. Clearly, as at the end of Part II, we take here an 'empirical' view of pedagogy – in conflict with the 'normative' view that axiomatic formulations are needed for precision. Here ends the discussion, and we turn to a:

Comparison with classical logic. Here functional incompleteness occurs, of course, only beyond the propositional level. For example, as Mostowski pointed out, the *notion* of a (finitary) general quantifier:

> mapping $(n + k)$-tuples of a set into n-tuples (invariant under permutation),

is clear enough. To be *logical*, the mapping should be defined on arbitrary sets (so to speak, defined for all possible worlds), for example, the cardinality quantifier $\exists_1$: there are uncountably many. This is treated in Keisler's monograph [6], with special stress on the fact that there is a simple set of rules which is deductively complete for $\{\neg, \wedge, \exists, \exists_1\}$. However, on present evidence, his formal system is *more* useful if it is not interpreted logically, but mathematically;

specifically, if one considers sets of real numbers, and means by $\exists_1 x$: there exist enough x to form a set of measure > 0. – Somewhat ironically, round about the same time as [6], there appeared a neat 'characterization' of the language $\{\neg, \wedge, \exists\}$ by Lindstrom [8], singling out this language among a very natural general class (of model-theoretic languages, also called 'abstract logics') by two properties of $\{\neg, \wedge, \exists\}$ which are used a great deal in the current literature. Naturally, $\{\neg, \wedge, \exists, \exists_1\}$ does not have (both) these properties. Lindstom's work confirms elegantly the experience of the sixties that there are useful languages beyond $\{\neg, \wedge, \exists\}$, but that

proofs about $\{\neg, \wedge, \exists\}$ can be fruitfully generalized only if they do *not* use those properties, in particular, compactness.

This was the (explicit) reason why, for example, the section on definability in [7] was set out in an unorthodox fashion, avoiding the use of socalled diagrammes: proofs concerning diagrammes of arbitrary structures always appeal to compactness.

(b) *Deductive completeness.* Since Troelstra's lecture contains a readable and up-to-date exposition of this topic, it is superfluous to restate the principal results. It is enough to complement his exposition by emphasizing parallels with completeness results in classical logic. As already mentioned, on present evidence this pedagogic use of the completeness results also seems to constitute their principal interest *sub specie aeternitatis*.

Since (deductive) completeness of a set of rules asserts the equivalence between

derivability and general (logical) validity,

the significance of completeness results stands or falls with that of general validity itself. To see the implications it is best to recall general experience in foundations.

Two foundational traditions (both evidently related to the fact, used throughout this paper as a principal – philosophical – lemma, that when we know very little, too little to discriminate between different areas of experience, the most general notion of its kind is also the most natural to study). *One* tradition assumes that the search for greater precision in the analysis of such general notions is a sure recipe for progress. The *second* most popular tradition assumes that those notions are bound to be inherently vague, and so can at best be replaced by precise notions (to be chosen, as one says, 'according to one's purposes'). Both assumptions are false; the second because we have plenty of convincing analyses, in particular, of general validity; the first because, as mentioned in II (c), what is valid in general, may be trivial in each particular case. But there are exceptions!

Paradigm: familiar, first order classical logic. Here, what is valid in general, is also of interest in some particular cases in the following way. Provided the 'particular cases' (= classes of structures considered in a particular branch of mathematics) include all number theoretic structures defined by socalled Δ_2^0-predicates, a formula is valid in the particular case only if it is valid in general. Of course, this fact can be read off the proof of Gödel's completeness theorem: but one will do so only if one is aware of the issue, if one is not hooked on the (first) foundational tradition which accepts general validity as an – obviously – significant object of study.

Exercise: Formulate the restatement above of the completeness theorem as a 'basis' result in the sense used in the exercise of III (a) on the operator ⊠. – The purpose of the present reformulation is slightly different here. In III (a) it was used to avoid genuine doubts about the extension of a class (that of arbitrary propositions), here it is used to generalize a result to cover more interesting situations. The familiar slogan 'the meaning of a proposition is its use' seems more appropriate when applied to the paradigm above than in its literal sense.

Understanding by contrast. As always, also the paradigm above becomes particularly memorable by looking at it from 'outside'. The first example below comes from classical, the second from constructive logic.

Example 1: A formula of *second* order logic (with quantifiers ranging over all subsets of the domain of the models considered) may be valid for all structures of cardinal less than, say, the first inaccessible uncountable cardinal, but not for all structures. The best-known example is the negation of current axiomatic set theory (of Zermelo–Fraenkel) when expressed by a single formula as follows: $\in$ is treated as an arbitrary binary relation on the domain of the model considered, and each axiom schema (such as comprehension: $\forall a \exists b \forall c (c \in b \leftrightarrow [c \in a \wedge F(c)])$ for all formulae of the set theoretic language not containing b) is reworded for arbitrary subsets of the domain (that is, arbitrary subsets in place of those defined by the list of formulae).

Specialists will know similar examples with 'measurable' in place of 'inaccessible' (this amplifies the *Reminder* in II (c) of Macintyre's lecture). – So to speak at the opposite extreme: a formula of predicate logic may be valid for all finite structures without being valid generally.

Example 2 (for intuitionistic logic). Here we have a parallel already at the *propositional* level: the set of valid formulae of $\{\neg, \wedge, \vee, \rightarrow\}$ is sensitive to whether

propositions about lawless sequences

are or are not included. Once again, the issue is not whether lawless sequences are 'legitimate' (tacitly: after one has given the matter some thought), but simply, whether we want to know about them. In brutal language:

> Far from being awe-inspiring, the notions of *legitimacy* and *precision* are far too crude to serve as criteria (here).

Historical remarks on well-known reservations in the literature with regard to *precise definitions of satisfaction* (or truth) and to *lawless sequences*.[3] Of course, there is nothing objectionable in theory to giving a definition of satisfaction: but, in practice, it draws attention away from the central problem (of the class of objects needed for a 'basis'). Similarly, if 'general validity' is to be taken literally, propositions about lawless sequences are certainly included. So, in theory they are not excluded, and the familiar formal laws for $\{\neg, \wedge, \vee, \rightarrow\}$ are complete. Thus, in practice, we have no reason to look for new laws which are valid for other classes of propositions, and may be more rewarding for the development of constructive mathematics. NB: This dependence of the set of valid logical formulae on the class of propositions – in the branch of mathematics – considered, is treated by Troelstra under the heading of 'interplay between logic and mathematics', a phrase which more often refers to the application of laws about general validity to specific mathematical problems. The (to date) most successful applications of this kind extract *bounds* from prima facie non-constructive or 'pure' existence theorems.

To conclude this (sub)section on deductive completeness it must be noted that actual research has not succeeded in following the specific strategy suggested by the analysis above, that is, in finding new laws that are valid for propositions not involving lawless sequences (though there are detailed albeit inconclusive discussions in the literature; cf. [14]). Instead, the following variant of the *interpretation of the logical operations* (intended by Brouwer and Heyting) has led to new logical laws. The variant *restricts* (some of) the

functions implicit in the logical symbolism

to be recursive, specifically, functions whose arguments and values are (in species isomorphic to the set of) natural numbers. In other words, one assumes Church's Thesis or, more pedantically, his thesis applied to the number-theoretic functions envisaged by Brouwer and Heyting in place of what Church may have meant. Not only the usual rules are incomplete, but *all* (sound) formal rules; for more precise information, cf. Troelstra's lecture.

Technical remarks. (i) The method of proof can be stated most memorably in terms familiar from the easy proof of the formal incompleteness of second order logic, specifically, for a suitable sequence $P \to A_n$ of formulae where P is the conjunction of Peano's axioms in their (original) second-order form. *The sequence has excessive expressive power* in the sense that

$$\{n: P \to A_n \text{ is valid}\} \text{ is not recursively enumerable;}$$

'excessive' because for any recursive sequence F_n of classical first order logic, $\{n: F_n \text{ is valid}\}$ is always recursively enumerable, In the case of intuitionistic logic, for interpretations satisfying Church's thesis, a more delicate argument (on disjoint sets which can only be separated by sets of relatively high degree) is used. (ii) The mere incompleteness of the usual rules of predicate logic is much easier (by use of the fact that they are a restriction of the classical rules). One simply writes down enough axioms Z to ensure that, from every model M of Z, a copy ω_M of the set of natural numbers can be extracted, and that the symbols A and B in Z denote disjoint recursively enumerable but not recursively separable sets (when restricted to ω_M). Then, for any predicate symbol Q not occurring in Z:

$$(Z \wedge \forall x[Q(x) \vee \neg Q(x)]) \to \neg \forall x \{[A(x) \to Q(x)] \wedge [B(x) \to \neg Q(x)]\}$$

is valid on Church's thesis, but not classically, and hence not derivable by the usual intuitionistic rules. (iii) While the need for negation to express recursiveness has long been known, it becomes particularly clear by Theorem 13 on p. 288sof [3] (proved more directly by H. Friedman) that the usual rules are complete for *minimal* predicate logic, that is, $\{\wedge, \vee, \to, \forall, \exists\}$ (provided, again, propositions about lawless sequences are considered). Incidentally the result also highlights the *defect* of the familiar notion of *proof-theoretic equivalence* between the current systems for $\{\wedge, \vee, \to, \forall, \exists\}$ and for $\{\neg, \wedge, \vee, \to, \forall, \exists\}$

where $\neg A$ is replaced by $A \to p$ for some new letter p: in the former case, derivability *is*, in the latter it is *not* equivalent to (intended) validity.

(c) *Constructive logical operations:* a special case of *extending operations beyond their familiar domain of definition.* Despite my – conscious – attempt in this paper to present the material as almost banal (and hence so to speak irrefutable) it has to be admitted that the conclusions are shocking to traditional expositions of the kind given by Dummett [3] or Prawitz [11]; inevitably so, since, by notes 1 and 2, their principal claim for the interest of constructive logic, the alleged conflict between two different views of the nature of mathematical existence and reasoning, is here related to some simple oversights. Quite generally – and almost totally independently of the particular individuals involved – such a situation would cast serious doubts on the conclusions unless those oversights have convincing precedents; preferably, not involving lack of acuteness, but lack of (intellectual) experience.

The precedent I have in mind is furnished by the – perhaps unusual – *juxtaposition* of two-separately-extremely *familiar extensions*[4] of (the ring) *operations on the natural numbers* or, more colloquially, answers to: What is the essence of natural numbers? To philosophers, the best-known extension, to (infinite) sets and well-orderings, is Cantor's definition of *cardinals* and *ordinals* resp. To mathematicians, the best known extension is the embedding of the natural numbers in the *field of complex numbers* (and, more recently, in other fields too, including homomorphisms into finite fields).

Warning. It is customary to assert, without further analysis, that the former is philosophically, the latter is mathematically interesting. We can do better by what Hilbert called *Tieferlegung der Fundamente*, that is, by giving the matter second thoughts, in particular, by stating explicitly some questions which are answered by one of those extensions, and not by the other.

(i) If we think of natural numbers in the narrow context of – or, in operational language, of using numbers for – *counting*, Cantor's analysis is very convincing. Also the distinction between cardinals and ordinals belongs here, showing that special properties of finite sets (all rearrangements of which have the same order type) permit the practice of checking by recounts. It is a discovery that this distinction becomes particularly memorable if one compares and contrasts the familiar case, of finite sets, with suitable infinite sets.

(ii) If we think of numbers and, in particular, the ring operations *geometrically* (as in Euclid on similar triangles), the extension to the plane and other vector spaces provides an adequate analysis or – as one says – 'captures' the meaning. These extensions are even formally different from (i) in that, for example, cancellation laws hold such as $x + a = x + b \to a = b$, which fail in general in (i).

Where then is the *link* between (i) and (ii)? Quite simply in this:

> What have we learnt from (i) and (ii) about natural numbers?

At the *present* time, we have learnt incomparably more from (ii), that is, from (various kinds of) analytic and 'basic' number theory than from (i). But there still remains the possibility that someday we shall learn something about numbers from Cantor's embedding in sets (if not from the arithmetic of infinite cardinals and ordinals). So we have a real issue here.

At this point some readers may have to be reminded of the warning above, because we seem to judge the two extensions by their mathematical, not philosophical use. But, *mutatis mutandis*, the question arises:

> What is the place of counting among all uses of natural numbers (in thought or action)?

and again

> How much need we know about numbers to count successfully?

In other words, how rewarding is *any* – mathematical or philosophical – analysis of numbers in the narrow context of counting? (where usually the important thing is not a knowledge of number theory but to – remember to – count at all, or what we count). Naturally, if one knows nothing about natural numbers except their use for counting, or if one chooses to ignore all one knows about them, all the questions above are very much easier.

IV. FOUNDATIONAL PROGRESS

Foundational progress is, trivially, measured differently according to different conceptions of the subject. In accordance with the rest of this paper, we use here the fact that foundational notions and questions belong to an *early* stage of knowledge. It will not have escaped the reader's notice that this is in line with general qualitative features of foundational discussions, for example, the dominant role of abstract, socalled *a priori* reasoning, and its appeal to the scientifically inexperienced or uninformed. (The question how such reasoning is possible leaves one speechless partly because one does not see how else to reason *prior* to much experience! This applies all the more to the metaphorical meaning of 'a priori' when our conclusions are less dubious then any grounds which we are able to make conscious to ourselves.)

(a) *Internal* progress in foundations (illustrated in this paper) is of two kinds. Some elementary, socalled conceptual distinctions have been found to apply to – and are easy to miss in – many branches of knowledge in their early stage, for example, between precision and usefulness of such general notions as validity. The generality involved has to do both with what is common to many different things, and also with what is apparent on superficial inspection of one thing. In addition, some 'genuine' techniques have been discovered which are of use in many different branches; the present paper, especially Part III, illustrates the techniques for by-passing uncertainties which are common at an early stage by means of the axiomatic method and also by means of basis results.

(b) *External* progress involves, above all, questions of perspective, specifically, concerning the place of foundational ideas and results in the body of later, advanced knowledge. This kind of progress requires of course a continuing activity, not unlike digestion. More specifically this applies when one recognizes simple features of some complex structure, and can use foundational notions (or techniques) to describe those features: being familiar since an early stage, such notions are particularly agreeable to handle. To avoid all misunderstanding, it seems worthwhile to repeat here a case in point (which is still not very well known), namely Artin's use of Sturm's treatment of polynomials in real algebra. Sturm's purpose was foundational: to avoid dubious infinitesimals in then-current continuity arguments. This purpose was soon superseded by Cauchy's treatment of convergence. Almost a century later Artin saw how to use Sturm's ideas to solve Hilbert's 17th problem (about non-negative polynomials); in other words, Artin made the decidedly non-trivial discovery that Hilbert's problem was much more elementary (that is, abstract) than it looked: the solution does not hold only for rational or real co-efficients, but for all orderable fields. – Not all truth is beautiful, and not all beauty true:[5] but what is (both true and) beautiful, is more manageable.

So far the positive has been accentuated. To state negative aspects, especially false expectations of foundations, the following distinction is useful.

(c) *Foundational* and *fundamental* interpretations of questions which have literally the same wording. The distinction is a particular case of the commonplace phenomenon that literally identical questions often have different answers in different situations; not because the wording is 'imprecise' or ambiguous in any practical sense, but because different interpretations are involved; either in the sense of *actually intended* or in the sense of *relevant* or *effective* for the general class of problems considered. It is this second alternative which is given most attention in modern mathematics, for example, in Part III (c) on extending the domain of operations. When, say, a functional equation occurs in some problem, it is a matter of *research* to discover which domain of the variables is useful. (And if, in the formalist tradition, this aspect is not considered to be mathematical, well, then mathematical aspects in this – formalist – sense are just not adequate to solve the particular problem). NB. Contrary to a wide-spread view there is no reason to regard effectiveness or usefulness as an *analysis* of the intended interpretation, let alone to doubt that there is such a thing. At the present stage of knowledge we can do something substantial about effectiveness, and not much about the dependence of the intended meaning on context. Furthermore, the latter seems to raise much the same issues whether we think of it in physiological or psychological terms: we don't know anything about new connections which are established in the nervous system, and not much more detail about the possibly unconscious background knowledge which affects the intended meaning. (Unconscious knowledge has come to be included here, simply because the domain of knowledge that we can make conscious to ourselves pretty patently does not lend itself to theory; no more than, say, the visible part of the physical world). The biological view, already mentioned in note 5, has the advantage of being less hackneyed, for example, in relating the extraordinary *specificity* of adaptations to molecular phenomena: though it may be false, it is not far-fetched to see here a parallel to the extraordinary specificity of the different meanings of identically worded formulations.

Returning to earth, in particular, to questions and notions at an early stage of knowledge, an interpretation is called *foundational* if it corresponds to the originally intended meaning; more specifically, if it is formulated by use of the background knowledge (more or less) available at an early stage. An interpretation, of the same wording, is called *fundamental* if it happens to fit quite advanced knowledge, and remains stable for, practically speaking, all further advances in sight; as atoms remain stable under all practically occurring forces. The standard example here is the question: What is matter? Note that, nowadays, knowing atomic structure we tacitly sharpen this to: What is matter made of? (which we should not do if we thought of substances as singularities in a field of force). It is by no means 'shocking' that, occasionally, foundational questions have fundamental interpretations too, and even that the foundational (*a priori*) style of reasoning is right at a very advanced stage; the background knowledge has become unmanageable, and it is best to make a fresh start: once again, *les extrèmes se touchent*. But unless one uses the doctrinaire terminology of calling only those conceptions 'fundamental' which happen to be introduced in the foundational tradition (as in the case of Einstein's special theory of relativity), it seems to me that relatively few foundational notions or categories, socalled modes of being, have turned out to be fundamental. The view behind the present paper is that much the same applies to modes (or kinds) of mathematical knowledge or 'understanding' too.

Stanford University

NOTES

[1] In my view the current (pious) objection to Brouwer's diatribes against formalization overlooks the following basic point. Any imaginative reader, presented with the formal laws which Brouwer knew, would immediately think of a great number of interpretations which are of roughly equal interest. There would be no particular confidence in any particular interpretation, for example, the one Brouwer intended. (He was far too perceptive to pretend that in ordinary reasoning we had his favourite interpretation in mind; he did not pretend to analyze that reasoning, but wanted to reform it). – Incidentally, Brouwer's practice was in conflict with his theory: hardly anyone has ever been as touchy about the *exact wording* in all his writings as Brouwer: certainly not Hilbert (whom Brouwer dubbed a 'formalist').

[2] Readers are reminded here of (i) the interpretation intended by Brouwer and Heyting, (ii) realizations in the sense of Kleene, (iii) operational, and (iv) game theoretic interpretations by Lorenzen (who considered particular games, in fact, debates or 'dialogues' according to tailor-made rules). The interpretations differ in the choice of *data* determining a proposition and, consequently, the operations (on those data) denoted by logical symbols.

[3] Cf. Troelstra's lecture for some textual criticism concerning Brouwer's own views on lawless sequences (which supplements footnote 2 on p. 224 of *Compositio math.* 20 (1968), 222–248). The discussion below is quite independent of these details inasmuch as it accepts the legitimacy of lawless sequences but asks: Can't we do better by ignoring them?

[4] It will not have escaped the reader's notice that the extension of the *truth functions* $\neg$ and $\wedge$ to the *set-theoretic operations* of complement and intersection presents analogous problems too (where truth functions are defined for the particular case of sets consisting of the 2 subsets of a set with a single element). What distinguishes those two set-theoretic operations? – The extensions considered in the text seem to me much more convincing because they involve an incomparably more substantial body of experience.

[5] The following example, from biology, should appeal to readers of this volume, the beautiful, and perhaps unsurpassably rational genetic code proposed 20 years ago by Crick, Griffith and Orgel [*Proc. Nat. Acad. Sc. USA* 43 (1957), 416–420]. Like the correct code it uses 3 letter words from a 4 letter alphabet. Unlike the correct code it is very 'economical': it is commaless and irredundant, and fits perfectly the observational fact that there are exactly 20 amino-acids. But it is quite false. – It does not seem to me far-fetched to use an example from biology in this paper on constructivist logics which claim to tell us something about mental operations.

BIBLIOGRAPHY

[1] L. E. J. Brouwer, *Collected Works*, A. Heyting (ed.), North-Holland, 1974; rev. *Bull. A.M.S.* 83 (1977), 86–93.

[2] C. Cellucci, 'Un connettivo per la logica intuizionista', *Matematiche* 29 (1974), 274–290.

[3] M. Dummett, *Elements of Intuitionism*, Oxford University Press, 1977.

[4] C. Goad, 'Monadic Infinitary Propositional Logic: a Special Operator', *Reports on Mathematical Logic* 10 (1978), 43–50.

[5] C. Jockusch, 'Ramsey's Theorem and Recursion Theory', *J. Symbolic Logic* 37 (1972), 268–280.

[6] H. J. Keisler, 'Logic With the Quantifier "There Exist Uncountably Many",' *Ann. Math. Logic* 1 (1970), 1–93.

[7] G. Kreisel and J.-L. Krivine, *Elements of Mathematical Logic*, North-Holland, 1971.

[8] P. Lindstrom, 'On Extensions of Elementary Logic', *Theoria* 35 (1969), 1–11.

[9] D. A. Martin, 'Borel Determinacy', *Ann. Math.* (2) 102 (1975), 363–371.

[10] J. Paris and L. Harrington, 'A Mathematical Incompleteness in Peano Arithmetic', in *Handbook of Mathematical Logic*, J. Barwise (ed.), North-Holland, 1977, pp. 1133–1142.

[11] D. Prawitz, 'Meaning and Proofs: On the Conflict Between Classical and Intuitionistic Logic', *Theoria* 43 (1977), 2–40.

[12] A. S. Troelstra, *Choice Sequences. A Chapter of Intuitionistic Mathematics*, Oxford University Press, 1977.

[13] D. M. Gabbay, 'On Some New Intuitionistic Propositional Connectives', *Studia Logica* 36 (1977), 127–139. This paper could not be discussed in the body of Part IIIa because I received a reprint only after the present article was typed. Like $\boxtimes$ in IIIa, the new operators are defined in the language of second-order propositional logic. But, in contrast to IIIa, the various meanings of 'new' are somewhat unorthodox (and not shown to be insensitive to the exact ranges of the propositional quantifiers, for example, by means of suitable 'basis' results). Specificially, by the mixed bag of conditions (1)–(6) on pp. 127–128, in Theorem A (of § 1) 'new' does not mean demonstrably indefinable in Heyting's system $\{\neg, \wedge, \vee, \rightarrow\}$, but rather the *consistency* of assuming such indefinability. In Theorem 3 (of § 2), where the 'new' (monadic) operator F is given in (c) of Def. 2.3 on p. 137, and the set of axioms T (given in the Cor. 27 on p. 138!) is valid by deductive completeness, F cannot be proved to be different from *True*

(by use of T): in fact, $\neg\neg\forall pF$ is asserted. Perhaps more conclusive indefinability results can be obtained from Gabbay's paper by attention to the pitfalls just mentioned." *Added in proof:* cf. also the review in *Zentralblatt f. Math.* **363** (1978), 17, No. 02027.

[14] H. Luckhardt, 'Über das Markov-Prinzip II', *Archiv f. math. Logik* **18** (1977), 147–157. In effect, this paper discusses the question whether $[\forall x(A \vee \neg A) \wedge \neg\neg\exists xA] \rightarrow \exists xA$ is valid for predicates A not depending on choice sequences.

[15] D. P. McCullough, 'Logical Connectives for Intuitionistic Propositional Logic', *J. Symbolic Logic* **36** (1971), 15–20.

[16] J. Zucker, *The Adequacy Problem for Inferential Logic*, Preprint 37, Dept. of Mathematics, University of Utrecht, 1976.

PS (*added July 1980*): Further information on the operator ☒ in Example 2 of III(a) will appear in [17] and [18]. By [17], ☒ has no basis in $\{\neg, \wedge, \vee, \rightarrow,$ ☒, $o\}$ under very general conditions on the range of propositions considered. In contrast, by [18], the validity of $\forall p[(\neg\neg p) \leftrightarrow$ ☒$(p)]$, even for propositions about projections of lawless sequences, can depend sensitively on the kind of projection (or, similarly, in the case of classical topological models: on connectedness properties of the topological space) considered. There is also unpublished work by Luckhardt on propositions involving (species of) both lawless and lawlike sequences, but required to satisfy Kripke's schema KS. Contrary to first impressions, for example, in § 3 of the PS to [17], his work is incomparable with [18] since KS is an implicit restriction on the species considered, requiring them to be enumerable (by certain lawlike functions).

[17] G. Kreisel, 'Monadic Operators Defined by Means of Propositional Quantification in Intuitionistic Logic', *Reports on Mathematical Logic* **12** (1980).

[18] A. S. Troelstra, 'On a Second Order Propositional Operator Intuitionistic Logic, *Studia logica*, to appear.

JON BARWISE

INFINITARY LOGICS*

We begin with two examples. The sentence "No one has more than a finite number of ancestors" might be written symbolically as

$$\forall x[A_0(x) \vee A_1(x) \vee A_2(x) \vee \ldots \text{etc.}]\,,$$

which would be read: for every person x ($\forall x$) either x has no ancestors ($A_0(x)$), or ($\vee$) he has one ancestor ($A_1(x)$), or he has two ancestors etc. Even if we interpret 'person' to mean past, present or future person, most of us would consider this sentence as being true. On the other hand, if one were to try to put an *a priori* upper bound n on the number of possible ancestors a person might have, and assert

$$\forall x[A_0(x) \vee A_1(x) \vee A_2(x) \vee \ldots \vee A_n(x)],$$

then we could no longer agree, for one could always conceive of man some-show surviving for another $n+1$ generations. Thus what we have is an infinitary sentence which is not logically equivalent to any of its finite approximations.

Another example, one which appears in most logic text books in the guise of a finitary sentence is "All men are mortal". If we define mortality in terms of, say, the number of heartbeats, writing $B_n(x)$ to mean that x has a life span of n heartbeats, then our example becomes

$$\forall x[B_1(x) \vee B_2(x) \vee B_3(x) \vee \ldots \text{etc}]\,.$$

Again, this sentence is not *logically* equivalent to any of its finite approximations.

I suppose the study of infinitely long formulas must strike anyone who is not a specialist in mathematical logic as being rather odd. There was a thirty year period, from about 1925 to 1955, when it struck most logicians the same way. But times and viewpoints change, so we will explain why the study of infinitary logics, far from being bizarre, is an important part of mathematical logic, that is, an important part of understanding the language and logic of mathematical experience.

We are going to use the phrase 'infinitary logic' to refer to any logical system which contains infinitely long disjunctions ('disjunction' means *or*, as

E. Agazzi (ed.), Modern Logic – A Survey, 93–112.

in the above examples) or conjunctions (*and*), or which has a rule of inference with an infinite number of hypotheses, or both. This eliminates some logics which one might call infinitary, but not many. We have attempted to write Sections 1–9 of this paper for someone not familiar with mathematical logic. A logic student should be able to read the first 11 sections. Except for some discoveries of an historical nature, the specialist will find nothing new until Section 12. There is an appendix related to Section 11.

1. Consider the very general situation where a person P uses S as a symbol for some other object O, which we abbreviate $\Delta(P, S, O)$. Various writers, starting with C. S. Peirce thru Susan Langer to Walker Percy have emphasized the importance of this basic triadic relation $\Delta(P, S, O)$ in studying all aspects of man as the symbol-using animal. Percy, the most eloquent of all, refers to this relation as the Δ-phenomenon and represents it by the following triangle.

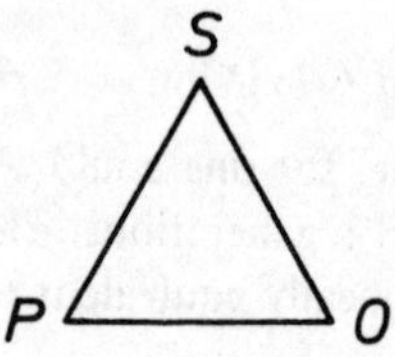

This simple diagram can be used quite effectively to illustrate some of the things that can happen when using symbols. The problem that is relevant to our topic is illustrated by the second of the following diagrams.

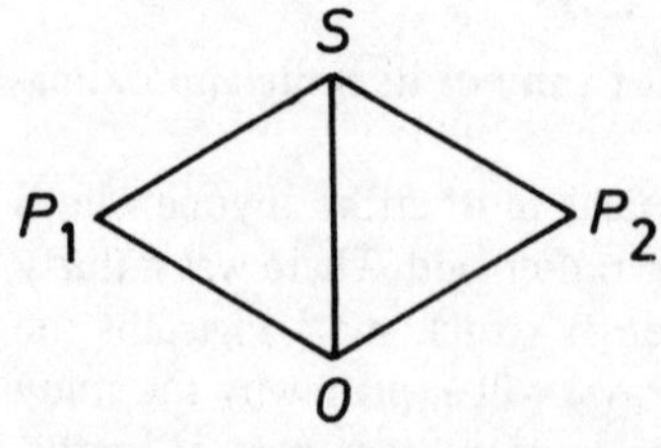

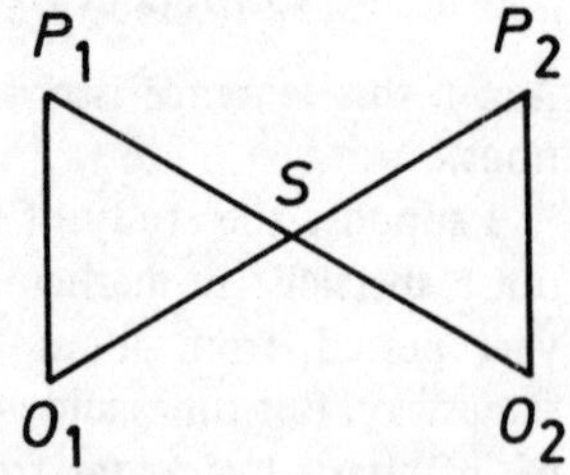

The first diagram indicates the hoped for a situation where two people P_1 and P_2 are using S as a symbol for one object O, whereas the second shows them using S for two distinct objects O_1 and O_2. In the latter situation there is every reason to suppose that confusion and misunderstandings may arise between P_1 and P_2.

2. Life and literature are full of confusion and chaos caused by people using symbols in different ways. A dramatic example arises in *Macbeth*. The pivotal point of the play, and its most terrifying scene, is the 'deed without a name' perpetrated by the witches. Murder, even 'murder most foul', at least has a name and is thus able to be understood. The deed of the witches, on the other hand, because it has no name, and because it in fact perverts the standard meanings of words, is ultimately irrational. Being beyond reason, Macbeth fails to understand and chaos follows from his misreading of the witches' symbols.

Walker Percy writes: "The word is that by which the thing is conceived or known." Carl Jung puts another light on it: "Because there are innumerable things beyond the range of human understanding, we constantly use symbolic terms to represent concepts we cannot fully understand." Jung didn't have mathematics in mind, but he probably would not have been surprised at how accurately this reflects the nature of mathematics.

One could go on giving examples, but the point is clear. Man understands reality through the symbols he uses to represent it, whether the symbols be words, pictures, music, psychological symbols of a personal sort, or the symbols of mathematics.

3. Symbolic logic attempts to explore, shape and understand the rational, conscious aspects of man's use of symbols, language and reasoning. It leaves to psychology, with its tools, the study of the irrational and unconscious aspects. The tools of symbolic logic are those from mathematics. At this meeting we will learn of progress in many parts of symbolic logic, of which mathematical logic is only one. Infinitary logic, at least as it is usually studied, is a part of mathematical logic.

4. Mathematical logic uses the tools of modern mathematics to study the language and logic of mathematics itself. Because the language of mathematics is incomparably simpler than natural language (contrary to popular opinion), mathematical logic is probably the most richly developed branch of symbolic logic.

Mathematical logic proceeds as follows. It takes as raw material the formulas, axioms, proofs and theorems of some branch of mathematics. It sets up a mathematical structure where this given material corresponds to abstract objects of the structure in a natural way. That is, it turns the formulas, axioms, and proofs into abstract objects on a par with the idealized points, lines and triangles of plane geometry, so that they can be studied by the precise tools of mathematics.

One aspect of mathematical logic is the analysis of those axioms and laws of logic used in a particular subject. This goes under the name of 'the deductive method' but it is only one part of mathematical logic as it is now understood. Another and more basic part is the study of the so called 'satisfaction relation', the relation between the syntactic way that an object is defined (that is, the 'shape' of its definition) and its mathematical properties. The satisfaction relation represents one aspect of the $S-O$ edge of the Δ-phenomenon in mathematics.

5. The most highly developed part of mathematical logic is called first-order logic. Here one studies only those *finite* expressions which can be built up from basic operations and relations (expressions like $x + y = z$ or $x < y$) by means of the following logical operation symbols:

$\wedge$ (and) $\vee$ (or) $\neg$ (not) $\rightarrow$ (implies) $\forall$ (for all) $\exists$ (there exists)

Using first-order logic, a large part of the language of mathematics can be treated *directly* as formal objects. For example, the informal axioms of plane geometry, as well as those of groups, rings and fields can be translated directly into first-order logic. One can then see which mathematical properties of these classes follow by virtue of the syntactic form of their definition, and which go beyond and say something genuinely novel about the class in question. Also, one can describe completely what it means for a first-order theorem to be provable from some list of axioms, thus partially solving an embarrassing old problem – namely, that mathematicians could always tell a proof when they saw one but, not too long ago, couldn't tell you precisely what one was.

6. However, there are many parts of mathematics that don't fit neatly within the confines of first-order logic. There are many things which are expressed in mathematics, things which are perfectly clear and unambiguous, but which cannot be expressed within first-order logic. Hence, as long as we restrict our symbolic expressions S to those of first-order logic, there are going to remain simple, mathematical instances of $\Delta(P, S, O)$ which are beyond our grasp. If this is the case, and if we are not going to give up a direct analysis of the logic of those parts of mathematics, then we must search for logics of greater expressive power.

The simplest examples of notions that lie outside the scope of first-order logic are those involving the notion *finite*. What is meant by the assertion

"There are a finite number of atoms in the universe"? Surely we all know. It means, for example, that if one were to assign distinct natural numbers 1, 2, 3, ... to all the atoms, this process would, in theory, stop. But this just hides the problems in the definition of the set N of natural numbers. How can we define N without using the word 'finite' which we are trying to explain?

We can't! At least not as long as we stay within those expressions that are part of first-order logic. In spite of the fact that we all know what finite means, we simply can't express it in the traditional framework. Put another way, any attempt to define the structure N of natural numbers by first-order axioms must fail. This is a direct consequence of the Gödel Incompleteness Theorem, which we will discuss later.

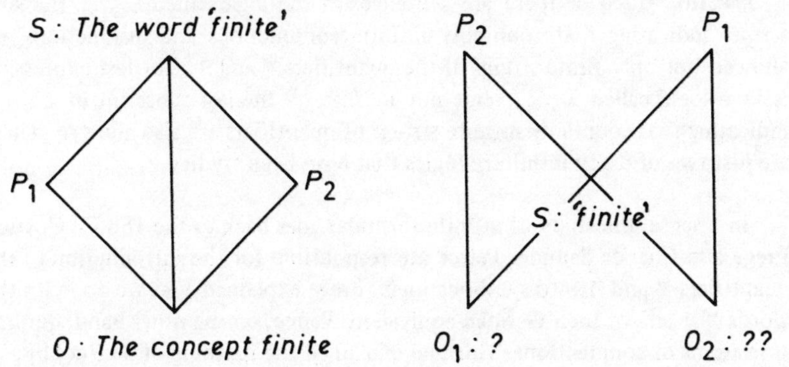

Mathematicians P_1, P_2 *First-order logicians* P_1, P_2

Anyone familiar with the manifold uses of the notions of finite and infinite in mathematics will realize the profound significance this fact has for logic. Here, for example, is a short list of some important notions from modern algebra that cannot be expressed directly within first-order logic: Archimedian field, torsion group, simple group, well-ordered set.

The past twenty years have seen a lot of experimentation with logics which go beyond first-order logic in various ways. It has turned out that the smoothest way to have a logic in which 'finiteness' can be expressed is the most obvious – namely, to allow infinite expressions. We list below some infinite expressions which, taken together with some additional first-order axioms, define the notion in question.

Natural numbers:

$$\forall x\,[x = 0 \vee x = 1 \vee x = (1+1) \vee x = (1+1+1) \vee \ldots]$$

Archimedian field:

$$\forall x\,[x < 1 \vee x < (1+1) \vee x < (1+1+1) \vee \ldots]$$

Torsion group:

$$\forall x\,[x = 0 \vee (x+x) = 0 \vee (x+x+x) = 0 \vee \ldots]$$

Well-ordering:

$$\forall x_1 \forall x_2 \forall x_3 \ldots [x_2 \geqslant x_1 \vee x_3 \geqslant x_2 \vee x_4 \geqslant x_3 \vee \ldots]$$

The first three of these are sentences of the logic called $L_{\omega_1\omega}$, the subscripts indicating that countably infinite conjunctions and disjunctions are allowed but only finite strings of the quantifiers $\forall$ and $\exists$. The last expression is in a logic called $L_{\omega_1\omega_1}$ but not in $L_{\omega_1\omega}$, the last subscript of $L_{\omega_1\omega_1}$ indicating that countably infinite strings of quantifiers are also allowed. These are just two of many infinitary logics that have been studied.

7. In a sense, the study of infinite formulas goes back to the 1880's. Gottlob Frege and Charles Saunder Peirce are responsible for the introduction of the quantifiers $\forall$ and $\exists$ into symbolic logic. Frege explained $\forall$ as we do, with the words 'for all', or their German equivalent. Peirce, on the other hand, defined $\forall$ in terms of conjunctions. Thus, he explained the meaning of $\forall x B(x)$ by:

$$B(a) \wedge B(b) \wedge B(c) \wedge \ldots$$

where $\wedge$ means 'and'. The conjunction is taken over all objects in one's domain of discourse, e.g., over all men if the statement is 'All men are moral'. This approach was anticipated by Albert of Saxony (1316–1390) but of course he wouldn't have considered the possibility of there being an infinite number of objects in the domain of discourse. Peirce was quite explicit about this possibility. Similarly, he defined $\exists\, xB(x)$ by

$$B(a) \vee B(b) \vee B(c) \vee \ldots$$

where $\vee$ means 'or'.

In his treatment of the quantifiers Peirce was followed by Schröder, Löwenheim, Wittgenstein, and Ramsey, among others. This view of the quantifiers was used very heavily in Löwenheim's proof of his famous theorem. Even though his theorem is about finite formulas, his proof made a detour through genuinely infinite formulas, a detour which several later generations found objectionable.

8. In spite of the encouraging beginning, the study of infinite formulas fell into disrepute. The reasons for this can be found in Hilbert's Program and the attendant position of formalism which dominated logic for many years. To understand Hilbert's Program, and its unfortunate influence on progress in infinitary logic, let us return to Ramsey's view of quantifiers and infinitary connectives.

In his 1925 paper, Ramsey argues that it is really an accident that an infinite formula cannot be written out explicitly, and that this accident should be ignored by logic. What he saw as accidental, however, Hilbert saw as necessary and as a possible foundation for mathematics. Hilbert, in his 1926 paper, hoped to exploit the finite nature of what mathematicians can write down, by setting up a program whose aim was nothing less than the complete understanding of mathematical activity in terms of manipulating finite sequences of formal expressions. We use the word expression here, rather than symbol, since for us symbols must have meanings, whereas his aim was to ignore the meanings of symbols entirely. In terms of the Δ-phenomenon, he attempted to reduce all of mathematics to the S vertex of the $P - S - O$ triangle, and with only first-order S.

It was a bold plan, and it took a firm hold on the mathematical imaginations of a generation, but it was too simple to work. Ramsey had a view much more in accord with the facts as they have emerged. In the same paper he writes, "But it does not seem to me in the least unlikely that there should be a tautology, which could be stated in finite terms, whose proof was, nevertheless, infinitely complicated ..."

The famous Gödel Incompleteness Theorem of 1931 produced just such a 'tautology', a statement of the form $\forall x A(x)$ about natural numbers such that each of $A(0)$, $A(1)$, $A(2)$, ... is provable from the first-order axioms about natural numbers, but such that there is no finite proof of $\forall x A(x)$ from the same axioms. Gödel's Theorem holds in such generality that it shows Hilbert's idea to be untenable. It shows, moreover, that one has to use some sort of infinitistic reasoning to prove certain true facts about finite natural numbers.

Karl Marx is supposed to have said, "Every time the train of history goes around a corner, the thinkers fall off." Gödel's Theorem was a very sharp corner on the logic line. In spite of the fact that Gödel's Theorem proved that Hilbert's Program could not succeed, that it could never provide a foundation for mathematics, there remained in many quarters a preoccupation with seeing just how far the program could be pushed. There would have been no harm in this, had it not been for the intolerance which some workers exhibited toward work that did not fit in with their views. It was as though Hilbert's Program were the ideal state of affairs, and the extent to which mathematics could not be squeezed into the narrow confines of first-order logic was somehow a measure of the inadequacy of mathematics, rather than of first-order logic. In the end, however, the train slowed for us to get back on board.

9. At this point our discussion splits into two parts, corresponding to two fairly distinct lines of work that eventually merged in modern infinitary logic. The first line was to stick with finite, first-order formulas, but to allow infinite proofs. This line was taken by several logicians, and culminated in the so-called ω-Completeness Theorem. The second line was to ignore the formalist tradition and to study infinitary formulas directly. The early work in this area was not received kindly, and much of it has been all but forgotten. For example, several works are not mentioned in any of the books on infinitary logic (mine included), in spite of the fact that they foreshadow many of the important developments of recent years. One of the aims of Section 11 is to draw attention to some of these forgotten papers.

The next two sections are devoted to the two lines of work mentioned above. The two lines merge in the so-called Omitting Types Theorem, a modern version of the ω-Completeness Theorem. Section 12 contains a technical discussion of the importance of this result for the study of infinitary logic. The moral is in Section 13.

10. The Gödel Incompleteness Theorem gave an example of a sentence $\forall x A(x)$ about natural numbers such that each of $A(0)$, $A(1)$, $A(2)$, ... is provable with a finite proof from the first-order version of the axioms for natural numbers, but such that $\forall x A(x)$ is not provable with a finite proof. This suggests adding the following infinitary rule of proof, called the ω-rule (in the past often called the rule of complete induction, or Carnap's rule): For any formula B, if each of $B(0)$, $B(1)$, $B(2)$, ... are provable, then conclude $\forall x B(x)$.

If the point of such a rule is lost on the reader, if he feels that there is no possibility of ever actually applying such a rule, he is in good company. The rule was first mentioned by Hilbert and Tarski, who both felt the same way. Tarski wrote in 1933 "... that such a rule, on account of its 'infinitistic' character, departs significantly from all rules of inference hitherto used, that it cannot easily be brought into harmony with the current view of the deductive method, and finally that the possibility of its practical application in the construction of deductive systems seems to be problematic in the highest degree."

The first person[1] to have taken the rule seriously seems to have been Rudolf Carnap in 1935 in his work on the syntax and semantics of language. His work is almost as hard for a modern logician to appreciate as it was for his contemporaries, but for entirely different reasons. Carnap had in mind a fixed countable universe of discourse where everything has a name, say $a_1, a_2, \ldots$. He wanted to develop syntactic rules of proof and semantical rules of truth in parallel, neither being more basic than the other. In particular, he wanted it to be the case that the only possible way to assign 'true' and 'false' to sentences in such a way as to preserve the rules of proof was to give all the logical operations their intended meanings. Thus, to make sure that $\forall$ has its intended meaning of 'for all', he had to have the rule of proof: if you can prove each of $B(a_1), B(a_2), \ldots$ then conclude $\forall x B(x)$.

It is obvious that if you are considering only the structure of natural numbers with the usual operation of addition and multiplication, then every true first-order sentence about natural numbers can be proved using the ω-rule. Rosser studied the ω-rule (or Carnap's rule as he called it in his 1937 paper) in the context of the axiom system P developed in Russell and Whitehead's *Principia Mathematica*[2], an axiom system that deals not just with natural numbers, but also with sets of natural numbers, sets of sets and so on. Rosser showed that the Gödel phenomenon is present even with the ω-rule. In particular, he showed that there is a sentence of the form

"there is a set X of natural numbers such that $A(X)$"

which is true, but which is not provable using the ω-rule, where $A(X)$ is a first-order sentence just about natural numbers, the operations of arithmetic, and membership in the set X.

There was some work of a proof-theoretic nature on the ω-rule carried out by Schütte and Lorenzen, but the next result of importance for infinitary logic had to wait for the mid 1950's with the proof of the ω-Completeness Theorem, by Henkin and Orey, independently. They showed that, in contrast to Rosser's results, any true sentence of the form

"for all sets X of natural numbers, $A(X)$"

is provable using the ω-rule.

This result was reformulated by the Polish logicians Grzegorczyk, Mostowski, and Ryll-Nardzewski in 1961, in a more general and more usable form. If we state their result in terms of infinite formulas, which they avoided, their version gives a condition for a first-order theory to be consistent with a simple infinite sentence of the kind we have seen before:

$$\forall x [A_0(x) \vee A_1(x) \vee A_2(x) \vee \ldots],$$

where each of the A_i are finite, first-order formulas. You get the ω-Completeness Theorem by taking $A_i(x)$ to be the formula $x = i$. Their result is now called the Omitting Types Theorem, and is one of the most basic results of infinitary logic.

11. The line of work dealing directly with infinitely long formulas is much less coherent than that dealing with the ω-rule. The earliest papers we know of are by the Russian mathematician P. S. Novikoff (1939 and 1943) and his compatriot, the logician D. A. Bochvar. These papers treat what we now call the *propositional part* of $L_{\omega_1\omega}$. That is, quantifiers are not discussed except as infinite conjunctions and disjunctions.

Novikoff's aim, which is not carried out in these papers, is to prove the consistency of arithmetic and the simple theory of types by working with infinitely long formulas within 'intuitionist mathematics'. Consistency statements are to be proved by translating, say, number theory into infinitary logic (replacing quantifiers by infinitary conjunctions and disjunctions), by quoting his theorem that an infinitary sentence which is provable is 'regular', and by noting that there are non-regular formulas (say a propositional letter) and hence unprovable formulas. This, in outline, is very much like the Gentzen–Schütte treatment of consistency through infinitary logic culminating in Tait's 1958 paper, though not formulated carefully enough to yield the kind of results Novikoff had in mind.

Novikoff's axioms and rules of proof consist of all finite tautologies, plus all of the following:

$$(11.1)\quad \begin{array}{l} (A_1 \wedge A_2 \wedge A_3 \wedge \ldots) \rightarrow A_i \text{ (for each } A_i \text{ in the list on the left)} \\ B_i \rightarrow (B_1 \vee B_2 \vee B_3 \vee \ldots) \text{ (for each } B_i \text{ in the list on the right)} \end{array}$$

His rules are those of modus ponens, substitution, and the following analogues of the ω-rule in this setting.

$$(11.2)\quad \begin{array}{l} \text{From each of } (A \rightarrow B_1) \text{ and } (A \rightarrow B_2) \text{ and } \ldots, \text{ infer } A \rightarrow (B_1 \wedge B_2 \wedge \ldots). \\ \text{From each of } (A_1 \rightarrow B) \text{ and } (A_2 \rightarrow B) \text{ and } \ldots, \text{ infer } (A_1 \vee A_2 \vee \ldots) \rightarrow B. \end{array}$$

Novikoff's notion of 'regular' amounted to being able to transform the given sentence into something which is obviously a tautology by means of the following distributive law:

$$A \vee (B_1 \wedge B_2 \wedge B_3 \wedge \ldots) \text{ is equivalent to}$$
$$(A \vee B_1) \wedge (A \vee B_2) \wedge (A \vee B_3) \wedge \ldots .$$

Another feature of interest in his papers is his use of the negation normal form. These papers are discussed further in the appendix.

Bochvar, in 1940, showed that Novikoff's rules were complete[3], that every tautology is provable – a result rediscovered by Scott and Tarski in their 1958 paper!

These papers were all reviewed in *The Journal of Symbolic Logic* and *Mathematical Reviews* soon after they appeared, but the reviews dealt primarily not with their achievements, but with their shortcomings, both actual and those of a strictly philosophical nature. Church, for example, in his review of Novikoff's 1939 paper, echoes Tarski's earlier remarks on the ω-rule. He writes, "In view of the non-effective nature of the rules of inference and of the formulas themselves ... it cannot be said that this calculus is a logic, or logistic system, in the proper sense of the word."

Carnap, in his 1943 book, decided to use infinite sentences, as well as his version of the ω-rule. He was apparently unaware of the Russian work discussed above. Carnap calls anything that is either a finite formula, or an infinite conjunction or infinite disjunction of finite formulas a *junctive*. He mentions the possibility of building up more complicated sentences out of junctives, but does not pursue the matter. What he does do, however, which is of historical interest, is to develop a notion like that of consistency property. He does this in the process of defining a notion 'A is a C-implicate of B' by requiring[4] (in essence) that every consistency property containing the junctive B also contains the junctive A.

Two works containing infinite formulas appeared in 1949. One, by the algebraist P. Jordan of Hamburg, is rather confused by modern standards. Some of the results are incorrect while others are intertwined with set-theoretic difficulties which apparently escaped the author. For example, E. Fisher[5] has recently shown that one of Jordan's 'theorems' is in fact equivalent to Vopenka's Principle, a strong axiom of infinity not generally accepted as true.

The other discussion of infinitary formulas in 1949 was by Abraham Robinson in his dissertation[6]. He mentions Carnap's book, defines $L_{\omega_1\omega}$ just as we would now, but only studies those formulas of the form

$$\forall x [A_0(x) \vee A_1(x) \vee A_2(x) \vee \ldots].$$

He too foreshadows important work to come by studying when such a formula is equivalent to one of its finite 'approximations':

$$\forall x A_0(x),$$
$$\forall x [A_0(x) \vee A_1(x)],$$
$$\forall x [A_0(x) \vee A_1(x) \vee A_2(x)], \text{ etc.}$$

Robinson uses his results to show that the concept of Archimedian field cannot be expressed in first-order logic.

There was another line of work in logic over the years which, while not dealing with infinitary logic, gradually produced the climate where the study of infinitary logic could flourish. This is the branch of logic known as model theory. It began with the theorem of Löwenheim referred to earlier. A number of people contributed to it but it was only about 1950 that, under the influence of Abraham Robinson and Alfred Tarski, it really became a coherent field of study. Tarski founded a school of model theory at Berkeley and this school eventually turned to the study of infinitary logic. This was only natural, as logic had become the study of the language and logic of mathematics, not just the study of deductive systems.

In the fall of 1956 Henkin and Tarski held a seminar on infinitary logic at Berkeley. This seminar marks the legitimatization of infinitary formulas. Carol Karp, then at work on her doctoral dissertation[8], discussed her results in this seminar. Other work from this seminar was presented to the world in the papers of Henkin, Tarski and Scott. These papers led to the dissertations of Hanf, Lopez–Escobar, Malitz, Kueker, Nebres and the author, all in California and all concerned with infinitary logic.

Of the many papers on infinitary logic that followed the Berkeley seminar, one seems to me to have been particularly important. That was the paper Dana Scott presented to the 1963 model theory symposium in Berkeley. In this paper Scott argued persuasively that of the host of infinitary logics then making the rounds, $L_{\omega_1 \omega}$ was the one most likely to produce a useful, interesting theory. This has certainly turned out to be the case.

It is not within the scope of this paper to go into any of the fascinating results in infinitary logic obtained in the past twenty years, or to predict the direction future work will take. The reader who wishes to learn more should consult the books of Keisler, Dickmann and the author listed in the references, or the *Handbook of Mathematical Logic*.

12. In this section we want to justify our claim, made in Section 10, that the Omitting Types Theorem is one of the most basic results of infinitary logic.

There are other extensions of first-order logic besides infinitary logics, namely those obtained by adding new quantifiers to the language of first-order logic, the new quantifiers usually expressing various mathematically precise versions of the informal notions of 'many' and 'most'. We mention in particular the logics $L(Q)$ where $QxA(x)$ means that there are uncountably many x satisfying $A(x)$ and the logic $L(aa)$ where $aaXA(X)$ means that $A(X)$ holds for almost all countable X. There are several others.

What is interesting is that whenever some new logic L^* like one of the above is developed and studied, it turns out that if L^* has nice properties, then so does the corresponding infinitary logic $L^*_{\omega_1\omega}$ which allows all the logical operations of L^* in addition to countably infinite conjunctions and disjunctions. The reason for this is that any proof of a Completeness-Compactness Theorem for an $\aleph_0$-compact logic L^* usually shows one how to obtain a version of the Omitting Types Theorem, and this alone is enough to allow one to obtain many important facts about the logic $L^*_{\omega_1\omega}$. In particular such a result can be used to read off a complete set of axioms and rules for $L^*_{\omega_1\omega}$ in a direct way.

The correct context for proving such a claim is given by abstract model theory, with which we assume the reader is more or less familiar. We assume also that L^* is a logic (in the sense of our 1974 paper) closed under the usual operations of first-order logic, and also closed under substitution of formulas $A(x_1 \dots x_n)$ for relation symbols $R(x_1 \dots x_n)$ in sentences $B(R)$. For any n, we use $true_n$, or simply *true* for some trivially true formula about $x_1 \dots x_n$.

We want to formulate a version of the Omitting Types Theorem which covers all of the known examples of Omitting Types Theorems. In particular, unlike other formulations in abstract model theory, it must not imply that every consistent sentence of L^* has a countable model, since this is not true about $L(Q)$ and $L(aa)$ which do satisfy versions of the Omitting Types Theorem. To formulate our condition, we introduce the following definitions.

A *test sentence* of L^* is a sentence $B(R)$ with the property that if $R = R_1 \cup R_2 \cup R_3 \cup \dots$ is a countable union of relations, and if $B(R)$ is true, then one of the $B(R_i)$ is true. (That is, if (M, R) is a model of $B(R)$, then for some i, (M, R_i) is also a model of $B(R)$.)

Let $\mathscr{B}$ be a set of test sentences, T a theory of L^*, and $\Sigma\,(x_1 \dots x_n)$ a set of formulas of L^*. We say that T *locally accepts* Σ *with respect* to $\mathscr{B}$ if the following holds: whenever $B(R)$ is a test sentence in $\mathscr{B}$, and R is an n-ary relation symbol not occurring in $T \cup \Sigma$, if $T + B(true_n)$ has a model then there is some σ in Σ such that $T + B(\sigma)$ has a model.

Finally, we say that a countable logic L^* has the *Omitting Types Property* if there is a set $\mathscr{B}$ of test sentences such that for all T and all $\{\Sigma_n(x_1, \dots, x_{k_n}) \mid n = 0, 1, \dots\}$, if T locally accepts each Σ_n with respect to $\mathscr{B}$, then there is a model of $T + \bigwedge_{n=0}^{\infty} \forall x_1 \dots x_{k_n} \vee \Sigma_n(\mathrm{x})$.

EXAMPLES. All of the most familiar examples of $\aleph_0$-compact logics satisfy this Omitting Types Property. For first-order logic the test formulas are those of the form

$$\exists x_1 \ldots x_n [A(\mathrm{x}) \wedge R(\mathrm{x})] .$$

For $L(Q)$, Keisler has proved an Omitting Types Theorem[8] where the test formulas are those that begin with a string of Q's and $\exists$'s, followed by a formula of the form

$$\exists \mathrm{x}[A(\mathrm{x}, \ldots) \wedge R(\mathrm{x})] .$$

There is a similar result for $L(aa)$, due to Kaufmann.

THEOREM. Let L^* be an $\aleph_0$-compact countable logic satisfying the Omitting Types Property with respect to a set $\mathscr{B}$ of test sentences. The following list of axioms and rules are complete for the logic $L^*_{\omega_1\omega}$.

Axioms: All valid sentences of L^*, the axioms in 11.1, plus, for every test sentence $B(R)$ in $\mathscr{B}$, all formulas of the form

$$B(\textstyle\bigvee_{i=1}^{\infty} A_i) \rightarrow \bigvee_{i=1}^{\infty} B(A_i).$$

Rules: The rules of modus ponens, generalization, substitution of formulas for relation symbols, plus the rules of 11.2.

The proof of this result is not difficult, but will be given elsewhere, where we will spell out more carefully exactly how the logic $L^*_{\omega_1\omega}$ is formed. We will also show how a number of other results about $L^*_{\omega_1\omega}$ follow from the same assumptions, e.g., the undefinability of well-orderings. The proof of the above is based on Keisler's proof ot he completeness theorem for $L_{\omega_1\omega}(Q)$ from his Omitting Types Theorem for $L(Q)$. What is interesting for us is how directly the additional axioms for $L^*_{\omega_1\omega}$ are from the set $\mathscr{B}$ of test sentences.

13. We use many normatives to describe the propositions of mathematics (true or false, provable or unprovable, interesting or uninteresting, significant or not) as though they all had equally absolute meanings. For better or worse, this is not the case. Our perception of the significance and interest of a result, or even of whole branch of mathematics, depends on certain consciously and unconsciously held beliefs about the nature of man, mathematics and the external world. Only by being aware of this dependence can we achieve the tolerance that is the catalyst for real advancement.

The history of infinitary logic shows the vicissitudes in one small part of mathematics caused by shifting philosophical attitudes as to the nature of mathematics and its proper relation to logic. It bears witness to the following remarks by Rudolf Carnap. The italics are his.

The history of science shows examples of ... prohibitions based on prejudices deriving from religious, mythological, metaphysical, or other irrational sources, which slowed up the developments for shorter or longer periods of time. Let us learn from the lessons of history. Let us grant to those who work in any special field of investigation the freedom to use any form of expression which seems useful to them; the work in the field will sooner or later lead to the elimination of those forms which have no useful function. *Let us be cautious in making assertions and critical in examining them, but tolerant in permitting linguistic forms.*[9]

It is fair to say that mathematical logic has grown in applicability by the study of infinitary logic, but that other parts of logic have yet to take advantage of this type of linguistic expression. The examples given in the introduction and in Section 6 show that infinitistic expressions can arise in formalizing ordinary English. It may well prove more fruitful to analyze them directly as above, rather than by the more traditional approach. If so, then perhaps in a future conference the subject of infinitary logic will really deserve to be considered as a part of pure (rather than applied) logic.

APPENDIX: NOVIKOFF'S THEOREM ON REGULAR FORMULAS

The reviews of Novikoff's papers do not inspire confidence in the correctness, let alone interest, of his main theorem, that every provable formula of propositional $L_{\omega_1\omega}$ is regular. Part of the problem is that these papers are not in the author's native language, so there are some mistranslations (like 'true' for 'provable'). There are also quite a few misprints. The main problem, though, is that Novikoff's proof is intrinsically difficult, for reasons which will become apparent.

Novikoff's definition of regular formula amounts to a second notion of provability, one with a form of the subformula property. Having given this definition, he then works syntactically and shows that the regular formulas contain all axioms and are closed under the rules of inference, including modus ponens. Thus, he is in effect giving a kind of cut elimination argument!

It seems worth giving Novikoff's definition of regularity, and showing that his theorem is correct. However, we will make life easy for ourselves by giving a semantic proof. It will become clear that one could use a careful syntactic analysis of Novikoff's proof as a substitute for cut-elimination in obtaining the ordinal-bound results obtained in Tait's paper.

Novikoff works with two kinds of propositional variables, $p_1, ..., p_n, ...$ which are as usual but also $q_1, ..., q_n, ...$ which are treated as non-logical axioms. A formula is in *negation normal form* (n.n.f.) – Novikoff uses the terms 'reduced' – if all negations apply directly to propositional variables, and if $\rightarrow$ does not occur in it. By using de Morgan's laws, one sees that every formula A is provably equivalent to a formula A^* in negation normal form.

In the following, we use $\mathscr{A}$, $\mathscr{B}$, and $\mathscr{C}$ to range over countable sets of propositional formulas of $L_{\omega_1\omega}$. If $\mathscr{A} = \{A_1, A_2, ...\}$ then $\bigwedge \mathscr{A}$ denotes the infinite conjunction $A_1 \wedge A_2 \wedge ...$, similarly for disjunctions.

The set of *regular n.n.f. formulas* is defined inductively as the smallest class of n.n.f. formulas satisfying:

(i) Each of the nonlogical axioms q_i is regular.
(ii) If for some i, both p_i and $\neg p_i$ are in $\mathscr{A}$, then $\bigvee \mathscr{A}$ is regular.
(iii) If A is regular and $A \in \mathscr{A}$ then $\bigvee \mathscr{A}$ is regular.
(iv) If each A in $\mathscr{A}$ is regular, then so is $\bigwedge \mathscr{A}$.
(v) If $\bigvee(\mathscr{A} \cup \mathscr{B})$ is regular, so is $\bigvee(\mathscr{A} \cup \{\bigvee \mathscr{B}\})$.
(vi) (Distributive law) If for each A in $\mathscr{A}$, the formula $\bigvee(\mathscr{B} \cup \{A\})$ is regular, then so is $\bigvee(\mathscr{B} \cup \{\bigwedge \mathscr{A}\})$.

An arbitrary formula A is regular if its negation normal form A^* is regular.

If one replaces '$\bigvee \mathscr{A}$ is regular' by '$\vdash \mathscr{A}$ is derivable' in above definition, then it is equivalent to Tait's treatment of Gentzen derivability for n.n.f. formulas. Thus Novikoff really is proving a cut-elimination theorem.

Church, in his review of Novikoff's second paper, wrote, "The author's definition of regularity, it should be remarked, has much the character of a definition of truth in the sense of Tarski, and his consistency proof belongs essentially in the category of those which make use of a truth definition." This does not seem correct, and is especially unfair given the trouble that Novikoff goes to in keeping his proof syntactic.

THEOREM (Novikoff). A formula is provable if and only if it is regular.

Proof. It is easy to see that every regular formula is provable, and that every provable formula is a tautology, that is, true under every truth assignment making all the q_i's true. Thus it suffices to show that every tautology is regular. Let C be a formula which is not regular, and let us show that C is not a tautology. We may assume that C is in negation normal form. For any formula B we let B' denot the negation normal for of $\neg B$. Note that C'' is C.

Let S be the set of all finite sets $s = \{B_1, ..., B_{k+1}\}$ $(k \geqslant 0)$ such that $(\bigwedge s)'$ is *not* regular. We will prove that S is a consistency property (see either

Keisler's or the author's book, with the obvious simplifications due to the fact that we are treating only propositional logic, for the definition of consistency property and the Model Existence Theorem) with the property that if $s \in S$ then $s \cup \{q_i\} \in S$, for each i. Thus by the Model Existence Theorem, there is a truth assignment making all the q_i's true as well as $\bigwedge s$, for any $s \in S$. But $\{C'\} \in S$ so C cannot be a tautology.

First, let us show that if $(\bigwedge \mathscr{A}) \in s \in S$, then for each $A \in \mathscr{A}$ $s \cup \{A\} \in S$. Using the notation from above, we let $B_1, ..., B_k$ $(k \geqslant 0)$ be the other formulas in S. We will show that for each $A \in \mathscr{A}$,' $\{B_1, ..., B_k, A\} \in S$, from which the conclusion easily follows. If this set is not in S, then

$$B_1' \vee ... \vee B_k' \vee A'$$

is a regular formula. Now it is easy to check that if $\mathscr{C}_0 \subseteq \mathscr{C}_1$ and $\bigvee \mathscr{C}_0$ is regular, so is $\bigvee \mathscr{C}_1$, so

$$\bigvee(\{B_1', ..., B_k'\} \cup \{D' \mid D \in \mathscr{A}\})$$

is regular. But then by rule (v)

$$B_1' \vee ... \vee B_k' \vee \bigvee\{D' \mid D \in \mathscr{A}\}$$

is regular, which is a contradiction, since this is $(\bigwedge s)'$.

Next we show the crucial clause, and leave the others to the reader. Assume that $\bigvee \mathscr{A} \in s \in S$. We must know that for some A in $\mathscr{A}$, $s \cup \{A\} \in S$. Now $(\bigwedge s)'$ is not regular, and has the form

$$B_1' \vee ... \vee B_k' \vee (\bigwedge\{D' \mid D \in \mathscr{A}\}),$$

so by the distributive law (vi), there must be some $A \in \mathscr{A}$ such that

$$B_1' \vee ... \vee B_k' \vee A'$$

is not regular, so $\{B_1, ..., B_k, A\} \in S$, from which it follows that $s \cup \{A\} \in S$. □

Novikoff draws the following consequence (and a generalization of it) from this theorem. It is a direct forerunner of the kind of existence proofs that are derived from cut-elimination arguments (see Schwichtenberg's Chapter D.2 in the *Handbook of Mathematical Logic*, e.g.).

COROLLARY. If each of $A_1, ..., A_n, ...$ is finite, and if $A_1 \vee ... \vee A_n \vee ...$ is provable, then one can find, from the proof, an integer k such that $A_1 \vee ... \vee A_k$ is provable.

Proof. Being provable, the formula is regular, and hence one can find a 'derivation' of it as a regular formula. It is easy to see that from any such 'derivation' one can read off a finite subderivation. The only clause that needs any consideration at all is the distributive law. So suppose that A_j is $B_1 \wedge \ldots \wedge B_r$, and that the derivation ends in the conclusion that $A_1 \vee A_2 \vee \ldots$ is regular because each of

$$A_1 \vee \ldots \vee A_{j-1} \vee B_i \vee A_{j+1} \vee \ldots$$

is regular, for $i = 1, 2, \ldots, r$. By induction, for each i there is an $n(i)$ such that the finite disjunction up to $A_{n(i)}$ is derivable, so one just lets k be the max of the various $n(i)$, for $i = 1, \ldots, r$. □

This corollary can be thought of as a syntactic 'effective' version.

University of Wisconsin, Madison
Stanford University

NOTES

* The preparation of this paper was partially supported by Grant NSF-MCS76-06541. We appreciate the suggestions of Janet Christen and H.J. Keisler on an earlier draft of the paper.

[1] See [7, 8, and 9].

[2] Gödel's Theorem was also in this context, but holds in first-order arithmetic, too, whereas Rosser's version needs a higher order theory.

[3] Having been unable to find the particular volume containing Bochvar's paper, I am forced to rely on the reviews of Church and Curry here. See [5].

[4] See, in particular, definitions 23-4 and 30-3 in [9].

[5] The 'theorem' in question is (ii) in [12].

[6] This appeared in print as [32].

[7] This appeared, in revised form, as [20].

[8] See the 'Strong Omitting Types Theorem' in [21], and the corresponding result about $L(aa)$ in [5].

[9] Page 221 of [10].

[10] We thank Mr. Robert Gray for drawing our attention to the relevance of [24] and [37] for our discussion.

BIBLIOGRAPHY

For ease of referencing, we have referred to all papers by their author and year of publication. This differs slightly from the dating system used in [15] below.

[1] J. Barwise, *Infinitary Logic and Admissible Sets*, Doctoral Dissertation, Stanford Univ., 1967. (Part of this appeared in *J. Symbolic Logic* 34 (1969), 226–252).

[2] J. Barwise, 'Axioms for Abstract Model Theory', *Annals of Math. Logic* 7 (1974), 221–265.

[3] J. Barwise, *Admissible sets and structures*, Springer-Verlag, 1975.
[4] J. Barwise (ed.), *Handbook of Math. Logic*, North-Holland, 1977.
[5] J. Barwise, M. Kaufmann, and M. Makkai, 'Stationary Logic', *Annals of Math. Logic* 13 (1978), 171–224.
[6] D. A. Bochvar, 'Über einen Aussagenkalkül mit abzählbaren logischen Summen und Produkten', *Matematiceskij sbornik*, n.s. Vol. 7, 1940, pp. 65–100. (Reviewed by H. Curry in *Math. Reviews* 11 (1940); and A. Church in *J. Symbolic Logic* 5 (1940), 119).
[7] Rudolf Carnap, 'Ein Gültigkeitskriterium für die Sätze der Klassischen Mathematik', *Monatshefte für Mathematik und Physik* 42 (1935), 163–190.
[8] Rudolf Carnap, *The Logical Syntax of Language*, (Orig., Vienna, 1934) London, 1937.
[9] Rudolf Carnap, *Formalisation of Semantics*, Cambridge, Mass., 1943.
[10] Rudolf Carnap, *Meaning and Necessity*, Second edition, Univ. of Chicago Press, 1956.
[11] M. A. Dickmann, *Large Infinitary Languages*, North-Holland, Amsterdam, 1975.
[12] E. Fisher, 'Vopenka's Principle, Category Theory and Universal Algebra', *Notices A.M.S.* (742-08-4) 24 (1977), A-44.
[13] A. Grzegorczyk, A. Mostowski, and C. Ryll-Nardzewski, 'Definability of Sets in Models of Axiomatic Theories', *Bull. Acad. Polon. Sci.* 9 (1961), 163–167.
[14] W. Hanf, 'Incompactness in Languages With Infinitely Long Expressions', *Fund. Math.* 53 (1964), 309–324.
[15] J. van Heijenoort (ed.), *From Frege to Gödel*, Harvard, 1967.
[16] L. Henkin, 'A Generalization of the Concept of ω-Consistency', *J. Symbolic Logic* 19 (1954), 183–196.
[17] L. Henkin, 'Some Remarks on Infinitely Long Formulas', *Infinitistic Methods*, Warsaw, 1961.
[18] D. Hilbert, 'On the Infinite', *Math. Annalen* 95 (1926), 161–190. Translated in [15].
[19] P. Jordan, 'Zur Axiomatik der Verknüpfungsbereiche', *Abh. Math. Sem. Univ. Hamburg* 16 (1949), 54–70. (Reviewed by T. Frayne, *J. Symbolic Logic* 23 (1958), 361; and by G. Birkhoff, *Math. Reviews* 11 (1950), 75).
[20] Carol Karp, *Languages With Expressions of Infinite Length*, North-Holland, Amsterdam, 1964.
[21] H. J. Keisler, 'Logic With the Quantifier "there exist uncountably many"', *Annals of Math. Logic* 1 (1970), 1–83.
[22] H. J. Keisler, *Model Theory for Infinitary Logic*, North-Holland, Amsterdam, 1971.
[23] G. Kreisel, 'Choice of Infinitary Languages by Means of Definability Criteria; Generalized Recursion Theory', in *The Syntax and Semantics of Infinitary Languages*, J. Barwise (ed.), Springer-Verlag, *Lecture Notes in Math.* 72 (1968), 139–151.
[24] L. Löwenheim, 'On Possibilities in the Calculus of Relatives', *Math. Annalen* 76 (1915), 447–470. Translated in [15].
[25] J. Malitz, *Problems in the Model Theory of Infinite Languages*, Ph.D. Thesis, Berkeley, 1965.

[26] P. S. Novikoff, 'Sur quelques theorems d'existence', *Comptes rendus (Doklady) de l'Académie des Sciences de l'URSS* 23 (1939), 438–440. (Reviewed by Church in *J. Symbolic Logic* V (1940), 69).

[27] P. S. Novikoff, 'On the Consistency of Certain Logical Calculus', *Matematiceskij sbornik* 12 (54), No. 2 (1943), 231–261. (This is an expanded version of [26]. It is reviewed by Church in *J. Symbolic Logic* 11 (1946), 129; and by McKinsey in *Math. Reviews* 5 (1944), 197.)

[28] S. Orey, 'On ω-Consistency and Related Properties', *J. Symbolic Logic* 21 (1956), 246–252.

[29] C. S. Peirce, *Collected Papers*, Harvard Univ. Press, Cambridge, Mass.

[30] Walker Percy, *The Message in the Bottle*, Farrar, Straus and Giroux, N.Y., 1975.

[31] Frank P. Ramsey, *The Foundations of Mathematics*, Proceedings of the London Mathematical Society, Ser. 2, Vol. 25, Part 5, 1925, pp. 338–384.

[32] A. Robinson, *On the Metamathematics of Algebra*, North-Holland, Amsterdam, 1951.

[33] Barkley Rosser, 'Gödel Theorems for Non-Constructive Logics', *J. Symbolic Logic* 2 (1937), 129–137.

[34] Dana Scott, 'Logic With Denumerably Long Formulas and Finite Strings of Quantifiers', in *The Theory of Models*, Addison, Henkin, and Tarski (eds.), 1965.

[35] D. S. Scott and A. Tarski, 'The Sentential Calculus With Infinitely Long Expressions , *Colloq. Math.* 6 (1958), 165–170.

[36] W. W. Tait, 'Normal Derivability in Classical Logic', in *The Syntax and Semantics of Infinitary Languages*, Springer Lecture Notes in Math., No. 72, 1968, pp. 204–236.

[37] A. Tarski, 'Some Observations on the Concepts of ω-Consistency and ω-Completeness', *Monatshefte für Mathematik* 40 (1933), 97–112; reprinted in translation in Tarski's book *Logic, Semantics, Metamathematics*, Oxford, 1956, pp. 279–295.

[38] A. Tarski, 'Remarks on Predicate Logic With Infinitely Long Expressions', *Colloq. Math.* 6 (1958), 171–176.

Added in Proof:

1. Wilfred Seig has drawn my attention to a little known anti-formalist paper of Zermelo which studies the propositional part of $L_{\omega,\omega}$: 'Grundlagen einer allgemeinen Theorie der mathematischen Satzsysteme', *Fundamenta Mathematica* 25 (1935), 136–146.
2. A technical version of this paper will appear as 'The Role of the Omitting Types Theorem in Infinitory Logic', in *Arch. f. math. Logik u. Grundl. Forschung*.

A. ROSE

MANY-VALUED LOGICS

I shall endeavour to cover as many branches of many-valued logic and as much of the work done in these branches as space permits. Much must, of course, be omitted, and I should therefore like to refer to an excellent bibliography of many-valued logics by Nicholas Rescher in his book (*Many-Valued Logic*, McGraw Hill 51893, 1969). This only covers publications to 1965, so I have given a few references (at the end of the text) to papers published since that date.

I should like to begin by outlining the solution to an independence problem in 2-valued logic. A complete formalisation of the 2-valued propositional calculus with material implication and the logical constant f as primitives is provided by the 2 axioms

(A1) $((p \supset q) \supset r) \supset ((r \supset p) \supset (s \supset p))$,
(A2) $f \supset p$,

together with the rules of substitution for propositional variables and *modus ponens*. The axiom (A1) may be shown to be independent by means of the following interpretation table for implication, the logical constant f being assigned the value 3.

	$P \supset Q$	Q: 1	2	3
	*1	1	2	3
P	2	1	1	2
	3	1	1	1

If (A1) is deleted the remaining axiom always takes the value 1 with respect to this interpretation and, if the premiss(es) of a primitive rule of procedure possess(es) this property, so does the conclusion. Thus every provable formula possesses the property. On the other hand (A1) does not possess the property and so it is independent.

$$((p \supset q) \supset r) \supset ((r \supset p) \supset (s \supset p))$$

2 23 12 2 2 12 2 1 22

E. Agazzi (ed.), Modern Logic – A Survey, 113–129.

This interpretation has, so far, no specifal significance other than that of providing a non-standard model yielding the independence proof, but I should like now to consider such tables in their own right. We shall consider an abstract universe in which propositions, instead of being divided into 2 categories – true and false – are divided into m categories, where $m \geqslant 2$ and m may even denote an infinite cardinal. The 2-valued truth-values T, F may be re-named, 1, 2 respectively and we shall, for the present, generalise this latter notation to denote the truth-values by $1, 2, ..., m$, assuming for the time being that $m < \aleph_0$. We shall not, at this stage, consider any particular interpretations of the truth-values, though, following Post, we shall regard i as more true than j $(1 \leqslant i < j \leqslant m)$.

Since interpretations are not yet under consideration we are under no obligation to give any particular names to the logical operations corresponding to particular m-valued truth-tables and we should be perfectly free to invent new names for them. In practice this does not normally occur, names being borrowed from the 2-valued propositional calculus in view of similarities in the properties of the operations, but there is, of course, nothing essential about this. The connection between 'or' of a many-valued logic and ordinary 2-valued disjunction is no stronger than the connection between the multiplication operation of an abstract group and that of the 3 times table. It is also important to remember that a particular notion of the 2-valued case may ramify into several different notions of the m-valued case. In the special case where $m = 2$ these all become the same as each other and as the 2-valued concept from which the name was borrowed.

We shall consider first the m-valued propositional calculi developed by Post for the cases where $2 \leqslant m < \aleph_0$ Post did not consider infinite-valued logics but we shall discuss these when we consider the alternative approach of Łukasiewicz. Post's m-valued propositional calculus has 2 primitive functors, for which the 2-valued names disjunction and negation are borrowed. If we re-write the conventional 2-valued truth-tables for these 2 functors using the above numerical notation we can see easily that if $P, Q, \sim P, P \vee Q$ take the

		Q		
	$P \vee Q$	1	2	$\sim P$
P	1	1	1	2
	2	1	2	1

truth-values $x, y, n(x), \mathrm{a}(x, y)$ respectively then

$$n(x) = x + 1 \quad (x \neq 2), n(2) = 1, a(x, y) = \min(x, y).$$

Post generalised these equations to the m-valued case, the generalised equations being

$$n(x) = x + 1 \ \ (x \neq m), n(m) = 1, a(x, y) = \min(x, y).$$

Thus, for example, if $m = 5$ the truth-tables are as follows:

	$P \vee Q$	Q: 1	2	3	4	5	$\sim P$
	1	1	1	1	1	1	2
	2	1	2	2	2	2	3
P	3	1	2	3	3	3	4
	4	1	2	3	4	4	5
	5	1	2	3	4	5	1

It follows easily that the commutativity and associativity of 2-valued disjunction are preserved, and, if we make the definitions

$$\sim^0 P =_{\text{df}} P, \sim^{i+1} P =_{\text{df}} \sim(\sim^i P) \ (i = 0, 1, ...),$$

the law of cancellation

$$\sim\sim P =_T P$$

of the 2-valued propositional calculus generalises to the law

$$\sim^m P =_T P.$$

The 2-valued propositional calculus with disjunction and negation as primitive functors is well known to be functionally complete and Post showed that this property holds in the *m*-valued case. To this end he established the definability of an alternative form of generalised negation and of a generalised conjunction. He considered also the assignment of truth-tables to generalised implication functors, though the definability of these was a consequence of his functional completeness theorem rather than a preliminary result. We note that if, in the 2-valued case, $P, Q, \sim P, P \,\&\, Q, P \supset Q$ take the truth-values $x, y, n(x), k(x, y), c(x, y)$ respectively then

	$P \,\&\, Q$	Q: 1	2	$\sim P$
P	1	1	2	2
	2	2	2	1

$P \supset Q$	Q: 1	2
1	1	2
2	1	1

$$n(x) = 3 - x, k(x, y) = \max(x, y), c(x, y) = \max(1, 1 - x + y).$$

The first 2 equations were generalized in a straightforward way, so that if, in Post's m-valued propositional calculus, P, Q, $\simeq P$, $P \& Q$ take the truth-values $x, y, n^*(x), k(x, y)$ respectively then

$$n^*(x) = m + 1 - x, \; k(x, y) = \max(x, y),$$

giving, as an example, in the case where $m = 4$, the following truth-tables:

$P \& Q$		Q: 1	2	3	4	$\simeq P$
	1	1	2	3	4	4
P	2	2	2	3	4	3
	3	3	3	3	4	2
	4	4	4	4	4	1

We note that the truth-table of the formulae $\sim P$, $\simeq P$ are distinct except in the case where $m = 2$, in which case they are both the conventional 2-valued negation truth-table. It follows easily that the commutative and associative properties of 2-valued conjunction and the distributive properties of 2-valued disjunction and conjunction are preserved. For the new generalisation (non-primitive) of negation the cancellation and deMorgan laws are preserved also,

$$\simeq\simeq P =_T P, \; \simeq(P \vee Q) =_T \simeq P \,\&\, \simeq Q, \; \simeq(P \,\&\, Q) =_T \simeq P \vee \simeq Q,$$

and, in corresponding fashion, Post made the definition

$$P \,\&\, Q =_{\mathrm{df}} \simeq(\simeq P \vee \simeq Q)$$

In some circumstances it is permissible, in the m-valued case, to use the equation

$$c(x, y) = \max(1, 1 - x + y)$$

given above, adopting truth-tables such as the following 5-valued one:

$P \supset Q$		Q: 1	2	3	4	5
	1	1	2	3	4	5
	2	1	1	2	3	4
P	3	1	1	1	2	3
	4	1	1	1	1	2
	5	1	1	1	1	1

Since, however, the rule of *modus ponens* is an almost standard rule in formalisations of propositional calculi, it seems essential to consider the choice of implication truth-tables in relation to formalisations of many-valued propositional calculi. In the proof of the independence of (A1) it was shown that, when (A1) is deleted, every provable formula takes the value 1 exclusively rather than that every provable formula takes the truth-value T always. This suggests that we may generalise the concept of a 2-valued tautology. We may, for an arbitrary integer s $(1 \leqslant s \leqslant m-1)$ divide the truth-values into 2 classes:

(i) the truth-values $1, \ldots, s$ which we shall refer to as the designated truth-values, i.e. those which are sufficiently true to warrant consideration.

(ii) the truth-values $s+1, \ldots, m$ which we shall refer to as the undesignated truth-values.

Since $1 \leqslant s \leqslant m-1$, neither class is empty and a generalised tautology will be defined to be a formula which takes designated truth-values exclusively. For example, if $m = 5$ and $s = 3$ then, using Post's notation, the formula $p \vee \sim\sim p$ is a generalised tautology.

$p \vee$	$\sim$	$\sim p$
11		
22	4	32
33	5	43
1	1	54
52	2	15

It seems obviously desirable that a formalisation of an m-valued propositional calculus with s designated truth-values should be drawn up in such a way that a formula is provable if and only if it is a generalised tautology. Thus the implication truth – table should be such that if the formulae $P, P \supset Q$ are both generalised tautologies, so is Q. The latter property will be ensured if we make the slightly stronger requirement that, whenever $x, c(x, y) \leqslant s; y \leqslant s$.

We must therefore consider the validity of the statement:

$$\text{if } x, \max(1, 1-x+y) \leqslant s \text{ then } y \leqslant s.$$

It follows easily that it is true in the case where $s = 1$. However, if $2 \leqslant s \leqslant m-1$,

$$2, \max(1, 1-2+(s+1)) \leqslant s \text{ but not } s+1 \leqslant s.$$

Thus the present generalisation of the conventional 2-valued implication truth-table appears to be suitable if and only if $s = 1$. Post therefore introduced different implication functors $\supset_m^s$ corresponding to the different permissible values of s. The implication functors $\supset_m^1$ are, in fact, those already considered. If P, Q, $P \supset_m^s Q$ take the truth-values x, y, $c_{sm}(x, y)$ respectively then

$$c_{sm}(x, y) = 1 \ (x \geqslant y),$$
$$c_{sm}(x, y) = y \ (x \leqslant s, x < y),$$
$$c_{sm}(x, y) = 1 - x + y \ (x > s, x < y).$$

Thus, for example, in the case where $m = 5$ and $s = 3$, the implication truth-table is as shown below.

	$P \supset_5^3 Q$	Q 1	2	3	4	5
	1	1	2	3	4	5
	2	1	1	3	4	5
P	3	1	1	1	4	5
	4	1	1	1	1	2
	5	1	1	1	1	1

It now follows easily that $c_{1m}(x, y) = c(x, y) \ (m = 2, 3, ...)$ and that

$$\text{if } x, c_{sm}(x, y) \leqslant s \text{ then } y \leqslant s \ (s = 1, ..., m-1; m = 2, 3, ...).$$

The Łukasiewicz propositional calculi have 2 primitive functors C, N which, if $2 \leqslant m < \aleph_0$, are the (defined) functors $\supset_m^1$, $\simeq$ of Post. However the truth-values $1, 2, ..., m$ were re-named by Łukasiewicz as $1, (m-2)/(m-1), ..., 0$ respectively so that, if x, x' are corresponding integral and rational truth-values,

$$x' = (m - x)/(m - 1), x = m - (m - 1)x'.$$

Thus, if P, Q, NP, CPQ take the (rational) truth-values x, y, $n^*(x)$, $c(x, y)$ respectively,

$$n^*(x) = 1 - x, c(x, y) = \min(1, 1 - x + y).$$

We note that the symbol m does not occur in the 2 latter equations so that the truth-value of a formula depends only on the truth-values of its propositional variables, not on the total number of truth-values, provided, of course, that the value of m is such that the truth-values of these variables are truth-values of the m-valued propositional calculus. Thus if $\mathscr{E} = \{0, 1\}$ and all propositional variables of a formula take truth-values in $\mathscr{E}$, the truth-value of the formula will be totally independent of the value of m and will always be that of the 2-valued case and therefore a member of $\mathscr{E}$. Since $\sim P$ takes the (rational) truth-value $(m-2)/(m-1)$ when P takes the truth-value 1 and $1 \in \mathscr{E}$, $(m-2)/(m-1) \notin \mathscr{E}$ $(m = 3, 4, ...)$, Post's primitive negation is not definable in the m-valued Łukasiewicz propositional calculus $(m \geqslant 3)$ and this calculus is therefore functionally incomplete. It will therefore be convenient, in future, to denote the truth-value of $\simeq P$(i.e. $1-x$) by $n(x)$ rather than by $n^*(x)$.

If $m'-1$ is a divisor of $m-1$, the m'-valued truth-value $i/(m'-1)$ may, of course, be re-written as $i\alpha/(m-1)$ where $\alpha = (m-1)/(m'-1)$. Thus all truth-values of the m'-valued propositional calculus may be regarded as truth-values of the m-valued propositional calculus and, if all propositional variables of a formula of the m-valued propositional calculus take truth-values of the form $i/(m'-1)$, the truth-value of the formula must itself be of this form by the above independence result. This is a fairly obvious restriction of the constructability of formulae of the m-valued Łukasiewicz propositional calculus and the question then arises whether further restrictions exist. McNaughton has shown that they do not.

If the syntactical variables $P_1, ..., P_n$ denote propositional variables, $\Phi(P_1, ..., P_n)$ is a formula containing no propositional variables other than those denoted by $P_1, ..., P_n$ and $\Phi(P_1, ..., P_n)$ takes the truth-value y $(= y(x_1, ..., x_n))$ when $P_1, ..., P_n$ take the truth values $x_1, ..., x_n$ respectively, $x_i = a_i/b_i$ where $(a_i, b_i) = 1$ $(i = 1, ..., n)$, $\{b_1, ..., b_n\} = c$ and $y = d/c$ $(d \in \{0, 1, ..., c\}$, $c = c(x_1, ..., x_n)$, $d = d(x_1, ..., x_n))$ for all the m^n n-tuples $(x_1, ..., x_n)$ then the formula $\Phi(P_1, ..., P_n)$ is constructable in the m-valued Łukasiewicz propositional calculus. In particular, as Rosser and Turquette have shown, we may define functors $J_1(\ ), ..., J_m(\ )$ such that if P, $J_i(P)$ take the (integral) truth-values x, $j_i(x)$ respectively,

$$j_i(i) = 1, j_i(x) = m\ (x = 1, ..., i-1, i+1, ..., m;\ i = 1, ..., m;\ m = 2, 3, ...).$$

Thus $J_i(P)$ may be read 'P takes the truth-value i'.

Since the symbol m does not occur in the equations

$$n(x) = 1 - x,\ c(x, y) = \min(1, 1 - x + y)$$

Łukasiewicz was able to generalise his finite-valued propositional calculi to the $\aleph_0$-valued and $\mathfrak{c}$-valued cases, taking the set of truth-values in the respective cases to be the sets of rational and real numbers x such that $0 \leqslant x \leqslant 1$, and retaining the equations. In the $\mathfrak{c}$-valued case McNaughton showed that necessary and sufficient conditions for the constructability of a formula $\Phi(P_1, ..., P_n)$ which takes the truth-value $\phi(x_1, ..., x_n)$ when $P_1, ..., P_n$ take the truth-values $x_1, ..., x_n$ respectively are

(i) $\phi(x_1, ..., x_n)$ is continuous

(ii) there exist a finite number of linear forms $\psi_i(x_1, ..., x_n)$ $(i = 1, ..., h)$ such that, for some integers $a_i, b_{i1}, ..., b_{in}$; $\psi_i(x_1, ..., x_n) = a_i + \Sigma_{j=1}^{n} b_{ij}x_j$ $(i = 1, ..., h)$ and to each n-tuple $(x_1, ..., x_n)$ there corresponds an integer i $(1 \leqslant i \leqslant h,\ i = i(x_1, ..., x_n))$ such that $\phi(x_1, ..., x_n) = \psi_i(x_1, ..., x_n)$.

Many-valued propositional calculi have, in many cases, been formalised. Normally, of course, a formalisation should be weakly complete, i.e. all generalised tautologies should be provable, and it should be plausible, i.e. all other formulae should be unprovable. A method of formalisation given by Rosser and Turquette has very wide application. It pre-supposes certain definability requirements, but these fall well short of the requirement of functional completeness.

A functor is, in general, said to satisfy 'standard conditions' if, after re-naming all designated (undesignated) truth-values by T (F), its truth-table becomes (with much repetition, but without contradiction) the 2-valued truth-table of that name. For example, Post's 5-valued disjunction truth-table becomes, in the case where $s = 2$, that shown on its right and it therefore satisfies standard conditions, but his 5-valued (primitive) negation functor's truth-table

	$P \vee Q$	Q: 1	2	3	4	5	$\sim P$
	1	1	1	1	1	1	2
	2	1	2	2	2	2	3
P	3	1	2	3	3	3	4
	4	1	2	3	4	4	5
	5	1	2	3	4	5	1

	$P \vee Q$	Q: T	T	F	F	F	$\sim P$
	T	T	T	T	T	T	(T)
	T	T	T	T	T	T	(F)
P	F	T	T	F	F	F	F
	F	T	T	F	F	F	F
	F	T	T	F	F	F	T

becomes contradictory, two contradictory entries being circled, so that this negation functor does not satisfy standard conditions. The general standard condition requirement for disjunction is, of course, that the truth-value of $P \vee Q$ is undesignated if and only if the truth-values of P, Q are both un-designated, since, in the 2-valued case, $P \vee Q$ takes the truth-value F if and only if P, Q both take the truth-value F. The functor $J_i(\ )$ (with no strict 2-valued counterpart) satisfies standard conditions if the truth-value of $J_i(P)$ is designated if and only if P takes the truth-value i $(i = 1, ..., m)$.

It is sufficient (though not always quite necessary), for the Rosser–Turquette method to be applicable, for the primitive functors $F_1(\;, ..., \;), ..., F_b(\;, ..., \;)$ of $n_1, ..., n_b$ arguments respectively ($b, n_1, ..., n_b \geqslant 1$) to have truth-tables such that functors $\vee$, $J_1(\;), ..., J_m(\;)$ satisfying standard conditions are definable. For the m-valued Łukasiewicz propositional calculi ($2 \leqslant m < \aleph_0$) the functors $J_1(\;), ..., J_m(\;)$ referred to earlier satisfy standard conditions irrespective of the value of s ($1 \leqslant s \leqslant m-1$) since $1 \leqslant s$ and $m > s$. Post's disjunction functor, which can easily be shown to satisfy standard conditions whenever $1 \leqslant s \leqslant m - 1$, is definable by the equation

$$P \vee Q =_{\mathrm{df}} (P \supset^1_m Q) \supset^1_m Q$$

since the formula $(P \supset^1_m Q) \supset^1_m Q$ may easily be shown to have the required truth-table. (Alternatively, by McNaughton's theorem, an appropriate definition of this functor must exist.)

It then follows that we must be able to define standard condition negation and disjunction functors as follows:

$$\sim P =_{\mathrm{df}} \Sigma^m_{i=P+1} J_i(P), P \supset Q =_{\mathrm{df}} \sim P \vee Q,$$

where Σ relates to summation (with a definite association convention) by the standard condition disjunction. We may then adopt any axiom schemes (of which there will now be additional instances) which, together with the rule of *modus ponens*, give a weakly complete formalisation of the 2-valued propositional calculus with disjunction and negation as the primitive functors, adjoining that rule and the additional axiom schemes

$$\Sigma^m_{i=1} J_i(P), J_i(P) \supset P \; (i = 1, ..., s),$$

and, if $f_i(x_1, ..., x_{n_i})$ is the truth-value of $F_i(P_1, ..., P_{n_i})$ when $P_1, ..., P_{n_i}$ take the truth-values $x_1, ..., x_{n_i}$ respectively and Γ relates to summation by the above standard condition implication functor with association to the right, the $\Sigma^b_{i=1} m^{n_i}$ axiom schemes

$$\Gamma^{n_i}_{k=1} J_{x_k}(P_k) J_y(F_i(P_1, ..., P_{n_i}))(x_1, ..., x_{n_i} \in \{1, ..., m\};$$
$$y = f_i(x_1, ..., x_{n_i});\; i = 1, ..., b).$$

The formalisations are plausible since all instances of the axiom schemes are generalised tautologies and, if $P, P \supset Q$ are generalised tautologies, so is Q. The generalised tautology property holds for the axiom schemes borrowed from the 2-valued propositional calculus since, in the proof that all (relevant) instances are 2-valued tautologies, we may, throughout, replace the words 'takes the truth-value T (F)' by 'takes a designated (an undesignated) truth-value'. For example, the proof that all instances of the axiom scheme $P \supset Q \vee P$ are tautologies may be adapted as shown below, where 'd' ('u') indicates that the relevant subformula takes a designated (an undesignated) truth-value.

$P \supset Q \vee P$	$P \supset Q \vee P$
$T\ TT$	$d\ \ dd$
$F\ T$	$u\ d$

The formalisations are weakly complete and this may be established by a generalisation of Kalmár's 'method of description of truth-tables'. The last axiom scheme (or, strictly, group of $\Sigma_{i=1}^{b} m^{n_i}$ axiom schemes) may be used to establish that if $P_1, ..., P_n$ denote propositional variables, $\Phi(P_1, ..., P_n)$ is a formula containing at most the values of $P_1, ..., P_n$ and this formula takes the truth-value $z(=z(x_1, ..., x_n))$ when $P_1, ..., P_n$ take the truth-values $x_1, ..., x_n$ respectively, then in all the m^n cases

$$J_{x_1}(P_1), ..., J_{x_n}(P_n) \vdash J_z(\Phi(P_1, ..., P_n)).$$

If $\Phi(P_1, ..., P_n)$ is a generalised tautology we may then infer, using the s axiom schemes $J_i(P) \supset P$ $(i = 1, ..., s)$, that

$$J_{x_1}(P_1), ..., J_{x_n}(P_n) \vdash \Phi(P_1, ..., P_n).$$

Having copied out, word for word, the derivation of the Deduction Theorem in the 2-valued case and also, in that case, of the hypothetical deduction

$$R_1 \supset S, ..., R_m \supset S, \Sigma_{i=1}^{m} R_i \vdash S$$

we may establish, by induction on α, that, in all the $m^{n-\alpha}$ cases,

$$J_{x_1}(P_1), ..., J_{x_{n-\alpha}}(P_{n-\alpha}) \vdash \Phi(P_1, ..., P_n) \ (\alpha = 0, ..., n)$$

from which weak completeness follows at once by considering the case where $\alpha = n$.

If we replace the axiom schemes by the corresponding axioms and adjoin the rule of substitution for propositional variables the formalisations remain, of course, weakly complete. In those cases where the functors $F_1(, ...,)$, ..., $F_b(, ...,)$ determine a functionally complete system the usual 2-valued proof that the formalisations are also strongly complete (i.e. that for all P, Q; if not $\vdash P$ then $P \vdash Q$) generalises without difficulty. For functionally incomplete systems the relationship between the 2 concepts of deductive completeness is more complex. In order to measure the 'distance apart' of the

2 concepts Tarski has introduced concepts of cardinal and ordinal degree of completeness and, more recently, several Polish logicians have considered a related concept of degree of maximality. To simplify matters somewhat let us suppose that, in relation to a formalisation $\mathscr{F}$, $P_1, ..., P_n$ are formulae such that

(i) not $P_1, ..., P_{i-1} \vdash P_i (i = 1, ..., n)$,
(ii) for all Q; $P_1, ..., P_n \vdash Q$

and that the value of n is bounded. In such a case the degree of completeness of $\mathscr{F}$ is said to be finite and its value is s the integer which is the successor of the least upper bound. Thus, for example, a strongly complete formalisation has degree of completeness 2. The degree of completeness of the above formalisations of Łukasiewicz propositional calculi is independent of the value of $s(1 \leqslant s \leqslant m-1)$ and is, in fact, equal to $1 + d(m-1)$, and therefore to 3 if $m-1$ is prime, but, for most other choices of $F_1(\;, ...,), ..., F_b(\;, ...,)$, its value is unknown. For some Łukasiewicz propositional calculi the degree of maximality has been evaluated.

The $\aleph_0$-valued Łukasiewicz propositional calculus with 1 designated truth-value may also be formalised by a Kalmár-type argument but, in this case, in order to keep the number of possibilities finite, the argument relates not directly to truth-values but to the linear forms considered by McNaughton. A non-constructive, but shorter, proof, using generalised Boolean algebra has since been found by Chang. Methods of proof translation may then be used to give corresponding results for the cases where the designated truth-values are the truth-values of the intervals $(r, 1]$ and $[r, 1]$, r being rational, though much remains to be done in the cases where r is irrational. Results relating to the ordinal degree of completeness of the formalisation of the $\aleph_0$-valued Lukasiewicz propositional calculus with 1 designated truth-value enable it to be inferred easily that if, to the 4 axioms of this formalisation (whose primitive rules of procedure are the rules of substitution and *modus ponens* with respect to C) a suitable fifth axiom is adjoined, then a weakly complete formalisation of the m-valued Łukasiewicz propositional calculus with 1 designated truth-value is obtained. An 'inner model' type of argument also shows that if the axiom *CCNpNqCqp* is replaced by the axiom *CCCpqCqpCqp*, a complete formalisation is obtained for the case where C is the only primitive functor. More recently an alternative proof was found, by McCall and Meyer, of a related result.

Many-valued propositional calculi with variable functors and with super-designated truth-values may be formalised by extensions of methods already outlined. When truth-values are divided into 3 classes, the super-designated truth-values $1, ..., t$, the designated truth-values $t+1, ..., s$ and the undesignated truth-values $s+1, ..., m$ $(1 \leqslant t < s < m)$, a generalised tautology is a formula which either

(i) takes designated truth-values exclusively, or

(ii) takes a super-designated truth-value under at least one assignment of truth-values to its propositional variables.

Thus, for example, if $m = 3$, $t = 1$, $s = 2$ and we use the notation of Post, the formulae

$$\sim((p \vee \sim p) \vee \sim\sim p), p$$

satisfy conditions (i), (ii) respectively. An extremely wide class of m-valued propositional calculi $(2 \leqslant m < \aleph_0)$ may be formalised by a generalisation, due to Shoesmith, of the methods of Rosser and Turquette.

m-valued predicate calculi of the first order $(2 \leqslant m < \aleph_0)$ have been formalised by Rosser and Turquette, the concept of standard conditions being extended to quantifiers, and the completeness proof being by a generalisation of the method used by Henkin in the 2-valued case. On the other hand Scarpellini has shown that it is impossible to obtain a complete formalisation of the first order predicate calculus corresponding to the $\aleph_0$-valued Łukasiewicz propositional calculus unless the only undesignated truth-value is 0. Nevertheless approximations to complete formalisations have been found by Louise Hay. The m-valued Erweiterter Aussagenkül with variable functors has been formalised by Watanabe, only 2 axioms being necessary $(2 \leqslant m < \aleph_0)$ but some infinite-valued versions of this calculus with the $\mathfrak{c}$ truth-values of the interval $[0, 1]$, can be shown, by an imitation of the methods of Gödel, to be incapable of formalisation. The method depends on defining the logical constant 1 and the functor H such that the truth-value of HP is half that of P and making $1, H$ correspond to the symbols $0, {}'$ of elementary number theory, a ternary primitive functor being closely related to Gödel's β function.

Apart from the Post systems already discussed, other m-valued functionally complete systems may be obtained from those of Łukasiewicz by adjoining to the primitives C, N the third primitive functor T where (if we use integer truth-values), TP always takes the truth-value 2 $(2 \leqslant m < \aleph_0)$. In the 2-valued propositional calculus there are only 2 binary functors, incompatability and joint denial, which alone determine functionally complete systems, and these are known as Sheffer functions. However, the number of Sheffer functions increases very rapidly with the value of m and is asymptotic to

m^{m^2}/e as m tends to infinity. Rousseau has shown that a binary functor is a Sheffer function unless there is an obvious reason, such as self-conjugacy, why it should not be and there are 3774 Sheffer functions in the 3-valued case of which 90 are commutative. Other important work on Sheffer functions has been done in recent years by several mathematicians.

For infinite-valued propositional calculi there can be no Sheffer functions or even functionally complete systems, since we cannot have only countably infinitely many formulae but non-countably infinitely many (generalised) truth-tables, but we can consider a weakened form of functional completeness known as local fullness. An infinite-valued propositional calculus is said to be locally full if to each partial truth-table specifying the truth-value of a formula under a finite number of assignments of truth-values to its propositional variables there corresponds a constructable formula and several functional completeness theorems may then be generalised. Among these are some which are themselves generalisations of Church's theorem concerning the existence of complete self-dual sets of independent connectives for the 2-valued propositional calculus. In its most general form, generalised duality extends to the form of arbitrary conjugacy, but these theorems relate to duality with respect to Post's (non-primitive) negation '$\simeq$'. Other generalised duality theorems relate to the corresponding concept of m-ality with respect to Post's primitive negation '$\sim$'. If $m = p_1^{a1} \dots p_k^{ak}$ where $p_1, \dots, p_k$ are distinct primes and $a_1, \dots, a_k$ are positive integers and a single self-m-a_1 functor determines a functionally complete system then then the minimum number of arguments of the functor is $p_1^{a1} + \dots + p_k^{ak}$ unless $k = 1$, in which case it is $p_1^{a1} + 1$ ($= m + 1$), the bounds being attained.

When we first discussed the Łukasiewicz propositional calculi we noted that the symbol m does not occur in the equations

$$n(x) = 1 - x, \; c(x, y) = \min(1, 1 - x + y).$$

It follows that, for all s $(1 \leqslant s \leqslant m-1)$, the m-valued Łukasiewicz propositional calculus is a sub-system of the 2-valued propositional calculus. This does not, however, apply to the Post systems or to the Erweiterter Aussagenkül, where there are additional tautologies such as (in the 3-valued case with 1 designated truth-value)

$$\sim\sim\sim(p \vee (\sim p \vee \sim\sim p)), \; \Sigma pCCCpNpNpNCCpNpNp.$$

If, however, we wish to use many-valued logics for independence proofs of non-logical axioms, then the propositional calculus must, in its entirety, satisfy the many-valued tables. This may be accomplished, as in the well-known independence proofs of Scott and Solovay in set theory, by using truth-values forming a Boolean algebra, so that they are preferably regarded as lattice-ordered rather than simply ordered, or by restricting functors to those satisfying standard conditions. As examples, the following 4-valued truth-tables for disjunction and negation illustrate the 2 approaches. In the first case the truth-values may be regarded as forming the lattice illustrated, the operations of disjunction and negation corresponding to lattice addition and complementation respectively. In both cases there is 1 designated truth-value.

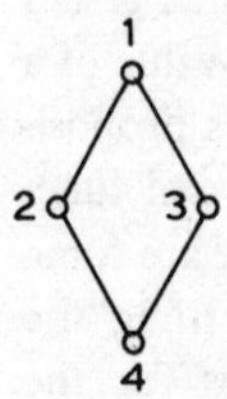

	$P \vee Q$	Q: 1	2	3	4	$\sim P$
P	1	1	1	1	1	4
	2	1	2	1	2	3
	3	1	1	3	3	2
	4	1	2	3	4	1

	$P \vee Q$	Q: 1	2	3	4	$\sim P$
P	1	1	1	1	1	4
	2	1	2	2	2	1
	3	1	2	3	3	1
	4	1	2	3	4	1

The latter approach may be used, in the 3-valued case with 1 designated truth-value, to establish, in Gödel set theory, the independence of the axiom of extensionality, even if it is restricted to non-empty sets.

The independence proofs do not, however, give an everyday meaning to many-valued logics. Post interpreted the m-valued logics by regarding an m-valued proposition as an ordered set of m-1 2-valued propositions, each of which implies all following ones, the ordered set taking the truth-value i if and only if all but the first i-1 2-valued propositions are true ($i = 1, ..., m$). Thus, if $p = (p_1, ..., p_{m-1})$, p takes the truth-value 1 if $p_1, ..., p_{m-1}$ all take the truth value T, the truth-value 2 if only p_1 takes the truth-value F, the truth-value $m-1$ if only p_{m-1} takes the truth-value T and the truth-value m if $p_1, ..., p_{m-1}$ all take the truth-value F and

$$p \vee q = (p_1 \vee q_1, ..., p_{m-1} \vee q_{m-1}).$$

Some logics with lattice-ordered truth-values may be regarded as interpreting incomplete mathematical theories. For example, since the continuum hypothesis and its negation are both consistent relative to the rest of set-theory, we may interpret the truth-values of the lattice discussed above as follows, retaining the disjunction and negation truth-tables already given, interpreting conjunction as corresponding to lattice intersection and assigning to $P \supset Q$ the truth-table of $\sim P \vee Q$.

1 = True under all circumstances,
2 = True if and only if the continuum hypothesis is true,
3 = True if and only if the continuum hypothesis is false,
4 = False under all circumstances.

As a further alternative we may, in the simply ordered case, apply many-valued logics to timetabling problems, the number of truth-values being the number of available lecture times during a week. When considering a proposition of the form

Professor A takes class B for the ith time

we are not concerned so much with its truth as with the time at which the even takes place. Thus the corresponding propositional variable p_{ABi} will take the truth-value k if this event occurs during the kth period of the week ($k = 1, \ldots, m$) and restrictions, such as the forbidding of clashes, may then be represented by formulae of the m-valued propositional calculus. The theory of 2-valued decision elements may then be generalised, but no new hardware is necessary since a formula of the m-valued propositional may, if $2^{n-1} < m \leqslant 2^n$, be represented as an ordered n-tuple of 2-valued formulae. For example, if $m = 4$, $1 = (F, F)$, $2 = (T, F)$, $3 = (F, T)$, $4 = (T, T)$ then

$$(\sim P)_1 = \sim P_1, (\sim P)_2 = P_1 \not\equiv P_2.$$

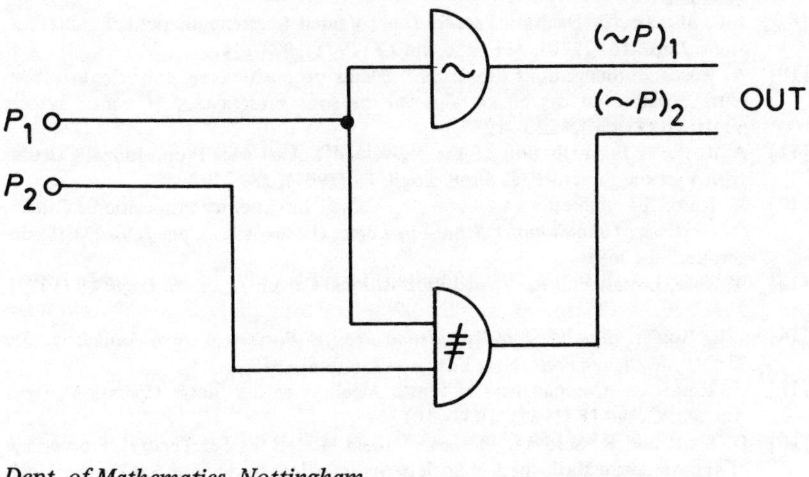

Dept. of Mathematics, Nottingham

BIBLIOGRAPHY

A complete list of publications on many-valued logics since 1965 would, of course, be far too long to he given here, but a few examples of the publications referred to in the text are given. Even a complete list of these publications would be somewhat lengthy and the omission of a paper from this list does not imply that it is considered to be unimportant. A few papers published before 1965 are included as they have considerable relevance to topics from many-valued logics discussed above, although they concern directly only 2-valued logic and are therefore omitted from Rescher's bibliography.

[1] R. O. Davies, 'Two Theorems on Essential Variables', *J. London Math. Soc.* **41** (1966), 333–335.

[2] R. O. Davies, 'On *n*-valued Sheffer Functions, *Z. Math. Logik* **25** (1979), 293–298.

[3] K. Gödel, 'Über formal unentscheidbare Sätze der Principia Mathematica und verwandter Systeme I', *Monatshefte Mathematik und Physik* **38** (1931), 173–198.

[4] K. Gödel, 'The Consistency of the Axiom of Choice and of the Generalised Continuum Hypothesis with the Axioms of Set Theory', *Ann. Math. Studies* **3**, Princeton, 1940.

[5] L. Henkin, 'The Completeness of the First Order Functional Calculus', *J. Symbolic Logic* **14** (1949), 159–166.

[6] L. Kalmár, 'Über die Axiomatisierbarkeit des Aussagenkalküls, Acta scientarum mathematicarum (Szeged)', 7 (1935), 222–243.

[7] S. McCall and R. K. Meyer, 'Pure 3-Valued Łukasiewiczian Implication', *J. Symbolic Logic* **31** (1966), 399–405.

[8,9] J. C. Munzio, 'A Decision Process for 3-Valued Sheffer Functions, I and II', *Z. Math. Logik* **16** (1970), 271–280 and **17** (1971), 97–114.

[10] A. Rose, 'Formalisations de certains calculs propositionnels polyvalents à foncteurs variables au cas où certains valeurs sont surdésignées', *Comptes rendus (Paris)* **262** (1966), 1233–1235.

[11] A. Rose, 'A Formalisation of the $\aleph_0$-valued Łukasiewicz Propositional Calculus with Variable Functors', *Z. Math. Logik* **13** (1967), 289–292.

[12] A. Rose, 'Formalisations of Some $\aleph_0$-Valued Łukasiewicz Propositional Calculi, *Proceedings of the Summer School in Logic*, (Leeds, 1967), pp. 269–271 (Springer, Berlin, 1968).

[13] A. Rose, 'Locally Full $\aleph_0$-Valued Propositional Calculi', *Z. Math. Logik* **18** (1972), 217–226.

[14] J. B. Rosser, *Simplified Independence Proofs, Boolean Valued Models of Set Theory*, Academic Press, New York and London, 1969.

[15] G. Rousseau, 'Completeness in Finite Algebras with a Single Operation', *Proc. Am. Math. Soc.* **18** (1967), 1009–1013.

[16] D. Scott and R. Solovay, 'Boolean Valued Models for Set Theory', Proceedings of the American Mathematical Society Summer Inst. Axiomatic Set Theory 1967, Univ. of California, Los Angeles, *Proc. Symp. Pure Math.* **13** (1969).

[17] D. J. Shoesmith, Ph. D. Dissertation, University of Cambridge, 1962.
[18] S. Watanebe, Ph. D. Thesis, University of Manchester, 1974.
[19] R. Wójcicki, 'The Logics Stronger Than Łukasiewicz's 3-Valued Sentential Calculus – the Notion of Degree of Maximality Versus the Notion of Degree of Completeness', *Studia Logica* **33** (1974), 201–214.

NUEL D. BELNAP, JR.

MODAL AND RELEVANCE LOGICS: 1977

If one looks at classical logic as reflected in an often-used textbook such as that of Mendelson (1964), it appears to divide into five central topics. The first four form a kind of tower. At the bottom is propositional logic, the logic of connectives, in this case solely truth-functional connectives. The second story adds quantifiers and perhaps identity. On the third floor resides arithmetic, with all its Goedelian incompleteness. At the top is set theory, under which rubric for present purposes I wish also to include type theory. Then along side the whole, perhaps acting as some kind of flying buttress, is that analysis and sorting of functions known as recursive function theory.

What I propose to do is have a look at modal and relevance logics according to this same division (but in a slightly different order): for modal logics, I will first look at propositional logics, then quantifiers, then set theory, then arithmetic, and finally, analysis of functions; and then do the same for relevance logics. I do not believe this classical tower represents the only satisfactory way of carving up the central problems of logic; for example, the alternative of Curry and his associates which fixes on combinatory logic instead of propositional logic as the foundation seems to me at least equally admissible. Nevertheless, some principle is needed, and I hope you will find my procedure suggestive. In each case my aim will be to draw some pictures in broad outline, offering a few citations as a monumentally unsatisfactory way of filling in details.

Two further words. In the first place, there is no settled meaning for 'modal logic'. In the context of this volume, with its other contributions on topics also sometimes called 'modal logic', I intend to invoke a narrower meaning: logics involving one-place connectives purporting to be associated with the concepts of necessity, possibility, impossibility, and the like. These are the *alethic* modalities of von Wright (1951). But it is still left open whether the necessity is to be logical, metaphysical, physical, or what have you. In the second place, I limit myself to mathematical as opposed to philosophical research, thus ignoring much of value.

1. PROPOSITIONAL MODAL LOGICS

Though there were some precursors, the first sustained investigations of modal

E. Agazzi (ed.), Modern Logic – A Survey, 131–151.

concepts were undertaken by C. I. Lewis (Lewis, 1918; Lewis and Langford, 1932) some several decades ago, with the explicit aim of getting a better account of the conditional or implication than that provided by truth-tables. That is, he wished to define that p strictly implies q by the formula which says that it is impossible that p be true and q not. These investigations were *principia* style, patiently using the method of substitution and detachment to see what followed from what, and the method of matrices, to see what didn't. Such methods are often belittled by mathematicians, but I must say that it seems to me that they are the only ones we have in the early stages of an enterprise, when in fact our intuitions are untutored and we do not see by the eye of the intellect or the intervention of semantics how various theses cohere.

In the course of his investigations, Lewis offered a number of alternative systematizations of modal logic, the best known being the systems, in order of increasing strength, S1–S5. Later researchers have added a variety of other systems, for example the system T, due independently to Feys (1937) (from an idea of Goedel (1932)) and von Wright (1951) (there known as M). And these later researchers figured out how all these systems fit together, and offered numerous formulations of each of them by the method which Halmos (1962) calls axiom-chopping. Again, though Halmos presumably intended to derogate the method, it seems to me a good one to use at a certain stage of the enterprise of intellectual exploration.

All along the way there were numerous philosophical discussions of the worth or unworth of modal logic in general or of various modal logics in particular, but since this paper is part of the portion of this program labeled 'pure logic', I shall ignore that topic altogether, except for mentioning two items: first, that W. V. O. Quine, the most influential philosophical logician currently practicing his trade, thinks, like Russell before him, that modal logic is a Bad Thing (see e.g., Quine, 1947); and second, that Arthur Prior, another distinguished philosophical logician, sadly now deceased, thought that modal logic was a Good Thing (see e.g., Prior, 1955).

A number of researchers involved themselves in the task of providing for modal logics formulations and results of a kind already available for truth-functional logic. A typical 'result' would be an appropriate deduction theorem for modal logic, first secured by Barcan Marcus (1946a). Or solution of various decision problems, as in Anderson (1954). Fitch (1952) showed how it was possible to give a natural deduction formulation of modal logic, while Curry (1950) began looking into Gentzen consecution ('sequenzen') calculus formulations. Work on the Hilbert-style, Gentzen consecution calculus, and semantic tableau formulations of modal logics is well summarized, organized, and enriched by Zeman (1973). There have also been some algebraic investigations, stemming from the work of McKinsey (1941). This work, as well as much else, and much that is new, is described in Hughes and Cresswell (1968). To this list should be added investigations concerning the expressive powers of modal languages such as the work on 'modalities' of Parry (1939) or the more recent work of Massey (1970), and connections between modal logic on the one hand and constructive or many-valued ideas on the other; Hughes and Cresswell (1968, p. 306), point to the work of Bull, Prior and Segerberg.

A significant event in the history of modal logic occurred in the 1950's when a young man then in high school in Omaha developed a satisfying semantic interpretation for modal logics. Though not without precursors (Meredith, 1956; Kanger, 1957; Bayart, 1958) it was the elegant work of this young man, first published in Kripke (1959), which had the effect of creating a surge of interest in modal logic. Kripke's idea had two parts. In the first place, on a fixed interpretation of the non-logical pieces of a sentence, the truth of the sentence is no longer absolute; instead, it is relative to an index of some kind, which most researchers call a 'possible world'. In the second place, a parameter of the semantic structure is a binary relation R, interpreted as relative possibility among the worlds; and the truth of the sentence 'Necessarily A' at a world w is to be identified with the truth of A itself at every world w' which is possible relative to w. By varying conditions on the relation R of relative possibility, conditions such as symmetry and transitivity, and in some cases by tinkering with other features of the semantic structures with which he was dealing, Kripke managed to provide a semantic analysis for a number of different modal logics. And in an independent project, Hintikka (1961) proposed a related type of semantics for modal logics in terms of so-called 'model sets', a proposal which, like Kripke's, has had a heavy influence on subsequent research.

The sport then became to try to extend these concepts and methods as far as possible. Partly this meant dealing with systems with which Kripke himself had not dealt, and partly this meant letting the semantic concepts themselves suggest new systems. Among the work of many others, that of Segerberg (1971) comes to mind. At the same time as the methods were extended, they were refined by the provision of a variety of alternate proof techniques, perhaps the most elegant of which were based on Henkin's idea of getting an interpretation by extending a given consistent theory, in a Lindenbaum way, to a complete and consistent theory (Kaplan, 1966; Hughes and Cresswell, 1968; Thomason, 1970).

I cannot keep from adding mention that the fundamental semantic ideas were applied outside of modal logic by such as Cochiarella, D. Lewis, Prior, Stalnaker, Thomason, van Fraassen, and many others, to areas such as deontic logic, the subjunctive conditional, and tense logic – but this already goes beyond my stated limitations.

2. MODAL LOGICS WITH QUANTIFIERS AND IDENTITY

There was a lapse of nearly fifteen years between the first full scale investigation of modal logic by Lewis and Langford and the first introduction of quantifiers in Barcan Marcus (1946). (Carnap published his work on quantified modal logic that same year.) In a way this represents a curious phenomenon, but from one point of view it is understandable: modal logic with quantifiers is an order of magnitude more difficult a topic than propositional modal logic, as I shall demonstrate. There seem to me to be three sources of difficulty. In the first place, as we can glean from the writings of Quine such as his 1947 piece, we are often more at sea in knowing what to make of ordinary language locutions which mix modal and quantifier expressions than is the case with modal locutions alone. To invoke an early example of Quine, we are given to wonder if there exists a possible fat man in the doorway; or whether there is a sense in which we can say that each man is necessarily rational such that in that same sense, it is not the case that each bicyclist is necessarily two-legged.

In the second place, although there are some choices to be made in propositional modal logic, the number of such choices seems to multiply enormously when quantifiers and identity are added. And I think it may fairly be said that it was not until the advent of Kripke's possible-worlds semantics about 1959 that we began to understand the nature of these choices. Let me give you just a sample of the possibilities from the possible-worlds semantics. (I omit citations here, because I would probably get them wrong.) We are given a number of possible worlds. We might give meaning to our quantifiers via the substitution interpretation, which does not require domains at all. If instead we appeal to domains, are we to assume that the domain of individuals is the same for each world? Suppose not; shall the relationship between the domains be influenced by the relationship of relative possibility, and if so, how? Further, the semantics for the quantifiers will doubtless be based on something amounting to assignments of values to the variables. Should the variables be assigned individuals straight off, or should the assignment to the variables of individuals be relative to worlds, as truth is relative to worlds? In the latter case, unless we get confused (as has happened), we have something equivalent to assigning to the variables what Carnap (1946, 1947) called an 'individual concept', i.e., a function from possible worlds to individuals. If we are assigning individual concepts, should we permit the assignment of individuals at a world which are not in the domain of that world? Indeed a similar choice can be seen even if we assign individuals directly.

Next, there are some choices to be made about predication. Take the case in which terms directly denote individuals. Then, what are we to do with a predication in which some argument-term denotes an individual not in the domain of the world at which we are evaluating the predication? Shall we call it always true, always false, always free of truth-value, or shall we allow more than one of these possibilities? And if we allow sentences without truth-values, we have, of course, many choices when we come to embedding them in larger contexts. And if instead we allow the assignment of individual concepts, or, equivalently, assignment of individuals relative to possible worlds, we must ask if the truth-value of the predication is to depend only on what the terms are assigned in that world, or on the whole range of their assignments; and perhaps in either case, but certainly in the former, in the situation when the term does not in that world denote an individual in the domain of that world, we must decide what is to happen.

Next, even having fixed what sort of assignments we are to make, and how predication works, there are still choices as to how the quantifiers shall be interpreted, or, except for the question of what to do with truth- value free expressions, perhaps there is only one way to go when assignments are directly to individuals. But when individual concepts are invoked, or, equivalently, when assignments are relative to worlds, the question remains as to *which* individual concepts shall be reckoned in computing the truth in a world of a quantified expression. All of them? Some fixed subset given by a semantic parameter? Some subset which depends on the domain of the world in question?

Further, there is the question of whether terms of various categories should be treated alike. Should variables and invidual constants and definite descriptions (if the language has them) be treated as semantically of a kind, or should they be given different semantic roles? For example, it is possible to allow individual constants to be assigned individual concepts, while individuals are directly assigned to variables.

With regard to identity, the chief decision has been as to whether to make it contingent, the truth of an identity statement varying like others with worlds, or noncontingent, never varying. And whether the sort of terms with which the identity is flanked should influence this decision. And in the direct-assignment case, how the absence of one or both of the individuals from the domain should influence the evaluation of the identity. And in the individual concept case, not only whether only the individuals assigned at the world of evaluation is enough to determine truth, but if not, whether the relational structure between the possible worlds should come in (I do not think this last alternative has as yet been explored).

Apart from all of this, though potentially miscible with much of it, is the question of whether the semantic structure should contain an element relating individuals in the various worlds on the pattern of what Lewis (1968) calls the 'counterpart' relation, so that an individual in the domain of one world might have one or more counterparts in the domain of another; and if so, just how this should figure in the clauses for the quantifiers and for the modalities.

It is not my purpose here to be complete or to survey these possibilities as other than bare possibilities, for I wish only to suggest the vast number of choices which are available. Much of the surveying is well carried out in Hughes and Cresswell (1968), though there have been many subsequent explorations, including the important ones of Thomason (1969), and of Bressan (1972), the latter for the first time adopting the alternative of nonextensional predication; and I should also like to mention the very recent and interesting invokation of sortal concepts into our understanding of quantification in the work of Gupta (1980), which partly relies on Bressan.

What sorts of work have been done on all these various systems of modalities with quantifiers and identity? Much of the work has been philosophical, and this, by agreement, I pass over. On the mathematical side, nearly everything has been of a kind with the work I surveyed on propositional modal logic. It does need saying, however, that in many cases obtaining results such as completeness theorems has required development of procedures neither required for ordinary quantification theory nor for propositional modal logic – the combination in this way, too, has brought with it a certain degree of richness not to be found in the components separately.

There are other sorts of work distinctive of quantified modal logic; these have to do with features which arise only when there is quantification into modalized contexts, thus giving rise to problems which philosophers treat under the heading of 'essentialism' and the distinction between *de dicto* modal statements, such as 'necessarily, each bicyclist is two-legged', and *de re* modal statements, such as 'each man is necessarily rational'. Such investigations were inaugurated by Parsons (1969), and furthered by the work of Tichy (1973) and Broido (1974; 1976). The former has to do largely with finding mathematically definable criteria for when a modal theory commits us to holding essentialist views, and the latter two with finding criteria for distinguishing sentences which make *de re* claims from sentences that don't (the syntax being an untrustworthy guide).

In the same vein, I should mention unusual results like that of Kripke (1962), which shows that undecidability in the modal case arises already with the monadic fragment.

3. MODAL TYPE AND SET THEORY

The pioneering work in raising modal logic somehow to the higher orders was carried out by Bayart (1958) and Fitch (1967). Neither of these caused much of a stir, perhaps rightly; the former stopped at the second order, while the latter, while giving us a theory interesting from a foundational point of view, postulated that membership implied necessary membership, thus drastically reducing the possibility of making distinctions of modality in a set-theoretical context.

Initial influential work in higher order modal logic was carried out independently by Montague (1970) and Bressan (1972). In each case a full-blown type theory of order ω was developed, though Montague and Bressan made somewhat different decisions in articulating their respective logics. (The two logics are doubtless strongly equivalent, although no one has as yet done the homework required to establish this.) Bressan (1972) gives a detailed development of his logic, including applications and an interesting relative completeness proof. Montague (1970) stops with defining the logic; mathematical work on the Montague logic has been carried out by Gallin (1972). Though by and large I have been concentrating on 'pure logic', it nevertheless needs saying that Montague developed his logic in order to permit applications in linguistics, applications which have led to an entire school of 'Montague grammarians', and that Bressan developed his logic in order to cope with certain applications to physics. My own view is that Bressan's language is the simpler of the two, and would be easier to use for either purpose; but as I said, I do believe them mathematically interchangeable.

Very recent work on modal type theory is to be found in Fine (1977), where a theory of intensional and extensional entities is presented which addresses such difficult questions as when an intension of a certain kind can reasonably be said to exist in a given world. As one tool Fine uses the existence of automorphisms, which he invokes in helping to give sense to the dependence of the identity of intensions on the identity of individuals. It seems to me likely that this study is the beginning of a worthwhile field of research, inasmuch as it combines interesting mathematical questions with philosophically perplexing ones.

There is a good deal of further work to be done on typed modal logic; for example, investigating how the presence or absence of the axiom of choice affects what is available in the first order fragment. But also much has been done, as e.g., Bressan's development of arithmetic in this context. But I leave the matter.

Next I pass on to modal set theory (using this phrase to suggest a type-free formulation). Perhaps you will be as surprised as I to learn that there is only one work – at least only one known to me – in which, unlike Fitch's, true membership statements can be contingent. I refer to the foundational work of Bressan (1973–74). As is obvious from a perusal of his work, Bressan deals with a great many concepts which have analogues neither in low-level modal logic nor in plain set theory but which rely on both – the combination offers great and interesting possibilities when treated in just the right way, as he does. As a tiny sample of the kind of question that arises, I choose the following: is it true that whenever A is a set, so is the class of x's which possibly belong to A? The threat of course is that such a class would be 'too big' – just how many possible fat men *are* in the doorway? In a satisfying and nontrivial theorem, however, Bressan shows in fact that this is not the case: happily, if the fat men in the doorway form a set, than so do the possible fat men.

I should like to commend modal set theory to the attention of investigators into set theory; naturally, they should begin with Bressan.

4. MODAL ARITHMETIC

Although interesting new things are known to happen when arithmetic is added to classical logic (without also adding some form of general set theory), I do not know any work that has been done on modal logic enriched by just arithmetic. And the reason is perhaps obvious: no one that I know has any intuitions which make modal distinctions among the truths or falsehoods of arithmetic, thinking of some as more necessary, or more possible, than others. I put the matter in this carefully historical way so as not to block the road to inquiry, but in fact I doubt that anything is likely to emerge.

I nevertheless include this level of the tower to which I referred in my introductory remarks in order to contrast the situation here not only with what happens in the case of classical logic on the one hand, but with what happens on the other in the case of relevance logic.

5. ANALYSIS OF MODAL FUNCTIONS

Modal ideas have not (so far as I know) themselves led to the addition of any new ideas to the classical analysis of functions as caught in recursion theory. However by a kind of double reflection through a program of research generated in the context of relevance logic, Helman (1977) has found that by fastening on the modal idea of the 'security' of necessary truths, a certain classification of functions into those which are *dependable* or not can be given smooth mathematical sense, and then related to historically given modal logics in interesting ways. It seems likely that there is much more to be built on Helman's seminal insights; I shall say something more about his program in Section 10 below.

This concludes my all too superficial survey of modal logic.

6. PROPOSITIONAL RELEVANCE LOGIC

What about relevance logic? Though, as always, having precursors, it begins with the seminal paper of Ackermann (1956), which suggested a calculus designed to catch the idea of a 'logischer zusammenhang' between propositions, so that a conditional, if A then B (which we will write $A \rightarrow B$), could only be true if in fact A were relevantly and necessarily connected to B. (I note that in what follows I pretty much suppress all citations, since virtually everything is either described or at least referred to in one of Anderson and Belnap (1975), Collier *et al.* (1980), or Anderson and Belnap (1980) – the last containing Wolf's complete and up-to-date bibliography).

It is helpful to begin with an unfortunately negative but still easily grasped characterization of what relevance logic is after: a relevant implication should avoid the so-called paradoxes of 'implication', paradoxes such as that a contradiction implies everything, or that absolutely anything implies a necessary truth. Since logicians had been saying for a long time that there was no mathematically stable idea of relevance to be grasped, it is little wonder that it took the genius of an Ackermann to devise a smoothly running logic which indeed provably avoided not only the classically known paradoxes, but a whole barnful of cousins.

Later work led to a pair of more positive characterizations of relevance. The first is more proof-theoretical in character: A relevantly implies B if A can be *used* as the premiss in an argument whose conclusion is B. But, you will say, what is this concept of 'use'? The clearest exposition of the idea relies on a natural deduction formulation of 'entailment', as one has come to call a relevant and necessary implication. In this formulation, one marks with numerals the hypotheses of natural deduction 'subordinate proofs' or 'subproofs', as Fitch calls them. These numerals then later indicate which steps in the proof relevantly depend on that hypothesis, in the sense that the hypothesis was actually used in obtaining that step. One also introduces a requirement which guarantees that subproofs always represent a necessary (as well as relevant) connection between their hypotheses and conclusions. There then turns out to be an excellent fit between Ackermann's calculus and the thus combined concepts of relevance and necessity.

At an early stage, Ackermann's calculus Π' was reformulated as the calculus E of entailment – at least it was conjectured that E was a reformulation of Π'. The principal obstacle in demonstrating the equivalence of the two calculuses lay in showing that E was closed under the rule, from $A \vee B$ and $-A$, to infer B, the rule Ackermann called (γ). This was no matter of axiom-chopping, since it can be shown that in a variety of senses, stronger than mere closure, (γ) is in fact *not* a rule of E. And the problem was left open for a number of years; I shall return to it below.

In the intervening years, this problem and others led to a good deal of instructive axiom-chopping, independence results, and the like, which resulted in the provision of a real feel for how the logic of entailment was put together. There were also investigations into the modal structure of E, for it turned out that necessity was definable in terms of entailment (but *not* in the Lewis way), and results were produced which related that modal structure to standard modal calculuses. On the other side of this coin was written the result that in fact entailment is not in any sense a modal logic – Meyer proved that the entailment connective could not be defined by applying any one-place modal connective, regardless of its properties, to any truth-functional combination. In this sense Meyer proved that entailment, because of its requirement of relevance, is an *essentially relational* concept.

It is also essentially relational in the sense that it is never the case that some non-relational property of A, even when conjoined with some non-relational property of B, suffices for A to entail B. And this observation leads me to the second positive characterization of relevance, promised above, this one with a more semantic flavor. For a long time, a few logicians have suggested that true implication should require some common meaning content – and of course others, who get nervous about 'meaning', have poked fun at this idea. In any event, in a propositional logic it is clear that a necessary condition for 'common meaning content' between formulas should be that at least one variable occurs in both, so that no semantic assignment of propositions to the variables could give them meanings which were totally disparate. And an early result established that indeed E and related relevance logics have the feature that if $A \to B$ is a theorem, then A and B share meaning in at least this minimal sense. It was said that logics not having this feature permitted 'fallacies of relevance', including of course that a contradiction like $p\&{-}p$ implies an arbitrary q. And while on the topic of fallacies, let me mention what were called 'fallacies of modality', which in fact also in their statement require a notion of relevance: a system was said to commit a fallacy of modality if (roughly) ever it permitted a formula asserting a claim to necessity to be relevantly implied by a formula which did not make such a claim. An early result of Ackermann's can be interpreted as demonstrating that his system permits no such shenanigans.

A spin-off from this program of research was the development of a number of cousins of E, together to be thought of as relevance logics. The most important, doubtless, is the calculus R of relevant implication – its implicative connective contains the idea of relevance, but unlike that of E, is divorced totally from modal concepts. In R, like E, $A \to B$ makes a claim that A is *relevantly* sufficient for B, but unlike E, there is no claim that there is *necessary* connection. R is therefore particularly instructive because it allows consideration of the concept of relevance *tout nu*.

Another interesting cousin is the system T of what was called 'ticket entailment', because it was designed to catch some aspects of Ryle's slogan that an implication is an 'inference ticket'. T is an even stricter system than E, partly by disallowing certain modal-like collapsing moves which E permits.

Much of the research on relevance logics, like that on modal logics, has been the provision of formulations and results analogous to those provided for classical logic; but in this case there remain some dramatically open problems, the most important of which I shall be mentioning in the course of these remarks.

One of the early results was the provision of an appropriate deduction theorem. As you might guess, what counts towards appropriateness is that the hypothesis to be discharged be actually *used* in obtaining the conclusion. I mentioned above the provision of natural deduction formulations for the various relevance logics – these playing, however, a conceptually analytic role which they did not, or not so much, in the case of modal logics. Then for various partial systems, Gentzen consecution calculuses were provided, including Dunn's for the entire positive system. But an outstanding open problem is the development of Gentzen consecution formulations for the whole of any of the relevance logics; at this point, no one has been able to solve this problem in an even remotely instructive way. Less related to this than one might by classical analogy think is the question of decision procedures. A good deal of work has gone into finding decision methods for various *subsystems* of the relevance logics, but perhaps the most important outstanding series of problems of this moment is constituted by the decision problems for the various *full* relevance logics. Indeed, at this stage he would be foolhardy who would conjecture that the systems are decidable, in spite of the teaching of history that every propositional logic which was not invented to be undecidable has so far turned out to be decidable. There is even a sort of 'reason' why relevance logics may turn out undecidable even on the propositional level: they alone among logics appear to involve an essentially relational idea, the idea of relevance; that is, they go beyond plain monadic ideas. And everyone knows that it is when we reach relations that things get sufficiently complicated as to lead to negative answers to the decision question. But on the other hand, relevance logics *look* so much like other logics known to be decidable that there is also "reason" to suppose them decidable. I myself do not now have a stable conjecture, but simply commend the problem to you. Let me add that there is a logic in the relevance family which is known to be undecidable; it was indeed invented by Meyer to be so, but still, unlike other such cases of which I know, it *looks* like a reasonably reasonable logic – no fishy rules, nor mysterious ways of generating axioms, nor even very many axioms. But Meyer has shown by an interesting argument that its decision problem reduces to the word problem.

Algebraic investigations have also played an important role in the development of relevance logics. Some of these logics turn out to answer to 'nice' algebraic structures when looked at in just the right way. And algebraic results have helped to solve various problems, such as partial decision procedures, some completeness results, and the like. Dunn has led the way in these investigations.

The development of relevance logic took a large step forward with the devising of the Meyer-Routley relational semantics, and the operational semantics independently offered by Urquhart and by Fine. I concentrate only on the relational semantics, beginning with the ways in which it departs from Kripke's ideas.

In the first place, the indexes at which formulas are to be evaluated can no longer be conceived of as 'possible worlds', for the good reason that logical falsehoods are to be true at some of the indexes, and that logical truths will be false at some. Routley and Routley introduced the term 'set-ups' to describe such indexes (see in Anderson and Belnap (1975) for anticipations of the idea by Dunn and by van Fraassen), and it has the right kind of neutrality to defuse any lingering nervousness which might be caused by talk of 'impossible worlds' or the like. Set-ups are drastically different from possible worlds in that they can either be *underdetermined* (incomplete) by including neither a sentence A nor its negation $-A$, or *overdetermined* (inconsistent) by including both A and $-A$. Such creatures are proper to the imagination, for surely we can imagine situations which are incompletely determined, or inconsistent. They are also proper to separating out the psychological content of mathematical propositions – for instance, one can imagine that the four color theorem is false, though it has been proved true. Of course, one wants to keep in mind that there are some indexes which behave normally, the 'real world' doubtless being among them – call these *normal* set-ups, and tie logical validity to truth not in all set-ups, but in all normal set-ups.

This first departure of Routley-Meyer from Kripke required considerable imagination. So did the second: in the analysis of relevant implications, one requires not a Kripkean *binary* relation, but instead a *three-termed* relation $Rxyz$. In analogy to Kripke's reading of the binary Rxy as 'y is possible relative to x', one may read $Rxyz$ as 'x and y are *compossible* relative to z', where compossibility itself is an essentially relational idea. Then one says that $A \rightarrow B$ is true at an index x just in case, for every y and z such that $Rxyz$, if A is true at y, then B is true at z. There are also appropriate clauses for other connectives.

When the two departures are put together, and an additional feature or two added, Meyer and Routley showed that by varying the postulates on the relational structure represented by the three-termed relation R of relative compossibility, it was possible accurately to model each of the important relevance logics so far considered, and as always happens in such cases, a number of others as well.

These semantics were deployed, mostly by Meyer, to solve a large number of problems about the relevance logics. New proofs of the admissibility of Ackermann's rule (γ) were forthcoming, it was shown that the various systems were not unreasonable in the sense of Halldén, all the appropriate conservative extension results were demonstrated, some partial decision procedures were engendered, and lots more.

Something else quite new was developed by Meyer to tackle certain problems concerning relevance logics; I refer to his 'coherence' method, a method which has application well beyond the area of relevance logics. The nub of the coherence method is to use membership of a formula in an antecedently given theory in an artful mixture with more standard truth-conditions in order to provide models with various desirable properties. Meyer has used this method to give a positively short proof that the relevance logics are closed under Ackermann's rule (γ), that where appropriate they are 'prime' in the sense of having either A or B as a theorem whenever $A \vee B$ is, and so forth. The method is elegance itself, and will doubtless see considerable use on a wide variety of problems.

Lastly, let me mention a type of exploration which has not as yet been much pushed but which will likely turn out fruitful: the investigation of relevance considerations in the context of a variety of non-extensional connectives. The most work has been done on combining relevant implication with alethic modalities, a little on combining it with deontic modalities, and a very little on its combination with epistemic ideas, but there is need for much more investigation of these possibilities, as well as need for consideration of other modalities such as those related to tense.

7. RELEVANCE LOGIC WITH QUANTIFIERS AND IDENTITY

One can take any one of the relevance logics and add a plausible looking set of axioms for existential and universal quantification at the level of individuals, thereby obtaining a quantified version of that logic. Early research relating such logics to natural deduction formulations, and parallel research of an axiom-chopping sort, compelled a belief in the stability of these quantified logics. In addition, it was shown that the various fragments had the sort of properties a quantified relevance logic might be expected to have, including Meyer's demonstration that monadic relevance logic is undecidable. Completeness theorems of an algebraic sort were also obtained for certain fragments of quantified relevance logic, and theorems having to do with fallacies of relevance and modality were extended to the quantified case. Significantly, the Meyer–Dunn proof of the admissibility of Ackermann's rule (γ) was extended to apply to the presence of quantifiers.

Furthermore, one can graft onto the Routley-Meyer semantics the simplest set of clauses for the quantifiers: namely, let each set-up have the same domain of individuals, and let assignments to variables be directly of individuals (not of individual concepts or of anything more complicated).

And one would expect not only that typical completeness and consistency claims tying those formal systems to these semantics would be true, but that proofs of them would be swiftly forthcoming. As it so far turns out, however, such is not the case. Just as the decision problem for propositional relevance logics remains open, so does the completeness question for quantified relevance logic. The techniques developed for generating completeness results for quantified modal logic do *not* work for relevance logic, at least not in any guise in which they have so far been tried.

No research of which I am aware has been done on adding quantifiers in one of the many, many other ways I described above in Section 2. There is doubtless some interesting work to be done in this area, for it would be odd if the most simple minded quantificational addition to relevance logic turned out to be satisfactory for all purposes.

No one has as yet investigated consecution formulations with quantifiers (except for some fragments), but that is probably because it looks so straightforward as to be pretty much uninformative.

Turning now to identity, it presents problems here even beyond those it engenders when it is added to modal logics, for if added without careful attention to its postulates, it can, by an observation of Bacon and of Dunn (see Freeman, 1974), lead to what might well be considered fallacies of relevance. For example, the most simple-minded postulates lead to the provability of $(c = b) \to (A \to A)$, for arbitrary c, b, A; from which no commonality of meaning content seems to leap at the eye. My own view of the situation is that more thought is required before we can see our clear way to the truth of the matter, and that very likely higher order relevance logic is the arena in which identity can most productively be investigated.

8. RELEVANT TYPE AND SET THEORY

There is a natural generalization of the simplest first order relevance logic to the simplest higher order relevance logic, adding the key property-existence schema as a co-entailment. Meyer has shown that in fact this logic is closed under Ackermann's rule (γ) even when the property-existence schema is limited in an arbitrary way. The simplest first order relational semantics can be generalized in a parallel way, and one asks if the system is complete relative to the Henkin secondary models based on these semantics. Aside from this important result and this important question, there is little that is definite about higher order relevance logic – it is a field calling for tilling.

On a more limited scale, something is known about quantification over propositions, which has been developed both axiomatically and algebraically. It would seem that our intuitions about relevance are on firmer ground here than in the area of higher order logic. To cite a minor but interesting recent result, one can show that adding a Hilbert epsilon operator to relevance logic with propositional quantifiers leads immediately to serious fallacies of relevance. And Grover has algebraic completeness results for formulas with not too many arrows.

One result along these lines is that of Daniels and Freeman (1977), who show that a certain relevance logic admitting quantifiers over both propositions and functions of propositions, as well as containing object-language analogues of certain semantic notions, is complete relative to a plausible relational semantics.

Nothing has been done to develop higher order relevance logics of a sophistication parallel to that of the higher order modal logics of either Bressan or Montague; all such investigations remain for future workers. In particular, it seems philosophically imperative that one look for relative completeness proofs such as those of Bressan or Gallin (to show the impossibility thereof would also be interesting). One can even conjecture that investigation of this problem would shed light on the recalcitrant completeness problem for relevance logics of the first order.

One might have supposed that relevance logic would give a quick 'solution' to the paradoxes, but such is surely not the case – Curry's paradox shows that once cannot retain even absolute consistency if one adds the naive class abstraction axiom to any of the relevance logics. Nevertheless, it does not follow and I think it is not true that relevance logics will shed no light on the paradoxes. The additional control they give us over what follows from what, if employed in just the right sort of way, may well help illuminate a murky and indeed gloomy corner.

I conclude by guessing that it may turn out that there is an interesting interaction between higher order relevance logic and the analysis of relevant functions, as described in Section 10 below.

9. RELEVANT ARITHMETIC

As Peirce, Russell, etc., pointed out, Aristotle gave us ways of *sorting* or *classifying* things, but it was reserved for modern logic to give us a language for *relating* things. Ironically, though not surprisingly, the contemporary study of arithmetic is in this sense largely Aristotelian: we are given ways of *sorting* arithmetic statements into those which are provable or not, while precious little attention is paid to how arithmetic statements are *related*. Relevance logic gives us the means to bring arithmetic up to date in this regard by permitting us to make statements about whether or not certain arithmetic statements are relevantly connected.

It is Meyer who has pursued this possibility, with fascinating results. His idea was to axiomatize Peano arithmetic in the context of relevance logic, putting the arrow of relevant implication where a real connection was wanted, and a mere truth-functional horseshoe where mere sorting sufficed. It became clear that the decision as to where to put the arrows was far from arbitrary, and that there could be definite intuitions about the matter. For example, a little thought-experiment sufficed to show that of two possible forms of induction,

$$[A(0) \,\&\, (x)(A(x) \rightarrow A(x'))] \rightarrow (x)A(x)$$

and

$$A(0) \rightarrow [(x)(A(x) \rightarrow A(x')) \rightarrow (x)A(x)]$$

only the former avoided arithmetic fallacies of relevance. For a second example, Meyer established results from which it follows that on plausible principles, one could show $0 = 1 \rightarrow 0 = 2$, but *not* conversely, even though one can certainly prove $-(0 = 2)$.

Following Meyer, let $R\#$ be the relevant codification of the Peano axioms (including the 'definitions' of addition and multiplication). It is easy to show that the arrow-free *axioms* of a formulation like that of Kleene (1952) follow therefrom. But recall that in relevance logic we do *not* have available, as primitive, detachment for the horseshoe (as opposed to the arrow), for that would be tantamount to Ackermann's rule (γ). So there is no automatic argument that the rest of the arrow-free theorems of (say) Kleene are provable in $R\#$. In fact, Meyer has shown, using the one-by-one method, in a series of proofs many of which are revelatory of the *relational, relevant* structure of arithmetic, that each of Kleene's numbered theorems is forthcoming in $R\#$. But the general question of relative completeness (is $R\#$ as complete as, say, Kleene, on arrow-free formulas?) remains open. It would be positively solved were it known that Ackermann's rule (γ) was admissible for $R\#$; but this, too, is an open question, even for arrow-free formulas.

In contrast, Meyer has shown that $R\#$ is (absolutely) consistent, and he has shown this not by some complicated transfinite induction, but rather by providing a very small finite model, with two numerical elements and three propositional values (in effect, three-valued arithmetic modulo two). This would have pleased Hilbert *enormously*.

Furthermore, by a result which Meyer communicated just a few weeks ago, there is a proof of (γ) for *R*##, the system which replaces Peano induction by infinite induction. Since the consistency proof for *R*# extends easily to *R*##, this result gives, among other things, a brand new proof of the consistency of classical Peano arithmetic.

Relevance logic was 'invented' with philosophical problems in mind, problems not having much to do with mathematics. With the advent of Meyer's work in relevant arithmetic, and keeping Kronecker's dictum in mind, it can be seen that the applicability of the ideas of relevance logic extends to the very foundations of mathematics. Still, no working mathematician has as yet felt a need for relevance in his mathematical life; relevance logic has not yet had its Brouwer. But it might.

10. RELEVANT ANALYSIS OF FUNCTIONS

One can pass from the ideas of relevance logic to those of relevant functions by a variety of paths; perhaps the easiest is this. There is the notion, derivative from several sources, that a useful representation of an implication is as a family of functions each of which takes one from a proof of the antecedent into a proof of the consequent. Suppose the implication to be represented is a relevant one; then harking back to first principles, not just any old function ought to count. What is evidently wanted is a notion of a function which 'really depends on its argument', one which really has to have a look at the proofs of the antecedent, which cannot ignore them completely in yielding a proof of the consequent. And so one is led to think independently about functions which are *strict*, in Scott's terminology, or *relevant*, as I shall say here – functions which really depend on their arguments.

The idea sounds perhaps mad, but research in pursuit thereof, building on some ideas of Scott, and much developed by Helman (1977), has led to a stable characterization of such functions.

Part of the evidence for stability comes through a semantic theorem of Helman's. Taking typed lambda terms in normal form (and including some operators not usually primitive in lambda systems), Helman gives *syntactic* criteria for dividing the relevant ones from the irrelevant. Then he shows that this division coincides in a satisfying way with the purely *mathematical* characterization of relevant function to which I referred above.

Furthermore, Helman shows that there is a strong sort of coherence between the logical and functional ideas of relevance; he establishes that a formula is provable in the relevance logic *R* just in case the type represented by that formula (thinking of $A \rightarrow B$, for instance, as representing the type of relevant functions from A into B) is the type of a syntactically relevant term.

And Helman also generalizes and enriches these ideas so as to apply to other relevance logics such as E and T. With regard to E, modal notions as well are involved, as I mentioned in Section 5 above.

In work quite independent of this, Pottinger (1977) has shown how lambda terms can be put to use in the analysis of proofs. Doubtless relevant lambda terms will be pressed into service when relevant proofs are wanted.

And with equal absence of doubt, it is easy to conjecture that there are lots more ideas to be discovered about the analysis of functions from a relevant or modal point of view, ideas extending well beyond those of recursion theory into brand new domains; for example, Dunn suggests that now is the time to invent relevant recursion theory – I close, then, by commending unto you this doubtless fascinating task.*

University of Pittsburg

NOTE

* Thanks are due the National Science Foundation for partial support via Grant SOC71–03594–A02, and to Chidgey, Dunn, and Gupta for valuable suggestions.

BIBLIOGRAPHY

Ackermann, W. 'Begrundung einer strengen Implikation', *J. Symbolic Logic* 21 (1956), 113–128.

Anderson, A. R., 'Improved Decision Procedures for Lewis's Calculus S4 and Von Wright's Calculus *M'*, *J. Symbolic Logic* 19 (1954) 201–214. Correction in *ibid.*, 20 (1955), 150.

Anderson, A. R. and Belnap, N. D., Jr., *Entailment: The Logic of Relevance and Necessity*, Vol. 1, Princeton University Press, Princeton, 1975.

Anderson, A. R. and Belnap, N. D., Jr., *Entailment: The Logic of Relevance and Necessity*, Vol. 2, Princeton University Press, Princeton, 1980.

Barcan M. and Ruth, C., 'A Functional Calculus of First Order Based on Strict Implication', *L. Symbolic Logic* 11 (1946), 1–16.

Barcan, M. and Ruth, C., 'The Deduction Theorem in a Functional Calculus of First Order Based on Strict Implication', *J. Symbolic Logic* 11 (1946a), 115–118.

Bayart, A., 'La correction de la logique modale du premier et second ordre S5', *Logique et Analyse* Vol. 1, 1958, pp. 28–44.

Bressan, A., *A General Interpreted Modal Calculus*, Yale University Press, New Haven and London, 1972.

Bressan, A., 'The Interpreted Type-Free Modal Calculus MC', *Rend. Sem. Mat. Univ. Padova* 49 (1973), 157–194; 50 (1973), 19–57; and 51 (1974), 1–25.

Broido, J., 'Von Wright's Principle of Predication – Some Clarifications', *J. Philosophical Logic* 4 (1974), 1–11.

Broido, J., 'On the Eliminability of *de re* Modalities in Some Systems', *Notre Dame Journal of Formal Logic* 17 (1976), 79–88.

Carnap, R., 'Modalities and Quantification', *J. Symbolic Logic* 11 (1946), 33–64.

Carnap, R., *Meaning and Necessity*, The University of Chicago Press, Chicago, 1947.

Collier, K. W., Gasper, A., and Wolf, R. G. (eds.), *Proceedings of the International Conference on Relevance Logics. In memorian: Alan Ross Anderson*. Forthcoming.

Curry, H. B., *A Theory of Formal Deducibility*. Notre Dame Mathematical Lectures, No. 6, Notre Dame University Press, Notre Dame, 1950. (Second Edition, 1955.)

Daniels, C. B. and Freeman, J. B., 'A Second-Order Relevance Logic With Modality', 1977. (Mimeographed.)

Feys, R., 'Les logiques nouvelles des modalities', *Revue neoscholastique de philosophie* 40 (1937), 517–553; and 41 (1938), 217–252.

Fine, K., 1975. *Proceedings of the Third Scandinavian Logic Symposium*, Universitet Uppsala, Uppsala, 1973, pp. 15–31. (Studies in logic and the foundations of mathematics, Vol. 82), North-Holland, Amsterdam.

Fine, K., 'Properties, Propositions and Sets', *J. Philosophical Logic* 6 (1977), 135–191.

Fitch, F. B., *Symbolic Logic*, The Ronald Press Company, New York, 1952.

Fitch, F. B., 'A Complete and Consistent Modal Set Theory', *J. Symbolic Logic* 32 (1967), 93–103.

Freeman, J. B., 'Quantification, Identity, and Opacity in Relevant Logic', 1974, Mimeographed. To appear in Collier, Gasper, and Wolf, 1980.

Gallin, D., *Intensional and Higher-Order Modal Logic*, University of California, Berkeley, Doctoral Dissertation, 1972.

Goedel, K., 'Zum intuitionistischen Aussagenkalkul', *Anzeiger der Akademie der Wissenschaften im Wein*, Vol. 69, No. 7, 1933, pp. 65–66. Reprinted in *Ergebnisse eines mathematischen Kolloguiums* 4 (1933), 40.

Gupta, A., *The Logic of Common Nouns: An Investigation in Quantified Modal Logic*, Yale University Press, New Haven and London, 1980.

Halmos, P., *Algebraic Logic*, Chelsea Publishing Company, New York, 1962.

Helman, G., *Restrictions on Lambda Abstraction and the Interpretation of Some Non-Classical Logics*, University of Pittsburgh, Doctoral Dissertation, 1977.

Hintikka, K. J. J., 'Modality and Quantification', *Theoria* 27 (1961), 110–128.

Hughes, G. E. and Cresswell, M. J., *An Introduction to Modal Logic*, Methuen and Co., London, 1968.

Kanger, S., *Provability in Logic*, Almqvist and Wiksell, Stockholm–Gotenborg–Uppsala, 1957.

Kaplan, D., 'Review of a 1963 Article by S. Kripke, *J. Symbolic Logic* 31 (1966), 120–122.

Kleene, S. C., *Introduction to Metamathematics*, Van Nostrand, New York, 1952.

Kripke, S. A., 'A Completeness Theorem in Modal Logic', *J. Symbolic Logic*, 24 (1959), 1–15.

Kripke, S. A., 'The Undecidability of Monadic Modal Quantification Theory', *Zeitschrift für mathematische Logik und Grundlagen der Mathematik* 8 (1962), 113–116.

Lewis, C. I., *A Survey of Symbolic Logic*, University of California Press, Berkeley and Los Angeles, 1918. Second edition, Abridged, Dover Publications, Inc. New York, 1960.

Lewis, C. I. and Langford, C. H., *Symbolic Logic*, The Century Co., New York and London, 1932. Second edition, Dover Publications, Inc., New York, 1959.

Lewis, D. K., 'Counterpart Theory and Quantified Modal Logic', *J. Philosophy* 65 (1968), 113–126.

Massey, G. J., *Understanding Symbolic Logic*, Harper and Row, New York, Evanston, and London, 1970.

McKinsey, J. C. C., 'A Solution of the Decision Problem for the Lewis Systems S2 and S4, With an Application to Topology', *J. Symbolic Logic* 6 (1941), 117–134.

Mendelson, E., *Introduction to Mathematical Logic*, D. van Nostrand Co., Princeton, 1964.

Meredith, C. A., *Interpretations of Different Modal Logics in the 'Property Calculus'*, 1956, Mimeographed. Christchurch, Philosophy Department, Canterbury University College (recorded and expanded by A. N. Prior).

Montague, R., 'Universal Grammar', *Theoria* 36 (1970), 373–398. Reprinted, with other relevant papers, in *Formal Philosophy: Selected Papers of Richard Montague*, R.. H. Thomason (ed.), Yale University Press, New Haven and London, 1974.

Parsons, T., 'Essentialism and Quantified Modal Logic', *Philosophical Review* 78 (1969), 35–52.

Pottinger, G., 'Normalization as a Homomorphic Image of Cut-Elimination', 1976. Mimeographed.

Prior, A. N., *Formal Logic*, Oxford University Press, 1955. (Second edition, 1961.)

Quine, W. V., 'The Problem of Interpreting Modal Logic', *J. Symbolic Logic* 12 (1947), 43–48.

Segerberg, K., *An Essay in Classical Modal Logic*, Vols. 1, 2, 3, Filosofiska Studier, No. 13, (Filosofiska Foereningen och Filosofiska Institutionen vid Uppsala Universitet, Uppsala, 1971.

Tichy, P., 'On *de dicto* Modalities in Quantified S5', *J. Philosophical Logic* 2 (1973), 387–392.

Thomason, R. H., 'Modal Logic and Methaphysics', in *The Logical Way of Doing Things*, K. Lambert (ed.), Yale University Press, New Haven, 1969, pp. 119–146.

Thomason, R. H., 'Some Completeness Results for Modal Predicate Calculi', in *Philosophical Problems in Logic*, K. Lambert (ed.), D. Reidel, Dordrecht, 1970.

von Wright, G. H., *An Essay in Modal Logic*, North-Holland, Amsterdam, 1951.

Zaman, J. J., *Modal Logic: The Lewis-Modal Systems*, Oxford University Press, Oxford, 1973.

PART 3

THE INTERPLAY BETWEEN LOGIC AND MATHEMATICS

E. CASARI

LOGIC AND THE FOUNDATIONS OF MATHEMATICS

To say something about the connections between logic and the foundations of mathematics in a meeting in which almost every topic concerning such a connection has undergone or will undergo a direct or indirect, analytical or cursory, theoretical or historical treatment is by no means an easy task.

Nevertheless, I will try to make on the proposed subject some remarks about some general features of this connection, in the hope of not merely confusing what has been clearly said. So I will start by remarking that if we try to rightly understand and correctly evaluate the role played by logic within that very complex phenomenon which is usually referred to as the investigation of the foundations of mathematics, it may be useful to distinguish in that phenomenon two main problem-complexes which, for lack of better terms, I will call the *rigorisation problematic* and the *justification problematic* respectively.

The rigorisation problematic, that is, roughly, all those themes and problems connected with the clarification, explicitation and systematisation of concepts, procedures and results, is in itself certainly not new. Recalling the name of Euclid should be sufficient to make anyone aware of the antiquity and nobility of its history. But it seems right to say that, beginning with the last century, this problematic undergoes such an impressive and rapidly increasing enlargement of horizons, problems and methods as to be, in its present form, hardly comparable with anything else in our history. It must be emphasized that this problematic was mainly developed within the world of mathematicians – although, particularly in some earlier phases of its history, some mathematically trained philosophers may have contributed to it.

There is a different situation where the second problem-complex is concerned: the one we have called justification problematic. The problems of explaining why mathematics is possible, whence its alleged security is derived, its place in the general frame or rationality, to give only a few examples, are old problems of the philosophical tradition, to which – even in modern times – much attention has been paid. One need only call to mind Kant's

E. Agazzi (ed.), Modern Logic – A Survey, 155–166.

philosophy of mathematics to see to what degree of complexity and sophistication these problems were developed in that tradition.

A very important phenomenon which began in the last decades of the past century and which has perhaps more than any other contributed, through its development, to the present form of foundational research, is the evolving of new ways of looking at the justification problematic starting from that of rigorization. Disregarding all other intermediate views – however important –, we may point out two somehow extreme positions which have been taken in the course of that development. On the one hand we have that according to which there is not really an independent justification problematic which goes beyond the rigorisation one, taking moreover the latter in a rather restricted sense; a view – in brief – which considers the task of justifying mathematical thought wholly incorporated in the task of rationally rigorising and systematising this thought. It was essentially along these lines that Peano moved at the end of the past century, and in this century, the Bourbaki-group.

The second position approaches the problem very differently. Rigorisation, especially in its more restricted sense, is not expected to provide in itself a completely satisfactory justification, and dealing directly with specific justificational problems becomes hence important. According to this view however, such problems cannot be dealt with along traditional paths and require for their discussion the same standards of rigor and 'mathematicality' used in the rigorization problematic. The Frege-Russell logicistic program as well as the Hilbert formalistic one are perhaps the two more refined and familiar concretizations of this view.

As a consequence of these new ways of looking at the justificational problematic we can observe the progressive contraction, if not indeed disappearance, of more traditional, autonomous reflections on justificational problems.

Though approximate, the introduced distinction between a rigorisation problematic and a justificational one allows us to appreciate better some different roles played by logic in the foundational discussion and, at the same time, helps us to see better some different ways through which such a problematic has influenced and modified logic itself.

Beginning with the rigorization problematic, we can say that the most striking and peculiar phenomenon which occurs in this field is just a generalized affirmation of logic as the basic tool for this kind of inquiry. It is true that closer historical consideration would show that the process through which this all-pervading presence of logic has come about was by r means a simple and straightforward one. It is also clear that even the mo superficial form of such a consideration would immediately force us to introduce some distinction and articulation as far as the real content of the word 'logic' is concerned.

Mention of the all-pervading presence of logic, cannot be taken as simply meaning that, for example, there are to-day very few examples of foundational works in which sooner or later, but rather sooner than later formal languages, well defined truth or provability notions for them, and so on are not introduced. This presence is indeed a much more complex and composite fact. What I want to stress, however, is that *within that part of the foundational work which was singled out as the rigorizational one*, problems are to-day approached along lines and – if I may put it thus – according to a mental style which has logic as an inseparable background.

Acknowledgement of this fact shows up the sense of the introduced distinction as it opens the way to a separate consideration of the role attributed to logic in dealing with those types of questions collected under the vague heading of "justificational problematic" and also of the consequences that the new ways of approaching such questions have had on logic itself.

The simplest case to be discussed in this perspective is obviously the Frege-Russell justification project.

In this project logic had not only to serve as a tool for classification and systematization but was also required to carry out the task of furnishing justification directly. It should be noted that the idea of logic underlying this project was certainly a much richer idea than the traditional one as it included, for example, fields of logic which the old logic had ignored, but nevertheless had retained some important characteristics of the old conception; in particular that of being somehow the science of necessary truths. It was precisely this characteristic that lay at the basis of the insights which inspired the whole project.

Considering mathematics primarily as the complex of the theories of finite and transfinite numbers, the justification of mathematics was conceived as translation of these theories into logic, that is as showing that the notions involved in those theories could be defined in pure logic in such a way that all theorems about them became theorems of logic. Logic having even those characteristics of security and unquestionability, this translation would have been a satisfactory answer to the main justification requirement.

Of the many consequences produced by the discovery that the logic used for such an undertaking was inconsistent, I would like to single out only one here. This has to do with the fact that the system worked out to overcome such inconsistencies had serious difficulties in being recognized as a logic in the original sense. I am not thinking at this moment so much of the predicativity and reducibility question as rather of the discussion about the 'logicity' of the axiom of infinity.

As a consequence we have had on the one hand an extension of the idea of logic and on the other – intimately connected with it – a certain shift of the crude justification problematic into the direction of what we have called the rigorisation problematic, that is to say, toward a much more refined analysis of notions such as "property" or "belonging to" which had been found not at all so ultimate and clear, as they used to be considered.

To be brief higher logic has tended to become more and more set-theory.

Not so simple is of course the question as to the role played by logic in the justificational part of Hilbert's project and as to the consequences of such a part on the growing out of our present image of logic.

If we restrict ourselves to contrasting such a project with that of Frege-Russell and disregard the whole structure of this project we may point out three features of it which, far beyond and often wholly independently from the peculiar justificational context in which they had merged, have exerted on the formation and evolution of the present image of logic an influence which can hardly be overemphasized.

The first one has to do with the direction into which justification is sought. Whereas in the logicistic project justification is sought *internally* as it were in a sort of *local* justification of the *single* notions involved in the theory – in the sense that one tried to logically analyse and define such notions – in the Hilbertian project, justification is sought *externally* in *a global* property (in particular, consistency) of the whole system of formulas which are provable in that formal system which is intended to translate the inquired theory into a form totally irreproachable from the rigorization point of view. The latter moreover being taken in its most restricted sense.

The second one has to do with the logical tools by means of which such a justification is sought. It is no longer general logic which is needed for such a task but only a very restricted part of it whose outlines were really not well defined but nevertheless sufficiently characterized as to allow reference to it as to the 'finitistic thought'.

The third one has to do with the particular methods envisaged for producing such a proof of consistency.

As contradiction could be expressed by logically very simple formulas, methods were sought to show that a simple formula can be proved if at all, then already by logically very simple tools. The underlying idea was then to use this simplicity of the proof to get the desired answer about consistency. The byproducts of such an approach were important (let us remember only the ϵ-theorems) but still more important was the type of problems it suggested, not only as far as the philosophy of mathematics is concerned – with which we will not deal here – but also as far as our more properly logical interests are concerned. Surely calling attention to global properties of systems and so opening – as it were – our metalogical eye, was not the work of Hilbertian school only. Post, to give an example, was certainly not influenced by Hilbert as he worked out the metalogic of propositional calculi; also the role played by Hilbertian themes on the developing of the *Polish* methodology of deductive sciences (even after its surely independent beginning) should, I think, be evaluated with very great caution. Not to mention the much earlier research, for example by Dedekind or Veblen or Hilbert himself on categoricity questions.

The same could be said about Hilbert's calling attention to a better understanding of our deeper and more elementary logical acitvity. Leaving aside Brouwer, to whom we will shortly return, it can hardly be maintained that for example Skolem was under Hilbert's influence as he began to work out the recursive number theory.

And finally even some features of all those subsequent topics connected with the question of what is really necessary, from a logical or from a descriptive point of view, to grant the truth of a proposition can be found in other different traditions.

Nevertheless it seems to be historically correct to recognize that owing to a very complex set of factors a certain prominence of Hilbert's influence cannot be denied. Through Hilbert's program and its difficulties pass most of the subsequent developments in the direction of an extraordinary expansion of our metalogical interests as well as in the direction of the deepening of our more properly logical knowledge both as knowledge of the behaviour of logical operations and as knowledge of the intrinsic logical force and complexity of propositions.

Having touched upon the subject of the great foundational projects it is of course impossible to pass over the name of Brouwer. At least some words must be said although in doing so it becomes clear how aproximate and rough our scheme is. If we stubbornly persist in using it, then we can say that Brouwer is the only one, of the great founders, for whom the justificational problematic is not somehow superimposed on the rigorizational but vice-versa. To put it differently: at the basis of his foundational work are some general answers to, or if you prefer it perhaps, some general assumptions about such problems as: what is mathematics, what is it concerned with? It is from this point, that Brouwer undertakes a deeper and deeper going analysis of the most important notions of mathematical tradition. This analysis is conducted along logical lines which are very different from those currently accepted elsewhere, but which ensue from precisely those assumptions. That, owing to a lot of reasons, including even personal Brouwerian idiosyncrasies and peculiarities, his ideas took a very long time to be progressively understood and appreciated is simply a question of fact; I think, however, that there are to-day very few logicians and foundationalists who are not convinced that Brouwer's work is a milestone in the entire history of their sciences and who are not willing to extend to him what von Neumann rightly said of Gödel: after him the subject of logic will never again be the same.

These very short and obviously fragmentary references to the three most celebrated justificational undertakings of our fathers are intended of course neither to give an outline of their real logical and philosophical content nor to constitute a generic historical premiss for many of the things we have heard, and will be hearing in this conference.

They were only intended as an explicit, though necessarily very superficial, calling of attention to the fact that in the forming process of the present image of logic a very important role has been played not only by the developments of all those foundational problems which we may be inclined to consider internal to mathematical thought, but also by the attempts to answer some very general philosophical problems or, rather, by the usurpation on the part of more mathematically minded scholars of the traditional justification problematic.

Leaving this subject aside, I would like to say something about the problem of the logic of mathematics or rather about that part of the problem which concerns the connections between logic and the realms of mathematical experience.

Approaching this question naively and with a strong feeling for content seems at first to lead to the following alternatives:

Either there is only one universally applicable logic which enters as the most general and uniform part in every theoretically organized system, *or* logic is – so to speak – system-dependent, that is, so intimately connected with the whole of the rational constructions constituting the system that it cannot really be separated from them unless in a purely formal and largely uninteresting way.

Experience shows that this alternative is really inadequate.

It should in fact be very difficult for anyone nowadays to maintain that there is ultimately only one logic of mathematics; at least unless the word 'logic' is given some particular sense very different from those usual to-day and for which in any case the idea of a deductively closed system of laws is essential.

But, on the other hand, it would not be a much easier task for anyone to rest consequently on the basis of the strong system-dependence of logic.

A reasonable way out of this difficulty seems to consist in considering another, intermediate possibility: that logic be – let us say – locally universal, that is universal for whole classes of organized rational systems.

Although so reasonable as to appear trivial, this way is not really simple to follow. Because as soon as one tries to specify and articulate it so that it become rationally palatable, numerous and sometimes difficult problems arise.

We will briefly touch upon one of them only, which could roughly be formulated thus:

Which are or should be the factors which determine the subdivision of mathematical experience in realms within which a certain logic is appropriate? Still proceeding naively one could at first think that such a factor is to be found in the objects. This seems however rather improbable, at least if objects are to be understood in a sufficiently narrow sense.

This is because, first of all, the particular objects about which some particular mathematical theory or a class of such theories do speak, are in general something very vaguely identifiable and moreover one of the main tasks of foundational research is precisely to give a better and more definite idea of these objects, but the reaching of such a goal presupposes in general a well-defined choice of logic.

Secondly, because merely on the basis of historical experience we can see that reflecting upon the objects does not lead to a universally acknowledged solution.

Even if we agree, for example, – and this is difficult – that natural numbers laid down by a plurimillenarian intellectual tradition are fairly well determined objects, we can hardly think that reflecting upon them will give us a univocal answer.

But if not the particular objects or the particular systems of objects, then perhaps some very general idea about what is in *general a mathematical object* or better about *possible ways of looking at objects* will give us a basis for determining the different realms of logic?

Now, it cannot be denied that historically it is precisely along this way, that we became aware of the possibility – not to use the word 'necessity' –

of distinguishing different logics to account better for the real content of the great mathematical ideas of our tradition.

Through a very complicated and interwoven process, the first conscious manifestations of which appear in the last decades of the past century but the deep roots of which may be traced back to much more remote times, two main general ways of looking at the question have – as is well known – gradually emerged and been consolidated, and to-day constitute the general background on which foundational work in mathematics is done. These two main perspectives are usually referred to by many names. I would prefer to use for them respectively the name of set-theoretical approaches and construction-theoretical approaches.

Others with much greater competence and authority have already spoken or will speak about the whole or about some parts of these two main perspectives and so I will therefore restrict myself to some very general remarks.

The first obvious remark is that the two main perspectives we have mentioned do not really present themselves as two well defined, uniquely determined conceptual schemata but rather as two different *ways of thinking* each giving rise to many different specifications not constituting in general a linear ordering under some type of inclusion but even perhaps presenting some incompatibilities. I would like to stress that this internal complexity and articulation of the two main perspectives should not be seen as a failing or a deficiency, but, on the contrary, as a natural consequence and significant demonstration of the density and wealth of their ground-insights.

The second remark I want to make is that in spite of all differences they both aim to furnish general conceptual tools for producing an intellectually satisfactory analysis of extant mathematical material and orienting work to be done.

As far as the strictly foundational problematic is concerned, in them both is inherent the old idea that logical analysis, conceived as the resolution of a concept in its more properly logical terms, is in any case the main if not – as I have already said – the only step in foundational work. Logic is here, of course, to be understood in a not too narrow sense, that is including not only a theory of logical operators but also concepts of property, of function, of law, of procedure even, possibly, of proof and so on.

The third and last remark concerns their most profound epistemological differences. It has often been maintained that the true differentiating point is to be found in a radically different view as far as the ontological status of mathematical entities in concerned.

Whereas the construction-theoretical approaches seem clearly to move on the basis of the view that the objects which mathematics is dealing with are in some way or other the result of constituting acts of our mind (and so can rightly be classified – in a general gnoseological frame – as conceptualistic views), the set-theoretical approaches were often seen, by their supporters but mostly by their opposers, as defensible only on the basis of very strong realistic assumptions as far as the ontological status of abstract entities is concerned. Precisely the refusal to accept such a doubtful philosophical position has often been used, especially in the past, to motivate a refusal of the set-theoretical approaches to the problem of foundations.

It is well known that the term 'platonism' is often used in foundational discussions as synonymous with what we call here set-theoretical approaches. Now, such a terminological identification, although useful in some cases, seems to me somewhat misleading as it may help to give credence to the existence of a necessary connection where perhaps only a contingent one is in operation.

That general platonistic assumptions are compatible with set-theoretical approaches is obviously true. It is also true that, in many cases, such assumptions have historically played an important role both in motivating as well as in *articulating* set-theoretical approaches. But this cannot be simply taken as a proof of the fact that such assumptions are a necessary constituent of those approaches. It seems indeed that such a necessity could be maintained only on the basis of a previous identification of all possible types of constituting acts of the mind with those which are studied within proper construction-theoretical approaches. But this is at least doubtful. Clearly such a purely negative assertion, cannot be translated into a trivial positive one which makes problems disappear, nor can it be seen as an attempt to diminish the general epistemological sense of construction-theoretical approaches. It may only be seen as an omen that the underlying question be not too simply explained away. Perhaps a critical reexamination of some general features and characteristics we have presumably incorporated in an idea of a constituting act may be of some use in this perspective.

This way of approaching the problem of the role and nature of logic within mathematical theories – or, to be more precise, the method so far followed in outlining some features of this problem – may however be somewhat misleading. This is because it can be taken as supporting the idea that ultimate foundational questions are not only, as is usually said, philosophical – which seems to be in all senses right – but may also be posed and adequately discussed along traditional paths.

The weakness of this idea is that it overlooks those features of to-day's foundational research which are precisely the most new and characterizing ones, that is it fails to account for that deep interaction between some, indeed, at least in part, traditional questions, and the highly developed equipment of methods, conceptual refinements, results which constitute the inheritance of more than one hundred years of *mathematische Grundlagenforschung*. Trying to separate within such a complex one or the other type of question is of course not only possible but even in many cases useful. This should however not be taken as an opportunity of forgetting the basic interactions.

And so I wish to conclude my talk by making some remarks about one of the many ways through which *present* foundational inquiry approaches the problem of the logic of mathematical theories. The way I mean is that consisting in setting up formal systems and studying them – with mathematical strength – in the light of the incorporated logic.

Clearly the types of problems one may encounter here are numerous and very varied too. Attempting to describe them one could introduce, for example, a distinction according to whether the consequences of the strength of the underlying logic are investigated *in* the theory or *about* the theory. Another distinction could be made according to whether those consequences are examined with regard to a particular theory such as number theory or analysis or with regard to a whole class of theories, such as first order or second order theories. It would also be important to make a distinction according to the type and power of the tools used to get the desired results. And so on.

The natural question about how such types of investigations can contribute to a solution or rather to a classification of the problems envisaged does not of course admit of a general answer, as the real foundational import of a particular research depends obviously on the specific nature of the questions posed and solved by the research; nevertheless one should not be too hasty in getting rid of such a question.

Clearly there are many cases in which the general foundational value of a result can immediately be seen.

Think, to give a simple example, of those results which concern the provability or non provability of certain schemata, or more generally the closure under certain rules of, let us say, elementary intuitionistic number theory.

It is easy to see that these results give us important information about what it means for example, for a poor natural number to exist intuitionistically. To give a different but also quite simple example, think of the generalisation of Henkin's completing procedure. As is well known, the proof devised by

Henkin to obtain Gödel's completeness theorem for first-order logic has a main step in showing that every consistent formal system can be extended to a formal system which is not only consistent but also complete and capable of exemplifying every existential proposition it can prove.

Now it has turned out that the basic lines of the argument do not really depend on the fact that the underlying logic is supposed to be the classical one and that some slight generalisation of the notions involved allows us to reproduce the main argument for example for the much wider class of so-called positive systems.

This crude fact has at least a twofold foundational value. On the one hand it gives us a better understanding of logics different from the classical one and opens the way to an extension to such logics of other notions, methods and results which have been primarily worked out for the classical situation; on the other hand, showing the inessentiality of certain assumptions it shows more clearly the points where such assumptions *have* a role and so contribute to a better understanding of their real contents and significance.

Think, to give a third example, of well known results about embeddings of classical formal systems into corresponding intuitionistic ones by means of so called negative translations. Every result in this field give us a well defined answer to some specification of the general problem not mentioned above but which naturally arises as soon as one has accepted the possibility of a plurality of logical systematization of a part or of the whole of mathematical inheritance: The problem of the relations between them. We could of course go further in this vein, but the three given examples should suffice to illustrate those situations in which the foundational interest of a particular technical result can almost immediately be seen.

Sometimes, of course, such an interest may be more hidden.

Typical in this way are, for example, those cases in which we proceed to investigate theories or classes of theories whose underlying logics are in some sense 'unnatural' either in themselves or in connection with the specific axioms of the theories. By a logic which is 'unnatural' in itself I mean, of course, a logic which does not allow itself at least immediately, to be conceived of as a formal precisation of an intuitive value of logical operations; such may be, for example, a particular intermediate logic taken at random.

By a logic which is 'unnatural' in connection with the specific axioms, I mean a logic which may perhaps be natural in itself but which is coupled with a system of axioms whose motivating insights do not seem to harmonize with the insights which render that logic meaningful: such may be, for example, a ZF-axiom system with minimal logic as basis.

I will not deny that some investigations of this sort may be (and in fact sometimes are) wholly superfluous and irrelevant: I think it is however important to emphasize – against a too reductive evaluation of the philosophical import of to-day's logical and foundational studies – that *at least in principle* such investigations are essential to the deepening and sharpening of our knowledge.

Such an undervaluation of this or similar types of investigation often expresses itself by attributing to them 'a purely mathematical interest'. This seems to me very misleading because those of the investigations which are really frivolous and trivial have no mathematical interest at all whereas those which have a real mathematical content do effectively contribute to our knowledge of the behaviour of the so-called logical constants as well as perhaps of the primitive concepts of the theories under discussion.

To get the deep meaning of logical operators, for example, is surely one of the tasks of every philosophically sustained logical investigation, and means in particular knowing the stability and invariance properties, the capabilities and the weakness of such operators. But purely abstract, let me say, combinatorial investigations are essential to determine this.

To put it frivolously: fancying about possibilities has always been a fundamental tool to get insights into realities. But are there anywhere such realities? Well, it depends upon what one means by this. If you overlead this question with too binding absoluteness requirements I am afraid that a satisfactory and not dogmatic answer will be rather difficult to find.

On the other hand, however, even the most sceptically oriented of us will have to acknowledge that in the whole of our mathematical inheritance there are some often recurring insights, uses and ways of arguing which claim for clarification, setting up of connections and breaking down into elements.

This is perhaps not all; but it is in any case enough to build a science on it.

University of Florence

GAISI TAKEUTI

LOGIC AND SET THEORY

In mathematics, our formation of sets is quite often of the form 'the set of all x satisfying a certain property'. Since logic is the calculus about the property, the nature of logic plays an intrinsic role in set theory. Here we take the classical logic, the intuitionistic logic, and the quantum logic and discuss the relation between each of them and set theory. Let us say a few words on these logic. The classical logic is the logic of the absolute. The intuitionistic logic is the logic of the mind. The quantum logic is the logic of the particles. The precise definition of the quantum logic is the logic of the closed linear subspaces of a Hilbert space.

The intuitionistic logic and the quantum logic form a striking contrast. The difference between the classical logic and the intuitionistic logic is that the law of the excluded middle and $\neg\neg p \rightarrow p$ do not hold in the intuitionistic logic. However, the intuitionistic logic and the classical logic become the same if one restricts the logic to the conjunction and the disjunction only. On the other hand, the law of the excluded middle and $\neg\neg p \rightarrow p$ hold in the quantum logic. Moreover, the quantum logic is quite different from the classical logic concerning the conjunction and the disjunction. For example, the distributive law does not hold in the quantum logic. The contrast goes further. In our opinion, the most important logical connective in the intuitionistic logic is the implication. However, there is no reasonable implication in the quantum logic. The best available definition of $p \rightarrow q$ in the quantum logic is $\neg p \vee (p \wedge q)$. This implication satisfies $p \wedge (p \rightarrow q) \rightarrow q$ and $(p \rightarrow q) \wedge \neg q \rightarrow \neg p$. But it does not satisfy $(p \leftrightarrow q) \rightarrow (r \wedge p \rightarrow r \wedge q)$ or $(p \leftrightarrow q) \wedge (p \vee r) \rightarrow (q \vee r)$. (See [5].)

Is there any reason for this marked contrast? Does this come from the contrast between the world of mind and the material world?

Now we come to set theory. First we consider set theory based on the intuitionistic logic. Set theory on the intuitionistic logic is quite different from the classical set theory i.e. Zermelo Fraenkel's set theory with the axiom of choice denoted by ZFC. It does not satisfy the axiom of regularity $\forall x(\exists z(z \in x) \rightarrow \exists y \in x(y \cap x = 0))$, the axiom of choice

$$\forall x(\forall y \in x\, \exists z(z \in y) \rightarrow \exists f(f: x \rightarrow \cup x \wedge \forall y \in x\,(f(y) \in y))),$$

E. Agazzi (ed.), Modern Logic – A Survey, 167–171.

and $\forall \alpha, \beta(\alpha \notin \beta \wedge \beta \notin \alpha \rightarrow \alpha = \beta)$ (α and β range over all the ordinal numbers) in the following sense. If intuitionistic set theory satisfies one of these properties, then its logic must satisfy the law of the excluded middle i.e. the logic must be the classical logic. (For these, see [2] for example.)

The set of all open sets of a topological space is a model of the intuitionistic logic i.e. if we take open sets as truth values, then the intuitionistic logic holds. In this sense, we can sometimes talk about the intuitionistic logic of a topological space. Let Ω be an intuitionistic logic obtained from a metric space and $V^{(\Omega)}$ be the intuitionistic universe of sets obtained by transfinite iteration of power sheaf construction over Ω. We define a real number by a Dedekind cut. If Ω is a two dimensional polyhedron, then the topology of Ω is characterized by the first order theory of the global real numbers in $V^{(\Omega)}$ in the following sense. If Ω' is another intuitionistic logic obtained from a metric space and $V^{(\Omega)}$ and $V^{(\Omega')}$ have the same first order global real number theory, then to topologies of Ω and Ω' are homeomorphic. This shows that the intuitionistic theory of $V^{(\Omega)}$ strongly reflects the topology of Ω. This is interesting since the Boolean algebras of the regular open sets of all positive dimensional polyhedra are the same therefore, the Boolean valued models made of them are all the same. In short, the set theory over Ω based on the classical logic does not reflect the topology of Ω at all. However, very little is known about the intuitionistic set theory.

Our notion of set is clearly based on the two-valued logic where the truth values are true and false. However, any complete Boolean algebra is a good model of the classical logic. Furthermore, Scott and Solovay found, in reformulating Cohen's forcing, that the Boolean valued model based on any complete Boolean algebra is a model of ZFC. The construction of the Boolean valued model based on a complete Boolean algebra $\mathscr{B}$ goes as follows. Instead of assigning the truth value true or false to $a \in b$, assign any member of $\mathscr{B}$ as a truth value of $a \in b$. Then we get a notion of $\mathscr{B}$-valued set. Iterate the $\mathscr{B}$-valued set construction transfinitely along all ordinals, i.e. construct $\mathscr{B}$-valued sets of $\mathscr{B}$-valued sets etc. Then we get the universe of all $\mathscr{B}$-valued sets, which is denoted by $V^{(\mathscr{B})}$. Since there are many different complete Boolean algebras and the theory satisfied by $V^{(\mathscr{B})}$ depends on $\mathscr{B}$, this is quite useful for proving independency of many statements from ZFC. For example, the independency of the continuum hypothesis from ZFC can be proved by this method. (See [3] and [7]).

Boolean valued models have not only many good applications for independence proofs but also interesting interpretations. In [4], Scott showed that there is a one-to-one correspondence between the real numbers in $V^{(\mathscr{B})}$

and the measurable functions if $\mathscr{B}$ is a measure algebra. This one-to-one correspondence is very natural so that the addition, the multiplication and the convergence are preserved. Now let us discuss another example. Let H be a Hilbert space. A set $\mathscr{B}$ of projections of H is called a Boolean algebra of projections if it satisfies the following conditions.

(1) Any two members of $\mathscr{B}$ are commutable.
(2) The identity operator I and the operator 0 belong to $\mathscr{B}$.
(3) If P_1 and P_2 belong to $\mathscr{B}$, so do $\neg P_1, P_1 \vee P_2$ and $P_1 \wedge P_2$, where $P_1 \vee P_2 = P_1 + P_2 - P_1 P_2, \neg P_1 = I - P_1$ and $P_1 \wedge P_2 = P_1 \cdot P_2$.

A Boolean algebra $\mathscr{B}$ of projections is said to be complete if $\mathscr{B}$ is not only complete as a Boolean algebra but also satisfies the condition

$$\mathscr{R}(\sup_\alpha P_\alpha) = \text{the closure of the linear space spanned by } \bigcup_\alpha \mathscr{R}(P_\alpha),$$

where $\mathscr{R}(P)$ is the range of P. Let $\mathscr{B}$ be a complete Boolean algebra of projections. A self-adjoint operator A is said to be in $(\mathscr{B})$ if every E_λ is a member of $\mathscr{B}$ in it spectral decomposition $A = \int \lambda \, dE_\lambda$. Then the real numbers in $V^{(\mathscr{B})}$ and the self-adjoint operators in $(\mathscr{B})$ have a nice one-to-one correspondence. The correspondence keeps the addition, multiplication, and the order-relation. Though the convergence is not necessarily preserved, $A_1, A_2, \ldots \longrightarrow A$ in the model implies $A_1, A_2, \ldots \longrightarrow A$ in the strong topology if $\|A_1\|, \|A_2\|, \ldots$ have a uniform bound. (See [5].) In the process of 'quantization' of a classical theory in physics, real quantities also become self-adjoint operators on Hilbert space and algebraic operations are preserved. Therefore M. Davis has proposed in [1] to use the model $V^{(\mathscr{B})}$ to give an interpretation of the formalism of quantum mechanics. More precisely he takes up N. Bohr's suggestion that there is an analogy with the instruments used in a measurement and an inertial frame in special relativity theory and interpretes quantum theory as a theory of relativity in which Boolean algebras of commuting operators serve as a frame. A measurement process is possible only with respect to a frame and truth values of statements about the results of such a measurement are simply such projections. Thus the famous 'collapse' of the wave packet is seen to be simply the effect of a Bollean-valued model. The following table presented by him is very suggestive.

Special Relativity	Quantum Mechanics
Inertial frame	Boolean algebra of projections generated by commuting observables
Lorentz Transformation	Fourier Transform
Lorentz Group	(Subgroup of) Unitary Group
Minkowski Metric (Invariant)	State Vector (ψ)

Let us add two more examples of application of the Boolean valued models using projection algebras. Let G be a locally compact abelian group. There is a one-to-one correspondence between the character groups of G in some Boolean valued model and the unitary representation of G. Though the Boolean algebra $\mathscr{B}$ depends on the unitary representation of G, it gives a general method transforming the theorems of harmonic analysis into different theorems of harmonic analysis involving the unitary representations. Our theory also gives a reasonable definition of a convergence of unbounded commuting self-adjoint operators. Thus it gives a nice way to reduce the differential equations with unbounded operators to the ordinary differential equations interpreting unbounded operators as constants in a model. (See [6]).

Now let us discuss set theory based on the quantum logic $\mathscr{L}$. As $V^{(\Omega)}$ and $V^{(\mathscr{B})}$, we can construct $V^{(\mathscr{L})}$ as the natural universe of $\mathscr{L}$-valued sets. However, the trouble here is that our notion of sets heavily depends on the equivalence class of properties and the quantum logic does not have any reasonable notion of implication therefore does not have any reasonable notion of equivalence. Therefore, even if we construct $V^{(\mathscr{L})}$, the set theory there does not satisfy the equality axiom. More specifically $a = b \rightarrow (a \in c \rightarrow b \in c)$ fails there. (See [5]). In this sense, there is no set theory in the traditional sense in the quantum logic. However, every complete Boolean algebra of projections can be isomorphically embedded in the quantum logic and the Poincaré group operates on the quantum logic and produces lots of isomorphisms among Boolean valued models inside the quantum logic valued model. One can interpret the Heisenberg relation as a relation between this type of isomorphism and Boolean valued models in $V^{(\mathscr{L})}$. Is there any possibility of a set theory in which the truth value is related not only with $\mathscr{L}$

but also with Poincaré group operations on $\mathscr{L}$? It seems to us that a completely new type of set theory is waiting for us.

Dept. of Mathematics, Urbana

BIBLIOGRAPHY

[1] M. Davis, 'Takeuti Models and Foundations of Quantum Mechanics', A talk given at Symposium on Abraham Robinson's theory of infinitesimal, Iowa City, 1977.

[2] R. Grayson, 'A Sheaf Approach to Models of Set Theory', Master thesis, Oxford, 1975.

[3] T. Jech, *Lectures in Set Theory*, Lectures Notes in Mathematics No. 217, Springer, 1971.

[4] D. Scott, 'Boolean Valued Models and Non-Standard Analysis', in *Applications of Model Theory to Algebra, Analysis and Probability*, Holt, Reinhart and Winston, 1969.

[5] G. Takeuti, *Two Applications of Logic to Mathematics*, Publications of the Mathematical Society of Japan No. 13, Iwanami and Princeton University Press, 1978.

[6] G. Takeuti, 'Boolean Valued Analysis', *Applications of Sheaves*, Edited by Fourman, Mulvey, and Scott, Lecture Notes in Mathematics No. 753, Springer, 1979.

[7] G. Takeuti and W. Zaring, *Axiomatic Set Theory*, Springer, 1973.

HANS HERMES

RECURSION THEORY

0. SURVEY

The theory of recursive functions can be characterized as a general theory of computation. It has been created in the twentieth century.

Sections 1 to 4 recall the historical background, establish some basic algorithmic concepts from the intuitive point of view and mention some related problems unsolved before 1936. Several exact mathematical notions which according to Church's Thesis (1936) correspond to the intuitive algorithmic concepts are introduced in 5 to 8. Based on Church's Thesis one has been able to solve these problems (always giving negative answers); this is reported in 9 to 12. The development of recursion theory itself is discussed in 13 to 18.

The literature concerning recursion theory and its applications is abundant. In the Bibliography* we name some of the fundamental papers which mark the origin of the theory; for the further development we have to confine ourselves to a choice of books or articles where the reader may find further references. He may also consult the *Journal of Symbolic Logic* (since 1936) which is the most important journal connected with the theory of recursive functions.

1. EARLY HISTORY

Computation is as old as mathematics itself. It often is based on a suitable codification of numbers. The so-called Arabic system of numerals which was introduced in Western Europe in the middle of the sixteenth century has at that time been named *algorism* or *algorithm*, recalling the famous Arabic mathematician Al Khwarizmi who lived in the first half of the ninth century. In more recent times we mean by an algorithm any system of rules describing a computation e.g. when speaking of the Euclidean algorithm. An algorithm often is referred to as a *calculus*, that name reminding the pebbles (calculi) which have been used in computation (calculation) by means of an abacus.

It has been mentioned before that the general theory of computation has originated in the twentieth century. Nevertheless we find earlier related ideas, often quite phantastic, with more or less mathematical background, and sub-

E. Agazzi (ed.), Modern Logic – A Survey, 173–195.

stantiated as often as marred with philosophical speculations. Raymundus Lullus in 1273 published a book with the title 'Ars magna'. This *ars magna* was supposed to be a combinatorial procedure which could be used to generate all 'truths'. Lullus' concept has had an astonishing influence during many centuries. Cardano in 1545 published his (and other people's) algebraic discoveries in a book 'Artis magnae seu de regulis algebraicis liber unus'. Lullus is cited in Leibniz's Dissertation de Arte Combinatoria (1666). Leibniz attempts to clarify the idea of an *ars magna* distinguishing many special *artes* as the *ars iudicandi* and the *ars inveniendi*[1].

It seems that mathematicians more or less have been guided by the idea that by trying hard enough they would be able to develop for any special class of problems an appropriate algorithm by which these problems could be solved. This primarily seemed to be the case for problems belonging to arithmetics. The gist of Descartes' 'La Géometrie' is his claim that by his methods he is able to reduce every geometrical to an arithmetical problem, and hence to submit it to well-known arithmetical algorithms.

Of course, mathematicians got conscious of the fact that there existed well-defined problems which could not (or not yet) be solved by known algorithms. Among the most famous of those problems may be mentionded the Entscheidungsproblem, Hilbert's tenth problem and the word problem of group theory.

2. THE ENTSCHEIDUNGSPROBLEM. DECIDABLE SETS

In the second half of the last century mathematicians have begun to study logic based on formal languages. A formula of such a language is called valid if it holds for every interpretation of the free variables occuring in it; it is called satisfiable if is holds for at least one interpretation. The *Entscheidungsproblem* for validity (resp. satisfiability) asks to find an algorithm which decides for every formula whether it is valid (resp. satisfiable). These problems are related to each other: A formula is valid iff its negation is not satisfiable. This connection gives us an algorithm to decide validity if we have an algorithm which decides satisfiability. In other words the decision problem for validity is *reduced* to that of satisfiability. In a similar way the decision problem for satisfiability can be reduced to that of validity. Hence both problems are equivalent.

Concerning decidability we have general the following situation: Let be given a finite alphabet A and let be A^* the set of all words built up from the letters of A[2]. Let S be a set of such words. A *decision procedure* for S is an algorithm which decides for every word of A^* whether it belongs to S. S (or the predicate which is defined by being an element of S) is *decidable* if there exists a decision procedure for S.

The Entscheidungsproblem (e.g.) for satisfiability for a certain class K of formulas is the question whether the set of the satisfiable formulas belonging to K is decidable. The Entscheidungsproblem has for the first time been formulated (and partially solved) by Schröder (1890–1905) to whom also is due the important concept of reduction. In later investigations mostly concerning first-order logic the Entscheidungsproblem has been solved for various classes K of formulas[3]. In another direction of investigations it has been shown that the Entscheidungsproblem for the class of all formulas of the predicate calculus is reducible to certain subclasses[4].

3. HILBERT'S THENTH PROBLEM. GENERATED SETS. THE WORD PROBLEM FOR GROUPS

A diophantine equation is of the form $f = 0$, where f is a polynomial (in several variables) whose coefficients are integers. Such an equation is called solvable if it holds for suitable integers. Hilbert (1900) in his tenth problem has asked whether the set of solvable diophantine equations is decidable.

The set of solvable diophantine equations can be generated (or listed) by an algorithmic procedure. Such a procedure may be described roughly as follows: Let be given a natural number $n \geqslant 1$. Then we can write down the finitely many diophantine equations in the variables $x_1, ..., x_n$ whose degrees and absolute values of coefficients are bounded by n. Furthermore we can write down the finitely many sequences $(a_1, ..., a_n)$ where the a_j are integers whose absolute values are bounded by n. For each of these diophantine equations and each of these sequences $(a_1, ..., a_n)$ we can check in a finite number of steps whether the sequence is a solution of the equation. We thus get effectively a finite number of solvable diophantine questions. By repeating this process for $n = 1, 2, 3, ...$ we generate (or list) every solvable diophantine equation. In this sense the set of all solvable diophantine equations is a *generated set* – a term which has been introduced by Post (1945)[5].

Very often in mathematics the problem arises whether a set is decidable which by its definition is known to be a generated set. That is also the case for the above-mentioned Entscheidungsproblem for validity, if validity is (or can be) defined by a calculus (as in first-order predicate calculus).

In many cases a generated set can be given by a calculus of a special kind. As an example the odd numbers may be given by the 'axiom' | and by the 'rule' $x \to x\,||$. Starting with the axiom and applying the rule several times, we get a deduction, e.g. |, |||, |||||, |||||||. The set of odd numbers coincides with the final words of deductions. Generalizing to a finite number of letters, axioms, variables, and premisses of the rules we get the so-called *calculi in canonical form* (Post, 1943). Special cases of such calculi have been considered much earlier. Thue (1914) introduced what to-day are called semi-Thue systems. The rules of a semi-Thue system are of the form $xUy \to xVy$, with variables x, y and for each rule fixed words U, V. If together with every rule there exists also the 'inverse rule' $xVy \to xUy$, we have a Thue system. The *word problem* for a semi-Thue system is the set of all pairs of words (W, W') s.t. taking W as an axiom we are able to derive W'. The word problem is a generated set. The question is whether this set is decidable.

The set of words built up from the letters of a given alphabet together with the juxtaposition (concatenation) is a semigroup whose unit elements is the empty word. If in a Thue system we define $W \sim W'$ iff (W, W') is an element of the word problem, we have a congruence relation which by factorization again yields a semigroup with a unit. If we assume that the alphabet is of the form $\{a_1, ..., a_n, b_1, ..., b_n\}$ and that all $xa_ib_iy \to xy$ and $xb_ia_iy \to xy$ belong to the rules of a Thue system, the factorization leads to a group. That is the method to present a group by 'generating elements and defining relations' (Dyck, 1882–83). The *word problem for groups* – first formulated by Dehn (1912), asks to find an algorithm which decides the word problem for this kind of Thue systems.

4. COMPUTABLE FUNCTIONS. THE BASIC ALGORITHMIC CONCEPTS

Let be A an alphabet and W_0, W_1 different fixed words over A. Then we can associate to S the *characteristic function* of S which has the value W_0 if the argument belongs to S and otherwise the value W_1. If S is decidable we have an algorithm which enables us to compute (calculate) the value of the characteristic function for any given argument. A function for which such an algorithm exists is called a *computable* (*calculable*) *function*. It is easy to see that a set is decidable iff its characteristic function is computable. Hence decidability may be defined by computability. Also the converse holds: A function f is computable iff the set of all pairs $(W, f(W))$ is decidable.

A set S is decidable iff S and the complement of S are generated. A set is generated iff it is void or the codomain of a computable function.

These relations show that the *three basic algorithmic concepts* of a computable function, of a decidable set and of a generated set are interdefinable.

As the 'substrate' for the algorithmic concepts we have taken the words over a finite alphabet. An arbitrary algorithm can be carried out only if it operates with 'manipulable objects'. These may not be primarily words but e.g. the beads of an abacus. But the significant positions of the beads of an abacus can be effectively represented by words and the original algorithm can be transferred to an algorithm operating with words. An analogue procedure can be used to represent effectively words by natural numbers so that one may, as it is often done, confine oneself to functions over natural numbers and to sets of natural numbers.

Effective representations of the described kind are often called *gödelizations* – Gödel (1931) has made an essential use of such representations in his famous paper on the incompleteness of certain logical calculi. A gödelization leading to natural numbers (Gödel numbers) is also called an arithmetization.

We have tacitly made use of gödelizations when speaking of decidable sets whose elements are pairs of words.

5. CHURCH'S THESIS. λ–DEFINABILITY

The basic algorithmic concepts are 'somewhat vague intuitive notions' (Church, 1936). A priori there is no reason to assume that these notions correspond to precise mathematical concepts. But to-day there exist a multitude of equivalent mathematical concepts which are believed to match the intuitive notions. The astonishing proposition that e.g. computability corresponds to a certain exact mathematical concept has first been published by Church (1936). To-day we are used to speak of *Church's Thesis* if we want to say that the intuitive algorithmic notions correspond to certain exact mathematical concepts. We indicate in the following some of these concepts and begin with λ–definability.

Church, when working on a logic without types, created (aided by Rosser and Kleene) the so called λ–calculus[6]. In this calculus we have terms built up from variables with the two operations of application and of abstraction. If T_1 and T_2 are terms, application leads to a new term $(T_1 T_2)$. If x is a variable and T a term, abstraction leads to a new term $\lambda x T$, where x is the so-called λ-operator. There are essentially two rules which lead to identification of terms: the renaming of bound variables leads e.g. to identify λxx with λyy, and the elimination of the λ-operator leads e.g. to identify (λxxy) with y[7]. Certain terms called numerals may be taken as representations of natural numbers, e.g. $\lambda y \lambda xx$ represents 0, $\lambda y \lambda x(yx)$ represents 1, $\lambda y \lambda x(y(yx))$ represents 2, etc.. It can be proved that numerals representing different numbers are not identified by the rules of the λ-calculus. A 1-place[8] function f whose arguments and values are natural numbers is represented by a term T if we have for all numbers n, m and all numerals N, M representing these numbers: $fn = m$ iff (TN) is identified with M. A function is called λ–*definable* if it is represented by a term. Regarding the algorithmic character of the rules it is evident that every λ-definable function is computable. After certain initial difficulties (mainly connected with the predecessor function) it was found that every computable function which was tried out was λ-definable. This fact ultimately led Church to claim that the computable functions coincide with the λ-definable functions[9].

6. RECURSIVE FUNCTIONS

The functions which are the exact counterpart of the computable functions are to-day mostly called recursive functions. This name dates from another line of investigations which started with Herbrand (1932) and Gödel (1934) and got its final form by Kleene (1936ff). Here we have terms built up from the symbol 0, variables (for numbers) and function symbols. We have the numerals $0, 0', 0'', \ldots$ (where $'$ is a 1-place function symbol) representing the numbers 0, 1, 2, ... Equations are of the form $T_1 = T_2$ where T_1 and T_2 are terms. We have two rules which allow to derive new equations from given ones: We may substitute numerals for variables and replace in an equation a term $fN_1 \ldots N_r$ by N, if $N_1, \ldots, N_r$ and N are numerals and if the equation $fN_1 \ldots N_r = N$ has already been derived. A function f is called *recursive* if there is a finite set E of equations and a function symbol F such for all n_1, ..., n_r, n and representing numerals $N_1, \ldots, N_r$, N we have $f(x_1, \ldots, x_r) = n$ iff $FN_1 \ldots N_r = N$ is derivable from E. Kleene (1936) has proved that a function is recursive iff it is λ-definable. The use of the word 'recursive' reminds the fact that originally the well-known process of recursion was believed to be the essential process to generate the class of recursive functions (see section 13).

7. TURING DEFINABLE FUNCTIONS

The processes which have been used in the definitions of λ-definability and of recursiveness are non-deterministic since in general in a step of a derivation we may apply several rules. To Turing (1936) is due an exact definition of the concept of a computable function using a process which has a deterministic character. Independently practically the same definition has been given by

Post (1936)[10]. When presenting the concept of what to-day is called a *Turing machine*, Turing has tried to give arguments in order to show that every computation which can be performed can also be performed using a Turing machine. In brief, his argumentation runs as follows: Computations are performed stepwise. It is sufficient to use a one-dimensional tape, divided into squares. It is sufficient to use a finite alphabet, called the alphabet of the Turing machine; two letters V and L of the alphabet are distinguished. In each step we have exactly one letter in each square of the tape (the 'void' letter V is used to indicate an empty square). We have a finite number of 'states of mind', in short 'states'. One state is distinguished as the 'initial state'. Each step is determined by a state and by the letter which is on a certain 'scanned' square. A step consists in ending the computation (stopping), or in changing the letter in the scanned square, or in changing the scanned square itself to the square immediately to the right or the left. In addition, if we have not a stop, we go over to a new state (which may be the old one). Hence, the behaviour of a Turing machine may be described by a finite matrix (Turing table), whose first two columns consist of all pairs of states and letters. A Turing machine is said to *halt* if after a finite number of steps the next step is the stop.

A 1-place function[8] f is called *Turing computable* if there is a Turing machine s.t. for all n, m we have $f(n) = m$ iff T, applied to n, halts on m. Here 'applying to n' means to start (1) with the initial state, (2) with a tape on which we have n successive letters L, and which is otherwise empty, and (3) with the last non-empty square as the initial scanned square[11, 12]. 'To halt on m' means to halt in such a way that m is the number of squares immediately to the left of the last scanned square which bear the letter L. – Turing (1936) has proved that the Turing computable functions coincide with the λ–definable functions.

8. OTHER EXACT ALGORITHMIC CONCEPTS. FINAL REMARKS CONCERNING CHURCH'S THESIS

Some of the other procedures by which recursive functions can be defined are related to the concept of a Turing machine but have a greater similarity to real computers. The tape of a Turing machine has an infinite number of squares; each square can have only a finite number of contents (namely the letters of the alphabet). We may introduce Turing machines with a finite number of tapes. This resembles the situation with computers where we have a finite number of registers and where we may idealize by assuming that each register can have an unlimited number of contents. Another concept which has been found very useful is the notion of a *register machine* (Minsky, 1967). In a register machine we have a finite number of registers. It operates stepwise. Before each step in each register is stored a natural number. A step is determined by one of a finite number of states. The step may be (1) to stop or (2) to add 1 to the content of a determined register or (3) to substract (if possible) 1 from the content of a determined register. If we have not a stop a new state is prescribed. In case (3) two different new states may be prescribed depending on the fact whether the content of the determined register before the step is 0 or not. This allows a branching of the algorithm.

The exact counterparts of the decidable resp. generated sets are called *recursive* resp. *(recursively) enumerable sets*.

Post (1943) has proved that a set S of words over an alphabet A is enumerable iff there is a calculus in canonical form[13] over an extension B of the alphabet A, and a finite set E of words over B, s.t. S concides with the set of words over A which are derivable from E in the canonical system.

Church's thesis is universally accepted. The main reason for this fact is the overwhelming experience which has shown that every example for one of the intuitive basic algorithmic concepts which has been checked also falls under the corresponding exact concepts. Some people are also convinced by Turing's argumentation. Finally the fact may be stressed that so many different approaches[14] undertaken in order to define exactly one of the basic algorithmic concepts have been proved to be extensionally equivalent[15].

9. A SPECIAL UNDECIDABLE SET: THE HALTING PROBLEM

Let be E a set of natural numbers[16], and T a Turing machine. We say that *T decides E* iff

$$(1)\quad \begin{cases} \forall n(En \leftrightarrow T, \text{ applied on } n, \text{ halts on } V), \text{ and} \\ \forall n(\neg En \leftrightarrow T, \text{ applied on } n, \text{ halts on } L). \end{cases}$$

(To halt on a letter X means to halt s.t. X is the letter on the last scanned square.) It is easy to prove that E is decidable iff there is a Turing machine T s.t. T decides E.

We want to define a special undecidable set connected with Turing machines. Two preliminary remarks: (1) It can be assumed without loss of generality that the (different) letters V and L occur in the alphabet of every Turing machine. (2) A Turing machine is given by its table which by gödelization can be described by a natural number. It can be assumed that every number is the Gödel number of a Turing machine[17]. Hence we can use T as a variable for natural numbers.

Let be E_0 the set of Turing machines defined by

(2) $E_0 T :\leftrightarrow T$, applied on T, halts on L.

(Applying T on T may be described as T studying itself.) E_0 *is not decidable*. Let otherwise T_0 be a Turing machine which decides E_0. Hence we have as a special case of (1):

(3) $\begin{cases} (\forall T)((E_0\, T \leftrightarrow T_0, \text{applied on } T, \text{halts on } V), \text{and} \\ (\forall T)(\neg E_0\, T \leftrightarrow T_0, \text{applied on } T, \text{halts on } L). \end{cases}$

Since $\forall T(E_0\, T$ or $\neg E_0\, T)$, we get from (3)

(4) $(\forall T)(T_0$, applied on T, halts on V or on $L)$.

If we replace in the first condition of (3) E_0 by its definition (2), we have

(5) $(\forall T)$ (T, applied on T, halts on $L \leftrightarrow T_0$, applied on T, halts on V).

Now we apply a diagonal procedure – such a procedure is typical for many proofs in recursion theory – by taking T_0 as the arbitrary T of (5). We get

(6) T_0, applied on T_0, halts on $L \leftrightarrow T_0$, applied on T_0, halts on V, which contradicts (4).

Let now E_1 be the set of Turing machines defined by

(7) $(\forall T)(E_1\, T \leftrightarrow T$, applied on 0, halts).

E_1 is called the *halting problem*.

One can associate in an effective way with every Turing machine T a Turing machine gT s.t. T, applied on T, halts on L iff gT, applied on 0, halts. Hence we have

(8) $(\forall T)\,(E_0 T \leftrightarrow E_1 gT)$.

By (8) we have reduced the decidability for E_0 so that of E_1, i.e. we have proved that E_0 is decidable if E_1 is decidable. Since we have already shown that E_0 is undecidable we get the undecidability of E_1. With other words: *The halting problem for Turing machines is undecidable.*

This undecidable problem has been used to show that many interesting predicates are also undecidable. Very often this is done by reducing the halting problem (or related undecidable problems) to the predicate in question. In the following we discuss some examples.

10. THE ENTSCHEIDUNGSPROBLEM CONTINUED. DOMINO PROBLEMS. UNDECIDABLE THEORIES

The Entscheidungsproblem for the first order predicate logic is undecidable. This result was one of the first applications of the theory, due to Church (1936a) and independently to Turing (1936). In the following we give a sketch of a later method due to Wang (1961) which was the origin of further important developments.

A domino is an oriented square plate. The edges of the upper sides are colored. Dominoes whose corresponding edges bear the same colours are called of the same type. In a 'corner game' D we have two finite sets D_0, D_1 (where $D_0 \subseteq D_1$) of domino types and infinitely many dominoes of each type. Let the game D be called a 'good' game if it is possible to cover the first quadrant with dominoes of the game in a way that matching edges have the same colour and that in the corner we have a domino belonging to D_0. It is possible to associate in a effective way with each Turing machine a domino game D s.t. T does not halt iff D is good. Therefore the (complement of the) halting problem is reduced to the goodness problem for dominoes and we have as a consequence: The goodness problem for corner domino games is not decidable. Now we associate in an effective way with each corner domino game D a formula α of the first-order predicate logic s.t. D is good iff α is satisfiable. Therefore the goodness problem for dominoes is reduced to satisfiability. Hence satisfiability is not decidable.

The formulas α associated with domino problems are of a special kind. Hence also satisfiablilty for formulas of this special kind is not decidable. Using more complicated domino games (the 'diagonal' games) Kahr, Moore and Wang proved that the class $\forall \exists \forall$ of formulas is undecidable, which was an open question for a long time[18].

In place of classifying formulas of the predicate calculus by the prefix of their normal forms (as it is the case for the class $\forall \exists \forall$), we may classify them as belonging to certain theories. A theory may be given by a set A of axioms. It is defined as the set of formulas which are derivable (or consequences) of A. Another way to define a theory is to give a model (or a class of models). In this case a theory is defined as the set of formulas which are satisfied by the model. Most of the common mathematical theories such as the elementary theory of groups are undecidable. Consult Tarski *et al.* (1953). Here the starting point is not the undecidability of the halting problem but the fact (obtained by diagonalization) that a consistent theory is undecidable if every recursive function is definable in it. For further results concerning undecidable theories cf. Ershov *et al.* (1965). For a remarkable decidable theory see Tarski (1948).[18a]

11. THE WORD PROBLEM FOR THUE SYSTEMS AND GROUPS. UNIVERSAL TURING MACHINES

The word problem for Thue systems was the first *classical* mathematical problem which was proved to be unsolvable. This fact was established by Post (1947) and Markov (1947). The idea is to associate with every Turing machine T in an effective way a Thue system S s.t. T, applied on n, halts iff in S a certain word W_0 is derivable from a word $W(n)$ which can be calculated if n is given. This reduction shows that there is no algorithm which decides the word problem for arbitrary Thue systems.

It is possible to construct a *universal Turing machine* U which 'simulates' arbitrary Turing machines. As a consequence we can associate in an effective way to each Turing machine T a number $N = N(T)$ s.t. T, applied on 0, halts iff U, applied on N, halts. This reduction shows the unsolvability for a halting problem for the special machine U and the unsolvability for the word problem for the special Thue system S which is associated with U.

Novikov (1955) and Boone (1957) have been the first to prove the unsolvability of the word problem for arbitrary groups (and for a special group). The attempts to get a better understanding of these results from the group-theoretic point of view has deeply influenced research in this topic[19].

It may be mentioned that semi-Thue systems are widely used in formal language theory (Chomsky and his successors)[20]

12. HILBERT'S TENTH PROBLEM (CONTINUED)

Hilberts's tenth problem (cf. Section 3) is unsolvable. In the following we give some outlines of the proof. It is sufficient to show the undecidability of the set D of diophantine equations which have solutions in natural numbers (originally: in integers).

A predicate P (for natural numbers $x_1, ..., x_n$) is called diophantine iff there exists a diophantine equation $f = 0$ where f is a polynomial in the variables $x_1, ..., x_n$ and certain additional variables $y_1, ..., y_m$, s.t.

$$(*) \qquad \forall x_1 \ldots \forall x_n (Px_1 \ldots x_n \leftrightarrow \exists y_1 \ldots \exists y_m f(x_1, \ldots, x_n, y_1, \ldots, y_m) = 0).$$

Theorem: A predicate is diophantine iff it is enumerable.

This remarkable connection between recursion theory and number theory has the following consequence: It is easy to see that the halting problem H is an enumerable set. Hence by (*) there exists a polynomial f in variables $x, y_1, \ldots, y_m$ s.t.

$$(**) \qquad \forall x(Hx \leftrightarrow \exists y_1 \ldots \exists y_m f(x, y_1, \ldots, y_m) = 0).$$

Let be x_0 an arbitrary number. If we assume that D is decidable we can decide whether the diophantine equation $f(x_0, y_1, \ldots, y_m) = 0$ (in the variables $y_1, \ldots, y_m$) has a solution. Hence, using (**), we can decide whether Hx. This contradicts the undecidability of the halting problem.

It remains to prove that every enumerable predicate is diophantine (the converse is trivial and not needed for the intended application). After several previous results Davis, Putnam and J. Robinson have proved in 1960 that it is sufficient to show that the exponential predicate E is diophantine where $Exyz \leftrightarrow x^y = z$. This was finally done by Matijasevič (1970) using properties of the Fibonacci sequence (also Pell's equation could be used i istead). A detailed account of the proof is given in Davis (1973).

13. PARTIAL RECURSIVE FUNCTIONS. μ-RECURSIVENESS

Until now we have considered only total functions i.e. r-place functions which are defined for all r-tuples of words. A r-place function whose domain is a subset of the set of all r-tuples of words is called a *partial function*. Every total funciton is a partial function. Kleene (1938) has remarked that in dealing with computability partial functions occur in a very natural way. This may be illustrated from the point of view of Turing machines. We can associate with *every* Turing machine T a partial function $f = f(T)$. f is defined for n[8] and has in this case the value m iff T, applied on n, halts on m. A partial function is called *Turing computable* if it is an $f(T)$[21].

We get the same functions if we associate with *every* term T of the λ-calculus a 1-place[8] function $f = f(T)$: f is defined for n and has in this case the value m iff (TN) can be identified with M (where N, M are numerals for n, m).

Starting in the realm of thought which has led to the Herbrand/Gödel/Kleene characterization of recursiveness Kleene (1943) has introduced the recursive partial functions in the following way: The arguments and values of these functions are natural numbers. Some very simple total functions are called 'initial functions', namely the 0-place function with value 0, the 1-place successor function $'$ and the identity (or projection) functions U^r_k $(1 \leqslant k \leqslant r)$, where $U^r_k(x_1, ..., x_r) = x_k$. Three processes are used to generate new partial functions from given partial functions, namely:

The process of substitution, which leads from $g, h_1, ..., h_r$ to $g(h_1, ..., h_r)$.

The process of recursion, which leads from g and h to f, where

$$f(x_1, ..., x_n, 0) \cong g(x_1, ..., x_n),$$
$$f(x_1, ..., x_n, y') \cong h(x_1, ..., x_n, y, f(x_1, ..., x_n, y)).$$

The process of the μ-operator, which leads from g to f, where

$$f(x_1, ..., x_r) \cong \mu y(g(x_1, ..., x_n, y) = 0).$$

The last equation is to be understood as follows: if for given $x = (x_1, ..., x_n)$ there is a y s.t. $g(x, 0), g(x, 1), ..., g(x, y)$ are defined and $g(x, y) = 0$, then $f(x, y)$ is the least such y. Otherwise $f(x, y)$ and $\mu y(g(x, y) = 0$ are undefined. ($\cong$ indicates that for given values both sides are undefined, or both sides are defined and equal.)

Kleene has called a partial function *μ-recursive* if it can be generated by applying the processes to the initial functions. The μ-recursive functions coincide with the Turing definable functions.

The total μ-recursive functions coincide with the recursive functions. They can be obtained from the initial functions using the three processes where the last is restricted to the case where for every x there is a y s.t. $g(x, y) = 0$.

If to-day a function is called a (partial) recursive function one thinks primarily at it being defined as a μ-recursive function.

In place of 'recursive partial function' it is customary to say 'partial recursive function', or only 'recursive function'.

Asser (1960) has extended the notion of μ-recursiveness to functions over words.

14. SOME FUNDAMENTAL THEOREMS ON PARTIAL RECURSIVE FUNCTIONS

We mention some fundamental theorems due to Kleene[22]. Kleene has called a function primitive recursive if it can be obtained by applying the substitution and the recursion processes to the initial functions. Every primitive recursive function is total. The definition of a primitive recursive function may be written down in the form of a 'schema' of equations. E.g. for multiplication we have the following schema[23]:

$$x + 0 = x$$
$$x + y' = (x + y)'$$
$$x \cdot 0 = 0$$
$$x \cdot y' = x \cdot y + x.$$

The set of all schemas for primitive recursive functions and hence the set of all primitive recursive functions can be generated. We may thus speak of the nth primitive recursive function f_n (this enumeration has repetitions). It is now possible to define a recursive function f by the following diagonal procedure: $f(n) = f_n(n) + 1$. This function cannot be primitive recursive. Otherwise there would be a number m s.t. $f = f_m$, and we would get the contradiction $f(m) + 1 = f_m(m) + 1 = f(m)$. Hence there exist total recursive functions which are not primitive recursive[24].

Also the set of all schemas for μ-recursive functions can be generated and we may speak of the nth μ-recursive function g_n. We can proceed as above and define a μ-recursive function g by postulating that $g(n) \cong g(n) + 1$. There exists a number m s.t. $g = g_m$. We get $g(m) + 1 \cong g(m)$. But 'by a kind of miracle' (Gödel, 1946) this does not lead to a contradiction: We only can infer that g is not defined for m.

n can be considered as a Gödel number which represents the partial recursive function g_n. That the partial recursive functions can be given in an effective way by numbers is made explicit by *Kleene's Normal Form Theorem* (1943). He has defined effectively a 1-place primitive recursive function U and for each n a $(n + 2)$-place primitive recursive function $T^{(n)}$ s.t.

$$U(\mu y T^{(n)}(t, y, x_1, ..., x_n) = 0)$$

runs through all n-place μ-recursive functions if t runs through the set of natural numbers. The tth function given by this formula is often abbreviated by $\{t\}$ (n being fixed) and t is called an index of $\{t\}$. The Normal Form Theorem shows that in order to generate every partial recursive function one needs to apply the process of μ-operation only once.

The fact that the partial recursive function $\phi(t, x_1, ..., x_n)$ defined by the formula mentioned above delivers every n-place partial recursive function by fixing the value of the variable t has been called by Kleene the Enumeration Theorem for partial recursive functions. Kleene has also proved that for each m, n there exists a primitive recursive function S_n^m with the following property: If T is an index of a $(m + n)$-place function f in the variables $y_1, ..., y_m, x_1, ..., x_n$ then $S_n^m\ (t, y_1, ..., y_m)$ is an index of the n-place function which we get from f by fixing the values $y_1, ..., y_m$. This theorem is called the S–m–n-Theorem (or parameter theorem or iteration theorem). Another remarkable theorem is the Recursion Theorem. It states that (given the number n) for each 1-place partial recursive function h there exists a number t s.t. t and $h(t)$ are indices of the same n-place partial resursive function[25].

The last-named theorems (and a few others) may be regarded as fundamental insofar as they can be taken as a basis for further developments of the theory. This fact has induced an axiomatic approach to recursion theory which still seems to be waiting for a final consolidation[26].

15. DEGREES OF UNSOLVABILITY

We have seen that in order to prove undecidability a concept of reducibility has been very useful, where A is reducible to B means that there exists a total recursive function f s.t. $\forall x(x \in A \leftrightarrow fx \in B)$. This special kind of reducibility has been called many-one reducibility ($A \leqslant_m B$)[27]. There exist other remarkable concepts of reducibility, among them especially what nowadays is called Turing-reducibility $\leqslant_T$ (Turing, 1939). We have $A \leqslant_T B$ iff there exists a Turing machine 'with an oracle for B' which decides A in the sense of Section 9. A Turing machine with an oracle for B is a Turing machine gifted with a special 'oracle state' s. If this state is reached during a computation the following step is determined by the state and the letter on the scanned square and two prescribed states s', s''. If we have on the tape the number n (meaning exactly n letters L immediately to the left of the scanned square), then s' is the next state if $n \in B$, otherwise s''. The question whether $n \in B$ is not answered by an algorithmic procedure carried out by the Turing machine but by an external agent called on 'oracle'. $\leqslant_m$ implies $\leqslant_T$. The converse does not hold[28].

The sets A and B are said to have the same *degree of unsolvability* if $A \leqslant_T B$ and $B \leqslant_T A$ (Post, 1944). Obviously the set D of degrees is a partial ordered set. In spite of very intensive investigations many questions concerning the structure of D remain open. Some results may be mentioned. D is an upper semi-lattice. It has a zero element 0 which is the set of all decidable sets. We have an operation (defined by a diagonal procedure) which associates to every degree d another degree d', the jump of d, s.t. $d < d'$[29]. The halting problem is an element of $0'$. A degree is called an enumerable degree if it contains an enumerable set. We have $d \leqslant 0'$ for every enumerable degree (but not every degree $d \leqslant 0'$ is enumerable).

For a long time it has been an open question whether there is an enumerable degree d with $0 < d < 0'$. This was answered positively by Friedberg (1957) and Muchnik (1957).[30]

Kleene (1952) and Davis (1958) have introduced a reducibility relation $\leqslant_T$ between total functions which later has been extended to partial functions by Belyakin (1970). We have[8] $f \leqslant_T g$ iff there exists a Turing machine 'with an oracle for g' which defines f in the sense of Section 7. If in this case we have the 'oracle state' s we ask whether $g(n) = m$, where n and m are numbers given on the tape. As before we have two prescribed states s', s''. The next state is s', if $g(n) = m$, otherwise s''. If g is undefined for n we stay in the oracle state s.t. in this case the Turing machine does not halt. As before $\leqslant_T$ leads to degrees, whose elements now are functions. If we confine ourselves to total functions and if we identify a function with its graph[31] we find that the partial order of these degrees is isomorphic to D.

Still another definition of D via functions can be obtained by generalizing the concept of recursiveness given in Section 6 (Kleene, 1952). We have $f \leqslant_e g$ iff there is a finite set E of equations s.t.[8] $fn = m$ iff $FN = M$ is derivable from $E \cup E_g$ in the sense of Section 6. N, M are the numerals for n, m. The function symbol F corresponds to f. E_g is a set of equations: An equation $GN_1 = M_1$ belongs to E_g iff $g(n_1) = m_1$ (where N_1, M_1 are the numerals for n_1, m_1 and G is a function symbol for g). If again we confine ourselves to total functions we find that $\leqslant_e$ leads to D.[32]

Reducibility relations such as $\leqslant_T, \leqslant_e$ are also called relations of relative recursiveness. Their coincidence in the case of total functions seems to indicate that there exists an intuitive notion of relative recursiveness for total functions which corresponds to the mathematical concept ('relativized Church's Thesis').

If we do not exclude partial functions we have $f \leqslant_T g \rightarrow f \leqslant_e g$ as before but not always the converse[33]. Hence in this case we have at least two (and indeed more) different notions of relative recursiveness. Nobody until now has found an intuitive reason to favour one of these notions. A survey of the fragmentary results obtained for these 'partial degrees' is found in Sasso (1975). It seems that $\leqslant_e$ is a kind of extremal relation of relative recursiveness[34].

16. HIERARCHIES. COMPLEXITY

The idea of computability has been used to introduce semi-order classifications or hierarchies in classes of functions or sets. In Section 15 we have already discussed hierarchies given by relative recursiveness. Here we mention two other hierarchies (there are many more). An n-place predicate for natural numbers is called arithmetical if it can be defined in first-order predicate logic starting with addition and multiplication. Beginning with the class of recursive predicates (all of which are arithmetical) we can exhaust the class of all arithmetical predicates by the process of prefixing. A n-place predicate P belongs e.g. to the class $\forall\exists\forall$ iff it can be written in the form $\forall x \exists y \forall Rxyzx_1 \ldots x_n$ where R is recursive. The class $\exists$ coincides with the class of enumerable predicates. The hierarchy of arithmetical predicates obtained by prefixing the recursive predicates is called the Kleene-Mostowski hierarchy[35]

The Kleene-Mostowski hierarchy can be considered as a classification of functions which in general are not recursive. Other hierarchies classify some or all recursive functions. Computability of a function is rather an idealistic concept which disregards the amount of time and/or space needed for the computation. We have the idea that some functions are 'easier to compute' or 'computational less complex' than others. Grzegorczyk (1953) has introduced a hierarchy in the class of primitive recursive functions. This is a sequence $E_0 \subset E_1 \subset E_2 \subset \ldots$ where (1) each E_r is a class of primitive recursive functions, (2) each primitive recursive function is an element of some E_r, and (3) the n-place functions belonging to E_r can be enumerated by a function belonging to E_{r+1}.

Cobham (1965) and Edmonds (1965) (among others) have proposed that from the point of view of 'efficient calculability' one should consider only the functions f for which there exists a Turing machine T and a polynomial p s.t. for each number n: T, applied on n, halts on $f(n)$ after having performed at most $p(l(n))$ steps. Here n and $f(n)$ must be given on the tape in decimal (or binary) representation, and $l(n)$ is the length of the representation of n. The class of these functions has been classified for the complexity of calculation.[36]

17. RECURSIVENESS CONNECTED WITH OTHER MATHEMATICAL CONCEPTS

Kleene's definiton of μ-recursiveness (cf. Section 13) makes use of the structure of the set of natural numbers which is mirrored in some initial functions and in the processes of recursion and μ-operation. This suggests to replace the set of natural numbers by other suitable mathematical structures as e.g. certain ordinals or sets.[37]

More generally we may consider any classical mathematical concept as e.g. the concept of fields (of characteristic zero). Here we have the basic functions addition and multiplication (in general: certain functions and predicates). We may postulate that the set of field elements (in general: of the structure) can be gödelized in such a way that the operations are recursive functions (and the predicates – if any – are recursive). This leads to the idea of a computable field (in general: of a computable structure). We now may investigate whether well-known algebraic processes remain valid if preservation of computability is required. So it can be proved that every computable field is 'computably embeddable' in an algebraically closed computable field[38].

University Freiburg

NOTES

* Notations like 'Author (1936)' or '(Author, 1936)' refer to the Bibliography.

[1] The *ars iudiçandi* may be identified with a decision procedure and the *ars inveniendi* with an enumaration procedure. Cf. Hermes (1969).

[2] An element of A^* is called a word over A.

[3] Cf. Ackermann (1954).

[4] Cf. Surányi (1959).

[5] It is convenient to include the void set among the generated sets.

[6] There are many different λ-calculi, whose difference is disregarded in the following remarks (which indeed refer to the so-called λ-*K*-calculus). For details see e.g. Curry and Feys (1968), and Curry, *et al.* (1972).

[7] These rules may be applied in the interior of terms.

[8] For simplicity we confine ourselves here to 1-place functions.

[9] Historical remarks are be found in Davis (1965) and Crossley (1975).

[10] Compare the critical remarks to Turing's concept in Post (1947).

[11] If $n = 0$ the initial scanned square may be an arbitrary square.

[12] Also other definitions are found in the literature.

[13] See Section 3.

[14] Including normal algorithms due to Markov, cf. (Markov, 1954), and the Basic Logic of Fitch, cf. (Fitch, 1956) and (Hermes, 1965).

[15] For the intuitionistic attitude towards Church's Thesis cf. (Troelstra, 1973), p. 95f, where especially papers by Kreisel are mentioned. Compare remarks by Kalmár which are cited in (Péter, 1967) and (Péter, 1976).

[16] In place of $n \in E$ we also write En.

[17] If by a method of gödelization we get $n_0 < n_1 < n_2$ ... as the Gödel numbers of Turing machines, we replace in an effective way $n_0, n_1, n_2, \ldots$ by 0, 1, 2, ...

[18] $\forall\exists\forall$ is the class of all formulas in the prenex formal form $\forall x \exists y \forall z \alpha$ where the kernel α has no quantifieres. For the early publications on the domino problem see Wang (1965). Wang's proof shows in addition that $\forall\exists\forall$ is a reduction type i.e. that the Entscheidungsproblem for the first-order logic can be reduced to the class $\forall\exists\forall$. For an elementary introduction to dominoes cf. Hermes (1970). The undecidability of the goodness for unrestricted domino games where we have only one class of domino types and the task to cover the whole plane was proved by Berger (1966). For a geometrical version see R. M. Robinson (1971).

[18a] Here it may be mentioned that a deeper understanding and even extensions of Gödel's incompleteness theorem (Gödel, 1931) have been obtained by the method of recursion theory (Rosser, 1936).
[19] See e.g. Boone *et al.* (1973).
[20] Cf. e.g. (Hopcroft and Ullmann, 1969).
[21] This definition coincides with the earlier given in Section 7, if the function is total.
[22] See the basic book (Kleene, 1952) and text books as e.g. (Davis, 1958), (Hermes, 1965) and (Rogers, 1967).
[23] The schema will be of more complicated form if we keep close to the form of processes indicated above.
[24] A very simple example has been given by Ackermann (1928).
[25] t can be calculated if an index for h is given.
[26] Cf. (Strong, 1968), (Wagner, 1969), (Moschovakis, 1971), and (Fenstad, 1974).
[27] The function f is in general many-one, not one-one.
[28] We always have $\bar{A} \leqslant_T A$ but not always $\bar{A} \leqslant_m A$.
[29] The jump operation was introduced by Kleene and Post (1954).
[30] For results on degrees consult Kleene and Post (1954), Sacks (1963), Rogers (1967), and Shoenfield (1971).
[31] The graph of a function f is the set of all pairs (x, fx) (for those x for which is defined).
[32] $\leqslant_e$ stands for 'enumeration reducibility' (Rogers, 1967). If $f \leqslant_e g$ then the graph of f (cf. Note 31) is in a certain sense enumerable in the graph of g.
[33] Skordev (1963).
[34] Hebeisen (1977).
[35] Cf. Mostowski (1954) and Kleene (1955).
[36] Cf. e.g. Aho (1973), Brainerd and Landweber (1947), Hopcroft and Ullman (1969), Schnorr (1974) and Specker and Strassen (1976).
[37] Cf. e.g. Fenstad and Hinman (1974).
[38] Cf. Rabin (1960) and Madison (1970).

BIBLIOGRAPHY

Ackermann, W., 'Zum Hilbertschen Aufbau der reellen Zahlen', *Math. Ann.* 99 (1928), 118–133.

Ackermann, W., *Solvable Cases of the Decision Problem*, North-Holland, Amsterdam, 1954, 121pp.

Aho, A. V. (ed.), *Currents in the Theory of Computing*, Prentice-Hall, Englewood Cliffs, N.J., 1973, 255 pp.

Asser, G., 'Rekursive Wortfunktionen', *Z. Math. Logik und Grundlagen der Mathematik* 6 (1960), 258–278.

Belyakin, N. V., 'Generalized Computability and Second Degree Arithmetic', *Algebra and Logic* 9 (1970), 255–243.

Berger, R., 'The Undecidability of the Domino Problem', *Memoirs Am. Math. Soc.* 66 (1966), 72 pp.

Boone, W. W., 'Certain Simple Unsolvable Problems in Group Theory', *Proc. Kon. Nederl. Akad.* A60 (1957), 22–27.

Boone, W. W., Cannonito, F. B., and Lyndon, R. C., *World Problems. Decision Problems and the Burnside Problem in Group Theory*, North-Holland, Amsterdam, 1973, 658 pp.

Brainerd, W. S. and Landweber, L. H., *Theory of Computation*, Wiley, New York, 1974, 357 pp.

Church, A., 'An Unsolvable Problem of Elementary Number Theory', *Am. J. Math.* **58** (1936), 345–363. (Reprinted in Davis, 1965).

Church, A., 'A Note on the Entscheidungsproblem', *J. Symbolic Logic* **1** (1936), 40–41. Corr. ibid. pp. 101–102. (Included in Davis, 1965.)

Cobham, A., 'The Intrinsic Computational Difficulty of Functions', in Y. Bar-Hillel (ed.), *Logic, Methodology and Philosophy of Science*, North-Holland, Amsterdam, 1965, pp. 24–30.

Crossley, J. N. (ed.), 'Reminiscenses of Logicians', in *Algebra and Logic*, Lecture Notes No. 450, Springer, Heidelberg, 1975, pp. 1–62.

Curry, H. B. and Feys, R., *Combinatory Logic I*, North-Holland, Amsterdam, 1968, 433 pp.

Curry, H. B., Hindley, J. R., and Seldin, J. P., *Combinatory Logic II*, North-Holland, Amsterdam, 1972, 534 pp.

Davis, M., *Computability and Unsolvability*, McGraw-Hill, New York, 1958, 235 pp.

Davis M. (ed.), *The Undecidable*. Raven Press, Hewlett, N. Y., 1965, (Basic papers of the theory of recursive functions by Gödel, Church, Turing, Rosser, Kleene, Post, commented by the editor.) 440 pp.

Davis, M., 'Hilbert's Tenth Problem is Unsolvable', *Am. Math. Monthly* **80** (1973), 233–269.

Dehn, M., 'Über unendliche diskontinuierliche Gruppen', *Math. Ann.* **71** (1912), 116–144.

Dyck, W., 'Gruppentheoretische Studien', *Math. Ann.* **20** (1882), 1–44 (II. ibid. **22** (1883), 70–108.)

Edmonds, J., 'Paths, Trees, and Flowers', *Canadian J. Math.* **17** (1965), 449–467.

Ershov, Yu. L., Lavrov, I. A., Taimanov, A. D., and Taitslin, M. A., 'Elementary Theories', *Russian Mathematical Surveys* **20** (1965), 35–105.

Fenstad, J. E., 'On Axiomatizing Recursion Theory', in J. E. Fenstad and P. G. Hinman (eds.), *Generalized Recursion Theory*, North-Holland, Amsterdam, 1974, pp. 385–404.

Fenstad, J. E. and Hinman, P. G. (eds.), *Generalized Recursion Theory*, North-Holland, Amsterdam, 1974, 464 pp.

Fitch, F. B., 'Recursive Functions in Basic Logic', *J. Symbolic Logic* **21** (1956), 337–346.

Friedberg, R. M., 'Two Recursive Enumerable Sets of Incomparable Degrees of Unsolvability', *Proc. Nat. Acad. Sci.* **43** (1957), 236–238.

Friedman, H. M., 'Axiomatic Recursive Function Theory', in R. O. Gandy and C. E. M. Yates (eds.), *Logic Colloquium '69*, North-Holland, Amsterdam, 1971, pp. 113–137.

Gandy, R. O. and Yates, C. E. M. (eds.), *Logic Colloquium '69*, North-Holland, Amsterdam, 1971, 465 pp.

Gödel, K. 'Über formal unentscheidbare Sätze der Principia Mathematica und verwandter Systeme I', *Monatsh. Math Phys.* **38** (1931), 173–198.

Gödel, K., *On Undecidable Propositions of Formal Mathematical Systems*, Princeton, N.J., 1934, 30 pp. (Included in Davis, 1965, with a postscriptum by Gödel, 1964.)

Gödel K., *Remarks Before the Princeton Bicentennial Conference on Problems in Mathematics 1946*. (Included in Davis, 1965.)
Grzegorczyk, A., 'Some Classes of Recursive Functions', *Rozprawy mat.* **4** (1953), 1–45.
Hebeisen, F., 'Charakterisierung der Aufzählungsreduzierbarkeit', *Achiv für math. Logik* **18**. (1977), 89–96.
Herbrand, J. 'Sur la non-contradiction de l'arithmétique', *J. reine angew. Math.* **166** (1932), 1–8.
Hermes, H., *Enumerability, Decidability, Computability*, Springer, Berlin, 1965, (2, 1969), 255 pp.
Hermes, H., 'Ideen von Leibzin zur Grundlagenforschung: Die ars inveniendi und die ars iudicandi', in *Akten des internationalen Leibnizkongresses Hannover, 14. – 19.11.1966, III,* Literatur und Zeitgescheben, Hannover, 1969, pp. 92–102.
Hermes, H., 'Entscheidungsprobleme und Dominospiele', in K. Jacobs (ed.), *Selecta Mathematica II*, Springer, Heidelberg, 1970, pp. 114–140.
Hermes, H., 'A Simplified Proof for the Unsolvability of the Decision Problem in the Case ∀∃∀', in R. O. Gandy and C. E. M. Yates (eds.), *Logic Colloquium '69*, North-Holland, Amsterdam, 1971, pp. 307–310.
Hopcroft, J. E. and Ullman, J. D., *Formal Languages and their Relation to Automata*, Addison-Wesley, Reading, Mass., 1969, 250 pp.
Kleene, S. C., 'General Recursive Functions of Natural Numbers', *Math. Ann.* **112** (1936), 727–742. (Reprinted in Davis, 1965.)
Kleene, S. C., 'On Notation of Ordinal Numbers', *J. Symbolic Logic* **3** (1938), 150–155.
Kleene, S. C., 'Recursive Predicates and Quantifiers', *Transactions Am. Math. Soc.* **53** (1943), 41–73. (Reprinted in Davis, 1965.)
Kleene, S. G., *Introduction to metamathematics*, North-Holland, New York, Amsterdam, 1952, (4, 1964), 560 pp.
Kleene, S. G., 'Hierarchies of Number-Theoretic Predicates', *Bull. Am. Math. Soc.* **61** (1955), 193–213.
Kleene, S. C. and Post, E. L., 'The Upper Semi-Lattice of Degrees of Recursive Unsolvability', *Ann. Math.* **59** (1954), 379–407.
Madison, F. W., 'A Note on Computable Real Fields', *J. Symbolic Logic* **35** (1970), 239–241.
Markov, A. A., 'On the Impossibility of Certain Algorithms in the Theory of Associative Systems', *C. R. (Dokl.) Acad. Sci USSR* (n.s.) **55** (1947), 583–586.
Markov, A. A., *Theory of Algorithms*, The Israel Program for Sci. Transl., Jerusalem, 1962, 444 pp. (Russ, original, 1954).
Matijasevitč, J. V., 'Enumerable Sets are Diophantic', *Soviet Math. Dokl.* **11** (1970), 345–357.
Minsky, M., *Computations. Finite and infinite machines*, Prentice-Hall, Englewood Cliffs, 1967, 334 pp.
Moschovakis, Y. N., 'Axioms for Computing Theories – First Draft', in R. O. Gandy and C. E. M. Yates (eds.), *Logic Colloquium '69*, North-Holland, Amsterdam, 1971, pp. 199–257.
Mostowski, A., *Development and Applications of the 'projective' Classification of Sets of Integers*, Proc. Intern. Congr. Math. Amsterdam, 1954, III. North-Holland, Amsterdam, 1956, pp. 280–288.

Muchnik, A. A., 'Negative Answers to the Problem of Reducibility of the Theory of Algorithms', (In Russian.) *Dokl. Adad. Nauk SSSR* **108** (1956), 194–197.

Novikov, P. S., 'On the Algorithmic Unsolvability of the Word Problem in Group Theory', (Orig. Russ.) *Am. Math. Soc. Transl.* **9** (1958), 122 pp. (Original 1955.)

Péter, R., *Recursive Functions*, Academic Press, New York, 1967. 300 pp.

Péter, R., *Rekursive Funktionen in der Komputer-Theorie*, Akadémiai Kiadó, Budapest, 1976, 190 pp.

Post, E. L., 'Finite Combinatorial Processes. Formulation I', *J. Symbolic Logic* **1** (1936), 103–105. (Reprinted in Davis, 1965.)

Post, E. L., 'Absolutely Unsolvable Problems and Relatively Undecidable Propositions', Account of an anticipation, 1941. (First published in Davis, 1965.)

Post, E. L., 'Formal Reductions of the General Combinatorial Decision Problem', *Am. J. Math.* **65** (1943), 197–215.

Post, E. L., 'Recursively Enumerable Sets of Positive Integers and Their Decision Problems', *Bull. Am. Math. Soc.* **50** (1944), 284–316 (Reprinted in Davis, 1965.)

Post, E. L., 'Recursive Unsolvability of a Problem of Thue', *J. Symbolic Logic* **12** (1947), 1–11. (Reprinted in Davis, 1965.)

Rabin, M. O., 'Computable Algebra, General Theory and Theory of Computable Fields', *Trans. Am. Math. Soc.* **95** (1960), 341–360.

Robinson, R. M., 'Undecidability and Nonperiodicity for Tilings of the Plane', *Inventiones Math.* **12** (1971), 177–209.

Rogers, Jr., H., *Theory of Recursive Functions and Effective Computability*, McGraw-Hill, New York, 1967, 501 pp.

Rosser, J. B., 'Extensions of Some Theorems of Gödel and Church', *J. Symbolic Logic* **1** (1936), 87–91 (Reprinted in Davis, 1965.)

Sacks, G. E., *Degrees of Unsolvability*, Univ. Press, Princeton, N.J., 1963, 180 pp.

Sasso, Jr., J. P., 'A Survey of Partial Degrees', *J. Symbolic Logic* **40** (1975), 130–140.

Schnorr, C. P., *Rekursive Funktionen und ihre Komplexität*, Teubner, Stuttgart, 1974, 191 pp.

Schröder, E., *Vorlesungen über die Algebra der Logik I*, Teubner, Leipzig 1880, 729 pp. II.1. Leipzig, 1891, 413 pp. III. Leipzig, 1895, 657 pp. II. 2. Leipzig, 1905, 234 pp.

Schoenfield, J. R., *Degrees of Unsolvability*, North-Holland, Amsterdam, 1971, 117 pp.

Skordev, D., 'Berechenbare und μ-rekursive Operatoren', *Bulgarska Akad. na Naukite Izvestija, Mat. Inst., Sofija* 7 (1963), 5–43. (Bulg., with Russ. and German summary.)

Specker, E. and Strassen, V. (ed.), *Komplexität von Entscheidungsproblemen*, Springer, Heidelberg, 1976, 217 pp.

Strong, H., 'Algebraically Generalized Recursive Function Theory', *IBM J. Research and Development* **12** (1968), 465–475. (With a Bibliography.)

Surányi, J., *Reduktionstheorie des Entscheidungsproblems im Prädikatenkalkül der ersten Stufe*, Ungar. Akad. der Wiss., Budapest, 1959, 216 pp.

Tarski, A., 'A Decision Method for Elementary Algebra and Geometry', Report Rand Corporation, 1948 (revised 1951), 63 pp.

Tarski, A., Mostowski, A., and Robinson, R. M., *Undecidable Theories*, Amsterdam, 1953, 109 pp.

Thue, A., 'Probleme der Veränderung von Zeichenreihen nach gegebenen Regeln', *Vid. Skrifter I. Mat.-Naturv. Klasse* **10** (1914), 34 pp.

Troelstra, A. S., 'Metamathematical Investigations of Intuitionistic Arithmetic and Analysis', Lecture Notes No. 344, Springer, Heidelberg, 1973, 502 pp.

Turing, A. M., 'On Computable Numbers, with an Application to the Entscheidungsproblem', *Proc. London Math. Soc. (2)* **42** (1936), 230–265. Corr. ibid. **43** (1937), 544–546. (Reprinted in Davis, 1965; compare the Appendix of Post, 1947.)

Turing, A. M., 'Systems of Logic Based on Ordinals', *Proc. London Math. Soc. (2)* **45** (1939), 161–228. (Reprinted in Davis, 1965.)

Wagner, E. G., 'Uniform Reflexive Structures: On the Nature of Gödelizations and Relative Computability', *Trans. Am. Math. Soc.* **144** (1969), 1–41.

Wang, H., 'Proving Theorems by Pattern Recognition II', *Bell Systems Technical Journal* **40** (1961), 1–41.

Wang, H.: 'Remarks on Machines, Sets and the Decision Problem', in J. N. Crossley and M. A. Dummett (eds.), *Formal Systems and Recursive Functions*, North-Holland, Amsterdam, 1965, pp. 304–319. (With a Bibliography.)

Note added in Proof: To note 26, also compare: Fenstad J. E., *General Recursion Theory*, Springer, Heidelberg, 1980, 225 pp.

A. S. TROELSTRA

THE INTERPLAY BETWEEN LOGIC AND MATHEMATICS: INTUITIONISM

1. HOW TO READ THE TITLE

There are several ways in which the title of this lecture can be interpreted, depending on our interpretation of 'logic', 'mathematics', and 'intuitionism'. For a start, let us remark that we take intuitionism here to refer to a certain body of concepts and principles which can be used in the development of mathematics, and which are in the line of L. E. J. Brouwer's reconstruction of mathematics; however, we do not claim exlcusiveness for these concepts and principles, that is to say we do not claim that they are the only legitimate and intelligible ones. In other words, intuitionism in regarded here as an interesting (and meaningful) object of study, not as an exclusive philosophy of mathematics.

1.1. If we take 'logic' in a very wide sense, including foundational discussions, we may ask how mathematics is affected by the intuitionistic viewpoint – or with less dogmatic overtones, what mathematics looks like when built up according to intuitionistic principles, and where it differs from classical mathematics. This is, one might say, the 'classical' interpretation of the title.

Here it certainly matters whether we are thinking of constructivism as represented by Bishop, where one tries to *limit* classical mathematics to concepts and proofs which are regarded as 'constructive', or intuitionism in Brouwer's line, where one may also envisage *new* objects and principles of proof which are meaningful in the intuitionistic approach, though not necessarily so from the viewpoint of classical mathematics.

This quite naturally leads to a discussion of the most outstanding examples of such concepts, i.e. various notions of *choice sequence*. It is a very well-known fact that the interpretation of infinite sequences of natural numbers as choice sequences results in unexpected and at first sight paradoxical theorems such as: "every real-valued function on [0, 1] is continuous".

In this lecture we shall concentrate on the possibility of new objects and thus we shall return to the topic of choice sequences at some length below (Sections 2–4).

1.2. On a second interpretation, logic is taken in a much narrower sense,

E. Agazzi (ed.), Modern Logic – A Survey, 197–221.

as referring to principles which can be formulated in the language of (first-order) predicate logic. (For 'first-order' we may substitute something more liberal, including possibly extra logical operations not definable in the standard ones; but to determine our thoughts and to illustrate the questions, 'first-order' will do for the moment.)

We may then ask which is the logic belonging to intuitionistic reasoning. Perhaps I should recall Brouwer's own attitude w.r.t. this problem, which can be summarized as follows: logic is part of mathematics, and what we call 'logical laws' are only the linguistic regularities observed when we describe certain very general operations on our mathematical constructions. Brouwer went as far as denying the reliability of a general law – each instance really ought to be checked separately (thereby denying the main advantage of formalization). We certainly can make a case (as we shall see) against the view of logic as something 'special' within intuitionistic mathematics, i.e. one cannot separate logic and mathematics inasmuch mathematics determines logic; and to that extent, Brouwer was right. However, we shall happily rely on formalization in our discussion. In connection with the logic appropriate to intuitionism, we observe

(A) We cannot assume every statement to have a definite truth-value, since intuitionistically only statements which have been proved are true; and we have no reason to assume that all statements can be either refuted or accepted. Therefore the truth-value interpretation of the logical operations, as e.g. used in explaining material implication, is of very limited application in intuitionism: it only makes sense where the constituting assertions have definite truth-values.

Thus if we want a concept of implication which can be generally applied to intuitionistic statements, we need something different. The intuitionistic explanation of implication which is commonly adopted is as follows: "a proof of $A \to B$ is given by presenting a construction which transforms any proof of A into a proof of B, together with the insight that the construction has this property". For some comments on this definition, see Note A, at the end of this paper.

(B) The set of 'universally valid' theorems depends on the set of possible proofs of a statement. Here 'universally valid' means: valid for all (intuitionistically meaningful) domains and relations over those domains. To be precise: if $A(P_1, ..., P_n)$ is a sentence of first order predicate logic, containing at most the r_i-ary predicate letters P_i, we say that A is universally valid ('Val(A)') if

$$\forall D\, \forall P_1^* \ldots \forall P_n^*\, A^D (P_1^*, ..., P_n^*)$$

where A^D is obtained from A by relativization of quantifiers to D and substituting P_i^* $(1 \leqslant i \leqslant n)$ for P_i; P_i^* is a r_i-ary relation over D. So the validity of A depends on the intuitionistic truth of A^D $(P_1^*, ..., P_n^*)$ and hence on the set of 'possible proofs' of such statements – and among other things, this is in turn determined by the *nature* of the objects in D – one has only to think of choice sequences again. The nature of the objects in D finds its (generally only partial) expression in the axioms we adopt for them in a formalization. In the case of classical predicate logic, the situation is somewhat similar, but simpler.

So here we have come across another aspect of the interplay between logic and (intuitionistic) mathematics: the class of possible domains and relations, and the possible proofs concerning the objects of such domains determine the set of universally valid sentences, hence the type of mathematical objects (and their properties) we are admitting influences the extent of validity. In the classical case, very little suffices: Δ_2^0-definable arithmetical predicates over the natural numbers are all we need to obtain completeness of the usual system of classical predicate logic, and therefore for any class of domains containing the natural numbers, and class of relations containing the Δ_2^0-definable ones, we have completeness. As we shall see later (Section 5), in the intuitionistic case this dependence on the objects admitted becomes both more subtle and more striking. As will have become clear, under this second interpretation of the title we have come very close to the subject-matter of G. Kreisel's talk at this conference.

1.3. On a third interpretation we regard logic as the theory of formalizing in the Frege–Hilbert sense (i.e. including the axioms of logic and the logical inference rules); then the title might be taken to refer to the formalization of (fragments of) intuitionistic mathematics and the utilization of this formalization to obtain results *in* intuitionistic mathematics. In the sequel, we shall disregard this somewhat artificial interpretation. Of course, the job of formalization is also relevant to the first and second interpretation of interplay between logic and mathematics.

The remainder of the paper is organized as follows. In sections 2, 3, 4 we discuss the principal example of 'deviant' objects: choice sequences, illustrating the first approach to our theme. In Section 5 we then turn to the second approach to our theme, which is in fact very closely related to the first approach; we mention some pertinent positive and negative results on completeness of first order intuitionistic predicate logic **IPC**. Section 6 briefly discusses another possibility for introducing new (classically meaningless) objects in intuitionism, in the controversial theory of the 'idealized mathematician'. Three notes are appended.

The main body of this paper assumes the reader has some elementary knowledge of mathematical logic, and has at least seen some of the most elementary 'classic' examples of how the requirements of constructivism affect mathematics (examplified by the rejection of the principle of the excluded third as a general principle of constructive reasoning). The notes at the end are slightly more technical and not independent from the references cited. They elaborate certain points made in the main body of the text, and provide some additional information.

2. INTERPLAY BETWEEN LOGIC AND MATHEMATICS: DEVIANT OBJECTS AND THEOREMS. CHOICE SEQUENCES

The theory of choice sequences might be said to be invented by L. E. J. Brouwer in order to bridge a gap[1] in the properties of a constructive continuum, consisting of reals given by a law, and the classical continuum. The naturalness of Brouwer's idea is easily understood if we consider the following example. Classically, a discontinuous function with a jump, e.g. the f defined by

$$\begin{array}{lll} f(x)=0 & \text{for} & x\leqslant 0 \\ f(x)=1 & \text{for} & x>0 \end{array} \quad (x \text{ ranging over } \mathbb{R})$$

is everywhere defined on $\mathbb{R}$. Constructively, we cannot assert this since for a real x for which we do not know whether $x \leqslant 0$ or $x > 0$ we cannot determine $f(x)$ to any required degree of accuracy. So one tends to feel that every real-valued f which we can prove to be everywhere defined on $\mathbb{R}$ has to be continuous.

Reals may be assumed to be introduced via the concept of Cauchy-sequences of rationals, hence ultimately depend on the concept of a number-theoretic function (= infinite sequence of natural numbers). Brouwer extended the concept of a sequence of natural numbers so as to include choice sequences, i.e. sequences which are not assumed to be determined completely by a law given in advance. When now an operation Φ is required to assign a definite (completely defined) object to each choice sequence, Φ must necessarily be continuous, i.e. the value of $\Phi(\alpha)$ depends on at most finitely many values of α. As a consequence, in a theory of real-valued functions based on choice sequences we now have as a *theorem*

THEOREM 1. Every real-valued function on $\mathbb{R}$ is continuous.

Refinement of the analysis yields:

THEOREM 2. A real-valued function is uniformly continuous on a closed interval.

A generalization for the case of separable metric spaces is

THEOREM 3. Every mapping from a complete separable metric space into a separable metric space is continuous.

This theorem can be appealed to at many places in the development of analysis, sometimes even simplifying theorems and proofs as compared with the classical case, since it has become redundant to state certain continuity conditions explicitly. (Example: for a function $f\colon \mathbb{R}^2 \to \mathbb{R}$ the existence of the partial derivatives f_x, f_y is sufficient to ensure that f is differentiable.) A still further generalization is contained in the

THEOREM 4. (Covering theorem). If Γ is a complete separable metric space and $\Gamma \subseteq \{V_i : i \in I\}$, $I \subseteq N$ is a covering by a sub-countable collection of pointsets (*not* necessarily open) then $\Gamma \subseteq \{\text{Interior}\,(V_i)\colon i \in I\}$.

From this theorem, Theorem 3 can be obtained as a corollary. Read classically, all these theorems are actually false. Certain other applications are of a different character: the theorems hold also classically, but their classical proof uses classical logic in an essential way, whereas the intuitionistic proof appeals to the continuity properties of choice sequences. A typical example is

THEOREM 5. A sequentially continuous mapping from a separable metric space into a metric space is continuous. (I.e. the two standard definitions of continuity are equivalent.)

All the examples given here (except Theorem 2) can be obtained axiomatically from the schema

$$\text{WC–N} \quad \forall\alpha\exists x A(\alpha, x) \to \forall\alpha\exists x\exists y\forall\beta\in\bar{\alpha}y A(\beta, x)$$

(α, β ranging over N^N,(the set of choice sequences) x, y varaibles for natural numbers, $\bar{\alpha}x = \langle\alpha 0, \ldots, \alpha(x-1)\rangle$, $\beta \in \bar{\alpha}x$ means $\bar{\beta}x = \bar{\alpha}x$).

The choice sequences as conceived here are the principal example of objects with properties which have no business in classical mathematics. The traditional theory has certain defects however.

3. CERTAIN DEFECTS AND THEIR REMEDY

There is one serious objection to Brouwer's theory of choice sequences one could make, namely that the notion is nowhere analyzed in any detail. Therefore it is not surprising that on closer scrutiny 'choice sequence' in Brouwer's writings seems to be a mixture of notions with occasionally conflicting properties. On the other hand, the idea of choice sequences is of considerable interest: it helps us in clarifying the problem of universal validity in intuitionistic logic, and as stressed by Kreisel it is of interest to note that there is a viable theory of such 'incomplete' objects at all.

Note also that the acceptance of objects such as choice sequences as legitimate objects in mathematics implies the denial of the view of a certain type of philosophy of constructive mathematics, in which all objects should be completely given and should be capable of some sort of linguistic representation (from which all their properties can be read off). This view is so to speak at the opposite extreme of Brouwer's view: that mathematics is (in principle, if not in practice) essentially a languageless activity, and that language is only needed in communicating with others. On the other hand, one does not have to accept Brouwer's view in order to accept choice sequences as legitimate.

However the lack of coherency in Brouwer's account of choice sequences forces us to look for a remedy. Several possibilities suggest themselves:

3.1. *First remedy: be satisfied with epistemological plausibility*. This 'remedy' consists in the observation that the consideration of choice sequences at least makes it plausible that a schema such as WC–N can be consistently adopted; of course, then a proposed axiomatization including WC–N ought to be supplemented by a consistency proof of WC–N relative to the other axioms.

This approach equally justifies the study of other axiom schemata incompatible with classical logic which at least have a certain plausibility even if we cannot give a rigorous (informal) justification. An example is the uniformity principle:

$$\text{UP} \qquad \forall X \exists x A(x, X) \rightarrow \exists x \forall X A(x, X)$$

for X ranging over sets of natural numbers; another familiar example is Church's thesis in the form

$$\text{CT}_0 \qquad \forall x \exists y A(x, y) \rightarrow \exists z \forall x A(x, \{z\}(x))$$

($\{z\}(x)$: the partial recursive function with code number z is applied to the argument x). In both cases relative consistency proofs are available (say, relative to second order arithmetic) and both are readily seen to conflict with classical logic (apply UP to $\forall X \exists x [(x = 0 \& X = \emptyset) \vee (x \neq 0 \& x-1 \in X)]$; and CT_0 to $\forall x [\exists y T(x, x, y) \vee \neg \exists y T(x, x, y)]$, where T is Kleene's T-predicate). For a survey of this approach, see Troelstra (1975).

There is something unsatisfactory about this remedy; where, in fact, the point to be demonstrated is the effect of introducing choice sequences as objects in mathematics, the remedy is no remedy at all. We can do slightly better by strengthening our 'first remedy' into the

3.2. *Second remedy: elimination of choice sequences*. Instead of only asking for a consistency proof one may attempt something more satisfactory: to explain quantification over 'dubious' objects as a 'figure of speech' by translation of every sentence involving quantification over choice sequences into a sentence involving only lawlike objects. This programme can be carried through completely for a theory of choice sequences **CS** which embraces all the applications of choice sequences in intuitionistic mathematical practice; the theory is conservative over its lawlike (= free of choice sequences) part. However, even if the idea of choice sequence turned out to be heuristically useful in this case, there is something unsatisfactory in thus having them explained away: this solution still does not permit us to regard choice sequences as objects, only as a figure of speech. And so we are led to attempt the

3.3. *Third remedy: a fresh start with a clear concept*. In this case the remedy is: extract from the mixture of notions a clearly delimited concept and develop its properties. Such a concept is that of a lawless sequence, which may be regarded as an extremely simple instance of a concept of choice sequence, at the opposite extreme of lawlike sequences (which are completely determined by a law given in advance). To some extent we shall have the best of two (or several) worlds: now we do have a clear concept, which *also* can be explained as a 'figure of speech' by means of the so-called elimination of lawless sequences. The concept is essential in clarifying the completeness problem for intuitionistic predicate logic; and it enables us to obtain many (though not all) mathematical consequences of the continuity schema WC–N by considering a certain universe $\mathscr{U}$ constructed from lawlike operations, and lawless sequences. The next section is devoted to a discussion of lawless sequences and the universe $\mathscr{U}$. It is also possible to formulate a more complex notion satisfying the main axioms of **CS** (Dummett, 1977, Chapter 7; Troelstra, 1977, Appendix C). The concept is more involved than the concept of a lawless sequence; for a description see Note B, at the end of this paper.

4. LAWLESS SEQUENCES

Lawless sequences may be thought of as processes for generating values such that at any moment we know only finitely many values, no general restrictions are made as to the choice of further values; moreover, we assume that to any given finite initial segment there is a lawless sequence beginning with that initial segment. For lawless sequences where the values have to be in $\{1, 2, 3, 4, 5, 6\}$ the sequence of the casts of a die is a good model, provided we permit finitely many deliberate placings of the die to begin with, so as to ensure that all possible initial segments *do* occur. Thus we should have in any case

$$\forall n\, \exists \alpha (\alpha \in n).$$

Another important principle which can be justified for lawless sequences is the axiom of open data

$$A\alpha \to \exists n\, [\alpha \in n \wedge \forall \beta \in n A\beta]$$

which can be justified as follows: assume we know $A\alpha$; then, since at any given moment we know only finitely many values of α, this must be on account of an intitial segment n of α only, and A should hold equally for all $\beta \in n$. (Here we must assume A not to contain lawless parameters besides α.) We can also justify

$$\forall \alpha\, \exists x A(\alpha, x) \to \exists \Gamma \forall \alpha A(\alpha, \Gamma\alpha)$$

where Γ stands for a continuous operation defined on *all* sequences of N^N (not only lawless ones) with natural numbers as values. 'Continuous' means

$$\forall \xi\, \exists x \forall \theta \in \bar{\xi} x (\Gamma\xi = \Gamma\theta).$$

Refinement of the analysis leads to justification of the fan theorem for lawless sequences ($\alpha \leqslant \beta \equiv_{\text{def}} \forall x (\alpha x \leqslant \beta x)$)

FAN $\quad \forall \alpha \leqslant \beta\, \exists x A(\alpha, x) \to \exists z \forall \alpha \leqslant \beta\, \exists y \forall \gamma \leqslant \beta (\bar{\gamma} z = \bar{\alpha} z \to A(\gamma, y))$

which has as a corollary the simpler

(*) $\quad \forall \alpha \leqslant \beta\, \exists\, x A(\bar{\alpha} x) \to \exists z \forall \alpha \leqslant \beta\, \exists x \leqslant z A(\bar{\alpha} x).$

The justification of the axioms for lawless sequences [2] is given in considerable detail in Chapter 2 of Troelstra (1977), to which we refer the reader for further information.

4.1. *The universe* $\mathcal{U}$. Lawless sequences as such are not directly suitable for real-valued analysis; the usual representation of reals via Cauchy-sequences of rationals (hence as sequence of natural numbers) would on restriction to lawless sequences yield a continuum without rationals. However, with the help of lawlike continuous operations $\Gamma: N^N \to N^N$ we can easily construct a more satisfactory universe of sequences to base our real-valued analysis on; namely the universe

$$\mathscr{U} = \{\Gamma(\alpha_1, \alpha_2, ..., \alpha_n): \alpha_i \text{ lawless}, 1 \leqslant i \leqslant n, n \in N\}$$

where $(\alpha_1, \alpha_2, ..., \alpha_n)$ indicates a single sequence coding $\alpha_1, ..., \alpha_n$. $\mathscr{U}$ is closed under continuous mappings, contains all lawlike sequences of natural numbers and permits us to obtain the Theorems 1–3, 5 in Section 2. (Theorem 4 does not hold in full generality relative to $\mathscr{U}$.)

5. THE PROBLEM OF COMPLETENESS FOR INTUITIONISTIC PREDICATE LOGIC

Let us very briefly recapitulate some general points. There are three steps in characterizing the untuitive concept of validity[3] for **CPC** (classical predicate logic):

(I) Provable sentences are intuitively valid. This is obvious, whatever the *precise* extension of the concept of a structure may be.

(II) If A is intuitively valid, then A is valid in all set-theoreitcal structures, hence a fortiori in all arithmetically definable structures. This is again obvious.

(III) For the converse to (I), one shows that for an underivable sentence there is a countermodel; it will be obvious that a proof of this fact actually yields *more*, namely a limited class of structures from which the countermodel be chosen. It turns out that Δ_2^0-definable arithmetical structures suffice in the case of **CPC**.

For substantial fragments of **IPC** (intuitionistic predicate logic) we can do something similar, but now the structures must include relations depending on *lawless* parameters. This also limits the usefulness of these completeness results for intuitionistic mathematical practice, since it also makes sense in intuitionistic mathematics to consider structures not depending on lawless parameters, and the completeness results do not apply to that class of structures. Completeness for A, A a formula of **IPC**, is defined as

$$\text{Val}(A) \to \exists x \, \text{Proof}_{\text{IPC}}(x, \ulcorner A \urcorner).$$

5.1. *Some positive results.* It has already been shown by Kreisel (1958) that for certain *decidable* fragments of **IPC** without function symbols (such as propositional and prenex (formulae) we have completeness in the following form:

THEOREM. If A is valid over the domain of natural numbers, relative to relations (for the predicate letters) which are r.e. in a single lawless parameter, then A is derivable in **IPC**.

The idea of the proof is to search for a proof tree for a sentence A (in some calculus of sequents); if the sentence is unprovable, the search continues indefinitely and we can read off a countermodel from the tentative proof trees.

THEOREM (Friedman, 1977). Let A be a sentence of **IPC** not containing $\perp$ (falsehood is assumed to be a primitive; alternatively we may drop negation); then completeness for A holds relative to the domain of natural numbers and relations depending on (in fact: recursively enumerable in) lawless sequences[4].

The proof uses a quite different idea and is very simple and elegant; in fact, Friedman constructs a single *Beth* model M such that for all $\perp$-free sentences A

$$M \models A \Leftrightarrow A \text{ is derivable in } \mathbf{IPC}.$$

(Validity in a single Beth model can be directly translated as validity in a set of structures indexed by a single lawless parameter; (see Troelstra, 1977, Chapter 7)). From the proof it also follows that the forcing relation in the Beth model is r.e. for *all* $\perp$-free forumulae. Friedman's result can also be obtained via an intuitionistic completeness theorem for so-called generalized Beth models; cf. Note C, Section 3.

To complete the picture, we mention that for certain classes $\mathscr{C}$ of formulae for which **CPC** is conservative over **IPC**, the completeness theorem for **CPC** yields weak completeness for formulae from $\mathscr{C}$ in the following form:

THEOREM (Kreisel, 1958, 1961). Let A be a negative formula or a negated prenex formula with a negated matrix (i.e. A is of the form $\neg Q \neg B$, B propositional, Q a string of quantifiers). Then, in intuitionistic arithmetic

$$\vdash \forall x \neg \mathrm{Proof}_{\mathrm{IPC}}(x, \ulcorner A \urcorner) \to \neg A(P_1^*, ..., P_n^*)$$

where $P_1^*, ..., P_n^*$ are certain arithmetically (in fact Δ_2^0-definable predicates of natural numbers, written without $\exists, \vee$ (see Section 4 of Note C).

It is not true that completeness holds for all A such that **CPC** $\vdash A \Rightarrow$ **IPC** $\vdash A$.

5.2. *Negative results*. G. Kreisel showed (Kreisel, 1970; van Dalen, 1973) that Church's thesis implies the incompletability of **IPC**. More precisely, on restriction to lawlike domains and relations and assumption of Church's thesis one can actually find a valid sentence not in **IPC**; moreover, on assumption of Church's thesis the set of valid sentences cannot be recursively enumerable. This clearly shows the sensitivity of the notion of validity to mathematical assumptions in the intuitionistic case.

Kreisel's result has been sharpened and improved by Friedman, who recently obtained a number of new results and improvements from which we quote an example: weak completeness of **IPC**, i.e.

$$\mathrm{Val}(A) \to \neg\neg\, \exists x\, \mathrm{Proof}_{\mathrm{IPC}}(x, \ulcorner A \urcorner) \text{ for all } A,$$

implies $\neg\neg Q$, where (R, S ranging over primitive recursive predicates)

$$Q \equiv \forall R \forall S (\forall nm (Rn \vee Sm) \to (\forall n Rn \vee \forall m Sm)).$$

6. ANOTHER EXAMPLE OF DEVIANT OBJECTS: THE THEORY OF THE IDEALIZED MATHEMATICIAN

We cannot take leave of our subject without commenting at least briefly on another, rather controversial source of 'deviant' objects in the intuitionistic mathematical universe: Brouwer's theory of the idealized mathematician, or, as Brouwer called him, the 'creative subject' (see e.g. Brouwer, 1948a, 1948c, 1949a, 1949b, 1952c, 1954, 1954b in Heyting (1975)). In the theory of the idealized mathematician ('IM' for short), it is possible to define constructions which refer explicitly to the mathematical activity of the IM, which is supposed to proceed in discrete stages (indexed by the natural numbers). The subject is highly controversial: many feel that the activity of the IM is itself not an object of mathematics, and moreover, there is no uniformity of opinion as to precisely which principles are to be adopted in this theory.

Notwithstanding these serious objections, it provides an interesting extreme example of how the intuitionistic viewpoint (now more particularly interpreted along Brouwerian lines) can give rise to new mathematical objects which have no place in classical mathematics. We limit ourselves here to a brief sketch, and refer the reader to Dummett (1977, Section 6.3.), and Troelstra (1969, Section 16) for further particulars, including a critical discussion and more references.

Let '$\vdash_n A$' for an assertion A, natural number n, mean: 'at stage n the IM has established A'. Then one assumes three axiom schemata:

C1 $\quad \vdash_n A \vee \neg \vdash_n A$

(the IM *knows* whether he has established A at stage n or not),

C2 $\quad \vdash_n A \;\&\; n < m \to \vdash_m A$

(knowledge is cumulative), and

C3 $\quad A \leftrightarrow \exists n(\vdash_n A)$

(A is regarded as true by the IM if and only if A is established at some stage of his activity).

Here, in this sketch I disregard controversial questions such as whether A itself may be defined involving $\vdash_n$ explicitly, or whether one ought to introduce levels of self-reflection. The genesis of new objects by C1–3 is examplified by the following definition. Let ϕ be any given function from N to N. Define ψ such that

$$\neg \vdash_n \forall x(\phi x = 0) \to \psi n = 1$$
$$\vdash_n \forall x(\phi x = 0) \to \psi n = 0.$$

Then obviously, by C1 ψn is defined for all n, and by C2, C3

(1) $\quad \forall x(\phi x = 0) \leftrightarrow \exists x(\psi x = 0).$

ψ is defined by reference to the creative subject, and it is easily seen that if ϕ ranges over total recursive functions, ψ cannot always be recursive.

On the other hand, no direct conflict with classical logic follows: introduce a function constant ψ_A for mathematical assertions A (we shall assume A to be free of $\vdash_n$, though A may possibly contain other ψ_B), such that

(2) $\quad \vdash_n A \leftrightarrow \psi_A n = 0, \qquad \psi_A n \leqslant 1.$

Then

(3) $\quad A \leftrightarrow \exists x(\psi_A x = 0).$

(3) can also be proved with help of classical comprehension axioms. As observed by van Dalen, we may now formally re-introduce $\vdash_n$ by

$$\vdash_m A \equiv_{\text{def}} (\exists n \leqslant m)(\psi_A(n) = 0).$$

Thus C1–3 become valid, and the theory based on C1–3 becomes a conservative extension of certain classical theories not containing $\vdash_n A$ in their language. This goes to show that the theory of the IM is not comparable to the theory of choice sequences as a source of deviant objects, since it does not, in itself, conflict with classical logic (reason why we preferred choice sequences as the principal illustration of our theme). The preceding discussion may also be interpreted as showing that all consequences of C1–3 not involving $\vdash_n$ in their statement can be obtained from instances of 'Kripke's schema'

KS $\quad A \leftrightarrow \exists x(\psi_A(n) = 0).$

KS does not contradict classical logic, but it does exclude certain interpretations for any universe $\mathscr{W}$ of functions containing the ψ_A. Church's thesis cannot hold for $\mathscr{W}$, as can be seen from (1). Similarly, an axiom of $\forall\alpha\exists\beta$-continuity cannot hold for $\mathscr{W}$ (cf. A6 in Troelstra, 1977).

NOTE A. ON THE BHK-INTERPRETATION OF INTUITIONISTIC LOGIC

1. L. E. J. Brouwer discusses in several papers (e.g. in 1908C, §1 of 1923C in Heyting (1975)) the intuitionistic validity of classical logical principles, and develops a calculus of 'absurdity'. The underlying interpretation of the logical constants (especially negation and implication) was afterwards formulated much more explicitly by Heyting (e.g. Heyting, 1930, 1931, and 1956); intuitionistic implication is explained as: $A \to B$ is established by a construction which transforms any given proof of A into a proof of B (and this property of the construction must itself of course be proved or be evident by its definition).

It was G. Kreisel (1962, 1965, 2.2) who explicitly drew attention to the decidability of 'c proves A' (the idea being that we *know* whether a given construction c establishes A or not), and that by this assumption the interpretation of intuitionistic logic can be reduced to a *logic-free* theory of (abstract) proofs and constructions. Thus, if $\pi_A(c)$ expresses 'c proves A', where the π_A are assumed to be decidable, implication is now explained as: $\pi_{A\to B}(d)$ if d is a pair $\langle d_1, d_2\rangle$ such that

$$\pi(d_1, \ulcorner \pi_A(x) \to \pi_B(d_2 x)\urcorner)$$

where x is a variable for proofs, d_2 is a construction on proofs, $\pi(d, \ulcorner C \urcorner)$ is read as 'd establishes C' (for C of the special type $\pi_A x \to \pi_B(d_2 x)$). π is again assumed to be decidable. Note that '$\to$' in '$\pi_A x \to \pi_B(d_2 x)$' may be read as classical truth-functional implication; because of the decidability of π_A, π_B, the statement $\pi_A x \to \pi_B(d_2 x)$ may be regarded as essentially quantifier-free.

A fairly detailed and leisurely sketch of this type of explanation of the logical operators may be found in Troelstra (1969, §2). In view of its historic origins, we have baptized it the 'Brouwer–Heyting–Kreisel interpretation' (BHK for short).

2. Because of its very abstract nature, and the impredicative character of the interpretation as exemplified in the case of → (a proof of A may very well refer to hypothetical proofs of $A \to B$ for example), one is naturally led to investigate the possibility of concrete models for the theory of constructions, which are sound for **IPC**. That is to say, we may ask for an arithmetically definable model, with the natural numbers as the domain of constructions, and decidable predicates P_A, P as interpretations of π_A, π.

It is easy to see the difficulty is in the decidability condition on P_A, P; if we drop this requirement, we may well take something close to 'x realizes A' (in the sense of Kleene's realizability for numbers) as our interpretation of π_A.

The construction of such concrete models promises to be an interesting research topic, to which we expect to return in the future. Here we shall limit ourselves to the presentation of a 'trivial' model for which we should like to claim some pedagogic interest.

3. *The trivial model.* We limit attention to **IIL**, intuitionistic implication logic here formalized as a calculus of natural deduction with rules of → introduction and → elimination (modus ponens). But in fact, the method of construction only uses the existence of a primitive recursive proof predicate, and the presence of modus ponens among the rules, and thus has a much wider range of application.

To each formula of **IIL** we assign a primitive recursive 'proof-predicate' Prf_A. For implications $\mathrm{Prf}_{A\to B}(x)$ is of the form

$$\mathrm{Prf}_{A\to B}(x) \equiv T_{A\to B}(j_1 x)\ \& \\ \&\ \mathrm{Prf}(j_2 x, \ulcorner \mathrm{Prf}_A(y) \to \mathrm{Prf}_B(t_{\bar{x}}(y))\urcorner),$$

where

(i) j_1, j_2 are primitive recursive inverses to a pairing function $j: N \times N \to N$, Prf is the proof predicate of a formal system containing at least primitive recursive arithmetic, T is also primitive recursive (intuitively $T_A(j_1 x)$ is to be read as 'x is of the right type').

(ii) $t_{\bar{x}}$ indicates a term with parameter y, the gödelnumber of which can be extracted primitive recursively from $j_2 x$, hence from x.

The model is now further specified by:

(iii) We assign to each propositional letter P a primitive recursive predicate $C_P(x)$ ('x is an elementary proof of P') and put

$$T_P(x) \equiv C_P(x)$$
$$\mathrm{Prf}_P(x) \equiv T_P(j_1 x) \,\&\, j_1 x = j_2 x.$$

(iv) $T_{A\to B}(x)$ is "x codes a deduction in **IIL** containing at most propositional letters as open assumptions, and an assignment of elements of C_P to the open assumptions P". For the special case where all C_P are empty, we may drop the second half.

Now we establish a

LEMMA. For each A, there is a primitive recursive f_A such that, provably in our meta-system,

$$T_A x \to \mathrm{Prf}_A(f_A x).$$

Proof. For a propositional letter P take $f_P(x) = j(x, x)$. Let $A \equiv B \to C$ and assume $T_{B\to C}(x)$, $\mathrm{Prf}_B y$. From x, y we obtain primitive recursively a deduction of C (since modus ponens is among the rules of **IIL**) together with an assignment of 'proofs' to possibly undischarged prime formulae in the deduction; the result is coded as $f(x, y)$, and thus $T_C f(x, y)$. By the induction hypothesis

$$\mathrm{Prf}_C(f_C f(x, y))$$

and thus provably

$$\mathrm{Prf}_B y \to \mathrm{Prf}_C(f_C f(x, y)).$$

This is proved, for fixed numeral $\bar{x}$, uniformly in y by a proof with number $g_C(x)$, and thus

$$\mathrm{Prf}(g_C x, \ulcorner \mathrm{Prf}_B y \to \mathrm{Prf}_C(f_C f(\bar{x}, y))\urcorner).$$

Now take

$$f_{B\to C}(x) \equiv j(x, g_C(x)).$$

Soundness is now trivial: if $\mathbf{IIL} \vdash F$, we can find a numeral $\bar{n}$ such that $T_F(\bar{n})$, hence also $\mathrm{Prf}_F(f_C \bar{n})$. Completeness follows in case we take all C_P empty.

We obtain a reformulation of the model setting

$$\mathrm{P}(x, \ulcorner C \urcorner) \equiv T_A(j_1 x) \,\&\, \mathrm{Prf}(j_2 x, \ulcorner C \urcorner),$$

then $\mathrm{Prf}_{A \to B}$ takes the form

$$P(x, \ulcorner \mathrm{Prf}_A(y) \to \mathrm{Prf}_B(t_{\bar{x}}(y)) \urcorner).$$

Now the model has indeed a form as requested: P, Prf_A may be taken as the interpretations of π, π_A.

From this model we may draw the conclusion that permitting very strong 'type-restrictions' T_A to be incorporated, or alternatively, putting no restrictions on the interpretation P of π besides being primitive recursively decidable, trivializes the problem of giving a concrete model. It also goes to show how little explanatory power the BHK-explanation possesses without being more specific on proofs, π_A, and π. Surely, intuitively one thinks of modus ponens as justified *because* of the intended interpretation of implication – one tends to feel it is cheating to *use* modus ponens itself to enforce the functional character of proofs of implication. For more interesting models, one should interpret π by a proof-predicate of a formal system (but then attempts at a soundness proof suggest the necessity of imposing extra restrictions, e.g. on the 'type' of $t_{\bar{x}}$).

4. The undesirable feature of including modus ponens in **IIL** is in itself easily removed. To see this, we construct a variant of the trivial model for a cut-free version **IIL*** (formulated as a calculus of sequents). Cut-elimination of **IIL*** + Cut-rule is primitive recursive and provable in primitive recursive arithmetic; from this we obtain a primitive recursive function assigning to a cut-free proof of $\Gamma \vdash A$ and a cut-free proof of $\Gamma \vdash A \to B$ a cut-free proof of $\Gamma \vdash B$; in other respects the details are as before.

NOTE B. CHOICE SEQUENCES VALIDATING MOST OF CS

1. In Troelstra (1969), and again more carefully in Troelstra (1977, Appendix C) I described a notion of choice sequence (GC-sequence, from: 'Generated by Continuous operations') intended to fulfill the more important axioms of the system **CS**: closure under continuous operations, continuity for numbers (i.e. $\forall\alpha\ \exists x$-continuity) and the axiom of analytic data. (No intuitive justification for continuity for functions, i.e. $\forall\alpha\ \exists\beta$-continuity was given.)

2. The notion is not all that hard to describe: we think of a GC-sequence α as a process of generating values *and* restrictions on future choices of values, as follows. We start choosing $\alpha 0, \alpha 1, \ldots$; at some stage, we may decide to make α dependent on certain other choice sequences $\alpha_0, \ldots, \alpha_n$ via a lawlike continuous operation Γ, i.e. we put from then onwards

$$\alpha = \Gamma(\alpha_0, ..., \alpha_n);$$

the choice of Γ is supposed to be compatible with the initial segment $\bar{\alpha}x$ already chosen. The freedom in choosing αx, $\alpha(x + 1)$, ... is from then on entirely given by the freedom of continuation of $\alpha_0, ..., \alpha_n$; these sequences may be either sequences 'freshly begun' in the course of the process of generating α, or sequences belonging to other independent similar processes started before. At the moment α is brought into connection with α_0, the latter sequence may itself already have been made dependent on $\beta_0, \beta_1, ..., \beta_k$; in a later stage, the $\beta_0, \beta_1, ..., \beta_k$ (and similarly for sequences β' on which $\alpha_1, \alpha_2, ..., \alpha_n$ are dependent) may in turn be made dependent on choice sequences γ_i, and so on. In this description we have taken notice of the discussion in Dummett (1977): it is necessary to state explicitly that α may be made independent at some stage on external, independent processes (after which the processes are not any longer independent of course), not just on choice sequences *newly* started in the course of generating α itself, for then we could not even justify closure of the GC-sequences under lawlike continuous operations.

3. We think the notion as outlined (more detail in the references given) is a rather natural one, though certainly not as simple as the concept of a lawless sequence: also, a rather convincing justification of the main axioms of **CS** can be presented. Then why are we not quite satisfied? It is mainly this: inspection of the justification of the axioms shows that certain (very plausible) assumptions are made which in principle should be capable of mathematical verification provided the concept of a GC-sequence itself could be presented more formally so as to make it amenable to mathematical treatment. In addition, there is the legitimate question whether we could not approximate the concept of a GC-sequence and its properties by means of certain sequences constructed from lawless sequences and lawlike operations, thereby reducing in a sense the GC-sequences to simpler basic notions. (Such a project is indicated in Appendix C of Troelstra (1977); work on it, by G. F. van der Hoeven and myself, is in progress.)

NOTE C. SOME REMARKS ON COMPLETENESS RESULTS FOR IPC

1. The basic fact that completeness results concerning **IPC** are very sensitive to the object admitted as legitimate in intuitionistic mathematics is very clearly demonstrated already by the two old results

(a) completeness of intuitionistic propositional logic if we admit lawless sequences;

(b) incompleteness of full **IPC** if we assume Church's thesis to hold. In this respect, the more recent refinements and sharpenings of these old results add little or nothing, even if these results are very interesting in their own right. The rest of this note is devoted to some remarks of a more technical nature which may be helpful to the reader in gaining some perspective w.r.t. the recent results. A survey of completeness for **IPC** is also contained in Troelstra (1976).

2. Beth's original completeness proof (Beth, 1959, Section 145) for **IPC**, carefully amended by Dyson and Kreisel (1961) yielded the completeness for *certain* (not all) decidable fragments of **IPC** (such as the propositional or prenex formulae). The proof is of the Gödel-type: one constructs, for a given formula A, a (search-) tree embodying all possible (tentative) proof trees in a certain sequent calculus; the tree may be viewed at the same time as a collection of tentative refutation trees. A non-terminating refutation tree shows that there cannot be a terminating proof tree; a Beth model on which A is invalid can be extracted from such a refutation tree. The reason that just decidability of a fragment is not enough is in the fact that the argument requires us, in case a formula is not decidable, to indicate a non-terminating refutation tree; it is not sufficient to establish 'not all refutation trees terminate' As observed in Kreisel (1958, p. 382), it is sufficient that the derivability of the sequents appearing at the nodes of the search tree (in our terminology) is decidable. A related (but different) result states

THEOREM. Every decidable consistent theory T formalized as a first order intuitionistic theory with a countable language has a recursive Kripke model (in fact, validity is recursive for all formulae).

As a corollary, by the standard transformation of Kripke models into equivalent Beth models (Kripke, 1965), and the equivalence between validity in Beth models and validity in structures with relations depending on lawless parameters (e.g. Troelstra, 1977, Chapter 7) we extract a completeness result for structures.

Note however, that e.g. the derivable prenex formulae of **IPC** do not constitute a decidable theory, so do not fall under this theorem.

The theorem is completely similar to the well-known classical result stating that every decidable theory has a recursive model; we have not found a statement of this theorem in the literature however, so we give a *sketch of the proof*. It suffices to give a slight modification of the usual Henkin-type Kripke model construction (due independently to several authors; as a reference one can use the presentation e.g. in Smorynski (1973, 5.1)).

The main idea is to modify the construction which assigns to a set Γ and a formula A with $\Gamma \nvdash A$ a saturated $\Gamma' \supseteq \Gamma$ such that $\Gamma' \nvdash A$, as follows.

Let $\mathscr{L}$ be a countable language, and let Γ be a set of sentences in $\mathscr{L}$, A a sentence in $\mathscr{L}$ such that $\Gamma' \nvdash A$. Let $C = \{c_0, c_1, c_2 ...\}$ be a set of constants not in $\mathscr{L}$; we put $\mathscr{L}' = C \cup \mathscr{L}$. We shall construct an $\mathscr{L}'$-saturated superset $\Gamma' = \cup \{\Gamma_k ; k \in \omega\}$ such that $\Gamma' \nvdash A$. At each step we construct Γ_k and an auxiliary formula F_k; the F_k satisfy $A \to F_k$ for all k, $F_k \to F_{k+1}$ for all k.

Let A_1, A_2, A_3 ... be an enumeration of all sentences in $\mathscr{L}'$. We put $\Gamma_0 = \Gamma$, $F_0 \equiv A$. Assume now Γ_k, F_k to be constructed. For the induction step we have to distinguish several cases:

Case 1. $\Gamma_k \nvdash F_k \vee A_{k+1}$. Then $\Gamma_{k+1} = \Gamma_k$, $F_{k+1} \equiv F_k \vee A_{k+1}$.

Case 2. $\Gamma_k \vdash F_k \vee A_{k+1}$, $A_{k+1} \equiv \exists x Bx$. Take $\Gamma_{k+1} = \Gamma_k \cup \{\exists x Bx, Bc_i\}$, c_i the first constant not in Γ_k, F_k, and let $F_{k+1} \equiv F_k$.

Case 3. $\Gamma_k \vdash F_k \vee A_{k+1}$, $A_{k+1} \equiv B_1 \vee B_2$. Let $\Gamma_{k+1} = \Gamma_k \cup \{B_1 \vee B_2, B_i\}$, for the least i such that $\Gamma_k \nvdash B_i \to F_k$; and let $F_{k+1} \equiv F_k$.

Case 4. Cases 1–3 do not apply. Then $\Gamma_{k+1} = \Gamma_k \cup \{A_{k+1}\}$, $F_{k+1} \equiv F_k$.

Now one readily verifies by induction on the construction that Γ' is $\mathscr{L}'$-saturated, and moreover, if $\Gamma \vdash C$ is a decidable relation (i.e. Γ axiomatizes a decidable theory) then so is $C \in \Gamma'$.

Now if T axiomatizes the consistent decidable theory, we construct a Henkin-Kripke model for T with the tree of all finite sequences of natural numbers as underlying partially ordered set; the nodes of length i are M_i-saturated theories (cf. Smorynski, 1973, 5.1), Γ_0 is an M_0-saturated superset of T with $\Gamma_0 \nvdash \bot$; to each $\mathscr{L}_{\text{1th}(n)}$-saturated node Γ_n we take as successors nodes $\Gamma_{n*\langle x\rangle}$, (saturated w.r.t. $\mathscr{L}_{\text{1th}(n)+1}$), one for each sentence G_x in $\mathscr{L}_{\text{1th}(n)}$, where $G_0, G_1, G_2, ...$ enumerates all sentence of $\mathscr{L}_{\text{1th}(n)}$ of the form $\forall x Hx$ or $H_1 \to H_2$ which are not derivable form Γ_n. If $G_x \equiv \forall x Hx$, then $\Gamma_{n*\langle x\rangle} \nvdash H_c$, for some c; if $G_x \equiv H_1 \to H_2$ then $\Gamma_{n*\langle x\rangle} \vdash H_1$, $\Gamma_{n*\langle x\rangle} \nvdash H_2$.

3. *Generalized Beth models and generalized structures*. Because of results by Kreisel and Gödel (of which the recent refinement by Friedman quoted above is a sharpening) that completeness for **IPC** (w.r.t. structures, Beth models or Kripke models) would imply some intuitionistically highly implausible assertions, results by Veldman (1976), Lopes-Escobar and Veldman (1975), and de Swart (1976) demonstrating completeness of **IPC** for so-called generalized Kripke and Beth models (in the form: validity in all models ⇒ provability)

have caused some excitement (see the lengthy discussion in Dummett (1977)). Now that the dust has settled, analysis of the matter shows that:

(a) there is no intuitive conflict between these results and the negative results of Gödel and Kreisel, and

(b) There is very close connection[5] between Friedman's result on the completeness of the $\perp$-free fragment quoted above and the completeness results for generalized models in the form obtained by de Swart. Below we shall describe this connection in some detail, thereby also illustrating (a). We assume some familiarity with the concept of a Beth model over a finitely branching, countable tree, with the natural numbers as domain, and the relationship between validity in Beth models and in structures with relations containing a lawless parameter. [Troelstra (1977, Chapter 7) or Dummett (1977) may serve as a reference; part of the discussion below is also to be incorporated in the Italian edition of Troelstra (1977)]. The models to be discussed are presented as triples $\langle K, \leq, \phi\rangle$, where K is a finitely branching tree of finite sequences of natural numbers, $\leq$ the obvious partial ordering on such sequences, and ϕ a model function which assigns to the nodes of K (denoted by $k, k', k'', \ldots$) sets of atomic sentences in the first order language considered (with constants for all elements in the domain of the model; we may restrict attention here to models with domain N). We shall assume

$$k \leq k' \Rightarrow \phi k \subseteq \phi k'.$$

For each of the different kinds of models discussed we then have to define $k \Vdash A$ ('k forces A' or 'k is true at A') by induction on the complexity of A; however, the clauses only differ for the case of atomic sentences, in all other cases they are the standard ones for Beth models.

For a *generalized Beth model* the clause for the atomic case is

(i) $k \Vdash P \equiv_{\text{def}} \forall \epsilon \in k\, \exists x (P \in \phi(\bar{\epsilon}x) \text{ or } \exists n(\perp \in \phi n))$ and for a (*proper*) *Beth model* or a *liberal Beth model* the clause is

(i)′ $k \Vdash P \equiv_{\text{def}} \forall \epsilon \in k\, \exists x (P \in \phi(\bar{\epsilon}x))$; in a proper Beth model $\forall k(\perp \notin \phi k)$, in a liberal Beth model we permit $\perp \in \phi k$, but require

(*) $\perp \in \phi k \rightarrow P \in \phi k$ for all atomic P.

Instead of requiring (*) for a liberal Beth model, we could alternatively have defined

(i)″ $k \Vdash P \equiv_{\text{def}} \forall \epsilon \in k\, \exists x (P \in \phi(\bar{\epsilon}x) \text{ or } \perp \in \phi(\bar{\epsilon}x))$.

Now observe:

(a) Generalized Beth models such that $\forall k(\perp \notin \phi k)$ are proper Beth models.

(b) Liberal Beth models may be viewed as Beth models where $\bot$ is interpreted as an ordinary propositional letter satisfying $\bot \to P$ for all atomic sentences, and thus validating **IPC**; if we drop (*) in the conditions of a liberal Beth model, we obtain a model for minimal logic only.

(c) Generalized Beth models correspond (bi-uniquely) to *particular* liberal Beth models, satisfying the additional condition

$$\bot \in \phi k \Leftrightarrow \exists k' (\mathrm{lth}(k) = \mathrm{lth}(k') \textit{ and } \bot \in \phi k').$$

To see this, associate to a generalized model $\langle K, \leq, \phi \rangle$ with forcing relation $\Vdash$ a liberal model $\langle K, \leq, \phi' \rangle$ with forcing relation $\Vdash'$ by stipulating

$$(\bot \in \phi k) \Leftrightarrow \forall k' (\mathrm{lth}(k) = \mathrm{lth}(k') \to \bot \in \phi' k');$$

one then readily proves by induction on logical complexity that

$$k \Vdash A \Leftrightarrow k \Vdash' A.$$

(d) There is a straightforward connection between validity in liberal models and validity in structures over N, with relations depending on a single lawless parameter (cf. Troelstra, 1977, 7.12). In the case of liberal models, the interpretation of $\bot$ corresponds to a zero-place relation $P_\bot^\epsilon$ (i.e. $P_\bot^\epsilon$ depends on ϵ alone) in the structure which may hold for certain ϵ. This of course disagrees with the *intended* interpretation in structures, where we simply require $\bot$ to be invalid, always and everywhere. For liberal models without condition (*) we obtain structures validating minimal logic.

We are now ready to describe the connection between de Swart's completeness theorem and the completeness of the $\bot$-free fragment.

(e) De Swart's proof, as analyzed in Troelstra (1977, Chapter 7) shows completeness (for single formulae A, or for $\Gamma \vdash A$, Γ recursively enumerable) relative to validity in generalized Beth models, hence relative to validity in a special class of liberal Beth models. As can be seen from the proof, the (generalized or liberal) Beth models considered depend on a choice parameter α (ranging over a finitely branching tree T) satisfying

$$\forall n \in T (\alpha \in n)$$
$$\forall \alpha\, \exists x A(\bar{\alpha}x) \to \exists z\, \forall \alpha\, \exists x \leq z A(\bar{\alpha}x) \quad (A \text{ primitive recursive}).$$

The forcing relations $k \Vdash P(n_1, ..., n_t)$, $P(...)$ atomic, are r.e. in α, k, $n_1, ..., n_t$, the domain of the models is N. Therefore, we may intepret α as ranging over lawless sequences in a tree. The Beth models themselves have (for given A, or given $\Gamma \vdash A$) a fixed finitely branching tree T' as underlying partially ordered structure.

By the previous observation under (d), this amounts to completeness relative to the class of 'liberal' structures ('liberal' in the sense that $\bot$ may possibly be interpreted as true) with domain N, and relations which are r.e. in lawless parameters $\epsilon_1 \in T$, $\epsilon_2 \in T'$ as interpretation of the predicate letters.

The two parameters can be contracted into a single lawless $\epsilon \in T \times T'$, where $T \times T'$ is a tree such that $n \in T \times T' \leftrightarrow k_1^2 n \in T \,\&\, k_2^2 n \in T'$ (in the notation of Troelstra (1977, 1.9)). To see this, one establishes by induction on the complexity of A, for arithmetic A:

$$\forall \epsilon \in n A(j_1 \epsilon, j_2 \epsilon) \leftrightarrow \forall \epsilon_1 \in k_1^2 n \, \forall \epsilon_2 \in k_2^2 n A(\epsilon_1, \epsilon_2).$$

Translating this back in terms of liberal Beth models we see that for each A (or $\Gamma \vdash A$ with r.e. Γ) we obtain via the contraction a *single* liberal Beth model M_A such that $(M_A \models A) \Rightarrow A$ is derivable in **IPC**; in M_A, $k \Vdash P(n_1, ..., n_t)$ is r.e. in $k, n_1, ..., n_t$.

(f) The validity of an $\bot$-free sentence in a liberal Beth model M is not affected by the set of nodes k for which $k \Vdash \bot$. In other words, replacing M by a proper Beth model M' on the same three satisfying $k \Vdash_M P \Leftrightarrow k \Vdash_{M'} P$ for all atomic $P \not\equiv \bot$ does not affect the validity of $\bot$-free sentences. Conversely, any proper Beth model for such a sentence A is a fortiori a liberal Beth model for the same sentence. If A is valid in all Beth models of a class $\mathcal{M}$, it is also valid on all liberal Beth models M' obtained from models $M \in \mathcal{M}$ by assigning an interpretation to $\bot$ such that (*) is satisfied (and vice versa). A fortiori, A is then valid on those liberal Beth models M' corresponding to generalized Beth models.

(g) Combining (e) and (f), we see that the completeness for generalized Beth models leads immediately to completeness of the $\bot$-free fragment for proper Beth models, with domain N, and r.e. forcing for atomic sentences.

(h) Completeness of the $\bot$-free fragment relative to structures with domain, N, and relations containing a lawless parameter, immediately yields completeness for minimal logic, for 'liberal' structures (not requiring $\bot \to P$ to hold, $\bot$ possibly valid): we only have to treat $\bot$ as an arbitrary propositional letter.

Friedman's construction in his proof of the completeness of the $\bot$-free fragment is essentially the construction of a 'universal' Beth model over a binary tree, domain N, and $k \Vdash P(n_1, ..., n_t)$ r.e. in $k, n_1, ..., n_t$ for predicate letters P; in the model A is valid iff A is provable in **IPC**, for all $\bot$-free A. In addition, the forcing relation $n \Vdash A$ is r.e. for all $\bot$-free A. A very slight adaptation of the proof (using an enumeration with infinite repetition of *all* formulae, instead of only $\perp$-free ones) yields a 'universal' liberal Beth model (though not a model corresponding to a generalized Beth model) thus we obtain almost de Swart's result; in addition, forcing is r.e. for *all* formulae in the liberal Beth model.

(i) The negative results on completeness for *intended* structures, where $\perp$ is actually interpreted as false, may now be viewed as indicating a lack of expressive power of **IPC**: no r.e. extension of **IPC** characterizes precisely the intended structures.

4. *Weak completeness for negations of prenex formulae with negative matrix*. In Kreisel (1958a) weak completeness for *negative* formulae was established. A very similar argument yields weak completeness for negations of prenex formulae with negated matrix (Kreisel, 1961).

Kreisel's argument makes it clear that the restriction of the matrix to negations is needed; Kreisel (1958a) shows by a counterexample that we cannot prove by intuitionistic means weak completeness for arbitrary negations of prenex formulae. Negations of prenex formulae with negated matrix are not always logically equivalent to their negative counterparts (obtained by application of the Gödel–Gentzen negative translation). Take e.g. $\neg\forall x\ \exists y\ \neg P(x, y)$, this is weaker than $\neg\forall x \neg\neg\ \exists y \neg P(x, y)$. (Example: let α, β range over choice sequences of 0, 1 such that $\alpha x = 1 \rightarrow \forall y > x(\alpha y = 1)$, put $\neg P(\alpha, \beta) \equiv \neg\neg[(\alpha = 0 \rightarrow \beta 0 = 0)\ \&\ \forall z(\alpha = (\lambda x \cdot 0)z * \lambda x \cdot 1 \rightarrow \beta 0 = z)]$, then by the fan theorem $\neg\forall\alpha\ \exists\beta\neg P(\alpha, \beta)$ holds, but also $\forall\alpha\neg\neg\ \exists\beta\neg P(\alpha, \beta)$.)

Mathematisch Instituut,
Universiteit van Amsterdam, The Netherlands

NOTES

[1] The gap consisted in the fact that intuitively speaking, the constructive continuum could be at most countable and could not be seen to be compact.

[2] In the literature lawless sequences first make their appearance in Kreisel (1958) (there called 'absolutely free choice sequences'). It has sometimes been maintained that Brouwer did not have the concept of a lawless sequence, nor would have considered it as legitimate. However, in a letter to A. Heyting dated 26–6–1924 he uses the concept of 'free' number of the continuum (described as reals which are approximated by successive intervals such that the choice of each next interval within the previous one remains completely free) in giving a counterexample. The counterexample can be reproduced on an axiomatic basis for lawless sequences.

[3] Our exposition here stresses the fact hat the *exact* extension of the class of domains and relations, and (in the intuitionistic case) the *precise* interpretation of the logical operators is not needed to characterize the set of valid theorems; in contrast, Tarski

(1936) emphasizes the precision obtained by specifying the possible domains and relations.

[4] The original announcement (Friedman, 1975) did not state clearly the need for lawless parameters.

[5] The fact that the Swart's result implied the completeness of the ⊥-free fragment of **IPC**, was observed independently by Dummett (1977).

BIBLIOGRAPHY

We have listed the main sources. References in the notes at the end of the paper *not* occurring below are to be found in the bibliography of Troelstra (1977).

de Swart, H., 'Another Intuitionistic Completeness Proof', *J. Symbolic Logic* **41** (1976), 644–662.

Dummett, M. A. E., *Elements of Intuitionism*, Clarendon Press, Oxford, 1977.

Friedman, H., 'Intuitionistic Completeness of Heyting's Predicate Calculus', *Notices Am. Math. Soc.* **22** (1975), A–648.

Friedman, H., 'The Intuitionistic Completeness of Intuitionistic Logic under Tarskian Semantics', Abstract, SUNY at Buffalo, N.Y., 1977.

Friedman, H., 'New and Old Results on Completeness of HPC', Abstract, SUNY at Buffalo, N.Y., 1977a.

Heyting, A., 'Sur la logique intuitionniste', *Académie Royale de Belgique. Bulletin de la Classe des Sciences, ser. 5,* **16** (1930), 957–963.

Heyting, A., 'Die intuitionistische Grundlegung der Mathematik', *Erkenntnis* **2** (1931), 106–115.

Heyting, A., 'La conception intuitionniste de la logique', *Les études philosophiques* **11** (1956), 295–297.

Heyting, A. (ed.), *L. E. J. Brouwer, Collected Works I. Philosophy and Foundations of Mathematics*, North-Holland, Amsterdam, 1975.

Kreisel, G., 'A Remark on Free Choice Sequences and the Topological Completeness Proofs', *J. Symbolic Logic* **23** (1958), 369–388.

Kreisel, G., 'Elementary Completeness Properties of Intuitionistic Logic with a Note on Negations of Prenex Formulae', *J. Symbolic Logic* **23**, (1958a), 317–330.

Kreisel, G., 'Note on Completeness and Definability', Technical Report No. 3, Applied Mathematics and Statistics Laboratories, Stanford University, 1961.

Kreisel, G., 'Foundations of Intuitionistic Logic', in *Logic, Methodology and Philosophy of Science*, (eds. E. Nagel, P. Suppes, A. Tarski), Stanford University Press, Stanford, California, 1962, pp. 198–210.

Smorynski, C. A., 'Applications of Kripke Models', in *Metamathematical Investigation of Intuitionistic Arithmetic and Analysis*, (ed. A. S. Troelstra), Springer-Verlag, Berlin, 1973, pp. 324–391.

Tarski, A., 'Der Wahrheitsbegriff in den formalisierten Sprachen', *Studia Philosophica* **1** (1936), 261–405.

Troelstra, A. S., 'Axioms for Intuitionistic Mathematics Incompatible with Classical Logic', Report 75–13. Department of Mathematics, University of Amsterdam, 1975. *Logic, Foundations of Mathematics and Computability Theory*, (eds. R. Butts and J. Hintikka), D. Reidel Publ. Co., Dordrecht, 1977, pp. 59–84.

Troelstra, A. S., *Choice Sequences, a Chapter of Intuitionistic Mathematics*, The Clarendon Press, Oxford, 1977. (An Italian translation is in preparation.)

Troelstra, A. S., 'Aspects of Constructive Mathematics', in *Handbook of Mathematical Logic*, (ed. J. Barwise), North-Holland, Amsterdam 1977a.

van Dalen, D., 'Lectures on Intuitionism', in *Cambridge Summer school in Mathematical Logic*, (ed. H. Rogers and A. R. D. Mathias), Springer-Verlag, Berlin, 1973, pp. 1–89.

Veldman, W., 'An Intuitionistic Completeness Theorem for Intuitionistic Predicate Logic', *J. Symbolic Logic* 41 (1976), 159–166.

Postscript added in proof (July 1980). Since this lecture was held, three years have elapsed and new material has become available. To help the reader, we indicate some directly relevant supplementary references below.

Troelstra, A. S., 'Some Remarks on the Complexity of Henkin-Kripke Models', *Indag. Math.* 81 (1978), 296–302.

Troelstra, A. S., 'A Supplement to "Choice Sequences"', report 79–04, Department of Mathematics, University of Amsterdam, 1979. (Contains corrections to Troelstra (1977) and expands the discussion of Note C, Section 3.)

van der Hoeven, G. F. and Troelstra, A. S., 'Projections of Lawless Sequences II', in *Logic Colloquium* 78, (eds. M. Boffa, D. van Dalen, and K. McAloon), North-Holland Publ. Co., Amsterdam, 1979, pp. 265–298. (A first instalment of the work referred to in Note B, Section 3.)

JENS ERIK FENSTAD

LOGIC AND PROBABILITY

I have been asked to give a survey of the various connections between logic and probability. As I am included in the section on logic and its relation to other parts of mathematics I will not enter into a discussion of 'inductive logic' and the foundation of statistical inference, but restrict myself to questions more 'mathematical' in nature. However, an insight into the mathematical structure is a prerequisite for any sound philosophic discussion of the foundations of probability.

My survey will be divided into three parts. In the first part I will discuss *probability functions defined on formal languages*. In the second part I will survey various connections between *randomness and recursion theory*. And in the final part I will give a glimpse into the recent applications of *non-standard methods* to the theory of stochastic processes.

PART ONE: PROBABILITY FUNCTIONS DEFINED ON FORMAL LANGUAGES

A *probability function* p on a formal language L is a mapping from formulas in L to the unit interval $[0, 1]$ satisfying the requirements

$$p(\varphi \vee \psi) + p(\varphi \wedge \psi) = p(\varphi) + p(\psi)$$
$$p(\neg\varphi) = 1 - p(\varphi)$$
$$p(\varphi) = p(\psi), \text{ if } \varphi \text{ and } \psi \text{ are equivalent in } L$$
$$p(\varphi) = 1, \text{ if } \varphi \text{ is provable in } L.$$

Assigning probabilities to sentences is not a new idea. It was adopted by J. M. Keynes in his treatise on probability [15] and also by H. Jeffreys in his well-known book [13], both being influenced by the Cambridge philosopher W. E. Johnson (see I. J. Good [11]).

The syntax of these earlier attempts was mostly left unspecified, H. Jeffreys very soon started to use sentences of the form '$dx\, d\theta$', and the authors only attended to the sentential structure of the language. In this way their studies were part of the more general study of measures on Boolean algebras [25], a topic I do not wish to enter into on this occasion.

R. Carnap in his study of inductive logic [2] was the first to go beyond

E. Agazzi (ed.), Modern Logic – A Survey, 223–233.

the propositional structure of language, but from a mathematical point of view his study was rather limited.

It was H. Gaifman who in 1960 for the first time used the full power of a first order language. Let L be a first order language and let C be the set of individual constants for L. A *probability model* $\langle U, p\rangle$ for L is an ordered pair where $C \subseteq U$ and p is a probability function on the quantifier free sentences, $S_0(U)$, of the language L extended by the constants in U.

THEOREM (H. Gaifman [9]), Let $\langle U, p\rangle$ be a probability model for L. There exists a unique extension p^* of p to $S(U)$, the set of all sentences, satisfying

$$(*) \qquad p^*(\exists x\varphi(x)) = \sup\{p^*(\varphi(a_1) \vee \ldots \vee \varphi(a_n)) \mid a_1, \ldots, a_n \in U\}$$

where the supremum is taken over all finite subsets of U.

The condition (*) has later been known as the 'Gaifman condition', and it and suitable generalizations of it have played an important rôle in the use of formal languages to extend probability measures.

The work of Gaifman was extended to richer languages in a study of D. Scott and P. Krauss [24]. Their basic language is $L_{\omega_1\omega}$ which allows countable conjunctions and disjunctions but retains finite quantification. A basic result in their study is an extension of Gaifman's theorem to the richer language. They also develop a rich model theory of probability models, for which we have to refer the reader to their paper [24].

But I do wish to mention, however briefly, another aspect of their work, viz. how to use a formal language to study the extension of probability measures. A stochastic process with index set T can be thought of as a probability space $\langle \mathbb{R}^T, \mathscr{B}^T, p\rangle$ where $\mathbb{R}$ is the two-point compactification of the reals, $\mathscr{B}^T$ is the product σ-field, and p a probability on $\mathscr{B}^T$. In general one wants to extend p to some larger σ-field in the product (note that, in general, the σ-field of Borel sets in $\mathbb{R}^T$ is a proper extension of $\mathscr{B}^T$).

It turns out that a 'Gaifman condition' in a suitable language for the process is the natural condition to consider.

In more detail, consider the infinitary language having a binary relation $<$ and a family of unary predicates P_q, indexed by rational numbers. Let the language be extended by individual constants which for convenience may be chosen equal to the index set T of the stochastic process.

One observes now that each function $x \in \mathbb{R}^T$ can be identified with a model of the language, viz. the system $\mathfrak{A}_x$ in which P_q is defined as $P_q = \{t \in T; x(t) \leqslant q\}$. Let $\mathsf{M}(\varphi)$ be the set of models of φ. A basic fact is now that $\mathscr{B}^T$ may be identified with the restriction of the set $\{\mathsf{M}(\varphi); \varphi \in S_0(T)\}$ to $\mathbb{R}^T$. Thus any probability on $\mathscr{B}^T$ induces a probability on $S_0(T)$ (modulo provability). Thus one may try to use the general existence theorem to extend the probability to some larger σ-field.

The matter is not entirely simple. The extension, if it exists, is unique. But even a 'Gaifman condition' is not always sufficient to ensure extendability. This is closely related to Doob's separability theorem. In fact, the separability condition of his theorem is a 'Gaifman condition' for a special class of sentences: Let $T = [0, 1]$ and consider $I = \langle t_1, t_2 \rangle \subseteq T$. Then one verifies that

$$\bigcap_{t \in I \cap T} \{x \in \mathbb{R}^T ; x(t) \leqslant q\} = \mathsf{M}(\forall v_0 [t_1 < v_0 < t_2 \to P_q(v_0)]) \cap \mathbb{R}^T.$$

Thus the separability condition is actually the Gaifman condition for the sentences

$$\forall v_0 [t_1 < v_0 < t_2 \to P_q(v_0)], q \in Q.$$

This type of extension problem has been further studied by K. Th. Eisele [4] who has obtained important extensions of the work of Scott and Krauss.

A somewhat different approach was taken by J. Łoś in 1962 [17] and extended further in Fenstad [5] and [6]. The given datum is once more a probability p on a first order language L. p assigns a value to both sentences and formulas of L with free variables. Let $\varphi(x)$ be a formula with one free variable, φ then expresses a property of or condition on the individual x. $p(\varphi(x))$ then gives the probability of the property φ.

Let M be the space of all models $\mathfrak{A}$ for L. Let ψ be any sentence of L. We define

$$\mathsf{M}(\psi) = \{\mathfrak{A} \in \mathsf{M} \mid \psi \text{ is true in } \mathfrak{A}\}.$$

The completeness theorem of logic tells us that we can without ambiguity define a set function λ on M by

$$\lambda(\mathsf{M}(\psi)) = p(\psi).$$

Since the space of models is compact λ can be extended to a σ-additive probability measure on the σ-field generated by the sets $\mathsf{M}(\psi)$, ψ a sentence of L.

This representation still belongs to the Boolean aspect of the theory. But it does point to the 'naturalness' of the notion of model in this context. A model for a formula $\varphi(x)$ with one free variable is an 'urn' containing 'white balls' (those individuals having the property φ) and 'black balls' (those individuals that do not have the property φ).

For each formula φ of L define a measure λ_φ on M by

$$\lambda_\varphi(\mathsf{M}(\psi)) = p(\varphi \wedge \psi).$$

Each measure λ_φ is absolutely continuous with respect to λ, hence by the Radon–Nikodym theorem it can be represented as

$$\lambda_\varphi(B) = \int_B f_\varphi(\mathfrak{A})\, \mathrm{d}\lambda(\mathfrak{A}).$$

λ is a probability on M, we would like to give a probabilistic interpretation of $f_\varphi(\mathfrak{A})$ in the model $\mathfrak{A}$. Let $\varphi[\mathfrak{A}]$ be the set of sequences satisfying φ in $\mathfrak{A}$. Is it possible to define a measure μ by the equation $\mu_{\mathfrak{A}}(\varphi[\mathfrak{A}]) = f_\varphi(\mathfrak{A})$? It almost is, but some measure theoretic difficulties enters. They can be overcome (most directly by using the theory of strong liftings, see Eisele [4]) and we have the following result.

THEOREM. Let L be a countable first order language and p a probability function on L. There exists a σ-additive probability measure λ on the space of models M for L, and for each model $\mathfrak{A} \in$ M a probability function $\mu_{\mathfrak{A}}$, such that for all formulas φ of L

$$p(\varphi) = \int_M \mu_{\mathfrak{A}}(\varphi[\mathfrak{A}])\,\mathrm{d}\lambda(\mathfrak{A}).$$

The use of the Radon–Nikodym theorem and a first version of the theorem is in Łoś [17]. His proof was not complete, the gap was filled in Fenstad [5]. The use of strong liftings is due to Th. Eisele [4].

This representation theorem can be regarded as generalization of de Finetti's theorem [8]. We explain how.

First one can show under certain mild symmetry assumptions that for a finite model $\mathfrak{A}$

$$\mu_{\mathfrak{A}}(\varphi[\mathfrak{A}]) = \mathrm{fr}(\varphi, \mathfrak{A}),$$

where $\mathrm{fr}(\varphi, \mathfrak{A})$ is the relative frequency of φ in $\mathfrak{A}$. If we now can restrict ourselves to finite models, de Finetti's theorem would follow.

This is best done by considering a family of conditional probability measures $p(\varphi \mid \psi)$, where φ can be any formula of L and ψ is a finite disjunction of sentences θ_n, which says that there are exactly n individuals in the domain.

In this special case we get for a formula $\varphi(x)$ with one free variable

$$p(\varphi \mid \theta_n) = \sum_{r=0}^{n} \frac{r}{n} \cdot \lambda_r^{(n)}$$

where

$$\lambda_r^{(n)} = \lambda(\{\mathfrak{A} \in \mathrm{M}(\theta_n);\ \mathrm{fr}(\varphi, \mathfrak{A}) = \frac{r}{n}\})/\lambda(\mathrm{M}(\theta_n)).$$

(One detail, in this case λ is a σ-finite measure on M. For technical details see Fenstad [6, 7].)

The numbers $\lambda_0^{(n)}, \ldots, \lambda_n^{(n)}$ define an atomic probability distribution Φ_n on the interval [0, 1] by

$$\Phi_n(t) = \sum_{r \leqslant t \cdot n} \lambda_r^{(n)}$$

Adjoining now a symmetry condition which is basically de Finetti's notion of exchangeability and which is intimately related to the notion of a sufficient statistics, we may prove that the distributions Φ_n converge to a probability distribution Φ consentrated on $[0, 1]$. In this way we obtain an absolute probability function p^* on L derived from the family $p(\cdot \mid \theta_n)$, $n = 1, 2, \ldots$, and hence the usual integral representations: Letting: $\varphi_r^{(n)}$ be a formula of L expressing that r out of n observed individuals have the property φ, we may calculate

$$p^*(\varphi_r^{(n)}) = \binom{n}{r} \int_0^1 t^r \cdot (1-t)^{n-r} \, \mathrm{d}\Phi(t).$$

For a further discussion we refer to [6] and [7].

I should like to end this part by drawing attention to some recent work of P. Hajek and Havranek [12] and H. Gaifman [10]. Gaifman studies probabilities defined on an arithmetical language (enriched by a class of 'empirical predicates'). In this way one can express inside the language more complex properties of the probability function and hence for special classes of probability measures obtain sharper results.

It has been a general feature of the various approaches described above that one tries to express a given 'probabilistic situation' in some formal language, and then use an appropriate blend of logic and probability to obtain specific results; recall e.g. the extension problem for stochastic processes as discussed by Scott and Krauss [24].

PART TWO: RANDOMNESS AND RECURSION THEORY

The idea of *randomness* is basic for all applications of probability and statistics. But a precise definition of what it means for a sequence to be random is no simple matter. R. von Mises [20] made it the basic notion in his axiomatic development of probability theory and of the theory of statistical inference [21]. But the notion of 'Kollektiv' was definitely in need of further clarification. A. Wald [27] gave in 1937 a consistency proof. But consistency is not the same as truth; soon afterwards J. Ville [26] constructed a sequence which is random according to von Mises, but which clearly ought not to be.

A. Church [3] was the first to apply notions from recursion theory to von Mises concept of a 'Kollektiv'. Let us consider infinite sequences x_1,

$x_2, \ldots, x_n, \ldots$ of 0's and 1's. Such a sequence is called *random* if first of all

$$\lim_{n \to \infty} \frac{1}{n}(x_1 + \cdots + x_n) = \tfrac{1}{2},$$

i.e. the limit frequence is equal $\frac{1}{2}$. The second requirement is that the limit frequence should also be equal $\frac{1}{2}$ for all subsequences $x_{i_1}, x_{i_2}, \ldots$ obtained in an 'effective' way from the original sequence.

It is here recursion theory enters: A subsequence $x_{i_1}, x_{i_2}, \ldots$ is *effective* if there is a recursive function f defined on finite binary strings and taking the values 0 and 1, such that i_1 = least n such that $f(x_1 \ldots x_{n-1}) = 1$, i_2 = least $m > i_1$ such that $f(x_1 \ldots x_{m-1}) = 1$, etc.

This is a precise definition, but it has the defects of Ville's example. Hence something more is needed. A first satisfactory definition was given by P. Martin–Löf [18], being inspired by earlier work of A. Kolmogorov.

We first notice that the set of sequences satisfying Church's definitions form a set of measure 1 in the product space 2^ω. Hence the set of sequences which fails this test of randomness has measure 0. But, as Ville's example shows, one has to consider a larger class of 'tests of randomness'. However, some restrictions are needed, as the intersection of all sets of measure one in 2^ω is empty.

Let $2 = \{0, 1\}$, 2^* be the set of all finite binary strings, and 2^ω the product space with the usual product measure μ. As is well known, a subset $A \subseteq 2^*$ determines a subset $[A] \subseteq 2^\omega$, $\alpha \in [A]$ if for some $n \in \omega$, $\alpha \restriction n \in A$.

A set $\mathbf{N} \subseteq 2^\omega$ is called a *recursive null set* if there is some r.e. set $Y \subseteq \omega \times 2^*$ such that

(i) $\mu([Y_i]) \leqslant 2^{-i}$, $i \in \omega$ (here $x \in Y_i$ iff $(i, x) \in Y$);

(ii) $\mathbf{N} \subset \bigcap_{i \in \omega} [Y_i]$.

The null-set generated by Y is $\mathbf{N}_Y = \bigcap_{i \in N} [Y_i]$. Y itself is called a *recursive sequential test*. It is now a basic fact, proved by P. Martin–Löf, that the class of all recursive sequential tests is recursively enumerable. And hence there exists an *universal* sequential test $U \subseteq \omega \times 2^*$ such that whenever Y is a recursive sequential test there is some $k \in \omega$ such that $[Y_{i+k}] \subseteq [U_i]$, $i = 1, 2, \ldots$.

Obviously if U is universal, then $\mathbf{N}_U$ contains every recursive null-set.

DEFINITION. Let U be a universal sequential test and let $\mathbf{N}_U$ be the associated (universal) null-set. A sequence $\alpha \in 2^\omega$ is called *random* if $\alpha \notin \mathbf{N}_U$.

Note that the set of random sequences has measure 1 in 2^ω and that no recursive sequence is random.

A rich mathematical theory has grown up, we refer the reader to the Springer Lecture Note by C. P. Schnorr [23]. Schnorr has himself sharpened Martin–Löf's definition in the following direction.

A function $f: \omega \to \mathbb{R}$ is called computable if there is a recursive function $g: \omega \times \omega \to Q$ such that $|f(n) - g(n,i)| \leqslant 2^{-i}$, $i \in \omega$. A recursive sequential test is called *totally recursive* when the function $f(n) = \mu([Y_n])$ is computable. Any subset $\mathbf{N} \subseteq \mathbf{N}_Y$ is called a *total recursive null-set*. And a sequence $\alpha \in 2^\omega$ is called *random* in this new sense when it belongs to no total recursive null-set.

An important distinction between the two notions is that the previously constructed universal recursive null-set is not a total recursive null-set, and it is possible given a total recursive null-set to effectively compute a recursive sequence in the complement, i.e. effectively to find a sequence which satisfies this property of randomness.

An extension in a different direction can be found in a later paper [19] of Martin–Löf. Again working in the space 2^ω he first notices that the intersection of all hyperarithmetical sets of measure one is a Σ_1^1 set of measure one. And he proposes to call this set the *set of random sequences*. In this connection one should note that hyperarithmetic corresponds to 'effective Borel'.

Obviously, a hyperarithmetic sequence is not random in this sense. And the set of random sequences is not hyperarithmetical. (If it were, it would as a set of measure one, contain a hyperarithmetic point.)

Thus recursion theory has given us a multitude of notions of randomness. And this is perhaps as it should be. Randomness is no 'physical phenomenon'. Your choice of a notion of randomness depends on the use you have in mind.

If one, as e.g. Schnorr [23], wants to stress "der intuitive Begriff des effektiv nachprüfbaren statistische Zufallsgesetzes", then ordinary recursion theory is a natural setting. If, however, the guiding idea is that a random sequence is a sequence where there is no law governing the behavior of the sequence, i.e. that there is no definable dependency between the elements of the sequence, then hyperarithmetical theory, as proposed by Martin–Löf [19], is a natural choice, – but by no means the only natural choice of underlying computation theory.

I should like to add one remark. In the recent work of Gaifman [10] there is an interesting mixture of the ideas of Martin–Löf on random sequences and the earlier work on probability measures defined on formal (in this case, arithmetical) languages.

PART THREE: NON-STANDARD METHODS

Non-standard methods is an alternative to the usual mathematical analysis in modeling 'large finite phenomena'. E.g. rather than consider an infinite sequence $x_1, x_2, \ldots, x_n, \ldots$ of tosses with an idealized coin, one studies a 'finite' (i.e. hyperfinite) extension of the sequence $x_1, x_2, \ldots, x_n, \ldots, x_\eta$, where η is a non-standard integer. The power of the method comes from the fact that the non-standard finite sequence $x_1, \ldots, x_\eta$ has many of the (algebraic and combinatorial) properties of a standard finite sequence $x_1, \ldots, x_n$.

Measure theory and probability was early studied within the context of non-standard analysis. It was, however, P. Loeb [16] who, in a paper published in 1975, first gave the 'correct' construction of a probability space associated with 'large finite phenomena'. (The reader should also consult the forthcoming paper of E. Nelson [22].)

Let $\eta \in {}^*N \backslash N$, i.e. η is some non-standard integer. Consider in a suitable non-standard extension the set of all binary internal sequences of length η, i.e. let $X = \{0, 1\}^\eta$. If the non-standard extension is ω_1-saturated, then any infinite sequence can be extended to an (internal) sequence of length η.

On X we may consider the usual counting measure, i.e. if $A \subseteq X$, and A is internal

$$\nu(A) = \frac{|A|}{2^\eta},$$

where $|A|$ is the (internal) cardinality of A. This is in complete analogy to the usual finite construction.

The Loeb construction is quite general. And the usefulness of it comes from the way Loeb [16] associated a standard measure space with the non-standard one. Let $(X, \mathfrak{A}, \nu)$ be an internal probability space, i.e. $\mathfrak{A}$ is an internal algebra of internal subsets of X, and ν is a finitely (hence hyper-finite but not σ-additive) measure on $\mathfrak{A}$. Let ${}^\circ\nu$ be the standard part of ν. It can be extended to a σ-additive measure $L(\nu)$ on the completion of the smallest σ-algebra, $L(\mathfrak{A})$, containing $\mathfrak{A}$, and the extension is unique. We now have a standard measure space $(X, L(\mathfrak{A}), L(\nu))$; however, in many cases on some unusual underlying set X.

In the coin-tossing example of Loeb [16] $X = \{0, 1\}^\eta$. Let A_n be the event "the first $n-1$ tosses are tails, the nth toss is a head". If we assume that η is even, the set $A = \cup_{n=1}^{\eta/2} A_{2n}$ corresponds to getting a head, the first one occurring at an even numbered toss. We calculate

$$\nu(A) = \sum_{n=1}^{\eta/2} \frac{1}{2^{2n}} = \frac{1}{3}\left(1 - \frac{1}{2^\eta}\right),$$

using the usual 'finite' algebra. Taking standard parts we see that $L(\nu)(A) = \frac{1}{3}$. This corresponds to the standard event $A' = \cup_{n=1}^{\infty} A_{2n}$ of getting at least one head, the first at an even numbered toss, in an infinite number of tosses.

This may be considered a curiosity. However, already Loeb gave in [16] an interesting application to Poisson processes. And a convincing proof of the power of the method came with the application of R. M. Anderson [1] to Brownian motion and stochastic integration (Itô's lemma).

A Brownian motion on a probability space $(\Omega, \mathscr{D}, P)$ is a function β: $[0,1] \times \Omega \to \mathbb{R}$ such that

(i) β is a stochastic process, i.e. $\beta(t, \cdot)$ is a measurable function;
(ii) for $s < t$, $s, t \in [0,1]$, $\beta(t,\omega) - \beta(s,\omega)$ has a normal distribution with mean 0 and variance $t - s$;
(iii) if $s_1 < t_1 \leqslant s_2 < t_2 \leqslant \cdots \leqslant s_n < t_n$, $s_i, t_i \in [0,1]$ then $\{\beta(t_1,\omega) - \beta(s_1,\omega), \ldots, \beta(t_n,\omega) - \beta(s_n,\omega)\}$ is an independent set of random variables.

Probabilists know how to construct a Brownian motion as a limit of random walks, see e.g. Section 12.2 of L. Breiman's well-known text. Let us, following Anderson [1], do this in a forthright non-standard way.

Let $\Omega = \{-1, 1\}^{\eta}$, $\eta \in {}^*N \backslash N$. Let $\mathfrak{A}$ be the algebra of all internal subsets of Ω, and for $A \in \mathfrak{A}$, set $\nu(A) = |A|/2^{\eta}$. On $(\Omega, L(\mathfrak{A}), L(\nu))$ we define explicitly a hyperfinite random walk by the formula

$$\chi(t,\omega) = \frac{1}{\sqrt{\eta}}\Big(\sum_{k=1}^{[\eta t]} \omega_i + (\eta t - [\eta t])\omega_{[\eta t]+1}\Big)$$

The factor $\eta^{-1/2}$ is explained in the following way. If we take a finite random walk with distance Δx and time unit Δt and want to go to a limit (both $\Delta x, \Delta t \to 0$) in such a way as to keep the variance finite, we easily see that Δx must be of the order $\sqrt{\Delta t}$. In the hyperfinite case we have chosen $\Delta t = \eta^{-1}$, hence the factor $\eta^{-1/2}$ since each $\omega_i = \pm 1$.

Let $\beta(t,\omega)$ be the standard part of $\chi(t,\omega)$. Then β is a Brownian motion on $(\Omega, L(\mathfrak{A}), L(\nu))$. And Anderson's proof of this is remarkably simple using the explicit construction of $\chi(t,\omega)$. The continuity of the process for almost all paths ω has also a reasonably simple 'combinatorial' proof. But for this we refer the reader to Anderson's paper, where also applications to stochastic integration can be found.

H. J. Keisler has in a forthcoming study, *Hyperfinite Model Theory* [14], given a systematic approach to this topic. He has introduced several formal languages appropriate to the study of stochastic phenomena and initiated their model theory.

Basic to this study is the notion of a *hyperfinite model*, i.e. a structure

$$\mathfrak{A} = \langle A, \mu, a_i, S_j \rangle_{i \in I, j \in J}$$

where $\langle A, \mu \rangle$ is a hyperfinite probability space (i.e. A is hyperfinite and μ an internal function $\mu: A \to {}^*[0, 1]$ such that $\Sigma_{a \in A}\, \mu(a) = 1$. For internal subsets B we set $\mu(B) = \Sigma_{a \in B}\, \mu(a)$). Each $a \in A$ and each S_j is an internal relation on A with finitely many arguments.

We promised only to give a glimpse into the non-standard approach. Let us therefore just conclude with stating the ultimate goal of the Keisler program: to create a hyperfinite model theory which stands in the same relationship to the theory of Brownian motions as ordinary model theory is related to the theory of algebraically closed fields.

We have surveyed a variety of approaches. They may seem to go off in all directions, but numerous interconnections exist. In this 'rounding off' I want to add, very briefly, a few remarks going beyond the purely mathematical aspects.

The motivation of some of the work reported on has been to use methods from logic and recursion theory to gain further understanding and insight.

It is e.g. a fundamental question of 'applied' probability theory to understand under which circumstances the notion of probability can be applied. Formal investigations cannot answer this question, but a representation theory may tell us what possibilities there are.

Formal methods may also help us build better models of 'natural phenomena'. In this respect recursion theory has been of the outmost importance in giving us precise models for notions of randomness.

And it is this model building aspect of 'hyperfinite' methods for large finite phenomena which offers intriguing possibilities for future investigations. There has been non-trivial applications in economics and physics, but more is certain to come.

University of Oslo

BIBLIOGRAPHY

[1] Anderson, R. M., 'A Non-Standard Representation for Brownian Motion and Itô Integration', *Israel J. Math.* 25 (1976), 15–46.

[2] Carnap, R., *Logical Foundation of Probability*, Chicago University Press, Chicago, 1951.

[3] Church, A., 'On the Concept of a Random Sequence', *Bull. Am. Math. Soc.* 46 (1940), 130–135.

[4] Eisele, K. Th., *Booleschwertige Modelle mit Wahrscheinlichkeitsmassen und Darstellungen stochastischer Prozesse*, Ph.D. thesis, Heidelberg, 1976.
[5] Fenstad, J. E., 'Representations of Probabilities Defined on First Order Languages', in Crossley (ed.), *Sets, Models and Recursion Theory*, North-Holland, Amsterdam, 1967, pp. 156–172.
[6] Fenstad, J. E., 'The Structure of Logical Probabilities', *Synthese* 18 (1968), 1–23.
[7] Fenstad, J. E., 'The Structure of Probabilities Defined on First Order Languages', to appear in R. Jeffrey (ed.), *Studies in Inductive Logic and Probability*, Vol. 2.
[8] Finette, B. de, 'Foresight: Its Logical Laws, Its Subjective Sources', in Kyberg and Smokler (eds.), *Studies in Subjective Probability*, J. Wiley, New York, 1964, pp. 95–158.
[9] Gaifman, H., 'Concerning Measures in First Order Calculi', *Israel J. Math.* 2 (1964), 1–18.
[10] Gaifman, H. and Snir, M., to appear.
[11] Good, I. J., *The Estimation of Probabilities*, MIT Press, Cambridge, Mass., 1965.
[12] Hajek, P. and Havranek, T., *Mechanizing Hypothesis Formation*, Universitext, Springer Verlag, to appear 1977.
[13] Jeffreys, H., *Theory of Probability*, 3rd. ed., Oxford University Press, Oxford, 1961.
[14] Keisler, H. J., 'Hyperfinite Model Theory', to appear in the *Proceedings of the 1976 ASL Summer Meeting*, Oxford 1976.
[15] Keynes, J. M., *A Treatise on Probability*, Macmillan, London, 1921.
[16] Loeb, P. A., 'Conversion from Non-Standard to Standard Measure Spaces and Applications in Probability Theory', *Trans. Am. Math. Soc.* **221** (1975), 113–122.
[17] Łoś, J., 'Remarks on Foundation of Probability', in *Proceedings of the International Congress of Mathematicians*, Stockholm, 1962, pp. 225–229.
[18] Martin–Löf, P., 'The Definition of Random Sequences', *Information and Control* 9 (1966), 602–619.
[19] Martin–Löf, P., 'On the Notion of Randomness', in *Intuitionism and Proof Theory*, North-Holland, Amsterdam, 1970.
[20] Mises, R. von, 'Grundlagen der Wahrscheinlichkeitslehre', *Math. Z.* **5** (1919), 55–99.
[21] Mises, R. von, *Mathematical Theory of Probability and Statistics*, Academic Press, New York, 1964.
[22] Nelson, E., *Internal Set Theory, a New Approach to Non-Standard Analysis*, to appear.
[23] Schnorr, C. P., *Zufälligkeit und Wahrscheinlichkeit*, Lecture Notes in Mathematics, No. 218, Springer-Verlag, Heidelberg, 1971.
[24] Scott, D. and Krauss, P., 'Assigning Probabilities to Logical Formulas', in J. Hintikka and P. Suppes (eds.), *Aspects of Inductive Logic*, North-Holland, Amsterdam, 1966.
[25] Tarski, A. and Horn, A., 'Measures in Boolean Algebras', *Trans. Am. Math. Soc.* 64 (1948), 467–497.
[26] Ville, J., *Etude critique de la notion de collectif*, Gauthier-Villars, Paris, 1939.
[27] Wald, A., 'Die Wiederspruchsfreiheit des Kollektivbegriffs in der Wahrscheinlichkeitsrechnung', *Ergb. eines math. Koll.* 8 (1937), 38–72.

GONZALO E. REYES

LOGIC AND CATEGORY THEORY*

In spite of the title, this paper deals with one aspect only of the interconnections between logic and category theory, namely the dialectics of 'concept' versus 'variable set' or, more precisely, the connections between model theory and topos theory. The connections between proof theory and category theory have been completely left out and the interested reader is referred to [22], where a full account of the work done in that area may be found. Furthermore, since a survey article on the connections between model theory and topos theory has recently appeared [10], I shall rather concentrate on one particular problem: to formulate rigourously the 'principle' that 'in the infinitely small, every function is linear' (Although this 'principle' was one of the fundamental intuitions that helped to develop calculus in the 17th Century, it did not survive the 'Arithmetization of Analysis' in the 19th and was swept out as hopelessly wrong along with infinitesimals, fluxions, etc.).

The solution (due mainly to A. Kock) will illustrate the use of topos-theoretical models as opposed to set-theoretical ones and will hopefully show the reader some of the possibilities of the use of the notion of 'variable set' in foundational studies.

I would like to thank A. Joyal, A. Kock, F. W. Lawvere, and M. Makkai for numerous discussions about some of the topics discussed here. Needless to say, I alone am responsible for the opinions, hopefully naive, expressed in the following pages.

§1. One of the most persistent dogmas of mathematics in the 20th Century has been the doctrine that, in the last analysis, only set theory can provide adequate foundations for all branches of mathematics. In practice (and independently of finer points arising from the notion of 'foundations') this doctrine forces us to consider all mathematical objects as sets and all constructions performed on these objects as set-theoretical. The example that comes most readily to mind is Analysis: integers, rational numbers and real numbers are all sets according to this doctrine, real-valued functions are sets of ordered pairs (of sets of natural numbers), etc., etc.

It is important to notice that, by 'embedding' mathematical objects in

E. Agazzi (ed.), Modern Logic – A Survey, 235–252.

the universe V of sets, these objects inherit the features of the surrounding universe. To analyse the specific features of V we shall follow Lawvere [13], taking advantage of the hindsight provided by the development of the theory of elementary topos (cf. [4, 24]).

As undefined terms we take those of the language of category theory: objects, morphisms, domain (of a morphism), codomain (of a morphism), composition (of morphisms). The intended interpretation is sets, functions, domain (of a function), codomain and usual composition of functions. As usual, we write $X \xrightarrow{f} Y$ for a morphism f with domain X and codomain Y. For basic terminology not explained here, we refer to [14].

There are four groups of axioms:

(I) *Axioms for Category*

These axioms state that objects and morphisms form a category (under compositions). One axiom, for instance, states that composition (whenever defined) is associative and has a left and a right unit, etc.

(II) *Structural Axioms*

This group describes the basic constructions whereby new sets are obtained from old ones. As an example, the product $X \times Y$ of X and Y in a category is defined as the unique (up to unique isomorphism) object Z together with morphisms (called projections)

$$X \xleftarrow{\pi_X} Z \xrightarrow{\pi_Y} Y$$

satisfying the following adjointness condition: via the projections, there is a bijection between morphisms $W \to Z$ and pairs of morphisms (obtained by composition with the projections) $W \to X$, $W \to Y$. (See e.g. [14].) Using a convenient notation reminiscent of Gentzen's we shall write

$$\frac{W \longrightarrow X \times Y}{W \to X,\ W \to Y}.$$

Similarly, the exponentation X^Y is defined (in any category) by the adjointness condition

$$\frac{W \longrightarrow X^Y}{W \times Y \longrightarrow X}.$$

The axioms of this group state the existence of finite $\varprojlim$, i.e., a terminal object 1 (defined by the condition that for any X there is a unique morphism

$X \to 1$), products of 2 objects and equalizers of pairs of maps $X \rightrightarrows Y$; the existence of exponentiation and the existence of a 'subobject classifier' Ω (which allows one to introduce 'characteristic functions').

We shall not describe these axioms further (see e.g. [24]) and we just point out the intended interpretation: 1 is a set with one element, product is the cartesian product and the equalizer of a pair of functions $X \rightrightarrows Y$ is the subset of X on which the functions coincide; exponentiation is the usual one and the subobject classifier Ω is a set with 2 elements.

(III) *Axiom on Natural Numbers*

This axiom states the existence of an object N with a 'successor' morphism $\mathrm{N} \xrightarrow{S} \mathrm{N}$ which satisfies a form of 'Peano's axioms'. We omit the exact formulation, since we shall not use it later (see e.g. [24]). The intended interpretation should be obvious.

(IV) *'Substantial' Axioms*

These axioms are designed to capture the most conspicuous character of a set: to be an aggregate or 'mob' of points which determine it completely. Furthermore each point is disconnected from the rest and may enter into any promiscuous collection of other points, collection which then splits the set into two disjoint pieces. To formulate these axioms, we first define, for each X, Points(X) = the set of all morphisms from 1 into X. Notice that whenever $X \xrightarrow{f} Y$ is a morphism, we may define a set-theoretical function Points(X) $\xrightarrow{\text{Points}(X)}$ Points(Y) by composition with f. Technically, Points is a functor, indeed the representable functor h^1. To say that a set is 'its substance', i.e., the collection of its points is to say h^1 is an equivalence of categories. No elementary set of axioms, however, can imply such an statement, although a few go some way towards this goal: 1 is a generator, i.e., whenever $X \overset{f}{\underset{g}{\rightrightarrows}} Y$ are two different morphisms there is a point $1 \xrightarrow{x} X$ such that $f \circ x \neq g \circ x$; 1 is irreducible, i.e., whenever $1 = U + V$, then $U = 1$ or $V = 1$ (where + is the 'disjoint union' operation characterized by the adjointness condition

$$\frac{X + Y \longrightarrow W}{X \to W,\ Y \to W}$$

which can be proved to exist on the basis of the axioms of the groups (I) and (II). As a last axiom of this group we add the axiom of choice (*AC*) Every epimorphism has a section, i.e., whenever $X \xrightarrow{f} Y$ is an epimorphism (see e.g. [14]) there is $Y \xrightarrow{s} X$ such that $f \circ s = 1_Y$.

It has been shown by Diaconescu (see e.g. [4]) that (*AC*) implies (on the base of the Axioms of groups (I) and (II)) the Boolean character of the category in the following sense: every subobject $X \rightarrowtail Y$ splits Y into 2 disjoint pieces, i.e. there is a subobject $X' \rightarrowtail Y$ such that the fibered product $X \times_Y X' = \emptyset$ (the initial object) and $X + X' = Y$.

This concludes our analysis. A category satisfying the axioms of groups (I) and (II) is called an *elementary topos*. If it satisfies (III) also, it is called an *elementary topos with natural number object*.

How do these features of V (the universe of sets) influence mathematical practice? By 'embedding' a given domain of mathematical objects in V, the objects become 'atomized' and these 'atoms' may be recombined to generate a host of new 'objects' and new 'operations' besides the intended one, 'objects' and 'operations' having nor relevance to the particular domain in question (E.g. square filling 'curves'). The standard solution is to devise principles of limitations in V to cut down this definitional pollution (E.g., only homeomorphs of the circle should count as 'curves', etc.). To the naive question why inflate to then deflate?, the answer seems to be that

(i) set theory provides a standard of (formal) correctness for mathematical statements.

(ii) by 'embedding' a given domain of objects in V we make sure that every conceivable extension of our domain is available when needed.

(iii) some global properties of V may explain specific problems in 'ordinary' mathematical practice (E.g. Shelah's work on the Whitehead's problem).

§2. Of course this dogma and the ensuing trend toward set-theoretical formalization has been challenged several times in this century. A powerful attack was launched by Brouwer and his followers who questioned the universality of logic (and set theory) and put forward explicitely the important doctrine that different domains of objects may require different logics (classical logic being the logic of the domain of finite sets and unsuitable for other domains of mathematical objects). In particular Brouwer thought that new objects and new principles of proof, not inherent in the universe of sets, were needed to develop Analysis and other branches of mathematics. (See Troelstra's contribution to this volume). Nevertheless, the resulting doctrine, Intuitionism, was mainly 'deviant' in the sense that it did not aim to provide foundations or justification for principles and constructions arising from the practice of mathematics, but to change mathematics itself to conform to a theoretical, a priori principle of 'constructivity'.

Less well-known that the intuitionist 'revolution' was the movement of 'civil disobedience' against the official doctrine which took place in Algebraic Geometry, specially under the lead of the Italian School. These workers ignored the new 'mot d'ordre' 'set-theorize' and continued to work in the style that was common before the advent of set theory. According to Shafarevich [21], "The style of thinking that was fully developed in Algebraic Geometry at that time was too far removed from the set-theoretical and axiomatic spirit, which then determined the development of mathematics". As a result, it became 'incomprehensible' and 'unconvincing', epithets that were not unknown to intuitionists (and for similar reasons). "Several decades had to lapse before the rise of the theory of topological, differentiable and complex manifolds, the general theory of fields, the theory of ideals in sufficiently general rings, and only then it became possible to construct Algebraic Geometry on the basis of the principle of set-theoretical mathematics".

From a foundational point of view, the most interesting development of this vast program of building Algebraic Geometry on set-theoretical basis was the emergence of a new notion of set with the creation of the theory of topos by Grothendieck and its school in the early 60's. It is fair to say, however, that this fact was not fully recognized until the work of Lawvere and Tierney on elementary topos in 69–70. I would like to add that particular toposes constructed from topological spaces had been introduced and studied in the mid 40's (for the history of topos theory we refer the reader to [1]). In the case of a topos constructed from a topological space X, this new notion of set, namely *sheaf* may be thought of (as a first approximation) as a '(continuously) variable set' or 'an X-indexed family of sets varying continuously with X'. More precisely, a sheaf is a couple of topological spaces E, X together with a local homeomoprhism $\pi: E \to X$ (i.e., via π, E and X 'look the same locally'). Notice that such a structure may be thought of as the X-indexed family $(E_x)_{x \in X}$ where $E_x = \pi^{-1}(x)$ is the 'fiber' over x. A morphism between the sheaves $E \xrightarrow{\pi} X$ and $E' \xrightarrow{\pi'} X$ is a continuous map $f: E \to E'$ preserving the fibers, i.e. such that the diagram

$$\begin{array}{ccc} E & \longrightarrow & E' \\ & {\scriptstyle\pi}\searrow \quad \swarrow{\scriptstyle\pi'} & \\ & X & \end{array}$$

is commutative. We let $\mathrm{Sh}(X)$ be the category of sheaves over the topological space X.

With this notion avialable, we can define a '(continuously) variable structure' as a 'structure in Sh(X)'. For instance, a '(continuously) variable ring' is a ring object in Sh(X). Spelling out the definition, such a ring object is the same as a sheaf $E \xrightarrow{\pi} X$ such that each fiber E_x is a ring and the ring structure varies 'continuously' in the sense that, e.g., if x is very near x' in X, then the zero element $0_x \in E_x$ should be very near the zero element $0_{x'} \in E_x$ in E. More precisely, the family $(0_x)_{x \in X}$ should be a continuous map $0\colon X \to E$ such that $\pi \circ 0 = 1_X$ (technically, a global section).

It is remarkable fact that the category Sh(X) of sheaves over X with continuous fiber preserving maps is an elementary topos in the sense of §1. In this case even with a natural number object N .

Only the 'substantial' axioms are not satisfied in this model. Sheaves have internal 'cohesion' just as open sets of a topological space have and just as open sets, they do not form a Boolean algebra and hence their 'logic' is not classical but intuitionistic.

To see what goes wrong with these axioms, let $X = S^1 = \{z \in \mathbb{C} \mid |z| = 1\}$. The following 2 sheaves have the same points namely no points at all, although they are utterly different:

(1) The sheaf on S^1 defined by $\emptyset \to S^1$ where $\emptyset$ is the empty set and $\to$ is the empty function in pictures:

S^1

(2) The double covering of S^1 defined by $S^1 \xrightarrow{q_2} S^1$ where $q_2(z) = z^2$ There is no global section since, essentially, there is no way of halving continuously all angles $0 \leqslant \theta < 2\pi$ (when θ tends to 2π, $\theta/2$ tends to π but it should also tend to $0/2 = 0$). In pictures:

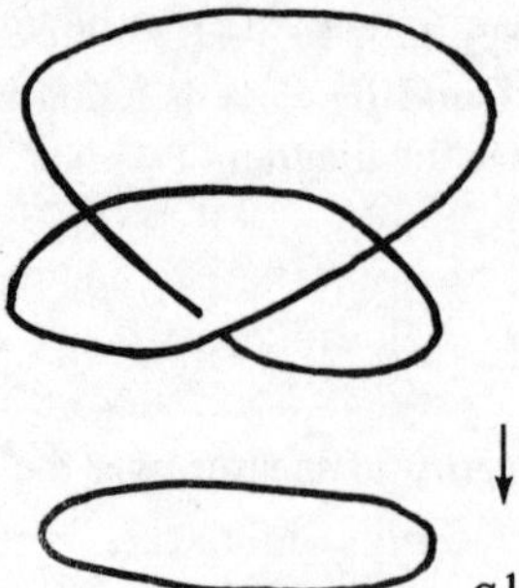

S^1

Notice that q_2 is an epimorphism without sections, i.e., (AC) fails in this model.

Intuitionism itself (or rather parts thereof) did not escape the trend towards set-theoretical formalization and the 60's in particular saw the appearence of Kirpke's semantics for first-order logic. Once again we may say, from the vantage point to topos theory, that the basic idea was to consider a new notion of set, namely the 'set in time'. The basic example of such a set was the growth of knowledge of an idealized mathematician. For the purpose of illustration we consider (cf. [24]) a simplified model of 'time' with two states: 'then' and 'now'. Using the language of category theory, we look at time as the category $\mathbf{2}$:

$$(\text{then} \longrightarrow \text{now})$$

A 'set in time' is then a functor X: $\mathbf{2} \to \text{Set}$ from $\mathbf{2}$ into the category of sets of functions. X is completely determined by the diagram (with the 'transition map')

$$X(\text{then}) \longrightarrow X(\text{now})$$

A 'function in time' $X \xrightarrow{\eta} Y$ is just a natural transformation, i.e., a couple of maps η_{then} and η_{now} compatible with the transition functions, i.e., such that the diagram

$$\begin{array}{ccc} X(\text{then}) & \longrightarrow & X(\text{now}) \\ \eta_{\text{then}} \downarrow & & \downarrow \eta_{\text{now}} \\ Y(\text{then}) & \longrightarrow & Y(\text{now}) \end{array}$$

is commutative.

The category of sets in time and functions in time is again an elementary topos with natural number objects. The 'substantial' axioms, however, are not satisfied.

Even the development of classical logic had witnessed a similar extension of the notion of set to provide models for infinitary logics (which lacked set-theoretical models) as in the work of C. Karp and others and to provide models of set theory to settle independence questions in set theory as in the work of Cohen, Scott–Solovay, etc. This new notion of set, the Boolean-valued set, was explicitely studied by Scott–Solovay.

It turns out, once again, that the category of Boolean-valued sets is an elementary topos with natural number object. Furthermore it satisfies (AC). (See [2].)

§3. In this section I shall discuss one specific problem arising in geometry (and differential calculus) and its solution in this context of elementary topos (with 'variable set' rather than 'set' as the basic notion). The following discussion is based on work done by A. Kock, G. Wraith, and myself (cf. [6, 7, 8, 11, 12, 19]), following a suggestion of F. W. Lawvere in 1967 (unpublished lecture at the University of Chicago).

One of the fundamental intuitions that helped to develop calculus was the 'principle' that, 'in the infinitely small, every function is linear'. Assuming this 'principle', it is obvious how to define the derivative of a function F at a point x_0. Indeed:

$$f(x_0 + d) = \alpha + \beta d$$

for every infinitesimal d. In particular (for $d = 0$) $\alpha = f(x_0)$ and we define $f'(x_0) = \beta$. In pictures:

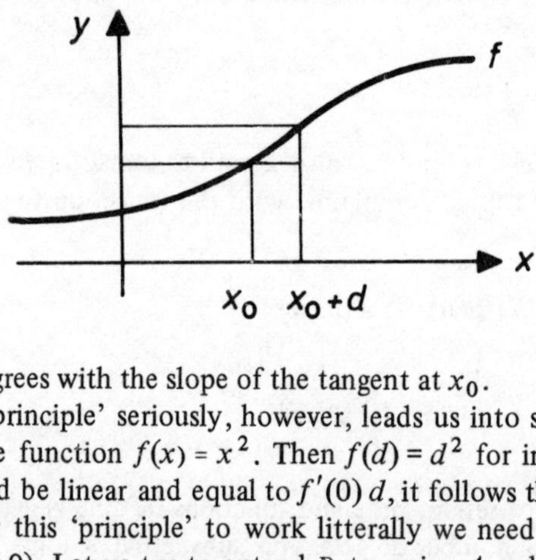

This obviously agrees with the slope of the tangent at x_0.

Taking this 'principle' seriously, however, leads us into some difficulties. Consider e.g. the function $f(x) = x^2$. Then $f(d) = d^2$ for infinitely small d. Since $f(d)$ should be linear and equal to $f'(0)\,d$, it follows that $f'(0) = 0$ and that $d^2 = 0$. For this 'principle' to work litterally we need real numbers of square 0 (and $\neq 0$). Let us try to extend $\mathbb{R}$ to a ring A and let us define the infinitesimals by $D = \{a \in A \mid a^2 = 0\}$. Then the function defined by

$$\varphi(d) = 0 \quad \text{if} \quad d \neq d_0$$
$$\varphi(d_0) = 1$$

(where $d_0 \in D - \{0\}$) cannot be linear, unless $A = 0$, the null ring. Indeed $\varphi(d) = \varphi(0) + d \cdot \beta$ implies that $\varphi(0) = 0$ and hence $d_0 \cdot \beta = 1$. Therefore $1 = 1^2 = d_0^2\, \beta^2 = 0$. Notice that in this argument (due to Lawvere) we are using the 'disconnected' character of the set D, namely d_0 splits D into two disjoint pieces $D = \{d_0\} + (D - \{d_0\})$, splitting which is essential to define φ.

Of course and in agreement with the use of principle of limitations discussed at the end of §1, we could try to define a topology on D and formulate a weaker 'principle' which makes reference to continuous functions only. However, we seem to be reproducing in the infinitely small the infinitely complex structure of $\mathbb{R}$ and the gain is doubtful! At any rate, let us change the context and consider an elementary topos $\mathbf{E}$ and a commutative ring object with unit A on $\mathbf{E}$. This means that there are morphisms

$$\mathbb{1} \overset{0}{\underset{1}{\rightrightarrows}} A \qquad A \times A \overset{+}{\underset{\cdot}{\rightrightarrows}} A \qquad A \xrightarrow{-} A$$

which satisfy the axioms for a commutative ring with unit. The associativity of +, e.g., is expressed by stating the commutativity of the following diagram

$$\begin{array}{ccc} A \times A \times A & \xrightarrow{\cdot \times A} & A \times A \\ {\scriptstyle A\times\cdot}\downarrow & & \downarrow{\scriptstyle \cdot} \\ A \times A & \xrightarrow[\cdot]{} & A \end{array}$$

(Intuitively: $(\cdot \times A)(a, b, c) = (a \cdot b, c)$, $(A \times \cdot) = (a, b \cdot c)$).

Let D be the subobject of A defined as the equalizer

$$D \rightarrowtail A \overset{(\,)^2}{\underset{0}{\rightrightarrows}} A.$$

In set-theoretical notation (that we shall use henceforth)

$$D = [\![a \in A \mid a^2 = 0]\!]$$

We shall think intuitively of A as 'the line' and of D as 'a point with an infinitesimal linear neighborhood'. In pictures:

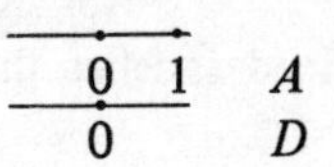

Since $\mathbf{E}$ is a topos, exponentials exist. In particular M^D exists for every object M and, furthermore, we have a morphism

$$\begin{array}{c} M^D \\ \downarrow{\scriptstyle \pi} \\ M \end{array}$$

obtained (via exponentials) from the map $\mathbb{1} \xrightarrow{0} D$ (Intuitively M^D are functions defined on D and π is just the evaluation at 0).

When M satisfies further properties (of being a 'manifold'), $M^D \xrightarrow{\pi} M$ will play the role of the 'tangent bundle' of M.

Notice that we also have a morphism

$$A \times A \xrightarrow{\alpha} A^D$$

which in set-theoretical notation associates to a couple (a, b) the linear function $\alpha(a, b)$ defined by $\alpha(a, b)(d) = a + b \cdot d$.

We are now in the position to state our 'principle' that every function in the infinitely small is linear:

α is an isomorphism.

This formulation is due to A. Kock [5] who defines A to be of *line type* if α is an isomorphism, i.e., if the 'principle' holds.

Let $A \xrightarrow{f} A$ be a morphism. We define the derivative of f, f', to be the new morphism obtained by composition:

$$A \xrightarrow{\hat{+}} A^D \xrightarrow{f^D} A^D \xrightarrow{\alpha^{-1}} A \times A \xrightarrow{\text{proj}_2} A, \qquad f' : A \to A \text{ (the composite)}$$

where $\hat{+}$ is obtained by adjunction from the morphism $A \times D \xrightarrow{+} A$ which in set-theoretical notation sends (a, d) into $a + d$.

In set-theoretical notation,

$\hat{+}(a) =$ the function sending d into $a + d = [d \to a + d]$,

$f^D(\hat{+}(a)) =$ the function sending d into $f(a + d) = [d \to f(a + d)]$.

Since this last function is linear (content of A being of line type) $f(a + d) = f(a) + df'(a)$ and so α^{-1} takes this function into $(f(a), f'(a))$ which, in turn, is sent into $f'(a)$ by proj_2. We got the right definition.

In [6], Kock proves that the derivative thus defined satisfies the usual laws:

$$(f + g)' = f' + g', (f \cdot g)' = f' \cdot g + f \cdot g', (f \circ g)' = (f' \circ g) \circ g'.$$

This is essentially the way that Fermat proceeded to find tangents to curves (cf. [5]). To handle questions of maxima and minima, Fermat proceeded as follows: if f has a minimum at x_0, say, the restriction of f to an infinitesimal neighborhood of x_0 (which is a line by the 'principle') is horizontal, i.e., $f(x_0 + d) = f(x_0)$ for all infinitesimal d. Hence $f(x_0 + d) = f(x_0) + df'(x_0) = f(x_0)$ and this implies that $f'(x_0) = 0$.

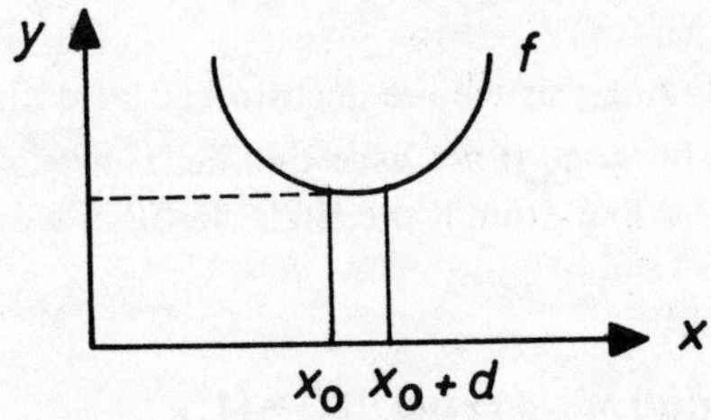

His arguments can thus be justified in this context. As a further example, consider the 'trigonometric' functions.

$$S^1 \underset{\text{Sin}}{\overset{\text{Cos}}{\rightrightarrows}} A$$

where S^1 is the circle defined by (in set-theoretical notation) $S^1 = [\![(x, y) \in A^2 \mid x^2 + y^2 = 1]\!]$ defined by Cos $(x, y) = x$, Sin $(x, y) = y$. It is well-known (since Gauss) that S^1 is a group object with the law $S^1 \times S^1 \xrightarrow{\oplus} S^1$ defined by $(x, y) \oplus (u, v) = (xu - yv, xv + yu)$ and the neutral element $\mathbb{1} \xrightarrow{\langle 1, 0\rangle} S^1$.

We obtain a morphism

$$S^1 \times D \xrightarrow{\oplus} S^1$$

defined by $((x, y), d) \mapsto (x, y) \oplus (1, d)$.

(Intuitively, we turn the circle by an infinitesimal angle.) By adjointness, we obtain a morphism

$$S^1 \xrightarrow{\oplus} S^{1D}$$

which may be thought of as the 'vector field of infinitesimal rotations' and we shall compute Cos′ the directional derivative of Cos along this 'vector field':

$$S^1 \xrightarrow{\oplus} S^{1D} \xrightarrow{\cos^D} A^D \xrightarrow{\alpha^{-1}} A \times A \xrightarrow{\text{proj}_2} A$$

(the composite being labelled Cos′)

In set-theoretical notation:

$$\theta = (x, y) \xmapsto{\oplus} [d \mapsto (x, y) \oplus (1, d)] = [d \mapsto (x - d \cdot y, y + x \cdot d)] \xmapsto{\text{Cos}^D} [d \to x - d \cdot y] \xmapsto{\alpha^{-1}} A \times A \xmapsto{\text{proj}_2} -y$$

i.e., Cos′ = – Sin.

Similarly $\mathrm{Sin}' = \mathrm{Cos}$.

Of course in 'real' Analysis we are accustomed to define sin as a function $A \xrightarrow{\sin} A$. This can be done if we have the 'helix' available, i.e., if we have a way of 'winding' the line around the circle. In other words, assume that we have

$$h: A \longrightarrow S^1$$

such that $h(a+d) = h(a) \oplus h(d)$ and $h(d) = (1, d)$.

Then we can define $A \overset{\cos}{\underset{\sin}{\rightrightarrows}} A$ by the composition $\cos = \mathrm{Cos} \circ h$, $\sin = \mathrm{Sin} \circ h$.

It follows at once that $\cos' = -\sin$, $\sin' = \cos$.

By using these infinitesimals in this context of 'variable sets', Kock and myself [12] showed how to justify an argument of E. Cartan to compute (and interpret) the Riemann–Christoffel curvature tensor by transporting a vector parallel to itself along the sides of an *infinite simal* parallelogram. It turns out that the operation of parallel transport has a very simple 'intrinsic' definition which seems quite in agreement with the intuitions of Levi–Civita and earlier geometers (including Cartan) who used infinitesimals in their formulations. Very roughly for objects M which are 'manifolds' and for morphisms $E \to M$ which are 'vector bundless', we have the following intuitive interpretation:

Object	*Elements*
M	(points)
M^D	(Infinitesimal notions)
E	(vectors)
E^D	(infinitesimal vector fields)
$E \times M^D$	
M	

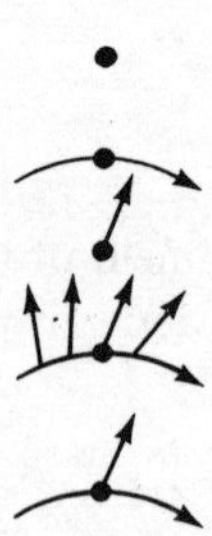

The operation ∇ of parallel transport should associate to a configuration

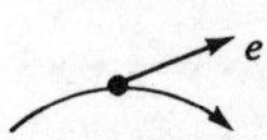 the result of transporting e parallel to itself along the infinitesimal curve γ, i.e., a configuration  Letting K be the (ob-

vious) operation which to an infinitesimal vector field 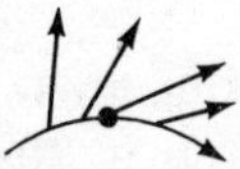 associates , we may express this as follows: ∇ is a splitting of

$$\begin{array}{ccc} E^D & \xrightarrow{K} & E \underset{M}{\times} M^D \\ & \pi \searrow \quad \swarrow \mathrm{Proj}_1 & \\ & E & \end{array}$$

Of course further linearity conditions should be imposed on ∇, but we shall not enter into this matter here.

We now turn to the discussion of models for the axiom stating that $A \times A \xrightarrow{\alpha} A^D$ is an isomorphism. Let **E** be the topos of functors from the category $\mathbb{A}$ of commutative rings with unit into the category of sets. The underlying set functor $\mathcal{U}$ (which associates the underlying set to a ring) is a ring object. Indeed the morphisms

$$\mathbb{1} \overset{0}{\underset{1}{\rightrightarrows}} \mathcal{U} \qquad \mathcal{U} \times \mathcal{U} \overset{+}{\underset{\cdot}{\rightrightarrows}} \mathcal{U}$$

are defined 'argument by argument'. E.g., + is the natural transformation $(+_A)_A$ which, on a ring A is just the + of that ring. The object D turns out to be the functor defined (on objects) by $D(A) = \{a \in A \mid a^2 = 0\}$. It has been shown by Kock [6] that $\mathcal{U}$ is of line type, i.e., $\alpha\colon \mathcal{U} \times \mathcal{U} \longrightarrow \mathcal{U}^D$ is an isomorphism. In this case a morphism $\mathcal{U} \xrightarrow{f} \mathcal{U}$ is just a polynomial $f \in \mathbb{Z}\,[X]$ and its derivative f' coincides with the 'formal' derivative as defined in Algebra.

Other models are the Zariski topos and the Etale topos (with the underlying set functor again as the ring object). Further models are discussed in the references.

To close this section, notice that these infinitesimals are quite different from those introduced by A. Robinson in his work on Non-Standard Analysis [20]. This is clear to start with since, as we saw, there are no models of our axioms in (the category of) sets. Very roughly, we can say that we weaken our structures and our logic (giving up the field structure of the reals and using intuitionistic logic in the surrounding universe) to introduce infinitesimals, whereas Robinson strengthens both the structures and the logic (using forms of (AC)) to introduce his. Furthermore, D usually behaves in our case as an 'atom', having no inner structure, in the sense that e.g. $(M + N)^D =$

$M^D + N^D$ (intuitively: there is no way of splitting D into disjoint pieces, even locally). In Non-Standard Analysis, on the other hand, the monad of 0 has a complicated set-theoretical structure. Finally let me point out that the intuitive notions of infinitesimals are quite different: in Non-Standard Analysis, the infinitesimals are those numbers which are smaller than all (finite) numbers. An order relation is essential to define them and whenever d is an infinitesimal, $d^2 > 0$. In our case, the infinitesimals are those numbers whose square is negligeable (i.e. is equal 0) and no order is necessary to define them.

It should be obvious that this program of 'algebro-geometrizing' Analysis has barely started and, for the time being, it is not clear how far we can proceed.

§4. Coming back to the discussion of the foundational role of set theory in §1, I would like to emphasize the fact that the principles of limitations (mentioned at the end of §1) are sometimes not only hard to formulate, but even harder to prove. An example is provided by Cantor's construction of a bijection between R and R^2 which he claimed had destroyed the theory of dimension. Even after the correct formulation of the limitation principle by Dedekind (that only homeomorphisms preserve dimension), it took years before Brouwer was able to prove it.

Furthermore, there is no a priori assurance that such principles can always be found and do their jobs. I suggested that a limitation principle in V to account for models of Kock's axioms would introduce in the infinitely small the complicated structure of $\mathbb{R}$ and this seems corraborated to some extend by the work on Non-Standard Analysis (cf. [20]).

Instead of a single 'universal' solution for the problem of providing satisfactory foundations for the whole of geometry (i.e., for geometry in all its guises: algebraic, differential, analytical, etc.), I would suggest a 'doctrinal' approach to this problem. This approach is not new and it is more or less explicit in recent publications on the subject.

Let me recall from [10], where further references can be found, that Grothendieck toposes (of which the category of sets is one instance) appear in categorical logic as one 'doctrine' among many others, namely as categorical formulations of (logical) theories described by Gentzen's sequents of the form $\Phi \Rightarrow \Psi$, where Φ and Ψ are finite sets of formulas built up from atomic ones by using $=$, $\wedge$, $\vee$, $\top$ (true), $\bot$ (false) W (infinitary disjunction) and $\exists$. Elementary Toposes, in the same vein, appear as categorical formulations of intuitionistic theories of types.

These formulation are 'invariant', in the sense that different choices of languages and axioms may lead to the same category. (The situation is analogous to that of matrices versus linear transformations). Under this 'logical' interpretation, a topos appears as a category of 'concepts': its objects are formulas in the theories in question and its morphisms are (equivalent classes of) provably functional relations. (Cf. [15].)

Many other 'fragments' of logic give rise to 'doctrines'. For instance, regular categories, i.e., categories with finite $\varprojlim$ and images which are stable under pull-backs are the categorical or 'invariant' formulation of theories of the form $\Phi \Rightarrow \Psi$, where Φ and Ψ are finite sets of formulas built up from atomic ones by using $=, \wedge, \top, \exists$.

With this notion of 'doctrine' available, my suggestion is simply this: formalize the intuitive notions and constructions under study in the weakest (or poorest) 'doctrine' where this formalization is possible. In the example of §3, this amounts to switching from the 'doctrine' of ringed elementary toposes (i.e., elementary toposes together with a ring object) to that of ringed categories with finite $\varprojlim$ and some exponentials. We may change the 'doctrine' whenever need arises. Notice that from a logical point of view such a ringed category is the invariant formulation of a theory of rings, although in a language with a highly unorthodox choice of logical connectives: $=, \wedge, \top$ are allowed as well as some higher order operations, but $\neg$ and $\exists$ are excluded. (Of course, this is the approach taken in the papers referred to in §3.)

I would like to point out a few consequences of this approach. Since no 'doctrine' is chosen once and for all to formalize all notions and constructions under study, 'structures' become relativized, since a given notion may live in several doctrines and hence have different 'structures'. As an example, a real vector bundle over a topological space X in (the category of) sets is the same as a free module over the ring C_X of germs of continuous functions in the topos of sheaves over X. We can say that 'structure + logic (of the doctrine)' is the absolute notion rather than 'structure' alone. Another consequence of this approach is the fact that usually 'constructive' versions of classical notions and 'constructive' proofs appear automatically as subproducts (since the 'doctrines' are usually very poor in logical means). From the point of view of this approach, the prop of these 'constructive' notions and proofs is not the idealistic longing for 'secure' results, but rather the more down to earth wish of 'proving more with less'.

In this context I would like to mention the work of Joyal on Constructive Algebra. Unfortunely, only fragments have been published [3].

As a last consequence of this approach, let me mention that new posibilities for proving theorems become now available. In fact, we can either prove diectly the theorem in the (weakest) 'doctrine' where it can be formulated, or we can change 'doctrines', proving it in another one and then 'coming back'. In the first case we can either use the (usually cumbersome) method of showing commutativity of diagrams or, more efficiently, use the logic of the doctrine by giving a syntactical proof and then interpreting the result in the doctrine. Alternatively, we can use the Kripke–Joyal semantics which allows us to work with generalized 'points' and use set-theoretical intuitions. (An example of this method to show the existence of the associated sheaf may be found in [23]). In the second case, we may embed the doctrine in a richer one in such a way that the logical structure of the doctrine is preserved and that the embedding is conservative (thus the richer 'doctrine' acts as an 'ideal' extension of the first one). Particularly useful are embedding of this type in the 'doctrine' of set theory, since all the resources of the category of sets are available for the proof. Several such embeddings are known (cf. [15]). Other possibility is to embed the category (doctrine) in question into a 'classifying topos' for the theory of which the category is the invariant formulation. This is a universe of 'variable sets' which contains a 'generic' model for the theory. Sometimes this 'generic' model has 'specific' properties in the full intuitionistic logic of the topos and these properties may simplify the proof of the original theorem (see e.g. [9] and [18]). This method may simplify classical proofs by using intuitionistic logic! Finally, a combination of these methods may be used. As an example (Cf. [16] and [17]), suppose that we want to prove Swan's theorem on real vector bundles over a compact topological space X. (The exact statement matters little.) Using our remark above, this reduces to a theorem about C_X-modules in the topos of sheaves over X. The 'structure' has been simplified, but at the expense of the 'logic' (which is now intuitionistic). However the statement of the new theorem (to be proved) is seen to be formalizable in the weaker doctrine of coherent categories for which embedding theorems in doctrines of sets are known. This shows that it is enough to prove the theorem in sets, but there is happens to be a well-known theorem of Kaplansky. We are done!

By way of conclusion, let me state the personal opinion that work on 'foundations' has been concentrated for too long on the field of Analysis and the dialectical contradiction of 'constructive' versus 'non-constructive'. It seems to me that it is high time to look for 'foundational' fields elsewhere and Algebraic Geometry with a much richer dialectics seems as good a choice as any. And who knows, it may even be the Ariadna's thread of the 'labyrinth of the continuum' ....

NOTE

* Research partially supported by a grant from the National Research Council of Canada.

BIBLIOGRAPHY

[1] Gray, J. W., 'Fragments of the History of Sheaf Theory', in *Applications of Sheaves* (Proceedings, Durham 1977), Lecture Notes in Mathematics No. 753, Springer-Verlag 1979, pp. 1–79.

[2] Higgs, D., 'A Category Approach to Boolean Valued Set Theory', preprint, 1973.

[3] Joyal, A., 'Les théorèmes de Chevalley-Tarski et remarques sur l'Algèbre constructive', *Cahiers de Topo et Géom. Diff.* **XVI** (3) (1975), 256–258.

[4] Johnstone, P. T., *Topos Theory*, Academic Press, 1977.

[5] Kline, M., *Mathematical Thought from Ancient to Modern Times*, Oxford Univ. Press, 1972.

[6] Kock, A., 'A Simple Axiomatics for Differentiation', *Math. Scand.* **40** (1977), 183–193.

[7] Kock, A., 'Taylor Series Calculus for Ring Objects of Line Type', *J. Pure Appl. Algebra* 12 (1978), 271–293.

[8] Kock, A., *Proprietá dell' anello generico*, Notes by Anna Barbara Veit Riccioli, Aarhus, 1977.

[9] Kock, A., 'Universal Projective Geometry Via Topos Theory', *J. Pure Appl. Algebra* 9 (1976), 1–24.

[10] Kock, A. and Reyes, G. E., 'Doctrines in Categorical Logic', in *Handbook of Mathematical Logic*, North-Holland, Amsterdam 1977, pp. 283–313.

[11] Kock, A. and Reyes, G. E., 'Manifolds in Formal Differential Geometry', in *Applications of Sheaves* (Proceedings, Durham 1977), Lecture Notes in Mathematics No. 753, Springer-Verlag 1979, pp. 514–533.

[12] Kock, A. and Reyes G. E., 'Connections in Formal Differential Geometry', in *Topos Theoretic Methods in Geometry*, Aarhus Various Publications Series No. 30, 1979, pp. 158–195

[13] Lawvere, F. W., 'An Elementary Theory of the Category of Sets', *Proc. Nat. Acad. Sci. U.S.A.* 52 (1964), 1506–1511.

[14] MacLane, S., *Categories for the Working Mathematician*, Springer-Verlag, Heidelberg, 1971.

[15] Makkai, M. and Reyes, G. E., *First Order Categorical Logic*, Lecture Notes in Mathematics, No. 611, Springer-Verlag, Heidelberg, 1977.

[16] Mulvey, C. J., 'Intuitionistic Algebra and Representation of Rings', in *Recent Advances in the Representation Theory of Rings and C*-Algebras by Continuous Sections*, Mem. Am. Math. Soc., No. 148, 1974.

[17] Reyes, G. E., 'Théorie des modèles et fais ceaux', *Advances in Math.* **30**, No. 2 (1978), 156–170.

[18] Reyes, G. E., 'Cramer's Rule in The Zariski Topos', in *Applications of Sheaves* (Proceedings, Durham 1977), Lecture Notes in Mathematics No. 753, Springer-Verlag 1979, pp. 586–594.

[19] Reyes, G. E. and Wraith, G. C., 'A Note on Tangent Bundles in a Category, with a Ring Object', *Math. Scand.* **42** (1978), 53–63.

[20] Robinson, A., *Non-Standard Analysis*, North-Holland, Amsterdam, 1966.

[21] Shafarevich, I. R., *Basic Algebraic Geometry*, Springer-Verlag, Heidelberg, 1974.

[22] Szabo, M. E., *Algebra of Proofs*, North-Holland, Amsterdam, 1977.

[23] Veit–Riccioli, A. B., 'Il forcing come principio logico per la construzione dei fasci', preprint, 1977.

[24] Wraith, G. C., 'Lectures on Elementary Topoi', in *Model Theory and Topoi*, Lecture Notes in Mathematics No. 445, Springer-Verlag, Heidelberg, 1975, pp. 114–206.

Added in Proof. Since the writing up of this paper, E. Dubric has built models for Kock's axiom as well as other axioms introduced in [11], which comprise 'classical' differential manifolds. For these developments see the book quoted in [12] as well as

[25] Reyes, G. E. (Editor), *Géometrie Différentielle Synthétique*, Fasciarles 1, 2, Rapport de Recherches du DMS Nos. 80–11, 80–12, Université de Montréal, 1980.

PART 4

THE RELEVANCE OF LOGIC TO OTHER SCIENTIFIC DISCIPLINES

EVANDRO AGAZZI

LOGIC AND THE METHODOLOGY OF EMPIRICAL SCIENCES

1. PRELIMINARY

For some time, one of the most typical (and emphasized) characteristics of 'modern' logic was that of qualifying as 'scientific', in contradistinction to traditional logic, which was meant to be simply 'philosophical'. We shall not be interested in analysing the hidden meaning underlying that distinction, which surely expressed, at an initial stage, a kind of mistrust of traditional logic: those times – which go back to the early stages of logical positivism – are quite far away by now, and a number of distinguished scholars openly declare themselves concerned with problems of 'philosophical logic'. What might still be worth remembering are rather the reasons why modern logic claimed to be 'scientific', and these are essentially twofold. On the one hand, the characteristic of scientificity appeared to be bound to the fact that the new logic had adopted the configuration of a respectable mathematical discipline, including the feature of having been explicitly axiomatized. On the other hand, its appurtenance to the family of sciences was evidenced by the fact that its aim was assumed to be, among others, that of providing an exact (and also practical) analysis of the processes of correct reasoning and rigorous argumentation actually employed or ideally to be adopted in scientific investigation and theory building. It is, obviously, this second aspect that made modern logic relevant to the methodology of science, with particular emphasis upon the methodology of formal sciences, i.e., mathematics. This close interconnection of logic with the problems of methodology and foundations of mathematics developed to such an extent that in the eyes of many people modern logic still appears as essentially identified with that task, but this fact should not prevent a careful observer from recognizing that a quite analogous task, with respect to the empirical sciences, had been attributed to modern logic (at least prospectively) from the early moments of its development in our century.

To clear up this point, it would be sufficient to recall that in his famous address to the International Congress of Mathematicians at Paris in 1900, titled *Mathematical Problems*, Hilbert explicitly indicated the following as one of the most significant problems that were to be faced by mathematicians in the then-beginning century: "A mathematical treatment for the axioms of

E. Agazzi (ed.), Modern Logic – A Survey, 255–282.

Physics."[1] In the presentation of this problem, he remarks that such a mathematical axiomatization is of paramount interest for every rigorous discipline and he suggests that, at least for such physical disciplines as mechanics and the probability calculus, times were already ripe for that kind of treatment, on analogy with what had already happened with geometry. Several years later, in an equally well-known paper on *Axiomatic Thinking*,[2] Hilbert starts from the consideration that logical and conceptual order lead by necessity to the axiomatic organization of a discipline. The accepted axioms, however, can usually undergo a deeper scrutiny, which enables one to reach more fundamental notions and assumptions that lie at the basis of the science concerned. All this amounts to a 'laying of the foundations' (*Tieferlegung der Fundamente*) of a science, especially as it allows one to formulate and handle such important problems as those of consistency and independence of the axioms (i.e., of the notions and of the basic principles accepted in a discipline).

These considerations are common to all kinds of sufficiently rigorous sciences, but Hilbert also adds something which is specific for the empirical sciences when he stresses that, in their case, the axiomatic treatment facilitates (beside the handling of these 'internal' features) also the important task of investigating the compatibility of a newly proposed theory with the already established and accepted ones. In conclusion, he expresses the view that

> Everything, that may be an object of consideration for the scientific thinking in general, undergoes as soon as it is mature for the construction of a theory, the competence of the axiomatic method and thereby of mathematics.[3]

In this way, axiomatization is being proposed as a kind of general paradigm of scientificity as such and, if one remembers that the specific kind of axiomatization Hilbert had in mind was a strict formalistic one, in which mathematical logic played a decisive role, one can easily see how formidable a task was being proposed for modern logic in the field of the methodology of empirical and non-empirical sciences.

As a matter of fact, the line of research that Hilbert was then sponsoring found significant applications in several domains of the empirical sciences and became somehow typical of the 'foundational' way of thinking, especially in physics. One surely need not recall the elaborate axiomatization of quantum mechanics provided by von Neumann[4], followed by other axiomatizations in more recent times, or to remember the axiomatic systems built up for different branches of physics by several authors: we shall not mention these researches, as another paper in this meeting is explicitly devoted to the foundations of physics. One might also remember that not only physics, but also biology, for instance, was axiomatized as early as 1937 in a well-known work by Joseph Woodger[5]. The reason why we do not intend to follow here the development of this trend is that the role of logic appears to be perhaps more directly perceivable along another path, which originated more or less inside the same intellectual atmosphere we have been considering thus far, but followed a course of development rather distinct from the axiomatization trend. This other line is that which considers logic as a 'tool for the analysis' of empirical theories, with special attention paid to the methodological problems that are posed by their construction and, especially, by their justification, testing, application, evolution, comparison and the like. In recent times, new stress has been laid upon these kinds of problems, which appear to hold at least as much interest as the traditional 'foundational' ones. It seems therefore reasonable to investigate in some detail the import of logic for these kinds of methodological issues in the field of empirical sciences.

2. EARLY NEOPOSITIVISM AND THE WORK OF CARNAP

It is easily recognized that employment of formal logic with the goal of clarifying the structure and methods of the scientific disciplines was completely within the spirit of the early neopositivistic movement, as a consequence of the basic components of its philosophical program. In fact, the victory against metaphysics was supposed to be possible by means of a careful application of mathematical logic to its statements, which would provide the evidence of their being either meaningless or logically incorrect. Beside this *pars destruens* the logical positivists envisaged a *pars construens* that was to consist in the promotion of a 'scientific worldview' (to put it in the words of the famous manifesto [6] of the Vienna Circle). This was thought to be possible along two different (though interconnected) pathways: (a) an effort at making more direct and efficient the impact of the actual results and discoveries of contemporary science on the shaping of the current and philosophical world pictures; (b) a careful and detailed examination of the cognitive structure of science, which should facilitate the proposal of a kind of generalized scientific pattern of knowledge to be applied in all fields which aim at genuine theoretical investigation. While the first path was somehow more typical of the Berlin branch of the neopositivistic movement (think, e.g., simply of the works devoted by H. Reichenbach to *Relativity Theory, Quantum Mechanics and Probability Theory*), the second rather characterized the researches of the representatives of the Vienna Circle, especially when they became involved in the disputes resulting from their original proposal to identify meaning with verification. As is well known, this proposal, expressed by the so-called 'verification principle', which was devised to discard metaphysical sentences as meaningless, turned out to discredit many genuine scientific sentences as well. The program of safeguarding the 'principle of empiricism', which had suggested the verification principle, together with some weakening of the latter which would allow all scientific sentences to be regarded as meaningful, necessarily led to a detailed analysis of the structure of the language of empirical scientific theories. In the philosophical debate about this issue, several members of the Circle (and also other scholars outside it) took part, but one can say that by far the most relevant work, as far as the actual application of *logical* tools is concerned, was performed by R. Carnap who, in this way, produced some of the most important results in the technical logical analysis of empirical theories.

As a matter of fact, Carnap's conspicuous effort to provide a more liberalized version of the verification principle led him to write *Testability and Meaning*[7], which, on the one hand, has remained a classic in the history of contemporary empiricism, representing the moment in which the more flexible criterion of 'confirmability' (wich is less strict not only than 'verifiability', but also than 'testability') was proposed as a prerequisite for meaningfulness. On the other hand, this essay is of special importance because, in order to define with the necessary exactness the notion of confirmation, distinguishing it from those of verification and testing, Carnap explicitly develops a 'logical analysis of confirmation and testing' that makes an 'empirical analysis of confirmation and testing' possible. This leads to a fully linguistic treatment of the problem, which clarifies through a number of formal logical theorems the exact syntactical features of the language that would correspond to different kinds of methodological requirements. Thus not only such well-known devices as 'reduction sentences' and 'introductive chains' for the insertion of new concepts in a theory make their first systematic appearance in this way, together with the demonstration that explicit definitions are insufficient for introducing a number of concepts in scientific disciplines, but a clear map is traced of the different kinds of languages which are admissible to formulate a theory and of the connections between features of these languages and the requirements of complete testability, complete confirmability, testability, and confirmability. In this way, e.g., one learns that complete confirmability would require a theory to be limited to molecular sentences and is therefore still too severe a requirement to be demanded in actual science.

The discourse of *Testability and Meaning* is an essentially syntactic one, even if it contains such important methodological results as the essential ineliminability of theoretical terms, by means of explicit definitions, in favor of the observational terms. The instruments provided are, however, insufficient to express how an empirical theory can handle its intended empirical objects. Such tools were basically introduced by Carnap himself a few years later in his *Introduction to Semantics*[8], in whose Preface he declares: "I believe semantics will be of great importance for the so-called theory of knowledge and the methodology of mathematics and of empirical science" (p. viii). In fact, by distinguishing between 'pure' and 'descriptive' syntax and semantics (§ 5), he provides the conceptual basis for the use of logic in the methodology of the *single* sciences, under the form, actually, of some 'descriptive' syntax and semantics, which are lucidly conceived as 'empirical' investigations: "Descriptive semantics describe facts; it is empirical science (p. 11) ... descriptive syntax is an empirical investigation of the syntactical features of given languages" (p. 12). A quite valuable remark, which seems to have been somehow neglected by many of the followers of the Carnapian line, is that, whereas 'pure' syntax and semantics are independent of pragmatics, their 'descriptive' counterparts do depend on it or even belong to it: "In this way, descriptive semantics and syntax are, strictly speaking, parts of pragmatics" (p. 13).

We are not going to mention here the terminological and technical instruments for semantics which were first introduced, or at least systematized, in this book, as well as the thematic development of the distinction between logical and descriptive signs to be found there: all that has become an integral part of current knowledge in basic mathematical logic. We simply stress that, thanks to this construction, a solid bridge appeared to be erected between the syntax of a language and the world of objects about which it was intended to speak and this provided the link for employing the sophisticated tools of formal logic in the methodology of actual sciences: "These concepts of different kinds of interpretations are useful for the logical analysis of science; for what is usually called the construction of a model for a set of postulates is the same as the semantical interpretation of a calculus" (p. 202).

The last quoted statement is typical of Carnap's approach to logic and explains why he could play so important a role in the methodological analysis of science: the fact is that he always had a special taste for 'applied logic' and this is significantly expressed also in the title of his book, *Introduction to Symbolic Logic and its Applications*[9], which, as a matter of fact, is devoted in its Part Two to applications. Some languages suitable to applications (like thing languages and coordinate languages) are presented there and it is shown how they apply to quantitative concepts. After a sketchy description of the axiomatic method, several axiomatic systems for particular sciences are exemplified (set theory, natural numbers, real numbers, topology, projective, affine and metric geometry, physical space-time topology according to different systems, biology at various levels), while abundant reference is made to several existing axiomatizations and formalizations of scientific theories. From this point of view, one must say that this book somehow integrates the two lines we have mentioned at the beginning: the 'foundational' one, focused on axiomatizations, and the 'methodological' one, based on the application of logical tools, and it still remains one of the quite few textbooks of mathematical logic which contain a significant part devoted to applications.

One would be right, of course, to remark that Carnap's contributions to applied logic abundantly surpass the few examples in this book: let us only think of his books on the foundations of probability, on inductive logic, on the philosophy of physics; but it will be the task of other papers in this meeting to mention them. We shall rather recall another paper by Carnap, *Meaning Postulates*[10], in which he faces the important problem of how to qualify inside a language the meaning of its descriptive terms: this problem is, of course, of special importance when one has to specify, e.g., the intended reference of at least some terms in the axiomatization of an empirical theory.

It will be only fair to stress, at this point, the obvious fact that, by devoting so much attention to Carnap's contributions, we do not mean to credit him alone with all the conceptual and technical innovations mentioned. It is Carnap himself, by the way, who frequently and honestly acknowledges how much he is indebted, e.g., to Popper's stimulating criticisms for his evolution from the verifiability to the confirmability theory of meaning, or to Tarski's work in his conversion to a full appreciation of the peculiar role and features of semantics (to limit ourselves only to two outstanding examples). Still it remains true that only after being assimilated and reformulated by Carnap were Popper's criticisms (which were of general philosophical and methodological character, without any formal apparatus) and Tarski's construction (which was formal, but rather abstract and more suited to mathematical theories) able to receive the form of tools ready for effective application to the methodology of empirical theories.

After having laid down, in a general way, the conceptual framework of the problematic we intended to discuss in this paper, we are now going to examine in some detail a few characteristic topics of it that have received more direct attention in recent times.

3. THE PROBLEM OF THEORETICAL CONCEPTS

Since the original researches by Carnap, this problem has never ceased to be central in the discussions of modern philosophy of science, especially in that trend of it which expressed the views of analytic philosophy and of the empiricist line of thought. By and large, one can say that it somehow splits into three subproblems, concerning the possibility of drawning, in a theory, a clear-cut distinction between: observational and theoretical terms, analytic and synthetic sentences, meaningful and meaningless statements. It is not necessary to recall here how the need to avoid criteria which would be at the same time 'too narrow' and 'too loose' gradually led to an attenuation of the original empiricist orthodoxy and eventually to an admission of the impossibility of such clear-cut distinctions. In particular, the question of meaningfulness was recognized to concern whole theories rather than isolated terms or sentences. Some papers by Hempel[11], Carnap[12], and Sellars[13] represent the well-known stages of this development, a general account of which can be found, e.g., in a couple of survey papers by Hempel[14].

All these investigations may truly be considered as 'classical' and to constitute a significant chapter in the history of contemporary philosophy, but perhaps because of this very fact, the problem they had been concerned with seemed to have been somehow exhausted some ten or fifteen years ago. That impression was, however, a quite transitory one and, as a matter of fact, this problem has shown an unexpected new vitality in recent years, owing to two factors: the first is that it has been reconsidered within philosophical views which are rather and even radically different from the analytic-empiricist views of the tradition; the second is that a considerable number of new logical tools have been carried into its discussion. The specific nature of this paper does not allow us to pay attention to the first of the two mentioned factors. Hence we shall not follow the process which has, e.g., highlighted the shortcomings of the 'partial interpretation' theory in establishing a rigorous semantical criterion for dividing scientific concepts into theoretical and observational.[15] Nor shall we examine how the dependence of the meaning of theoretical terms on theories, rather than on their relation to observational terms, has been stressed.[16] Nor shall we look at criteria that have been proposed for considering theoretical statements as factually true in the full sense,[17] not to mention some extensive vindications of scientific realism which originated within philosophy of science and developed into full-fledged philosophical theories.[18] We shall, instead, lay some stress on the fact that what distinguishes the new approaches to the problem of theoretical concepts is the substantial employment of technical logical tools. This does not imply that the 'classical' authors were unaware of these tools, or of the relevance of some results in mathematical logic to the problems they were investigating – indeed, they used to mention and discuss such results – but they did not employ them in their discourse which remained therefore essentially philosophical rather than technical in its style. This can be easily perceived, e.g., if one compares the extensive and by no means superficial, but still non-formal, discussion of Craig's and Ramsey's elimination techniques for theoretical terms in the last sections of Hempel's paper *The Theoretician's Dilemma* (which is carried on in the form of a philosophical discussion of the theoretical implications and relevance of those results) with the wide technical exploitation of Craig's interpolation theorem,[19] together with Hintikka's theory of distributive normal forms[20] and of Ramsey's proof-theoretic and model-theoretic elimination theory,[21] found in the important book recently devoted to theoretical concepts by Tuomela[22]. But this is, of course, no exclusive feature of this book, nor does it depend on its author being a 'scientific realist', for an equally detailed attention to the implications of Craig's and Ramsey's results on the methodological issues of empirical sciences can be found, e.g., in an instrumentalistically inspired author like Cornman,[23] or in scholars more in line with the traditional Carnapian line, like Stegmüller,[24] Essler,[25] or Rozeboom.[26] In other words, this increased attention paid to the results and techniques of mathematical logic does not express (what is after all quite natural) a reorientation in the philosophical attitude towards these problems, but rather a new style in the methodology of the discussion, which allows old and recent philosophical approaches to come to a confrontation on the basis of a richer, more rigorous and more sophisticated set of arguments.

Another aspect in which the most recent researches appear to have reaped substantial benefits from a closer interplay with logic is in the theory of definition. As a matter of fact, the problem of theoretical concepts was approached from the outset as a problem of how to provide some kind of 'definition' of them in terms of observational concepts, and it is therefore a little astonishing that only in recent years have modern results in the logical theory of definition been adequately taken into account. Actually, it is only with the books of Przelecki[27] and Essler[28] that a detailed reference to the theory of definition has been presented as a general background for discussing problems in the methodology of the empirical sciences along semantic lines of analysis. In the aforementioned book by Tuomela[29], an analogous theme is investigated along different lines, which are rather of a syntactical character, having to do with the extensional interconnections of the primitive concepts of a theory in virtue of the logical form of the sentences of the theory itself. Many interesting results are presented there, partly based upon previous work by Tuomela himself and by Hintikka[30], and partly on some purely logical investigations, such as those of Kueker[31]. Speaking of the Tuomela book, one should also say that in its last two chapters one can see what impressive strides can be made toward an improved understanding of the methodological role of theoretical concepts in virtue of a deeper appreciation of the logical features of deductive explanation and inductive systematization.[32]

The mention of inductive systematization calls to mind the role that inductive logic (besides the more traditional deductive logic) is now playing in these methodological issues. Although inductive logic is the specific topic of another paper in this conference, it may be appropriate to remember that it has some interesting connections with a classical problem in the field we are concerned with here, i.e., the problem of the introduction of 'dispositional predicates', as discussed, e.g., in a book by Essler[33]. All this indicates not only that philosophical analyses can receive significant help from the adoption of logical techniques, but also that new perspectives may thereby be obtained on 'technical' questions that might have been too hastily conceived of as 'closed'. A typical case of this kind is the theory of reduction sentences, which goes back, as we have seen, to some early Carnap papers, but which has been the subject of recent investigations, e.g., by Traff[34] and Essler[35].

In concluding this section, we shall point out that the problem of theoretical concepts has recently been approached in a completely new light in a very important book by J. Sneed[36]. The main feature of this book is that the traditional observational-theoretical dichotomy, which was conceived as a kind of 'absolute' epistemic distinction, is consciously ignored in the logical analysis of physical theories, being replaced by a distinction between *T*-theoretical and *T*-non-theoretical terms, which is only a 'relative' one, in the sense of being relativized to any particular theory *T* under consideration. The criterion for distinguishing between these two classes of terms is (roughly speaking) the following: a concept is *T*-theoretical if its application always presupposes some kind of validity of *T*, while it is *T*-non-theoretical if at least in some cases its application does not presuppose the validity of *T*. In some simplified way, we could say that *T*-non-theoretical terms offer the basis for 'testing' the theory *T*, while *T*-theoretical ones play a role in systematizations, explanations and predictions.[37]

Problems connected with the possibility of concretely applying the said criterion led Sneed to face the question of the eliminability of theoretical terms and here too he has original solutions. Starting from his proposal of axiomatizing physical theories by means of a set-theoretic predicate (rather than by means of sentences of a first-order calculus), he can introduce a powerful generalization of Ramsey's method, whose most important feature is that the existential quantifier in the usual Ramsey sentence for a theory ranges over variables for models of the theory. These models need to be somehow made more precise and this is done by taking into account three characteristics of the empirical content of a theory: multiplicity of its applications, 'constraints' corresponding to conditions expressing interrelations among these applications, and 'special laws' associated with some particular constraints (as distinct from the 'general laws' formulated as defining conditions of the set-theoretic predicate which characterizes the theory). All this leads to a quite complex existentially quantified sentence which, besides playing the role of a Ramsey sentence, provides much more information about the empirical models the theory admits. It is not possible to give here more than this very general idea about Sneed's work, whose technical complexity is on the one hand an indispensable condition for an adequate understanding of the novelty and of the soundness of the proposed views, but makes on the other hand an informal account quite insufficient. If one considers, however, the concrete applications of the perspectives that Sneed brings to classical particle mechanics in Chapter VI and to comparisons between Newtonian, Lagrangian, and Hamiltonian mechanics in Chapter VII, one could become persuaded that general philosophy of science, when developed with exactness and rigor, can be relevant to a better understanding of concrete scientific theories, besides having an intellectual value in itself. We shall have the opportunity of referring again to Sneed's book later on in this paper for some other questions. Let us now mention that not all points in this book are equally clear, convincing and uncontroversial; the author himself has contributed to a clarification and reformulation of some of them in subsequent papers, but a particularly significant discussion, clarification and development of Sneedian perspectives has been advanced by Stegmüller[38], whose contributions on several questions are so original that the corresponding positions are by now correctly labelled as the 'Sneed-Stegmüller conception'.

4. THE SEMANTICS OF EMPIRICAL THEORIES

An obvious assumption, which holds as a tacit presupposition in all the discussions surveyed thus far, is that empirical theories, in contradistinction to formal ones, speak 'about' some domain of objects and aim at being somehow 'true' of them: it is quite clear, e.g., that the problem of theoretical concepts may be considered, in a broad sense, as that of making clear how far these concepts are necessary or dispensable in order for a theory to fulfill those tasks. On the other hand, it is also clear that such a presupposition need not remain tacit and unexplored. On the contrary, one can expect a number of useful results to come from analysing *how* a theory does actuallly speak about its objects, that is to say, from an explicit investigation of the semantics of empirical theories. This problem was, of course, not completely overlooked in the traditional methodological investigations and it has led, in particular, to the original Carnapian approach, in which a theory was conceived of as an uninterpreted logical calculus, to which some possible interpretation could be provided by means of meaning postulates or correspondence rules. But the analytic work turned out to concentrate on syntactic, rather than on semantic issues. In more recent times, however, a new line of research has been developing in which the preceding analytic work has been preserved, but supplemented by a detailed semantical analysis that has made systematic use of tools and results from model theory. In other words, the domain of objects about which an empirical theory purports to speak has been considered as one of the possible 'models' of the calculus formalizing the theory, and the central problem has appeared to be that of characterizing (among the infinity of such possible models) the specific 'intended model' of the theory. This problem is in turn strictly connected with (and actually presupposes) the possibility of assigning well-defined interpretations to the descriptive constants of the language used for formalizing the theory, and it is here that most of the novelties come out. As a matter of fact, the intuitive view, according to which the observational terms can receive in an immediate way their unambiguous interpretation, from which a 'partial interpretation' for the theoretical terms can be obtained, turned out to be so oversimplified as to be altogether untenable. This appeared as a consequence not only of the known difficulties in establishing a clear-cut dichotomy between observational and theoretical terms, but also of intrinsic difficulties with the various methods for assigning an interpretation to terms, even if such a dichotomy could be taken for granted. The consequence appeared to be that one has to accept an ineliminable measure of 'semantic ambiguity' in the interpretation of practically all the terms of an empirical theory, and this inevitably led to the consequence that the sentences of an empirical theory can only turn out to be partially or 'approximately' true of their objects. The features we have been briefly summarizing here have been pointed out through extensive use of model-theoretic notions and results, as well as through results in the logical theory of definition and through a formal analysis of actual concept formation in the exact sciences (which involves, among other things, taking into account measurement procedures and the expression of their results in the form of mathematical functions). M. Przełęcki and R. Wójcicki have done perhaps the most systematic work in this direction,[39] but important contributions have come also from other sides.[40]

Almost if not all of the researches just mentioned in the semantics of empirical theories were inscribed in a general framework characterized by two essential features: the adoption of a basically empiricist ontology (often recognizable under the form of the 'partial interpretation' theory for theoretical terms) and a reliance on extensional semantic techniques which is typical of model theory. It was therefore to be expected that some new approaches would appear if one or both of these two presuppositions were dropped.

This is actually the case, e.g., with the aforementioned book by Tuomela, which develops a thorough criticism of the empiricist viewpoint, and presents an alternative view based on the acceptance of a scientific realism that he shares in common with, among others, Bunge.[41] This alternative gives rise to a 'holistic thesis' concerning the meaning of extralogical terms in a scientific theory, which makes them depend (in a sense which is properly specified) on the whole logical, mathematical and axiomatic structure of the theory, and offers several technical and methodological advantages.[42] As for the replacement of the extensional viewpoint with a more effective intensional one, an indication has been given, e.g., in a paper by Agazzi[43] which advocates the introduction of meanings for 'basic predicates' by means of operational definitions, that, working as 'criteria' for the indefinitely open applicability of predicates, do not presuppose the existence of domains or subdomains of objects on which descriptive constants should extensionally be interpreted. One of the main features of this intensional approach is that, by explicitly pointing out the pragmatic component (i.e., the operations) included in the reference of some basic concepts, it provides a tool for eliminating the semantic ambiguity typical of the extensional approach. In particular, it turns out to be possible, according to this perspective, to assign to a theory its 'intended model', which is a practically unsolvable problem inside extensional semantics, as can be seen, e.g., from the intelligent but scarcely successful efforts at overcoming this difficulty in the first part of the last chapter of the aforementioned book by Sneed.[44]

When speaking of 'approximate truth', it is natural to think of the well-known Popperian thesis, according to which scientific theories, though being in themselves almost inevitably false, replace one another in a process of progressive approximation to truth, new theories being more 'verisimilar' or 'closer to truth' than their predecessors. One must say, however, that such an association has no intrinsic justification, for the 'approximate truth' of which we have spoken before has primarily to do with the *semantic* indeterminacy of the concepts involved in sentences, while the Popperian concept of verisimilitude is an *epistemic* or even a *methodological* one, having to do with critera for coming closer to a hypothetical objectively existent realm of scientific truth. This does not imply, on the other hand, that the notion of verisimilitude is unable to undergo a rigorous formal explication. As a matter of fact, Popper himself outlined one such[45] in terms of logical consequence and in terms of logical probability. These attempts were shown to be defective by Tichy, who was also able to propose a satisfactory formal redefinition of verismilitude, along a line which seems worthy of further deepening in the direction of a general characterization of concepts like those of degrees of truth and of comparability of the truth content of theories.[46]

5. SPECIAL LOGICS

So far, we have been tacitly understanding by 'logic' only the standard classical logic. As a matter of fact, if one looks at the actual applications of logic to the methodology of empirical theories, one must recognize this to be by far the most frequent case. Some important exceptions must however be considered which are, loosely speaking, the consequence of an affirmative response to the following question: if a particular domain of inquiry shows such peculiar features that they are hardly expressible or explainable by adhering faithfully to the received logical patterns, should we not try to modify those patterns, or to introduce new ones, in order to accommodate them to our domain of investigation? As is well known, a problem of this kind was one of the basic reasons that led Lukasiewicz to introduce many-valued logics in an explicit and formal way and, in particular, the very same exigency led Birkhoff and von Neumann to propose a special logic for quantum mechanics as early as 1936.[47] Both fields have known an impressive development since then and we are not going to add any word about them, as they lie completely within the scope of other papers in this conference. But in more recent years some new theories have been proposed that are of interest in view of some problems mentioned in the section devoted to the semantics of empirical theories: as was noted there, a drawback which is characteristic of the combined extensionalist and empiricist semantics for these theories is the 'vagueness' or 'ambiguity' in the denotation of concepts, seemingly in violation of the requirements of an 'exact science' and making the application of traditional logical tools somehow problematic. It happens, however, that much attention has been recently devoted to the treatment of this kind of problem, i.e., so to speak, to the question of how to get an exact science out of inexact concepts. This question is, by the way, a quite general one, as ordinary discourse is full of such concepts (like 'long', 'short', 'bald', etc.), the use of which has been known to give rise to paradoxes since antiquity. Contemporary solutions of these paradoxes have been proposed by providing a suitable semantic interpretation of these concepts, upon which a plausible syntax can be based. The proposed semantics uses so-called 'fuzzy sets', an expression under which it has become customary to designate sets which are not sharply defined in the following sense: for any usual set X and any given object x, it is determinate whether $x \in X$ or $x \notin X$. This is no longer a requirement for 'fuzzy sets'. That is to say, between a truth value (say 1) corresponding to the situation $x \in X$ and a truth value (say 0) corresponding to the situation $x \notin X$, a whole spectrum of intermediate truth values is admitted, which correspond to different degrees in the determinacy of X and, consequently, to different degrees in the truth assignments to sentences of the kind $P(x)$, P being the predicate denoting X. Without going into details, it is already apparent from the above (and it can be shown by a technical presentation) that some significant analogies are involved here with the techniques of Boolean-valued sets and with topics in category theory. Other analogies, which seem intuitively immediate, are instead rather superficial. Such is, e.g., the analogy with probability theory, which may be suggested by the presence of truth functions with values in the 0–1 interval. But the difference in 'spirit' is, so to speak, rather clear, since the purpose in the present case is to handle vagueness, ambiguity and ambivalence, rather than to handle likelihood, and this fact has its due consequences also on the technical plane. Something similar must be repeated for analogies with many-valued logics: it is true, on the one hand, that the theory of fuzzy sets yields a multi-valued logic, but it is also true, on the other hand, that this differs substantially from customary many-valued logics in its operations. If one really wants to find a close affinity, this would be found in intuitionistic logic, formalized by a complete Brouwersche lattice.

Anyway, we are not going to pay any more attention to this theory, whose main applications lie elsewhere (e.g., in the theory of pattern recognition) and which has an interest of its own as an area of pure mathematical investigation. Its applications to the logic of empirical theories seems to us, at least up to now, still of a limited scope. We shall therefore simply mention a few other peculiar features, in addition to the already sketched ones. As a consequence of the fact that truth-values can themselves be defined as fuzzy subsets of the unit interval 0–1, it follows that the truth-value set is not closed under the usual sentential operations. This means that, besides having fuzzy truth-values (corresponding to expressions of the ordinary language like 'true', 'very true', 'rather true', 'not true', 'false', 'not completely true' and 'not completely false', etc.), we also have imprecisely defined truth-tables. These semantical features are reflected in corresponding syntactic peculiarities and, as can be expected, fuzzy premisses also have fuzzy and not uniquely defined consequents. But this is due also to the fact that rules of inference as well have only approximate validity. One consequence is, e.g., that the result of a long chain of only slightly unreliable deductions can turn out to be very unreliable.

But not wanting, for the above reasons, to give a thorough account of this recent trend of research, we prefer to make reference to a couple of significant papers which will provide the reader with a substantial introduction and bibliographical information about this 'logic of inexact concepts' or of 'approximate reasoning'.[48] It must be noted, however, that the usefulness of fuzzy sets in the semantics of empirical theories is far from being generallly accepted, even by authors who believe in the 'vagueness' of extension of empirical concepts. Some of them have tried to elaborate alternative approaches to this problem based upon the traditional model-theoretic semantics.[49]

6. INTER-THEORETIC RELATIONS AND THEORY CHANGE

An important separate chapter in the methodology of empirical sciences has always been represented by problems of inter-theoretic (rather than intra-theoretic) relevance, that is by problems posed by the existence of several theories historically and/or logically capable of showing mutual relationships of different kinds. Among the most relevant of such problems, we could mention the following: what does it mean to say that two theories are identical or equivalent; that one is a subtheory of the other; that one is reducible to the other; that one has been superseded by the other; that one is better than the other; etc. In particular, it is clear from the last mentioned questions that the problems of theory change and of 'progress in science' are directly involved in these issues.

One can say that two positions had essentially dominated the stage until recently. The first has been characteristic of the analytic-empiricist tradition, which considered scientific theories as sets of sentences and was inclined therefore to envisage inter-theoretic relationships from the view point of logical derivability. In such a way, identity or equivalence of theories was considered as formal identity or as the possibility of getting the axioms of one theory as theorems in the other and vice versa; while a theory T was supposed to be a subtheory of another theory T' if it was possible to deduce T from T' but not vice versa. This fact expressed the view that T' was more comprehensive than T and also allowed one to say that T was 'reducible' to T' (with the help of some appropriate boundary conditions). As is intuitively clear, one can express this circumstance by saying that T' must be able to deductively explain everything that was explainable by means of T and something else 'in addition'. In such a way, a criterion was also supplied for justifying theory change and for making the notion of scientific progress precise: when a theory T is found defective for being unable to explain some facts, a new theory T' is to be looked for, with respect to which T has to be reducible in the just mentioned sense and this automatically implies T' to be 'better' than T and that cumulative progress of science be granted. The sketch of the traditional position presented here is very rough and oversimplified, but this view is so well known and easy to find in much more accurate accounts[50] that we do not fear it being misunderstood. On the other hand, we are not going to give it in more detail because, despite the fact of relying so much on the notion of logical deduction, it did not involve many logical techniques in its actual presentation.

The second position, which has some elements in common with the first (in particular, the fact of considering theories as sets of sentences), but differs from it in many respects, is the Popperian doctrine according to which, when theories are 'falsified' by a negative impact with experience, they are condemned as false and superseded by others which do not appear as a kind of extension of them. On the contrary, they are incompatible with them, though being more comprehensive. How this kind of non-cumulative progress is possible is explained by Popper in terms of increasing empirical content and verisimilitude. Having hinted at some formal treatments connected with these notions in a preceding section of this paper, we feel dispensed of the task of giving further details here, while we shall come back to some aspects of the Popperian approach later on.[51]

What has recently led the whole problem of inter-theoretical relationships to be investigated under a new light can perhaps be expressed in a few words by saying that in the traditional identification of such relationships with deducibility links a basic requirement had too hastily been taken for granted. For, in order that a deductive link between T and T' be meaningful, it is necessary that the descriptive vocabulary of T occurs in T' 'essentially and with approximately the same meaning', as was correctly pointed out, e.g., by Nagel.[52] Otherwise, we are confronted with a preliminary problem of 'translation' of the concepts, which could change the status of the question completely. As a matter of fact, this turned out to be actually the case and this is why the well-known positions upheld by Kuhn and Feyerabend (quite apart from more general contexts of discussion and related polemics) have shown a non-extrinsic link with this area of methodological problems: they are among the most typical and sharp claims that concepts are strictly theory-dependent in their meaning and that the previously mentioned 'translation' from one theory to another is hardly, if at all, possible.

The way for the formal treatment of the whole question has been paved in the book by Sneed[53], whose Chapter VII considers the problems of identity, equivalence and reduction between theories. The novelty is that different theories can, in Sneed's account, be considered as equivalent if, although differing in their theoretical superstructures, they have exactly the same empirical (in the sense of non-theoretical) systematizations. As for reduction, the requirement of this partial homogeneity does not even appear (sharply distinguishing it in such a way from any 'subtheory-like' approach). The only condition to be assumed is the possibility of an application from the models of the 'reducing' theory to those of the 'reduced' one.

In order to clarify the details of these proposals, one would have to present the notions of 'core' and 'expanded core' of a theory, with all their technicalities, which certainly lie outside the scope of this paper. The interested reader is referred either to Sneed's book or, for a better presentation, not only from an expository viewpoint but also for some substantial improvements, to an already quoted book by Stegmüller.[54]

A particularly interesting aspect of this Sneed-Stegmüller formulation of the reduction problem is that it yields new prospects also for the problem of theory change, and it is at this point that Kuhnian views come to a direct interplay with this highly formal research and receive a logical reconstruction capable of showing them in a more exact, less controversial and less polemic form. The reason for their coming into play is that, in order to make the notion of 'intended applications of a theory' precise, Sneed needs to refer to a primary subset of 'paradigmatic applications'; he tries in addition to provide an analysis of the Kuhnian idea of scientific revolution. Anyway, it is exactly on this point that Stegmüller especially improved Sneed's original account.[55] To give a brief account of the more salient points of this interpretation, we could say that its intention is that of justifying the fact that, in the presence of some empirical difficulties, a theory can often be modified without being discarded or abandoned. In order to give an exact determination of this intuitive fact, the technical notions of 'structural core' and 'expanded core' of a theory are introduced and the idea is proposed that modification in the different expanded cores of a theory can take place without affecting its structural core and leaving the theory itself, in such a way, constant. But what really leads to a modification of the expanded cores of a theory are their relationships with the 'intended applications' of the same and here, while Sneed takes a somehow platonistic attitude considering them as something given in themselves, Stegmüller tries to identify them by means of the concept of 'availing oneself of a theory'. This has to do with historically determined communities of scientists who, by the fact of adhering to a common 'paradigm' in the Kuhnian sense, accept a structural core K and a certain basic set I_0 of intended applications of a theory. In this sense they 'avail themselves of the same theory', but their positions do differentiate about the problem of which particular expansions could be succesfully introduced with respect to the commonly agreed K and I_0. One of the major consequences of this view is that the Popperian doctrine of the falsification of a theory appears untenable (for falsification can only affect particular 'extensions' of a theory which, as we have seen, do not compromise it). It follows that a theory can be changed only as a whole, by a substitution of paradigm in a sense close to the Kuhnian one, because what characterizes it is, in the last analysis, its 'structural' mathematical core. This leads in particular to the 'incommensurability' of theories, as their concepts are totally dependent in their meaning on the mathematical structure in which they are embedded (the 'structuralist' perspective of Sneed-Stegmüller is therefore a special kind of the already mentioned 'holistic' conceptions of meaning). Nevertheless, such an incommensurability is compatible with a new kind of 'reducibility' and with an evaluation of 'progress', based on the concept of successful performance of theories in terms of explanations, predictions, and systematizations. In this sense, a theory T' could admit among its models the models of T and be more successful because its extended core has successful expansions to which no analogous successful expansions of the extended core of T correspond.

One should not get the impression from the aforesaid that the more 'traditional' views about inter-theoretic relations and theory change have been somehow totally refuted or proven incapable of satisfactory logical analysis by the powerful formal treatment which came to support the more recent and 'revolution-like' approaches. Although nothing comparable to the complexity of the Sneed–Stegmüller elaboration has been put forth to sponsor them, one should not underestimate, e.g., the quite respectable treatment of comparison between theories that has been recently proposed in a paper by Harris[56]. The main idea developed there is to define comparability of two theories, say V and W, with respect to a 'comparison set' of sentences C. The first problem is that of specifying what can be meant by saying that theory W agrees better with set C than does theory V, and this is shown to be possible according to different methods, based on distinct cases in which logical relations of entailment hold between those sets of sentences. One such method appears to qualify as 'fundamental' and the paper proves theorems, discusses criticisms and provides some examples from physics which fit rather well in the proposed approach. The general aim conforms to the Popperian doctrine of verisimilitude, according to the formal amendments of it we already mentioned.

7. THE PROBLEM OF MEASUREMENT

We cannot conclude this paper without at least mentioning a question which has played a central role in the methodology of empirical science for a very long time: the question of measurement. To indicate how early it has concentrated on itself the attention of scientifico-philosophical investigation, it would be sufficient to point out that a celebrated paper by Helmholtz on *Counting and Measuring*, which appeared in 1887, is still considered important and often mentioned in today's literature.[57]

In our century, the importance of a clear understanding of the different issues implied in measurement has been greatly emphasized in the field of quantum mechanics, when the appearance of Heisenberg's indeterminacy relations dramatically posed the problem of the uncontrolled modification induced in a microsystem by the very fact of performing measurements on it. Actually, it would not be exaggerated to say that almost all the philosophical, methodological and logical researches about quantum theory could be grouped together as different chapters of a single investigation to be titled 'the problem of measurement in quantum mechanics'.

A second powerful impulse to the development of measure-theoretical investigation has come from the field of behavioral sciences. As is well known, they have known in our century not only a tremendous development in the sense of the quantitative expansion of their areas, but also an effort toward a better intellectual qualification. In other words, their 'scientific' status or dignity being often questioned, they felt somehow pushed on the one side to defend themselves by stressing some basic analogies with other well-established and recognized sciences; on the other hand, they felt obliged to improve their level of exactness by introducing all possible kinds of measurement and scales in their domains. Psychology, sociology, economics are among the disciplines in which such attempts have been significant. We are not interested here in discussing the reasons why measurement and quantities are considered of such decisive importance to qualify a discipline as a 'science'. Besides some objective reasons (e.g., the fact that general laws of phenomena may turn out to be easier to find out and formulate if their properties can be expressed numerically), others are surely less justified and rather express an intellectual subordination toward the patterns of physical sciences. Anyway, the consequence of all that has been the development of a large amount of research in the field of the most abstract and general theory of measurement, with the goal (at least implicitly) of finding out some pattern of measurement that could prove more useful and significant than the rather unsuccessful methods hitherto adopted.

The first class of problems, being directly connected with quantum mechanics, lies inside the scope of another paper in this conference. The second class, being of a quite general character, is of genuine interest for the methodology of empirical sciences and, as a matter of fact, it has traditionally received due attention both in connection with problems of concept formation and of theory construction. In this sense, most of the genuinely methodological problems connected with measurement have been incorporated in the discussions about observational, operational, theoretical concepts, and about the semantics of empirical theories, which have been surveyed in the previous sections.

What would remain still to be presented are the specific features of the general theory of measurement proper that has received in the last decades a highly formalized treatment. But at this point one has to admit that logic as such does not play a very significant role in these developments which are rather of a genuine and specialized mathematical character: algebra and topology are by far the two disciplines that must be credited with the most significant novelties, approaches and tools which have been recently introduced in the formal treatment of the theory of measurement.

We think it therefore advisable, instead of giving here a rough and inadequate sketch of some characteristic topics of this branch of research, to address the reader to some publications where he can find useful orientations and references.[58]

8. CONCLUSION

From the preceding sections of this paper it appears quite clearly that the methodology of the empirical sciences is an area in which the interplay between logic and philosophy of science is perhaps most direct and significant. This fact, however, must be appreciated in a correct way to avoid possible misunderstandings, and this means, more or less, that one must be aware of the circumstance that logic plays here the typical role of an instrument.

In particular, it should be borne in mind: (a) That the use of logical formalism and tools does not necessarily yield any philosophical superiority: deep philosophical insights have often been expressed with clarity and exactness without any significant contribution of logical formalism, while there are plenty of papers in which the complexity of logical techniques is a poor replacement for the triviality of the underlaying ideas.[59] (b) That also among people who are particularly fond of formalization and technical reasoning there are quite a few who find their tools in branches of mathematics (like set theory or algebra) rather than in logic proper.[60] This is to remind us that formal logic does not exhaust even the domain of formal rigor. (c) That logical analysis and formal development of philosophical perspectives, while providing an extremely valuable clarification of the different issues, are not expected to have the final word in the most serious controversies.[61]

These quite obvious reminders should in particular help one appreciate the kind of survey provided in this paper. Being devoted to the presence of *logic* in the methodology of empirical sciences, it did not take into consideration many contributions which, although of great philosophical value, did not make relevant use of formal logic as an instrument for their developments. Non-mention in this paper does not therefore mean underestimation.

Let us remark, finally, that although it seemed correct to point out that logical technicism cannot replace philosophical insight, this remark was not meant to minimize the relevance of logic to philosophical investigation in this field. Actually, it is hardly possible, without technical logical analysis, to show explicitly how far certain assumptions can go, into what difficulties they can run, which positive developments they allow, which implicit presuppositions they hide, how some paradoxical aspects can be circumvented, how criticisms by opponents can be answered, and so on. As a matter of fact, we had the opportunity of seeing in this paper how some old philosophical views have found new vitality and interest as a consequence of deepenings made possible by logical inquires that opened new vistas and motives for philosophical meditation.

University of Genova

NOTES

[1] See Hilbert (1901).
[2] See Hilbert (1918).
[3] See Hilbert (1918), p. 156.
[4] See von Neumann (1932).
[5] See Woodger (1937).
[6] See Carnap–Hahn–Neurath (1929).
[7] See Carnap (1936).
[8] See Carnap (1942).
[9] See Carnap (1958).
[10] See Carnap (1952).
[11] See especially Hempel (1952) and Hempel (1958).
[12] See Carnap (1956).
[13] See Sellars (1961).
[14] See Hempel (1950) and Hempel (1951). These two essays have been combined with some omissions and changes in a chapter: 'Empiricist Criteria of Cognitive Significance: Problems and Changes' of Hempel (1965), pp. 101-119.
[15] One could consider, on this point, the papers by Putnam (1962), Maxwell (1963), Achinstein (1965), and the book by the same author, Achinstein (1968); Spector (1966).
[16] See, e.g., Feyerabend (1965). This view has rather close affinity with the analyses about 'context-dependence' of the meaning of theoretical terms, which is to be found, e.g., in the already quoted papers by Achinstein (1965) and Spector (1966).
[17] Consider e.g. the complex speculation of W. Sellars and his 'scientific realism', as it is proposed in Sellars (1963) and Sellars (1967). In this last book, e.g., the paper *Scientific Realism or Irenic Instrumentalism* (1965) is reprinted which is of particularly direct interest for the problem we are mentioning here.
[18] The most remarkable example of this kind may be considered M. Bunge, whose work Bunge (1967a) expresses a realistic and anti-empiristic perspective within philosophy of science, which has been deepened with regard to physics in the book Bunge (1967b) and has given rise to a treatise on general philosophy of which the first volumes have already appeared (Cf. Bunge [1974]). Among other things, he has so radically challenged the current empiristic view that he simply denies physical theories to contain any observational concept, by remarking that the notion of an 'observer', being a pragmatical and not a semantical one, has no proper place inside a scientific theory. For a concise presentation of this point see, e.g., his paper Bunge (1969). A philosophical attitude of scientific realism, implying a particular evaluation of the role of theoretical concepts, especially in connection with the explanatory task of scientific theories, and assigning them a full ontological denotation, is developed in the book by Agazzi (1969).
[19] The relevant original papers in which this theorem is presented and some of its applications in scientific methodology are discussed are the following: Craig (1953, 1956, 1957, 1960) and Craig-Vaught (1958).
[20] See Hintikka (1964, 1965).
[21] See Ramsey (1931).
[22] See Tuomela (1973).
[23] See Cornman (1972).
[24] See Stegmüller (1970).

[25] See Essler (1970a).
[26] See Rozeboom (1960, 1963).
[27] See Przełęcki (1969).
[28] See Essler (1970a).
[29] See Tuomela (1973), Chapter IV.
[30] See Hintikka–Tuomela (1970).
[31] See Kueker (1970).
[32] See the said two chapters also for further references to relevant papers on these topics.
[33] See Essler (1970b).
[34] See Trapp (1975).
[35] See Essler (1975). For a complete survey of the discussion about the problem of the introduction of dispositional predicates, see Stegmüller (1970), pp. 213 and ff.
[36] See Sneed (1971).
[37] A view similar to this has been proposed in the form of a philosophical viewpoint by E. Agazzi in the book Agazzi (1969) and in some other papers. A more formal presentation of some aspects of it is to be found in the paper by Agazzi (1976), where a way is indicated of introducing 'operational predicates' which can be applied independently of the theory for which they build up the referential basis.
[38] This can perhaps be appreciated in a most significant way in Stegmüller (1973).
[39] See, in particular, the systematic account provided in the book by Przełęcki (1969) and the papers by Wójcicki (1973, 1974a, 1975), Przełęcki-Wójcicki (1969, 1971). A systhematic book has been recently published in Polish by Wójcicki (1974b).
[40] Let us only mention in this connection the paper by Dalla Chiara and Toraldo di Francia (1973), who independently proposed some views in good agreement with those of the Polish authors just mentioned; or the paper by Hilpinen (1976), which analyses several different approaches to the problem of 'approximate truth'. It is however quite difficult to do justice to a number of valuable but somehow scattered contributions pertaining to this topic; an acceptable alternative to that may perhaps be to refer the interested reader to the volume edited by Przełęcki-Szaniawski-Wójcicki (1976), which contains the proceedings of a Conference held in 1974 and, by its 34 papers, offers a rather reliable survey of the present status of the research in the field.
[41] See Tuomela (1973). We are not maintaining however, by stressing the relevance of this book, that *all* its criticisms of the empiricist 'received view' nor *all* its claims in favor of an alternative view are equally succesful and well grounded.
[42] A quite similar holistic view had been proposed in a detailed way, but without technical developments, in Agazzi (1969).
[43] See Agazzi (1976).
[44] See Sneed (1971).
[45] See in particular Popper (1972).
[46] See Tichy (1974) for the criticism of the Popperian formulation and Tichy (1974) for the redefinition of the concept of verisimilitude.
[47] See Birkhoff–von Neumann (1936).
[48] The most recommendable papers are perhaps those by Goguen (1968) and Zadeh (1975). The last is included in a special issue of *Synthese* **30**, No. 3/4, 1975), which is devoted to 'The Logic Semantics of Vagueness' and also contains several other interesting philosophical and logical contributions to the topic.

[49] See e.g. Przełęcki (1969, 1976) and Fine (1975). A more detailed account of these methods had already be given in a less known paper by Przełęcki (1964) published in Polish.

[50] It may be sufficient to mention here, for a reliable presentation of that position, the works by Nagel (1960, 1961).

[51] Anyhow, for an account of Popper's position on the problems envisaged here, see, e.g., Popper (1962).

[52] See Nagel (1960), p. 291.

[53] Sneed (1971).

[54] Stegmüller (1973), Part I.

[55] Besides the already mentioned book, one could very profitably read Stegmüller (1975): in this paper a brief, clear, and self-contained presentation is made of the Sneedian notions that are necessary and sufficient for the application to the problem of scientific change and to the discussion of the Kuhnian viewpoint; and the original Stegmüller approach to these questions is outlined. It would be out of place to add here references to the works by Kuhn, Feyerabend and other people, related to the topic we are discussing. Pertinent and detailed references of this kind, on the other hand, are provided especially in Stegmüller (1973).

[56] See Harris (1975).

[57] See von Helmholtz (1887).

[58] Very good books of a general character are those by Ellis (1966), Pfanzagl (1968), Krantz–Luce–Suppes–Tversky (1971). Excellent and well known is also Suppes–Zinnes (1963). In these works the reader will find different axiomatizations for measurement. In order to give some references also to publications more directly concerned with methodological problems, we shall mention: a book by Suppes (1969), which contains several selected papers, some of them relevant to the general methodology of measurement; a very important paper by Kanger (1972); a recent issue of *Synthese* 33, 1976), which contains two interesting articles, by J. O. Ramsey and by D. K. Osborne, devoted to measurement theory. We want to stress, anyway, that other publications not mentioned here are by no means less important than the few titles we have listed.

[59] As an example of outstanding work in philosophy of science, in which formal logic plays only a secondary role, one could mention such an important contribution as Popper's.

[60] An author for whom this remark seems particularly appropriate might be M. Bunge.

[61] We have had the opportunity of seeing, in fact, how practically every major position upheld in the philosophy of empirical sciences has proven able to develop its formal armaments, from empiricism, to anti-empiricism, from Carnapian, to Popperian, and to Kuhnian views, etc. In so doing, every 'school' can show the best of the positive achievments it is able to reach, and can stress some shortcomings of the opposite viewpoints, but it would be quite unrealistic to think that this can really lead to contriving, 'decisive' arguments in favor of or against any of the classical conceptions involved in the methodological dispute.

BIBLIOGRAPHY

Achinstein P., 'The Problem of Theoretical Terms', *American Philosophical Quarterly* 2 (1965), 193–203.

Achinstein, P., *Concepts of Science. A Philosophical Analysis*, Johns Hopkins Press, Baltimore, Maryland, 1968.

Agazzi, E., *Temi e Problemi di Filosofia della Fisica*, Manfredi, Milano, 1969; Reprint: Abete, Roma, 1974.

Agazzi, E., 'The Concept of Empirical Data. Proposals for an Intensional Semantics of Empirical Theories', in Przełęcki, Szaniawski, and Wójcicki (1976), 143–157.

Birkhoff, G. and von Neumann, J., 'The Logic of Quantum Mechanics', *Annals of Mathematics*, 1936 pp. 823 ff.

Bunge, M. (ed.), *Quantum Theory and Reality*, Berlin–Heidelberg–New York, Springer, 1967a.

Bunge, M., *Foundations of Physics*, Berlin–Heidelberg–New York, Springer, 1967b.

Bunge, M., 'What Are Physical Theories About?', *American Philosophical Quarterly* 3 (1969), 61–99.

Bunge, M., *Treatise on Basic Philosophy*, 4 Vols., D. Reidel, Dordrecht, Holland, 1974–79.

Carnap, R., 'Testability and Meaning', *Philosophy of Science* 3 (1936), 419–471; and 4 (1937), 1–40.

Carnap, R., *Introduction to Semantics*, Harvard University Press, Cambridge, Mass., 1942.

Carnap, R., 'Meaning Postulates', *Philosophical Studies* III (1952), 65–73.

Carnap, R., 'The Methodological Character of Theoretical Concepts', in Feigl, Scriven, and Maxwell (1956), pp. 38–76.

Carnap, R., *Introduction to Symbolic Logic and its Applications*, Dover, New York, 1958.

Carnap, R., Hahn, H., and Neurath, O., *Wissenschaftliche Weltauffassung, Der Wiener Kreis*, Wien, 1929.

Colodny, R. G. (ed.), *Beyond the Edge of Certainty*, Prentice Hall, Englewood Cliffs, 1965.

Cornman, J. W., 'Craig's Theorem, Ramsey-Sentences and Scientific Instrumentalism', *Synthese* 25 (1972), 82–128.

Craig, W., 'On Axiomatizability Within a System', *Journal of Symbolic Logic* 18 (1953), 30–32.

Craig, W., 'Replacement of Auxiliary Expressions', *Philosophical Review* 65 (1956), 38–55.

Craig, W., 'Linear Reasoning: A New Form of the Herbrand–Gentzen Theorem', *Journal of Symbolic Logic* 22 (1957), 250–268.

Craig, W., 'Bases for First-Order Theories and Subtheories', *Journal of Symbolic Logic* 25 (1960), 97–142.

Craig, W. and Vaught, R. L., 'Finite Axiomatizability Using Additional Predicates', *Journal of Symbolic Logic* 23 (1958), 289–308.

Crossley, J. and Dummett, M. (eds.), *Formal Systems and Recursive Functions* North-Holland Publ. Co., Amsterdam, 1965.

Dalla Chiara, M. L. and Toraldo Di Francia, G., 'A Logical Analysis of Physical Theories', *Rivista del Nuovo Cimento, Serie 2,* 3 (1973), 1–20.

Danto, A. and Morgenbesser, S. (eds.), *Philosophy of Science*, Meridian Books, New York, 1960.

Ellis, B., *Basic Concepts of Measurement*, Cambridge University Press, London, 1966.

Essler, W., *Wissenschaftstheorie I. Definition und Reduktion*, Alber, Freiburg-München, 1970a.

Essler, W., *Induktive Logik. Grundlagen und Voraussetzungen*, Alber, Freiburg-München, 1970b.

Essler, W., 'Die Kreativität der Bilateralen Reduktionssätze', *Erkenntnis* 9 (1975), 383–392.

Feigl, H., Scriven, M., and Maxwell, G. (eds.), *Minnesota Studies in the Philosophy of Science*, University of Minnesota Press, Minneapolis, Vol. I (1956), Vol. II (1958), Vol. III (1963).

Feigl, H. and Maxwell, G. (eds.), *Current Issues in the Philosophy of Science*, Holt, Rinehart, and Winston, New York, 1961.

Feyerabend, P., 'Problems of Empiricism', in Colodny (1965), pp. 145–260.

Fine, K., 'Vagueness, Truth and Logic', *Synthese* 30 (1975), 265–300.

Goguen, J. H., 'The Logic of Inexact Concepts', *Synthese* 19 325–373.

Harris, J. H., 'On Comparing Theories', *Synthese* 33 (1975), 29–76.

Hempel, C. G., 'Problems and Changes in the Empiricist Criterion of Meaning', *Revue Internationale de Philosophie* 11 (1950), 41–63.

Hempel, C. G., 'The Concept of Cognitive Significance: A Reconsideration', *Proceedings of the American Academy of Arts and Sciences* 80 (1951), 61–67.

Hempel, C. G., *Fundamentals of Concept Formation in Empirical Science*, Chicago University Press, 1952.

Hempel, C. G., 'The Theoretician's Dilemma', in Feigl, Scriven, and Maxwell (1958), pp. 37–98. Reprinted in Hempel (1965).

Hempel, C. G., *Aspects of Scientific Explanation*, Free Press, New York, 1965.

Hilbert, D., 'Mathematische Probleme', Reprinted in Hilbert (1965), III (1901), 290–329.

Hilbert, D., 'Axiomatisches Denken', Reprinted in Hilbert (1965), III (1918), 146–156.

Hilbert, D., *Gesammelte Abhandlungen*, Chelsea, New York, 1965 (Reprint).

Hilpinen, R., 'Approximate Truth and Truthlikeness', in Przełecki, Szaniawski, and Wójcicki (1976), pp. 19–42.

Hintikka, J., 'Distributive Normal Forms and Deductive Interpolation', *Zeitschrift für Math. Logik u. Grundlagen der Mathematik* 10 (1964), 185–191.

Hintikka, J., 'Distributive Normal Forms in First-Order Logic', (1965), in Crossley and Dummett (1950), pp. 47–90.

Hintikka, J. (ed.), *Rudolf Carnap, Logical Empiricist: Materials and Perspectives*, D. Reidel, Dordrecht, Holland, 1975.

Hintikka, J. and Suppes, P. (eds.), *Information and Inference*, D. Reidel, Dordrecht, Holland, 1970.

Hintikka, J. and Tuomela, R., 'Towards a General Theory of Auxiliary Concepts and Definability in First-Order Theories', in Hintikka and Suppes (1970), pp. 298–330.

Kanger, S., 'Measurement: An Essay in Philosophy of Science', *Theoria* 38 (1972), 1–44.

Krantz, D. H., Luce, R. D., Suppes, P., and Tversky, A., *Foundations of Measurement*, Vol. 1, Academic Press, New York, 1971.

Kueker, D. W., 'Generalized Interpolation and Definability', *Annals of Mathematical Logic* 1 (1970), 423–468.

Maxwell, G., 'The Ontological Status of Theoretical Entities', in Feigl, Scriven, and Maxwell (1963), pp. 3–27.

Nagel, E., 'The Meaning of Reduction in Natural Science', in Danto and Morgenbesser (1960), pp. 288–312.
Nagel, E., *The Structure of Science*, Harcourt, Brace and World, New York, 1961.
Nagel, E., Suppes, P., and Tarski, A. (eds.), *Logic, Methodology and Philosophy of Science*, Stanford University Press, Stanford, 1962.
Pfanzagl, J., *Theory of Measurement*, Wiley, New York, 2nd edition, 1968. Phisica-Verlag, Würzburg-Wien, 1971.
Popper, K. R., *Conjectures and Refutations*, Basic Books, New York, 1962.
Popper, K. R., *Objective Knowledge*, Clarendon Press, Oxford, 1972.
Przełęcki, M., *The Logic of Empirical Theories*, Routledge and Kegan Paul, London, 1969.
Przełęcki, M., 'Z semantyki pojeć otwartych', *Studia Logica* **15** (1964), 189–220.
Przełęcki, M., 'Fuzziness as Multiplicity', *Erkenntnis* **10** (1976), 371–380.
Przełęcki, M. and Wójcicki, R., 'The Problem of Analiticity', *Synthese* **19** (1969), 374–399.
Przełęcki, M. and Wójcicki, R., 'Inessential Parts of Extensions of First-Order Theories', *Studia Logica* **28** (1971), 83–99.
Przełęcki, M., Szaniawski, K., and Wójcicki, R. (eds.), *Formal Methods in the Methodology of Empirical Sciences*, D. Reidel, Dordrecht, Holland, 1976.
Putnam, H., 'What Theories are Not', in Nagel, Suppes, and Tarski (1962), pp. 240–251.
Ramsey, F. P., 'Theories', in *The Foundations of Mathematics and Other Logical Essays*, 1931. Reprint: Littlefield, Adams, and Paterson, N.J. (1962), pp. 212–236.
Rozeboom, W., 'Studies in the Empiricist Theory of Scientific Meaning I–II', *Philosophy of Science* **27** (1960), 359–373.
Rozeboom, W., 'The Factual Content of Theoretical Concepts', in Feigl, Scriven, and Maxwell (1963), pp. 273–357.
Sellars, W., 'The Language of Theories', in Feigl and Maxwell (1961), pp. 57–77.
Sellars, W., *Science, Perception and Reality*, Routledge and Kegan Paul, London, 1963.
Sellars, W., *Philosophical Perspectives*, Thomas, Springfield, Ill., 1967.
Sneed, J. D., *The Logical Structure of Mathematical Physics*, D. Reidel, Dordrecht, Holland, 1971.
Spector, M., 'Theory and Observation I–II', *The British Journal for Philosophy of Science* **7** (1966), 1–20; 89–104.
Stegmüller, W., *Probleme und Resultate der Wissenschaftstheorie und Analytischen Philosophie*, Band I: Wissenschaftliche Erklärung und Begründung, Springer, Berlin–Heidelberg–New York, 1969.
Stegmüller, W., *Probleme und Resultate ...*, Band II: Theorie und Erfahrung. Erster Halbband: Begriffsformen, Wissenschaftssprache empirische Signifikanz und theoretische Begriffe, Ibidem, 1970.
Stegmüller, W., *Probleme und Resultate ...*, Band II: Theorie und Erfahrung. Zweiter Halbband: Theorienstrukturen und Theoriendynamik, Ibidem, 1973.
Stegmüller, W., 'Structures and Dynamics of Theories', *Erkenntnis* **9** (1975), 75–100.
Suppes, P., *Studies in the Methodology and Foundations of Science*, D. Reidel, Dordrecht, Holland, 1969.
Suppes, P. and Zinnes, J., 'Basic Measurement Theory', in R. D. Luce, R. R. Bush, and E. H. Galanter (eds.), *Handbook of Mathematical Psychology*, Vol. 1, Wiley, New York, 1963, pp. 3–76.

Tichy, P., 'On Popper's Definitions of Verisimilitude', *British Journal for Philosophy of Science* 25 (1974), 155–160.

Tichy, P., 'Verisimilitude Redefined', *British Journal for Philosophy of Science* 27 (1976), 25–42.

Trapp, R., 'Eine Verfeinerung des Reduktionsverfahrens zur Einführung ven Dispositionspradikanten', *Erkenntnis* 9 (1975), 355–382.

Tuomela, R., *Theoretical Concepts*, Springer, Wien–New York, 1973.

von Helmholtz, H., 'Zählen und Messen erkenntnistheoretisch betrachtet', in *Philosophische Aufsätze E. Zeller gewidmet*, Leipzig, 1887.

von Neumann, J., *Mathematische Grundlagen der Quantenmechanik*, Springer, Berlin, 1932.

Wójcicki, R., 'Set Theoretical Representation of Empirical Phenomena', *Journal of Philosophical Logic* 3 (1974a), 337–343.

Wójcicki, R., *Metodologia formalna nauk empiryczych*, Wydawnictwo Polskiej Akademii Nauk, Warszawa, 1974b.

Wójcicki, R., 'Basic Concepts of Formal Methodology of Empirical Sciences', *Ajatus* 35 (1973), 168–195.

Wójcicki, R., 'The Factual Content of Empirical Theories', in Hintikka (1975), pp. 55–82.

Woodger, J., *The Axiomatic Method in Biology*, Cambridge University Press, Cambridge, 1937.

Zadeh, L. A., 'Fuzzy Logic and Approximate Reasoning', *Synthese* 30 (1975), 407–428.

JAAKKO HINTIKKA

STANDARD VS. NONSTANDARD LOGIC: HIGHER-ORDER, MODAL, AND FIRST-ORDER LOGICS

Model-theoretical (semantical) treatments of modal logic have enjoyed spectacular success ever since the pioneering work by Stig Kanger in 1957.[1] Quine and others have admittedly proffered sundry philosophical objections to modal logic and its semantics but they have not impeded the overwhelming progress either of the semantical theory of intensional (modal) logics or of its applications.

There nevertheless exists an important *prima facie* objection to more of the current versions of this approach which quite surprisingly has not been presented in its full generality in the literature. (For partial exceptions, see above, note 1, and see below, especially notes 6 and 7.) It is directed primarily against the current treatments of *logical* modalities in semantical terms. In order to see what this objection is, let us first recall the key idea on which the whole possible-worlds semantics is based. This basic idea is to require for the truth of

(1) Nec p

(where 'Nec' expresses necessity) in a world w_0 nothing more and nothing less than the truth of p (i.e., p *simpliciter*) in all worlds alternative to w_0. Likewise, the truth of

(2) Poss p

in w_0 (where 'Poss' expressed possibility) amounts to the truth of p is at least one such alternative. These characterizations presuppose that, instead of considering just one world (model) at a time, we are considering a set of models on which a two-place relation (the relation of being an alternative to) has been defined.

So far, so good. But what *are* these alternative worlds (models)? Here we come to a veritable skeleton in the cupboard of semanticists of modal logic: to a problem which is of the utmost importance both historically and systematically but which has scarcely been discussed in the literature. Kripke has always assumed that any old subset of some given set of models will do as the set of alternatives, as long as it contains w_0.[2] Or strictly speaking, he has assumed that any set w_0 of models together with an arbitrary reflexive

E. Agazzi (ed.), Modern Logic – A Survey, 283–296.

relation of alternativeness defined on it is a *frame* in which a modal sentence can be evaluated for truth (with respect to each member w_0 of W_0). I shall refer to a truth-definition of this sort (for modal sentences) as a K-type truth-definition. ('K' for Kripke, of course.)

Almost all subsequent logicians have followed Kripke here, who was anticipated among others by Guillaume and Hintikka.[3]

However, the arbitrariness of the choice of alternatives involved in a K-type truth definition appears completely unmotivated, especially in the case of logical modalities. When we say that something is logically necessary, we do not mean just that it is true in each member of some arbitrary set of alternatives. Rather, we mean that it is true in each *logically possible* alternative. In other words, it seems that we ought to impose much more stringent requirements on frames than is the case in a K-type semantics for modal logics. We ought to require at the very least that W_0 contains an instance of each logically possible kind of model with a fixed set of individuals I_0 (or with a subset of I_0) as its domain of individuals. By a logically possible type of model we of course mean a model reachable by choosing the extensions (interpretations) of nonlogical symbols in some suitable way. Moreover, an instance of every such model type must occur among the alternatives of each member of W_0. We shall call such frames L-frames. ('L' stands for logically possible worlds.) The semantics based on them will be called L-semantics.

This was the semantics presupposed by Kanger in 1957 and also by Montague in his earliest work on modal logic.[4] Thus we have in fact not only one but two quite unlike traditions in the foundations of modal logics, the one relying on K-semantics and the other on L-semantics. Later, however, Montague switched over from L-semantics to K-semantics, without discussing his reasons.[5] L-semantics has nevertheless made a couple of brief appearences in the writings of Montague's associates and former students, especially David Kaplan[6] and Nino Cocchiarella.[7]

The two traditions are connected with a number of other issues. K-semantics was initially made interesting mathematically by being a natural extension of earlier work by Tarski and his associates on Boolean algebras with operators.[8] K-semantics is indeed unproblematic in connection with intensional logics in the narrower sense, e.g., in connection with epistemic logic, doxastic logic, and the logic of other propositional attitudes. It is mostly in connection with logical modalities and with whatever analytical modalities are involved in the analysis of linguistic meanings that K-semantics loses its plausibility.

Almost all the actual work in the semantics of modal notions has been based on K-semantics rather than L-semantics. It is therefore in order to ask what will happen if we impose similar requirements in ordinary modal logic of logical modalities? The details of the situation require a more extensive study than can be undertaken here. I shall make only a few general comments.

First, it may be observed that the additional requirement that is imposed on frames by L-semantic go way beyond all the requirements that can be imposed on frames in K-semantics by putting further conditions on the alternativeness relation. For instance, it is pretty generally agreed that in the case of logical modalities alternativeness relation must also be transitive and symmetric, i.e., an equivalence relation. These additional requirements do not change the picture essentially but only complicate it in certain ways which I shall not try to discuss here.

The next main point is an obvious one. It can be expressed in the form of an analogy:

$$\frac{\textit{L-frames}}{\text{K-frames}} = \frac{\textit{standard semantics}}{\text{nonstandard semantics}}$$

In more picturesque terms we can put the same equation as follows.

$$\frac{\textit{Kanger}}{\text{Kripke}} = \frac{\textit{Tarski}}{\text{Henkin}}$$

For the terms 'standard' and 'nonstandard' are here used in the sense of Henkin.[9] These notions were defined by him to apply in the first place only to models for higher-order logics. In a standard model M_0 quantification over (say) one-place predicates of individuals is understood as quantification over *all* (and only) extensionally possible subsets of some given set of individuals I_0. In a nonstandard model M_1, such quantifiers range over some fixed (i.e., fixed relative to M_1) subset of the power set of I_0. (This difference extends naturally to other kinds of higher-type variable.) The analogy with L-frames vs. K-frames is obvious.

This is an instance of a much more sweeping point. The distinction Henkin made has so far been applied only to higher-order logics. It is true that the labels 'standard' and 'nonstandard' have occasionally been used also in the connection with different first-order models, especially models of arithmetical and other mathematical axiom systems. These uses are not all connected with each other or with Henkin's definition in any systematic manner, however. Often, it would be less misleading to use the terms 'intended' and 'unintended' instead of 'standard' and 'nonstandard' for these models. It is not my purpose here to try to capture this variety of different nonstandard models in terms of any one concept. I don't think that it can be done, and some of the other kinds of nonstandard conceptions of models definitely deserve a separate treatment.

In this respect, a radical change has been brought already by the game-theoretical semantics for first-order logic (and parts of natural languages) which I have outlined in earlier writings.[10] It would take me too far to study this new semantics in its entirety here or even to give a explicit definition of it. Suffice it to say that this semantics yields a translation of first-order logic into a fragment of second-order logic, possibly (depending on certain fine points in the semantical interpretation of propositional connectives) into a fragment of higher-order logic (simple type theory). Given a prenex first-order sentence p, its translation asserts the existence of such associated Skolem functions as make the quantifier-free part of p true for any choice of the values of the universally quantified variables. For instance,

(4) $(\forall x)(\exists y)(\forall z)(\exists u)\, M(x, y, z, u)$

will translate into

(5) $(\exists f)(\exists g)(\forall x)(\forall z)\, M(x, f(x), z, g(x, z))$.

Returning for a moment to the game-theoretical semantics for first-order languages, we can think of the value of existentially quantified variables as being chosen successively by myself in a little game against Nature who chooses the values of universally bound variables. Then (5) will say that I have a winning strategy in the game associated with (4). This will be the general form of the definition of truth in game-theoretical semantics: a sentence is true if I have a winning strategy in the correlated game, false if Nature has one. (Since it is not in general true that either player has a winning strategy in an infinite two-person game, we see already here how a door is opened by game-theoretical semantics for treating such nonclassical logics as are not subject to the law of bivalence.)[11]

The game just sketched is readily extended to propositional connectives and to quantifiers in a noninitial (nonprenex) position. For instance, a disjunction marks my move. I choose a disjunct with respect to which the game is then continued. Similarly for conjunctions, except that Nature chooses the conjunct.

A possible elaboration of these games is obtained by dividing them into subgames.[12] After such a subgame, one of the players divulges his strategy in the subgame. (We know from game theory that to play a game is to choose a strategy for it. Hence to play out a game to the bitter end is to divulge one's strategy in it.) Then a player's subsequent moves may depend on that strategy. Since a strategy in the subgame is the function that tells one which moves to make depending on what has happened earlier on the game and since a player's overall strategy will be defined by a functional (function whose arguments are functions). In this way various functional interpretations of first-order sentences can be obtained, depending on the details of the game rules.[13]

Independently of these details, the explicit truth-condition for each first-order sentence can always be expressed by a second-order or higher-order sentence. For what this truth-condition amounts to is the existence of a winning strategy for myself, i.e., a strategy which wins against *any* strategy of Nature's. Since strategies are represented by functions or functionals, the truth-condition can be expressed in higher-order logic.

This translation makes the standard-nonstandard distinction automatically applicable to first-order logic, too, independently of the details of the game-theoretical interpretation. Depending on whether the second-order translation (or the higher order translation) of a first-order sentence is given standard or nonstandard interpretation, we likewise obtain a similar distinction between standard and nonstandard interpretations of *first-order* logic. Moreover, to both these interpretations my game-theoretical semantics assigns not only a clear *semantic* meaning but a concrete *pragmatic* content.[14]

Conversely, any distinction along these lines between standard and nonstandard interpretations of ordinary (linear) first-order logic induces as a matter of course a distinction between the corresponding interpretations of the logic of finite partially ordered quantifiers. As I have pointed out elsewhere,[15] the logic of such quantifiers (called f.p.o. quantification theory) is 'almost' as strong as second-order logic, in the sense that the decision problem for the latter reduces to the decision problem for the former. Hence the standard-nonstandard distinction, when made along the lines I am suggesting for linear first-order sentences, in effect forces us to a Henkin-type distinction in higher-order as well.[16]

The first main point I am making in this paper is thus that the standard-nonstandard distinction also carries over to modal logics and to first-order logic in an important way.

But is it a distinction with a real difference? For instance, is there any bite in the putative criticism of the modal logic mentioned in the beginning of this paper? Does the difference between K-interpretation and L-interpretation really matter?

It is obvious that quite a number of changes take place already in propositional logic when we switch from K-logic to L-logic. For whenever a complex sentence F is satisfiable, the modalized sentence Poss(F) will be logically true (valid) in L-semantics. In propositional logic, L-logic is nevertheless axiomatizable.[17] Obviously, modalized predicate logic (quantification theory) with L-semantics cannot be completely axiomatized. For otherwise we could decide the logical truth of any plain first-order sentence F by grinding out theorems of the complete axiomatization until F or Poss($\sim F$) has made an appearance. Of course such a decision method is known to be impossible.

This does not yet say very much of the expressive power of, say, a first-order quantification theory *cum* modality with L-semantics. Does the switch from K-semantics to L-semantics matter greatly here?

At first sight, the answer might seem to be negative. In some parts of customary modal logics, the choice between the K-interpretation and the L-interpretation apparently does not affect expressive power greatly. However, in other cases there seem to be important differences. The whole matter is complex, and requires a fuller investigation than it can be given here. Suffice it to point out some connections between this problem and certain other important issues concerning the foundations of modal logics.[18]

As the reader can gather from any explanation of Henkin's standard-nonstandard distinction, the crucial question is whether an L-semantics enables us to quantify over all the subsets of a given set (and of course over them only). At first blush, this seems easy to do. For the sentence

(6) $(\forall x)(\text{Poss}(Ax) \supset Ax)$

says that all individuals that possibly are A's actually are A's. Hence the set of all A's in any one alternative to the given (actual) world is a subset of the set of actual A's. Since these alternatives encompass all logically (extensionally) possible worlds, each subset will show up in some alternative. Hence to quantify over these alternatives is in effect to quantify over all the subsets of the set of actual A's – or so it seems – and over them only. And such quantification over alternatives is precisely what modal operators do.

This line of thought has a gaping hole in it, however. It is seen by asking: What are the values of the bound variable 'x' in (6)? The above argument remains valid if it is assumed that all the individuals that can be members of an alternative world are also members of the actual world. Merely allowing these individuals to fail to exist in some worlds does not affect its validity, for we can then change (6) to say that any individual that exists and is an A is some alternative exists also in the actual world and is in it an A.

However, I have argued for independent reasons that the most natural way of looking at (6) is to take 'x' to range over individuals which not only exist in but can be cross-identified between the worlds as a member of which x is being considered in (6). These worlds are obviously the actual one and the relevant alternative. But to quantify over such cross-identifiable individuals leaves it completely open as to what we want to say of individuals which exist in an alternative w_1 to the actual world w_0 but which cannot be cross-identified between w_1 and w_0. Such individuals cannot be ruled out by a *fiat*, and they may include plenty of A's. Hence in this kind of semantics (6) does not enable us to consider all the subsets of the set of all the actual A's.

Thus the introduction of L-semantics brings out a remarkable fact about the interpretation of quantifiers in modal logics. Far from having only philosophical motivation and philosophical implications, the problems of quantifying in and cross-identification have remarkable technical repercussions as well. On these problems apparently hangs the question whether standard modal logics of the conventional sort reduce to nonstandard ones.

One can look at the relation of standard and nonstandard modal logics from a slightly different viewpoint, viz. in terms of what the syntax of conventional modal logics enables us to express. The basic reason why the difference between K-frames and L-frames does not seem to matter in much ordinary modal logic (with a suitable interpretation of quantifiers) is that certain kinds of dependence of the domain d_1 of individuals of an alternative world (model) w_1 on the domain d_0 of a world w_0 to which it is an alternative cannot be expressed in the language of conventional modal logic. We can say in such a language that individuals existing in w_0 also exist in some or every w_1, and that these individuals have (absolutely or at certain conditions) certain properties in w_1. However, we cannot express any converse dependence. We cannot take some individual in some particular w_1 and go on to say what it is like in the actual world. (The world of conventional modal logic is like Thomas Wolfe's: In it, you cannot go back home again.) Hence d_1 can for instance by any old superset of d_0. The effects of this one-sided dependence seem to be quite subtle, and they sometimes eliminate some of the relevant differences between K-frames and L-frames.

However, the situation is changed radically by the introduction of the so-called backwards-looking operators.[19] They enrich our syntax in precisely the way needed here. What they accomplish is just to enable us to take an individual in one of the worlds alternative to w_0, say in w_1, and to bring it back to the actual world, that is, to say something about it, *qua* member of w_0. For instance if 'D' is such an operator.

(7) $\quad \text{Poss}\,[(\forall x)(Ax \supset \text{D}Bx)]$

says that there is at least one alternative world such that whatever is there A is actually B. Likewise,

(8) $\quad \text{Nec}\,[(\forall x)(Ax \supset \text{D}Ax]$

says that the set of A's in any alternative is a subset of all the actual A's.

The latter example shows how, in the presence of backwards-looking operators L-semantics enables us to quantify over all the subclasses of a given class (and over them only). Thus it is fairly clear that a modal logic with the usual (linear) first-order quantifiers *and* backwards-looking operators is in effect as strong as the whole second-order logic with standard interpretation. If a detailed argument is needed, my 1955 reduction of higher-order logics to a fragment of second-order logic[20] (both with the standard interpretation) produces a reduct which is expressed without too much trouble in quantified modal logic with backwards-looking operators. The nerve of the translation is to replace quantification over all subsets of a given set by a use of the necessity-operator. And that can readily be accomplised by the means envisaged. For instance, a standard second-order sentence

(9) $(\forall X)F(X)$

where 'X' is a one-place predicate variable (ranging over predicates of individuls) and where F does not contain any higher-order quantifiers will translate as something like the following:

(10) $\text{Nec}\, F'(X) \wedge \text{Nec}\, (\forall x)\, [X(x) \supset \text{D}X(x)] \wedge \text{C}$

where F' is like F except that all quantifiers have been relativized to X and where C is a conjunction of sentences of the form

$$\text{Nec}\, (\forall x)\, [Rxy \equiv \text{D}Rxy]$$

which say that the different predicates R in F obtain between exactly the same individuals in the actual world and all of its alternatives. The second conjunct of (10) says that the extension of X in the alternatives is a subset of its extension in the actual world. Since we are dealing with an L-logic, each such subset is the interpretation of X in some alternative or other, and hence the first conjunct of (10) ensures that $F(X)$ is true for all values of X.

The transition from (9) to (10) or *vice versa* obviously preserves satisfiability. Such a transition does not work when the quantifier is in a noninitial position. What the reduction just mentioned[20] accomplishes is to bring (*salva* satisfiability) every higher-order sentence to a form in which the maneuver exemplified by the transition from (9) to (10) is possible. For its upshot is in each case a formula which contains only one one-place bound second-order variable (bound to an initial universial quantifier) over and above free predicates and which is satisfiable if the original formula is.

One may still have legitimate compunctions about the intepretation of quantifiers in (10). However, a simple change rectifies the situation. One of the *prima facie* problems with (10) is that in the second conjunct x is apparently being considered as a member *both* of a selected alternative world and of the actual one. Hence 'x' apparently should be restricted to only such values as can be reidentified in the actual world and the given alternative. A slight modification of the second conjunct removes this defect, however. We can write it as follows:

(11) $\text{Nec}(\forall x)\,[X(x) \supset (\exists z)\,(z = x \wedge \text{D}X(z))]$

Likewise, each conjunct in C can be rewritten as follows:

$$\text{Ncc}\,[(\forall x)(\forall y)(Rxy \supset (\exists z)(\exists u)(z = x \wedge u = y \wedge \text{D}Rzu))]$$
$$(\forall x)(\forall y)(Rxy \supset (\exists z\,(\exists u)(z = x \wedge u = y \wedge \text{Nec}\,Rzu))$$

It follows *inter alia* that a system of quantified (first-order) modal logic with backwards-looking operators (call it B) with the L-interpretation cannot be axiomatized. What its semantics is is obvious at once, however, on the basis of what has been said.

The following general point is suggested by our observations. It has sometimes been said or thought that the logic of logical modalities is somehow more powerful or philosophically deeper than the usual first-order logic. Historically speaking, such claims have often been formulated in terms of the alleged superiority of intensional logic over extensional logic. Most of the earlier treatments of modal logics have nevertheless failed to lead to the deepest problems of logic. The main exceptions to his negative judgement, for instance intuitionistic logics, have, in my opinion, moved much more in the direction of epistemic concepts than in the realm of logical or analytical modalities. Now we can see how these old claims for the special significance of intensional logic can perhaps be partly vindicated. This vindication is predicated on two separate ideas: (i) the standard interpretation of modal logic (i.e., L-semantics); (ii) the idea of a backwards-looking operator. Of these, (i) is essentially based on an extension of Henkin's distinction between standard and non-standard interpretation to modal logic, and (ii) has gradually evolved from the work of Hans Kamp, David Kaplan, Esa Saarinen, and others.

The relation of the distinction standard vs. nonstandard to the old contrast of intensions with extensions is riddled with ambivalences, however. There is a sense in which the *standard* interpretation of higher-order logics turns on an *extensional* viewpoint. This sense is seen by observing that on the standard interpretation predicate variables (higher-order variables) range over all extensionally possible values. A vindication of the intensionalistic position which depends essentially on the standard interpretation therefore smacks of a Pyrrhic victory.

But if B-logics are essentially (i.e., as far as their decision problems are concerned) equivalent to second-order logic (with the standard interpretation), what possible uses does their study promise? An obvious answer is that studying them will be an important part of any attempt to clarify the concept of logical necessity. Over and above this obvious purpose, there nevertheless is another direction which appears to be worth a serious investigation. Virtually all the most important set-theoretical problems are tantamount to the question of the logical truth of some second-order sentence. One difficulty in trying to solve these problems is the difficulty of finding intuitions which would somehow enable us to see which assumptions are acceptable and which ones are not. It may be worthwhile to attempt to see whether a 'translation' of second-order logic into a modal logic with backwards-looking operators will sharpen our perception in this difficult field. I do not consider this very likely, but in view of the great potential payoff I think an attempt should be made. The best chance we have is probably to wed modal logic with backwards-looking operators to game-theoretical semantics. Game-theoretical intuitions have elsewhere yielded new ways of approaching strong set-theoretical hypotheses. Maybe my B-logics will offer a framework for systematizing some of this work.

An even more general point that can now be better appreciated is the potential generality and importance of the standard-nonstandard distinction, which is seen to permeate not only higher-order logics but first-order logic and modal logics as well.

An important qualification to – or perhaps rather an elaboration of – this claim is nevertheless in order. I have been speaking as if there existed such a thing as *the* nonstandard interpretation. Now the only sense in which this is the case is so trivial as to be uninteresting. The only patently unique nonstandard interpretation is the minimal one, viz. the one in which literally *any* subset $S \subseteq P(I)$ of some power set $P(I)$ is acceptable as the value range of predicate variables or on which *any* set of models is acceptable as the set of alternatives to a given model in a frame. This is in many ways a trivial interpretation, which comes very close to reducing all higher-order logics and modal logics to many-sorted first-order logic, at least insofar as purely logical (deductive and model-theoretical in contradiction to pragmatical) aspects of the situation are concerned. Usually some conditions, for instance closure with respect to Boolean operations and projective operations, are imposed on $S \subseteq P(I)$. For instance, in this case we obtain the usual higher-order logics with nonstandard interpretation. In contrast to traditional higher-order logics, in first-order logic a different condition on S is eminently natural. There game-theoretical semantics strongly encourages us to limit S to *recursive* sets, and *mutatis mutandis* for other higher-type entities, especially for functions representing players' strategies. The motivation should be clear: how can anyone expect to play a game using nonrecursive strategies?

Other restrictions on S (or on its counterparts of in modal logics) are of course possible. The question as to what the natural, important, or otherwise interesting restraints on S are is connected in many interesting ways with the central problems in modern logic and the foundations of mathematics. I have in this paper established connections between the different manifestations of this question (of the choice of a nonstandard interpretation) in the realm not only if higher-order logics but also of first-order logic and modal logics. These connections may be hoped to be useful in throwing light on the choice of the right interpretations.

One especially interesting further question is the following. In discussing the distinction between K-frames and L-frames I have spoken apparently as a matter of course of a fixed domain I of individuals shared by all members of a frame W_0. (Admittedly, not all members of I have to exist in all the members of W_0.) This assumption is not unproblematic, however, and has in effect been challenged for philosophical reasons. What happens if the assumption of a fixed I is given up? I don't know, but it is obvious that an inquiry into this matter promises results which are relevant to the philosophical controversies concerning 'prefabricated' individuals, 'possible individuals', and similar matters. It is very likely that leaving I completely open results in incoherence. If it does, then philosophical arguments which one can easily give for the freedom of the choice of I for different members of one and the same frame tend to make suspect the unlimited and unqualified notion of purely *logical* modality.

In spite of the programmatic character of the last few remarks, it seems to me that we have seen enough to appreciate the great interest of the generalization of the standard-nonstandard distinction which has been outlined in this paper.

A couple of complementary remarks may serve to throw this whole complex of issues into a firmer perspective. The standard vs. nonstandard distinction has recently played an interesting role in *propositional* modal logics (and propositional tense logics). The reason is that in modal logics a propositional variable is usually taken to range over all subsets of the frame.

This corresponds to the standard interpretation. For many reasons, it may be more natural to let them range over some subset of the power set of the frame. This step, which has been taken by S. K. Thomason and others,[21] leads us to a counterpart of the nonstandard interpretation. The resulting distinction is different from what is drawn in this paper, however, even though it, too, serves to illustrate the great importance of the difference between standard and nonstandard interpretations in Henkin's sense.

But do we need the distinction in the applications of modal logic and of first-order logic? The following ingenious observation, which is due to Lauri Carlson,[22] illustrates the relevance of the distinction by means of a small example. In many languages, for instance in English, there is a construction which amounts to second-order quantification (over the subsets of a given set). It is the following construction:

> Some X's are such that – Y_1 – each one of them – Y_2 some one of them – Y_3,

A case in point could be

(12) Some fleas are such that for each of them we can find some one of them who is smaller than it.

If the relation of being smaller than is asymmetric and transitive, the only viable choices for 'some fleas' which make (12) true are infinite classes of fleas.

A moment's thought convinces one that the construction (12) amounts to second-order quantification, and my 1955 results suggest that the specific kind of quantification involved in it is enough to capture the full complexity of second-order logic, as far as questions of satisfiability are concerned.

From this fact it follows that the interpretation of second-order quantifiers (standard vs. nonstandard) is relevant to the semantics or ordinary English. This observation is independent of game-theoretical semantics, which in its own way puts a premium on the standard-nonstandard distinction.

Another main door through which the standard-nonstandard distinction enters recent applications of logic to linguistics is Montague semantics.[23] Its logic is higher-order intensional logic. Being higher-order logic, it is highly sensitive to the difference between standard and nonstandard semantics. Yet I cannot find any traces of awareness of the difference in the secondary literature over and above those already mentioned (see notes 6 and 7 above). Here is another important task for applied logicians. I doubt that the adequacy of Montague semantics as a viable model of natural language can be assessed without close attention to the standard-nonstandard distinction and to the problem of choosing between different varieties of nonstandard interpretation.

Florida State University

NOTES

[1] Stig Kanger, *Provability in Logic*. Stockholm Studies in Philosophy, Vol. 1, Stockholm, 1957. Kanger deserves much more credit for developing a viable semantics for modal logics than is given to him in the literature. For instance, the main novelty of such semantics as compared with Carnap's old ideas is the use of the alternativeness relation. (See below for an explanation of this concept.) Kanger introduced this idea in the literature and used it in his work before anyone else, e.g., five years before Kripke.

[2] See Saul Kripke, 'A Completeness Theorem in Modal Logic', *J. Symbolic Logic* **24** (1959), 1–4; 'Semantical Considerations on Modal Logic', *Acta Philosophica Fennica* **16** (1963), 83–94; 'Semantical Analysis of Modal Logic I', *Zeitschrift für mathematische Logik und Grundlagen der Mathematik* 9 (1963), 67–96; 'Semantical Analysis of Modal Logic II', in J. W. Addison, L. Henkin, and A. Tarski (eds.), *The Theory of Models*, North-Holland, Amsterdam, 1965, pp. 206–220; 'The Undecidability of Monadic Modal Quantification Theory', *Zeitschrift für mathematische Logik und Grundlagen der Mathematik* **8** (1962), 113–116; 'Semantical Analysis of Intutionistic Logic', in J. N. Crossley and Michael Dummett (eds), *Formal Systems and Recursive Functions*, North-Holland, Amsterdam, 1965, pp. 92–130.

[3] Marcel Guillaume, 'Rapports entre calculs propositionels modaux et topologie impliqués par certaines extensions de la méthode des tableaux: Système de Feys–von Wright', *Comptes rendus des séances de l'Academie des Science (Paris)* **246** (1958), 1140–1142; 'Système S4 de Lewis', *ibid.*, 2207–2210; 'Système S5 de Lewis', *ibid.*, **247** (1958), 1282–1283; Jaakko Hintikka, 'Quantifiers in Deontic Logic', *Societas Scientariarum Fennica, Commentationes humanarum litterarum*, Vol. 23, 1957, No. 4; 'Modality and Quantification', *Theoria* **27** (1961), 119–128; 'The Modes of Modality', *Acta Philosophica Fennica* **16** (1963), 65–82.

[4] See Richmond Thomason (ed.), *Formal Philosophy: Selected Papers of Richard Montague*, Yale University Press, New Haven, 1974, Chapters 1–2.

[5] *Op. cit.*, Chapters 3–8.

[6] David Kaplan, UCLA dissertation, 1964.

[7] Nino Cocchiarella, 'On the Primary and Secondary Semantics of Logical Necessity', *Journal of Philosophic Logic* **4** (1975), 13–27; 'Logical Atomism and Modal Logic', *Philosophia* 4 (1974), 40–66.

[8] Alfred Tarski and Bjarni Jonsson, 'Boolean Algebras with Operators I–II', *American Journal of Mathematics* **73** (1951), and **74** (1952).

[9] See Leon Henkin, 'Completeness in the Theory of Types', *J. Symbolic Logic* **15** (1950), 81–91. (Please note that Peter Andrews has discovered a flaw in Henkin's original argument and has shown how to repair it.)

[10] See especially Jaakko Hintikka, 'Quantifiers in Logic and Quantifiers in Natural Languages', in S. Körner (ed.), *Philosophy of Logic*, Blackwell's, Oxford, 1976, pp. 208–232; 'Quantifiers vs. Quantification Theory', *Linguistic Inquiry* 5 (1974), 153–177; *Logic, Language-Games, and Information*, Clarendon Press, Oxford, 1973. Much of the relevant literature has now been collected in Esa Saarinen (ed.), *Game-Theoretical Semantics*, D. Reidel, Dordrecht, 1978.
[11] Cf. here Jaakko Hintikka and Veikko Rantala, 'A New Approach to Infinitary Languages', *Annals of Mathematical Logic* **10** (1976), 95–115.
[12] For an explicit discussion of this idea see Jaakko Hintikka and Lauri Carlson, 'Conditionals, Generic Quantifiers, and Other Applications of Subgames', in A. Margalit (ed.), *Meaning and Use*, D. Reidel, Dordrecht, 1978.
[13] As Dana Scott has pointed out in an unpublished note, one can in this way also obtain Gödel's functional interpretation of first-order logic and arithmetic. See Kurt Gödel, 'Eine bisher noch nicht benützte Erweiterung des finiten Standpunktes', in *Logica: Studia Paul Bernays Dedicata,* Ëditions du Griffon, Neuchatel, 1959, pp. 76–83.
[14] Cf. my paper 'Language Games', in *Essays on Wittgenstein in Honour of G. H. von Wright* (Acta Philosophica Fennica, Vol. 28, Nos. 1–3), North-Holland, Amsterdam, 1976, pp. 105–125.
[15] 'Quantifiers vs. Quantification Theory', *Linguistic Inquiry* 5 (1974), 153–177.
[16] Of course this is not the only nor the most natural way of imposing the distinction on second-order logic.
[17] See David Kaplan, *op. cit*. (note 6 above).
[18] I have discussed these issues in the essays collected in *Models for Modalities*, D. Reidel, Dordrecht, 1969, and *The Intentions of Intentionality and Other New Models for Modalities*, D. Reidel, Dordrecht, 1975.
[19] For backwards-looking operators, see Esa Saarinen, 'Backwards-Looking Operators in Tense Logic and Natural Language', in Jaakko Hintikka *et. al* (eds.), *Essays on Mathematical and Philosophical Logic*, D. Reidel, Dordrecht, 1978, pp. 341–367; and Esa Saarinen, 'Intentional Identity Interpreted', *Linguistic and Philosophy* 2 (1978), 151–223, with further references to the literature. The initiators of the diesa seem to have been Hans Kamp and David Kaplan.
[20] 'Reductions in the Theory of Types', *Acta Philosophica Fennica* 8 (1955), 56–115.
[21] See S. K. Thomason, 'Semantic Analysis of Tense Logics', *J. Symbolic Logic* 37 (1972), 150–158; 'Noncompactness in Propositional Modal Logic', *ibid*., 716–720; 'An Incompleteness Theorem in Modal Logic', *Theoria* **40** (1974), 30–34.
[22] Personal communcation.
[23] Barbara Hall Partee (ed.), *Montague Grammar*, Academic Press, New York, 1976, and note 4 above.

CORRADO BÖHM

LOGIC AND COMPUTERS

Combinatory Logic as Extension of Elementary Number Theory

1. INTRODUCTION

1.1. Historical Background

Shortly after the appearance of the first computers, that is computing machines with stored programs, there arose the problem of how to communicate efficiently with them, especially how to simplify the writing of coded instructions. Zuse (1949) was probably the first to suggest that machines should be employed to facilitate this work using logical propositional methods. Shortly after, the author of this article (1951–52) devised a 'language'. Its phrases were to have a double meaning: for mathematicians they signified the description of some algorithm and for the computer they signified a list of instructions to be obeyed in order to implement that algorithm. Moreover the computer was to take upon itself the task of translating these phrases into sequences of instructions written in its own code (Böhm, 1954).

It was the beginning of construction of 'high level' programming languages, as FORTRAN (1954), ALGOL (1958) etc. together with the relative translation programs (compilers).

The next step was to mechanize the construction of the compilers (1960–1970), i.e., to write compiler compilers. A programming language became a real formal system, the correctness of which was first 'syntactically' checked (programs acting as recognizers, parsers) secondly 'semantically' checked by constructing machines or interpreters which accepted phrases of a source programming language as commands. In order to perform this last step all known computability schemes were revisited, like Turing machines (Shepherdson and Sturgis, 1963) Markof algorithms (De Bakker, 1964) combinatory logic and λ-calculus (Burge and Landin, 1964; Böhm and Strachey, 1964).

The λ-calculus theory of equality attracted the interest of both computer scientists and logicians because:

(i) It was partially implemented as the programming language LISP McCarthy, 1962) especially constructed for the recursive treatment of non-numerical entities such as lists, symbolic expressions, etc.

(ii) It has the ability of expressing easily minimal fixed point solutions

E. Agazzi (ed.), Modern Logic – A Survey, 297–309.

to recursive equations involving functionals or functions (Kleene, 1950; Morris, 1968; Park, 1970; De Bakker and Scott, 1969; and many other researchers).

(iii) It possesses set-theoretical models (Scott, 1971; Plotkin; Scott, 1976) which gave rise to a beautiful mathematical theory of comtation.

The λ-calculus theory of reduction has not yet received much attention in the computer science because of its greater intrinsic difficulty. Abstract machines attempting the reduction to the normal form were described by Church (1941), Curry (1958), Wadsworth (1971), Böhm and Dezani (1972–73) and are still being studied by many people.

1.2. Summary

The aim of this paper is to sketch the introduction of combinatory logic and λ-calculus in a way that I hope will be satisfactory either from a tutorial or from an aesthetic point of view for both mathematicians and computer scientists. The idea is to extend the concept of integer in order to reach that of *bominatory integer* or, adding variables to this concept, that of *combinatory integer form.*

As rational, real, complex numbers cause results of division, limit operations, square roots of negative numbers etc., always to exist, combinatory integers or integer forms render the representation of effectively constructable functions or functionals on their own set always possible.

Non-negative integers are given together with addition multiplication and power-elevation operations. To this there is to add an infinite set of variables with the replacement property. A combinatory entity **C** and a limited logarithmic function with a variable as basis are then introduced, together with a convenient set of axiom schemes, defining the set of combinatory integer forms as the smallest set to which all axiom schemes apply.

All explicitly definable functions on this set are then proved to be represented by elements still belonging to the same set (Section 2).

Implicit or recursive defined functions are still proved to be representable. Finally, combinatory integer forms are proved to build a multiplicative monoid in more than one way and the relevance to concepts of computer science will also be discussed (Sections 3 and 4).

2. COMBINATORY INTEGERS AND INTEGER FORMS

Computers as well as computer science itself probably originated from the decision to put into the same registers or memory cells either numerals (coded integers) or coded instructions.[1] That was the starting point to program stored computers. A program is a sequence of instructions the meaning of which is the input-output function it describes. The idea to use the same constant to represent either an operand or an operator, the distinction between them being based only on their relative position inside one expression (left for operator, right for operand), was done many years before by Schönfinkel, Curry and Church (1921–40) to found combinatory logic.

To introduce combinatory logic and this section at the same time let us describe *another* way of looking at the number expression 2^7. We may consider 7 as an operator acting on 2 as operand in order to obtain 128 as result. x^7 then represents the raising of x to the 7th power and in this context 7 represents the corresponding unary function.[2] Since functions are usually written to the left of their argument(s) as in $f(x)$ or $f(x, y)$ we will slightly deviate from the common usage writing ${}^7 2$ instead of 2^7 and so on.

To enter the subject we will consider a mathematical structure based on the set N of non-negative integers extended by a new constant **C** (the combinatory constant) with the binary operations of: addition (+), multiplication ($\circ$) power-elevation ${}^{\cdots}\ldots$ and with the equality relation (=).[3] All objects obtained operating on integers and by means of the three given operations will belong to the class CN of combinatory integers. We will extend further the structure by allowing (an infinite set of) variables obtaining then the class CNF of combinatory integer forms.

As it was done in the classical introduction of relative, rational and complex numbers we will employ a more restricted set of axioms than Peano axioms (without mathematical induction) for integers but, joining also one axiom for **C** and one derivation rule for the equality, we will extend the meaning of the old operations warranting that the new extension be conservative, i.e., recovering the old meaning for integers and their operations.

2.1. Axioms and their Discussion

The axiom system can be summarized as follows: 6 (usual) axioms on integers and forms, asserting some known equalities on powers (3rd–6th), the replaceability of equal forms (1st) and the invariance of the equality w.r.t. the simultaneous replacement of all occurrences of the same variable by any form into another arbitrary form (2nd). The 7th axiom introduces or eliminates the constant **C**. The 8th rule states that if the same variable is raised to two forms (not containing that variable) and the two results are equal then the two forms are equal too.

The structure achieves a more constructive shape if we observe that all non-negative integers are generated from 0, 1 by means of the + operator. The set $C\mathrm{N}$ of combinatory integers is thus finitely presented. Formally we have:

$$C\mathrm{N} \equiv (=;\ {}^{\cdots}\!\ldots, \circ, +, 0, 1, \mathbf{C})$$
$$C\mathrm{N}F \equiv (=;\ {}^{\cdots}\!\ldots, \circ, +, 0, 1, \mathbf{C}, x, y, z, \ldots).$$

In the sequel v will denote an arbitrary variable, a and b arbitrary (combinatory integer) forms not containing v and $\alpha, \beta, \gamma, \delta$ will denote unrestricted arbitrary forms.

The set of axiom schemes and axiom rules is the following:

(1) $\alpha = \beta, \gamma = \delta \rightarrow {}^{\gamma}\alpha = {}^{\delta}\beta$[4]

(2) $\alpha = \beta \rightarrow [\gamma/v]\alpha = [\gamma/v]\beta$

(3) ${}^{\gamma \circ \beta}\alpha = {}^{\gamma}(\beta_{\alpha})$

(4) ${}^{\gamma + \beta}\alpha = {}^{\gamma}\alpha \circ {}^{\beta}\alpha$

(5) ${}^{0}\alpha = 1$

(6) ${}^{1}\alpha = \alpha$

(7) ${}^{{}^{{}^{\mathbf{C}}\gamma}\beta}\alpha = {}^{{}^{\gamma}\alpha}\beta$

(8) ${}^{a}v = {}^{b}v \rightarrow a = b.$

We state here some results whose proof succeeds without the help of the 'strange' axiom (7):

(i) $\circ$ and + become associative operators, but not commutative, in general, and moreover axiom rules similar to (1) are valid for $\circ$ and +.

(ii) $\alpha \circ 1 = 1 \circ \alpha$ and $\alpha + 0 = 0 + \alpha$.

(iii) $0 \circ \alpha = 0$ but not $\alpha \circ 0 = 0$, in general.

(iv) $(\alpha + \beta) \circ \gamma = \alpha \circ \gamma + \beta \circ \gamma$
but not $\alpha \circ (\beta + \gamma) = \alpha \circ \beta + \alpha \circ \gamma$ in general.

(v) $0 \neq 1 + \alpha$.

Let us prove the last assertion with a *per absurdum* argument. If $0 = 1 + \alpha$ then by (1) ${}^{0}0 = {}^{1+\alpha}0$. The l.h.s. is by (5) equal to (1). The r.h.s. by (4) becomes ${}^{1}0 \circ {}^{\alpha}0$ and by (i) and (6) ${}^{1}0 \circ {}^{\alpha}0 = 0 \circ {}^{\alpha}0 = 0$ the last result being done by (iii). Then $0 = 1$, contradiction.

In order to simplify the writing let us give a name to two very useful combinatory integers:

$$\mathbf{K} \overset{\mathrm{DF}}{\equiv} {}^{\mathbf{C}}0 \quad \text{and} \quad \mathbf{C}_{*} \overset{\mathrm{DF}}{\equiv} {}^{\mathbf{C}}1.$$

Using axiom (7) twice we have

(9) $\quad {}^{{}^{\mathbf{K}}\beta}\alpha = {}^{{}^{0}\alpha}\beta = {}^{1}\beta = \beta$

(10) $\quad {}^{{}^{\mathbf{C}_*}\beta}\alpha = {}^{{}^{1}\alpha}\beta = {}^{\alpha}\beta$

which may be used to eliminate or introduce **K** and $\mathbf{C}_*$. One may ask the reason for restricting axiom rule (8). Without the restriction the system becomes inconsistent, as it is visible by the following counterexample:

First: $x \neq {}^{\mathbf{C}_*}x$. Otherwise we would have e.g. and ${}^{1}0 = {}^{{}^{\mathbf{C}_*}1}0$ that is $0 = {}^{0}1 = 0$, a contradiction.

Second: ${}^{x}x = {}^{{}^{\mathbf{C}_*}x}x$ as becomes evident from (10). The last equality is the counterexample we have been seeking.

In order to show how the whole system works let us prove that **C** is a 'square root' of (1)!

First: ${}^{2}\mathbf{C} = {}^{1+1}\mathbf{C} = {}^{1}\mathbf{C} \circ {}^{1}\mathbf{C} = \mathbf{C}\circ\mathbf{C}$

Second: ${}^{{}^{{}^{\mathbf{C}\circ\mathbf{C}}x}y}z = {}^{{}^{{}^{\mathbf{C}}({}^{\mathbf{C}}x)}y}z = {}^{{}^{{}^{\mathbf{C}}x}z}y = {}^{{}^{x}y}z$

Third: ${}^{{}^{{}^{1}x}y}z = {}^{{}^{x}y}z$ then it is

$${}^{{}^{{}^{\mathbf{C}\circ\mathbf{C}}x}y}z = {}^{{}^{{}^{1}x}y}z$$

and by a triple application of (8) the result follows.

Before examining more deeply rule (8) let us introduce a new useful constant:

$$D \overset{\mathrm{DF}}{\equiv} \mathbf{C}\circ\mathbf{C}_*$$

which enables us to present an equality supposed to be new:

(11) $\quad {}^{\beta}\alpha = {}^{{}^{\mathbf{C}_*}\beta\,\circ\,D}\alpha$.

Rule (8) may be interpreted as the assertion of the *existence of a logarithmic function* of a power whose basis is a variable and whose exponent is a form not containing that variable.

The counterexample proves that without that restriction the logarithmic function is no more univalent.[5]

Let us give solidity to the existence of the special logarithmic function just discussed by denoting it as *λ-ogarithm* (as hommage to Church) *in basis v* and by rewriting rule (8) as a new equality:

(12) $\quad \lambda v \cdot {}^{a}v = a$.

2.2. *Combinatory Integer Forms as Function Designators*

We are now able to justify the introduction of the notion of combinatory integer form. The aim of this section is to prove that combinatory integer forms can represent functions from CNF into CNF or functions from $CNF \times CNF$ into CNF, etc.

Let us concentrate first on unary functions. Naturally associated to each combinatory integer from α is the function which maps every form β into the form $[\beta/v]\alpha$ (here β and v are arbitrary combinatory integer form and variable.

If, *as a special case* $\alpha \equiv {}^{a}v$ then $\lambda v \cdot \alpha = \lambda v \cdot {}^{a}v = a$ represents such a function: in fact by (2)

$$(13) \qquad [\beta/v]\alpha = [\beta/v]\, {}^{a}v = {}^{a}\beta = {}^{\lambda v \cdot \alpha}\beta,$$

that is, the equality

$$[\beta/v]\alpha = {}^{\lambda v \cdot \alpha}\beta$$

can be rephrased stating that $\lambda v \cdot \alpha$ maps β into $[\beta/v]\alpha$ and this shows a strict analogy to a unary function-mapping an argument β into $f(\beta)$.

The main theorem is the following:

COMPLETENESS THEOREM (Curry and Feys, 1958).
The λ-ogarithm of any form α in any basis v still exists and satisfies (13), for any form β.

Proof. The proof is *constructive* (a good feature for computer scientists!) since it is done by structural induction on (or, what is the same, on the number of symbols of) α.

$$\begin{array}{llll} \text{Basis: } \alpha \equiv b & \text{then } \lambda v \cdot b = {}^{\mathbf{K}}b & \text{check: } & {}^{{}^{\mathbf{K}}b}v = b, \\ \qquad\;\; \alpha \equiv v & \text{then } \lambda v \cdot v = 1 & \text{check: } & {}^{1}v = v. \end{array}$$

Inductive step: let $\lambda v \cdot \alpha$ and $\lambda v \cdot \beta$ exist, then:

$$\lambda v \cdot \alpha \circ \beta = \lambda v \cdot {}^{\lambda v \cdot \alpha}v \circ {}^{\lambda v \cdot \beta}v = \lambda v \cdot {}^{\lambda v \cdot \alpha + \lambda v \cdot \beta}v = \lambda v \cdot \alpha + \lambda v \cdot \beta,$$

$$\begin{aligned} \lambda v \cdot {}^{\beta}\alpha &= \lambda v \cdot {}^{\mathbf{C}_*}\beta \circ {}^{D}\alpha = \lambda v \cdot {}^{\mathbf{C}_*}\beta + \lambda v \cdot {}^{D}\alpha = \lambda v \cdot {}^{\mathbf{C}_*}({}^{\lambda v \cdot \beta}v\, {}^{\mathbf{C}_*}({}^{\lambda v \cdot \alpha}v), \\ &= \lambda v \cdot {}^{\mathbf{C}_* \circ \lambda v \cdot \beta}v + \lambda v^{D \circ \lambda v \cdot \beta}v = \mathbf{C}_* \circ \lambda v \cdot \beta + D \circ \lambda v \cdot \alpha. \end{aligned}$$

We shall omit the steps needed to prove the last result:

$$\lambda v \cdot \alpha + \beta = {}^{\mathbf{K}}({}^{\mathbf{C}_*}\lambda v \cdot \alpha + {}^{\mathbf{C}_*}\lambda v \cdot \beta) + D.$$

Since each combinatory integer form is either a variable v or a form non-containing v or a power or a sum or a product of two 'smaller' forms, the proof is completed.

Summarizing, we proved that the representation power of combinatory integer forms is very great since they represent all possible unary functions obtained thinking any variable as argument and the result of replacing that variable by any form as value (explicit definition).

We will soon see that combinatory integer forms can do more. First, since $\lambda y \cdot \alpha$ do not contain y any more,[6] we may iterate the λ-ogarithm function by constructing, e.g., $\lambda x \cdot \lambda y \cdot \alpha$. As a consequence of the completeness theorem the last combinatory integer form may represent a function of (2) variables; and so on.

EXAMPLE. We next compute $\lambda x \cdot \lambda y \cdot {}^{x}y$ and $\lambda x \cdot \lambda y \cdot x \circ y$

$$\lambda x \cdot \lambda y \cdot {}^{x}y = \lambda x \cdot x = 1$$

$$\lambda x \cdot \lambda y \cdot x \circ y = \lambda x \cdot (\lambda y \cdot x + \lambda y \cdot y) = \lambda x \cdot {}^{\mathbf{K}}x + 1 =$$
$${}^{\mathbf{K}}({}^{\mathbf{C}*}\mathbf{K} + {}^{\mathbf{C}*}0) + D\,.$$

Before doing anything else let us make a slight change of notation for the sake of both the printer and combinatory logician! We will put all exponents on the same line writing, e.g., $\mathbf{C}_*((\lambda v \cdot \beta)v)$ instead of ${}^{\mathbf{C}*}({}^{\lambda v \circ \beta}v)$, adding some parentheses, if needed.

2.2. *Toward a Fusion with Combinatory Logic and λ-calculus*

The last rewriting convention enables us to put into evidence that what we described is nothing else than a mixture of combinatory logic and λ-calculus with equality.

Following Curry (1958) a combinatory *term* is either a variable or **K** or **S** or a *combination* (MN) of two combinatory terms.

Axioms are: $\mathbf{K} \neq \mathbf{S}$, $((\mathbf{K}x)y) = x$ (to compare with (9)) $(((\mathbf{S}x)y)z) = ((xz)(yz))$.[7]

(8) is called *weak extensionality rule* and it is written $(av) = (bv) \to a = b$. The completeness theorem follows very easily.

Following Church (1941a) λ-term is either a variable or an *application* (MN) of two λ-terms or an *abstraction* $(\lambda x \cdot M)$ of a term with respect to a variable. There are three equalities:

$\lambda v \cdot (av)$	$= a$	rewriting of (12)	η-rule,
$((\lambda v \cdot M)N)$	$= [N/v]M$	rewriting of (13)	β-rule,
$\lambda v \cdot M$	$= \lambda z \cdot [z/v]M$[8]		α-rule.

Church's interpretation of $\lambda x \cdot M$ was the function with argument x and value M.

The difference between λ-calculus and combinatory logic is, very roughly phrased, that the former does not eliminate the λ-notation since this is the only way to express constants: it follows that integer n is represented by the term $\lambda x \cdot \lambda y \cdot x(x(\ldots x(xy) \ldots))$ (Church numeral), etc.

To sum up, our approach to combinatory logic and λ-calculus seems to be more mathematically oriented than the conventional ones. Natural numbers and elementary operations on them are here basic, the operations of power-elevation and its limited inverse, the λ-ogarithm, have more intuitive appeal than application and abstraction.

3. APPLICATIONS TO COMPUTER SCIENCE

3.1. The Fixpoint Theorem

With reference to our last statement, it seems conceptually less objectionable to elevate a combinatory integer form to itself than to apply a function to itself. This is just what must be done to express a solution of the equation $X = FX$ where F is a known combinatory integer form. First we have:

$$xx = (\lambda v \cdot vv)x = (\lambda v \cdot \mathbf{C}_* v \circ Dv)x = (\mathbf{C}_* + D)x\,.$$

Then it is easy to prove that a solution is

$$X = (\lambda x \cdot F(xx))(\lambda x \cdot F(xx)).$$

In fact

$$\begin{aligned} \lambda x \cdot F(xx) &= \lambda x \cdot F((\mathbf{C}_* + D)x) = \lambda x \cdot (F \circ (\mathbf{C}_* + D))x \\ &= F \circ (\mathbf{C}_* + D) \end{aligned}$$

and we have

$$\begin{aligned} X &= (F \circ (\mathbf{C}_* + D))(F \circ (\mathbf{C}_* + D)) = F((\mathbf{C}_* + D)(F \circ (\mathbf{C}_* + D)) \\ &= F((F \circ (\mathbf{C}_* + D))(F \circ (\mathbf{C}_* + D))) = FX. \end{aligned}$$

Since F is arbitrary we may consider the found solution as depending on F in a uniform way

$$X = \mathbf{Y}F \quad \text{where} \quad \mathbf{Y} = \lambda y \cdot (\lambda x \cdot y(xx))(\lambda x \cdot y(xx)).$$

3.2. The Representability of Recursive Functions

It is very easy to prove that

$$Dxyz = zxy, \text{ i.e. } D = \lambda x \cdot \lambda y \cdot \lambda z \cdot zxy .$$

Since $DXY0 = 0XY = 1Y = Y$ and $DXY\mathbf{K} = \mathbf{K}XY = X$. DXY can be considered as a formalization of an ordered pair $DXY \overset{\text{DF}}{\equiv} \langle x,y \rangle$ together with the projection functions $\mathbf{C}_*\mathbf{K}$ and $\mathbf{C}_*0$.

Defining the predecessor function π we have

$$\pi 0 = 0,$$
$$\pi(1+n) = n.$$

A way to represent π is to consider πn as the result of iterating n times starting on $\langle 0,0 \rangle$ the transform of $\langle X,Y \rangle$ into $\langle 1+X,X \rangle$, thus obtaining $\langle n, \pi n \rangle$, and finally taking its second projection. Formally we write:

$$\pi n = nM(D00)0 \quad \text{where} \quad M \equiv \lambda z \cdot D(1+z\mathbf{K})(z\mathbf{K}),$$

A representation of π is then

$$\pi = \lambda x \cdot xM(D00)0 .$$

The successor function σ is represented by $\lambda x \cdot 1 + x$. If we represent *true* by $\mathbf{K}$ and *false* by 0 the predicate Z such that $Z0 = \mathbf{K}$ and $Z(\sigma n) = 0$ is represented by $Z = \lambda x \cdot x0(\mathbf{KK})0$ since by (iiii)) $00 = 1$ and $\sigma x0 = 0$. The unary function ζ whose value is always 0 is represented by $\mathbf{K}0$.

To prove that recursive functions can be represented by combinatory integers it is sufficient to prove that ordered pairs, successor and predecessor functions, zero function and predicate are representable, as we just showed, and moreover that some functional operators such as **if then else fi, while do od** and composition operator are representable too (Robinson, 1950; Böhm, 1964; Böhm and Jacopini, 1966).

Let P represent a unary predicate and $\underline{f}, \underline{g}$ two unary functions on $\mathbb{N}$. Then the operator

if P **then** f **else** g **fi** is represented by
$\lambda x \cdot px(fx)(gx)$.

The iteration **while** P **do** f **od** represents the minimal fixpoint of the equation

$$h = \lambda x \cdot Px(h(fx))x = (\lambda t \cdot \lambda x \cdot Px(t(fx))x)h$$

whence

$$h = Y\lambda t \cdot \lambda x \cdot Px(t(fx))x.$$

Finally, the composite function obtained applying first a function represented by f and after a function represented by g is simply represented by

(14) $g \circ f$.

3.3. Combinatory Integer Forms as a Multiplicative Monoid

We follow here the development indicated by Church (1937).

Church discovered the two equalities

(15) $\mathbf{C}_*(xy) = \mathbf{C}_* y \circ \mathbf{C}_* x \circ B,$

(16) $\mathbf{C}_* x \circ \mathbf{C}_* = x,$

where $\mathbf{B} \equiv \lambda x \cdot \lambda y \cdot \lambda z \cdot x(yz)$. Since combinators (combinatory integers) are generated by iterated application of **S** and **K** only, it follows that they build a multiplicative monoid (see (ii)) having as finite basis $\mathbf{C}_*\mathbf{S}$, **CK**, $\mathbf{C}_*$ and **B**. This fact has been applied in computer science by constructing translators with a minimum of syntactical check (Böhm and Dezani-Ciancaglini, 1972; Bert and Petrone, 1977).

Here we will briefly show how the basis can be reduced to only H and $\mathbf{C}_*$ (see also Klop, 1975). In fact

$$H \equiv D(\mathbf{K} \circ \mathbf{C}_*\mathbf{K})\mathbf{S}$$

$$H \circ \mathbf{C}_* = \mathbf{C}_*\mathbf{K},\ \mathbf{C}_*\mathbf{K} \circ \mathbf{C} = \mathbf{K},\ H \circ \mathbf{K} = \mathbf{C}_*\mathbf{S} \circ \mathbf{C}_* = \mathbf{S}$$

and

$$\mathbf{S} \circ \mathbf{K} = \mathbf{B}.$$

The infinite basis H, $\mathbf{C}_*$, $\mathbf{C}_*x$, $\mathbf{C}_*y$, $\mathbf{C}_*z$, ... presents therefore a basis for the multiplicative monoid of combinatory integer forms.

4. CONCLUSION

Somebody could ask why the equality (11), conveniently rewritten as

(17) $xy = \mathbf{C}_* x \circ Dy,$

has not be chosen as basic for the multiplicative monoid. This objection is very reasonable. The corresponding equality in Church's monoid is

(18) $xy = \mathbf{C}_* y \circ \mathbf{C}x;$

while 'our' equalities, corresponding to (15) and (16), would be

$$(19) \quad D(xy) = \mathbf{C}_*(2(\mathbf{CB})) \circ Dx \circ Dy$$
$$(20) \quad \mathbf{C}_* 1 \circ Dx = x\,.$$

The answer is that we just discovered (17) or (11) working on this paper. A more general and more uniform treatment is still being studied (Böhm and Dezani-Ciancaglini, 1977).

The two monoids are not totally equivalent with respect to computer science applications. The last one seems promising more, at least for two reasons:

(i) A 'natural' order of scanning multiplicative terms is from right to left as was visible also from term (14), and moreover, in general, operands should be scanned before operators. These conditions are satisfied by (19) and (20) but not by (15) and (16).

(ii) The entity D formalizes the concept of ordered pair which is a very important data structure especially with relation to LISP and APL (Iverson, 1962) programs and primitive recursive operations (Venturini-Zilli, 1965). Moreover the information about the components is lost in $\mathbf{C}_* x(\mathbf{C}_* y) = xy$ but not in $Dx(Dy) = R$ since $(D \circ \mathbf{C}_*\mathbf{K})R = Dx$ and $(\mathbf{C}_* 0)R = Dy$.

ACKNOWLEDGMENTS

I am grateful to Lidia Sciama and to Emy Rosenfeld for helping me to polish the English text of the whole paper including this statement!

University of Rome

NOTES

[1] This idea is attributed to Von Neumann even if it was implicitly realized in the concept of universal Turing machine.

[2] This function, considered as mapping from N to N, is informally described as 'raising to the 7th power'.

[3] An alternative way would be to introduce a combinatory class of algebras, to consider equality as a congruence relation w.r.t. power-elevation and to eliminate variables by means of unique extensions of homomorphisms induced by a free algebra into *ad hoc* algebras belonging to the original class.

[4] To be complete one should add reflexive symmetric and transitive properties of equality.

[5] It is easy to prove that a (multivalent) logarithm of any form β with basis α always exists: it is simply $^{\mathbf{K}}\beta$, as it comes out reconsidering (9).
[6] We note that $\lambda y \cdot \alpha = \lambda z \cdot [z/y]\alpha$ if z is not in α.
[7] It is easy to prove that $((\mathrm{S}x)y) = \mathbf{C}_* \circ x + D \circ y$.
[8] The conditions on z and M are a generalization of what is done at note 6.

BIBLIOGRAPHY

de Bakker, J. W., 'Formal Definition of Programming Languages', Mathematics Centrum, Amsterdam, 1967.

de Bakker, J. W. and Scott, D., 'A Theory of Programs', Unpublished Notes, IBM Seminar, Vienna, 1969.

Böhm, C., 'Du déchiffrage des formules logico-mathématiques par la machine même dans la conception du programme', *Ann. Math. Pura Appl.* 37 (1954), 5–47.

Böhm, C., 'On a Family of Turing Machines and the Related Programming Language', *ICC Bulletin* 3 (1964), 187–194.

Böhm, C., 'The CUCH as a Formal and Description Language', in T. B. Steel (ed.), *Formal Language Description Languages for Computer Programming*, North-Holland, Amsterdam, 1966, pp. 179–197.

Böhm, C. and Dezani, M., 'A CUCH Machine: The Automatic Treatment of Bound Variables', *Int. J. Computer Inf. Sci.* 1 (1972), 171–191.

Böhm, C. and Dezani, M., 'Notes on "A CUCH Machine: The Automatic Treatment of Bound Variables" ', *Int. J. Computer Inf. Sci* 2 (1973), 157–160.

Böhm and Dezani-Ciancaglini, M., 'Can Syntax be Ignored During Translation?', in M. Nivat (ed.), *Automata, Languages and Programming*, North-Holland, 1973, pp. 197–207.

Böhm, C. and Dezani-Ciancaglini, M., 'Combinatory Logic as Monoids', in preparation, 1977.

Böhm, C. and Gross, W., 'Introduction to the CUCH', in E. R. Caianiello (ed.), *Automata Theory*, Academic Press, New York, 1966, pp. 35–66.

Böhm, C. and Jacopini, G., 'Flow-Diagrams, Turing Machines and Languages with Only Two Formation Rules', *Comm. ACM* 9 (1966), 366–371.

Burge, W. M., 'The Evaluation, Classification and Interpretation of Expressions', ACM Nato Conference, 1964.

Church, A., 'Combinatory Logic as a Semigroup', (abstract), *Bull. Am. Math. Soc.* 43 (1937), 333.

Church, A., 'The Calculi of Lambda-Conversion', *Ann. Math. Studies* 6, Princeton Univ. Press, Princeton, N.J., 1941.

Curry, H. B. and Feys, R., *Combinatory Logic*, vol. I, North-Holland, Amsterdam, 1958.

Iverson, K., *A Programming Language*, Wiley, New York, 1962.

Kleene, S. C., *Introduction to Metamathematics*, Van Nostrand, New York, 1950.

Klop, J. W., 'On Solvability by λ*I*-Terms', in C. Böhm (ed.), *Lambda-Calculus and Computer Science Theory*, Computer Science, Springer-Verlag, New York, 1975.

Landin, J. P., 'The Mechanical Evaluation of Expressions', *Computer Journal* 6 (1964), 308–320.

McCarthy, J., *The LISP 1.5 Programmers Manual*, MIT Press, Cambridge, Mass., 1962.

Morris, J. H., 'Lambda Calculus Models of Programming Languages', Ph.D. Thesis, MIT, Cambridge, Mass., 1968.

Park, D. M. R., 'Fixpoint Induction and Proofs of Program Properties', in B. Meltzer and D. Michie (eds.), *Machine Intelligence*, vol. 5, American Elsevier, New York, 1970, pp. 59–78.

Petrone, L. and Bert, M. N., 'Relaxing Syntax to Simplify Syntax-Directed Translations', *Proc. of 'Informatica 77'*, Bled, 1977.

Plotkin, G. D., 'A Set Theoretical Definition of Application', Memo, MP–R–95, School of Artificial Intelligence, Univ. of Edinburgh.

Robinson, J., 'General Recursive Functions', *Proc. Am. Math. Soc.* 1 (1950), 703–718.

Shepherdson, J. C. and Sturgis, H. E., 'Computability of Recursive Functions', *J. ACM* 10 (1963), 217–255.

Scott, D., 'Continuous Lattices', *Proc. 1971 Conference, Lecture Notes in Mathematics*, No. 274, Springer-Verlag, New York, 1972, pp. 311–366.

Scott, D., 'Data Types as Lattices', *Siam J. Computing* 5 (1976), 522–587.

Strachey, C., 'Toward a Formal Semantics', in T. B. Steel (ed.), *Formal Language Description Languages for Computer Programming*, North-Holland, Amsterdam, 1966, pp. 198–220.

Venturini-Zilli, M., 'λ-K-formulae for Vector Operators', *ICC Bulletin* 4 (1965), 157–174.

Wadsworth, C. P., 'Semantics and Pragmatics of the Lambda-Calculus', Ph.D. Thesis, Oxford Univ., Oxford, England, 1971.

Zuse, K., 'Ueber den allgemeinen Plankalkul als Mittel zur Formulierung schematisch kombinatorischer Aufgaben', *Arch. Math.* 1 (1948–49), 441–449.

FORTRAN, 'The Fortran Automatic Coding System', by J. W. Backus *et al.*, *Proc. of the WJCC*, I.R.E., New York, 1957.

ALGOL, 'Report on the Algorithmic Language ALGOL 60', P. Naur (ed.), *Comm. ACM* 3 (1960), 299–314.

GERALD J. MASSEY

LOGIC AND LINGUISTICS

The paths of logic and linguistics, long divergent, were reunited in 1957. The publication in that year of Chomsky's *Syntactic Structures* ushered in a new and exciting era in linguistics.[1] Equipped with methods adequate to deal with the creative aspects of language, methods bequeathed to them by logicians, modern linguists attacked with zest problems whose outlines had been perceived by their forerunners centuries ago.[2] In particular, the problem of logical form, the problem of accounting structurally for logical consequence relations among the sentences of a natural language, was soon restored to its place as one of the central problems of linguistics. With the restoration came new demands. Hitherto, grammarians could rest content with taxonomic descriptions of sentence structure; thereafter, they would be obliged to supply theoretical explanations.

Logical form is not the private problem of linguistics. It is also a central problem of logic and, in a wider sense, of philosophy itself.[3] Through two millenia logicians have set themselves the task of demarcating valid arguments from invalid ones, and justifying the demarcation. Whereas linguists had neglected logical form to address more tractable problems, in the 80 years preceding the publication of *Syntactic Structures*, and in the last 20 years as well, logicians and philosophers made unprecedented progress. The problem of logical form was virtually solved for mathematical discourse by the development of the logic of truth functions and quantifiers.[4] Progress went well beyond mathematics, however. For example, tense, though irrelevant to mathematics, received illuminating theoretical treatment.[5] Even modal idioms, a source of confusion since logic's infancy, received their theoretical due.[6] Substantial inroads were made on problems posed by sentences of propositional attitude: belief, knowledge, and the like.[7] Even causal statements and action sentences yielded some of their secrets.[8] A solution to the vexing problem of indexical expressions was fashioned after the one given to modal constructions.[9]

So rapid was the pace of progress that theory construction often outstripped application to natural language. As evidence theoref, consider such developments as many-valued logics, infinitary logics, the theory of multigrade connectives, the logic of individuals or parts-wholes (mereology), deontic

E. Agazzi (ed.), Modern Logic – A Survey, 311–329.

logics, and entailment systems. Efforts, sometimes tentative, sometimes philosophical, have been made to apply these systems and theories. Nevertheless, most logicians value them for their own sakes, not for the sake of any presumptive application or relevance to natural language. In the case of these developments, and unlike the case of those mentioned a paragraph ago, theoretical or intrinsic interest far exceeded their practical or extrinsic interest. Such at least was the case until quite recently when some of these 'offbeat' theories found applications within linguistics. Theories previously considered little more than quaint formal curiosities made their entrance on the stage of empirical linguistics and won acclaim in their practical roles.

These last-mentioned episodes in linguistics are reminiscent of episodes in physics wherein mathematical theories deemed formal curiosities received important empirical applications. One need look no further than non-euclidean geometry for an apt illustration. The nineteenth century saw non-euclidean geometry carried to a high state of development, but purely as a formal theory. From its inception, mathematicians, physicists, and philosophers recognized the empirical potential of non-euclidean geometry; they even set about to determine whether the structure of real space and time was euclidean or non-euclidean. When all attempts to detect non-euclidean features of real space and time failed, most thinkers drew what seemed to be the obvious conclusion, namely that non-euclidean geometry lacked empirical application. That is, whatever might have been the case, the fact was that the actual structure of real space and time was euclidean.

There were minority opinions, of course. Poincaré, for example, believed that the geometry of real space and time was a matter of convention or choice. One could assure a non-euclidean structure for space by adopting non-standard coordinating definitions, a maneuver that he thought complicated geometry without effecting off-setting simplifications within physical theory. Poincaré thus concluded that mathematical simplicity would forever dictate the choice of geometry to be euclidean.[10]

A dramatic turn-around was effected in the 20th century by relativity physics. Einstein recognized that piecemeal simplicity considerations need not square with overall simplicity considerations. The physicist's primary concern should be the simplicity of the total theory, $P + G$ (physics plus geometry), not with P or G taken separately. Local complications in P or G can lead to global simplifications in the complex $P + G$. Utilizing non-euclidean geometries already at hand, Einstein created an explanatorily powerful and elegant system of physics, general relativity, in which the structure of real space and time is non-euclidean.[11] Non-euclidean geometry remained no longer a speculative curiosity of merely formal or intrinsic interest. Incorporation within the GTR gave non-euclidean geometry empirical relevance equal to that enjoyed by euclidean geometry in classical physics.

I have stressed the parallelism of the aforementioned episodes in linguistics and physics for a reason. The parallelism is, I believe, no happenstance. Rather, it reflects an underlying or deeper parallelism which may be summarized thus: *with respect to their natural domains of application, logic bears to linguistics* (*more exactly, to grammar*) *the same relationship that geometry bears to physics*. For support of this thesis, we need only look at the linguistic theories spawned in the epoch since 1957.

As everyone knows, Chomsky's principal innovations in linguistics lie within grammar. As early conceived by Chomsky, grammar was tripartite, consisting of syntax, phonology, and semantics. Though tripartite, this conception was decidedly non-trinitarian; the three branches of grammar were inherently unequal. The basic branch was syntax. Syntax generated the objects that were converted into sounds by phonology and into meanings by semantics. The objects of phonic interpretation and semantic interpretation were different, however. In the former case, phonology, the objects of interpretation were the *surface structures* of sentences of natural language. In the latter case, semantics, the objects of interpretation were postulated entities called *deep structures*. Accordingly, syntax (or grammar in a narrower sense) contained two very different components: a *base component* which was essentially a phrase-structure grammar that recursively generates the objects of semantic interpretation, and a *transformational component* that converts deep structures, by such operations as movement, addition, and deletion of elements, into the surface structures of the language. In addition to thus pairing sound with meaning, grammar was expected to do a variety of tasks, among them the following:

(i) To account for grammaticalness and degrees thereof;

(ii) to explain amphiboly (by showing that amphibolous surface structures can be transformationally derived from several deep structures);

(iii) to account for evident logical equivalence of distinct surface structures (by showing that they are transformationally derivable from a single deep structure);

(iv) to account for logical consequence relations among surface structures (presumably by showing that their deep structures are so related that no interpretation could simultaneously turn the 'implying' structures into true sentences and the 'implied' structure into a false sentence);[12]

(v) to explain, in conjunction with psychology, how human beings can learn their native languages from infantile exposure to a small and corrupted set of utterances.

Chosmky and his early co-workers concentrated on syntax. Phonology was already highly developed, so their relative neglect of it was both understandable and justified.[13] But their neglect of semantics, however understandable, was not similarly justified. Logicians and philosophers such as Frege, Russell, Tarski, Carnap, Wittgenstein, and Austin had already made important contributions to semantics, but they produced no semantical theory that could be brought to bear upon the deep structures of transformational grammar in the same straightforward way that extant phonological theory could be brought to bear upon surface structures. From hindsight one can see that the unsatisfactoriness of the semantic component stemmed less from the often alleged immaturity of semantics than from the eccentricities of the base component of transformational grammar. The base component was modeled upon the recursive formation rules of familiar logical systems, but only to a certain point. Whereas in the logical systems each formation rule is typically accompanied by a semantical rule, so that the meaning of a wff becomes a function of the meaning of its wf parts (*Frege's principle*), in transformational grammar the phrase-structure rules were framed independently of semantics and irrespective of whether an associated semantical rule could be given. (This casualness about or indifference to semantical rules has prompted Pieter Seuren to refer to transformational grammar as *autonomous syntax*. Autonomous syntax contrasts with *semantic syntax* which seeks a semantic explanation or justification for each rule of grammar.)[14] Not surprisingly, the deep structures generated by the base component proved recalcitrant to semantic interpretation. There was simply no way to interpret them conformably to both intuition and Frege's principle. However well transformational grammar might meet such objectives as (i)–(iii), it evidently was impotent to effect (iv). That is to say, tranformational grammar could not hope to solve the problem of logical form.

Recognition that the problem of logical form is central to linguistics, coupled with the realization that attempts to solve it in transformational grammar were doomed to failure, caused many young linguists to become disenchanted with transformational grammar and to develop a rival theory called *generative semantics* (or *semantic syntax*).[15] (The label *generative semantics* contrasts with *generative syntax* or *generative grammar*, generic names for the transformational grammars produced by Chomsky's school.) The proponents of generative semantics (Lakoff, McCawley, Postal, Ross, Seuren) attributed the shortcomings of transformational grammar to its postulation of a level of syntactical deep structure distinct from logical form. By identifying syntactical deep structure with logical form, they hoped to provide a grammatical account of language that succeeded where transformational grammar had failed, namely in providing a grammatical explanation of the logical consequence relations among sentences of natural language. The rules of grammar were taken to be simply 'the rules relating logical forms to the surface forms of sentences'.[16] For their logical forms, these linguists turned to logic, both philosophical and mathematical. Sentence connectives, quantifiers, individual variables, and scope indicators began to appear in grammatical deep structures. But their borrowings were not limited to these devices; modal connectives and possible-world semantics for modalities and propositional attitudes found their way into grammar. Lakoff, for example, purported to explain the alleged ungrammaticalness of the expression "It is possible that Sam will find a girl and certain that he will kiss her" as a violation of the general principle that "an antecedent must have a referent in all the worlds in which the anaphoric noun phrase (or pronoun) has a reference".[17] Even the theory of speech acts left its mark on grammar; Ross advanced the thesis that the main predicate of every sentence is a performative verb, notwithstanding surface impressions to the contrary.[18] A place was found even for such esoteric devices as multigrade connectives; McCawley argued that they were needed for an adequate theory of presupposition.[19]

Some linguists complained that the generative semanticists did not carry their program far enough. Bartsch and Vennemann, for example, recently pointed out that many of the deep structures of generative semantics bear only a superficial resemblance to the wffs of systems of symbolic logic.[20] Such forms are logico-syntactical hybrids no more interpretable conformably to Frege's principle than are the syntactic deep structures of transformational grammar, and for the same reason. Many of the formation rules of generative semantics lack semantic correlates. Bartsch & Vennemann compared generative semantics unfavorably to the grammars developed by Montague for fragments of English.[21] Montague's grammars embodied Frege's principle perfectly, the wffs receiving model-theoretic interpretations within higher-order intensional logic. In the spirit of Montague grammar, Bartsch and Vennemann proposed that "a true goal of linguistics is to adjust the theory of grammar in such a way that discourse can be represented in logic".[22] What they meant by this is that linguists should take seriously the identity to which generative semanticists gave only lip service, namely the identity of syntactic deep structure with logical form, where logical forms are taken to be the wffs of logical systems that satisfy Frege's principle. As in generative semantics, the transformational rules of grammar will be the rules that carry these logical forms into the surface structures of natural language.

This brief account of recent work in linguistics confirms, I think, my hypothesis that linguistics bears to logic much the same relationship that physics bears to geometry, so far as their natural domains of application are concerned. What predictions follow from this hypothesis? First, that linguists will employ the methods of logic in the construction of their grammars, a fact to which we have already alluded. Second, that, as Quine put it, logic will serve as a source of syntactical insights.[23] By rendering conspicuous in artificial symbolic languages grammatical functions quite inconspicuous in natural language, (for example, indication of scope) logic draws the linguists' attention to these phenomena and provides an articulated theory of them to guide the construction of grammars. Third, that logic provides linguistics with a veritable gold mine of logical systems that might play the theoretical role of the base component in transformational grammar. That is to say, the wffs of these logical systems can serve as the 'deep structures' that transformations carry into surface structures. Unlike Chomsky's deep structures that resist interpretation in accordance with Frege's principle, the wffs of these logical systems were designed to be so interpretable and to account for the logical consequence relations among the resulting sentences. One would expect, therefore, to see these logical systems being incorporated into grammars that are used to explain consequence relations among sentences of natural language. This, of course, is exactly what has been happening in generative semantics, most faithfully perhaps in Bartsch and Vennemann's version called *natural generative semantics*. Fourth, that not every logical system will thus find its way into grammar, anymore than every system of geometry appears as part of some physical theory or other. Recent work in linguistics bears out all of these predictions.

It might seem that logic has much to offer linguistics but little or nothing to receive in return. Again, my hypothesis predicts that work in linguistics will suggest new directions of logical research, just as progress in physics has from time to time stimulated mathematical discovery. (Recall, for example, how Newton was led to invent the infinitesimal calculus to deal with problems growing out of his physical ideas.) The development of a logic of adverbs by Parsons, Montague, and Clark would be a good instance of this phenomenon, but I prefer to relate a somewhat more pale instance, namely recent efforts to articulate a logic of phrasal conjunctions and group quantifers. In 1964 Katz and Postal proposed a significant simplification of transformational grammar which eliminated all many-place transformations (transformations that operate on more than one phrase-marker); only singulary or one-place transformations were retained.[24] The acceptability of their proposal turned on showing that the grammar of coordinate conjoined structures can be handled without appeal to many-place transformations. Because phrasal conjunctions are the thorniest species of coordinate conjoined structures, they consequently merited special attention by transformational grammarians. Hence, my preference for this example.

Phrasal conjunctions are expressions of the sort that appear as the surface grammatical subjects of (1), (2), and (3).

(1) Tom, Dick, and Harry weigh 300 kilograms.
(2) Tom, Dick, and Harry are partners.
(3) Tom, Dick, and Harry are philosophers.

Lakoff and Peters proposed a grammar of coordinated conjoined expressions in which the deep structures of (1) and (2) exhibit phrasal subjects 'Tom, Dick, and Harry', whereas the deep structure of (3) does not.[25] Sentence (3) is derived from an underlying sentential conjunction of threee sentences by a conjunction reduction transformation. By thus segregating (3) from (1) and (2), Lakoff and Peters hoped to explain their differential logical behavior, e.g., the fact that (3) logically implies (4)

(4) Tom is a philosopher.

although (1) does not logically imply (5).

(5) Tom weighs 300 kilograms:

Similarly, (3) is logically equivalent to (6)

(6) Tom and Dick are philosophers, and Dick and Harry are philosophers.

whereas (2) logically implies, but is not logically implied by, (7).

(7) Tom and Dick are partners, and Dick and Harry are partners.

Lakoff and Peters' grammar properly segregates (3) from (1) and (2), and provides a satisfactory analysis of (3). It errs, however, in lumping (1) and (2) together, for in logical behavior (1) is as unlike (3) as it is unlike (2). Notice, for example, that although (2) logically implies (7), (1) does not logically imply (8).

(8) Tom and Dick weigh 300 kilograms, and Dick and Harry weigh 300 kilograms.

A satisfactory grammar, therefore, must assign different logical forms to each of (1)–(3).

Gleitman has proposed a grammar wherein all phrasal conjunctions are mere surface traces of underlying sentential conjunctions.[26] Her grammar, consequently, cannot provide a satisfactory account of (1) and (2).

Dougherty has constructed a grammar of coordinate conjoined structures that, like Lakoff and Peters' grammar, posits both phrasal and sentential conjunctions in deep structure.[27] By means of a set of features, [± individual], [± total], [± disjunctive], and [± negative], Dougherty tries to account for the differential semantical and syntactical behavior of different kinds of phrasal conjunctions. But his grammar is unsatisfactory for several reasons. It assigns different deep structures to (3) and (9)

(9) Tom is a philosopher, Dick is a philosopher, and Harry is a philosopher.

without providing a convincing reason to believe these structures logically equivalent. It is artificially restricted to conjoined noun phrases at least one of whose constituents is semantically singular; there is no apparent way to extend the grammar to all conjoined noun phrases. Finally, it seems to make false predictions even within its limited domain of applicability.[28]

In their 1940 paper 'The Calculus of Individuals', Leonard and Goodman showed in effect how handle sentences like (1) and (2) within mereological predicate logic.[29] Where '+' is the sum operator of their logic of individuals, sentence (1) may be recast as (10).

(10) (Tom + Dick + Harry) weighs 300 kilograms.

But (10) fails to imply (5) because of the non-validity of formula (11).

(11) $(x)(y)(z)[F(x+y+z) \supset F(x+y) \cdot F(y+z)]$.

Leonard & Goodman's ingenious rendering of (2) as (12)

(12) Tom, Dick, and Harry each stand in the partnership relation to each of the others and to any sum of the others.

guarantees that (2) will imply (7), but not conversely.[30]

Building on this early work of Leonard & Goodman, I have tried to supply linguists not only with a logic of phrasal conjunction, but also and more importantly with a logic of group quantification, that explains certain puzzling phenomena noticed by linguists, e.g., the apparent scopelessness of group quantifiers.[31] (Group quantifiers are quantificational analogues of phrasal conjunctions. For example, the expression 'all the men' functions as a group quantifier in (13) and (14).)

(13) All the men weigh 300 kilograms.
(14) All the men are partners.

Here is a logical theory, however modest, that owes much of its development to problems and puzzles encountered by linguists who were trying to fashion a grammar of phrasal conjunctions and group quantifications. It demonstrates, I think, my contention that work in linguistics will from time to time prompt developments in logic.[32]

Physical ideas sometimes stimulate mathematical developments. This is an important service that physics renders to mathematics, but it is not the most important one. The principal service rendered by physics is to make abstract mathematical theories relevant to the real world, i.e., to turn abstract theories into empirical theories. Exactly the same is true of logic and linguistics, i.e., linguistics makes logical theories relevant to natural language.

It might seem, however, that logic is directly applicable or relevant to natural language. The business of logic, we have long been told, is the evaluation of arguments, the principled sorting of arguments into the valid and the invalid. The arguments in question are natural language arguments, those advanced by people in everyday life, in the empirical sciences, in mathematics, and in logic itself. Logic textbooks are replete with exercises that require the student to show that certain natural language arguments are valid, and that certain others are invalid. Anyone who thinks that 'ought' implies 'can' would seem driven to conclude that logic can establish, wholly apart from linguistics or any other science, the validity of some arguments and the invalidity of others. The relevance of logic to natural language seems to be a truism, safe even from skeptical assault.

I have argued elsewhere that the appearance and the reality are far apart.[33] No argument, I claim, has ever been shown invalid as a matter of logical theory, save in an accidental and uninteresting sense. Further, every demonstration that an argument is valid incorporates intuitive judgments about paraphrase in such a way that the verdict of validity rests as much on undisciplined linguistic intuition as it does upon logical theory. I will briefly rehearse my arguments for these claims.

Consider argument (A):

(A) (15) Tom and Dick are philosophers.
(16) Tom is a philosopher.

The customary way of showing that (A) is valid goes like this. First, one selects and appropriate system of logic in which to represent the premisses and conclusion. In the case of (A), one might choose the logic of truth functions and then let 'p' and 'q' represent 'Tom is a philosopher' and 'Dick is a philosopher' respectively, while correlating 'and' with the dot of truth-functional conjunction. Then, viewing 'Tom is a philosopher and Dick is a philosopher' as a paraphrase of (15), one represents the form or structure of (A) by (B).

$$\text{(B)} \qquad \frac{p \cdot q}{q}.$$

The theory of truth functions is then brought to bear to show that (B) is a valid argument form in that no assignment of truth values to its variables yields a true premiss and false conclusion. Then, by appeal to the *master theorem* that says that an argument is valid if it instantiates at least one valid argument form, one concludes that argument (A) is valid.

The foregoing procedure is so smooth that appeal to intuitions about paraphrase almost escapes notice. But the appeal becomes manifest when we contrast (A) with (C) and (D).

(C) (17) Tom and Dick weigh 200 kilograms.
(18) Tom weighs 200 kilograms.

(D) (19) Tom and Dick are partners.
(20) Tom is a partner.

Though they are remarkably similar to (A), no one would claim that (C) and (D) are valid by virtue of instantiating (B). Given our readiness to represent (15) as a conjunction '$p \cdot q$', what explains our unwillingness to so represent (17) and (19)? Clearly, our intuitive judgment that 'Tom weighs 200 kilograms and Dick weighs 200 kilograms' is not a paraphrase of (17), and that 'Tom is a partner and Dick is a partner' is not a paraphrase of (19). In short, intuitions about paraphrase were as instrumental in our decision to apply the logic of truth functions to (A) as they were in our decision to refrain from applying it to (C) and (D). It follows that the validity of (A) is not a matter of logic alone; it is rather the joint verdict of logic and undisciplined linguistic intuition. What is thus true of (A) holds quite generally. *All demonstrations that natural language arguments are valid depend no less on undisciplined linguistic intuition than on logical theory, no matter how sophisticated the latter might be.*

The unsatisfactoriness of this situation hardly needs emphasis. That the application to natural language of the powerful and sophisticated systems of modern logic should depend crucially upon intuitions about paraphrase is, when recognized, intolerable. The remedy is as formidable as it is obvious: to devise a theory or science of paraphrase that relates sentences of natural language to the formulas of logical systems. One might dub such a science *the theory of the logical form of natural languages*. There is, however, no need for a baptism since this science already has a venerable name, *grammar*.

However bad off proofs of validity may be, proofs of invalidity are far worse off, with one exception. If one can show that all its premisses are true but its conclusion false, one has proved an argument invalid. But this method is indifferent to logic, save when logic happens to be used to establish the truth value of a premiss or the conclusion. Beyond this trivial, logic-indifferent method of showing invalidity, there are at present no others.

Many will think I am exaggerating. They will recall times when they themselves applied logic to convict an argument of invalidity. Or they will point to the exercises in logic textbooks that oblige the student to use logical theory to show the invalidity of numerous arguments of natural language. All such applications and exercises are bogus, or so I claim. I will try now to convice you of it.

I have already reviewed the standard method of proving validity. Let me now do the same for invalidity. Most textbooks say very little about proving invalidity. Their authors seem to assume that proving validity and proving invalidity are two sides of the same coin; whoever can do the one can do the other. A few treat explicitly of the topic, and perhaps the best of these treatments is Copi's. In a section of *Symbolic Logic* entitled 'Proving Invalidity' that follows his presentation of the elementary theory of truth functions, Copi states that "We can establish the invalidity of an argument by using a truth table to show that its form is invalid."[34] The method Copi has in mind is this. First, translate or paraphrase a given argument into the notation of truth functions in such a way that all its intuited truth-functional structure is rendered explicit. Second, use a truth table to test the resulting argument form, the symbolic rendition of the given argument, for validity. Third and finally, characterize the given argument as invalid just in case the aforementioned argument form turns out to be invalid. Applied to argument (C), this method yields the invalid argument form (E).

$$\text{(E)}\quad \frac{p}{q}$$

So Copi's method correctly characterizes (C) as invalid. Notice, however, that Copi's method also generates (E) as the relevant argument form of (D), thereby condemning (D) as invalid. But (D) is a valid argument, a fact revealed by its translation into the valid argument form (F) of mereological predicate logic.

$$\text{(F)}\quad \frac{P(t, d) \cdot P(d, t)}{(\exists x)P(t, x)}.$$

Copi's method yields correct judgments about arguments, i.e., judgments that conform to our intuitions about validity and invalidity, in countless cases. Unfortunately, it also yields incorrect judgments in countless other cases. Copi credits his method with the power to show the invalidity of any argument whose invalidity can be established by a truth table. His claim is true but wholly uninteresting. What makes it true is not its substance but its vacuity: there is no argument whatsoever whose invalidity can be established by means of a truth table.

The defect in Copi's method does not stem from the relative poverty of the background logical theory, truth-functional logic in the cases examined above. Appeal to a richer logic, mereological predicate logic, saved argument (D) from being pronounced invalid. But does paraphrase into that richer logic convict (C) of invalidity, since the most structure-revealing paraphrase of (C) into mereological predicate logic is the invalid argument form (G)?

$$\text{(G)}\quad \frac{W(t + d)}{Wt}.$$

I don't dispute the invalidity of (C). My quarrel is only with the claim that optimal paraphrase of (C) into mereological predicate logic convicts (C) of invalidity. For, just as in the case of truth-functional logic, countless valid arguments would thereby be incorrectly classified as invalid, e.g., argument (H).

$$\text{(H)}\quad \frac{\text{Necessarily, Tom and Dick are partners.}}{\text{Tom and Dick are partners.}}$$

Let me return for a moment to what I called the *master theorem*, i.e., the thesis that an argument is valid *if* it instantiates a valid argument form of some (correct) logical theory. Proofs of invalidity turn on a putative *converse master theorem*, to wit: an argument is valid *only if* it instantiates a valid argument form of some (correct) logical theory. Together, these two theses make instantiation of a valid argument form of a correct logical theory to be both sufficient and necessary for argument validity. But it is one thing to claim on the basis of one's linguistic intuitions that a natural language argument is paraphraseable into a particular valid argument form of some extant logical theory, quite another to claim that there is no valid paraphrase of it into any correct logical theory, extent or otherwise. The latter is a general claim that requires theoretical backing. Short of a general theory of logical form, i.e., short of a grammar that assigns 'deep structures' to all the sentences of natural language, 'proofs' of invalidity amount to little more than disingenuous restatements of one's intuitions or pre-theoretical beliefs about validity. So far as the application of logic to natural language goes, then, grammar really comes into its own when invalidity is at issue. Grammar is useful but not indispensable to proofs of validity; its value consists in supplanting piecemeal intuitions about paraphrase by a general theory. In the process, it turns the *art* of validating arguments into a *science*. But there is not even an art of proving arguments invalid. By nature this task is theoretical throughout. Grammar does not merely improve on proofs of invalidity; it makes them possible.

One final point. I have taken intuitions about paraphrase and logical consequence at face value. In fact, these notions are quite problematic. Consider, for example, argument (I)

$$\text{(I)}\qquad \frac{\alpha \text{ is a part of } \beta \text{, and } \beta \text{ is a part of } \gamma.}{\alpha \text{ is a part of } \gamma.}$$

Someone who paraphrased the part relation this way:

$$\text{(21)}\qquad \text{Part}\,(x, y) =_{\text{Df}} (z)\,[\text{Overlap}\,(z, x) \supset \text{Overlap}\,(z, y)]$$

might argue that (I) was valid by virtue of instantiating a valid argument form of mereological predicate logic. Yet someone who rejects the overlap paraphrase of 'part of' might claim that (I) was invalid, accounting for its intuited goodness as an enthymeme with a suppressed premiss that asserts the transitivity of the part relation. Which is right? Apart from a general theory of paraphrase, i.e., a grammar, the question seems ill-formed.[35]

Nor are intuitions about logical consequence much better off. Does (22)

(22) The least noise bothers Tom.

logically imply or merely conversationally implicate that any noise bothers Tom? Does it presuppose a scale of sound intensity according to which a sound bothers someone only if any louder one does too?[36] It is questionable whether these questions can be well put, let alone answered, apart from a general theory of logical form, i.e., apart from a grammar.

I mentioned earlier Poincaré's conviction that the geometry of physics would remain forever euclidean. An analogous thesis, in the guise of a constraint on grammatical theory, has lately been advanced by Gilbert Harman.[37] Harman argues that departures from first-order predicate logic as the logic of natural language should be kept to an absolute minimum. Stripped of inessentials, Harman's argument for preserving first-order logic closely resembles Poincaré's case for euclidean geometry. But first-order-logic chauvinism deserves no more place in grammar than euclidean chauvinism deserved in physics. Indeed, Montague, by employing higher-order intensional logic in his grammars of fragments of English, may already have discredited Harman's thesis in the same way that Einstein discredited Poincaré.[38]

University of Pittsburgh

NOTES

[1] The revolution in linguistics associated with Chomsky had already begun well before the publication of *Syntactic Structures*. Yet such was the fame and influence of this petite monograph that it is both proper and convenient to regard 1957 as the first year of the new era in linguistics.

[2] Chomsky is himself fond of attributing some of the leading ideas of transformational grammar, in particular the conception of meaning-bearing grammatical forms somehow underlying surface grammatical forms, to thinkers of the 17th century Port-Royal school. See Chomsky's monograph *Current Issues in Linguistic Theory*, pp. 15ff., for a discussion of anticipations of transformational grammar by earlier students of language, and of limitations under which these thinkers labored.

[3] Logicians and philosophers have, from ancient times to the present, taken a keen interest in logical form. Substantial progress on the problem, however, could not have been made apart from the revolutionary advances made within logic during the late 19th century and the 20th century, roughly from Frege onward. For a superb statement of the problem of logical form, as that problem is understood in this paper, see Davidson and Harman's introduction to their anthology *The Logic of Grammar*.

[4] The suggestion implicit in this remark is that one look upon Frege's *Die Grundlagen der Arithmetik* and *Grundgesetze der Arithmetik* and Whitehead and Russell's *Principia*

Mathematica as proposed solutions to the problem of logical form for the language of mathematics.

[5] See, for example, the work of Prior and especially that of Cocchiarella on the logic of tensed discourse. An excellent bibliography of tense logic appears in Pizzi's anthology *La Logica del Tempo*.

[6] So much valuable work in modal logic has been done in the past twenty years that one is hard put to mention only a few names and works, though the investigations of Saul Kripke have assumed paramount importance. Hughes and Cresswell's *An Introduction to Modal Logic* provides a reasonably comprehensive survey of the field, as well as a useful bibliography.

[7] I have in mind especially the work set in motion by Jaakko Hintikka's seminal tract *Knowledge and Belief*.

[8] Davidson's analyses of causal and action sentences were constructed with the problem of logical form in view. Not surprisingly, then, linguists have recently begun to use them in their attempts to frame a grammar of natural language. Some of the relevant papers of Davidson are reprinted in the anthology mentioned in note 3.

[9] As Thomason remarks on p. 63 of his introduction to *Formal Philosophy*, pragmatics, thought of as the theory of indexical expressions, owes much of its formal development to Montague, his students and associates. Thomason there explains in what sense pragmatic theory represents a generalization of possible-worlds semantics of modal logic. Chapters 3 and 4 of *Formal Philosophy* are reprints of two of Montague's seminal contributions to the theory of indexical expressions.

[10] See his *The Foundations of Science* for a forceful statement of Poincaré's belief that scientists would unfailingly choose euclidean geometry over alternatives. Chapter 4 of Grünbaum's *Philosophical Problems of Space and Time* contains an account and critique of the philosophies of geometry of both Poincaré and Einstein.

[11] See Einstein's 'Geometry and Experience' for a clear and simple statement of his views on local and global simplicity of physical theories.

[12] One will look in vain among Chomsky's works for a statement equivalent to objective (iv). Nevertheless, I believe that (iv) represents a natural thrust or extension of Chomsky's overall approach to grammar, a belief confirmed not only by developments within such breakaway movements as generative semantics (for example, Lakoff's program to articulate a 'natural logic' or McCawley's program for logic) but also within Chosmky's own school (for example, Katz's conception of the semantic component of a transformational grammar). Katz himself describes his conception of semantic theory, according to which "the study of grammatical structure in empirical linguistics will eventually provide a full account of the logical form of sentences in natural language", as the natural next step of Chomsky's general approach to linguistics and grammatical theory (*Semantic Theory*, p. xxiv).

[13] In collaboration with Halle and Lukoff, Chomsky has in fact made noteworthy contributions to phonology, but these have been overshadowed by his contributions to syntax.

[14] See Seuren, 'Autonomous versus Semantic Syntax', in his *Semantic Syntax*, pp. 96–122, as well as his introduction to that book, pp. 1–27.

[15] See any of the works mentioned in notes 12 and 14. Bartsch and Vennemann's *Semantic Structures* contains an informative comparison and critique of transformational grammar and generative semantics. Chomsky has argued that 'standard theory'

transformational grammar (the theory described in this paper) and generative semantics are 'intertranslatable' in the sense of being 'mere notational variants' of one another ('Deep Structure, Surface Structure, and Semantic Interpretation', p. 187). Surprisingly, then, he goes on to argue that generative semantics cannot handle phenomena associated with substitution of equivalent expressions in opaque context, whereas a relatively minor modification of the standard theory seems to accomodate them (*Ibid*., pp. 197ff.). If the standard theory and generative semantics were really notational variants of one another, one would expect them to fare equally in the face of recalcitrant phenomena.

[16] The quotation comes from Lakoff's 'Linguistics and Natural Logic', p. 588, but the idea is common to all the generative semanticists.

[17] See Lakoff, 'Linguistics and Natural Logic', pp. 618ff.

[18] See Davis, *Philosophy and Language*, pp. 122ff. for an instructive discussion and critique of Ross' performative thesis.

[19] McCawley argues ingeniously ('A Program for Logic', pp. 519ff.) that an adequate account of presupposition must posit an exclusive disjunction connective that takes any number n of arguments, $n \geqslant 2$, and that the combinatory possibilities of the sentence connectives for conjunction and inclusive disjunction in no way differ from those of the exclusive disjunction connective. Connectives such as these that can take varying numbers of arguments have been called *multigrade*. See Hendry and Massey, 'On the Concepts of Sheffer Functions', pp. 288ff. for the rudiments of a general theory of multigrade connectives.

[20] See Bartsch and Vennemann, *Semantic Structures*, pp. 14ff. While I agree generally with Bartsch and Vennemann's criticism of generative semantics, I dissociate myself from the implicit attribution of logical naivety to generative semanticists. It would be difficult, for example, to find someone whose grasp of modern logic is more sophisticated than McCawley's.

[21] *Ibid*., pp. 31ff.

[22] *Ibid*., p. 16.

[23] See Quine's 'Logic as a Source of Syntactical Insights'.

[24] See Chomsky's *Topics in the Theory of Generative Grammar*, pp. 60ff., for a lucid discussion of the significance of Katz and Postal's proposed elimination of many-place or generalized transformations (transformations that operate on several phrase-markers simultaneously) in favor of amending the rules of the base component to permit sentence embedding, i.e., to allow the category symbol '*S*' to appear on the right side of a rewrite rule (phrase-structure rule).

[25] See Lakoff and Peters, 'Phrasal Conjunction and Symmetric Predicates'. The attentive reader will have noticed that my present examples, as well as most of those that follow, are ambiguous in the sense that they are susceptible of several different readings. My comments are meant to apply with respect to that reading which is the most likely, given what the world is like. For example, on one reading sentence (1) attributes a weight of 300 kilograms to each of Tom, Dick, and Harry. But extralinguistic information would normally cause a reader unconsciously to dismiss this reading as unintended.

[26] See Gleitman, 'Coordinating Conjunctions in English'.

[27] See Dougherty, 'A Grammar of Coordinate Conjoined Structures: I and II'.

[28] A much expanded account of my criticisms of the grammars of Lakoff and Peters,

Gleitman, and Dougherty can be found in my paper 'Tom, Dick, and Harry, and All the King's Men'.

[29] By *mereological predicate logic* I understand ordinary first-order predicate logic supplemented by the devices of the calculus or logic of individuals. In mereological predicate logic one quantifies over a domain D' of individuals induced by the domain D of individuals of ordinary predicate logic. Typically, D' will consist of the union of D with the set of all sums of members of D. The semantics of mereological predicate logic is the same as that of an ordinary first-order predicate logic whose domain is D'.

[30] Sentence (2) can of course be rendered in a way that uses, rather than mentions, the predicate for the partnership relation. But since (12) is more perspicuous in structure to the untutored eye than Leonard and Goodman's actual rendering that uses the partnership predicate, I have presented (12) as a concession to the reader.

[31] The rudiments of this logic of phrasal conjunction and group quantification are set forth in the paper mentioned in note 28.

[32] Logical work of other sorts is directly stimulated by work in linguistics. For example, the very construction of formal grammars raises metatheoretical questions about their generative capacity, the equivalence of grammars, etc. But the questions thus posed, however interesting in themselves, are not peculiar to grammar; the same questions are raised by formal theories generally.

[33] See may paper 'Are There Any Good Arguments That Bad Arguments Are Bad?' and its sequel 'In Defense of the Asymmetry' which addresses objections to, and clears up possible misunderstandings about, the first paper.

[34] Copi, *Symbolic Logic*, pp. 51ff. See also *ibid*., pp. 91ff. Two footnotes (p. 268 and p. 338) in his elementary textbook *Introduction to Logic* show that Copi is at least partially aware of the asymmetrical character of proving validity and proving invalidity.

[35] What was just done for 'part of' in terms of 'overlap', namely to provide a paraphrase that turns specified truths expressed in terms of 'part of' into logical truths, can be done quite generally. Building on earlier work of Nelson Goodman and himself, Quine has shown how to supply paraphrases that will convert any finite number of truths into truths of arithmetic. See Quine's 'Implicit Definition Sustained'.

[36] The example (22) is taken from a fascinating paper 'Pragmatic Scales and Logical Structure' by Gilles Fauconnier who puts it and its ilk to quite different use.

[37] See Harman, 'Logical Form'.

[38] Thomason's 69-page introduction to *Formal Philosophy* contains a clear and comprehensive account of Montague's approach to grammar. The book itself includes all of Montague's contributions to grammatical theory.

BIBLIOGRAPHY

Bartsch, R. and Vennemann, T., *Semantic Structures*, Athenäum Verlag, Frankfurt/Main, 1972.

Chomsky, Noam, *Syntactic Structures*, Mouton & Co., The Hague, 1957.

Chomsky, Noam, *Current Issues in Linguistic Theory*, Mouton & Co., The Hague, 1964.

Chomsky, Noam, *Topics in the Theory of Generative Grammar*, Mouton & Co., The Hague, 1966.

Chomsky, Noam, *Aspects of the Theory of Syntax*, MIT Press, Cambridge, Mass., 1965.
Chomsky, Noam 'Deep Structure, Surface Structure, and Semantic Interpretation', reprinted in Steinberg and Jakobovits, *Semantics*, pp. 183–216.
Chomsky, N., Halle, M., and Lukoff, F., 'On Accent and Juncture in English', in Halle, Hunt, and MacLean (eds.), *For Roman Jakobson*, Monton & Co., The Hague, 1956.
Cocchiarella, Nino, *Tense Logic: A Study of Temporal Reference*, Ph.D. dissertation, U.C.L.A., 1966.
Copi, Irving, *Introduction to Logic* (4th edition), Macmillan Co., New York, 1972.
Copi, Irving, *Symbolic Logic* (3rd edition), Macmillan Co., New York, 1967.
Davidson, D. and Harman G. (eds.), *The Logic of Grammar*, Dickenson Publishing Co., Inc., Encino, California, 1975.
Davidson, D. and Harman, G. *Semantics of Natural Language*, D. Reidel Publishing Co., Dordrecht, 1972.
Davis, Steven, *Philosophy and Language*, The Bobbs-Merrill Co., Inc., Indianapolis, 1972.
Dougherty, Ray, 'A Grammar of Coordinate Conjoined Structures: I and II', *Language* **46** (1970), 850–898, and **47** (1971), 298–339.
Einstein, Albert, 'Geometry and Experience', reprinted in Feigl and Brodbeck (eds.), *Readings in the Philosophy of Science*, pp. 189–194.
Fauconnier, Gilles, 'Pragmatic Scales and Logical Structure', *Linguistic Inquiry* **6** (1975), 353–375.
Feigl, H. and Brodbeck, M. (eds.), *Readings in the Philosophy of Science*, Appleton-Century-Crofts, Inc., New York, 1953.
Frege, Gottlob, *Die Grundlagen der Arithmetik. Eine logisch-mathematische Untersuchung über den Begriff der Zahl*. Breslau, 1884.
Frege, Gottlob, *Grundgesetze der Arithmetik. Begriffschriftlich abgeleitet*. Jena, 1893–1903.
Grünbaum, Adolf, *Philosophical Problems of Space and Time*, Alfred A. Knopf, Inc., New York, 1963.
Gleitman, Lila, 'Coordinating Conjunctions in English', *Language* **41** (1965), 260–293.
Harman, Gilbert, 'Logical Form', in Davidson and Harman (eds.), *The Logic of Grammar*, pp. 289–307.
Hendry, H. and Massey, G. J., 'On the Concepts of Sheffer Functions', in K. Lambert (ed.), *The Logical Way of Doing Things*, pp. 279–293.
Hintikka, Jaakko, *Knowledge and Belief*, Cornell Univ. Press, Ithaca, 1962.
Hughes, G. E. and Cresswell, M. J., *An Introduction to Modal Logic*, Methuen & Co., Ltd., London, 1968.
Jacobs, R. and Rosenbaum P. (eds.), *Readings in English Transformational Grammar*, Ginn Publ. Co., Waltham, 1970.
Katz, Jerrold J., *Semantic Theory*, Harper & Row, Pubs., New York, 1972.
Katz, J. J. and Postal P. M., *An Integrated Theory of Linguistic Descriptions*, MIT Press, Cambridge, Mass., 1964.
Lakoff, George, 'Linguistics and Natural Logic', reprinted in Davidson and Harman (eds.), *Semantics of Natural Language*, pp. 545–665.
Lakoff, G. and Peters, S., 'Phrasal Conjunction and Symmetric Predicates', in Reibel and Schane (eds.), *Modern Studies in English*, pp. 113–142.

Lambert, Karel (ed.), *The Logical Way of Doing Things*, Yale Univ. Press, New Haven, 1969.

Leonard, H. and Goodman, N., 'The Calculus of Individuals and its Uses', *J. Symbolic Logic* 5 (1940), 45–56.

Massey, Gerald J., 'Tom, Dick, and Harry, and All the King's Men', *American Philosophical Quarterly* 13 (1976), 89–107.

Massey, Gerald J., 'Are There Any Good Arguments That Bad Arguments Are Bad?', *Philosophy in Context* 4 (1975), 61–77 (published by Cleveland State University).

Massey, Gerald J., 'In Defense of the Asymmetry', *Philosophy in Context, Supp.* 4 (1975), 44–56.

McCawley, James, 'A Program for Logic', in Davidson and Harman (eds.), *Semantics of Natural Language*, pp. 498–544.

Montague, Richard, 'Pragmatics', reprinted in Thomason (ed.), *Formal Philosophy*, pp. 95–118.

Montague, Richard, 'Pragmatics and Intensional Logic', reprinted in Thomason (ed.), *Formal Philosophy*, pp. 118–147.

Montague, Richard, 'English as a Formal Language', reprinted in Thomason (ed.), *Formal Philosophy*, pp. 188–221.

Montague, Richard, 'Universal Grammar', reprinted in Thomason (ed.), *Formal Philosophy*, pp. 222–246.

Montague, Richard, 'The Proper Treatment of Quantification in Ordinary English', reprinted in Thomason (ed.), *Formal Philosophy*, pp. 247–270.

Pizzi, Claudio (ed.), *La Logica del Tempo*, Boringhieri, Turin, 1974.

Poincaré, Henri, *The Foundations of Science*, The Science Press, Lancaster, 1946.

Prior, Arthur N., *Time and Modality*, The Clarendon Press, Oxford, 1957.

Prior, Arthur N., *Past, Present, and Future* The Clarendon Press, Oxford, 1967.

Quine, W. V. O., 'Logic as a Source of Syntactical Insights', reprinted in Davidson and Harman (eds.), *The Logic of Grammar*, pp. 75–78.

Quine, W. V. O., 'Implicit Definition Sustained', reprinted in Quine, *The Ways of Paradox and other Essay*, pp. 195–198.

Quine, W. V. O., *The Ways of Paradox and other Essays*, Random House, New York, 1966.

Reibel, D. and Schane S. (eds.), *Modern Studies in English*, Prentice-Hall, Inc., Englewood Cliffs, 1969.

Ross, James R., 'On Declarative Sentences', in Jacobs and Rosenbaum (eds.), *Readings in English Transformational Grammar*, pp. 222–273.

Seuren, Pieter, *Semantic Syntax*, Oxford Univ. Press, Oxford, 1974.

Steinberg, D. and Jakobovits L. (eds.), *Semantics*, Cambridge Univ. Press, Cambridge, 1971.

Thomason, Richmond (ed.), *Formal Philosophy: Selected Papers of Richard Montague*, Yale Univ. Press, New Haven, 1974.

Whitehead, A. N. and Russell, B., *Principia Mathematica*, 3 volumes, Cambridge Univ. Press, Cambridge, 1910–1913.

M. L. DALLA CHIARA

LOGICAL FOUNDATIONS OF QUANTUM MECHANICS

It is very natural to recognise a strict analogy between the main problems concerning the logical foundations of quantum theory and most fundamental problems which have arisen in the field of the foundations of mathematics. In both cases (physics and mathematics) three fundamental classes of conceptual difficulties seem to have played a particularly relevant role:

(1) The discovery of paradoxes, which led, in a natural way, to the attempt to axiomatise and formalise the theories under investigation.

(2) The arising of some doubts concerning the adequacy and the legitimacy of classical logic. As is well known, these doubts have suggested the creation of intuitionistic logic and other 'weak' logics (in the field of the foundational researches about mathematical theories) and of quantum logic (in the framework of quantum theory).

(3) The recovery, in connection with the foundational problems, of some traditional gnoseological questions concerning the dilemma 'realism or idealism?'.

A characteristic logical difficulty of quantum mechanics (which, so far, seems to distinguish the logical status of quantum theory from a number of mathematical and physical theories) is the following: the deductive structure of quantum theory in its present forms seems to be essentially founded on a kind of 'mixture' od different logics. Naturally, the coexistence of different logics, in the domain of one and the same theory, is bound to cause, at least on a first judgment, a lot of perplexity. In this particular case, it gives rise to a number of logical, physical and epistemological problems. We will try and discuss some of these problems in the framework of a general 'empirical semantics',[1] which appears to be a somewhat realistic metatheoretical description of 'concrete' physical theories.

1. A GENERAL SEMANTICS FOR PHYSICAL THEORIES

As is well known, in standard model theory, a *formalised theory* T is usually represented by a pair $\langle FS, K\rangle$ consisting of a *formal system* FS and the class K of all the *models* of FS. A formal system FS is determined by a triple $\langle L, A, D\rangle$ consisting of a *formal language* L, a particular set A of sentences

E. Agazzi (ed.), Modern Logic – A Survey, 331–351.

of L corresponding to the *axioms* of *FS* and finally a set of rules of inference D, which together with the *logical axioms* (contained in A) determine the *logic* of *FS*. *A model* of *FS* is defined as an abstract structure (of a certain type) in which the axioms are *true*.

This kind of idealization of the concept of 'scientific theory', which, so far, has been mainly applied to the logical analysis of mathematical theories, admits of an interesting application also to the case of physical theories. However, in order to obtain a somewhat realistic description of concrete physical theories, one has to take into account some specific features of such theories. To this end, it appears necessary to render explicit a number of formal aspects of physical theories, which are generally neglected in standard model theory.

A *formalised physical theory* T can be identified, as in standard model theory, by the usual pair $\langle FS, K\rangle$ where *FS* is a *physical formal system* and K the class of the physical models of *FS*. But the notion of physical model requires a specific definition. Let us first define a *physical structure* $\mathcal{M}$ by

(1) $\mathcal{M} = \langle \mathcal{M}_0, S, Q_0, ..., Q_n, \rho\rangle,$

where

(a) $\mathcal{M}_0$ represents the *mathematical part* of $\mathcal{M}$ (ordinarily the *standard model* of a mathematical theory);

(b) $\langle S, Q_0, ..., Q_n\rangle$ represents the *operational part* of $\mathcal{M}$: S is a set of *physical situations* consisting of *physical systems* in specified *states* and each Q_i represents a *physical quantity operationally defined* on a subset of S^2. We suppose that, generally, in one and the same physical situation $s \in S$ one may carry out for a quantity Q_i more than one measurement (for instance, one might have to measure different masses or different times). We denote these different results for Q_i, measured in s, by $Q_{i_1}[s], Q_{i_1}[s], ...$. A result $Q_{i_l}[s]$ may be represented either by an interval I of real numbers (whose length depends on the resolving power ϵ^A of the instrument A used for our measurement) or more generally (in the case where s is a statistical ensemble of physical systems) by a probability distribution of real numbers. This probability distribution is experimentally determined only up to a double 'error' depending both on the resolving power ϵ^A of the apparatus used and on the accuracy ϵ^P with which we measure probability. As a consequence, the graphical representation of our result will consist of a curved strip Σ, whose size depends both on ϵ^A and ϵ^P.[3] We define an *ideal value of* $Q_{i_l}[s]$ either as a real number belonging to the interval I (if $Q_{i_l}[s]$ is the interval I) or as a function representing a probability distribution which is comprised in

Σ (if $Q_{i_l}[s]$ is the strip Σ). In these two different cases we will speak respectively of *results* (*ideal values*) of *first* and of *second type*.

(c) ρ is a function which associates a mathematical interpretation in $\mathscr{M}_0$ with any term of the operational part of $\mathscr{M}$.

(2) A physical structure as $\mathscr{M}$ will be called a *realisation* of a formal language L, when:

(a) $\mathscr{M}_0$ is a realisation of the mathematical sublanguage L_0 of L; that is to say that every (mathematical) symbol of L_0 has an interpretation in $\mathscr{M}_0$, according to the standard model theoretical conventions.

(b) L contains, for each quantity Q_i a double denumerably infinite list of *special physical variables* $\mathbf{d}_{i_1}, \mathbf{d}_{i_2}, \ldots; \mathbf{p}_{i_1}, \mathbf{p}_{i_2}, \ldots$. For the sake of simplicity, we will suppose that Q_0 represents in all cases the quantity *time*, and we will write also, $\mathbf{t}_1, \mathbf{t}_2, \ldots$ instead of $\mathbf{d}_{0_1}, \mathbf{d}_{0_2}, \ldots$. From the semantical point of view, the t_k's are supposed to range over all ideal values of the quantity time (i.e. real numbers). The $\mathbf{d}_{i_k}$'s are supposed to range over all functions which associate to any time a first-type ideal value for the quantity Q_i. Finally the $\mathbf{p}_{i_k}$'s range over all functions which associate to any time a second-type ideal value for the quantity Q_i.

By *elementary physical term* we will understand any term of the language L which has one of the following forms $\mathbf{t}_k$, $\mathbf{d}_i(\mathbf{t}_k)$, $\mathbf{p}_j(\mathbf{t}_k)$. A sentence of L will, in general, have the form

$$\alpha[\mathbf{t}_k, \mathbf{d}_i(\mathbf{t}_r), \mathbf{p}_j(\mathbf{t}_s)],$$

where $\mathbf{t}_k$, $\mathbf{d}_i(\mathbf{t}_r)$, $\mathbf{p}_j(\mathbf{t}_s)$ stand each for a (possibly empty) finite sequence of physical elementary terms of that type, and where at most the physical variables may occur free.

Let $\mathscr{M}$ represent a realisation of the language L. We want to define the *truth* of a sentence α of L with respect to a physical situation s of $\mathscr{M}$ ($\models_s \alpha$). Let us first determine when α is *defined* with respect to a physical situation s. Roughly speaking, α will be considered as defined in s, when what α asserts 'has a meaning' with respect to s. This requires that for each physical variable occurring in α the corresponding physical quantity is operationally defined with respect to s. More formally:

(3) $\alpha[\mathbf{t}_k, \mathbf{d}_i(\mathbf{t}_r), \mathbf{p}_j(\mathbf{t}_s)]$ is said to be defined in s iff:

(a) for each time variable $\mathbf{t}_h$ occurring in α a corresponding result

for the quantity time (Q_0) can be obtained in s; let us denote this result by $Q_{0_h}[s] = t_h \pm (\epsilon^{At}/2)$ (where t_h is a real number and ϵ^{At} represents the precision of our clock);
(b) for each first-type term $\mathbf{d}_i(\mathbf{t}_r)$ (second-type term $\mathbf{p}_j(\mathbf{t}_s)$) occurring in α, a corresponding first-type result (second-type result) for the quantity Q_i (Q_j) can be obtained in s at time $t_r \pm (\epsilon^{At}/2)$ ($t_s \pm (\epsilon^{At}/2)$). Let us denote this result by $Q_i[s(t_r)]$ ($Q_j[s(t_s)]$).

Now we can put:

(4) $\models_s \alpha[\mathbf{t}_k, \mathbf{d}_i(\mathbf{t}_r), \mathbf{p}_j(\mathbf{t}_s)]$ iff:
(a) α is defined in s;
(b) for each time result $Q_{0_h}[s]$ there exists an ideal time value, i.e. a real number t_h belonging to $Q_{0_h}[s]$; for each first-type result $Q_i[s(t_r)]$ (second-type result $Q_j[s(t_s)]$) there exists an *ideal first-type value*, i.e. a real number $d^{(i)}$ belonging to the interval $Q_i[s(t_r)]$ (an *ideal second-type value*, i.e. a probability distribution $p^{(j)}$ belonging to the strip $Q_j[s(t_s)]$) such that:
$\models_{\mathcal{M}_0} \alpha[t_h, d^{(i)}, p^{(j)}, p^{(j)}]$.[4]

Finally for the concept of truth in $\mathcal{M}$, we will put:

(5) $\models_{\mathcal{M}} \alpha$ iff:
(a) α is defined for at least one s of $\mathcal{M}$;
(b) for any s of $\mathcal{M}$ for which α is defined, $\models_s \alpha$.

Any formal language which admits of a physical realisation will be called a *physical formal language*. By *physical formal system* we will mean a triple $\langle L, A, D\rangle$ consisting of a physical formal language, a set of axioms A, and a set of rules of inference D.

Any physical formal system FS has a mathematical subsystem FS_0; any element of the set A_0 of the axioms of FS_0 will be either a *logical* or a *mathematical* axiom of FS; any element of $A - A_0$ (which is not a logical axiom) will be called a *physical axiom* of FS. The concept of *theorem* of a physical formal system ($\vdash_{FS} \alpha$) is defined as usually.

(6) A *model* of a physical formal system FS is a physical realisation of the language of FS such that:
(a) $\mathcal{M}_0$ is the standard model of the mathematical subsystem of FS;[5]
(b) $\mathcal{M}$ verifies all the axioms of FS, and the truth in $\mathcal{M}$ is pre-

served by all the rules of inference of *FS*; in other words, if α is an axiom, $\models_{\mathcal{M}} \alpha$; further if $(\alpha_1, ..., \alpha_n)/\alpha$ is a rule of inference and $\models_{\mathcal{M}} \alpha_1, ..., \models_{\mathcal{M}} \alpha_n$ then also $\models_{\mathcal{M}} \alpha$.

A *physical theory* is determined as a pair $\langle FS, K\rangle$ consisting of a physical formal system *FS* and the class *K* of all its models. The theorems and the models of *T* are assumed to be the theorems and the models of the corresponding formal system. A sentence α of *T* will be called a *valid* sentence of $T\,(\models_T \alpha)$ iff α is true in every model of *T*.

As in standard model theory, one can prove trivially a *soundness theorem* for any physical theory *T* (i.e. for any sentence α, if $\vdash_T \alpha$ then $\models_T \alpha$). But, unlike what happens in standard model theory, a *completeness theorem* (i.e. for any sentence α, if $\models_T \alpha$ then $\vdash_T \alpha$) seems to be improvable. Indeed, *K* does not represent, as in the standard case, the class of all 'possible worlds' which satisfy the theory, but only the class of all physical (i.e. 'real') worlds which verify the theory. In this situation, a formal completeness property would mean that our theory represents an intuitively 'complete' description of the real world; in other words, whatever empirically happens in all parts of the physical world, which correspond to a model of the theory, should be theoretically predicted by the theory. This may have appealed to some strictly rationalistic philosophers of the past, but to day represents of course a too strong epistemological requirement. There are also purely logical reasons, speaking against this completeness property. For we have seen that every physical model $\mathcal{M}$ includes the same mathematical part $\mathcal{M}_0$. Now, owing to Gödel's incompleteness theorem, the mathematical subtheory of *T* will generally[6] contain some sentences which are true in $\mathcal{M}_0$ and undecidable in *T*: as a consequence some mathematical sentences of *T* will be true in any physical model of *T*, yet be not provable in *T*.

From an intuitive point of view, the notion of truth we have defined represents a sort of *empirical truth*, and it is worthwhile to notice that it has some formal properties that are not shared by the classical and standard notion of truth. For instance for a given sentence α and for a given physical situation *s*, we may have both $\models_s \alpha$ and $\models_s \neg\alpha$, but not $\models_s \alpha \wedge \neg\alpha$. In other words, α and $\neg\alpha$ can be both true, nevertheless the contradiction $\alpha \wedge \neg\alpha$ is not true. Indeed, in this kind of empirical semantics, the logical connectives turn out to be not *truth-functional*.[7] It is of interest to notice that the failure of the truth-functionality property does not prevent that the logic of a physical theory be classical logic. For it is quite possible that all classical laws (expressed in the language of *T*) are true in any physical model of *T*, and consequently valid in *T*.

2. A FORMAL VERSION OF QUANTUM THEORY

We want now to sketch, in the framework of this empirical semantics, a formal version of quantum mechanics.[8] As any other physical theory, quantum theory (QT) is determined as a pair consisting of a formal system FS and the class K of all its models. The models $\mathcal{M} = \langle \mathcal{M}_0, S, Q_0, ..., Q_n, \rho \rangle$ will satisfy the following conditions:

(8.1) $\mathcal{M}_0$ is the standard model of functional analaysis.

(8.2) For any physical system σ occurring in S, the mathematical interpretation $\rho(\sigma)$ of σ is a Hilbert space H in $\mathcal{M}_0$.[9] Further, the mathematical interpretation of the set $\Omega(\sigma)$ of all states that σ may assume is the set of all *statistical operators* in H. We will call this set $\rho(\Omega(\sigma))$ the set of all *ideal states* that σ can take.[10]

(8.3) For any quantity Q_i (different from the quantity time Q_0) and for any system σ (for which Q_i is defined) $\rho_\sigma(Q_i)$ is a selfadjoint operator in $\rho(\sigma)$.

(8.4) If W is an ideal state and b is a Borel-set of real numbers, the probability that, by performing a measurement for the quantity Q_i in the state represented by W, one can find an ideal first-type value which is contained in b, is calculated by means of the standard Born-rule of QT. We will denote this probability (which is usually called the *Born-probability*) by $\text{Prob}_w^{Q_i}(b)$.

(8.5) We will assume that there exists at least one *ideal translation* τ, such that, for any system $\sigma, \tau(\sigma)$ is a function $\hat{W}$ which associates to any ideal time-value t a statistical operator $W \in \rho(\Omega(\sigma))$. W represents an ideal state of σ at the ideal time t. We will write also: $\tau(\sigma)(t) = \hat{W}(t) = W$. If the state of σ at time $t(\omega[\sigma(t)])$ is characterized by the results $\langle Q_1[\sigma(t)], ..., Q_m[\sigma(t)] \rangle$ an ideal state W associated with $\omega[\sigma(t)]$ will satisfy the following conditions:

(a) for any quantity Q_i, which is defined for $\sigma(t)$, W determines (according to the Born-rule) a probability distribution p_i^w which represents a possible ideal (second-type) value for Q_i; let $\Delta_{p_i}^w$ represent the dispersion of p_i^w (which is supposed to be defined in some standard way);

(b) if $Q_i[\sigma(t)]$ is a first-type result which has the form $r_i \pm (\epsilon^{A_i}/2)$ then $\Delta p_i^w \leqslant (\epsilon^{A_i}/2)$ and $\bar{x}_i \in Q_i[\sigma(t)]$ (where $\bar{x}_i$ represents the mean value of p_i^w);

(c) if $Q_i[\sigma(t)]$ is a second-type result, then $p_i^w \in Q_i[\sigma(t)]$.

(8.6) If σ_1 and σ_2 are two physical systems and $\sigma_1 + \sigma_2$ represents the compound system, then $\rho(\sigma_1 + \sigma_2) = \rho(\sigma_1) \otimes \rho(\sigma_2)$, where $\otimes$ is the tensor product of Hilbert spaces.

(8.7) The ideal translation of a physical state *after* the performance of a measurement concerning a physical quantity is determined by von Neumann's projection postulate.

As to the formal system *FS* which is characteristic of QT we will suppose that

(9) the mathematical axioms of *FS* are the axioms of functional analysis; the set of physical axioms can be described by a unique metatheoretical schema corresponding to the Schrödinger equation;

(10) the logical axioms and the rules of inference of *FS* are the axioms and the rules of classical logic (CL).

As a consequence, according to our approach, the general logic of QT is CL and not quantum logic (QL). Indeed, the general logic of *QT* must govern, at the same time, the mathematical and the physical part of *FS*; and it seems quite improbable that it is convenient to formalise the mathematical subtheory of QT in a quantum logical calculus. QL will be introduced later and will regard only a particular physical sublanguage of QT. It is worth while noticing that in this formal context, the principles which are usually called in the literature 'the axioms of QT' have been distinguished in two different classes: (a) specific physical axioms (described by a unique metatheoretical schema); (b) metatheoretical rules concerning the interpretation-function ρ (which correlates the operational part with the mathematical part of any model of QT).

3. QUANTUM LOGIC IN QUANTUM THEORY

In order to understand, in an intuitive way, the arising of QL in QT, it is expedient to make a formal comparison between *QT* and the classical-particle mechanics (CPM). If $\mathscr{M} = \langle \mathscr{M}_0, S, Q_0, ..., Q_n, \rho \rangle$ represents a model of CPM, ρ will satisfy the following requirements (which are clearly different from the corresponding conditions of QT):

(a) for any physical system σ occurring in S, $\rho(\sigma)$ is a *phase-space* P (if σ consists of a single particle, P will be R^6 (where R is the set of all real numbers).[11] Any point p of P represents a *pure ideal state*, which σ may assume.

(b) For any quantity Q_i (which is defined for σ), $\rho_\sigma(Q_i)$ is a function whose domain is P and whose range is R.

In this framework it is very natural to assume that, from an intuitive point of view, the power set $\mathscr{P}(P)$ of P represents the set of all possible properties of the (pure) ideal states that σ might take. Now let us consider a particular sublanguage L^* of the language L of CPM: L^* is the smallest sublanguage of L which contains all atomic well formed formulas of the form $\mathbf{d}_i(\mathbf{t}) \in b$, $\mathbf{d}_i(\mathbf{t}) \in z_k$ (where b is a constant for a Borel set and z_k is a variable ranging over the set B of all Borel sets of real numbers and which is closed, according to the standard syntactical conditions, with respect to the classical logical constants ($\neg, \wedge, \vee, \rightarrow, \forall, \exists$). Since the time dependence of the $\mathbf{d}_i$'s will, in this context, be generally inessential, we will write simply $\mathbf{d}_i \in b$ ($\mathbf{d}_i \in z_k$) or also $P_i b$ ($P_i z_k$), because the expression $\mathbf{d}_i \in \ldots$ can be represented as a monadic predicate of the object language L^*.

We can associate, in a natural way, to any sentence α of L^* an element $v(\alpha)$ of $\mathscr{P}(P)$, which represents intuitively the 'meaning' of α in $\mathscr{P}(P)$, in other words the *physical world* where α holds. We will call $v(\alpha)$ also the *proposition* associated with α. The natural definition of $v(\alpha)$ is the following:

(11)
$$
\begin{aligned}
& v(\mathbf{d}_i \in b) = [p \in P / \rho(Q_i)(p) \in b] \\
& v(\neg\beta) = -v(\beta) \\
& v(\beta \wedge \gamma) = v(\beta) \cap v(\gamma) \\
& v(\beta \vee \gamma) = v(\beta) \cup v(\gamma) \\
& v(\beta \rightarrow \gamma) = -v(\beta) \cup v(\gamma) \\
& v(\forall z_k \beta) = \cap \{v(\beta(z_k/b))\}_{b \in B} \\
& v(\exists z_k \beta) = \cup \{v(\beta(z_k/b))\}_{b \in B}
\end{aligned}
$$

In other words, v associates, as a meaning, to any atomic sentence $\mathbf{d}_i \in b$ the class of all states whose value for the quantity Q_i is in b; whereas the connectives and the quantifiers are interpreted, in a natural way, as the corresponding (boolean) set-theoretical operations.

On this ground, one may define the truth of α with respect to an ideal state p ($\models_p \alpha$) as follows:

(12) $\underset{p}{\models} \alpha$ iff $p \in v(\alpha)$

More formally, we can say that the structure $\mathscr{R} = \langle \mathscr{B}^P, B, v \rangle$ (where $\mathscr{B}^P$ is the complete boolean algebra defined on $\mathscr{P}(P)$ and B is the set of all Borel sets of real numbers) represents an *algebraic boolean realisation* for the language L^* (of course, we will put $\underset{\mathscr{R}}{\models} \alpha$ iff $v(\alpha) = P$).

The concept of truth with respect to the ideal states represents clearly a kind of *ideal truth*, which can be correlated, in a natural way, with our concept of *empirical truth*. If s is a physical situation consisting of a single state of the physical system σ and α is an atomic sentence of the language L^*, we will have:

(13) $\models_s \alpha$ iff there exists an ideal state p associated with s such that $\models_p \alpha$

In perfect analogy with the case of QT (see (8.5)), in CPM we will say that a state $\omega[\sigma(t)]$, which is characterized by the first-type results $\langle Q_1[\sigma(t)], ..., Q_m[\sigma(t)]\rangle$ admits p as a possible *ideal state* when

$$\rho_\sigma(\mathcal{Q}_1)(p) \in Q_1[\sigma(t)], ..., \rho_\sigma(Q_m)(p) \in Q_m[\sigma(t)].$$

Let us now go back to the case of QT, where, as we have seen, the role of the phase-space P, is played by a Hilbert space and the role of the ideal states is played by the statistical operators in H, the pure states being represented by the normalised vectors of H (i.e. the vectors with length 1). Now let us ask: what kind of structure does correspond in this case to the boolean algebra $\mathcal{R}^P$, and does consequently represent the structure of all quantum properties? One can easily realise that the power-set of H is not very significant in this case. Think for instance that there are infinitely many subsets of H which do not contain any ideal state; consequently infinitely many sets should represent the 'impossible property'. A more lucky candidate seems to be represented by a proper subset of $\mathcal{P}(H)$, namely the set C of all closed subspaces of H. Since the singleton $\{0\}$ of the null vector is the only subspace which does not contain any ideal quantum state and $\{0\}$ is included in all other subspaces, it would be reasonable to maintain that $\{0\}$ represents in C the 'impossible quantum property'.

However, C is not closed under the set theoretical operations: namely the complement of a subspace is not generally a subspace, and the union of two subspaces is not generally a subspace. As a consequence, one cannot trivially define a boolean structure on C, by using the set theoretical operations. Nevertheless C can be extended, in a natural way, to an algebraic structure which is a complete lattice, and which, in a sense, simulates a 'quasi-boolean' behaviour. This structure $\mathcal{L}^H$ can be defined as follows:

(14) $\mathcal{L}^H = \langle C, \perp, \sqcap, \sqcup, \prod, \bigsqcup, \mathbf{1}, \mathbf{0}\rangle$,
where
$X^\perp = [a\langle\psi \in H \,/\, \forall \varphi \in X(\langle\psi, \varphi\rangle = 0)]$ (for any $X \in C$)
(in other words, $X^\perp$ contains all the vectors which are orthogonal to any element of X).

$X \sqcap Y =$ the greatest subspace $Z \in C$ such that $Z \subseteq X \cap Y$ (for any $X, Y \in C$);

$X \sqcup Y =$ the smallest subspace $Z \in C$ such that $X \cup Y \subseteq Z$ (for any $X, Y \in C$);

$\sqcap\{X_i\}_{i \in I} =$ the greatest subspace $Z \in C$ such that $Z \subseteq \cap\{X_i\}_{i \in I}$ for any class of subspaces X_i belonging to C);

$\sqcup\{X_i\}_{i \in I} =$ the smallest subspace $Z \in C$ such that $\cup\{X_i\}_{i \in I} \subseteq Z$ (for any class of subspaces X_i belonging to C);

$\mathbf{1} = H$ (i.e. **1** represents the total space);

$\mathbf{0} = \{0\}$ (where 0 represents the null vector in H).

One can easily show that: $X^\perp$ is a subspace such that $X^\perp \subseteq -X \cup \{0\}$; $X \sqcap Y = X \cap Y$, $\sqcap\{X_i\}_{i \in I} = \cap\{X_i\}_{i \in I}$.

Further one can show that:

(15.1) $\mathscr{L}^H$ is a *complete lattice with maximum and minimum* (where the lattice-relation is the set theoretical inclusion);

(15.2) $\mathscr{L}^H$ is *orthocomplemented* (i.e. the operation $\perp$ satisfies the following conditions: $X \sqcap X^\perp = \mathbf{0}$; $X \sqcup X^\perp = \mathbf{1}$; $X^{\perp\perp} = X$; $X \subseteq Y \Rightarrow Y^\perp \subseteq X^\perp$);

(15.3) $\mathscr{L}^H$ is *orthomodular;* that means $X \subseteq Y \Rightarrow Y = X \sqcup (X^\perp \sqcap Y)$

(15.4) $\mathscr{L}^H$ is *not* distributive (hence $\mathscr{L}^H$ is not a boolean algebra).

Let us now discuss the question whether it is reasonable to claim that this non boolean structure $\mathscr{L}^H$ represents, in a sense, the structure of all properties of our ideal quantum states. In order to answer this question, we will first point out some consequences which can be derived from our hypothesis. In perfect analogy with the case of CPM, the structure $\mathscr{L}^H$ can be extended to an algebraic realisation $\mathscr{R} = \langle \mathscr{L}^H, B, v \rangle$ of a given language, whose atomic sentences have the form $\mathbf{d}_i(\mathbf{t}) \in b$ (where Q_i is supposed to be defined in the physical system whose mathematical interpretation is represented by H). Since the operation in $\mathscr{L}^H$ are not boolean, we cannot expect that the logical constants which correspond to such operations behave as the classical logical constants. Now, as we have seen, the system of the logical constants of QT ($\neg, \wedge, \vee, \rightarrow, \forall, \exists$) is supposed to obey classical logic; as a consequence, in order to avoid any theoretical confusion, one has to enrich the language of QT with a new system of logical constants which we will call *quantum logical constants* (and denote by $\sim, \&, \curlyvee, \supset, \bigwedge, \bigvee$). Let L' represent this extension of L, and let $L^\#$ be the smallest sublanguage of L' whose atomic formulas have the form $\mathbf{d}_i(\mathbf{t}) \in b$, $\mathbf{d}_i(\mathbf{t}) \in z_k$ and which is closed with respect to the quantum logical constants (as in the case of CPM we will write also $\mathbf{d}_i \in b$ or $P_i b$ instead of $\mathbf{d}_i(\mathbf{t}) \in b$; similarly for $\mathbf{d}_i(\mathbf{t}) \in z_k$). The definition of the function v is not so obvious as in the case of CPM. Indeed here, unlike what happens in the case of CPM, we cannot refer to a natural two-valued valuation for the predicates P_i with respect to the ideal states ψ's$\in H$: the Born rule provides only, for any predicate P_i and any state ψ, a probabilistic valuation. In this situation, a reasonable choice seems to be the following: to claim that 'having a certain property for an ideal state' simply means that 'the property holds for that state with probability 1'.

As a consequence, we will state that $v(P_i)$ is a function which associates to any Borel set b the value $[\psi \in H/\mathrm{Prob}_{\psi}^{Q_i}(b) = 1]$ (which is an element of $\mathscr{L}^H$). For the sentences of $L^{\#}$, we will then state, in perfect analogy with CPM, the following conditions:

(16) $v(P_i b) = v(P_i)(b)$ for any atomic sentence $P_i b$.

$v(\sim\beta) = v(\beta)^{\perp}$.

$v(\beta \mathbin{\&} \gamma) = v(\beta) \sqcap v(\gamma)$.

$v(\beta \vee \gamma) = v(\beta) \sqcup v(\gamma)$.

$v(\beta \supset \gamma) = \begin{cases} \mathbf{1} & \text{if } v(\beta) \subseteq v(\gamma); \\ \mathbf{0} & \text{otherwise.}^{12} \end{cases}$

$v(\bigwedge z_k \beta) = \sqcap \{v(\beta(z_k/b))\}_{b \in B}$.

$v(\bigvee z_k \beta) = \sqcup \{v(\beta(z_k/b))\}_{b \in B}$.

Finally we will say that:

(17) a sentence α of $L^{\#}$ is *quantum logically true* in an ideal state ψ ($\models_{\psi} \alpha$) iff $\psi \in v(\alpha)$; and α is *quantum logically true* in the realisation $\mathscr{R}(\models_{\mathscr{R}} \alpha)$ iff $v(\alpha) = \mathbf{1}$.

We will have of course: $\models_{\mathscr{R}} \alpha$ iff for any state ψ, $\models_{\psi} \alpha$.

Let us now point out some immediate consequences of the definition of quantum logical truth.

The strong *tertium non datur-principle*, i.e. the metatheoretical assertion according to which 'for any sentence α, either α or its negation is true', is here generally violated. Indeed, we may have for a certain α and a certain ψ:

(18) not $\models_{\psi} \alpha$ and not $\models_{\psi} \sim\alpha$.

This will hold when $\psi \notin v(\alpha)$ and $\psi \notin v(\alpha)^{\perp}$ (recall that $X \cup X^{\perp}$ is properly included in H, if both X and $X^{\perp}$ are different from H). Nevertheless the weak *tertium non datur-principle*, i.e. the theoretical assertion 'α or not-α must be true for any sentence α. In other words:

(19) $\underset{\psi}{\models} \alpha \vee \sim\alpha$.

Indeed, $v(\alpha) \sqcup v(\alpha)^{\perp} = H$.

As a consequence of (18) we will have that the 'non truth of a sentence' does not coincide with the 'truth of the negation of the sentence'. In other words, there are three possible *states of truth* for a given sentence α, with respect to a physical state ψ: *true* (when $\models_{\psi} \alpha$), *false* (when $\models_{\psi} \sim\alpha$), *indetermined* (when neither $\models_{\psi} \alpha$ nor $\models_{\psi} \sim\alpha$).

The conjunction of condition (18) and (19) gives rise to an apparently curious logical situation. However, such situation is historically not new. As is well known, already Aristotle had recognized that when we are interested in a *contingent* sentence concerning the *future*, the application of the metatheoretical *tertium non datur* becomes critical. According to a modern interpretation of Aristotle's *De Interpretatione*, one may suppose that Aristotle himself did, in some sense, realize the possibility of a logical situation, founded on the conjunction of (18) and (19).

Conditions (18) and (19) show at the same time that the truth of a disjunction does not generally imply the truth of at least one of the members of the disjunction. In other words:

(20) $\underset{\psi}{\models} \alpha \vee \beta \nRightarrow \underset{\psi}{\models} \alpha$ or $\underset{\psi}{\models} \beta$.

On the other hand there holds:

(21) $\underset{\psi}{\models} \alpha$ or $\underset{\psi}{\models} \beta \Rightarrow \underset{\psi}{\models} \alpha \vee \beta$.

Whereas for the conjunction we have:

(22) $\underset{\psi}{\models} \alpha \,\&\, \beta$ iff $\underset{\psi}{\models} \alpha$ and $\underset{\psi}{\models} \beta$.

This asymmetrical behaviour of conjunction and disjunction causes the failure of the *distributivity*-laws. Indeed, we will have:

(23) $\underset{\psi}{\models} (\alpha \,\&\, \beta) \vee (\alpha \,\&\, \gamma) \supset \alpha \,\&\, (\beta \vee \gamma)$

But, generally, not the other way around!

And dually:

(24) $\underset{\psi}{\models} \alpha \vee (\beta \,\&\, \gamma) \supset (\alpha \vee \beta) \,\&\, (\alpha \vee \gamma)$.

But generally, not the other way around!

On can easily find a number of physical examples, which show that (18)–(24) are quite reasonable principles in the framework of QT; this examples confirm, at the same time, that the choice of $\mathscr{L}^{H}$ to represent the structure of all properties of the ideal quantum states appears to be, from an intuitive point of view, a correct choice.

Recognizing the essential presence of the quantum logical constants, in the deductive structure of QT, permits to solve, in a very elegant and economical way, a class of much debated 'logical anomalies' of quantum mechanics. Such anomalies are characteristic of a sort of physical situations, where a physical system seems to satisfy a certain alternative property, whereas both members of the alternative must be *strongly indetermined* for that system. For instance, in the famous 'two-slits experiment', one deals with a physical situation where, for a certain particle ψ, it is true that 'either ψ has gone through a slit A or it has gone through a slit B' ($\models_\psi \alpha \vee \beta$); nevertheless one can neither maintain that it is true that 'the particle ψ has gone through A' nor that it is true that 'it has gone through B' (not $\models_\psi \alpha$ and not $\models_\psi \beta$). Such a situation, which has been described for a long time as intuitively paradoxical,[13] represents nothing but a particular instance of condition (20).

Unfortunately, not all conceptual difficulties of QT belong to this class of 'logical anomalies'!

As we have seen, our concept of quantum logical truth can violate some laws of classical logic (CL) (for instance, the distributivity-laws). What is the logic which governs this particular subtheory of QT, which we have expressed in the language $L^\#$? The answer is: quantum logic, which turns out to be weaker than CL. From a purely logical point of view, the most intuitive way of characterizing QL can be obtained, in this framework, as a natural generalization of our physical starting point.

As we have seen, in any Hilbert space H we can define a complete orthomodular lattice $\mathscr{L}^H$, and this lattice can be extended in a natural way to an algebraic realisation for the language $L^\#$. Now, any $\mathscr{L}^H$ represents nothing but a particular case in the class of all abstract structures, which are called *complete orthomodular lattices.* We will say that an abstract structure of the kind

(25) $\mathscr{L} = \langle A, \perp, \sqcap, \sqcup, \bigsqcap, \bigsqcup, \mathbf{1}, \mathbf{0} \rangle$

is a complete orthomodular lattice when:

(a) A is a non-empty set;

(b) the substructure $\langle A, \sqcap, \sqcup \rangle$ is a *lattice* (i.e. $\sqcap$ and $\sqcup$ are binary operations in A which satisfy both the associative and the commutative property; further there holds: $a \sqcap (a \sqcup b) = a$ and $a \sqcup (a \sqcap b) = a$. We call $a \sqcup b$ ($a \sqcap b$) also the *supremum* (the *infimum)* of a and b. One can define a *lattice-relation* $a \leqslant b$ as: $a \sqcap b = a$;

(c) **1** and **0** represent respectively the *maximum* and the *minimum* of

$\mathscr{L}$ (i.e. for any $a \in A$, $a \leqslant \mathbf{1}$ and $\mathbf{0} \leqslant a$);

(d) the 1-ary operation $\perp$ is an *orthocomplement* (i.e. $a \sqcup a^{\perp} = \mathbf{1}$, $a \sqcap a^{\perp} = \mathbf{0}$, $a = a^{\perp\perp}$, $a \leqslant b \Rightarrow b^{\perp} \leqslant a^{\perp}$);

(e) the *completeness*-property means that any set X of elements of A has in A an *infimum* $\sqcap X$ (i.e. the greatest element with respect to $\leqslant$, which is smaller or equal than any element of X) and a *supremum* $\sqcup X$ (i.e. the smallest element which is greater or equal than any element of X);

(f) the *orthomodularity*-property means that for any $a, b \in A$: $a \leqslant b \Rightarrow b = a \sqcup (a^{\perp} \sqcap b)$.

One can easily recognize that our *concrete* orthomodular lattice $\mathscr{L}^H$ does satisfy the properties (a)–(f).

Let us now refer to a generic first-order language L with n-adic predicates P^n_m and with the quantum logical constants. We can define the concept of *algebraic orthorealisation* for L as follows: an algebraic orthorealisation for L is a structure

(26) $\mathscr{R} = \langle \mathscr{L}, D, v \rangle$ where:

(a) $\mathscr{L}$ is a complete orthomodular lattice;

(b) D is a non-empty set (the set of individuals of $\mathscr{R}$); let $L^{\bullet}$ be an extension of L containing an individual name **d** for any $d \in D$;

(c) v interprets the non-logical constants of $L^{\bullet}$ and associates to each sentence α of $L^{\bullet}$ a value $v(\alpha)$ in A. For any $\mathbf{d}$, $v(\mathbf{d}) = \mathrm{d}$. For any predicate P^n_m, $v(P^n_m)$ is an *n-ary attribute* in $\mathscr{R}$, that is a function which associates to any n-ple $\langle d_1, \ldots, d_n \rangle$ of elements of D an element of A. Further, for any sentence α of L, $v(\alpha)$ is determined as follows:

$$v(P^n_m \mathbf{d}_1 \ldots \mathbf{d}_m) = v(P^n_m)(v(\mathbf{d}_1), \ldots, v(\mathbf{d}_n))$$

$$v(\sim\beta) = v(\beta)^{\perp}$$
$$v(\beta \,\&\, \gamma) = v(\beta) \sqcap v(\gamma)$$
$$v(\beta \vee \gamma) = v(\beta) \sqcup v(\gamma)$$
$$v(\beta \supset \gamma) = \begin{cases} \mathbf{1} & \text{if } v(\beta) \leqslant v(\gamma) \\ \mathbf{0} & \text{otherwise} \end{cases}$$
$$v(\bigwedge x\, \beta) = \sqcap \{(v(\beta(x/\mathbf{d}))\}_{d \in D}$$
$$v(\bigvee x\, \beta) = \sqcup \{(v(\beta(x/\mathbf{d}))\}_{d \in D}\,.$$

(27) A sentence α will be said *true* in an orthorealisation $\mathscr{R}(\models_{\mathscr{R}} \alpha)$ iff $v(\alpha) = \mathbf{1}$; α will be said to be *quantum logically valid* or also a *quantum logical law* ($\models_{\mathrm{QL}} \alpha$) iff for any algebraic orthorealisation $\mathscr{R}$, $\models_{\mathscr{R}} \alpha$.

In this way, we have completely characterized QL by means of an algebraic semantics. The same logic admits of some alternative semantical descriptions (for instance a Kripke-style semantics,[14] a dialogical semantics[15]) and a number of different axiomatisations which turn out to be sound and complete with respect to the different semantics.[16] These syntactical and semantical descriptions have made fairly clear the *logical status* of QL, as well as its precise place in the vast class of the logics weaker than CL. As a consequence, the doubts set forth in the past by some scholars, concerning the 'authentic nature' of logic of QL, seem today to be completely dispelled.

A characteristic metalogical feature of QL (which, so far, seems to distinguish this logic from most 'weak' logics) concerns the strong impossibility or proving, for this logic, a 'Lindenbaum theorem'. Namely, if *FS* is a consistent quantum logical formal system (i.e. a formal system whose logic is QL), generally *FS* does not admit any consistent and *complete* quantum logical extension (in other words, there exists no consistent logical extensions of *FS*, which for any sentence α, either proves α or $\sim\alpha$. This consequence can be derived from a result proved by Kochen and Specker,[17] according to which an orthomodular lattice does not generally admit any homomorphism on a two-valued boolean algebra. One can guess that the 'boolean two valued homomorphism-property' represents an important dividing-line between different modes of being 'a logic weaker than CL'. A logic, which (like QL) does not satisfy this property, must be, in some sense, 'semantically incompatible' with CL, even if, syntactically it turns out to be theoretically included in CL.

In spite of this kind of 'semantical incompatibility' between QL and CL (which, up to now, seems to require further investigations) one can ask whether or not it is possible to describe the 'meaning' of the quantum logical constants, with the 'eyes' of a classical logician, that is within a theoretical framework, where we are using CL and not QL. This is a crucial logical question for QT, since, as we have seen, QT gives rise to a logical situation, where every logical constant splits into two different interpretations: the classical and the quantum logical one. Actually, when somebody is arguing in quantum mechanics and is claiming, for instance, that 'something is not the case', one should ask him "please what kind of 'not' are you using on this particular occasion?'"?. Can we compare the different systems of logical constants used in QT, or does this situation represent only a kind of unavoidable 'logical schizophrenia'? Fortunately, the answer to this question is 'yes, a formal comparison can be made'; namely, one can give a classical interpretation of the quantum logical constants, by using a particular superlogic of CL, which is represented by a form of modal logic. This modal interpretation of QL is, formally, very similar to the well known modal interpretation of intuitionistic logic, proposed by Gödel, Tarski and other authors.[18]

One can refer to a modal logic ML (which turns out to be a superlogic of the so called 'Brouwer's modal system') and define a translation τ of the language of QL into the language of ML such that:

(28) for any sentence α of QL, α is quantum logically valid iff its modal translation $\tau(\alpha)$ is a valid sentence of ML.

This result can be obtained, in a semantical way, by proving that any algebraic orthorealisation $\mathscr{R}$ of the language of QL can be transformed into a modal realisation $\mathscr{M}^{\mathscr{R}}$ of the language of ML, such that:

(29) $\models_{\mathscr{R}} \alpha$ iff $\models_{\mathscr{M}^{\mathscr{R}}} \tau(\alpha)$ for any sentence α of QL.

And viceversa, any modal realisation $\mathscr{M}$ of ML can be transformed into an algebraic orthorealisation $\mathscr{R}^{\mathscr{M}}$ of QL such that:

(30) $\models_{\mathscr{M}} \tau(\alpha)$ iff $\models_{\mathscr{R}^{\mathscr{M}}} \alpha$ for any sentence α of QL.

These results give a complete answer to our question concerning the classical meaning of our quantum logical constants.

Let us now go back to QT and ask what is the physical meaning of the modal realisation $\mathscr{M}^{\mathscr{R}^H}$ which we have associated, in this way, to any algebraic realisation $\mathscr{R}^H$ of the sublanguage $L^{\#}$ of QT. As a consequence of the proof of (29), we obtain that the *possible worlds* of the modal realisation $\mathscr{M}^{\mathscr{R}^H}$ are represented by all non-null subspaces of H; in other words, any non-null subspace represents, in the modal realisation, $\mathscr{M}^{\mathscr{R}^H}$, a 'possible physical world'. Among the physical worlds it is interesting to consider the *unidimensional* physical worlds X_ψ, which contain only one normalized vector. There holds: for any sentence α of $L^{\#}$, α is quantum logically true in the ideal state ψ, iff the modal translation $\tau(\alpha)$ is *classically true* in the physical world X_ψ.

One can ask whether these model-theoretical results may have some bearing on the general philosophy of quantum mechanics. It seems to me that all this can lead, in a natural way, to the following claim: from a purely logical point of view, quantum logic is not really *essential* to the logical development of quantum mechanics, since the role played by this logic can be equivalently replaced by a form of classical modal logic. Perhaps, this conclusion can give some psychological help to those people who think that a theoretical situation essentially founded on a *mixture of logics*, is very disagreeable. As a logician, I must say that I do not feel any particular allergy to a situation of mixture of logics. On the contrary, it seems to me that, generally, a form of plurality of logics cannot be avoided in modern science. In any case, even if, philosophically, we do not trust a unique privileged logic, from a logical point of view any reduction of a logic to another logic represents a relevant result. However, in this particular case, concerning quantum logic, can we really assert that we have completely reduced quantum logic to classical logic? As we have seen, we have only proved the following metatheorem: $\models_{QL} \alpha$ iff $\models_{ML} \tau(\alpha)$. But ML is not *simply* classical logic. Indeed it represents a very particular extension of classical logic. One could ask: why just the modal system ML fits with quantum mechanics?

The modal interpretation of QL, seems to solve, at least partially, the problem of the 'logical schizofrenia' of QT. However, an important metalogical problem seems to remain, at this point, still open: the problem concerns what we could call the 'double truth-question' of QT.

So far, we have defined the concept of quantum logical truth only with respect to the ideal states. But one can extend this definition, in a natural way, also to the physical situations s consisting of a single state. If α is a sentence of $L^{\#}$ we will say that:

(31) α is *quantum logically true in s* ($\underset{s}{\models\!\!\!=}\alpha$) iff
(a) α is defined in s;
(b) there exists and ideal state ψ of s such that $\underset{\psi}{\models\!\!\!=}\alpha$.

One may wonder what is the relation between the concept of quantum logical truth and that of empirical truth (defined in (4)). Of course, this comparison makes sense only for the case of atomic sentences which belong both to L and $L^{\#}$. One can recognize that the quantum logical truth represents a stronger concept than the empirical truth. Namely there holds:

(32) $\underset{s}{\models\!\!\!=} \mathbf{d}_i \in b \Rightarrow \underset{s}{\models} \mathbf{d}_i \in b.$

But generally not the other way around! [3]

Hence, the perfect symmetry between the ideal and the empirical truth, which as we have seen, holds in the case of CPM (see (13)), breaks down in the case of QT.

From the intuitive point of view, the quantum logical truth means (in the case considered in (32)): *we know with certainty* (i.e. with probability 1) that if we made a measurement for the quantity Q_i in the physical situation s, we would find as a result a value contained in b. In other words, the notion of quantum logical truth corresponds to a kind of *a priori-certainty*. On the contrary, the empirical truth means: *we do* a measurement and *we find* that the value of Q_i is in b. One could say that by means of relation (32), we have simply recovered, on a formal level, that 'in QT events may happen without being certain'. This has been observed on many occasions by Jauch,[19] and is, in some sense the basic idea of Van Fraassen's modal interpretation of quantum mechanics.[20]

The distinction between two essentially different concepts of truth within QT has a bearing on a much debated question of quantum mechanics, which involves some paradoxical consequences, namely the 'measurement problem'. As is well known, in spite of the vast literature devoted to this problem, from a semantical point of view the measurement problem seems to represent, in a sense, still an open question of quantum mechanics,[21] which requires further investigations.

However these questions go beyond the limits of the present paper. As a final remark, let me only stress the following: one can hardly hope to solve the semantical difficulties which are connected with the measurement problem, if one implicitly adheres to an hypothesis which simply identifies the concept of *truth* in QT with that of *quantum logical truth*. Apparently, the logical analysis of physical theories cannot be carried out, in a satisfactory way, by using a unique concept of truth; the definition of 'physical truth' seems to be, so far, much more critical and ambiguous than the corresponding concept of 'mathematical truth'.

University of Florence

NOTES

[1] See [1], [2], [3]. A similar approach has been proposed independently in Wójcicki [4].

[2] These concepts admit of a formal description in the metatheory of T (see [3]). According to this approach, we assume that the terms 'physical system' and 'procedure of measurement' are primitive terms of the metatheory; on this ground one can define the following notions: *operationally defined quantity, measurement, result of a measurement, (operational) physical state, physical situation*.

[3] This notion can be made more precise in the following way: if $p(x)$ is a continuous probability distribution, we can plot it against x, in rectangular coordinates, and obtain a continuous curve. If from each point z we trace a cross, centered at z, whose horizontal and vertical arms are ϵ^A and ϵ^P in length, respectively, we obtain a strip Σ. The result of the application of a probabilistic procedure to a statistical ensemble is represented by the set of all probability distributions $p'(x)$, whose curves lie entirely within Σ.

[4] $\models_{\mathscr{M}_0} \alpha$ represents the standard notion of mathematical truth. For the sake of simplicity (and to avoid a more heavy logical formalism) we suppose that the language contains a name for any real number and for any probability distribution of real numbers. We will not distinguish the object-language names from the metatheoretical names.

[5] In the most common cases, the mathematical subsystem FS_0 of FS admits of a standard model. If FS includes an *abstract* mathematical theory (with *no* standard models) it is convenient to take as $\mathscr{M}_0$ a standard model of set theory.

[6] T must be a 'well behaved' theory, in the sense that it must satisfy some standard formal requirements.

[7] See [5].

[8] More details can be found in [3].

[9] A notice for the reader who is not familiar with the theory of Hilbert spaces: the main arguments developed in this paper can be understood, even if one is not acquainted with the precise definitions of the mathematical concepts here involved. The non-mathematical reader should only recall that, if $\mathscr{C}$ is an operational concept, $\rho(\mathscr{C})$ (or $\tau(\mathscr{C})$) can be conveniently defined in the mathematical part of our physical structures.

[10] If W has the form P_ψ, where P_ψ is the projection-operator along a normalized vector ψ of H (i.e. a vector with length 1), we will say that W represents a *pure state*, otherwise it represents a *mixture*. Owing to the one-to-one correspondence between the set of all P_ψ's and the set of all normalized vectors in H, we may say also that a pure state is represented by a normalized vector ψ of H.

[11] If $\langle r_1, ..., r_6\rangle \in R^6, r_1, r_2, r_3$ are supposed to represent the three coordinates of *position*, whereas r_4, r_5, r_6 represent the three coordinates of *momentum*.

[12] It is worth while to notice that our semantical characterization of the quantum-logical implication corresponds better to a kind of 'entailment-connective' than to a 'material implication'. For a general discussion of the 'implication-problem of QL' see [6].

[13] A logical analysis of the 'two-slits experiment' can be found for instance in [7], [8], [9].

[14] See [10], [11], [12].

[15] See [13], [14], [15].

[16] A Hilbert–Bernays-style axiomatisation of QL can be found in [9].

[17] See [16].

[18] See [17], [11], [12].

[19] See [18].

[20] See [19], [20].

[21] "The proper conclusion to draw from the semantic problem of measurement is that the orthodox semantic interpretation of the state vector conflicts with the interpretation of the statistical operators as defining conditional probabilities on a non-boolean structure. The solution to this problem requires an alternative semantics consistent with the statistical interpretation of the pure statistical operators." [21]

BIBLIOGRAPHY

[1] M. I. Dalla Chiara and G. Toraldo di Francia, 'A Logical Analysis of Physical Theories', *Rivista del Nuovo Cimento* 3 (1973), 1–20.

[2] M. L. Dalla Chiara and G. Toraldo di Francia, 'The Logical Dividing Line between Deterministic and Indeterministic Theories', *Studia Logica* XXXV (1976), 1–5.

[3] M. L. Dalla Chiara and G. Toraldo di Francia, 'Formal Analysis of Physical Theories', in G. Toraldo di Francia (ed.), *Problems in the Foundations of Physics*, North-Holland, Amsterdam, 1979.

[4] R. Wójcicki, 'Set Theoretic Representation of Empirical Phenomena', *Journal of Philosophical Logic* 3 (1974), 337.

[5] M. L. Dalla Chiara, 'A Multiple Sentential Logic for Empirical Theories', in M. Przełęcki, K. Szaniawski, and R. Wójcicki (eds.), *Formal Methods in the Methodology of Empirical Sciences*, Ossolineum, Warsaw, 1976.

[6] G. Hardegree, 'The Conditional in Quantum Logic', in P. Suppes (ed.), *Logic and Probability in Quantum Mechanics*, D. Reidel Publ. Co., Dordrecht, Holland, 1976.

[7] H. Putnam, 'Is Logic Empirical?', in R. Cohen and M. Wartowski (eds.), *Boston Studies in the Philosophy of Science*, V, D. Reidel Publ. Co., Dordrecht, Holland, 1969.

[8] A. Fine, 'Some Conceptual Problems of Quantum Theory', in R. Colodny (ed.), *Paradigms and Paradoxes*, University of Pittsburg Press, Pittsburg, 1972.

[9] M. L. Dalla Chiara, 'A General Approach to Non-Distributive Logics', *Studia Logica* XXXV (1976), 139–162.

[10] H. Dishkant, 'Semantics for the Minimal Logic of Quantum Mechanics', *Studia Logica* XXX (1972), 23–36.

[11] R. I. Goldblatt, 'Semantic Analysis of Orthologic', *Journal of Philosophical Logic* 3 (1974), 19–35.

[12] M. L. Dalla Chiara, 'Quantum Logic and Physical Modalities', *Journal of Philosophical Logic* 6 (1974), 391–404.

[13] P. Mittelstaedt, *Philosophical Problems of Modern Physics* (*Boston Studies in the Philosophy of Science*, XIII), D. Reidel Publ. Co., Dordrecht, Holland, 1976.

[14] P. Mittelstaedt and E. W. Stachow, 'Operational Foundation of Quantum Logic', *Foundations of Physics* 4 (1974), 355–366.

[15] P. Mittelstaedt, 'Quantum Logic', in G. Toraldo di Francia (ed.), *Problems in the Foundations of Physics*, North-Holland, Amsterdam, 1979.

[16] S. Kochen and E. P. Specker, 'The Problem of Hidden Variables in Quantum Mechanics', *Journal of Mathematical Mechanics* 17 (1967), 59–87.

[17] M. L. Dalla Chiara, 'Some Logical Problems suggested by Empirical Theories', *Boston Studies in the Philosophy of Science*, (to be published).

[18] J. M. Jauch, *Foundations of Quantum Mechanics*, Addison-Wesley, 1968.

[19] B. van Fraassen, 'A Formal Approach to Philosophy of Science', in R. Colodny (ed.), *Paradigms and Paradoxes*, University of Pittsburg Press, Pittsburg, 1972.

[20] B. van Fraassen, 'The Einstein–Podolski–Rosen Paradox', in P. Suppes (ed.), *Logic and Probability in Quantum Mechanics*, D. Reidel Publ. Co., Dordrecht Holland, 1976.

[21] J. Bub, 'The Measurement Problem of Quantum Mechanics', in G. Foraldo di Francia (ed.), *Problems in the Foundations of Physics*, North-Holland, Amsterdam, 1979.

[22] M. Jammer, *The Philosophy of Quantum Mechanics*, John Wiley, New York, 1974.

[23] G. Birkhoff and J. von Neumann, 'The Logic of Quantum Mechanics', *Annals of Mathematics* 37 (1936), 823–843.

L. JONATHAN COHEN

INDUCTIVE LOGIC 1945–1977

I

The seventeenth century saw the beginnings of two powerful and important ways of conceiving one proposition to support another in cases where the truth of the former is formal-logically consistent with the falsehood of the latter. Early in the century Francis Bacon urged the possibility of discovering causal uniformities from tables of presence and absence – lists of circumstances present, and circumstances absent, when the phenomenon under investigation was found. Bacon thought that natural laws which were so discovered would become more and more certain as they increased in comprehensiveness and subsumed a greater and greater variety of known uniformities, provided that these laws also lead us to new knowledge. A little later Pascal and Fermat laid down principles for a mathematical calculus of chance that Leibniz and Bernoulli interpreted as binding normal judgements of probability – in the law courts, for example, as well as in games of chance.

For a couple of centuries these two systems of ideas tended to be considered apart from one another.

Like a good Baconian Leibniz considered one scientific hypothesis to be more probable than another if it was simpler, explained a larger number of phenomena from a smaller number of postulates, and allowed the prediction of as yet unknown phenomena.[1] But, apparently, he never tried to represent or elucidate these criteria within the calculus of chance, despite his application of the calculus to other kinds of probability-judgment. Hume actually went on to distinguish two different types of probability when he argued that

> probability or reasoning from conjecture may be divided into two kinds, *viz*. that which is founded on *chance*, and that which arises from *causes*.[2]

William Whewell, J. F. W. Herschel and J. S. Mill reformulated Bacon's ideas in the light of post-Baconian scientific developments, but never attributed a Pascalian structure to judgements about how much this or that variety of evidential data supports a stated universal generalisation about causal processes.

Equally, when mathematicians refined and developed the theory of Pascalian probability, they pointed out its value *within* science, in calculations

E. Agazzi (ed.), Modern Logic – A Survey, 353–375.

aimed at drawing out the best value for a quantitative parameter from a multitude of varying measurements.[3] Or they argued that an empirical hypothesis increased its probability with the mere number of observed instances irrespective of their variety.[4] But they did not normally propose applying Pascalian principles to the main logical problem *about* science with which the Baconian tradition had been grappling – viz. the problem of how to assess the strength of the support that is given by experimental variations of evidential circumstances to a universal hypothesis about causal connections.

Nevertheless, in the latter half of the nineteenth century, as the mathematics of Pascalian probability became better and better understood, while the logical structure of Baconian induction remained wholly unformalised, the temptation to treat the former as a theory of the latter became more and more obviously attractive. W. S. Jevons certainly succumbed to this temptation;[5] and in the 1920's J. M. Keynes[6] in England, and Jean Nicod[7] in France, found it quite natural to assume without question that judgements of inductive support from variations of evidential circumstance should conform to Pascalian principles. A great part of the more recent history of the subject has also consisted of work done on the basis of this unquestioned assumption. But, as we shall see, the assumption has turned out to be a rather frustrating one, and its rejection permits a breakthrough into some rewardingly new areas of logico-mathematical analysis.

II

It would be a mistake to suppose, however, that the only important constraints on recent development in inductive logic have been set by Pascalian ideas about probability, on the one side, and scientists' norms of evidential assessment, on the other. In addition to those two factors, certain well-known puzzles or paradoxes have made a major contribution towards determining the direction that developments have taken. These paradoxes have been as important for inductive logic as have other paradoxes, like the Liar and Russell's antinomy, for deductive logic: I shall mention just three of them.

In 1945 C. G. Hempel pointed out,[8] in effect, that three apparently plausible assumptions about the concept of confirmation are not co-tenable. These assumptions are as follows: –

(1) If the antecedent and consequent of a generalized conditional are conjointly satisfied, this confirms the generalisation to at least

some extent. For example, an object that is both a raven and black confirms the generalization 'Anything, if it is a raven, is black.'

(2) Logically equivalent propositions are equally confirmed by the same evidence. So evidence that confirms 'Anything, if it is a raven, is black' must also confirm its contrapositive equivalent 'Anthing, if it is not black, is not a raven'.

(3) A typical object that is neither black nor a raven, like a white handkerchief, does not confirm 'Anything, if it is a raven, is black' (despite the fact that it confirms the contrapositive equivalent of this generalisation).

Obviously one or other of these assumptions has to be modified and Hempel's own proposal was to replace (1). Another proposal[9] has been to sidestep (2), by saying that evidence which satisfies a generalisation like 'Anything, if it is a raven, is black', will selectively confirm the generalisation only if it also disconfirms the generalisation's contrary, viz. 'Anything, if it is a raven, is not black.' Yet another proposal[10] has been to reject (3), on the ground that, because so many more things are not ravens than are ravens, the finding of some non-black things that is not a raven is merely of very low, not null, confirmatory value. But it is unprofitable to discuss the merits of any one such solution of this paradox except as part of a general theory of inductive reasoning which is also competent to solve all other relevant paradoxes also.

In 1953 N. Goodman propounded[11] another paradox about the same criterion of confirmation. Suppose that all emeralds examined before a certain time *t* are green. Then at time *t*, according to this criterion, all our past observation of emeralds confirm the hypothesis that all emeralds are green. But the same observations also confirm the hypothesis that all emeralds are grue, where the novel predicate 'grue' is defined as applying to all things examined before *t* just in case they are green and to other things just in case they are blue. Hence our observations appear to confirm equally well two inconsistent predictions: the prediction that all emeralds subsequently examined will be green and the prediction that all emeralds subsequently examined will be blue.

Goodman's own solution of his paradox was to supplement Nicod's criterion by a linguistic requirement. He proposed to evaluate rival hypotheses in accordance with their 'degree of projectibility', where one hypothesis is said to be more projectible than another if the predicates in terms of which it is formulated – or predicates co-extensive with them – have occurred more often in successfully predictive hypotheses. (Also, if a predicate P applies only to certain mutually disjoint classes, and Q applies to one of these classes, then P, or any predicate co-extensive with P, is said to be as good as Q for these purposes.) If two inconsistent hypotheses were equally well instantiated by our observations, the more projectible of the two was to be regarded as the better confirmed. But it is arguable that, if the founders of modern chemistry had behaved as Goodman suggests, we should still be talking about earth, air, fire and water, instead of about hydrogen, lithium, beryllium, boron, etc.[12]

A third paradox of fundamental importance to the subject was formulated in 1961 by H. E. Kyburg.[13] This paradox is not concerned with the relation between evidence and hypothesis, but with how one may treat a hypothesis once it has achieved a satisfactory degree of evidential confirmation. Again three apparently plausible assumptions are not co-tenable: –

(1) It is reasonable to accept any hypothesis H that, after thorough enquiry, retains a Pascalian probability (on the available evidence) of $1 - \epsilon$ (where ϵ is as small a positive number as you care to make it).

(2) It is reasonable to accept any logical consequence of a set of hypotheses that it is reasonable to accept.

(3) It is not reasonable to accept an inconsistent set of hypotheses.

These assumptions are not co-tenable in relation to, say, a lottery that sells a million tickets, only one of which can win the prize. In the case of each of the million tickets it is reasonable to accept the hypothesis that that ticket is not the winning one. But this conjunction of hypotheses is inconsistent with another hypothesis, which it is also reasonable to accept, viz. the hypothesis that just one ticket will win. Kyburg's own solution of the paradox was to restrict (2), by confining its application to logical consequences of individual hypotheses, as determined by some original partition of possibilities. Other philosophers have modified (1) in various ways, and some have even been prepared to reject (3). But no solution can be satisfactory unless it has a rationale that is independent of its ability to resolve this particular paradox. *Ad hoc* solutions, which are justifiable only by their possession of that ability, cannot provide us with adequate intellectual compensation for having to give up the conjunction of three such plausible assumptions.

III

R. Carnap[14] was the first philosopher in the post-1945 period to undertake a large-scale systematic investigation of inductive reasoning. Suppose a language to have one or more families of mutually incompatible primitive predicates (e.g. the family 'red', 'blue', 'white', etc.). Then a state-description, for a given domain of objects, may be defined as a conjunction of propositions that ascribe to each individual object exactly one primitive predicate of each family. A weight is to be assigned to each state-description so that all the weights sum to unity. Different ways of thus assigning weights to state-descriptions are conceivable: one such would be to assign each the same weight. The range of a proposition p is defined as the set of all the state-descriptions in which p occurs. Once a measure m has been defined for these ranges, as the sum of the weights assigned to the various state-descriptions in the range, it is possible to define the degree of confirmation that one proposition e gives another h, which is written $c(h, e)$, as the ratio of $m(h \& e)$ to $m(e)$. The intuitive idea is that e's support for h is measured by how far the various possible states of affairs in which both h and e hold good overlap with the various possible states of affairs in which e holds good. And, since range-measures of this kind conform to the principles of Pascalian probability, the resultant confirmation-functions do also, in virtue of Bayes' law. Out of a continuum of desirable range-measures Carnap preferred those producing a higher and higher degree of confirmation for the hypothesis that an object has a certain property according as the evidence comes to include more and more objects that already have the property. Indeed, as J. Humburg and H. Gaifman[15] later showed, it can be proved in Carnap's final version of his system (with the help of a plausible additional axiom) that the confirmation of a singular statement h_1 is always increased when, in addition to original evidence stated in e, which is consistent with h_1, we accept a new evidential statement h_2 which reports another instance of the same property as h_1 reports.

But the discovery of a proof for this principle, though welcomed by Carnap, was in fact a heavy blow to his claim to be explicating natural-scientific modes of discourse about inductive support. The discovery showed that this 'principle of instantial relevance', as Carnap called it, is rather deep-rooted in his confirmation-theory. And the harsh truth is that functions for which the principle is provable are cut off therewith from granting the support that reports of successful experimental tests are supposed to give to the hypotheses tested. The reason is that e might already report an instance of the property described by h_1, and h_2 cannot be regarded as stating evidence that increases the support for h_1 merely because it describes yet another instance of the same property. Admittedly a test-result has to be replicable in order to count as genuine evidence in favour of the hypothesis concerned. But the test-result's actual replication (perhaps in another laboratory at a later date) merely confirms its replicability. To get stronger confirmation for the hypothesis itself one would have to construct a different experiment, either testing a different consequence of the hypothesis, or testing the same consequence more thoroughly – i.e. with better controls and greater safeguards against the interference of factors not mentioned in the hypothesis. So, because Carnap's type of confirmation theory requires $c(h_1, h_2 \& e) > c(h_1, e)$ in the circumstances described above, it cannot avoid being closer to what Bacon contemptuously described as induction by simple enumeration than to the induction by variation of circumstances that Bacon, Whewell, Herschel and Mill rightly took to be characteristic of scientific reasoning about the probative force of experimental results.

Carnap's inductive logic has often been criticised for its failure to assign plausible values to confirmation-functions where the hypothesis to be confirmed is a universal generalisation. If the hypothesis is a singular proposition or conjunction of proposition the logic allows a wide spread of possible vaues, in the closed interval $\{0, 1\}$, to the function $c(h, e)$, so as to vary with the actual relation of e to h. But, if h is a universal proposition, its degree of confirmation from favourable instances gets very small as its domain increases, and for domains of infinite size its value is always zero. Since some domains of scientific enquiry may be infinite, this seems a flaw in Carnap's logic. But Carnap himself did not think that it was one. Carnap argued that, for a scientist or engineer to construct his predictions on the rational basis of past evidence, it was not necessary for him to route his inferences via appropriate generalisations. Indeed, while a man who had seen many white swans and no non-white swans might be willing to bet on the next swan's being white, he might well be unwilling to bet that every swan in the universe is white.

Carnap's attitude here was curiously the inverse of Karl Popper's. Popper denied that science had any need for inductive logic, and claimed that scientists sought instead to discover the boldest and simplest hypotheses that resisted falsification. Thus while high prior probability could help a hypothesis to achieve a high degree of confirmation by Carnapian criteria, it was high prior *im*probability that helped a hypothesis to qualify for scientific esteem according to Popper's corroboration-functions.[16] Correspondingly each philosophy, as a logic of science, had both a merit and a defect that the other philosophy lacked. Carnap could claim to represent a certain way of measuring evidential support for the singular predictions that are essential to technology: an engineer must know how reliable, on the evidence of past experience, will be the bridge that he is actually building. But Carnap could not represent a plausible way of measuring evidential support for the highly general propositions that are needed for theoretical explanation and system-building in natural science, like Newton's laws of motion. Popper, on the other hand, could offer a plausible criterion for choosing between one system of scientific theory and another, if the only thing at issue was explanatory power. But he could not provide any adequate guidance for the technologist on questions of reliability. Hypothesis h_2 may be so much bolder than h_1 that we cannot yet test it as thoroughly as h_1 has been tested; and then, even if h_2, like h_1, has not yet been refuted, we can scarcely regard it as being more reliable than h_1 merely because it is bolder. Popper claimed that his falsificationist methodology had solved Hume's problem about induction: there was no need to try and *prove* propositions about the future. But he could only maintain this claim by systematically ignoring the intellectual needs or engineers, navigators, agriculturalists and other technologists. Again, Carnap's adoption of a range-measure ratio, to evaluate degree of confirmation, rendered his inductive logic relatively immune to Hempel's paradox and his prior choice of language protected him, albeit artificially, from Goodman's. But an acceptance-criterion constructed in terms of one of his confirmation-functions would certainly be hit by Kyburg's paradox. On the other hand, while a defender of Popper's views about the logic of science has to work very hard indeed to show that they are not hit by analogues of Goodman's paradoxes, Popper's exposure to Kyburg's paradox is substantially reduced by the fact that he seeks high *im*probability and seeks it for general theories.

IV

J. Hintikka contributed an important new idea[17] to range-based inductive logic in 1964. He reviewed the difficulty about getting adequate confirmation for universal propositions in Carnap's system, and traced it to the way in which the measure of a proposition's range comes to depend on the number of individuals in the domain.

Carnap measured the range of a proposition by the sum of the weights of the different state-descriptions in which the proposition held good. He preferred not to assign equal weights to every state description, however, because this led to a confirmation-function that was indifferent to the accumulation of favourable evidence. Instead he proposed assigning equal weights to every structure-description, where each structure-description is a disjunction of all the different state descriptions that can be transformed into each other by permuting the names of individuals. Suppose, for example, that the language consists of a family of just two primitive monadic predicates, and just two names of individuals, plus the usual logical connectives: in such a language four state-descriptions can be constructed but only three structure-descriptions. Carnap's idea was then to divide the weight which a structure-description receives into equal parts, one for each of the state-descriptions that it disjoins.

But this still makes the measure of a universal proposition's range depend in part on the number of individuals in the domain, and as Hintikka remarked, it is rather perverse to start one's inductive logic by assuming that one is already sufficiently familiar with the whole of one's universe to know its cardinality. Accordingly Hintikka proposed a type of range-measure that was, in the case of universal propositions, independent of this number.

Suppose that we are given k primitive monadic predicates. By means of these predicates and propositional connectives we can partition our domain, whatever its size, into 2^k different kinds (empty or non-empty), distinguished by the various complex predicates that describe them. Then we can describe a possible world by a sentence describing all the non-empty kinds of individuals in it. Such a sentence, which Hintikka calls a 'constituent', will be a consistent conjunction of existentially quantified complex predicates, conjoined with a universal quantification of their disjunction. An equal weight may be given to each constituent (or kind of possible world), and the weight of each constituent may be divided among all the state-descriptions that make it true. But, since every consistent universally quantified sentence has an equivalent (its distributive normal form) that is a disjunction of constituents with the same predicates, the measure of a universal proposition's range is independent of the number of state-descriptions that make any particular constituent true and thus quite independent of the numbers of individuals of various kinds in the universe or of the total number of individuals. Hintikka also showed how his system could in principle cover sentences with polyadic predicates or more than one quantifier. His confirmation-functions, like Carnap's conformed to the principles of Pascalian probability. But they nevertheless resembled Popper's corroboration-functions in allegedly recommending to us the simplest generalisation compatible with the evidence because, for Hintikka, the simplicity of a generalisation varied inversely with the structural complexity of its distributive normal form, rather than with its probability.

Hintikka's inductive logic is thus a definite improvement on Carnap's. But it still suffers from a number of serious disadvantages.

(1) As we have already seen, neither type of logic captures the characteristic scientific attitude towards the bare replication of existing evidence – viz. that it confirms the legitimacy of the evidence but not the hypothesis itself.

(2) Neither type of logic can in practice yet go any distance towards measuring degrees of confirmation for hypotheses that contain polyadic predicates, because of the difficult problems that arise in combinatorial arithmetic. Neither type of logic, therefore, is yet able to provide a reconstruction of scientific inference beyond a very elementary level. Treatment[18] of the role of theoretical concepts in scientific inference can hardly be very convincing if the language of analysis is confined to first-order monadic predicates. Hintikka's confirmation-functions are also subject to those restraints on computability that derive from the non-existence of a decision-procedure for the logic of polyadic predicates.

(3) Hintikka's inductive logic seems at first sight to be better than Carnap's at avoiding Kyburg's paradox. But in fact it is not. Hintikka and Hilpinen[19] seek to avoid the trouble that Carnap's theory encounters here by treating the fundamental unit of acceptance as a universal proposition, not a singular one. No analogue of the lottery paradox can then be constructed. But a singular proposition is then said to be acceptable if and only if it is a substitution instance of an acceptable generalisation – as if one ought not to accept that it will rain to-morrow unless one accepts that it will rain for all eternity.

(4) Perhaps the most serious flaw is this. Both Carnap's and Hintikka's logic assume a pre-existing language, and the confirmation-assessments that they derive therefrom are accordingly analytic and *a priori* in character, (as also are Popper's assessments of the degree to which one proposition corroborates another). Consequently all expressions of a given linguistic category have to be put on a level with one another. At some point equipartitions of weight are assumed – between all state-descriptions, or all structure-descriptions, or all constituents – as if all circumstances in nature are equally important (at the appropriate level of complexity). Hintikka's logic is sensitive to variations of evidential circumstances, but it treats all such variations alike, at any particular level of complexity. Yet in the actual

conduct of scientific reasoning some evidential circumstances (i.e. some families of predicates) may be deemed to be much more important than others in relation to hypotheses of a particular kind. A patient's previous medical history turns out to be more important than the colour of his eyes in relation to most hypotheses about the safety of a drug for medical purposes. Not surprisingly, therefore, most scientists take assessments of how well a certain experiment's results support a given hypothesis to be empirically corrigible. When pharmacologists learned that some drugs like thalidomide had teratogenic properties, they learned thereby to incorporate trials on pregnant rats in any experimental test on drugs of that kind. At the same time they had to revise any assessments of the support given by previous test-results to hypotheses about the non-toxicity of this or that drug. So, if we want to represent inductive assessments in natural science by a two-place function $c(h, e)$ that maps ordered pairs of propositions on to numbers, we ought not to treat values for the function as emerging analytically from some independently existing sub-language. The fashioning of the relevant sub-language is an indispensable part of the process of scientific reasoning. Both Bacon and Whewell implicitly recognised this long ago, when they emphasised the siginificance, for inductive purposes, of the invention of new concepts. It is quite understandable that some modern logicians should have hoped an inductive logic might issue in analytic, *a priori* truths which would be comparable with the analytic, *a priori* truths of standard deductive logic. Particular equations of the form $c(h, e) = r$ were to be comparable with particular instantiations of Russellian theorems. But, though that kind of inductive logic may conceivably have a useful application elsewhere, it certainly misses essential features of inductive reasoning in experimental science. If there is any parallelism between deductive logic, on the one hand, and the inductive logic of experimental reasoning, on the other, it has to be sought along another dimension.

V

I. Levi has proposed[20] a rather different approach to the problems of inductive logic. He too supposes, like Popper and Carnap and Hintikka, that a sub-language is given which determines the kinds of hypothesis and evidential report that can be considered. But he considers the inductive reasoner as a man who ought rationally to choose that option which bears maximum expected utility, and the utilities involved are understood to be epistemic ones. These cognitive options are ordered by two rules. Correct answers ought to be epistemically preferred to errors; and correct answers, or errors, that afford a high degree of relief from agnosticism ought to be preferred to correct answers, or errors, respectively, that afford a low degree of relief from agnosticism. In order to determine the degree of relief from agnosticism that a given sentence affords, Levi constructs a measure of a sentence's content that is based on the ultimate partition of the sub-language into available hypotheses. It then becomes possible to determine, relative to a given statement of evidence, the cognitively optimific choice of hypothesis.

Levi's content-measures are Pascalian improbabilities, and his system therefore has obvious affinities to Popper's theory of corroboration as a reconstruction of the intellectual basis for acceptance. But Levi can justifiably claim that his own decision-theoretic system establishes a much closer rational connection than Popper or Hintikka does between his proposed criteria for evidentially-warranted acceptance, on the one hand, and certain plausibly supposed ends of scientific enquiry, on the other. He can explain why people should want hypotheses that score well by his criteria. Also, Levi's system is as immune as Carnap's or Hintikka's to the paradoxes of Hempel and Goodman, because it has replaced their simple, qualitative criterion of confirmation for hypotheses in every day language by an appropriately sophisticated quantitative criterion for hypotheses in a rather restricted artificial language. But his resolution of Kyburg's paradox seems to be entirely *ad hoc*. Levi proposes to limit the application of his acceptance rule to propositions composing an ultimate partition of the domain of assessment, such as 'Ticket 1 will win' and 'Ticket 1 will not win'. In this way no conjunction of propositions from different ultimate partitions will be eligible for assessment and the lottery paradox cannot be constructed. But the trouble is that Levi's restriction seems to have no other motivation or rationale than its capacity to avoid difficulties about a possible lottery. If it were not for those difficulties, we might well feel that all conjunctions of propositions should be just as eligible for assessment as their conjuncts. In the complexities of practical life we need constantly to combine and recombine beliefs about different issues.

Levi's system has the same overall defect of apriorism that taints Popper's ideas about corroboration-functions, and vitiates the Carnap-Hintikka theory as a logic of experimental resoning. Inductive assessments are derived from a postulated sub-language but nothing is said about the extralogical terms of this language except that there will be 'as many ... as the occasion demands'.[21] So, in a period (1950–1970) when inductive logicians gave such cavalier treatment to the actual facts of scientific reasoning and typically justified their theories by appealing to their own or their readers' 'intuitions',[22] it is scarcely surprising that many philosophers came to be rather sceptical about the extent to which logical analysis can shed any light on the nature of science. Indeed, if Popper, Carnap, Hintikka, Levi and others had produced more convincing analyses, the anti-analytical reaction of philosophers like Hanson, Kuhn, Feyerabend and Toulmin would perhaps hardly have got off the ground. But, as has so often happened before in human intellectual history, the reaction was overdone. The limitations inherent in a certain one-sided approach to a subject were attributed to the subject itself. Instead of finding fault just with apriorist versions of inductive logic, these critics supposed no logic at all to be capable of representing actual scientific reasoning.

VI

M. Hesse's account of scientific inference[23] avoids the fallacy of apriorism. She interprets the (Pascalian) probability of a hypothesis on given evidence in personalist terms; so that in the long run, when all evidence that is directly or indirectly relevant has been taken into account, different scientists' probability-assessments may reasonably be expected to coincide, if each scientist treats all his assessments at any one time as if they were the elements of a coherent betting strategy. One proposition e is then said to confirm another h, if positively relevant to it, i.e. if $p(h, e) > p(h)$; and the extent of such confirmation may be measured by the extent to which $p(h, e)$ exceeds $p(h)$. In this way degree of confirmation becomes sensitive to the changing state of scientists' information, rather than just to the structure of some arbitrarily assumed sub-language. Of course, a personalist interpretation of Pascalian probability-functions ought not to be considered available where universal propositions over an unbounded domain are taken as possible arguments for the function. A reasonable man does not envisage betting on the truth of such a universal proposition, since a single observable event might demonstrate that he had lost his bet but no determinate sequence of observable events could ever demonstrate that he had won it. However, Hesse, like Carnap but unlike Popper or Hintikka, does not envisage a scientific hypothesis that acquires inductive confirmation as being a universal proposition over an unbounded domain. Instead she thinks of it has having some such form as 'All the next n P's in a limited region of space and time are Q.' Consequently, like Carnap also, Hesse argues that enumerative induction is more fundamental than induction by variation of circumstance. But she does make rather more allowance for the latter than Carnap does. First, she emphasises that, where a finite list of hypotheses is assumed, the elimination of some hypotheses makes a disjunction of the others more probable. Secondly, she points out that, where there is a substantial analogy between the phenomenon described by one hypothesis and the phenomenon described by another, each increases the probability of the other.

Hesse's choice of restricted generalisations, rather than truly universal propositions, as candidates for confirmation, is in fact motivated by her adoption of positive Pascalian relevance as the criterion of confirmation – even though her personalist interpretation of probability-functions also compels this choice. The point is that her positive relevance criterion compels her to accept the so-called converse entailment condition. Where one hypothesis, h, entails another, g, and we have both $1 > p(h) > 0$ and $1 > p(g) > 0$, Bayes's theorem gives her $p(h, g) = [p(h)/p(g)] > p(h)$, and so g confirms h. But an intolerable paradox results if anyone accepts both this converse entialment condition and also the so-called special consequence condition, viz. if f confirms h and h entails g, then f confirms g. For, by accepting both conditions, it is possible immediately to prove that any two propositions confirm one another: if $f \& g$ is logically equivalent to h, then by the converse entailment condition f confirms h and so, by the special consequence condition f confirms g. Accordingly Hesse rejects the special consequence condition. Yet that condition has a good deal of plausibility in its application to general scientific theories. For example, one might well suppose that the confirmation afforded to Newton's theory of gravitation by the Keplerian (or quasi-Keplerian) laws of planetary orbits and the Galilean (or quasi-Galilean) law of falling bodies flows down to that theory's predictions about the orbits of comets or of space-satellites. In order to avoid countenancing such a source of plausibility for the special consequence condition Hesse proposes to reject theories like Newton's as candidates for confirmation and to treat them rather as rules for analogical inference from one kind of restricted generalisation to another. The inductive strength of the theory will then presumably be measured by the increase of probability that one such generalisation can give to another.

Here at last we have a confirmation-measure that is not only sensitive to changes in scientific opinion and to differences in the degree of relevance between one piece of evidence and another, but also tries to grapple realistically with the part played by theoretical systematisation in inductive reasoning. This latter factor was emphasised long ago by Bacon; and Whewell, calling it the 'consilience of inductions', was able to furnish a number of impressive illustrations of it from the history of science between Bacon's day and his own. But it was never treated adequately in the work of Carnap, Hintikka or Levi. Nevertheless Hesse's inductive logic still suffers from at least three major implausibilities as an analysis of actual scientific reasoning.

One of these is the logic's refusal to treat general theories like Newton's as propositions that can be either confirmed or disconfirmed. It is natural to suppose, as Bacon did, a kind of spectrum in people's hypotheses about nature, beginning at one extreme with hypotheses about obvious, large-scale phenomena in a man's immediate spatio-temporal environment, and going on, through more and more extensive speculation, to hypotheses about laws that control the fundamental constituents of reality throughout the universe. Inductive logic, we might suppose, can deal more easily with hypotheses of the more limited type of scope. But its domain can scarcely be restricted to these. Nor is this conception just a prejudice of philosophers or logicians. Hesse invites us to accept a kind of discontinuity in the pattern of scientific reasoning that has no warrant whatever in the ways in which any leading chemists or physicists have expressed themselves.

A second difficulty about Hesse's inductive logic arises from her use of a positive relevance criterion that is formulated in terms of Pascalian probability. Where, say, $p(g) = p(h) = 0.2$, and $p(g, e) = 0.9$, and $p(h, e) = 0.1$, we shall have to hold, according to Hesse's criterion, that e confirms g and disconfirms h. Yet, if g and h here are independent of one another, e will confirm the conjunction of g and h. Hence, so far as our inductive logic is to afford a basis for our technological judgements, we are told here that there is confirmation for exploiting the conjunction of g and h in constructing our bridges or airplanes, despite the fact that there is disconfirmation for h on its own. It is difficult to think that an inductive logic which issues in such judgements could ever be much used in practice.

A third difficulty is that though Hesse's logic is not hit by Hempel's or Goodman's paradox it has no way of meeting the challenge of Kyburg's, unless perhaps in the same *ad hoc* way as that in which Levi tried to meet it. In fact Hesse herself prefers to suppose that inductive logic can afford no basis for a criterion of rational acceptance. But to suppose this is to sacrifice one of the major purposes that might be thought to make investigation of the subject worthwhile.

VII

All the above-mentioned post-1945 logicians have shared one assumption.

They have all assumed that any function which assesses evidential support must either itself conform to the principles of Pascalian probability, like Carnap's and Hintikka's confirmation-functions, or must at least be built up from functions which so conform, like Popper's corroboration-function or Hesse's confirmation-measure. Yet this was an assumption which writers in the classical, Baconian tradition did not share, as we have already seen. Correspondingly these recent writers have envisaged the aim of inductive reasoning in natural science as some kind of maximisation in relation to truth. The aim is either to know as much of the truth as possible, or to be as near as possible to the true answer for a certain question, or to have as large a chance as possible that one has got hold of that answer, or at any rate to have a larger chance than one would have had without the evidence. But again, the aim of classical inductive logic was a different one. It sought the discovery of laws, not just of truths. It was interested in what causes what, not just in what happens. Bacon's terms for such a law was a 'form', and knowledge of the form of heat, on his view, would enable a man to superinduce heat under suitable conditions. The propositions stating such laws he called axioms, and the higher a scientist mounts on the latter of axioms the greater the certainty he could have. And all this was to be achieved by studying tables of presence and absence.

At the heart of Bacon's inductive logic, therefore, lies a marriage between the idea of induction by variation of the evidence, traces of which are to be found earlier in the writings of Robert Grosseteste, William of Ockham and others, and the idea of intellectual progress through a hierarchy of forms, which we owe to Plato. Correspondingly, if we wish to develop and systematise Bacon's logic, our theory[24] will need to have two main components. First, it needs to embrace what I shall call 'the method of relevant variables', as a representation of the way in which, in any particular field of enquiry, the reliability of a hypothesis may be graded in the light of appropriately varied experimental evidence. Secondly, it nees to embrace a generalised modal logic which will represent those grades of inductively attestable reliability as steps on a ladder that mounts towards the statement of a law.

In experimental science the reliability of a hypothesis is identified with its capacity to resist falsification under cumulatively more and more challenging conditions. So, in relation to each given category of scientific hypotheses, it is necessary to form a higher-order empirical hypothesis about the variables – non-exhaustive sets of mutually exclusive circumstance-types – that are inductively relevant to them, where a variable is said to be relevant if each circumstance-type (or 'variant') in that variable has falsified at least one generalisation of the category in question. This list of relevant variables must also be ordered, in accordance with the supposed falsificatory potential of the various variables. The list is then extended by prefacing that variable which contains all the circumstances mentionable by the antecedents of generalisations in the category. A scientific hypothesis may be supposed to be tested with first grade thoroughness when every variant of the first variable in the final list is present in turn, so far as this is possible, but no variant of any other relevant variable is present. A hypothesis is tested with second grade thoroughness when each possible combination of a variant of the second variable with a variant of the first (and no variant of any other relevant variable) is present in turn. And so on, with cumulatively more and more complex tests. Accordingly at least first-grade inductive reliability may be inferred for a generalisation from a proposition reporting, in effect, that it has passed a test of first-grade thoroughness, and higher grades of reliability may be inferred from propositions reporting successful test-results of correspondingly higher grades. But failure to pass, say, a third-grade test implies that a generalisation has at most second-grade reliability.

The replicability of test-results is assumed. So that if contradictory gradings are inferable from true evidential reports, we need to revise either the list of relevant variables (as in the thalidomide case) or the terminology from which hypotheses are constructed (as when new scientific concepts are introduced). The discovery of such a contradiction is not a deep blow to the whole system of inductive logic, as it would be for an apriorist theory like Carnap's or Hintikka's, but represents a fruitful stimulus to scientific imagination and research.

Moreover this mode of grading inductive reliability – by the method of relevant variables – can be applied *mutatis mutandis* to causal generalisations, to correlations between quantitative variables, and to comprehensive scientific theories, as well as to elementary generalisations about qualitative characteristics. It produces a very straightforward analysis of consilience. And it can also be applied to appropriately modified versions of hypotheses, where the unmodified versions meet unfavourable test results. Thus if a generalisation is falsified by certain variants of a relevant variable but not others, a mention of the latter can be introduced into the antecedent of the generalisation as so to exclude falsification by the former. In this way a higher grade of inductive reliability can be maintained for a hypothesis, though at the cost of accepting a lower grade of simplicity for it. Nor is the method of relevant variables restricted in any way to monadic predicates.

But, unlike Carnap's, Hintikka's, Levi's or Hesse's system, the method of relevant variables does not *measure* anything. It merely *ranks* inductive support, by mapping ordered pairs of propositions, of a particular category, on to the first n integers ($n \geqslant 0$) where there are $n - 1$ relevant variables. Consequently the method can have no pretensions to be able to compare the grades of support that two hypotheses have if they belong to quite different fields of scientific enquiry, except in the limiting cases of no support or full support. On the other hand the method does not apply only to the natural sciences. It applies equally well to other fields of inductive enquiry, such as to jurisprudences that rely on precedent and derive rules of law from previous judicial decisions.

If inductive reliability is graded in this way, the principles that govern compatibilities an incompatibilities between such gradings are demonstrably incapable of being mapped on to the Pascalian calculus of probabilities. They are representable instead within a generalisation of the C. I. Lewis modal logic S4. For example, the so-called special consequence condition emerges, as with confirmation-functions that determine Pascalian probabilities. We also get a similar uniformity principle, or principle of symmetry, whereby the inductive reliability of a singular proposition is invariant under any unform transformations of its individual constants. But the logic has certain importantly non-Pascalian features. A hypothesis can have greater than zero reliability even when the evidence includes some counter-examples to it; and the conjunction of two hypotheses has the same grade of reliability as either of its conjuncts, if they are equally reliable, or as the less reliable of the two if they are unequal in reliability. Also, mere multiplicity of instances – repetition of precisely the same test-result – neither increases nor decreases inductive support for a generalisation.

This kind of inductive logic supplies both a dyadic function $s[H, E]$ that grades the support given by E to H, and a monadic one $s[H]$ that grades the natural reliability of H – i.e. the strength of its resistance to falsification by relevant variables. But in addition to dyadic and monadic support-functions for propositions of a given category, the logic also generates dyadic and monadic probability-functions of a characteristically non-Pascalian type, viz. $p_I[S, R]$ and $p_I[S]$. Any first order generalisation of the form $(x_1)(x_2)$ ... $(x_n)(R \to S)$ – where $x_1, x_2, ...$ and x_n are all the individual letters free in R and S – provides us with a rule of inference from the satisfaction of its antecedent to the satisfaction of its consequent, and the strength of such a rule may be graded by the inductive reliability of the generalisation. Hence the inferability of the consequent from the antecedent may be regarded as a form of probability that is graded by the reliability of the covering generalisation. For example, $p_I [Sa, Ra] = s[(x)(Rx \rightarrow Sx)]$.

Moreover, just as the inductive reliability of a generalisation may be raised by introducing appropriate modifications into its antecedent, so too the inductive probability of *Sa* on *Ra* & *Va* may be higher than on *Ra* alone. Inductive probability-functions thus capture the principles behind that kind of everyday probability-judgement in which the probability of a conclusion rises as the weight of evidence – the extent of relevant information – increases, where the balance of the evidence in any case favours the conclusion. These functions are therefore particularly well suited to the task of providing a foundation for rules of rational acceptance. After all, there are very many kinds of issues on which it is both folly to make up one's mind until one has enough information, and also impracticable to wait for certainty. We need, as it were, a high but non-maximal grade of inductive probability on available evidence. At the same time inductive probability-functions can afford a basis for rational acceptance, even in relation to predictions about one's not winning a lottery. This is because by inductive standards one needs considerably more information than the number of tickets in order to be justified in believing that one will not win: for example, information that the draw is likely to be rigged in favour of the organiser's nephew might suffice. So Kyburg's paradox does not arise here.

The logical syntax of inductive probability-judgements derives directly from that of inductive reliability, but the dyadic probability-function does not behave in quite the same way as the dyadic support-function. For example, though $p_I [Sa, Ra]$ conforms to the same conjunction principle as $s[H, E]$, it does have zero-value in normal cases in which *Ra* contradicts *Sa*. But a monadic probability-function may be defined that makes $p_I [Sa]$ equal to $p_I [Sa, Sa \vee -Sa]$. It then turns out to be demonstrable that a monadic inductive probability-function always has precisely the same value, for a given argument, as a monadic inductive support-function. I.e., $p_I [Sa] = s[Sa]$. Note also that the prior inductive probability of a proposition is its intrinsic capacity to resist falsification by relevant variables, while the posterior inductive probability is the falsification-resisting capacity of its implication by certain other factors. So it can easily happen that $p_I [Sa] = 0$ while $p_I [Sa, Ra] > 0$. This is an important property of inductive (Baconian) probability, as distinct from mathematical (Pascalian) probability, in those legal systems or forensic situations in which it is desired to assign a zero prior probability to the guilt of an accused person – the presumption of innocence prior to evidential proof of guilt. The point is that Baconian probability graduates proof on a scale that runs from provability to non-provability, while Pascalian probability graduates it on a scale that runs from provability to disprovability.

VIII

The balance-sheet for neo-Baconian inductive logic therefore looks something like this. On the credit side it sticks closely to the characteristic methods of experimental reasoning in natural science and is responsive to their empirical flexibility. It is quite unrestricted in its application to scientific hypotheses, however rich or complex these may be. It has no difficulty in handling Kyburg's paradox as well as Hempel's and Goodman's. And it can satisfy Levi's requirement that we should be able to see why people want hypotheses about the world which score well by its criteria. Where certainties are unobtainable, such hypotheses tell us of laws whose operations are relatively resistant to interference. They strengthen our power to plan our lives successfully. But on the debit side ability to compare support-grades in different fields is severely restricted, and it can only rank support-grades, not measure them. Also it cannot be interpreted in terms of familiar Pascalian principles, and seems to complicate our intellectual life by introducing non-Pascalian principles into an area of reasoning where Pascalian principles have often seemed to hold a monopoly of power.

Nevertheless, the first of these three disadvantages is not a very serious one. Neo-Baconian inductive logic is not more modest in its ambitions with regard to inter-field comparisons than are natural scientists themselves.

Also, on the second point it seems in any case preferable to have a ranking-function that is not restricted in application to assessing first-order generalisations about monadic attributes, rather than a measure-function that is so restricted. Moreover it is doubtful whether any measure is possible for support-grades that are evaluated by the toughness of the experimental tests on which they are grounded. This is because the conditions requisite for additivity do not seem to obtain here. The nature of causality is such that the toughness of a test that manipulates two relevant variables does not depend only on the several toughnesses of tests manipulating each variable separately but also on the various kinds of further effects that the variants of the two variables may combine to produce.

The third point, however, raises some deep issues about the nature of probability and about the relationships between Pascalian and non-Pascalian systems. It is certainly clear that if one thinks of probability, from the semantical point of view, as a generalisation on the notion of provability, then, for the following reasons, at least one important kind of non-Pascalian system must be accepted. Just as proof rules may be pigeon-holed in a classificatory matrix in accordance with whether they are singular or general, extensional or non-extensional, and necessary or contingent, so too the familiar forms of Pascalian probability, as relative frequency, logical relation, propensity, degree of belief, etc. may all be seen as generalisations on such different kinds of provability.[25] For example, a relative-frequency conception of probability may be seen as being analogous to provability in a deductive system of which the rules are general, extensional and contingent. But all these forms of generalisation on the concept of provability – even if only comparative and not measure-theoretic – are based on an assumption of completeness about the proof system, in the sense that h is provable if and only if $-h$ is not provable. Hence arises the familiar Pascalian principle of complementationality: $p[x, y] = 1-p[-x, y]$. Yet very many proof-systems are *in*complete, in this sense, so that in an analogous system of probability it would be possible to have $p[x, y] = 0 = p[-x, y]$. The generalised scale would then run down from proof to no-proof, rather than from proof to disproof; and such a probability-function would grade how complete the evidence is when on balance it stands in favour of a particular conclusion, rather than how large a proportion of the presumptively complete evidence stands in favour of that conclusion.

So some fairly abstract considerations about the nature of probability expose the existence of a conceptual niche which inductive probability-functions are admirably suited to occupy, since, as we have seen, they grade the weight of evidence. Correspondingly probability-functions that are regulated by Baconian modal logic are just as legitimately entitled 'probability-functions' as the functions regulated by Pascalian mathematics. Indeed, the seeds of both theories were sown within a short while of one another in the seventeenth century, even though Pascalian theory came earlier to maturity. If Pascalian theories have hitherto appeared to monopolise the systematic analysis of probability-judgements, we must put this down to an accident of human intellectual history rather than to a necessary principle of rationality.

The underlying connections, and underlying differences, between the Pascalian inductive logic of Carnap and Hintikka and the neo-Baconian inductive logic that is generated by the method of relevant variables may also be illuminated by reference to the appropriate models that can be constructed in terms of alternative possible worlds, at least so far as the possible-world metaphor is intelligible.

The model suggested by Carnap and Hintikka's inductive logic is straightforward enough, since each state-description may obviously be taken as true for just one possible world. But how is such a model to be constructed for Baconian induction?

A logically possible world, W_1, should be said to be subject to the uniformities of another, W_2, in regard to generalisations of a particular category, if and only if (i) every such generalisation that is true and instantiated in W_2 is also true, whether vacuously or by instantiation, in W_1, and (ii) every such generalisation that is vacuously true in W_2 is also vacuously true in W_1. A logically possible world should be termed 'physically possible' if and only if it is subject to the uniformities of the actual world. A physically possible world would then be termed a t_1 world if and only if every variant of the first relevant variable, and no variant of any other relevant variable, is instantiated in it. A physically possible world W would be termed a t_2 world if and only if every t_1 world is subject to the uniformities of W and every admissible combination of a variant of the first relevant variable with zero or more variants of the second is instantiated in W, but no variant of any other relevant variable. And so on for t_3, t_4, t_{n-1} worlds. The actual world, or indeed any t_n world, would be assumed to contain a plenitude of relevant events, whereby every physically possible combination of a variant of the first relevant variable with zero or more variants of other relevant variables is instantiated in it. So, for all i and j, each t_i world is subject to the uniformities of each t_j world, where $j \geqslant i$, as well as to the uniformities of the actual world.

A generalisation may then be said to have at least ith grade inductive reliability if it is true in all t_i worlds, and the characteristic principles of Baconian induction emerge. For example, since a t_i world is subject to the uniformities of a t_j world where $j \geqslant i$, it follows that if one generalisation holds good in all t_i worlds and another in all t_j worlds, their conjunction must hold good in all t_i worlds. Similarly a high grade of inductive reliability is compatible with the existence of anomalies, since a generalisation may hold good in all t_i worlds, for every $i < n$, even though it is falsified in our actual world: the relation of being 'subject to the uniformities of' is not symmetrical. Indeed an experimental test of ith grade throughness can be thought of as a simulated minimal t_i world; and the idealised domain to which some scientific generalisations apply – e.g. the domain of bodies moving in a vacuum – can also be though of as a t_i world for some appropriate i. Finally, the relation of being 'subject to the uniformities of' constitutes a relation of inductive accessibility or knowability that holds between some possible worlds in the model and not others. Since this relation is transitive and reflexive but not symmetrical, the appropriate formalisation could be expected (in the light of Kripke's work[26] on modal logic) to relate to C. I. Lewis's system S4, as indeed it does.

Hence the prior inductive probability (which equals the inductive reliability) of a generalisation can be viewed as a ranking of inductive range, by contrast with Carnap and Hintikka's conception of a proposition's prior mathematical probability as a measure of its logical range. The inductive range of a generalisation is ranked by reference to the fullest kind of physically possible world – i.e. the highest grade of relevantly eventful world – in which the generalisation always holds good, while the logical range of a proposition is measured by reference to the sum of the values severally assigned to the various logically possible worlds in which the proposition holds good. Neo-Baconian inductive logic looks at physically determined qualities of possible worlds: Carnap's and Hintikka's systems look at logico-linguistically determined quantities of them. That is ultimately how they differ, and that is ultimately why neo-Baconian inductive logic provides a better representation of experimental reasoning in natural science.

The Queens College, Oxford, England

NOTES

[1] Letter to Couring, March 19, 1678, in *Die philosophischen Schriften von Gottfried Wilhelm Leibniz*, ed. by C. I. Gerhardt, Vol. I, 1875, p. 195f.

[2] D. Hume, *A Treatise of Human Nature*, 1739, Bk I, Pt. III, Sec. XI.

[3] E.g. P. S. de Laplace, *A Philosophical Essay on Probabilities*, tr. F. W. Truscott and F. L. Emory, 1951, Pt. II, Ch. ix.

[4] E.g. James Bernoulli, letter to Leibniz of April 20, 1704, in *Leibnizens mathematische Schriften*, ed. by C. I. Gerhardt, Vol. III, 1855, p. 87f.

[5] *The Principles of Science: A Treatise on Logic and Scientific Method*, 1874, Vol. I, p. 276ff.

[6] *A Treatise on Probability*, 1921.

[7] *Le problème logique de l'induction*, 1924, Eng. transl. in *Foundations of Geometry and Induction*, 1930.

[8] 'Studies in the Logic of Confirmation', *Mind* liv, 1945, p. 1ff and p. 97f.

[9] E.g. I. Scheffler, *The Anatomy of Inquiry*, 1963, p. 289.

[10] E.g. J. L. Mackie, 'The Paradoxes of Confirmation' *British Journal for Philosophy of Science* 13 (1963), 265–77.

[11] In lectures subsequently published as Chapters II–IV of *Faction, Fiction and Forecast*, 1954. This may be regarded as a modern form of Leibniz's curve-fitting paradox: however many points are given, an infinity of different curves may still be drawn through

them. Cf. Leibniz's letter to James Bernoulli of December 3, 1703, in *Leibnizens mathematische Schriten*, ed. by C. I. Gerhardt, Vol. III, 1855, p. 83f.

[12] Cf. also the rather more *ad hominem* argument that Goodman's solution is intrinsically incoherent: A. Zabludowski, 'Concerning a fiction about how facts are forecast', *Journal of Philosophy* lxxi (1974), p. 97ff.

[13] *Probability and the Logic of Rational Belief*, 1961, pp. 196–9.

[14] Cf. in particular his *Logical Foundations of Probability*, 1950. Carnap (ibid. p. 83) attributes the seminal idea of his theory to L. Wittgenstein, *Tractatus Logico-Philosophicus*, 1922. But I. Hacking, *The Emergence of Probability*, 1975, p. 134ff., traces it to Leibniz.

[15] In R. Carnap and R. C. Jeffrey (eds.), *Studies in Inductive Logic and Probability*, Vol. I, 1971, p. 227ff.

[16] *The Logic of Scientific Discovery*, 1959, For Popper's 'degree of corroboration' as a measure of acceptability cf. pp. 388, 392, 394, etc.

[17] 'Towards a Theory of Inductive Generalisation', in *Proceedings of the 1964 International Congress for Logic, Methodology and Philosophy of Science*, pp. 274–288.

[18] E.g. I. Niiniluoto and R. Tuomela, *Theoretical Concepts and Hypothetico-Inductive Inference*, 1973.

[19] J. Hintikka and R. Hilpinen, 'Knowledge, Acceptance and Inductive Logic', in *Aspects of Inductive Logic*, ed. by J. Hintikka and P. Suppes, 1966, pp. 1–20.

[20] *Gambling with Truth*, 1967.

[21] Ibid. p. 25.

[22] These appeals to intuition are referenced and criticised in L. Jonathan Cohen, 'How Empirical is Contemporary Logical Empiricism?', *Philosophia* 5 (1975), pp. 299–317.

[23] *The Structure of Scientific Inference*, 1974. In a more extensive coverage it would also be necessary to discuss those writers (e.g. H. Reichenbach, *The Theory of Probability*, 1949, p. 429ff.) who take induction about scientific generalisations to be just the limiting-case of some mode of statistical reasoning about non-universal correlations. Their general fault is to attach greater value to enumerative induction than is compatible with good scientific practice.

[24] This theory was first presented in detail in L. Jonathan Cohen, *The Implications of Induction*, 1970, and was further extended (with some minor revisions) in *The Probable and the Provable*, 1977.

[25] Cf. L. Jonathan Cohen, *The Probable and the Provable*, 1977, Secs. 1–9.

[26] S. Kripke, 'Semantical analysis of modal logic I, normal propositional calculi', *Zeitschrift für mathematische Logic und Grundlagen der Mathematik* 9 (1963), 67–96.

PART 5

LOGIC AND PHILOSOPHICAL TOPICS

CZESLAW LEJEWSKI

LOGIC AND ONTOLOGY

My discussion of the topic prescribed by the title of the paper will consist of two parts. In Part I, I propose to discuss, in very general and informal terms, the nature of logic and ontology, and the relationship that seems to connect these two disciplines. In Part II, I intend to examine, in some detail, a certain specific problem, which concerns logicians as well as ontologists, a problem which has been with us for about forty years, and which lacks a generally acceptable solution. Now, without further preliminaries let us turn at once to Part I.

I

The strange thing about logic is that it is by no means easy to delineate its province. According to some scholars logic can be described as the study of formal systems, often referred to as calculi or algebras or algorithms. A formal system consists of formulae generated in a certain way while formulae consist of signs or symbols. If the symbols are ordered in accordance with explicitly stated rules of formation, the formula is said to be well-formed. Otherwise the formula is not well-formed and cannot be part of the system. Some of the well-formed formulae, usually finite in number, are chosen, to provide the starting point for the construction of the system. They are called primitive formulae. By applying to them explicitly stated rules of transformation we can obtain new formulae and incorporate them into the system. Well-formed formulae which cannot be obtained in this way do not belong to the system. Constructing a formal system in accordance with rules of formation and transformation has been likened to playing a sort of game. The comparison is apposite. For moves in a game, say in chess, are also determined by what may be called rules of formation and transformation. The question as to what the formulae say or what they are about, is of little interest to the pure formalist. He constructs his formal systems in order to study their structure and establish various truths about it. Thus, logic conceived as the study of formal systems in the sense just explained seems to be part of metamathematics. For the metamathematician, too, studies the structure of various formal systems. The fact that some formal systems lend themselves to interpretation, in other words the fact that the formulae

E. Agazzi (ed.), Modern Logic – A Survey, 379–398.

which constitute a system, turn out to be true if interpreted in an appropriate way, is to the formalist of secondary significance. For him it only proves the applicability of the system, and should attract the attention of the practitioners of applied sciences.

Logic conceived as a study of formal systems does not seem to have much in common with ontology unless accidentally; for instance, a formal system may, for some reasons, happen to be of interest to the formalist, and, at the same time, happen to lend itself to an ontological interpretation.

However, there are logicians and philosophers who argue that the central topic of logic is not the structure of formal systems but rather the theory of proof or the theory of deductive inference. But this is what semantics, which is part of metalogic, is about. If the theory of deductive inference were to be regarded as the central topic of logic then deductive systems such as Frege's, or the one constructed by the authors of *Principia Mathematica*, or the logical systems of Leśniewski, would have to be placed either outside the province of logic proper or at its periphery away from the centre. A conception of logic with such implications would not be compatible with the views of those who regard the systems just mentioned as paradigms of logic. In this dilemma an acceptable compromise can be achieved by distinguishing between logic in its narrow sense as exemplified by, say, *Principia*, and logic in a wider sense, comprising, in addition, not only the theory of deductive inference but the whole of metalogic.

For the sake of completeness I should perhaps mention yet another conception of logic, but only in order to disown it. In accordance with this conception the principal task of logic is to discover and systematise the fundamental laws of thought. Surely, if logic were indeed to be concerned with the study of the laws of thought then logic would have to be regarded as part of psychology, a conclusion which is acceptable neither to contemporary psychologists nor to comtemporary logicians.

Within the framework of the present discussion it is the relationship between logic in the narrow sense of the term (in what follows I shal refer to it simply as logic) and ontology that is our main concern. But, before we proceed, let me try and replace my ostensive definition of logic by a definition which seems to be a little more informative. Speaking generally, we can characterise a theory either by specifying the vocabulary peculiar to it or by determining its subject matter. Needless to say, the two methods are not exclusive of each other. For our purpose the method of specifying the vocabulary peculiar to logic appears to be more convenient at this stage, although the specification that can be offered may turn out to be imcomplete, indeed, incapable of completion.

It seems to be generally accepted that the vocabulary of logic contains, in the first place, terms such as 'if ... then', 'or', 'and', 'it-is-not-the-case-that'; secondly, we have terms such as 'is-identical-with' (Frege, the authors of *Principia*) and 'is' or 'is-a' (Leśniewski); finally, for the purpose of formulating statements or theses of logic use is made of variables and of quantifiers. With the aid of this very modest conceptual apparatus a host of other logical terms can be defined, among them terms which accommodate the notions of object (or entity), existence, difference, equinumerosity, numerical infinity, to mention only a few. The vocabulary of this sort has the following property. No discipline can do without it. Every discipline other than logic includes, in its vocabulary, a portion, greater or smaller, of the logical vocabulary. This means that every discipline other than logic presupposes logic and makes use, implicit or explicit, of logical principles in inferences or proofs within its own framework. Logic, on the other hand, is in no need of similar support from other disciplines. Deduction within the framework of logic rest on logical premisses alone, and logical premisses are formulated exclusively in terms of the logical vocabulary. Thus, logic shows itself to be the most general, that is to say, universal theory.

Now, a claim to universality has also been put forward on behalf of ontology and that at the very inception of the discipline. In Book IV of his *Metaphysics*, at 1003^a21–1003^a26, Aristotle writes that:

There is a science which investigates being as being and the attributes which belong to this in virtue of its own nature. Now this is not the same as any of the so-called special sciences; for none of these others treats universally of being as being. They cut off a part of being and investigate the attributes of this part; this is what mathematical sciences for instance do. (*The Works of Aristotle*, Vol. VIII, *Metaphysica*, The Clarendon Press, Oxford, 1966.)

Centuries later the name of ontology was given to this science of being as envisaged by Aristotle. Its distinguishing mark is universality. In the case of zoology the universe of discourse can be said to be constituted by animals, and in the case of botany – by plants; the ontological universe of discourse contains everything that there is. In describing this universe an ontologist who accepts Aristotle's conception of the science of being should look, in the first place, for attributes or properties which belong to everything that exists.

If both logic and ontology are universal disciplines then one would expect them to make use of the same conceptual apparatus at least in some of their pronouncements, and one would expect them to share the same subject matter. Indeed, affinity between logic and ontology was already appreciated by Aristotle. According to him it befits the science of being to study the first principles of demonstration (αἱ ἀρχαὶ ἐξ ὧν δείκνυσι πάντες, 995^{b}8) and syllogism (αἱ συλλογιστικαὶ ἀρχαί, 1005^{b}8) and also the principles which in mathematics are called axioms (τὰ ἐν τοῖς μαθήμασι καλούμενα ἀξιώματα, 1005^{a}20), and this on account of the universality of the principles. For they apply to everything that exists and not only to one kind of being apart from other kinds of being. And it is the business of ontology to study the notions of identity and difference, and other notions of dialectical discourse (995^{b}21), which, as I hinted earlier, are embedded in the logical vocabulary. It is significant that the principle of non-contradiction and the principle of excluded middle, which are logical principles, were discussed by Aristotle within the framework of his science of being, i.e. within the framework of his ontology.

Neither the principle of non-contradiction nor the principle of excluded middle seem to have any special property which would warrant their inclusion among the principles of ontology while justifying, at the same time, the exclusion from ontology of any other logical principles. However, Aristotle did not go to the length of suggesting that syllogistic as expounded by him in the *Prior Analytics* fell within the boundaries of the science of being. For him logic as a whole remained a sort of propaedeutic to every scientific enquiry.

It did not so for Heinrich Scholz, a distinguished philosopher, logician and theologian, formerly of Münster. In his 1944 paper 'Logik, Grammatik, Metaphysik' (H. Scholz, *Mathesis Universalis*, 2nd edition edited by H. Hermes, F. Kambartel, and J. Ritter, published by Schwabe & Co., Basel/Stuttgart, 1969, pp. 399–436) he claims that there are formalised systems of logic which can be interpreted in such a way as to make it sensible and appropriate to describe them as systems of metaphysics. I do not think that he would object if in this context I replaced the word 'metaphysics' by the word 'ontology' to be understood as synonymous with Aristotle's 'science of being'. For by a metaphysical truth Scholz understands a truth that universally holds in every *possible world* and thus also in the actual world. The term 'possible world' is Leibnizian but Scholz gives it a somewhat different meaning. A possible world seems to be for him what other philosophers and logicians describe as universe of discourse. In any case, for Scholz, every possible world contains at least one individual appropriate to it, and in this sense a possible world is a real one, and the individuals which constitute it fall within the purview of ontology. To be sure, the notion of possible world requires further clarification, but to this problem I will address myself later.

Scholz's views on the relationship between logic and ontology (metaphysics) can be summarised as follws. A logical system, as he understands it, consists of propositional formulae containing free variables among other means of expression. Concerning such formulae one can ask whether or not they are applicable in a given non-empty world. The answer is 'yes' if and only if on replacing the free variables by appropriate constant terms that are meaningful in the world under consideration, the same variable by the same constant term, we always obtain a true proposition. A further question that can be asked, is whether or not a logical formula which is universally true in a given possible world, is also true in every other non-empty possible world. If the answer is in the positive then the formula is said to be an ontological (metaphysical) propositional formula, and its ontological (metphysical) character is revealed by the truth of the proposition which results from binding the free variables of the formula with the universal quantifier. An example will make this line of thinking clearer.

Consider the formula

(5) if for some *a*, *F*(*a*) then for all *a*, *F*(a)

In a possible world constituted by one and only one object (or individual) formula (5) is universally applicable, i.e. it turns out to be true irrespective of the interpretation we assign to '*F*', provided the interpretation is meaningful in the possible world under consideration. However, formula (5) is not universally applicable in a possible world containing more than one object whereas, for instance, the formula

(6) if for all *a*, *F*(*a*) then for some *a*, *F*(*a*)

is universally applicable in any possible world. It can, therefore, be described as an ontological (metaphysical) propositional formula. Its ontological (metaphysical) character results, according to Scholz, from the truth of the proposition which says that

(7) for all *F*, if for all *a*, *F*(*a*) then for some *a*, *F*(*a*).

Scholz seems to regard it as obvious that (7) belongs to ontology or to metaphysics as he would put it. And, Aristotle, too, would have to find a place for it in his science of being. For being true in every possible world proposition (7) must be true of everything that there is, and consequently it belongs to the most general discipline.

Propositional formulae

(8) if *F*(*a*) then for some *b*, *F*(*b*)

and

(9) (for some *a*, it-is-not-the-case-that *F*(*a*)) if and only if it-is-not-the-case-that for all *a*, *F*(*a*)

can serve as further examples of ontological formulae paralleled by the following ontological truths:

(10) for all *F* and *a*, if *F*(*a*) then for some *b*, *F*(*b*)
(11) for all *F*, (for some *a*, it-is-not-the-case-that *F*(*a*)) if and only if it-is-not-the-case-that for all *a*, F(*a*)

Briefly, on Scholz's view, the logical system of Frege and the logical system of the authors of *Principia* must be regarded as systems consisting of ontological (metaphysical) propositional formulae whereas the logical system developed by Leśniewski should be described simply as ontological (metaphysical) since it allows for no free variables in its theses and thus consists of what Scholz calls metaphysical truths.

Earlier in the paper I decided to use the term 'logic' and its derivatives in the narrow sense, but at that time I said nothing about the possibility of narrowing the sense of the term even further and understanding by logic what is commonly called the logic of propositions or sentential logic. Now, the question is whether the propositional formulae of the logic of propositions can be described as ontological. The answer is not as obvious as we would wish it to be. Following Scholz's intuitions one is tempted to suggest that these propositional formulae of the logic of propositions, which were applicable in every possible world, deserved to be called ontological, and that the propositions which resulted from quantifying such formulae deserved to be counted as ontological truths. For to be true is to be related in some way to what there is. But I do not propose to press the point. On closer investigation the problem may turn out to be one of terminology to be settled by convention.

Another question that comes to one's mind is this: if logic is an axiomatised and formalised part of ontology, is every ontological statement a logical truth? In its informal description of what there is, ontology appears to need a vocabulary which is richer than the logical vocabulary, since it contains terms which cannot be defined in logic. Thus, for instance, ontology may be concerned with the problem of whether or not every object has a proper part, or with the problem of whether or not every object lasts, that is to say, whether or not it is extended in time; or with the problem of whether or not every object is bulky, that is to say, whether or not it is extended in space.

One way of dealing with this query would be to say that to consider problems of this nature would amount to trespassing into the fields of disciplines other than logic. For no answer to any of these problems can, in fact, be described as ontological simply because no such answer can be meaningful for every possible world. According to some, to say that a number lasts or does not last, or to say that a number is bulky or is not bulky, is, with reference to the possible world of numbers, just talking nonsense.

But suppose, for the sake of argument, that the theses of a theory of part-whole relations (there is such a theory, it is called mereology and was worked out by Leśniewski) were true in every possible world; in that case, would mereology be a logical theory? Leśniewski considered it to be a mathematical theory. It presupposed logic but itself was not a logical theory. However, in his published papers there does not seem to be any hint at the rationale of this distinction. It would appear that the distinction between logic and other deductive theories which presupposed logic could be based on the following criterion. Given appropriate rules of definition, logic determines the syntactical variety of a standardised or canonic language. Non-logical theories can only expand the vocabulary of the language; they bring with them no new syntactical forms. Thus, mereology exhibits the use of terms not definable within the framework of logic, but the parts of speech (semantical categories) exemplified by these terms are already available in logic. Unfortunately, this neat criterion falls short of its purpose. For it turns out that with the aid of the primitive notions of Leśniewski's logic in conjunction with the primitive notions of his mereology one can define a notion such that if, in turn, it were used as a primitive term, it would prove to be sufficient for the purpose of defining both the relevant notions of logic formerly used as primitive and the primitive notions of mereology. This means that the boundary between logic and mereology vanishes. Whether the same can be said about other theories which Leśniewski would call mathematical, must remain, for the time being, an open question.

We have seen that for Scholz a statement is ontological (metaphysical) if it is true in every possible world, and that a possible world, as Scholz understands it, is in fact a real world since it contains at least one individual. There are no empty possible worlds for Scholz. But what about his non-empty possible worlds? How are they related to one another? As far as I can judge, the term 'possible world' lends itself to at least two distinct interpretations.

In 'Logik, Grammatik, Metaphysik' we find a number of passages which differentiate between various possible worlds on account of the number of individuals they contain. We can distinguish, so we are told, possible worlds each constituted by only one individual or by at least one individual, or by *n* individuals or by at least *n* individuals. This way of talking about possible worlds reminds one of Russell, who in his *Introduction to Mathematical Philosophy* (Allen & Unwin, London, 1919, p. 203) writes that "Among 'possible' worlds, in the Leibnizian sense, there will be worlds having one, two, three, ... individuals", and he continues by pointing out that "There does not even seem any logical necessity why there should be even one individual – why, in fact, there should be any world at all". Thus, unlike Scholz, Russell might have been prepared to entertain an empty possible world. But this is only by the way.

Now, we can conceive of an all-embracing possible world containing all individuals from all possible worlds. There would be only one such world, and it seems to be reasonable to identify it with the world in which we live. A predicate that is significant with respect to the individuals constituting any of the possible worlds, could significantly be predicated of any individual belonging to the all-ambracing world and vice versa, the result of such a predication being either true or false. On this view, whatever exists, that is to say, whatever there is, is of one kind. Individuals which constitute various possible worlds represent only one category of being. It is, therefore, appropriate, so it seems, to describe the ontology which underpins such an interpretation of the notion of possible world as a unicategorial ontology.

However, certain other remarks made by Scholz in the same paper suggest a different interpretation of the notion of possible world. For it follows from what he says occasionally, that there are predicates which can be used significantly with reference to individuals in one possible world whereas they cannot be so used with reference to individuals in another possible world. In accordance with this view expressions

(12) Socrates is-an-even-number

and

(13) number two is-a-philosopher

are meaningless. They are simply incoherent sequences of words. And if this is the case then in the propositions

(14) Socrates is-an-individual

and

(15) number two is-an-individual

the predicate 'is-an-individual' is used in two different senses. Its occurrence in (14) must exemplify a part of speech (semantical category) which is not the same as the part of speech (semantical category) exemplified by its occurrence in (15) because the terms 'Socrates' and 'number two' exemplify two different parts of speech. And this last statement follows from the fact that the expressions

(16) Socrates is-a-philosopher

and

(17) number two is-an-even-number

are syntactically coherent whereas (12) and (13) are not. The individuals in the sense in which the term is used in (14) constitute one possible world while the individuals in the sense in which the term is used in (15) constitute a different possible world. The individuals belonging to the former represent a certain category of being while an entirely different category of being is represented by the individuals belonging to the latter. There is no possible world embracing the individuals of both possible worlds just distinguished. An ontology which envisages several categories of being and underpins this alternative interpretation of the notion of a possible world, can appropriately the described as multicategorial. Interestingly enough, the groping for a multicategorial ontology goes back to Aristotle and his distinction between primary and secondary substances (*πρῶται οὐσίαι*, *δεύτεραι οὐσίαι*, Categoriae, 2^a11-2^b28).

Our tentative identification of the notion of possible world with that of category of being raises at once the question

(18) what categories of being are there?

or

(19) what kinds of things are there?

as G. E. Moore once formulated what he regarded as the main problem of philosophy or

(20) what is there?

which is Quine's version of the ontological problem.

In Part II, which follows, I offer no answer to these questions, since I have done so already elsewhere (see my 'Outline of an Ontology', *Bulletin of the John Rylands University Library of Manchester* **59** (1976/77), 127–147).

Instead, I propose to discuss a preliminary problem, which is a challenge to the logician rather than to the traditional ontologist. The problem is this. How can we express, in terms of a logically standardised language, our answers to the ontological question 'What is there?' And since answers to ontological questions are likely to be controversial, how are we to negate the answers of our opponents? Briefly, how are we to express our ontological commitment, be it positive or negative?

According to Quine, our final answers to the ontological question 'What is there?' should be read off from our use of the quantifiers. For him, to be is to be a value of a variable. Thus, if what we are prepared to assert implies universal generalisations (i.e. statements of the form: for all $a_1 \ldots a_n$, $F(a_1 \ldots a_n)$) or indefinite particularisations (i.e. statements of the form: for some $a_1 \ldots a_n$, $F(a_1 \ldots a_n)$) then thereby we are committed to allowing for the existence of the values of the quantified variables. Could not statements of the form: a's exist, adequately express our ontological commitment? Perhaps they could, but the notion of existence embedded in the constant term 'exist' is, in Quine's view, more ambiguous than the notion of existence embedded in the quantifiers. However, the quantifiers, too, seem to lend themselves to various interpretations, and it is to this point in particular that I intend directing my attention in the rest of my paper.

II

Let us begin by considering the formula

(21) $(\exists b) \centerdot b = a$

where 'a' stands for a singular name. The formula is said to be true if and only if

(22) there-exists-exactly-one a,

this last proposition meaning the same as

(23) a is-an-individual-object

Thus, formula (21) defines or explicates the notion of individual or singular existence, and I do not know of any logical system within the framework of which formula (21) could not be interpreted as doing exactly that.

Since formula (21) exhibits the use of three notions, the notion of quantification, the notion of identity, and the notion of singular name, it is reasonable to ask which of them carries with it existential import, that is to say, which of them makes the formula commit its propounder to the existence of something or other. And it is necessary for our purpose to examine the notion of quantification under two headings: indefinite particularisation and universal generalisation. So, in the end, we have four possible bearers of existential import to consider.

It would not be rewarding to exhaust all the combinations in the possible answers to our query. Let us, however, consider in some detail the following three cases:

Case 1. each of the four notions, the notion of indefinite particularisation, the notion of universal generalisation, the notion of identity, and the notion of singular name, has existential import.

Case 2. only the notion of indefinite particularisation has existential import.

Case 3. only the notion of identity has existential import.

As far as I can judge, Case 1 is characteristic of what, out of respect for history, can be called Frege–Russellian language. Allowing for some streamlining this is the language of the traditional, some would say classical, theory of quantification with identity or rather the language of the full system of the simplified theory of types. In this language by singular names we are to understand singular referential names, i.e. proper names, that name something, and definite descriptions that describe something. Singular names in this sense form a semantical category which, in conjunction with the semantical category of propositions, gives rise to other semantical categories within the framework of the language. Singular names that fail to name anything and definite descriptions that fail to describe anything are not allowed in the language. Instead, recourse is had to predicates that fail to apply to anything. Thus, for instance, instead of the singular name 'Pegasus' we can have the predicate 'is-Pegasus' (or 'Pegasises'). Consequently, in the Frege–Russellian language the mere use of singular names commits one to entertaining the existence of whatever the names purport to name or of whatever the descriptions purport to describe.

In the Frege-Russellian language the notion of identity has also existential import. This is evident from *14.28 of *Principia*, which reads as follows:

(24) $E!(\iota x)(F(x)) \,.\equiv.\, (\iota x)(F(x)) = (\iota x)(F(x))$.

We learn from (24) that definite descriptions satisfy the law of reflexivity for '=' if and only if they do not fail to describe something. It is true that

(25) the author of Waverley = the author of Waverley

but it is not the case that

(26) the winged horse of Bellerophon = the winged horse of Bellerophon.

'The primitive propositions' in *Principia Mathematica* – writes Russell in his *Introduction to Mathematical Philosophy*, p. 203[1] – "are such as to allow the inference that at least one individual exists". He evidently refers, to use his own way of talking, to propositions of the form "the propositional function so-and-so is sometimes true', i.e. to propositions of the form

(27) $(\exists a) . F(a)$.

In his view propositions of this form assert existence, and for this reason, he thought, they cannot occur in logic as complete asserted propositions. They can only occur as antecedents or as consequents of complete asserted propositions. At the time of writing the *Introduction* his considered opinion was that no logical principle should assert or imply the existence of anything. For him, indefinite particularisation had existential import, and he went on to suggest that asserted propositions of logic should "all be such as to affirm that some propositional function is *always* true", i.e. that they should all be of the form

(28) $(a) . F(a)$.

'We may lay it down', Russell concludes (see p. 204 of the *Introduction*) "that, if there were no universe, *all* general propositions would be true; for the contradictory of a general proposition is a proposition asserting existence, and would therefore always be false if no universe existed."

As regards the logical system of *Principia*, and this also applies to the traditional theory of quantification with identity, the argument is not quite sound. For the contradictory of a proposition of the form (27), i.e. a proposition of the form (28) implies a proposition which asserts existence (see *10.25 of *Principia* and proposition (6) of the present paper). This means that a proposition of the form (28) also asserts existence, be it implicitly. The outcome is that if we wanted to free the contradictory of an existential proposition of the form (27) from any existential implications and make it hold even if there were no universe then we should replace some of the primitive propositions of *Principia* (and of the traditional theory of quantification with identity) by different principles. Now, this problem takes us to Case 2 and to the language of so-called free logic, various systems of which have been worked out by Karel Lambert and his associates.

In the language of free logic by singular names we are to understand singular names and definite descriptions that name or describe something as well as singular names and descriptions that fail to name or describe anything at all. Thus, from the mere occurrence of a singular name or definite description in a proposition formulated in the language of free logic we cannot draw any existential conclusions. Nor can we draw any existential conclusions from the notion of identity favoured by free logicians. Since this notion differs from the one available in the Frege–Russellian language, I shall use the symbol '$\cong$' to express it. While in the Frege–Russellian language the variable '*a*' in the formula

(29) $a = a$

stands for a singular name that names something or for a definite description that describes something, such names and such descriptions being the only allowable substituends for variables of the first order, the free logic formula

(30) $a \cong a$

holds irrespective of whether the name or the definite description for which '*a*' stands, names or describes anything or not. Thus, whereas (29) implies the existence of *a*, (30) does not.

As regards the use of the indefinite particularisation in connection with variables of the first order, there is no difference between free logicians and the logicians who employ the Frege–Russellian language. They differ, however, in their interpretation of the universal quantifier, and in order to acknowledge the difference I shall use the crossed brackets "$\{$' and '$\}$" to express universal generalisation in the language of free logic. The nature of the difference will become clear later. At this stage suffice it to note that the formula

(31) $(a) \cdot F(a) \cdot \supset \cdot (\exists a) \cdot F(a)$

is universally applicable in any universe including the empty one, whereas the formula

(32) $\{a\} \cdot F(a) \cdot \supset \cdot (\exists a) \cdot F(a)$

is not. It fails if the possible world for which it is meaningful, happens to be empty.

Case 3 is characteristic of the language which in a paper read at the International Colloquium in Salzburg in 1965, I described as L_4 ('A Theory of Non-Reflexive Identity and its Ontological Ramifications', in *Grundfragen der Wissenschaften und ihre Wurzeln in der Metaphysik*, ed. by Paul Weingartner, Salzburg/ München 1967, pp. 65–102). Like the language of free logic L_4 accommodates singular names and definite descriptions irrespective of whether they name or describe anything or not. Unlike systems of free logic the system of non-reflexive identity in L_4 uses, as the only primitive notion other than quantification, the notion of identity with existential import, i.e. it is based on '$=$' and not on '$\cong$'. Neither the particular nor the universal quantifier has existential import in L_4. To emphasise this peculiarity I symbolise them, following Leśniewski, with the aid of square brackets. And the way I interpret them, has much in common with the way Leśniewski interpreted quantified expressions in his logical language.

From what I have said, one can infer that in my view there are, in respect of the first order variables, at least three different interpretations of the universal quantifier, symbolised by '$(a) \,.\, F(a)$', '$\{a\} \,.\, F(a)$', and '$[a] \,.\, F(a)$', and at least two different interpretations of the particular quantifier, symbolized by '$(\exists a) \,.\, F(a)$' and '$[\exists a] \,.\, F(a)$'. One way of showing what these different interpretations are, is to relate them to each other in propositions that one is prepared to put forward as truths. This has been done, in part, by Karel Lambert, who in a paper written in collaboration with Thomas Scharle related a first order fragment of my system of non-reflexive identity, System A, with his own system of free logic, System FL and its extension. (See 'A translation theorem for two systems of free logic', *Logique et analyse* **10** (1967), 328–41.) Quite naturally, Lambert discusses my 'square' quantification (I owe this expression to Michael Dummett) from the point of view of his System FL and in the light of quantification as it is used in FL. What I propose to do now is to relate the various senses of the two quantifiers within the framework of my System A, appropriately extended.

System A presupposes the logic of propositions, and is based on the following single axiom:

(33) $[a\,b] : a = b \,.\!\equiv\!.\, [\exists c] \,.\, c = a \,.\, c = b.$

The system is developed in accordance with the following directives or rules of procedure: (a) *rules of inference*: substitution, quantification, detachment, (b) *rules of definition*: the rule for defining constant functors which directly or indirectly form propositions, the rule for defining constant singular names or functors which directly or indirectly form definite descriptions, (c) *rules of extensionality*.

For the purpose of the present discussion we ought to keep in mind that among the substituends for the first order variables we have any singular name whether it names anything or not. The rule of quantification is such as to allow us to prove 'square bracket' analogues to all these quantificational formulae derivable in the traditional theory of quantification in which no constant terms occur other than the constant terms of the logic of propositions. Thus in a sense, one can say that 'square bracket' quantification does not *formally* differ from the traditional 'round bracket' quantification. It is in relation to certain constant terms other than the constant terms of the logic or propositions that the differences in the meaning of the quantifiers become apparent.

The axiom (33) is inferentially equivalent to the following two theses:

(34) $[a\,b] : a = b \,.\supset.\, b = a$
(35) $[a\,b\,c] : a = b \,.\, b = c \,.\supset.\, a = c.$

This shows that the functor '=' is symmetrical and transitive. It is not, however, reflexive.

By applying the rules of definition we can introduce into the system the following theses:

(36) $[a\,b] \therefore a \cong b \,.\equiv:\, [c] : c = a \,.\equiv.\, c = b$
(37) $[a] : \mathrm{ob}(a) \,.\equiv.\, [\exists b] \,.\, b = a$ or $[a] : \mathrm{ob}(a) \,.\equiv.\, a = a$
(38) $[a] \therefore a = \wedge \,.\equiv:\, \sim(a = a) : [b] : \sim(a = b) \,.\supset.\, a = b.$

And among the theses provable in the system we have:

(39) $[a] \,.\, \sim(a = \wedge)$
(40) $\sim(\wedge = \wedge)$
(41) $\wedge \cong \wedge$
(42) $\sim(\mathrm{ob}(\wedge))$
(43) $[F] : [a] \,.\, F(a) \,.\supset.\, F(\wedge)$
(44) $[F] : F(\wedge) \,.\supset.\, [\exists a] \,.\, F(a).$

Definition (36) defines the notion of identity which is reflexive, symmetrical, and transitive. It is this notion that is made use of in systems of free logic.

Definition (37), in either of its forms, introduces into the system the functor of individual or singular existence (see (21), (22) and (23)).

Definition (38) introduces into the system the singular name '$\wedge$'. As is evident from (42), '$\wedge$' does not name anything. We can read it as "the-object-which-does-not-exist".

Now, the following theses characterise, in terms of 'square' quantification, the quantifiers as used in free logic and in the traditional theory of quantification:

$$(45) \quad [F] : (\exists a) \cdot F(a) \cdot \equiv \cdot [\exists a] \cdot \mathrm{ob}(a) \cdot F(a)$$

$$(46) \quad [F] \therefore \{a\} \cdot F(a) \cdot \equiv : [a] : \mathrm{ob}(a) \cdot \supset \cdot F(a)$$

$$(47) \quad [Fc] :: \mathrm{ob}(c) \cdot \supset \therefore (a) \cdot F(a) \cdot \equiv : [\exists b] \cdot \mathrm{ob}(b) : [b] : \mathrm{ob}(b) \cdot \supset \cdot F(b).$$

I hesitate to call these theses definitions. In particular, this applies to (47). They do not conform with the rules of definition as laid down for System A. But I am prepared to assert them axiomatically, and thus extend System A. In the extended system we can now prove that

$$(48) \quad [F] : [\exists a] \cdot F(a) \cdot \equiv : F(\wedge) \cdot \vee \cdot (\exists a) \cdot F(a)$$

$$(49) \quad [F] : [a] \cdot F(a) \cdot \equiv \cdot F(\wedge) \cdot \{a\} \cdot F(a)$$

$$(50) \quad [F] \therefore [a] \cdot F(a) \cdot \equiv \cdot F(\wedge) \cdot (a) \cdot F(a) : \vee : [a] \cdot F(a) \cdot \equiv \cdot F(\wedge).$$

These theses can be said to characterise the 'square' quantification in terms of quantification as used in free logic and in the traditional theory of quantification. Note, however, that the notion of '$\wedge$' had to be made use of in the characterisation.

It has been found helpful, as we all know, to explain the notion of quantification in terms of so-called expansions, and it is with this sort of informal explanation that I wish to conclude my enquiry into the meaning of the quantifiers.

Assume, for the sake of argument, a possible world consisting of exactly n individual objects, $a_1, a_2, \ldots, a_n$. Assume further that in our language we have singular referential names, 'a_1', 'a_2', ..., 'a_n', and a singular non-referential (empty) name '$\wedge$'. On these assumptions we would be justified in asserting equivalences of the following form:

$$(51) \quad (\exists a) \cdot F(a) \cdot \equiv : F(a_1) \cdot \vee \cdot F(a_2) \cdot \vee \cdot \ldots \cdot \vee \cdot F(a_n)$$

$$(52) \quad [\exists a] \cdot F(a) \cdot \equiv : F(a_1) \cdot \vee \cdot F(a_2) \cdot \vee \cdot \ldots \cdot \vee \cdot F(a_n) \cdot \vee \cdot F(\wedge)$$

$$(53) \quad (a) \cdot F(a) \cdot \equiv \cdot F(a_1) \cdot F(a_2) \cdot \ldots \cdot F(a_n)$$

$$(54) \quad \{a\} \cdot F(a) \cdot \equiv : \mathrm{ob}(a_1) \cdot \supset \cdot F(a_1) : \mathrm{ob}(a_2) \cdot \supset \cdot F(a_2) : \ldots : \mathrm{ob}(a_n) \cdot \supset \cdot F(a_n) : \mathrm{ob}(\wedge) \cdot \supset \cdot F(\wedge)$$

$$(55) \quad [a] \cdot F(a) \cdot \equiv \cdot F(a_1) \cdot F(a_2) \cdot \ldots \cdot F(a_n) \cdot F(\wedge).$$

If we want our assertions to apply to a non-finite possible world then we have to replace the equivalences by implications schematised in this way:

(51′) $F(b) \cdot \supset \cdot (\exists a) \cdot F(a)$, where '$b$' stands for a singular referential name

(52′) $F(b) . \supset . [\exists a] . F(a)$ where '*b*' stands for any singular name whether it is referential or not

(53′) $(a) . F(a) . \supset . F(b)$ where '*b*' stands for a singular referential name

(54′) $(\!\!-a-\!\!) . F(a) . \supset : \text{ob}(b) . \supset . F(b)$ where '*b*' stands for any singular name

(55′) $[a] . F(a) . \supset . F(b)$ where '*b*' stands for any singular name

Every proposition corresponding to one of the above schemata is provable within the framework of one or another theory of quantification so far considered.

It is time now to try and answer the principal question of Part II, namely the question concerning ontological commitment of theories formulated in terms of a standardised logical language. And, in the first place, let us consider the case of unicategorial ontology, which presupposes one all-embracing universe or possible world.

For the purpose of expressing the existence of something the language of the traditional theory of quantification with identity, the language of free logic, and L_4 are all adequate.

Statements formulated in the language of the traditional theory of quantification carry with them ontological commitment if they imply propositions of the form '$(\exists a) . F(a)$'. *A fortiori* the statements '$(\exists a) . \text{ob}(a)$' and '$(a) . \text{ob}(a)$', which are provable within the framework of the traditional theory of quantification with identity, commit the theory to an ontology with individual objects. This sort of commitment, innocuous though it may appear, offends those who like Russell care for the purity, i.e. ontological neutrality of logic. Strictly speaking, the ontological commitment of the theory of quantification in its traditional form is traceable to the pre-systematic and informal decision that what we want to state within the framework of the theory, will concern a *non-empty* universe or possible world, and that in our language we shall not make use of any singular names that fail to name or of any definite descriptions that fail to describe.

Statements formulated in the language of free logic also carry with them ontological commitment if they imply propositions of the form '$(\exists a) . F(a)$'. But free logic as a whole remains ontologically netural, since no proposition of the form '$(\exists a) . F(a)$' is provable within its framework. Its language is adequate for expressing commitment to the existence of something. There is, however, no pre-systematic or informal stipulation as to the non-emptiness of the universe of discours or otherwise.

Statements formulated in L_4 have existential import if they imply propositions of the form '$[\exists a] \cdot \text{ob}(a)$' or '$[\exists a] \cdot a = a$', but no such propositions are provable within the framework of the theory of non-reflexive identity. Thus, the theory is ontologically neutral and, in this respect, is comparable with free logic. While in the language of the latter ontological commitment is traceable to the use of the particular quantifier, in the former ontological import is originally encapsulated in the constant term '='.

The problem of committing oneself to the existence of classes or the problem of denying the existence of classes presents no difficulty to the unicategorial ontologist. It is exactly the same as the problem of asserting or denying, say, the existence of lions or unicorns. For this purpose we need the notion of general existence, which can be defined as follows:

(56) $(F): \text{ex}(F) . \equiv . (\exists a) . F(a)$ or $[F] : \text{ex}(F) . \equiv . [\exists a] . \text{ob}(a) . F(a)$.

However, the problem of denying the existence of the whole universe of discourse, in other words, the problem of saying that nothing exists, is a little more complicated. Within the framework of the traditional theory of quantification one cannot assert that nothing exists, '$(a) . \sim(\text{ob}(a))$ in symbols, or that something does not exist, '$(\exists a) . \sim(\text{ob}(a))$' in symbols, without contradicting oneself. Perhaps it would be more correct to say that within the language of the traditional theory of quantification a proposition that nothing exists is not really expressible. Both '$(a) . \sim(\text{ob}(a))$' and '(F): $(a) . \sim (F(a))$' lead to a contradiction, and the same is true of the proposition that something does not exist, '$(\exists a) . \sim(\text{ob}(a))$' in symbols. Note, however, that '$(\exists F) . \sim(\text{ex}(F))$' is provable.

In the language of free logic the proposition that nothing exists can be expressed as follows: $(a) . \sim(a \cong a)$. But I do not know how to say, in this language, that something does not exists, i.e. that it-is-not-the-case-that something is-an-individual-object.

In L_4 the proposition which says that nothing exists, '$[a] . \sim(\text{ob}(a))$' in symbols, is not self-contradictory, and the proposition which says that something does not exist, '$[\exists a] . \sim(\text{ob}(a))$' in symbols, is provable.

To sum up, one can, if one wants to, deny the existence of the whole universe of discourse in the language of free logic and in L_4. For either of these languages is ontologically neutral. Understandably enough, one cannot deny the existence of the whole universe of discourse in the language of the traditional theory of quantification with identity since the theory and its language is based on the assumption that the universe of discourse is not empty.

Ontological neutrality of a standardised language becomes significant when we turn to the problem of expressing ontological commitment of a multicategorial ontologist. According to Quine the problem is quite simple. Quantification involving first order variables commits us to an ontology with individual objects; quantification involving higher order variables, unless we can get rid of it, commits us to an ontology with higher categories of being.

We have seen that if the universe of discourse or the possible world is constituted by individual objects then Quine's first assertion is correct provided we adhere to the language of the traditional theory of quantification. It is also correct if we express our ontology in the language of free logic and by quantification understand the use of the particular quantifier. But the assertion is not correct in application to L_4. Quantification in L_4 like quantification in Leśniewski's language carries with it no ontological commitment. But does the quantification involving variables of higher order express ontological commitment to the existence of categories of being other than the category of individual objects? According to Quine it does. But I beg to differ. Quine's doctrine to the effect that it does, stands or falls with what can be called *designator – designatum* semantics. In accordance with the latter every constant term names an entity of an appropriate category of being; singular names name individual objects, one place predicates name properties or classes, and so on. In accordance with the former to every quantified variable there corresponds not only a range of substituends but also a range of values, i.e. a range of extra-linguistic entities. The doctrine of the *designator – designatum* semantics, once espoused by Russell of *The Problems of Philosophy*, is now rejected even by Quine, who attributes it to the confusion of meaning with naming. As far as I can judge, the *variable – value* conception of quantification should also be rejected. To first order variables there corresponds a range of substituends and there may also correspond a range of values which could be identified with a universe of discourse or a possible world. To variables of a higher order there corresponds a range of substituends only. Thus, quantifying variables of various orders does not necessarily commit one to a multicategorial ontology.

In line with the traditional theory of quantification we are entitled to infer the proposition '$(\exists F) \cdot F$(Socrates)' from the premiss 'Socrates is wise'. Now, if, as Quine tells us, the premiss does not commit us to the existence of properties but the conclusion does then the inference cannot be valid. I agree that the premiss carries with it no commitment to the existence of properties but I prefer to regard the inference as valid and reject the view that quantifying predicate variables commits us, within the framework of the traditional theory of quantification, to an ontology with properties or any other abstract entities.

If that is the case, how can the multicategorial ontologist present his doctrine in a standardised language? In my view he can still use any of the three languages we have distinguished, each time specifying informally the universe of discourse (the possible world) he is describing. Every statement of his theory will be about entities belonging to one universe of discourse or possible world. No proposition referring to more than one possible world will be expressible in any of the three languages at his disposal. Moreover, the language of the traditional theory of quantification will not enable him to deny the existence of any possible world as a whole. If he wanted to do that, he would have to turn to the language of free logic or to L_4 both appropriately re-interpreted. For the existence of a possible world can only be denied in an ontologically neutral language.

However, logic can offer a better way of helping the multicategorial ontologist in his predicament, a way which is also acceptable to his opponents. It consists in constructing an ontologically neutral multicategorial language. As far as I know, Kazimierz Ajdukiewicz, the Polish logician, was the first to see the possibility of such a language. Independently, some work in this field has been done by propounders of many-sorted theories (A. Schmidt, Hao Wang). For a concrete example of a standardised language for bicategorial ontology may I refer those who are interested to a paper of mine which I read at another Salzburg Colloquium, held in 1973? ('A System of Logic for Bicategorial Ontology', *Journal of Philosophical Logic* 3 (1974), 265–283)

Department of Philosophy, University of Manchester, England

GEORG HENRIK VON WRIGHT

PROBLEMS AND PROSPECTS OF DEONTIC LOGIC
A SURVEY

1. "There is no such thing as philosophical logic", Wittgenstein said in a letter to C. K. Ogden.[1] In spite of his *veto* the term now has an established use. It could be defined as signifying the applications of the tools of formal logic to the analysis of concepts and conceptual structures in which philosophers traditionally have taken interest. Pursuits in this spirit sometimes shed interesting light on old problems. More often perhaps they give rise to new problems and steer the interest of philosophers in new directions.

The rebirth of modal logic in the mid-century was a singularly consequential event for the development of philosophical logic. This was so chiefly because the structures which modal logic had traditionally studied turned out to possess formal analogies within several important types of discourse of widely differing content. One could speak of a General Theory of Modality embracing all these structurally analogous conceptual fields: chronological discourse, the families of basic doxastic and epistemic notions known from traditional theory of knowledge, the deontic concepts of normative discourse, – even the study of the quantificational notions of 'classical' non-modal logic can be regarded as different provinces within this vast realm of formal inquiry.[2] Here I shall deal with that province of analogical modal logic which has acquired for itself the established name Deontic Logic.

2. When a new discipline has been born it often appears more novel than it actually is. This impression may be due partly to ignorance of past history and partly to initial difficulties in assessing the relevance of new discoveries.

Today, a quarter of a century or more after its birth, it is obvious that deontic logic has a not uninteresting prehistory. I hope someone will before long record this history in a book.

Broadly speaking, one can distinguish two trends in the prehistory of deontic logic. One goes back to Leibniz, the other to Bentham. The first exploits the analogy between deontic and modal concepts. The second relates the deontic ideas to the notion of the *will*.

Leibniz's thoughts on the matter are found in an early fragment *Elementa Juris Naturalis*, probably written in 1671.[3] Leibniz notes that the terms

E. Agazzi (ed.), Modern Logic – A Survey, 399–423.

licet, non-licet, and *debet* are analogous to possibility, impossibility, and necessity. Leibniz, moreover, was also aware that the two triads are analogous to the quantifiers 'some', 'no', and 'all'. This I find particularly gratifying in view of the fact that my General Theory of Modality took its origin from the observation of analogies between modalities and quantifiers.[4]

As far as I know, Leibniz did not pay special attention to the fact that the members of the triads[5] are themselves interdefinable. By taking one member as primitive one can, through a process of successive negations, define the others. The first to have made this quite clear for the deontic concepts seems to have been Alois Höfler in a paper written in the 1880's, but not published until 1917.[6]

Bentham's efforts to build what he calls a Logic of Imperation or of the Will take their point of departure in the view that norms express 'aspects' of the will of a legislator.[7] Command, prohibition and permission answer to the legislator's wish that something be the case, that something be *not* the case, and to his *not* wishing that something be *not* the case respectively.

Virtually, Bentham's logic takes what may be called the orthodox view of the interrelatedness of the basic deontic notions. Permission consists in the absence of a prohibition, and prohibition being 'a negative aspect to a positive act' is equipollent with 'an affirmative aspect towards the correspondent negative act', *i.e.* with a command not to do.[8]

Bentham also acknowledges a principle to the effect that no act can be both commanded and prohibited (relative to the same 'will'). This is the first genuine 'axiom' of a deontic logic ever formulated. Accepting that permission is absence of prohibition, it is equivalent to saying that, if something is commanded, it is permitted – and also to saying that either the positive or the corresponding negative act or both must be permitted.

Bentham's 'imperational logic' dates from the 1780's but remained virtually unknown until the 1970's. Ernst Mally did not know any predecessor when in 1926 he published his book *Grundgesetze des Sollens: Elemente der Logik des Willens*. As indicated by the title, Mally follows Bentham in regarding the normative Ought as an expression of will. He also calls the logic of willing *Deontik*. (Bentham had used the term 'deontology' for the entire theory of morality.)

Mally tried to give to his *Deontik* an axiomatic *Aufbau*. In this regard his efforts were much more systematic than Bentham's. But it can hardly be said that Mally succeeded very well.[9] A good many of the theorems of his system are counter-intuitive – *befremdlich* as he says himself. The deepest reason for this is that the symbolic language which he employs is an unhappy blend of expressions for *Is* and for *Ought*.

An advance beyond Bentham is that Mally's *Deontik* knows the distribution principle for the obligation- or ought-operator. One of Mally's axioms, moreover, says that the negation of something which ought to be cannot itself be obligatory (*gefordert*). This answers to Bentham's principle mentioned above. Furthermore: in his deductions Mally relies on the interchangeability of equivalent expressions. These features of his system mean that it, in fact, contains all the ingredients of a fullyfledged deontic logic. Unfortunate. is only that it also has ingredients which undermine and trivialize the whole enterprise.

The line inaugurated by Bentham's Logic of the Will must be said to have been abortive. When deontic logic was definitely born in the early 1950's, this happened in the tradition which goes back to Leibniz. It is an interesting coincidence that all the three independent contributions – by Oskar Becker[10], Jerry Kalinowski[11], and myself[12] – from which deontic logic in its modern form took its start were based on a conscious exploitation of the analogy between deontic and modal concepts. (Less so, however, with Kalinowski than with Becker and myself.) All three authors showed awareness of previous work. Becker and Kalinowski mention Leibniz. Peter Geach had drawn my attention to some observations by Aquinas. But essentially I thought of my work as a start from scratch.

3. By a *normal* modal logic I shall understand a formal system which we obtain by adding to a set of axioms and the rules of inference of 'classical' propositional logic (PL) *at least* the following axioms and rules (or their equivalents):

A1. $N(p \,\&\, q) \leftrightarrow Np \,\&\, Nq$
A2. $Np \rightarrow p$
A3. Nt

Rule of Extensionality: Formulas which are provably equivalent in the system are interchangeable *salva veritate*.

The letter 't' stands for an arbitrary tautology, *e.g.* $p \vee \sim p$. The operator 'N' is read 'it is necessary that'. An operator 'M' for 'it is possible that' is introduced by the definition 'M' $=_{df}$ '$\sim N \sim$'.

With the aid of A3 and the Rule of Extensionality one proves a metatheorem which says that, if a formula f is a theorem of the system, then the formula Nf is a theorem too. This is sometimes called a Rule of Necessitation.

By adding further axioms one gets stronger systems of normal modal logic, such as S4 and S5. The system without such additional axioms is also called the System *M* or *T*.

The shift to deontic logic is now made by substituting for the necessity operator '*N*' the obligation operator '*O*'. This is read 'it ought to be the case that'. Corresponding to '*M*', we have the permission operator '*P*', 'it may be the case that'.

It is easy to see that a sound system of deontic logic cannot be (an analogue of) a normal modal logic as defined above. At least we must give up A2. Its deontic analogue $Op \rightarrow p$ says that if something ought to be the case then it is the case. This may be said to run contrary, not only to 'experience', but also to the philosophic idea of a sharp separation between the Is and the Ought.

There is, however, a weaker form of A2 which may be considered logically valid. This is the formula $\sim N \sim t$ or Mt of modal logic, corresponding in the deontic interpretation to $\sim O \sim t$ or Pt. If we have A2 we can prove Mt, but not conversely. Replacing A2 by Mt in modal logic leads to systems which are weaker than the normal ones, but in many ways interesting to study.

The deontic formula $\sim O \sim t$ says that a contradictory state of affairs is not obligate or, alternatively, that a tautologous state is permitted. Putting $p \vee \sim p$ for t and applying the distribution axiom A1, we can write $\sim O \sim t$ in the form $\sim(Op \,\&\, O \sim p)$ or, alternatively, in the form $OP \rightarrow Pp$, or in the form $Pp \vee P \sim p$. This is the principle which Bentham envisaged as a basic law of a 'logic of the will'. (Cf. above p. 400.) In my 1951 paper I called this the Principle of Permission.

The deontic analogue of A3 is Ot. It says that a tautologous state of affairs ought to obtain. This sounds strange. Moreover, from the deontic analogue of A3 we could, with the aid of the extensionality rule prove the deontic analogue of the Rule of Necessitation. This would mean that everything which is provably true in deontic logic ought to be true. I don't think this makes good sense either. Since, on the other hand, the Rule of Extensionality seems unobjectionable, I think we had better drop the deontic analogue of A3.

Some logicians disagree with me on this. One can argue as follows: If Ot is not logically true, then its negation $\sim Ot$ or, which means the same, $P \sim t$ might be contingently true. But $P \sim t \rightarrow Pp$ is a theorem of (most systems of) deontic logic. This formula means that if a contradictory state of affairs were permitted, then just any state of affairs would be permitted. This argument does not impress me very much, however. Therefore I cannot agree with those logicians wo think that Ot should be logically valid in a deontic system.

I propose that by the Standard System of Deontic Logic[13] we understand a system built on two-valued propositional logic with the addition of the deontic axioms

A1. $O(p \& q) \leftrightarrow Op \& Oq$
A2. $\sim O \sim t$

and the inference rule of extensionality and the definition 'P' $=_{\text{df}}$ '$\sim O \sim$'. Because of this definition, we can also state the axioms in the terms of the permission operator, as follows:

A′1. $P(p \vee q) \leftrightarrow Pp \vee Pq$
A′2. Pt.

It should be noted that this Standard System differs in two important respects from the system proposed in my 1951 paper. First, it admits 'mixed' formulas formed of propositional variables, sentential connectives, and deontic expressions. For example: $p \rightarrow Oq$ is a well-formed formula of the standard system. Secondly, the system admits iteration of the deontic operators. *POp*, for example, is well-formed.

For the sake of convenience I shall, somewhat egocentrically, refer to my 1951 system as the Classical System of Deontic Logic. This system did not admit 'mixed' formulas, nor iteration. There was a clear reason for this restriction. In the classical system the variables are not regarded as schematic letters for sentences but as schematic representations of names of categories or types of action. We shall later have occasion to comment on this difference in basic conceptions.

4. At the time of publishing my 1951 paper I realized that something new had been started which was going to be taken up by others. But I did not anticipate that developments would be as extensive and rapid as has been the case. (A recently published Bibliography by Amedeo G. Conte and Giuliano di Bernardo lists 1460 contributions.[14]) Nor did I anticipate that the subject would turn out to be controversial. As a matter of fact, however, almost every formula which at the time seemed to me clear and uncontroversial has subsequently been subjected to doubts. Also, the very idea of building a deontic logic in analogy with modal logic remains open to debate. (See the last section of this essay.)

There are branches of formal study which are very closely related to deontic logic – so much so that they may be regarded as extensions of offshoots of it. I am thinking, in particular, of the formal theory of *action* and of *ability* (the 'Can do'). This subject is still in a *statu nascendi*. In my opinion it represents a promising new venture in logic.[15]

In the rest of my paper I shall make a survey of some principal themes which have evolved in the course of the recent history of deontic logic. I shall, on the whole, not evaluate the work done by others but rather try to formulate a personal stand on controversial and debated questions. I single out for discussion the following seven topics:

The question of a prescriptive *versus* a descriptive interpretation of deontic logic, the proposed 'reduction' of deontic logic to alethic modal logic, the relevance to a logic of norms of the distinction between *Seinsollen* and *Tunsollen*, the formulation of hypothetical norms, the status of permissions, the iteration of the deontic operators and the building of a hierarchy of norms, the treatment of some 'anomalies' or 'paradoxes' which have intrigued deontic logicians.

In the end section of the paper I shall sketch an alternative approach to the entire subject of deontic logic.

5. In discussions in the late 1930's and early 1940's – in certain ways the aftermath to Mally's pioneering work – some philosophers raised doubts about the "possibility" of a logic of imperatives and norms.[16] The doubts reflected the then prevailing climate of opinion of logical positivism and empiricism, partly also a characteristic Scandinavian tradition in legal and moral philosophy, *viz*. the 'value-nihilism' of the Uppsala School.

The criticism was founded on three premisses. The first was that relations of logical consequence and consistency can subsist only between true or false propositions.[17] The second was that imperatives are not true or false, and the third that norms (and value-judgements too) are disguised imperatives.[18] From these premisses it seemed to follow that there can be no such thing as a logic of imperatives or of norms or of value-judgements. In the late 1940's this was still a firmly established and widely accepted position.

The turning of the tide which took place a few years later did not proceed from a considered counter-criticism of the premisses of the 'value-nihilists'. I for my part simply by-passed the problem – and the same has been true, I think, of most subsequent workers in the field. But soon the problem began to nag me, and the difficulties I have felt here have coloured much of what I have written since and also been responsible for many shifts in my position.

Bentham already made a distinction which is helpful here. He separated imperatives proper, *e.g.* 'you shall not kill!', from sentences which describe what the legislator has enjoined or permitted, *e.g.* 'it is prohibited to kill'. Sentences of the latter kind are 'an improper mode of expression' when they occur in the law: "the legislator speaking as it were in the person of another man who is considered as explaining the state which things are in, in consequence of the arrangements taken by the legislator".[19] In the 1940's the Swedish philosopher Ingemar Hedenius made the very same distinction in a clearcut way and coined for it the terms 'genuine' and 'spurious' legal sentences.[20] In *Norm and Action* I distinguished between *norms* and *norm-propositions.*[21] The linguistic form used for enunciating a norm I called *norm-formulation*. One and the same form of words in the indicative mood, a deontic sentence, can be used both for enunciating a norm and for expressing a norm-proposition. For example, the above sentence 'it is prohibited to kill' can be used as norm-formulation for prohibiting killing, or it can be used for stating a proposition that there is a norm to this effect.

Norm-propositions are true or false. That there can exist logical relations between them is unproblematic. In view of this it might be suggested that deontic logic is a logic of norm-propositions, and that there is no such thing as a logic of norms proper. This suggestion is not unproblematic, however. There are at least two reasons why this is so. One is that the status of norm-propositions themselves is not without problems. They are propositions to the effect that certain norms exist. But what does it mean that a norm 'exists'? This is far from clear. The second reason why the above suggestion is problematic is the following: If a logic of norm-propositions is to be of special interest, then it must have peculiarities which distinguish it from the logic of just any propositions. These peculiarities, it seems, must reflect logical features of the *norms* themselves.[22] But if norms have 'characteristic logical features', does this not mean that there is after all, *also* a logic of norms proper?

In *Norm and Action* I took the view that deontic sentences and their compounds have both what I called a *prescriptive* and a *descriptive* interpretation.[23] I hardly succeeded in making clear how the two interpretations are related. But the idea was that there is both a logic of norms *and* a logic of norm-propositions and that the former is, somehow, *basic* in relation to the latter.[24] Some other authors, who accept the distinction, notably Alchourrón and Bulygin, are anxious to separate the two 'logics' even more sharply than I did in *Norm and Action.*[25]

A prescriptive interpretation of deontic logic assumes that sentential connectives, when applied to norm-formulations, yield new norm-formulations. It is not certain that this assumption is justified. A difficulty is caused by disjunction. If I am told that I ought to open the window *and* ought to shut the door, I know what I have to do. But if I am told that I ought to open the window *or* ought to shut the door, it is not clear what I am expected to do. I am not given a compound rule of action. The situation is rather like this: I am given *incomplete information* about what rules there are. I might, on the basis of what I have been told, hazard a guess that I ought to open the window and act accordingly. But if my guess was mistaken I may in fact then be doing something forbidden. And similarly for shutting the door.

How could a disjunction of two deontic sentences be anything but a sentence to the effect that there is at least one of two norms? Is not, in other words, the function of the sentential connective here to express a disjunctive norm-proposition? I think the answer has to be affirmative. And if this is right, it wrecks the possibility of a prescriptive interpretation of deontic logic.

This seems to me now to be the right attitude to take. Deontic logic *is* a logic of norm-propositions. But we shall still have to account for the fact that norm-propositions have a *peculiar* logic. That is: we must show why the principles of deontic logic are valid for these propositions. To maintain that they just *are* valid would be dogmatic. In order to justify them we must say something about the norms themselves. This we can do, I think, without having to fall back on an underlying 'prescriptive interpretation' of the deontic formulas.

6. One of the most momentuous events in the history of modern deontic logic was A. R. Anderson's proposal for a reduction of deontic to alecthic modal logic.[26] Anderson suggested a reduction schema $Op =_{df} N(\sim p \rightarrow S)$, where '$N$' is the necessity operator of a normal modal logic and 'S' a propositional constant. It is further postulated that it is not necessarily true that S, *i.e.* $\sim NS$ or $M \sim S$.

Anderson called S 'the bad thing' and said that it could be, for example, a punishment or sanction consequent upon neglect of duty. Punishment should of course be avoidable, *i.e.* something which does not of necessity befall agents. Therefore the stipulation $M \sim S$ seems reasonable.

When translated in accordance with the Andersonian schema the axioms and theorems of Standard Deontic Logic become theorems of a normal modal logic to which has been added the axiom $\sim NS$. Under the proposed 'reduction' the deontic analogue of A3, *i.e.* the doubtful principle Ot, also turns out to be true. One can avoid this by imposing the further requirement that the variable in Op should stand for a possibly false proposition. This too seems natural in view of the intended meaning of *S*. Punishment should indeed be avoidable, but it should also be *possible* to 'sin'. Otherwise norms would not be needed.

Anderson's idea has caused philosophic controversy. Some have accused it of committing the 'naturalistic fallacy'.[27] Others have found it 'unrealistic'; neglect of duty does not necessarily lead to 'the bad thing' – some sinners happily escape punishment.

When, some ten years after Anderson, I took up the same thread myself, I substituted for the idea of punishment or sanction the notion of *liability*, and the correlated idea of *immunity*.[28] To satisfy one's obligations is a necessary condition of immunity to legal punishment. This is a conceptual observation; therefore the implication involved in the reduction schema is *logically* necessary.

But are not the notions of immunity and liability themselves deontic notions? If they are, what is the 'reduction' worth philosophically – if they are not, are we not then guilty of a 'naturalistic' fallacy? These questions should be answered as follows:

Against a person who is liable to punishment certain legal measures may or ought to be taken. Such procedures are usually themselves regulated by norms. But whether a person *is* liable to punishment depends upon what he has in fact *done* and upon the norms which there in fact *are*. In this regard it is a 'naturalistic' property of an agent to be immune or liable to punishment. What is partially defined in the reduction schema is the *existence* of obligations. Neither circularity nor a fallacy is involved in the reduction.

It may be objected that the reduction is, at best, of limited relevance only. Immunity, liability, and sanction are typically legal notions. But far from all norms are legal norms. To this objection one could answer by pointing out that the three notions have analogical counterparts also in the moral sphere. Blame, disapproval, and various retributive reactions are moral sanctions. Whether a person is immune or liable to them depends partly on his behaviour and partly on the constitution of the moral code of the community of which he is a member.

The 'point' of the Andersonian reduction, as I see it, is that it provides a *rationale* for the specific principles of deontic logic. The need for a *rationale* is particularly strong in the case of the principle which, in one of its versions, says that a thing and its contradictory cannot both be obligatory. (Cf. above p. 400 and p. 402.)

Is this principle a 'logical truth', or is it not? One thing is clear: if the principle is true at all, then it is true only in relation to a given 'system' of norms.

Nothing in logic can exclude that something is obligatory in one, say, legal code and its contradictory in another. But can logic exclude this from being the case within one and the same code? Can there not exist 'contradictions' in the law?[29] The answer is Yes or No depending upon what counts as constituting the 'existence' of an obligation, *i.e.* upon how we lay down the truth-conditions of norm-propositions. It can happen that one and the same norm-authority, *e.g.* a parliament or a head of state, *promulgates* two contradictory norms both of which have been *enacted* in due order and both of which are thereafter *enforced* by various sub-authorities within the legal order. Everybody would agree, I think, that this is a highly unsatisfactory situation. If it arises, one would probably soon try to remedy it. The law may even provide means for an 'automatic' correction. But is the case we are envisaging contrary to logic, *i.e.* can we 'in the name of logic' refuse to admit that both norms really (co-)*exist*? The existence of both is, to be sure, contrary to one of the laws of deontic logic. But what gives to deontic logic the authority of Logic?

I think this last question demands an answer. In order to answer it we must step beyond deontic logic itself. This is what happens in the Andersonian reduction by relating the notion of a norm (an obligation) to that of a *necessary requirement* for something which can, in a broad sense, be characterized as an *end*. But then one must also ask which conditions requirements for ends should reasonably satisfy. Two such conditions seem to be that the end is something which one can secure and that the requirements are something which one may fail to fulfil. If both conditions are satisfied, the 'logic' involved in the Standard System is normal modal logic, and this seems as good a *rationale* for deontic logic as one could possibly wish for. But the conditions themselves, be it observed, are got from considerations relating to what may be termed the *raison d'être* for norms and for the activity of issuing them.

Bentham and Mally thought of 'deontic logic' as a Logic of the Will. (Cf. above p. 400.) This is a related position to the one which I am advocating here. Giving norms and willing are related activities. The conception of norms as expressions of a will is limited and one-sided if taken literally, but contains an important grain of truth if understood in an analogical or extended sense.

As we have seen, the principles of deontic logic can claim to be valid only provided certain rationality-requirements are imposed on norms. The same holds true for a Logic of the Will. 'Bare' willing need not obey any logic at all – but a Rational Will can aspire only after attainable things and demand only that which is not of necessity already there.

7. It is significant that all the three 'founding fathers' of modern deontic logic, *viz*. Becker, Kalinowski, and myself, regarded *actions* (and not states of affairs) as the 'contents' pronounced obligatory, permitted or forbidden in deontic sentences.[30] I thought, moreover, that these 'contents' were *types* of action, such as murder or smoking, and not *individual* actions, as for example the murder of Caesar. Kalinowski seems to have favoured the opposite view. Becker did not note the distinction. In a deontic logic using quantifiers it is natural to regard the contents as individual actions performed by such and such agents on such and such occasions. This avenue was first explored by Hintikka.[31]

Deontic logic was thus originally conceived of as a logic of what ought to or may or must not *be done* – and not as a logic of what ought to or may or must not *be*. It was thus a logic of what in German is called *Tunsollen* (*-dürfen*) as distinct from a *Seinsollen* (*-dürfen*).

Under a strict *Tunsollen*-conception, the formal language of deontic logic is subject to noteworthy restrictions. If the variables *p, q, etc*. represent verbs for action, for example 'to steal' or 'to smoke', then neither 'mixed' expressions such as, *e.g.*, $p \rightarrow Oq$, nor 'higher order' expressions such as, *e.g.*, OPp will make sense. These restrictions were carefully observed in my 1951 paper. The Classical System of deontic logic was, therefore, formally a very poor system. (Cf. above p. 403.)

Subsequent authors on deontic logic soon shifted to a *Seinsollen*-conception. The contents of norms were regarded as states of affairs which ought to or may or must not *be*. The variables, in other words, represent sentences expressing propositions. A. N. Prior[32] and A. R. Anderson[33] were two outstanding pioneers for this change from the 'Classical' to the 'Standard' system of deontic logic.

The special problems connected with a *Tunsollen*-logic, however, retain their interest. It can, for one thing, be doubted whether the 'founding fathers' were entirely successful with their interpretation of the variables in deontic sentences. They took for granted that the sentential connectives *apply* to names or verbs for action – just as I had taken it for granted that the connectives applied to norm-formulations. These assumptions can be challenged. In the case of symbols for actions, the chief trouble-maker is negation. I thought that, if 'p' signifies an action, '$\sim p$' must signify the omission or forbearance of that action.[34] It did not then occur to me that one can and must make a distinction between merely denying that an agent performs a certain action and affirming that he omits it. A person who *cannot* read, does not read a text presented to him. But he does not *omit* reading it either. He, so to say, neither reads nor not-reads.

Since the early system of deontic logic did not pay needed attention to the problem of compound symbols for actions, one can rightly say that none of these systems wa successful as an attempt to build a formal logic of the *Tunsollen*. This defect can, however, be remedied. I hope to have been able to show[35] that one can build a Logic of Action which makes unobjectionable use of the sentential connectives for joining verb-phrases for actions. By attaching deontic operators to schematic letters for action-verbs and their compounds one forms deontic sentences in which the operator '*O*' should be read 'one ought to' and '*P*' 'one may'. These atomic deontic sentences can in their turn be combined by connectives to form molecular compounds. The language of this deontic calculus is the language of the Classical System.

Which are the axioms of such a *Tunsollen*-logic? There are several alternatives. The simplest is to regard as axioms simply the two axiomatic principles of the Classical System.[36] The deontic logic thus constructed could be said to capture the intentions behind my 1951 paper. The provable formulas would not be exactly the same, however. Thus, for example, the Ross's Paradox formula $Op \rightarrow O(p \vee q)$ is not in its general form provable in this amended version of the Classical System.

Regrettably few people working in the field have paid special attention to the problems connected with a logic of the *Tunsollen*. The problems are often brushed aside by simply assuming that the logic of *Tunsollen* is obtained from the logic of *Seinsollen* by stipulating that the variables *p*, *q*, *etc*. stand for sentences describing actions.[37] This way out, however, is too easy to be successful. If '*p*' is a schematic representation of an action-*sentence* (not of an action-*verb*), '$\sim p$' will represent the negation of that sentence. But the negation of an action sentence must be distinguished from a sentence to the effect that a certain action is forborn or omitted. (Cf. above p. 409.) Therefore, only at the expense of obliterating the distinction between not doing and omitting can one 'transform' a logic for the *Tunsollen* into a logic for the *Seinsollen* by stipulating that the variables which occur in deontic sentences represent action sentences.

The relation between the two types of norm and, consequently, between the two types of deontic logic remains in my opinion an open logico-philosophical problem. I have no good suggestion of how to solve it. I shall only make one observation about it here:

Let the norm be to the effect that it ought to be the case that *p*, for example that a certain window is closed. And let us assume that this norm is addressed by some norm-authority to a certain norm-subject. That the norm is "addressed" shall mean that the subject is expected to extract for himself a *Tunsollen* out of the given *Seinsollen*. How is he to do this? In the first instance, the norm seems to tell him that he *ought to see to it that* the window is closed. How does he do this? If the window is open, he can do this by shutting the window. If it is already closed, he can do it by omitting to open it. These, however, are not the only possibilities. He can also order, persuade or urge another person to shut the window or to refrain from opening it and in this way 'see to it' that what *ought to be* also *is the case*.

These considerations show that there is no unique way of 'extracting' a *Tunsollen* from a *Seinsollen*. The *Tunsollen* which may be extracted depends upon circumstances which prevail in the world – in our example upon whether the window (already) is closed or is open. What ought to be done is not univocally determined by what ought to be the case. Norms of the *Tunsollen* type are inherently conditional, one could also say. This takes us to a now major problem area in deontic logic, *viz*. the theory of *conditional norms*.

8. There has been much confusion and debate about the best way of formalizing conditional norms.[38] Some writers have vested hopes in the possibility of overcoming the difficulties by constructing a *dyadic* deontic logic. In it the deontic operators are prefixed to *pairs* of schematic letters *p, q, etc.* or their molecular compounds. One member of the pair represents the condition under which the action or state represented by the other member ought to or may be realized.

There are many systems of dyadic deontic logic. The pioneers were, I think, Rescher and myself – and each of us made several attempts.[39, 40] They have been criticized and interestingly discussed above all by Bengt Hansson, who has also contributed independently to the development of this line in the history of deontic logic.[41]

I am less confident now than I used to be in the value of a dyadic deontic logic. *One* reason for this is that it now seems to me possible to build a satisfactory theory of conditional norms using simpler and more conventional logical tools. I think that the notion of *material implication* will actually serve the purpose. The norm to the effect that, when it is the case that p, it ought to be the case that q may be rendered by $p \rightarrow Oq$.

Against this proposal there is a standard objection which must be met. The formula $\sim p \rightarrow (p \rightarrow Oq)$ is a logical truth. Hence, the objection goes, if it is *not* the case that p, then, if it is the case that p it ought to be the case that q. The falsehood of the condition seems to validate the conditional norm.

This objection, however, is not serious. It is not even clear wherein the 'objection' really consists. The truth of the formula $\sim p \rightarrow (p \rightarrow Oq)$ does not warrant the reading 'if it is not the case that *p*, then if it *were* the case that *p* - - -'. What the formula says is that either it is the case that *p* or that $\sim p$ or that it ought to be the case that *q*. This is a trivial truth of propositional logic and has no bearing on any norm, whether conditional or unconditional. But the shorter disjunction which says that either it is not the case that *p* or ought to be the case that *q has* such bearing. Because it says that if it is the case that *p* it ought to be the case that *q, i.e.* it states a conditional obligation.

If the variables are understood as representing *generic* propositions (states of affairs), there are various ways of introducing quantifiers into the formulas. A very common and natural way of formulating a conditional norm would be to say that *whenever* it is the case that *p*, it ought to be the case that *q*. If the variables represent *individual*, true or false, propositions it would be more natural to say that the formula represents a conditional *command* (imperative) than a conditional *norm*.

Primarily, norms are rules of action. As we already noted (p. 411), it is not clear by itself which action the norm expressed by '*Op*' enjoins, when '*p*' describes a state of affairs. If this state does not obtain, the norm enjoins us to produce it or not to prevent its coming into existence. If this state obtains, the norm enjoins us to forbear its destruction or, as the case may be, actively to preserve it. The presence and absence of the state constitute the two *conditions of application*, as I shall call them, for the norm.[42] Generally speaking: the conditions of application of a categorical norm are the set of all possible 'state-descriptions' in the terms of the given norm-content. Thus, for the norm expressed by '$O(p \vee q)$' the four conditions of application are the states described by '$p \,\&\, q$', '$p \,\&\, \sim q$', '$\sim p \,\&\, q$', and '$\sim p \,\&\, \sim q$'.

If a norm is designed to guide action only under *some* but not *all* of its conditions of application, this will have to be stated in a full formulation of the norm. (In the case of singular imperatives it is usually clear from the context and often also from the wording which the conditions of application are; therefore the norm may be formulated in a categorical disguise.) Thus, if *Op* enunciates an order to see to it that a state which is not yet there shall prevail, the form of the norm is, in fact, $\sim p \rightarrow Op$. If the order is to apply under all conceivable circumstances, it can be split into two, *viz.* $\sim p \rightarrow Op$ and $p \rightarrow Op$. The conjunction of these two formulas is equivalent with $p \vee \sim p \rightarrow Op$ and this reduces to *Op*. Categorical norms may thus be regarded as a *limiting case* of conditional norms.[43]

One can make a distinction between two types of conditional norm. Some norms are made conditional upon the prevailing of *some* only of all conceivable conditions of application of the corresponding categorical norm – as in $p \rightarrow Op$. Other norms are conditional upon the prevailing of some state which is logically independent of the conditions of application of the corresponding categorical norm – like $p \rightarrow Oq$.

Often the two types occur mixed. The formula $p \,\&\, {\sim}q \rightarrow Oq$, for example, says that if it is the case that p but not also that q, then q ought to be the case. What ought an agent to whom this norm is addressed to do? Normally, he should act in such a way that it comes about that q. Suppose, however, that instead he acts so that it is no longer the case that p. If the order is 'if fire breaks out sound the alarm!' and fire breaks out, the best thing to do may be to extinguish it at once, thus annihilating the condition under which the order applies. If there is no categorical norm enjoining that it be the case that q, this may be a thoroughly reasonable reaction to the *situation*. But it is not the adequate reaction to the *order*.

9. A notorious problem in legal philosophy has been the status of permissive norms. It is natural that the difficulties surrounding the concept of permission should also have been reflected in debates within deontic logic.

There are two main stands on the disputed questions. According to the one position, permission just consists in the absence of a ('corresponding') prohibition. According to the opposed view, permission is something 'over and above', absence of prohibition.

In the first view, the two deontic operators, O and P, are interdefinable. In the second view, it is at least uncertain whether they are interdefinable.[44] It is not surprising if logicians, for reasons of simplicity and elegance and maybe also under the impact of the analogy with modal logic, have been strongly attracted by the first view. It has been the dominant view in deontic logic. From this does not follow that it is the philosophically most satisfying view.

The controversy between the two positions is related to the debate about 'gaps in the law'. If we accept the interdefinability view, every state of affairs or action will, within a given system of norms, have a determined 'deontic status', *i.e.* will be either forbidden or permitted. The system is necessarily deontically *closed*. In the opposite view, a system of norms may be deontically *open, i.e.* there can exist states or actions which, although they are not forbidden by any norm of the system, are nevertheless not permitted either. Their deontic status is left *undecided* by the system.

If one is anxious to cater for the possibility of open systems, one can introduce a distinction between *strong* and *weak* permission.[45] Anything which is not forbidden can be said to be, by definition, 'permitted' in the weak sense. But within an open system, weak permission does not count as a deontic status. Only strong permission does.

It is reasonable to think that a good many, if not all, legal obligations lay down necessary conditions of immunity to punishment. The well-known juristic principle *nulla poena sine lege* or *nullum crimen sine lege* can serve as a norm permitting all non-forbidden acts. It may be regarded as a characteristic of a *Rechtsstaat* that the principle should function in this way. The purpose of the norm is then to close the legal order with regard to all actions. Thereby the distinction between strong and weak permission becomes superfluous.[46]

It is of some interest, I think, to study systems of deontic logic which reject the interdefinability of the operators O and P and reckon with two deontic primitives. In order to be reasonable, such systems would have to accept the formula $Pp \to \sim O \sim p$ which says that if something is permitted it is not forbidden. This would presumably be an axiom of such systems. The converse formula $\sim O \sim p \to Pp$ is rejected.

If one wanted to build a system with two deontic primitives but otherwise deviating minimally from the received systems of deontic logic, then the following axioms seem feasible:

A1. $O(p \,\&\, q) \leftrightarrow Op \,\&\, Oq$
A2. $P(p \vee q) \leftrightarrow Pp \vee Pq$
A3. $Op \to Pp$
A4. $Pp \to \sim O \sim p$

The formula $\sim O \sim t$ which is an axiom of the standard system, is now a theorem. The decision problem of the system is easily solved.

10. As noted, the standard system allows iteration of the deontic operators. This, however, is a purely 'formal' admission and does not, by itself, warrant a meaningful use of iterated deontic modalities in prescriptive and other kinds of normative discourse.

On the formal level, the admission of higher order deontic expressions challenges the question whether such formulas obey peculiar logical laws in addition to the laws of first order formulas. Are, for example, reduction principles corresponding to those of the modal systems S4 and S5 valid for the deontic modalities?

Such questions, obviously, cannot be answered by appealing to 'intuition' but only on the basis of considerations of 'interpretation'. The following initial observation of a formal logical character, however, should be mentioned:

The system S5 of normal modal logic contains the system S4. In S5 all higher order modal expressions are reducible to first order expressions. The distinguishing axiom of S5 is the formula $MNp \rightarrow Np$. That of S4 is $Np \rightarrow NNp$. The deontic analogues of these formulas are $POp \rightarrow Op$ and $Op \rightarrow OOp$ respectively. Standard deontic logic, it should be remembered, is *not* the analogue of a normal modal logic but of a deviant one. (Above p. 402.) In the modal system which corresponds to standard deontic logic, the formulas $MNp \rightarrow Np$ and $Np \rightarrow NNp$ are independent. If, therefore, we wanted to build a deontic logic containing the principle $POp \rightarrow Op$, this would not commit us to accept also the principle $Op \rightarrow OOp$. Nor would $POp \rightarrow Op$ entail that all deontic expressions are reducible to expressions of the first order.

I do not think, incidentally, that either one of the two formulas just mentioned can claim for itself the status of a truth of (deontic) logic. But it seems to me that some systems of norms might satisfy one or the other of the formulas. That a system satisfies $POp \rightarrow Op$ means that everything which may be obligatory *is* in fact obligatory, – for example because a norm-authority actually has enjoined all those things which he is entitled to enjoin. That this should be the case is perhaps not unreasonable, in particular if the norm-authority in question holds his permission to issue orders from some superior source.

The problems in this region deserve a much more throughgoing study than they have so far received. Of particular interest would be to investigate hierarchies of norms to which correspond hierarchies of superior and subordinate norm-giving authorities. A promising beginning of such study is made in a paper by W. H. Hanson.[47] In order to express in a symbolic language the hierarchical relations, however, means are needed which are essentially richer than those of the standard system or of any extension of it known to me. It also seems to me doubtful whether a deontic logic built in analogy with a modal logic will be adequate for the purpose.

11. All through its modern history deontic logic has been beset by some 'anomalies' or 'paradoxes' which have engendered much controversy and discussion.

Oldest of these anomalies is presumably the one known as Ross's Paradox. It was first noted by the eminent Danish jurist and legal philosopher Alf Ross and was used by him as a counter-argument against the very possibility of building a logic of norms.[48]

As is well known, the 'paradox' is the fact that the formula $Op \rightarrow O(p \vee q)$ is a theorem of most systems of deontic logic. If one ought to mail a letter, one ought to mail or burn it – to use Ross's famed example. Or, speaking in the language of *Seinsollen*: If it ought to be the case that a letter is mailed, it ought also to be the case that it is mailed or burnt.

It is no exaggeration to say that the literature dealing with this anomaly is enormous. To a great extent it has been spilled ink. Many systems of deontic logic have been constructed in which the Ross's Paradox formula is not provable.[49] Some such systems may have special virtues – but the mere fact that they avoid the paradox cannot, in my opinion, be regarded as highly meritorious. The best attitude to the problem is one which I propose to call 'relaxed'. What I mean can be explained as follows:

An order has been given to someone to mail a letter. If he does not mail the letter but does something else instead, he has not satisfied *that* order. If the order was seriously meant, he may have to suffer evil for neglect of duty. He cannot excuse himself on the ground that he carried out *another* order which, he claims, was entailed by the order to mail the letter. The giver of the order can agree that that other order was entailed; the question whether it is or not is irrelevant to what he wanted the recipient of the order to effect. Perhaps the other thing which the agent did was something prohibited. Then he can be reproached or punished for having done it as well as for not having mailed the letter. Again he cannot excuse himself by saying that in doing the forbidden thing he carried out an order which, by implication, had been given to him. He ought indeed to have carried out that other order too, – but by mailing the letter and not by doing something else. Admitting that Op entails $O(p \vee q)$ is of no consequence for the way orders function or for the ground on which they are issued. This is what I mean by saying that we can take a 'relaxed' attitude to Ross's Paradox.

The much discussed paradoxes of Commitment and the Good Samaritan can be regarded as versions of Ross's Paradox. The first then consists in the provability of the formula $O{\sim}p \rightarrow O(p \rightarrow q)$ and the second in that of the formula $O{\sim}p \rightarrow O{\sim}(p \,\&\, q)$. But these two paradoxes can also be presented in more elaborate versions which are interesting and deserve special attention. I shall not discuss them here.

Another, and in my opinion much more serious, puzzle which I wanted to mention concerns norms with disjunctive content. For example: 'it ought (is permitted) to be the case that p or that q' – and the corresponding *Tunsollen*-norm 'one ought (is permitted) to p or to q'.

Consider first the permissive norms. On the normal understanding of language, the form of words 'you may read or write' would be understood as a permission to choose freely between the two actions, or do both of them. A permission, thus understood, I have called *free choice permission.*[50] Permissions of this nature seem to obey a distribution rule which in the formal language is expressed by the equivalence $P(p \vee q) \leftrightarrow Pp \,\&\, Pq$. Its introduction into the classical or standard systems, however, instantly leads to absurdities.

A similar observation can be made on obligation norms. If I tell somebody that he ought to read or write, the normal way of understanding this is that he ought to do at least one of the two things and may do either. The obligatory character of the disjunctive action entails its permitted character; and that the disjunctive action is permitted entails that the agent is free to choose whether he is going to avail himself of the one or the other of the alternatives offered him.

Some logicians and philosophers see no genuine difficulty here at all.[51] The appearance of a puzzle is attributed to an accident of language. 'Or' sometimes simply means 'and'. This observation may, as such, be correct. But I do not think it enough to resolve the puzzle.[52] This is, in my opinion, convincingly shown by the example with disjunctive obligations. 'You ought to *p* or to *q*'. Surely 'or' here stands for disjunction and *not* for conjunction. The order is to do at least one of two actions, the presumption being that the choice between them is free, *i.e.* that one may choose the one, but also the other, or do both.

That the puzzle must be taken seriously is also shown, I think, by the following consideration: If I am ordered to *p* or to *q* and cannot take it for granted that both actions are allowed, then one of the actions may be forbidden – and I run the risk that, in doing my duty, I do what is forbidden. The situation is *not* analogous with the case in Ross's Paradox. If I am ordered to *p* but as a matter of fact do *q* which is forbidden, I cannot excuse myself with the pretext that an order to *p* entails an order to *p* or *q* and that by *q*'ing I was satisfying this second order. (Cf. above p. 416f.) The giver of the order may admit that in ordering *p*'ing to be done he was ordering *p*'ing or *q*'ing to be done. But he had also made it quite clear what the recipient of the order had to do, *viz*. to *p* – and thereby to satisfy both the explicitly given and any implicitly entailed order. But if I am ordered to *p* or to *q* and cannot assume that it is up to me to choose between the two actions, then I simply do not know what I am supposed to do. If I am not allowed this assumption, the order sounds like a cheat or, at best, a riddle.

How then shall one resolve the difficulty? One can build a

contradiction-free deontic logic in which permission distributes conjunctively over disjunctive contents. But it is doubtful whether this construction does not itself give rise to new anomalies and complications, if it is carried out using the same conceptual and symbolic apparatus as the one employed in traditional deontic logic either of the *Seinsollen* or of the *Tunsollen* variety. I shall conclude this essay with a sketch of a deontic logic which departs radically from the traditional models and which seems to possess some advantages over them.

12. The proposal which I am going to make is that permittedness and obligatoriness be treated, not as modal operators, but as *properties* of *individual actions*. Individual actions will be represented by variables *x*, *y*, *etc*. The properties of permittedness and obliagatoriness will be symbolized by $\mathscr{P}$ and $\mathscr{O}$ respectively. The variables *p*, *q*, *etc*. shall represent *generic states* – for example that a man is killed or a door is open or a cigarette lit.

$\mathscr{P}x$ says that x is permitted, $\sim\mathscr{P}x$ that x is not permitted. It will be assumed that not-permitted means the same as forbidden.[53] The formula $[p]x$ shall mean that the action x results in the state of affairs that p, – for example in that a certain door is open. It is important to distinguish between $\sim[p]x$ which says that the action x does not result in the state that p, and $[\sim p]x$ which says that the action results in the contradictory state – for example in that the door in question is closed (= not open).

For action sentences I propose the following set of axioms:[54]

A1. $[\sim p]x \rightarrow \sim[p]x$

A2. $[\sim\sim p]x \leftrightarrow [p]x$

A3. $[p \,\&\, q]x \leftrightarrow [p]x \,\&\, [q]x$

A4. $[\sim(p \,\&\, q]x \leftrightarrow [\sim p]x \vee [\sim q]x$

The rules of inference are those of substitution and detachment and, if quantifiers are introduced, the usual rule for binding free variables. Furthermore, all tautologies of PL are theorems of this logic, when action sentences are substituted for the variables. By definition, '$p \vee q$' shall mean the same as $\sim(\sim p \,\&\, \sim q)$.

Consider now the formula $(x)([p]x \rightarrow \mathscr{P}x)$. It says that every action is permitted which results in that (it is the case that) p. That is: (all) actions of this category or type are permitted.

If in the formula which says that actions of a certain type are permitted we substitute '$p \vee q$' for 'p' and distribute the expression $[p \vee q]x$ according to A4 of our action logic, then we obtain by the rules of propositional and predicate logic the following result: Actions resulting in that at least one of two states obtains are permitted if, and only if, actions resulting in that the one state obtains *and* actions resulting in that the other state obtains are permitted. This agrees with the common way of understanding disjunctive permissions: they present the agent with a choice between permitted alternatives. (Above p. 416f.)

That actions of a certain type are forbidden is expressed by the formula $(x)([p]x \rightarrow \sim \mathscr{P} x)$. If actions of a certain type are forbidden, then one ought to see to it that all individual actions are such that they do not result in the forbidden state (*i.e.* the state which is such that actions resulting in it are forbidden). This is *one* sense of 'obligation'.

Consider the formula $(x)(\sim[p]x \rightarrow \sim \mathscr{P} x)$. It says that every action is forbidden which does not result in that (it is the case that) p. When everything one does is such that it is forbidden unless it results in that p, then actions resulting in that p are in yet another and stronger sense obligatory.

It is easy to see that a conjunctive state is, in this strong sense, obligatory if, and only if, each conjunct is obligatory. $(x)(\sim[p \& q]x \rightarrow \sim \mathscr{P} x)$ is equivalent with $(x)(\sim[p]x \rightarrow \sim \mathscr{P} x) \& (x)(\sim[q]x \rightarrow \sim \mathscr{P} x)$. This is what answers in the deontic logic we are now building to the distribution principle $O(p \& q) \leftrightarrow Op \& Oq$. Some people have expressed doubts about this formula.[55]

The above obligation concept may be thought too strong to be of much significance to a theory of norms. This is probably true. But when applied to an individual action a, the formula $\sim[p]a \rightarrow \sim \mathscr{P} a$ makes perfectly good sense. It is the norm-proposition which answers to the imperative 'do p!'. Within the framework of the new deontic logic one can also construct a logic of *imperatives* (as distinct from *norms* or *rules*).

The formula $(x)([p \& q]x \rightarrow \mathscr{P} x)$ does not entail $(x)([p]x \rightarrow \mathscr{P} x)$. From the fact that the state or action is permitted which consists in the conjunction of two states or actions it does not follow that each conjunct by itself is permitted. This is in harmony with our intuitions and explains why people sometimes doubted the formula $P(p \& q) \rightarrow Pp$ which is a theorem of standard and classical deontic logic.[56]

The distribution properties and related features of permissions and obligations follow from the definitions of the deontic notions in combination with principles of action logic alone. No specific deontic axioms are needed.

It is different with the Principle of Permission, answering to A2 of the standard and classical systems. It cannot be proved on the basis so far sketched. It must be assumed axiomatically, if we wish to have it in our deontic logic at all.

In action logic we can prove $\sim[p \,\&\, \sim p]\, x$. No action is such that it results both in a state and its contradictory. Since this is provable, $(x)([p \,\&\, \sim p]\, x \rightarrow \mathscr{P}\, x)$ is also provable. This means that, on our definitions, actions which result in contradictory states are permitted. But this is no reason for concern. Such actions cannot be performed and, moreover, their permittedness does not – as in traditional deontic logic – entail the permittedness of actions resulting in just any state. (Cf. above p. 402f.)

The formula $[p \vee \sim p]\, x$ is *not* a theorem of action logic. Not just any action is one which either result in that p or in that $\sim p$. Hence $(x)(\sim [p \vee \sim p]\; x \rightarrow \sim \mathscr{P} x)$ is *not* a logical truth. If one calls the action 'tautologous' which results either in a certain state or in its opposite, one can say that it is a feature of our new deontic logic that it does not commit us to regard 'tautologous' actions as obligatory.

The deontic logic which I have been sketching differs considerably from the traditional one. It accords much better, it would seem, with our 'intuitions' concerning normative discourse. It is also much more powerful in that it from the very start allows quantification.

Further discussion of the proposed new logic will have to center, I think, round two questions. One concerns the notion of a *result of action*. What does it mean to say that an action results in a certain state? This is a question for the philosophy of action to answer. I shall not say anything about it here. The other question concerns the feasibility of treating permittedness and obligatoriness as *properties*. On this question I shall only say the following:

If the ground for pronouncing individual actions permitted or obligatory is that they instantiate characteristics which stand in conditionship (requirement) relations to certain other characteristics ('ends'), then it is certainly quite in order to regard permittedness and obligatoriness as properties of those individual actions. If in the Andersonian reduction schema we substitute '$[p]\, x$' for 'p' we get $O[p]\, x =_{\text{df}} N(\sim[p]\, x \rightarrow S)$. It says that it is obligatory that an action x results in the state that p if, and only if, the fact that the action does not result in this state necessarily implies a certain other state of affairs, the Andersonian 'bad thing'. We can now introduce the property 'obligatoriness' by means of the definition $\mathscr{O}\, x =_{\text{df}} (Ep)([p]\, x \,\&\, (x)(\sim[p]\, x \rightarrow S))$. According to this an individual action is obligatory if, and only if, its performance results in some state such that any action which does not result in that state implies the 'bad thing'.

Traditional deontic logic was born as an off-shoot of modal logic. Was this a happy birth or a miscarriage? I am afraid we must say that it was not an *altogether* happy birth. Perhaps a reason why deontic logic has aroused such lively interest has been an implicit feeling that the whole enterprise was problematic. The symptoms of illness were the existence of various anomalies and the fact that doubt could be raised on intuitive grounds about the validity of so many of its formulas. It remains to be investigated whether the new conception which I have here proposed and which treats of the basic deontic categories as properties instead of as modal operators perhaps represents a sounder and more fertile approach to the logical study of normative discourse.

Helsinki, Finland

NOTES

[1] Ludwig Wittgenstein, *Letters to C. K. Ogden*, Basil Blackwell, Oxford and Kegan Paul, London 1973, letter of 23 April, 1922, p. 20.

[2] It was the vision of such a General Theory that inspired my first and major contribution to modal logic, *An Essay in Modal Logic*, North-Holland Publ. Co., Amsterdam, 1951.

[3] In Leibniz, *Sämtliche Schriften und Briefe*, ed. by Preussische Akademie der Wissenschaften, 6. Reihe, Vol. I, Otto Reichl Verlag, Darmstadt, 1930.

[4] Leibniz, *op. cit.*, p. 469; *An Essay in Modal Logic*, p. v.

[5] With Leibniz actually a quadruple of concepts, since he also noted the analogy between the facultative and the contingent.

[6] A. Höfler, 'Abhängigkeitsbeziehungen zwischen Abhängigkeitsbeziehungen', Sitzungsberichte der kaiserlichen Akademie der Wissenschaften in Wien, *Philosophisch-historische Klasse* 181 (1917).

[7] The main sources among Bentham's works are *An Introduction to the Principles of Morals and Legislation*, ed. by J. H. Burns and H. L. A. Hart, London, 1970, and *Of Laws in General*, ed. by H. L. A. Hart, London, 1970.

[8] *Of Laws in General*, p. 95.

[9] A good critical account of Mally's ideas is the essay by D. Føllesdal and R. Hilpinen, 'Deontic Logic: An Introduction', in *Deontic Logic: Introductory and Systematic Readings*, ed. by Risto Hilpinen, D. Reidel Publ. Co., Dordrecht, Holland, 1971.

[10] *Untersuchungen über den Modalkalkül*, Westkulturverlag Anton Hain, Meisenheim am Glan, 1952.

[11] 'Théorie des propositions normatives', *Studia Logica* 1 (1953).

[12] 'Deontic Logic', *Mind* 60 (1951).

[13] This notion of Standard System differs from the one proposed by Bengt Hansson in 'An Analysis of some Deontic Logics', *Noûs* 3 (1969) in that it does not accept *Ot* as an axiom.

[14] Published as an appendix to *Logica deontica e semantica*, Atti del Convegno tenuto a Bielefeld 17–22 marzo 1975, ed. by G. di Bernardo, Società editrice il Mulino, Bologna, 1977.

[15] My own contributions to it are embodied, chiefly, in *Norm and Action*, Routledge and Kegan Paul, London, 1963, in *An Essay in Deontic Logic and the General Theory of Action*, North-Holland Publ. Co., Amsterdam, 1968, and in the paper 'Handlungslogik' in *Normenlogik*, ed. by H. Lenk, Verlag Dokumentation, Pullach bei München, 1974.

[16] See J. Jørgensen, 'Imperatives and Logic', *Erkenntnis* 7 (1937–1938) and Alf Ross, 'Imperatives and Logic', *Theoria* 7 (1941).

[17] Cf. W. Dubislaw, 'Zur Unbegründbarkeit der Forderungssätze'. *Theoria* 3 (1937), especially p. 238ff. Also Ross, *op. cit*., p. 55.

[18] The following quotation from Carnap, *Philosophy and Logical Syntax*, Psyche Miniatures, London, 1935, p. 23 is revealing of a tendency to assimilate to each other value judgements, norms, and imperatives: "Is it easy to see that it is merely a difference of formulation, whether we state a norm or a value judgment. A norm or rule has an imperative form. - - - actually a value statement is nothing else than a command in a misleading grammatical form."

[19] Bentham, *Of Laws in General*, p. 154.

[20] I. Hedenius, *Om rätt och moral*, Tidens Förlag, Stockholm, 1941.

[21] *Op. cit*., Ch. VI, pp. 93–106.

[22] Cf. *Norm and Action*, p. 134.

[23] *Op. cit*., p. 132ff.

[24] *Ibid.*

[25] C. E. Alchourrón, 'Logic of Norms and Logic of Normative Propositions', *Logique et Analyse* 12 (1969), and C. E. Alchourrón and E. Bulygin, *Normative Systems*, Springer Verlag, Wien, 1971.

[26] A. R. Anderson, 'A Reduction of Deontic Logic to Alethic Modal Logic', *Mind* 67 (1958). A very similar proposal had been made by Stig Kanger in an unpublished paper from the year 1950.

[27] Cf. P. H. Nowell-Smith and E. J. Lemmon, 'Escapism: The Logical Basis of Ethics', *Mind* 69 (1960).

[28] 'On the Logic and Ontology of Norms', *Philosophical Logic*, ed. by J. W. Davis, D. J. Hockney, and W. K. Wilson, D. Reidel, Publ. Co., Dordrecht, Holland, 1969.

[29] This problem is discussed, for example, by Hans Kelsen in his classic works *Reine Rechtslehre*, Deuticke, Wien, 1934; and *General Theory of Law and State*, Harvard University Press, Cambridge, Mass., 1949; and in the paper 'Recht und Logik', *Neues Forum* 12 (1965). See also O. Weinberger, *Rechtslogik*, Springer Verlag, Wien, 1970.

[30] Becker, *op. cit*., p. 41; Kalinowski, *op. cit*., p. 147, 'Deontic Logic', p. 2.

[31] 'Quantifiers in Deontic Logic', Societas Scientiarum Fennica, *Commentationes Humanarum Litterarum* 23 (1957).

[32] A. N. Prior, *Formal Logic*, Oxford University Press, London, 1955.

[33] A. R. Anderson, 'The Formal Analysis of Normative Systems', Technical Report No. 2, Contract No. SAR/Nonr-609 (16), Office of Naval Research, Group Psychology Branch, New Haven, 1956, reprinted in *The Logic of Decision and Action*, ed. by N. Rescher, University of Pittsburgh Press, Pittsburgh, 1967.

[34] The same view was expressly taken by Becker, *op. cit*., p. 41.

[35] Cf. my papers 'Deontic Logic Revisited', *Rechtstheorie* 4 (1973); and 'Handlungslogik' in *Normenlogik*, ed. by H. Lenk, Verlag Dokumentation. Pullach bei München, 1974.

[36] Deviant systems of a *Tunsollen*-logic are presented in 'Deontic Logic Revisited' and in my essay 'Normenlogik' in *Normenlogik*, ed. by H. Lenk.
[37] Cf. D. Føllesdal and R. Hilpinen, 'Deontic Logic: An Introduction', p. 14.
[38] Cf. H. Lenk, 'Zur logischen Symbolisierung bedingter Normsätze', in *Normenlogik*, ed. by H. Lenk, Verlag Dokumentation, Pullach bei München, 1974.
[39] Rescher's earliest dyadic system was presented in 'An Axiom System for Deontic Logic', *Philsophical Studies* 9 (1958).
[40] My first attempt was in 'A Note on Deontic Logic and Derived Obligation', *Mind* 65 (1956).
[41] 'An Analysis of some Deontic Logics', *Noûs* 3 (1969).
[42] On this notion see *Norm and Action*, p. 74f., p. 178f., and *passim*.
[43] *Ibid.*, p. 177f.
[44] Rejecting the interdefinability of the operators in the sense of the classical system does not exclude restoring their interdefinability within some richer system of deontic logic. Hintikka has argued, I think convincingly, that only in a deontic logic which allows quantification over act-individuals can one capture correctly the intended meaning of the definition 'O' $=_{\text{df}}$ '$\sim P \sim$'. Cf. his paper 'Some Main Problems of Deontic Logic' in *Deontic Logic: Introductory and Systematic Readings*, ed. by Risto Hilpinen, D. Reidel Publ. Co. Dordrecht, Holland, 1971.
[45] As far as I know, this distinction was first made in my paper 'On the Logic of Negation', Societas Scientiarum Fennica, *Commentationes Physico-mathematicae* 22, 1959.
[46] The problem of 'gaps' and of open and closed systems is extensively and penetratingly discussed in C. E. Alchourrón and E. Bulygin, *Normative Systems*, Springer-Verlag, Wien, 1971.
[47] W. H. Hanson, 'A Logic of Commands,' *Logique et Analyse* 9 (1966).
[48] The *locus classicus* is Ross's paper 'Imperatives and Logic', *Theoria* 7 (1941).
[49] In any reasonable logic of the *Tunsollen* it is almost certain that the Ross's Paradox formula will, not in its *general* form, be derivable. How small this gain is, however, can be seen from the paper by I. Ruzsa, 'Semantics for von Wright's Latest Deontic Logic', *Studia Logica* 35 (1976).
[50] *An Essay in Deontic Logic and the General Theory of Action*, p. 22.
[51] Cf. D. Føllesdal and R. Hilpinen, 'Deontic Logic: An Introduction', p. 22f.
[52] For further discussion of the problem, see H. Kamp, 'Free Choice Permission', *Proceedings of the Aristotelian Society* 74 (1973–1974).
[53] If one wants to build a deontic logic which distinguishes between strong and weak permission, one must use a predicate logic in which one can distinguish between ('merely') denying that a thing has a certain property and affirming that a thing lacks a certain property. For a predicate logic satisfying this requirement, see my paper 'Remarks on the Logic of Predication', *Ajatus* 35 (1973).
[54] The axioms are the same as those of my papers 'Deontic Logic Revisited' and 'Handlungslogik' referred to above, but with the following difference: here the variables *p, q, etc.* represent states of affairs and not types of action, and the variables *x, etc.* represent individual actions and not individual agents.
[55] Cf. L. Bergström, 'Utilitarianism and Deontic Logic', *Analysis* 29 (1968).
[56] Cf. 'Deontic Logic Revisited', p. 31f. and 'Normenlogik', p. 44f.

BAS C. VAN FRAASSEN

REPORT ON TENSE LOGIC*

ABSTRACT. Tense logic is a very young subject; in its current form it began with Prior's book *Time and Modality* (1957). An excellent chronological bibliography can be found in Rescher and Urquhart *Temporal Logic* (1971). I shall here survey important recent developments with special attention to two problems: how can tense be combined with modal operators and conditionals, and, can the past and future operators be eliminated in favour of operators which 'pay no attention' to the direction of time? As final preliminary, we must distinguish between temporal logic and tense logic. In this report I am concerned with the latter. By 'a tensed proposition' I mean whatever is expressed by such sentences as 'Professor Cohen has been happy', 'I am happy', and 'The translator will always be happy'.

Most of the topics covered in this paper are treated more fully in my other papers listed in the bibliography.

1. MODELS FOR TENSE LOGIC

The history of tense logic proper began with Prior's insight:

1. Tensed propositions are propositional functions, with times as arguments.

The values of a propositional function are propositions of course. A model for tense logic needs therefore two main ingredients: a model *T* for time and a model *P* for the family of propositions. The family of tensed propositions can then be constructed, by making a number of decisions about them, answering such questions as:

(1) (a) are they full or partial functions?
(b) are they one-place functions, or many-place?

In answer to 1(a), R. H. Thomason used partial functions (produced by supervaluations) to accommodate the indeterminacy seen in Aristotle's sea battle example. Hans Kamp, in effect, made tensed propositions two-place functions in his study of 'now'. But in most work on tense-logic, tensed propositions have been treated as full, one-place functions; let me call this *orthodox* tense logic.

In orthodox tense logic, most of the effort went to attempts to describe the structure of tensed propositions given different models of time. The

E. Agazzi (ed.), Modern Logic – A Survey, 425–438.

simplest structure has the real line as T; the most reasonable general structure (or most general reasonable structure) makes T a partially ordered set. In that case, branches in T are viewed as belonging to different possible histories; but this seems to amount to exactly the same thing as keeping T linearly ordered and saying that the propositions are about world histories.

This brings us to propositions. These have been reified most simply as truth values one and zero; less simply as sets of possible worlds; and these possible worlds may have structures or relations on them, or historical structure. In all cases, however, as far as I know, the family of propositions has been taken to be a Boolean algebra, possibly with additional operators.

To make this account concrete, I shall construct two tense logical models; the second, more complex one will be used through the remainder of the paper.

FIRST MODEL. Time is the real line R, and the propositions are the truth values 1 and 0. The tensed propositions are all the functions from R into $\{0, 1\}$; let us call this family *TP*. The following operators can be defined for A, B in *TP*:

$$
\begin{aligned}
\neg A:&\quad \neg A(t) = 1 - A(t)\\
A \& B:&\quad (A \& B)(t) = A(t) \cdot B(t)\\
FA:&\quad FA(t) = 1 \text{ iff } \exists t' > t(A(t') = 1)\\
GA:&\quad GA(t) = 1 \text{ iff } \forall t' > t(A(t') = 1)\\
PA:&\quad PA(t) = 1 \text{ iff } \exists t' < t(A(t') = 1)\\
HA:&\quad HA(t) = 1 \text{ iff } \forall t' < t(A(t') = 1)
\end{aligned}
$$

We can read 'FA' as "It will (at some time) be the case that A" and 'GA' as "It will always (henceforth) be the case that A"; the past tense operators P and H can be read analogously; and of course, G is $\neg F \neg$ and H is $\neg P \neg$.

SECOND (GENERAL) MODEL. Time is still the real line R, but the propositions are now the subsets of a set K of possible worlds, and each world x in K has associated with it a history h_x, which is a map of R into a certain set H, the space of possible instantaneous states of the worlds. The state of world x at time t is $h_x(t)$.

A proposition may be called *historical* if a world belongs to it or not depending on its history – that is, if $h_x = h_y$ then x belongs iff y does. Other propositions are *ahistorical*. The tautology K is, trivially, a historical proposition, but the proposition that the world is created by God is ahistorical if we assume that for each (or some) possible world created by God there is another, uncreated one with the same history. Another example is provided by two worlds, in one of which certain regularities hold due to physical laws (laws of nature), and in the other exactly the same things happen by chance. Less metaphysical propositions may be ahistorical in the model if in describing H we leave out constant factors. For instance, if H is the phase-space of a pendulum bob, we leave out such details as the material of which the bob is made.

Let $X \subseteq H$. Then a *prime historical proposition* is

$$X_t^* = \{x \in K: h_x(t) \in X\}.$$

There is a corresponding (present-) tensed proposition

$$X^*: X^*(t) = X_t^*.$$

So X^* is true in world x at time t exactly if $h_x(t)$ is in X. Other historical propositions will be discussed below.

What are arbitrary tensed propositions like? Well, if A is tensed, and t a time, then $A(t)$ is a set of worlds. Hence we can induce operations:

$$\begin{aligned}
\neg A(t) &= K - A(t)\\
(A \& B)(t) &= A(t) \cap B(t)\\
FA(t) &= \{x: \exists t' > t(x \in A(t'))\}\\
GA(t) &= \{x: \forall t' > t(x \in A(t'))\}\\
PA(t) &= \{x: \exists t' < t(x \in A(t'))\}\\
HA(t) &= \{x: \forall t' < t(x \in A(t'))\}.
\end{aligned}$$

Of course we call *A true in x at t* exactly if x is in $A(t)$.

As I said above, K is a historical proposition. It is a limiting case, a *constant* proposition. Such propositions can be constructed by such phrases as "was from the beginning, is, and always shall be":

(2) $$(HA \;\&\; A \;\&\; GA)(t) = \{x: (\forall t)(x \in A(t))\}$$

which has a truth value independent of t.

2. TENSED MODALITIES

Kit Fine, Hans Kamp, Peter Schotch, Richmond Thomason, Roger Woolhouse, and various other writers have discussed tensed modalities. The central insight, explicitly expressed by Woolhouse, is, it seems to me:

(II) Modal qualifiers in general turn untensed sentences into tensed ones.

Expressed about models, this means that modal operators turn constant tensed propositions into non-constant ones; and deeper yet, ahistorical propositions into historical ones.

Of course, some modalities do not act like this. If something is logically necessary then it always was and always will be so. But this is not typical:

(3) (a) In 1930 it was still possible to avert the population explosion, but by 1950 it was too late.

(b) I did not always believe that $2.2 = 4$ and I do not believe Fermat's last theorem, though I may do so yet.

Belief is surely the most general modality in this respect. I shall now discuss briefly Thomason's 'settled', Woolhouse's 'physically necessary', and belief; then address a problem about the introduction of conditionals recently raised by Thomason.

2.1. *What is Historically Settled*

Let us say that worlds x and y *agree through* time t exactly if their histories are the same up to and including t. *Settled at* time t in world x are exactly those propositions to which belong all worlds agreeing with x through t.

We have a corresponding operator on propositions:

(4) $SA(t) = \{x\colon \forall y (\text{if } y \text{ agrees through } t \text{ with } x \text{ then } y \text{ is in } A(t))\}$.

Since agreement through t is an equivalence relation, S is a sort of tensed S5 necessity. Moreover, what is settled is true:

(5) $SA(t) \subseteq A(t)$

Explicating Aristotle's seabattle, Thomason took a tensed proposition to be true if and only if settled, and false iff its denial is settled.

2.2. *What is Physically Necessary*

If the possible worlds are also exactly those which are physically possible, then being settled at t is one possible candidate for being physically necessary at t. But Woolhouse pointed to a different meaning, in which what is physically necessary may not remain so. This allows for a tacit *ceteris paribus* clause in the modal operator.

One example comes from a certain interpretation of quantum mechanics. Suppose we say that something about system X is physically necessary at t, iff it receives probability 1 given the quantum mechanical state of X at t. Von Neumann allowed, besides the usual deterministic evolution of state also 'acausal transitions', notably during measurement. Hence predictions based on the present state may be false when tested, namely if one of these acausal transitions has meanwhile occurred.

Another example, not so exciting, is this: suppose we say that this bell must ring when pushed, or this computer must solve a certain problem if that is fed to it. In that case there is a tacit 'because' ("because the bell is in working order, because the computer has been programmed in a certain way"). This 'because' may become false. Pure present tensed propositions are true if necessary (in this sense), but future or past tensed ones need not be.

We can explicate this by introducing a relation of being physically ideal with respect to world x at t, which world y bears to it if $h_x(t) = h_y(t)$ and x and y are 'programmed' in the same way at t, but in addition, this program is 'carried out' in y. Let us call this relation R_t. The corresponding operator is

$$(6) \qquad LA(t) = \{x: \forall y \text{ (if } xR_ty \text{ then } y \in A(t))\}.$$

We know very little about this relation; it is certainly not intended to be an equivalence relation. But recalling the prime historical proposition X^* (with $X \subseteq H$, the state space), we see that $LA(t) \subseteq GLA(t)$ is not the case in general, nor is $LA(t) \subseteq A(t)$; but

$$(7) \qquad LX^*(t) \subseteq X^*(t)$$

does hold. (Note: this short sketch leaves out some main features of Woolhouse's formal language in which present tense and necessity are combined with chronologically definite propositions. Also, Woolhouse in effect chose a weaker relation than R_t, so that present tense propositions need not be true if necessary.)

2.3. *What is Believed*

Lines 5 and 7 above show that 'settled' and 'necessary' obey certain rules connecting modalized propositions with what actually happens. No such rule can hold for belief, since logically there is no relation between truth and belief at all.

However, as Hintikka first explained, belief can be modelled by introducing the relation a world bears to this one exactly if it is compatible with what is believed here. Properties of this relation will only connect propositions about belief with other propositions about belief; for example, perhaps if something is believed then it follows that it is believed that this is indeed believed. That compatiblity relation can of course be seen to change with time, so we may call it B_t and define the corresponding operator:

(8) $BA(t) = \{x: \forall y \text{ (if } xB_t y \text{ then } y \in A(t))\}$.

For example if X^* is the proposition that it is raining then $FBFX^*$ is the proposition that it will be believed that it will rain: world x is in $FBFX^*(t)$ exactly if it is believed in x at some time t' after t that it will rain at some yet later time t'' after t'. (As I shall discuss below, this is not the only, and perhaps not the most obvious meaning of that English sentence which I used to express the proposition.)

3. COUNTERFACTUAL CONDITIONALS COMBINED WITH TENSE AND MODALITY

In each of the above cases we introduced a single new modality, and there is no guarantee that the story will stay so simple if several are introduced at once. Indeed, that is does not was found by Thomason when he brought counterfactual conditionals into his logic of what is historically settled.

By means of examples, he argues that the following conditions must be fulfilled (where I shall now write '$A, B \Vdash C$' for '$A(t) \cap B(t) \subseteq C(t)$ for all times t' when A, B, C are tensed propositions):

(A) $\neg S \neg A,\ SB \Vdash A \rightarrow B$
(B) $S \neg A,\ S(A \rightarrow B),\ A \rightarrow SA \Vdash A \rightarrow SB$
(C) $S \neg A,\ S(A \rightarrow B) \Vdash A \rightarrow S(A \supset B)$
(D) $S \neg A,\ S(A \rightarrow B) \nVdash A \rightarrow SB$.

Note that the last one is a case of a principle which is said *not* to hold. The crucial example is: Suppose it is settled that I shall not take the local bus (at any time to come), and also settled that if I were to take the local 20 minutes from now, I would be late for work; it does not follow that if I were to take the local in 20 minutes it would be settled that I would be late. For the possibility of modus ponens clearly shows that the consequent is about *now*, and the antecedent does not say that *it is settled* that I shall take the local – only that it happens to be true. (Please note that in the present discussion I am not taking *true* to be equivalent to *settled*, but am allowing a future tense statement to be true on the basis of the actual future history of the world; the propriety of doing this follows from the way Thomason handles these distinctions, and the example is essentially the same as his.)

In order to fulfill desiderata (A)–(D) Thomason decided to change (or rather, add to) the meaning of 'settled': he proposed that this also have counterfactual content, and that SA means that, even if the actual future histories of the relevant possible worlds were different from what in fact they are, A would still be true in all of them.

There may be independent reasons to consider this stronger notion of what is historically settled. But I shall attempt here to satisfy (A)–(D) for the old meaning of 'settled'.

In Stalnaker's (untensed, general) theory of conditionals, a *selection function* is introduced, so that if x is a world and Y is a non-empty proposition, then $s_x Y$ is also a world, 'the most similar Y-world', such that

(a) if x is in Y then $s_x Y = x$
(b) $s_x Y$ is in Y
(c) if $s_x Y$ is in Z and $s_x Z$ is in Y then $s_x Y = s_x Z$.

The conditional is defined by

$$x \text{ is in } Y \rightarrow Z \text{ iff either } Y \text{ is empty or } s_x Y \text{ is in } Z.$$

Turning now to tensed propositions $Y = A(t)$, we shall need to make the selection depend on time, so that the function and definition will be:

$$x \text{ is in } (A \rightarrow B)(t) \text{ iff } A(t) \text{ is empty or } s_x^t A(t) \text{ is in } B(t).$$

Note that in this formulation, the other world is inspected for the truthvalue of B at exactly the same time t at which the counterfactual is evaluated in x. I do not believe, for instance, that if A was true in x at some other time, we should look to the truthvalue of B in x at that other time. For instance, if I were to see a handsome pair of shoes (now), I would buy them; although on myriad occasions I have not done so.

Yet there must be special conditions on the selection function that relate to time. The first I propose is

(d) if $H_x^t \cap Y$ is not empty then $s_x^t Y$ is in H_x^t,

where H_x^t is the family of worlds in agreement with x through t. The intuitive reason is that, other things being equal, those worlds are to be considered at t as much more like x than other worlds, no matter how similar the others are to x in the future.

This new condition (d) establishes principle (A); for if x is in $\neg S \neg A(t)$ then $H_x^t \cap A(t)$ is not empty, so $s_x^t A(t)$ agrees with x through t; hence if x is in $SB(t)$, then it is in $(A \rightarrow B)(t)$. Indeed, the following stronger principle holds:

$$\neg S \neg A,\ SB \Vdash A \rightarrow SB$$

in which I would be inclined to read the conclusion as "so, *even* if A were true, B would still be settled".

The second new condition is more complicated, it is a *global* condition on the model, and does not simply relate x to the effect of a selection based on x.

(e) If $z = s_x^t Y$ then $H_z^t \cap Y \subseteq s^t Y[H_x^t]$.

Here I use the set function:

$$s^t Y[X] = \{s_x^t Y : x \in X\}.$$

So the new principle (e) says:

> if $z = s_x^t Y$ then z agrees through t with another world z' also in Y only if $z' = s_w^t Y$ for some world w which agrees through t with x.

This second principle is a consequence of the first (d) when x is in $\neg S \neg A(t)$, for in that case, all the worlds considered in the calculation agree through t with each other. Therefore the new principle is of use exactly when x is in $S \neg A(t)$; and indeed, it serves to validate (C).

For suppose that x is in $S \neg A(t)$, and in $S(A \to B)(t)$. We ask now whether $z = s_x^t A(t)$ is in $S(A \to B)(t)$. Well, if w agrees with z through t, and w is in $A(t)$, then by (e) there must be some world y such that $w = s_y^t A(t)$ and y agrees through t with x. By the second premise, $A \to B$ is also true in y at t. Hence w is in $B(t)$. So we see that $A \supset B$ is true in every world that agrees through t with z, and the answer to our question about z is yes.

We have not violated (D), for $H_z^t - A(t)$ may not be empty, and its members need not all be in $B(t)$. On the other hand (B), the remaining principle, follows from (C) provided we have

$$A \to SA,\ A \to S(A \supset B) \Vdash A \to SB,$$

and that is validated provided we have

$$SA, S(A \supset B) \Vdash SB,$$

which is certainly the case. Thus the proposed alternative theory fulfills Thomason's conditions; of course there may be further desiderata which will upset this conclusion.

We must note that in this treatment of conditionals, the allowance for ahistorical propositions (hence, the use of the logical space H) plays a significant role. This can be shown by considering the issue of determinism.

A world x is *deterministic* at t if only one possible future history is open for it at t. It is tempting to gloss this as: H_x^t has x as its only member. But that would assume that if two worlds have the same history they are identical. So we should say: x is *deterministic* at t exactly if any world y which agrees with x through t, also agrees with it through all later times (that is, $h_x = h_y$).

Let us suppose now that $B(t)$ is the proposition that determinism holds at t, let x be deterministic at t, and let us look at the world $z = s_x^t \neg B(t)$. Clearly z is not deterministic, so there is at least one historical proposition C which is true but not settled in z at t, hence we have a world w which agrees with z through t, while z is in $C(t)$ and w is in $\neg C(t)$. Obviously w is also not deterministic at t, so w is in $\neg B(t)$, and our postulate (f) now requires a world y, agreeing with x through t, such that $w = s_y^t \neg B(t)$.

At this point we realize that $h_x = h_y$, but $x \in (\neg B \to C)(t)$ and $y \in (\neg B \to \neg C)(t)$. It follows that the conditional $(\neg B \to C)(t)$ is an *ahistorical* (if you like, a *metaphysical*) proposition.

It should perhaps be added that the problem and solution are rather general, for we could have used some other necessity-type connective instead of S, with corresponding access relation R_t and replaced H_x^t by $\{y: xR_t y\}$. However, the meaning of the connective would determine whether the analogues of (d) and (e) could reasonably be imposed.

4. GRAMMAR OF TENSED MODALITIES

I have so far concentrated on tensed propositions, and mentioned tensed sentences in passing only. It seems easy enough to interpret each tensed sentence A as standing for a tensed proposition $A(t)$, and hence at each time t for an untensed proposition $A(-)$. But there are some features of tensed discourse that are obliterated in this simple picture. For instance, consider the sentences:

(9)(a) He believed that it would rain.
(b) He believed that it will rain.
(10)(a) He believed that it was raining.
(b) He believed that it is raining.

As was pointed out by Prior, Montague, and Kamp in connection with the word 'now', we can in orthodox tense logic symbolize only (9)(a) and (10)(a), namely as *PBFA* and *PBA* respectively. The others are equivalent to:

(9)′(b) He believed that it will rain now.
(10)′(b) He believed that it is raining now.

The word 'now' refers to the time of speaking, and it does this no matter where it appears – no matter how deeply it is embedded inside tense or modal operators.

A related problem occurs with cross-references to times as in:

(11) Sue had a high temperature and Bill believed that she was going to be ill.

This also has a tacit reference to a specific time in it and cannot be symbolized simply as $PA \,\&\, PBFA'$. Indeed, (11) is equivalent to:

(12) Sue had a high temperature and Bill believed *at that time* that she was going to be ill.

The cross-reference cannot be made explicit in orthodox tense logic.

In the prehistory of tense logic, we find Reichenbach's theory about tensed propositions. According to him, each tensed sentence is related to three times:

time of utterance
time of reference
time of the event

In many cases, some of these are identical. The times of reference of two sentences may be co-ordinated through cross-reference, or the time of the event of one identified as the time of reference of another. This is done by '*locator words*': 'then', 'at that time', 'when', and also by special ones that relate to the time of utterance: 'now', 'yesterday', 'tomorrow'.

There is an obvious place to attach locator words in tense logic, for the meaning of P and F contains an existential quantification. So we can introduce 'it was the case at u' and 'it will be the case at u':

$$P_uA(t) = \{x\colon u < t \text{ and } x \in A(u)\}.$$
$$F_uA(t) = \{x\colon t < u \text{ and } x \in A(u)\}.$$

The locator word may be chronologically definite, as in 'Napoleon died in 1815' or more like a pronoun, as in 'Napoleon died then'.

The cross-reference in (12) can now be symbolized:

(13) $P_uA \,\&\, P_uBFA'$.

Indefinite cross-reference can be established by a dyadic connective *once ... when*:

(14) Once, when Sue had a high temperature, Bill believed that she was going to be ill.

(15) $[\textit{once A when A}\ ](t) = \{x : \exists u < t\,(x \in A(u)\ \&\ x \in BFA'(u))\}$

All this is rather inelegant, but it works as long as the locator words can be regarded as having a definite reference which can be fixed beforehand. Really, of course, they do not: their reference is fixed by the context. For example, the reference of 'at that time' in (12) was fixed by the event described in the first conjunct; and the reference could be quite different if that same second conjunct appeared as part of another sentence. This brings us to contextual tense logic.

5. CONTEXTUAL TENSE LOGIC

If we make the assumption that there is, for each world, a context which determines the reference of the locator words, and this context is itself a function of time, we arrive at *two-dimensional* or *contextual* tense logic. This subject and more generally two-dimensional or doubly-indexical modal logic have been developed by Klamp, Vlach, Åqvist, Segerberg, Kaplan, and others.

The context is generally determined by the time of utterance, so that 'now' refers to the time of the context. But the context also determines the reference of the other locator words. Once these references are fixed we can of course also ask whether the sentence, *as presently* (at t_0) *interpreted*, is true at some other time t.

(16) I was ill then but am better now.

Will (16) be true tomorrow? That question is ambiguous: *what it says now* will still be true tomorrow if it is true today; but tomorrow these words would appear in a different context, if they were spoken then. We introduce:

> x is in $A(t_0, t)$ exactly if A, as interpreted in x at t_0, is true in x at t,

thus switching to dyadic propositional functions (but obviating the need for functions of more than two time arguments).

In ordinary sentence combinations the time t_0 of the context remains fixed. Note that $A(t_0, -)$ is itself a one-place propositional function, hence an orthodox tensed proposition. The orthodox operators therefore have natural generalizations:

$$\neg A(t_0, t) = \{x: x \text{ is not in } A(t_0, t)\}$$
$$(A \,\&\, B)(t_0, t) = A(t_0, t) \cap B(t_0, t)$$
$$PA(t_0, t) = \{x: \exists t' < t(x \in A(t_0, t'))\}.$$

But now we can introduce 'now' and also the reference $u(x, t_0)$ of locator word u in x at time t_0:

$$\textbf{Now}\, A(t_0, t) = A(t_0, t_0)$$
$$P_u A(t_0, t) = \{x: u(x, t_0) < t \text{ and } x \in A(t_0, u(x, t_0))\}.$$

For example, "He had telephoned the day before, and (hence) was expected" refers to the time of reference and to the day before that, and is in the past tense; it is true of any time between the time of reference and today, if it is true today. "He believed that it would rain now" is symbolized PB **Now** A, and we have:

$$\begin{aligned} x \text{ is in } PB\,\textbf{Now}\,A(t_0, t) \quad &\text{iff} \quad \exists s \angle t(x \in B\,\textbf{Now}\,A(t_0, s)) \\ &\text{iff} \quad \exists s \angle t(\forall y)(\text{if } xB_sy \text{ then} \\ &\qquad y \in \textbf{Now}\,A(t_0, s)) \\ &\text{iff} \quad \exists s \angle t(\forall y)(\text{if } xB_sy \text{ then} \\ &\qquad y \in A(t_0, t_0)). \end{aligned}$$

Hence as interpreted at t_0, with reference to time t, the sentence says that, sometime before t, he believed that it would rain at t_0. In most ordinary cases the reference would be to $t = t_0$, and this shows how we can recapture the propositions of orthodox tense logic: these are the one-place functions $A(t_0, t_0)$.

6. CONTEXTUAL REDUCTION OF TENSE OPERATORS

In English we use expressions like "That time is past", "That was in the past", "That is still in the future" to locate events described in other (preceding) sentences.

With a little extrapolation we can introduce special sentences P and F, which are true, as interpreted now, at exactly those times which are earlier (respectively, later) than now:

$$P(t_0, t) = \{x: t < t_0\}$$
$$F(t_0, t) = \{x: t_0 < t\}.$$

Recalling the above two-dimensional generalization of the operator P, we find that this can now be eliminated by definition for the orthodox propositions.

First we generalize '*once ... when*' to make it apply equally to past, present, and future:

$$(A \,♀\, B)(t_0, t) = \{x: \exists u(x \in (A \,\&\, B)(t_0, u))\}$$

which can be read as "At some time, both A and B".

$$(17) \qquad (P ♀ A)(t_0, t) = \{x: \exists t'(x \in (P \& A)(t_0, t'))\} = \{x: \exists t'(t' < t_0 \,\&\, x \in A(t_0, t'))\} = PA(t_0, t_0).$$

A slightly more complicated construction allows us also to cover the more general case of P applied to genuinely dyadic functions:

$$(18) \qquad (A \circ B)(t_0, t) = \{x: \exists u\, (x \in A(t, u) \cap B(t_0, u))\}$$

$$(19) \qquad (P \circ A)(t_0, t) = \{x: \exists u\, (x \in P(t, u) \cap A(t_0, u))\} = \{x: \exists u < t\, (x \in A\, (t_0, u))\} = PA(t_0, t).$$

I have here used the dual of the implication operator which I used elsewhere to reduce non-logical necessities.

So we may conclude that the tense operators P and F, and hence also G and H, can be eliminated in favour of special sentence constants plus operators which do not depend on the direction of time. Those sentence constants have however an irreducibly context dependent meaning.

University of Toronto
University of Southern California

NOTE

* The author gratefully acknowledges support of the Canada Council. Since the presentation of this report I have published the theory described in Section 3; see van Fraassen (1980).

BIBLIOGRAPHY

Åqvist, L., 'Modal Logic with Subjunctive Conditionals and Dispositional Predicates', *J. Philosophical Logic* 2 (1973), 1–76.

Åqvist, L, 'Formal Semantics for Verb Tenses as analyzed by Reichenbach', in T. A. van Dijk (ed.), *Pragmatics of Language and Literature*, North-Holland, Amsterdam, 1976.

Kaplan, D., 'Demonstratives', presented *American Philosophical Association*, Pacific Division, April 1977.

Kamp, H., 'Formal Properties of "Now" ', *Theoria* 37 (1971), 227–274.
Prior, A. N., 'Now', *Noûs* 2 (1968), 101–119.
Prior, A. N., *Time and Modality*, Oxford, 1957.
Reichenbach, H., *Elements of Symbolic Logic*, New York, 1947.
Rescher, N. and Urquhart, A., *Temporal Logic*, New York, 1971.
Segerberg, K., 'Two-dimensional Modal Logic', *J. Philosophical Logic* 2 (1973), 77–96.
Stalnaker, R., 'A Theory of Conditionals', in N. Rescher (ed.), *Studies in Logical Theory*, American Philosophical Quarterly, Monograph Series, Oxford, 1968.
Thomason, R. H., 'Indeterminist Time and Truthvalue Gaps', *Theoria* 36 (1970), 264–281.
Thomason, R. H., 'A Theory of Conditionals in the Context of Branching Time', *Philosophical Review*, January, 1980.
van Fraassen, B. C., 'The Only Necessity is Verbal Necessity', *J. Philosophy* 74 (1977), 71–85.
van Fraassen, B. C., 'A Temporal Framework for Conditionals and Chance', *Philosophical Review*, January, 1980.
Woolhouse, R. S., 'Tensed Modalities', *J. Philosophical Logic* 2 (1973), 393–415.

R. STALNAKER

LOGICAL SEMIOTIC

Semiotic was Charles Morris's term, borrowed from Charles Peirce, for the general theory of signs of communication.[1] Morris divided semiotic into three divisions – syntax, semantics, and pragmatics – and this trichotomy has become a standard way of subdividing the study of language and speech. The idea of the division was something like this: syntax concerns relations among linguistic expressions; semantics concerns relations between linguistic expressions and the objects to which they refer; pragmatics concerns relations among expressions, the objects to which they refer, and the users of the expressions. This characterization is vague and not accurate without qualification. Different theorists have interpreted it in different ways, and some have denied that it reflects any useful division. At best, it is a rough guide for the development of theory. If a precise explanation of the differences among the branches of semiotic can be given at all, it will be given in the context of the development of particular syntactic, semantic and pragmatic theories. So I will begin my discussion by saying something about the theoretical presuppositions of some of these theories – presuppositions on which the distinctions among the branches of semiotic depend. Then I will focus my attention on the most speculative and least well developed branch of semiotic, the branch to which the tools of logic have only recently begun to be applied – pragmatics. Although pragmatics is a more tentative field of study than syntax or semantics, I believe the shape of a theory which is capable of rigorous development and fruitful application is beginning to emerge from the work of a number of philosophers, linguists and logicians. I will sketch some of the central concepts of this theory, some of the formal apparatus which I think will be useful in explicating and developing these concepts, and some of the problems that fall within the domain of the theory.

PRESUPPOSITIONS OF SEMANTICS AND PRAGMATICS

When a person says something, what he says normally has a *content*; in Frege's terminology, it expresses a thought. It is the central theoretical presupposition of pure semantics as an autonomous discipline, and so of the traditional trichotomy, that this content, thought, or proposition can be abstracted both from the linguistic form in which it is expressed – the *means*

E. Agazzi (ed.), Modern Logic – A Survey, 439–456.

used to express it – and also from the force and purpose with which it is expressed – the *end* of its expression. Pure semantics is the study of these abstract propositions, the relations among them and between them and other objects of reference. In particular, semantics is concerned with the way in which the contents of complex expressions are a function of the referents and contents of their simpler parts.

Pure pragmatics, as I shall understand it, is the study of the relation between propositions and the contexts in which they are expressed. At least three different kinds of problems fall under this general description. First, expressions are often context dependent. What is said – what proposition is expressed in a linguistic act – depends not just on the meanings of the words used, but also on extra-linguistic facts about the situation in which the act takes place. Context dependence is most obvious in the use of personal pronouns, tenses and demonstratives: when such expressions are used, what is said may depend on who says it and to whom, when it is said, what the speaker is pointing at. But there are many other kinds of context dependence: the contents of sentences containing quantified expressions like *someone* or *everyone* depend on contextually determined domains; the contents of sentences containing adjectives like *large* and *cold* depend on contextually determined comparison classes; the contents of modal and conditional sentences depend on semantic determinants which may vary with changes in context. The study of the way context constrains or determines content in all of these cases is a problem in pragmatics.[2] Second, it is standard to analyze a speech act like assertion into two parts, the content and the force. While the analysis of content falls within the domain of semantics, the analysis of force is a problem in pragmatics. What, for example, is it to *assert* a proposition? How is it different from supposing it or questioning whether it is true? How does an assertion alter the context in which it is made? How is it related to the beliefs and intentions of speaker and audience?[3] Third, there are, or seem to be, rules governing discourse which cannot be explained entirely in terms of semantic rules that determine contents of what is expressed in discourse. A speech act may be anomalous, even though the sentence used is meaningful and a coherent proposition is expressed. An assertion may be inappropriate even though true. An inference may be reasonable in context, even though not semantically valid, or semantically valid, but not reasonable in context. The tasks of formulating such rules of conversation and of showing how they can be exploited to communicate something different from what the semantic rules determine that one has said are problems in pragmatics.[4]

Now the central presupposition of pragmatics, as a unified field of study, is that there is a single concept of *context* relevant to the solution of all of these kinds of problems. The context that context dependent utterances are dependent on should be the same context in terms of which speech acts are analyzed, and rules of conversation and constraints on appropriateness stated. Only if one can develop a single concept of context which plays all of these roles can one hope to give systematic explanation of the interaction between context and content. It is intuitively obvious that a speech act changes the context in which it is made, and that the changed context in turn affects both what it is appropriate to say subsequently, and also the means that can be used to say it. So the state of a context, at a given time, is both an *effect* of previous linguistic actions and a *cause* of subsequent linguistic actions. If one can find systematic relations of both kinds between utterances and contexts, then one may be able to use the context as a kind of intervening variable to give explanations of relations between utterances at different points in a discourse which are simpler and more natural than those that might be given within syntactic or semantic theory.

POSSIBLE WORLDS AND CONTEXTS

Formal pragmatic theory begins, as do the semantic theories that have been most fruitfully applied to natural languages, with possible worlds. Possible worlds semantics is an appropriate framework for pragmatic theory, not just because it has proved to be an elegant, flexible and technically fruitful apparatus, but because it makes possible an explanation of content and context in terms of an essential feature of discourse, and more generally of rational activity. It is a common, and I think defining feature of rational activities – inquiry, deliberation, communication – that they involve agents distinguishing among alternative possibilities. Possible worlds theory is just a theory that takes alternative possibilities as its basic primitive notion. The theory is philosophically controversial: some philosophers have been skeptical about the theory because it is alleged to make extravagant and implausible ontological commitments. But to begin with possible worlds is not necessarily to make a metaphysical commitment to possible worlds as ultimate irreducible entities. All one commits oneself to is the methodological presumption that one can usefully theorize at a certain level of generality. The foundation of the theory need not be a particular ontology, but only the assumption that a common structure underlies a range of human activities. It is obvious that to make sense of the activity of communicating, one must admit the existence, in some sense, of alternative possibilities. Whether or not they can be analyzed away in some more comprehensive psychological or metaphysical theory is a question we can set aside.[5]

A *proposition* is defined, in possible worlds theory, as a set of possible worlds, or, equivalently, as a function from possible worlds into truth values. To express a proposition, the definition suggests, is essentially to distinguish certain possibilities from others; to assert, suppose or believe a proposition is to assert, suppose or believe that the world is located in a certain part of a conceptual space of possibilities. The definition implies that any division of a set of alternative possibilities is a candidate to be an object of belief or the content of a speech act. It also implies that two speech acts or propositional attitudes that divide the same set of possible worlds in the same way have the same content. There are some problems with these consequences, but they seem appropriate to the purposes for which propositions are expressed and entertained: to distinguish the way the world is from various other ways that it might have been, or to help bring it about that certain possible worlds rather than others are actualized.

In any situation in which propositions, understood in this way, are expressed, there must be a domain of possibilities which the expressions distinguish among. This need not be a domain of all logically or ontologically possible worlds; it need include only the possibilities which are regarded, in the particular situation, as the live options – the possibilities which it is the point of the discourse to discriminate among. These possibilities will be the ones compatible with all the information which is taken for granted in the conversation – with the presumed common background knowledge of speaker and audience.[6] This set of possible worlds, which I will call the context set, is crucial to the understanding and explanation of a discourse for several reasons. First, it represents the information about the context which is available to be exploited in the use of context dependent sentences. Second, it is at least one thing which the speech acts that make up a discourse are intended to change. Speech acts are designed to communicate information, and if the communication is successful, it will change the presumed common knowledge of the parties to the transaction. Third, the context set constrains the appropriateness of speech acts. Obviously what is taken for granted limits what it is appropriate to say, as well as the means that it is appropriate to use to say it.

In this very simple concept of a context set we have a unifying concept around which to build a pragmatic theory – a theory of the dynamics of speech. We have a representation of context, or of the state of a context, which has intuitive motivation, which connects with well articulated semantic theories, and which promises to bring out the connections among the various ways that speech interacts with context. After saying just a little about the intuitive content of this notion, I will try to relate it to some theoretical developments in pragmatics.

A context set represents what an individual speaker or addressee takes to be the common background of the discourse he is participating in. So each party to a linguistic transaction will have his own context set at each moment. But since an individual's context set represents what he believes to be the information held in common between himself and the others, there is a presumption that the context sets are all the same. The states of *belief* of different parties in a discourse need not converge – people can agree to disagree – but their beliefs about their common background beliefs can differ only in case of misunderstanding, and will tend to converge as misunderstandings are discovered and corrected in the course of a conversation. Call a context *defective* if the context sets of the various participants are different. A defective context is in disequilibrium and will tend to adjust toward the equilibrium position of a non-defective context.

Context sets are constantly changing for a least three different reasons. First, and most simply, they change in response to observable changes in the environment of the discourse. If someone enters the room or begins to speak, or if all the lights go out, this fact will normally become part of the mutually recognized background knowledge. Second, contexts adjust in response to evidence that the context is defective – that the presuppositions of the different participants are not the same. Clues as to what is being taken for granted are continually being dropped in the course of a conversation which enables the participants to keep the context close to its equilibrium Third, contexts change in response to explicit speech acts. For example, normally, if I tell you something, then unless you overtly reject what I say, it will become a presupposition of subsequent conversation.

This notion of context – a set of individuals, the participants in a conversation, each with a context set changing from moment to moment in response to the events of the conversation – is an abstract skeleton on which to hang the substantive principle of pragmatic theory. Analyses of force, general conversational maxims, specific linguistic rules relating content to the extra-linguistic situation, lexical presupposition constraints, can all be stated as relations between speech and context, where context is defined this way. Let me now review some pragmatic problems that philosophers and linguists have discussed and some substantive developments of pragmatic theory. I will try to relate both to this framework.

PRESUPPOSITION

Statements, questions, and other speech acts are often said to have *presuppositions*. When I say "the book on the table is interesting", I presuppose that there is exactly one book on a certain contextually determined table. When I say 'Harry regrets poisoning his grandmother", or ask "Why did Harry poison his grandmother?" I presuppose that Harry poisoned his grandmother. When I say "Even Elmer enjoyed the play" I presuppose, among other things, that people other than Elmer enjoyed the play. The examples are clear enough, but it is less clear what they are examples of. It is easier to recognize instances of the phenomenon than to characterize it.

Until recently, it was taken for granted by linguists and philosophers that the relation of presupposition is a semantic relation between sentences or propositions, a relation to be explained in terms of truth conditions. A definition in this tradition is the following: a sentence A presupposes a proposition φ if and only if, for any possible world i, if A expresses a proposition that is either true of false in i, then φ is true in i. A sentence lacks a truth value when any of its presuppositions is false. In such cases, the question of truth 'does not arise'.

The problem for formal semantics posed by this characterization of presupposition was to give an account of truth-value gaps, and more generally, of gaps in the semantic values of expressions. Most formal semantic theories are constructed on the assumption that interpretations are complete and determinate. Semantic rules explaining how the value of a complex expression is a function of the values of its parts do not say what to do if the value of one of the parts is undefined. For example, the semantics for classical propositional calculus does not say whether a disjunction should be true or neither true nor false if one disjunct is true and another truth-valueless. Various three-valued logics have been applied to this problem, and linguists have constructed various solutions to what they have called the projection problem: the problem of relating the presuppositions of complex expressions to the presuppositions of their parts. It proved difficult to find a solution that was either theoretically satisfactory or adequate to the phenomena.

From a theoretical point of view, the most promising general theory of semantic presupposition was Bas Van Fraassen's theory of supervaluations.[7] The idea of the theory is this. Truth-value gaps arise because of underdetermination of semantic interpretation. An underdetermined or partial semantic interpretation can be represented by a class of complete interpretations, all the different ways of arbitrarily completing the partial interpretation. Call this class the class of *classical valuations* associated with a partial interpretation. The *supervaluation* is then defined in terms of the classical valuations as follows: a sentence is true if it is true in all the classical valuations, false if false in all the classical valuations, and undefined if it is true in some of the classical valuations and false in others.

One reason this theory has proved the most successful theory of truth-value gaps is that it offers a completely general procedure for explaining the relationship between gaps in the semantic values of complex expressions and gaps in the values of their parts. Ordinary three-valued logics would have to be extended piecemeal to languages containing new operators, but the theory of supervaluations provides a single method for extending any determinate two-valued semantical theory (predicate logic, modal, epistemic, deontic or tense logics, logics of conditionals) to an underdetermined version of that theory. It gives us a unified account of truth-value gaps, whatever their source: vagueness of predicates, category mistakes, future contingents, underdetermination of one or another contextual determinant.[8]

The theory of supervaluations is also an intuitively well motivated account of truth-value gaps. It assumes that language aims at a two-valued ideal. Deviations from the ideal arise because one or another semantic determinant is not fully specified by the conventions or intentions of the language users. It seems natural to assume that where the incomplete specification does not matter – where the value of an expression determined by the ideal semantics would be the same no matter how the specification were completed – one can ignore the deviation. That is just what the supervaluation account allows one to do.

Finally, the theory of supervaluations is an attractive theory because it preserves two-valued logic. Whatever two-valued semantical theory the supervaluation method is applied to, a sentence will be true in all supervaluations if and only if it is true in all classical valuations. So the same sentences will be valid in the theory of supervaluations as are valid in the idealized, determinate semantical theory. This is an intuitive virtue, and not just a technical convenience, since standard two-valued logics provide an intuitively compelling account of reasoning. The theory of supervaluations allows us to reconcile the explanatory power of two-valued logic with the fact that semantic underdetermination is a pervasive feature of the use of natural language.

Unfortunately, the theory of supervaluations, interpreted as a complete account of the presupposition phenomena identified by linguists, fails to fit the facts. That is, if we define presupposition in terms of truth-value gaps, and use the supervaluation account to explain the relation between the truth-value gaps in complex sentences and those in their component parts, we get results that conflict with speakers' intuitions about presuppositions. Let me give two examples of well supported generalizations about presuppositions that conflict with the supervaluation account. First, normally, if a sentence *A* presupposes a proposition, then so do sentences like 'It might be that *A*', and 'If *A*, then *B*'. "The Queen of Switzerland is bald" presupposes that Switzerland has a queen, as does "the Queen of Switzerland might be bald", and "If the Queen of Switzerland were bald, she would wear a wig". But it will not, in general, be true on the supervaluation account, that whenever *A* in fact lacks a truth-value, modal and conditional statements containing *A* will also lack a truth-value. Second, examples suggest that a statement of the form '*A* and *B*' will have all the presuppositions of *A* and of *B* (except those presuppositions of *B* entailed by *A*). "The Queen of England is bald, and so is the Queen of Switzerland" seems to presuppose that both England and Switzerland have queens. But on the supervaluation theory, that statement has a truth value despite the fact that its second conjunct lacks one. It is straightforwardly false.[9]

One response to this conflict between theory and fact would be to look for a different account of truth-value gaps, but an alternative response that has proven more fruitful is to look for a different way to characterize the presupposition phenomena. It may be argued that presupposition is a pragmatic phenomenon and that it distorts the facts to characterize it in purely semantics terms. The concept of context sketched above gives us a ready made characterization of *speaker* presupposition: a speaker presupposes a proposition if and only if it is entailed by (true in all possible worlds in) the speaker's context set. One can then use this notion to describe various ways in which sentences or utterances have or make presuppositions. For example, one might say that a sentence (type) presupposes a proposition if and only if the appropriate use of that sentence requires, for one reason or another, that the speaker presuppose the proposition. One might then use pragmatic maxims constraining the appropriateness of speech acts to explain why various sentences have the presuppositions they have. It has been shown that the generalization about the presuppositions of conjunctive sentences mentioned above can easily be explained in this way, using independently motivated assumptions about the relation of speech acts to context.[10]

The supervaluation theory and the pragmatic account of presupposition need not be thought of as competing expianations of a single notion. The proper understanding of the relation between them seems to me to be this: the phenomenon of presupposition is best *described* as a pragmatic phenomenon – as a constraint on the contexts in which sentences are appropriately used. But there may be various different *explanations* for the pragmatic phenomenon, various different reasons why a speaker is required to make a certain presupposition in order to use a certain sentence appropriately. *One* possible explanation for a presupposition requirement is that the sentence used *semantically* presupposes the proposition: that is, the sentence fails to express a proposition which is true or false in possible worlds in which the presupposed proposition is false. Semantic presuppositions explain pragmatic presupposition requirements in virtue of the following truistic pragmatic maxim: speaker are required to use sentences that express determinant propositions relative to their context sets. This maxim implies that a truth-value gap is sufficient, but not necessary, for presupposition failure. Semantic presuppositions provide one possible explanation for an independently characterized pragmatic phenomenon. The independent characterization shifts some of the burden of explanation of speech from semantics to pragmatics, allowing for more flexibility in the construction of semantic theory and more natural explanations of the diverse range of presupposition phenomena.

CONTEXT DEPENDENCE

The first attempts to develop a rigorous formal pragmatic theory, by Richard Montague and some of his associates, began with analyses of tenses, demonstratives, and personal pronouns – expressions whose extensions depend on the extra-linguistic situation in a relatively clear and straightforward way.[11] But Montague did not use a notion of context such as I have sketched, and did not attempt to relate context dependence to other pragmatic phenomena. His strategy was to represent the *context of use* of the expressions of a pragmatic language (a constructed language containing context dependent expressions) by an *n*-tuple whose terms were all the features of the situation on which the extensions of any of the expressions were dependent. The interpretation of a pragmatic language assigned to the expressions functions from these *n*-tuples (which Montague called *indices*) into ordinary extensions (individuals, classes of individuals, truth values, etc.). Indices thus played a role exactly analogous to the role of possible worlds in the semantics for modal language. Pragmatics was viewed by Montague as a generalization of modal logic, with the more abstract and general notion of an index replacing the notion of a possible world. If the language contained modal operators, the index might include a possible world as one of its terms, along with time of utterance, speaker, addressee, location, and perhaps others. To take a simple example, one might construct a pragmatic language with just two context dependent expressions, the personal pronouns 'I' and 'you'. An index would then be an ordered pair of individuals drawn from a domain of potential language users, first a speaker and second an addressee. The value of 'I' would be a function taking an index into its first term, and the value of 'you' a function taking an index into its second term. 'I love you' is then true when said by *a* to *b* (that is, relative to index $\langle a, b \rangle$) if and only if *a* loves *b*, just as one would hope.

Critics of the simple index theory of context dependence argued that it pressed the analogy between possible worlds and features of context of use too far, and in doing so missed some of the interesting complexity of context dependence.[12] They argued that the way the truth-value of what is said depends on context is different from the way it depends on the circumstances the statement is about – on which alternative possibility is actualized. To capture the difference, one must separate the factors on which extensions depend into two parts and distinguish the *meaning* or *semantic value* of an expression from the *content* it expresses in a given context (both being different from the *extension* of the expression). The *character* of a context dependent expression (to use David Kaplan's terminology) is a function taking a context of use, not into an extension, but into a *content*. Content is itself a function taking a possible world, or possible circumstances, into an extension. (If the expression is a sentence, the extension will be a truth-value, and so the content will be a proposition.) David Kaplan, in developing his theory of demonstratives, argued that these distinctions are needed to explain the peculiar status of sentences like 'I am here now'. It is evident from the meanings of the words in this sentence that in any normal context of use, it will express a truth, but the truth it expresses will be a contingent one, since the speaker might not have been where he was at the time he spoke. It seems that a logic of personal pronouns and demonstratives should make that sentence logically true, but not necessary. Using *two* indices, one to represent the context that determines content, and one to represent the circumstances that determine the truth-value of the content, we can get this result. Let the context consist of a time, a place, a speaker, and a possible world, related so that in that possible world that speaker is at that place at that time. Now the value of the sentence 'I am here now', relative to any context $\langle t, p, s, w \rangle$ will be the proposition that *s* is at place *p* at time *t*. Because of the relationship among the elements of a context, this proposition will always be true in *w*, the world of the context, but since it may be false in other possible worlds, it is a contingent truth. So we have the result we want. The sentence is valid because true relative to every context, but it may at the same time be contingent since the content determined by the context need not be the necessary proposition.

The distinctions between character and content and between context of use and circumstances are important not just because they help to explain some peculiarities in the interaction of modal and indexical expressions. It is important for pragmatics to identify the *content* of an expression since it is the point of discourse to communicate content. Pragmatic rules constraining language use can be motivated in terms of the purposes of discourse only if we can represent *what is said* in an utterance in abstraction from the means used to say it.

Kaplan's theory of demonstratives does go further toward a unified pragmatic theory than Montague's simple index theory by making this important distinction, but the concept of context used in this theory is similar to Montague's: contexts of use are represented by *n*-tuples consisting of all the elements on which the contents of context dependent expressions depend. How does this notion of context relate to the notion of context sketched above? The connection can be made by the following very simple and obvious pragmatic maxim: to speak appropriately, a speaker must believe or assume that his audience will understand what he is saying – what the *content* of this utterance is. This means that all the elements of the situation on which content depends (all the relevant terms of the *n*-tuple which is the context in Kaplan's sense) must be fixed by the presumed common knowledge of speaker and audience (by the speaker's *context set*).

To see what this comes to, consider an example. O'Leary says "You look tired" to Daniels. It will obviously be part of the presumed common knowledge of speaker and audience that this utterance was produced. This means that in each of the possible worlds in the speaker's context set, he (or someone) produces that utterance. Now in this example, the content expressed by the sentence used depends on who the addressee is. For each of the possible worlds in the context set, the facts about the speaker's intentions in that world will determine an addressee for the utterance token, and so will determine the content of the utterance when produced in that world. What the simple and obvious pragmatic maxim stated above implies is that the addressee must be the same in each of these possible worlds.

To give a little more detail to the example, consider three possible worlds, *i*, *j* and *k*. In each of these worlds. O'Leary produces the utterance quoted above. In *i*, he refers to Daniels, who in fact looks tired. In *i* he also refers to Daniels, but in that world Daniels does not look tired. World *k* is just like *i* except that there O'Leary refers to someone else, say Schultz, who does not look tired in any of the three possible worlds. We can represent the two different ways that the truth-value of what is said depends on the way the worlds is in the following two-dimensional diagram:

	i	*j*	*k*
i	T	F	T
j	T	F	T
k	F	F	F

The horizontal lines represent the contents expressed in the utterance in the various possible worlds in which the particular utterance is produced. The whole diagram represents a *propositional concept* – a function from possible worlds into propositions, propositions being, in turn, functions from possible worlds into truth-values. What the pragmatic maxim requires is that the propositional concept be a *constant* function with respect to the possible worlds in the speaker's context set. So, if the context set in our example consists of just worlds *i* and *j*, O'Leary's statement will conform to the maxim. If, on the other hand, world *k* is compatible with O'Leary's presuppositions as well, then the maxim will be violated. (This would happen, for example, if O'Leary made his statement to Daniels, knowing that Daniels would be in doubt about whether O'Leary was talking to him or to Schultz.)[13]

To summarize this point: two truisms about context dependence set the stage for the use of propositional concepts to relate indexical semantics to the kind of pragmatic theory that I have been discussing. First, context dependence is dependence of content on certain *facts* about the possible world in which the utterance is produced. Second, if the utterance is to be appropriate to its purpose – the communication of its content – those facts must be available, and known or assumed to be available, to the speaker and his audience.

Let me make one clarification before I give an example of the way this two-dimensional framework can help to explain some facts about context dependence. There are two different kinds of two-dimensional semantical objects involved in the account of context dependence that I have been sketching. It is important to see, first that they are different, and second that they are not alternative accounts of the same thing, but complementary parts of a single account. The first kind of two-dimensional semantical object is a function taking an *index* into a proposition, where a proposition takes a possible world into a truth-value. This kind of function, which Kaplan calls a *character*, is assigned by an indexical semantical theory to a sentence *type*: it is the *meaning*, or *semantic value* of the sentence. The index may include, as one of its elements, a possible world, but it will normally include additional elements as well (a time, a place, speaker and audience, etc.). A possible world alone could not do the work of an index, since the same sentence with the same meaning or character may be used in different contexts (relative to different indices) within the same possible world. The second kind of two-dimensional semantical object is a function from possible worlds into propositions. This kind of function, which I have called a *propositional concept*, is determined by a particular utterance *token* rather than by a sentence type, and its arguments are not indices, but simply possible worlds. One does not need additional elements to determine the content of the utterance, since all the relevant contextual features are fixed by the facts surrounding the production of the utterance. Propositional concepts are not assigned by a semantic theory for a language to the utterance tokens; they are instead determined by the assignment of a character (a function from indices to propositions) to the sentence used, and by the facts surrounding the particular use of the sentence in the various possible worlds compatible with the context of that use. The first kind of double dependence of extension on the facts arises because the same indexical sentence can be used on different occasions to say different things. The second kind of double dependence arises because a particular concrete utterance token, indexical or not, occurs in many different possible worlds – in all the possible worlds compatible with the beliefs or presuppositions of anyone who believes or presupposes that that particular utterance was produced – and the proposition expressed in the utterance need not be the same in all of those possible worlds.

The interesting applications of the two-dimensional notion of a propositional concept come when there are apparent violations of the pragmatic maxim that a constant propositional concept is expressed, relative to the context. Suppose, in response to O'Leary's question, "What time is it?" Daniels says, "It is now three o'clock". According to the standard, straightforward semantic accounts of this sentence, it will express a necessary, eternal truth when used at three o'clock, and a necessary, eternal falsehood when used at any other time. So if we assume, for simplicity, that O'Leary and Daniels presuppose that it is either three or four o'clock – the question is which one – then the following propositional concept will be determined by Daniels's utterance:

	i	*j*
i	T	T
j	F	F

Possible world *i* is the world in which Daniels' utterance takes place at three o'clock; world *j* is the world in which it takes place at four.

There are two anomalous consequences of this semantic account. First, since the content expressed is either necessary or impossible, it is either already presupposed or incompatible with what is presupposed. So the assertion of it will be either unnecessary or self-defeating. Second, the pragmatic maxim that a speaker should believe or assume that the addressee knows what he is saying will be violated. One must know what time it is to know what is being said, and obviously in any normal use of the sentence the addressee will not, prior to the assertion, know what time it is. These anomalies suggest that the semantic account cannot be right. One strategy for responding to them would be to tinker with the semantics, for example to look for a different, perhaps more complicated analysis of *now*. But this would mean abandoning a semantic analysis that has been very successful at explaining the behaviour of that word in other contexts.[14] An alternative strategy is available if we make one general *pragmatic* assumption about the influence of context on content. This strategy enables us to reconcile the simple semantic analysis with the phenomena, in this as well as many other cases. The assumption is that blatant violations of pragmatic maxims force a re-interpretation of what is said. When there is a violation of the maxim in question – that a constant propositional concept is expressed relative to the context – there is a natural re-interpretation that suggests itself, a re-interpretation which is obained by performing a certain two-dimensional modal operation on the propositional concept determined.

For any propositional concept, there is a unique proposition determined, which I have called the *diagonal proposition*, which may be different from any of the horizontal propositions expressed. This is the proposition which, for any possible world *i* is true at *i* if and only if the horizontal proposition expressed at *i* is true at *i*. In the propositional concept expressed by Daniels's statement, the diagonal proposition is the *contingent* proposition which is true at *i* and false at *j*. Now we might re-interpret Daniels's statement, taking him to be expressing *that* proposition rather than the necessary or impossible proposition determined by the semantical rules. More generally, we might say that when this particular pragmatic maxim is violated, interpretation normally shifts to the diagonal proposition. In the example I have given, as well as in others, this operation yields a result that seems right intuitively: it seems obvious that what Daniels is trying to say in the situation as described is that the actual world is i, and not j.

The diagonalization operation has parallel application in a wide range of cases: it can, for example, explain how identity statements and analytic truths can be informative, and how negative existentials using proper names can be both meaningful and true.[15] The general strategy which this kind of example illustrates is to use pragmatic theory to reconcile simple semantic analyses with complex facts about usage.

CONCLUSION

Once upon a time, formal syntax was a rigorous, well developed theory, while semantics was just an informal intuitive commentary on it. At that time, anyone who liked to theorize rigorously tended to push semantical problems into syntax. The study of the logical syntax of language was really a method for studying semantics by constructing languages in which semantic relations were clearly reflected in syntax. Given the state of the development of theory at that time, this was a reasonable procedure, although it may have contributed to some conceptual confusion about the relation between syntax and semantics. Later, when semantics was a rigorous, well developed formal theory but pragmatics was a speculative informal subject, there was a tendency to try to let semantics – the study of content – explain as much about the use of language as it could. This too was reasonable methodological procedure, but it carried the risk of distorting the phenomena. It is intuitively clear that the context in which language is used has a strong influence on the content language is used to convey, and a fully adequate semantic theory must take account of that influence. Pragmatics is still a speculative field of study, but I have tried to suggest some developments which may provide part of a theory which can contribute to a complete account of the use of signs of communication.

Cornell University

NOTES

[1] See Morris [20].
[2] See Bar Hillel [3], Montague [18] and other papers in [19], Kaplan [10], Kamp [8] and [9], Lewis [16].
[3] See Austin [2] for the classic discussion of speech acts and Searle [23].
[4] See Grice [7] and Searle [23]. In Stalnaker [29] I try to give a analysis of a pragmatic concept of *reasonable inference* which does not coincide with semantic entailment.
[5] See Lewis [17], pp. 84–91 for a metaphysical defense of possible worlds, and Stalnaker [28] for a less metaphysical defense.
[6] This notion of speaker presupposition is discussed more extensively in Stalnaker [26] and [27]. Related notions of common knowledge and mutual knowledge are developed and discussed in Schiffer [22] and Lewis [15].
[7] See Strawson [31], pp. 175–79 and Van Fraassen [34] and [35], pp. 153–63.
[8] For examples of the range of application of the supervaluation idea, see Fine [6], Field [5], Thomason [32] and [33].
[9] See papers by the linguists Karttunen [11], [12] and [13] and Morgan [21] for discussion of these generalizations and more generally, the problem of relating presuppositions of compound sentences to the presuppositions of their parts.
[10] See Stalnaker [26] and [27] and Karttunen [12] for attempts to give a pragmatic explanation of this generalization. See also Kempson [14] for extensive discussion of semantic and pragmatic presupposition.
[11] See Montague [18], Lewis [16], Cresswell [5], pp. 109–119, for discussion of index theory.
[12] See Kaplan [10] and Stalnaker [25].
[13] A number of logicians have studied the formal properties of what I have called propositional concepts in abstraction from their application to pragmatic theory. They have constructed two-dimensional modal logics with propositional concepts(functions taking a *pair* of possible worlds into a truth value) as the semantic value of the formulas, and various two-dimensional sentence operators interpreted by functions from propositional concepts into propositional concepts. Two such operators which are of interest to pragmatics, represented by a dagger and an upside down dagger, are defined as follows:

(1) $v_{i,j}(\dagger A) = v_{j,j}(A)$,
(2) $v_{i,j}(\downarrow A) = v_{i,i}(A)$.

See Segerberg [24], Åqvist [1] and Lewis [17], pp. 63–64n. The notation is Lewis's.
[14] See Kamp [18] for a detailed exposition and defense of the analysis.
[15] Diagonalization is discussed in more detail in Stalnaker [30], and is applied to identity statements and singular negative existentials.

BIBLIOGRAPHY

[1] Åqvist, L., 'Modal Logic with Subjunctive Conditionals and Dispositional Predicates', *J. Philosophical Logic* 2 (1973), 1–76.
[2] Austin, J. L., *How to Do Things with Words*, Harvard Univ. Press, Cambridge, Mass., 1965.

[3] Bar Hillel, Y., 'Indexical Expressions', *Mind* **63** (1954), 359–79.
[4] Cresswell, M., *Logics and Languages*, Methuen & Co., London, 1973.
[5] Field, H., 'Theory Change and the Indeterminacy of Reference', *J. Philosophy* **70** (1973), 462–481.
[6] Fine, K., 'Vagueness, Truth and Logic', *Synthese* **30** (1975).
[7] Grice, H. P., 'Logic and Conversation', in D. Davidson and G. Harman (eds.), *The Logic of Grammar*, Dickenson Publ. Co., Encino, California, 1975, pp. 64–75.
[8] Kamp, J. A. W., 'Formal Properties of "Now"', *Theoria* **37** (1971), 227–273.
[9] Kamp, J. A. W., 'Two Theories about Adjectives', in E. L. Keenen (ed.), *Formal Semantics of Natural Language*, Cambridge Univ. Press, Cambridge, 1975, pp. 123–155.
[10] Kaplan, D., 'Demonstratives', *Mimeo*, 1977.
[11] Karttunen, L., 'Presuppositions of Compound Sentences', *Linguistic Inquiry* **4** (1973), 169–193.
[12] Karttunen, L., 'Remarks on Presupposition', in A. Rogers (ed.), *Proceedings of the Texas Conference on Performatives, Presupposition and Conversational Implicature*, Univ. of Texas Press, Austin, 1973.
[13] Karttunen, L., 'Presupposition and Linguistic Context', *Theoretical Linguistics* **1** (1974), 181–194.
[14] Kempson, R. M., *Presupposition and the Delimitation of Semantics* Cambridge Univ. Press, Cambridge, 1975.
[15] Lewis, D., *Convention*, Harvard Univ. Press, Cambridge, Mass., 1969.
[16] Lewis, D., 'General Semantics', in D. Davidson and G. Harman (eds.), *Semantics of Natural Language*, D. Reidel Publ. Co., Dordrecht, Holland, 1972, pp. 169–218.
[17] Lewis, D., *Counterfactuals*, Basil Blackwell, Oxford, 1973.
[18] Montague, R., 'Pragmatics', 1968 in [19], pp. 95–117.
[19] Montague, R., *Formal Philosophy*, ed. by R. H. Thomason, Yale Univ. Press, New Haven, 1974.
[20] Morris, C., *Foundations of the Theory of Signs*, Univ. of Chicago Press, Chicago, 1938.
[21] Morgan, J., 'On the Treatment of Presupposition in Transformational Grammar', in R. Binnick *et al* (eds.), *Papers from the Fifth Regional Meeting of the Chicago Linguistics Society*, Chicago, 1969.
[22] Schiffer, S., *Meaning*, Clarendon Press, Oxford, 1972.
[23] Searle, J., *Speech Acts*, Cambridge Univ. Press, Cambridge, 1969.
[24] Segerberg, K., 'Two-Dimensional Modal Logic', *J. Philosophical Logic* **2** (1973), 77–96.
[25] Stalnaker, R., 'Pragmatics', in D. Davidson and G. Harman (eds.), *Semantics of Natural Language*, D. Reidel Publ. Co., Dordrecht, Holland, 1972, pp. 380–97.
[26] Stalnaker, R., 'Presuppositions', *J. Philosophical Logic* **2** (1973), 447–457.
[27] Stalnaker, R., 'Pragmatic Presuppositions', in M. Munitz and P. Unger (eds.), *Semantics and Philosophy*, New York Univ. Press, New York, 1974, pp. 197–214.
[28] Stalnaker, R., Possible worlds', *Noûs* **10** (1976), 65–75.
[29] Stalnaker, R., 'Indicative Conditionals', *Philosophia* **5** (1975), 269–86.
[30] Stalnaker, R., 'Assertion', *Syntax and Semantics* **9** (1978), 315–332.
[31] Strawson, P. F., *Introduction to Logical Theory*, Methuen & Co., London, 1952.

[32] Thomason, R. H., 'Indeterminist Time and Truth-Value Gaps', *Theoria* **36** (1970), 246-281).

[33] Thomason, R. H., 'A Semantic Theory of Sortal Incorrectness', *J. Philosophical Logic* **1** (1972), 209–258.

[34] Van Fraassen, B. C., 'Singular Terms, Truth-Value Gaps and Free Logic', *J. Philosophy* **63** (1966), 481–95.

[35] Van Fraassen, B. C., *Formal Semantics and Logic*, The Macmillan Co., New York, 1971.

CH. PERELMAN

LOGIC AND RHETORIC

PRELIMINARY REMARKS

In the last fifty years we have seen an enlargement of the scope of logic from syntax to semantics and pragmatics. But the question remains: How do we go from logic to rhetoric? In other words, is there a relationship between the study of formal systems and that of style and figures of speech?

As a logician, I was very much interested by the fact that people disagree on questions of value. From the point of view of empirical logical positivism, such disagreements arise because value judgments are subjective and therefore cannot be substantiated; but I could not accept this conclusion. This suggests the problem: Is there a logic of value judgments? Can they be justified through reasoning?

As a simple example, when at the beginning of this conference Father Bochenski restricted his definition of logic to the study of formal reasoning and excluded all other conceptions of logic, he was implicitly making a value judgment. Now, did he merely assert without giving any reasons that logic should be defined in this manner, or did he attempt to justify his definition as being a reasonable one, that is, as being preferable to alternative formulations? Here we have an example of the problem of choice, which we resolve, not by arbitrary, subjective decisions, but by an appeal to *reasonableness*. This manner of reasoning is employed not only in law and philosophy, but in the sciences as well, whenever one must choose between competing methodologies or definitions.

Thus I began to investigate the logic of value judgments, proceeding empirically, much as Frege had done a century ago; but whereas Frege had analyzed the method of deduction in mathematics, I examined how people justify reasonable choices. After several years of work, I came to the disappointing conclusion that a logic of value judgments simply does not exist. I finally realized something which as a logician I had completely ignored: there are tools of reasoning *other* than those studied in formal logic, tools which Aristotle had called *dialectical* reasoning, but which I preferred to term *argumentative reasoning*. (People often forget that Aristotle is the father not only of formal logic, which he terms *analytical reasoning*, but also of dialectical reasoning to which he devoted his *Rhetoric*, his *Topics* and the *Sophistical Refutations*)

E. Agazzi (ed.), Modern Logic – A Survey, 457–463.

When the results of my inquiry began to coalesce into a field in its own right, it was time to choose a name for it: the most natural choices were Rhetoric and Dialectic, the two main branches of Aristotle's study of dialectical reasoning. (They are discussed in his *Rhetoric* and his *Topics*, respectively.) Rhetoric seemed the wiser choice, for Hegel and Marx have used 'dialectic' in a very different sense. Moreover, the concept of the *audience*, which I considered vital to an understanding of argumentative reasoning, was completely absent from the *Topics*, playing an explicit role only in the *Rhetoric*.

As I began to study the history of the subject, I noticed that in the Middle Ages and the Renaissance, the important distinction that Aristotle had drawn between analytic and dialectical reasoning had, inexplicably, been forgotten. Both forms of reasoning were known as Dialectic but some logicians stressed formal logic, others rhetoric. For example, Professor Bochenski alluded to Valla's three volume treatise, *De inventione dialectica*, 'invention' being the principal component of rhetoric. (The other components are disposition, elocution, memory and action). Other important logicians, in the rhetorical tradition, were Sturm and Agricola.

Dialectic continued to display this lack of unity until Ramus, the well-known sixteenth century French logician who died in the Saint-Bartholomew's Day Massacre. Ramus conceived Dialectic as the study of *all* forms of reasoning and thus included both analytic and dialectical reasoning in his ambitious work, drawing no distinction between them. He reserved the term 'rhetoric' for those components of persuasive communication (elocution, memory and action) which cannot strictly be called reasoning: these topics he left to his friend, Omer Talon, who conceived rhetoric in the narrow sense of *ars ornandi,* the art of ornate speech. And so, from Talon's time onward, rhetoric was regarded as nothing more than the study of literary form and expression; as such, it gradually disappeared as a branch of philosophy.

In contrast, modern logic, which has greatly expanded upon Aristotle's analytics, has flourished. But what of the discipline which Aristotle had called dialectical reasoning? And which I have tried to revive under the name "Rhetoric"?

One question that interested me greatly was how to connect persuasive discourse with rhetoric (used in the sense of Ramus and Talon) on the one hand, and with formal logic on the other. Clearly, Ramus was mistaken in his assertion that figures of speech are merely ornamental and cannot be characterized as reasoning. They are, in fact, condensed arguments: this explains why figures of speech are used as effective methods of persuasion.

What of the connection with formal logic? A dialectical argument can be judged strong or weak, relevant or irrelevant, but it does not possess the quality of incontrovertibility or self-evidence which characterizes an analytical argument. Also, in formal logic, everything which gives rise to controversy must be eliminated, necessitating the invention of an artificial language with formal rules for manipulating symbols and forming well-defined sentences.

After this brief introduction, I would like to present my own ideas on '*the new rhetoric*'.

The reduction of logic to formal logic, which became widespread under the influence of Frege, Russell and those logicians who had received a mathematical training, resulted in the neglect of the large field of non-demonstrative reasoning, of those reasonings which enable us to choose among a set of opinions that which seems the best, the most acceptable, the most reasonable. It is the vast field of reasoning relating to controversy, criticism and justification of every kind, reasoning by means of which we attempt to convince and persuade, to find reasons for and against some thesis in the course of a deliberation, whether individual or collective. It is therefore not surprising that to remedy the baneful effects of the aforesaid reduction, we should endeavour to complete formal logic – regarded as the theory of demonstrative proof – by a rhetoric conceived of as a theory of argumentation.

Let us quickly examine the features which mark the differences between the two.

An essential condition for the establishment of a system of formal logic necessitates the preliminary removal of any difficulty which could only be solved by having recourse of a power of interpretation or decision. This is the reason why the 'language' of formal logic must exclude every ambiguity right from the start. In saying that '$x = x$' or that '$p \rightarrow p$', we are not stating a law of nature but simply asserting that in each of these propositions the same values must be substituted for symbols 'x' and 'p' as they are not liable to receiving two interpretations.

When it comes to a natural language, this condition is not necessarily satisfied. It is presumed that the same word has the same meaning, but proof of the contrary is admissible. Thus it seems normal to derogate from the presumption to univocity whenever the latter could be preserved only at the cost of resulting incoherence, triviality or unacceptability.

We normally hesitate to believe that an intelligent man asserts something which at first sight strikes us as a contradiction. When Heraclitus says that "we step and do not step twice into the same river", we try to avoid the apparent contradiction by interpreting "the same river" in two different ways. When we hear such a proposition as "war is war" we understand that we are faced with a "pseudo-tautology" aiming at the justification of a piece of behaviour which would be shocking in peace time: this we could not do had we considered the proposition as a mere application of the principle of identity. When in his *Pensées*, Pascal tells us that 'When God's word, which is true, is false literally, it is true spiritually", he thereby urges ut to look for a new interpretation of the biblical text in order to safeguard its truth.

In a natural language, the univocity of signs is not, as in an artificial language, a condition required under all circumstances. As a result, a reinterpretation of signs is always possible, and this prevents us from deciding, once and for all, whether a thesis is true or false by means of a formal criterion. Law and theology supply numerous cases in which, for some reason or other, the literal interpretation of a legal or a sacred text is unacceptable.

A system of formal logic contains rules of deduction which make it possible to transfer a property (truth, probability, modality) from the premisses to the conclusion. However, where is the warrant that the premisses possess the property in question? The classical logicians trusted self-evidence as a guarantee of the truth of the axioms which were considered as the principles of a science. But Aristotle had already pointed out (*Topics*, 101) that when the interlocutor refused to regard these principles as true, recourse to argument was indispensable in order to persuade him. This enables me to emphasize the distinction between argumentation and demonstrative reasoning: whereas a formal, logical or mathematical system can be developed independently of any reference to whoever's agreement, argument can only proceed by taking into consideration adherence to a given thesis.

The explicit reference to adherence, which is always somebody's adherence, is the only way to explain why the *petitio principii* is no logical fault, whereas it *is* a fault of argumentation. Whereas the principle of identity, expressed "if p, then p", is an indisputable law in any logic, presupposing the adherence to a thesis when the purpose of the argument is to gain such adherence constitutes undeniably a *petitio principii*.

I must add, in this respect, that adherence to a thesis may vary from one individual to another, and that its intensity may differ.

Whereas the presupposition on which any usable logic is built is that the truth of a thesis of the system is objective and cannot by virtue of the principle of contradiction be contradicted by any other thesis, in argumentation there is not guarantee that a thesis to which one agrees will not turn out to be incompatible with another thesis to which one also adheres. By incompatibility, I do not mean the existence of a formal contradiction but the fact that two theses cannot be simultaneously applied to a given situation. Thus the two moral rules "one may not lie" and "one must obey one's parents" become incompatible if one of the parents orders a child to lie. There are numerous antinomies in law and morals. When an incompatibility is unavoidable, we are forced to make a choice which limits the field of application of at least one of the theses. We shall restrain the field of validity of the thesis which is of less import for us.

Insofar as argumentation aims at reinforcing adherence to a thesis by an audience, be it the individual who deliberates, the interlocutor in a discussion, an assembly listening to a speech, or the universal audience – an ideal audience composed of all men qualified to judge of the matter – it must rely on an explicit or presumed adherence to other theses which will serve as starting points. The latter will have to be expressed in a language, whether natural or technical. Agreement on such theses implies agreement on the meaning of the terms used. This constitutes a preliminary given. If agreement on the terms of a thesis is accompanied by disagreement as to their interpretation, argumentation will aim at making one of them prevail. Thus the distinction between that which is given and that which must be the object of argumentation is not preliminary to the discussion. It will emerge as a result of the participants' attitudes and the latter will often only come to light in the course of the debate.

The theses accepted at the beginning of an argumentation make up a more or less indeterminate body among which the speaker, the person who presents the argument, will have to choose those which seem most relevant for his purpose. The choice of the type of theses will be determined by the subject matter and the audience. Sometimes they can be limited to commonplaces, to facts or to commonly accepted values, sometimes they will have to cover a whole field, scientific, legal or theological. They may even include sacred texts of the works of authoritative writers.

It may happen that in a controversy or in a political debate each of the speakers relies on different theses while trying to lend them *presence* in the minds of their audience. Often their argumentation will lead to incompatible conclusions. In such cases, the discussion will turn either on the value of the arguments leading from the accepted to the controverted theses, or it will require greater precision or eventually the confrontation of the theses which have served as premisses to the speakers. Very often, the matter at stake, the very object of disagreement, will only be revealed when the opposed theses have been fully developed.

When we compare formal logic to rhetoric, demonstrative methods and the techniques of argument, we realise that demonstration unfolds within a closed univocal system, problems of interpretation and choice having been eliminated beforehand. Argumentation, on the other hand, concerns a body of presumably accepted theses which is indeterminate and equivocal, containing elements which could, each of them, be questioned again if the need were to arise. That is the reason why an argumentation is never impersonal, mechanical and compelling, correct or incorrect, but rather stronger or weaker, for its value is the result of the confrontation of different, even opposite points of view. Whereas demonstration unfolds inside a system, like a monologue, typical argumentation makes up a controversy, the confrontation of opposed theses and discourse, which the listener, who is also often the judge, will have to compare before taking a decision. This explains why in a lawsuit a balanced judgment presupposes that both parties have been heard. The judgment will bear either on the procedure or on the substance of the debate. The issue will lead to individual or collective action or simply to an adherence to a general thesis, whether political, legal, moral, philosophical or religious.

Education aims at creating a state of mind, at instilling some general theses transmitted from adults to children, masters to pupils, the initiated to the non-initiated, the purpose being to obtain the adherence to theses which will serve as premisses for further argumentation with ultimately concrete situations in view. This difference between general theses and their application to particular situations is referred to in ancient rhetoric as the well-known distinction between '*quaestio*' and '*causa*'.

In the treatise of argumentation we published over twenty years ago with the title *The New Rhetoric*[1], we produced a detailed analysis of the various types of arguments and of the specific problems which arise through recourse to argumentation. I cannot dwell on those points here. It will suffice to point out that we distinguished arguments of association (quasi-logical arguments, arguments based on the structure of reality and relations establishing the structure of reality) and dissociation of concepts. But it may be worth our while to end this talk with a few remarks concerning a problem of interest to all logicians: "Can the various types of arguments be reduced to purely formal structures?" It is impossible to give a wholly general answer to such a question. But we could try enumerating the conditions which are required to make the reduction of argumentation to formal operations possible.

The first would be that the theses which are accepted at the beginning of an argumentation should be made univocal, so as to ensure that different interpretation of a phrase and any possibility of further interpretations is excluded. It should be necessary that all clarified theses should possess a property (truth, probability or modality) which would guarantee their independence from the adherence of any audience. Further, all the theses accepted at the start should be enumerated without exception, so as to avoid any surprise – and the whole thus constituted should be coherent. It would also be indispensable for the various arguments which are not formally valid to lead to conclusions regarding the probability of which there should be no disagreement, at this probability should be ascertained independently of the parties' opinions.

Such conditions could be satisfied in some disciplines for which the recourse to argumentation could be replaced by a recourse to the logic of induction and to the theory of probability. However, although the reduction could eventually succeed in those fields where arguments of association are used, be they of a quasi-logical nature or relative to the structure of the real, it is out of question that the dissociation of concepts should be amenable to formalization whenever the concepts about which argumentation takes place call for restructuration. We are in the presence of such a typical case when, from a single concept, we are led to create a philosophical couple. The stock example is that of the opposition between *appearance* and *reality*.

The purpose this opposition serves is to eliminate an incompatibility by specifying a criterion which makes it possible to subordinate one aspect of experience to the other when they seem incompatible. For example, if happiness is presented as opposed to virtue, we may disqualify this kind of happiness by calling it *apparent*.

That is the reason why I hold that the methodology proper to the elaboration of philosophical thinking is supplied by rhetoric, not by formal logic[2]

University of Brussels

NOTES

[1] Ch. Perelman and L. Olbrechts-Tyteca, *The New Rhetoric: A Treatise on Argumentation*, University of Notre-Dame Press, 1969 (French edition 1958).

[2] Cf. Ch. Perelman, 'Philosophy, Rhetoric, Commonplaces', in *The New Rhetoric and the Humanities*, D. Reidel, Dordrecht, Holland, 1979, pp. 52–61.

INDEX OF NAMES

INDEX OF SUBJECTS

SYNTHESE LIBRARY

Studies in Epistemology, Logic, Methodology, and Philosophy of Science

1. J. M. Bochénski, *A Precis of Mathematical Logic*. 1959.
2. P. L. Guiraud, *Problèmes et méthodes de la statistique linguistique*. 1960.
3. Hans Freudenthal (ed.), *The Concept and the Role of the Model in Mathematics and Natural and Social Sciences*. 1961.
4. Evert W. Beth, *Formal Methods. An Introduction to Symbolic Logic and the Study of Effective Operations in Arithmetic and Logic*. 1962.
5. B. H. Kazemier and D. Vuysje (eds.), *Logic and Language. Studies Dedicated to Professor Rudolf Carnap on the Occasion of His Seventieth Birthday*. 1962.
6. Marx W. Wartofsky (ed.), *Proceedings of the Boston Colloquium for the Philosophy of Science 1961-1962*. Boston Studies in the Philosophy of Science, Volume I. 1963.
7. A. A. Zinov'ev, *Philosophical Problems of Many-Valued Logic*. 1963.
8. Georges Gurvitch, *The Spectrum of Social Time*. 1964.
9. Paul Lorenzen, *Formal Logic*. 1965.
10. Robert S. Cohen and Marx W. Wartofsky (eds.), *In Honor of Philipp Frank*. Boston Studies in the Philosophy of Science, Volume II. 1965.
11. Evert W. Beth, *Mathematical Thought. An Introduction to the Philosophy of Mathematics*. 1965.
12. Evert W. Beth and Jean Piaget, *Mathematical Epistemology and Psychology*. 1966.
13. Guido Küng, *Ontology and the Logistic Analysis of Language. An Enquiry into the Contemporary Views on Universals*. 1967.
14. Robert S. Cohen and Marx W. Wartofsky (eds.), *Proceedings of the Boston Colloquium for the Philosophy of Science 1964-1966. In Memory of Norwood Russell Hanson*. Boston Studies in the Philosophy of Science, Volume III. 1967.
15. C. D. Broad, *Induction, Probability, and Causation. Selected Papers*. 1968.
16. Günther Patzig, *Aristotle's Theory of the Syllogism. A Logical-Philosophical Study of Book A of the Prior Analytics*. 1968.
17. Nicholas Rescher, *Topics in Philosophical Logic*. 1968.
18. Robert S. Cohen and Marx W. Wartofsky (eds.), *Proceedings of the Boston Colloquium for the Philosophy of Science 1966-1968*. Boston Studies in the Philosophy of Science, Volume IV. 1969.

19. Robert S. Cohen and Marx W. Wartofsky (eds.), *Proceedings of the Boston Colloquium for the Philosophy of Science 1966-1968.* Boston Studies in the Philosophy of Science, Volume V. 1969.
20. J. W. Davis, D. J. Hockney, and W. K. Wilson (eds.), *Philosophical Logic.* 1969.
21. D. Davidson and J. Hintikka (eds.), *Words and Objections. Essays on the Work of W. V. Quine.* 1969.
22. Patrick Suppes, *Studies in the Methodology and Foundations of Science. Selected Papers from 1911 to 1969.* 1969.
23. Jaakko Hintikka, *Models for Modalities. Selected Essays.* 1969.
24. Nicholas Rescher *et al.* (eds.), *Essays in Honor of Carl G. Hempel. A Tribute on the Occasion of His Sixty-Fifth Birthday.* 1969.
25. P. V. Tavanec (ed.), *Problems of the Logic of Scientific Knowledge.* 1969.
26. Marshall Swain (ed.), *Induction, Acceptance, and Rational Belief.* 1970.
27. Robert S. Cohen and Raymond J. Seeger (eds.), *Ernst Mach: Physicist and Philosopher.* Boston Studies in the Philosophy of Science, Volume VI. 1970.
28. Jaakko Hintikka and Patrick Suppes, *Information and Inference.* 1970.
29. Karel Lambert, *Philosophical Problems in Logic. Some Recent Developments.* 1970.
30. Rolf A. Eberle, *Nominalistic Systems.* 1970.
31. Paul Weingartner and Gerhard Zecha (eds.), *Induction, Physics, and Ethics.* 1970.
32. Evert W. Beth, *Aspects of Modern Logic.* 1970.
33. Risto Hilpinen (ed.), *Deontic Logic: Introductory and Systematic Readings.* 1971.
34. Jean-Louis Krivine, *Introduction to Axiomatic Set Theory.* 1971.
35. Joseph D. Sneed, *The Logical Sstructure of Mathematical Physics.* 1971.
36. Carl R. Kordig, *The Justification of Scientific Change.* 1971.
37. Milic Capek, *Bergson and Modern Physics.* Boston Studies in the Philosophy of Science, Volume VII. 1971.
38. Norwood Russell Hanson, *What I Do Not Believe, and Other Essays* (ed. by Stephen Toulmin and Harry Woolf). 1971.
39. Roger C. Buck and Robert S. Cohen (eds.), *PSA 1970. In Memory of Rudolf Carnap.* Boston Studies in the Philosophy of Science, Volume VIII. 1971.
40. Donald Davidson and Gilbert Harman (eds.), *Semantics of Natural Language.* 1972.
41. Yehoshua Bar-Hillel (ed.), *Pragmatics of Natural Languages.* 1971.
42. Sören Stenlund, *Combinators, λ-Terms and Proof Theory.* 1972.
43. Martin Strauss, *Modern Physics and Its Philosophy. Selected Papers in the Logic, History, and Philosophy of Science.* 1972.
44. Mario Bunge, *Method, Model and Matter.* 1973.
45. Mario Bunge, *Philosophy of Physics.* 1973.
46. A. A. Zinov'ev, *Foundations of the Logical Theory of Scientific Knowledge (Complex Logic).* (Revised and enlarged English edition with an appendix by G. A. Smirnov, E. A. Sidorenka, A. M. Fedina, and L. A. Bobrova.) Boston Studies in the Philosophy of Science, Volume IX. 1973.
47. Ladislav Tondl, *Scientific Procedures.* Boston Studies in the Philosophy of Science, Volume X. 1973.
48. Norwood Russell Hanson, *Constellations and Conjectures* (ed. by Willard C. Humphreys, Jr.). 1973.

49. K. J. J. Hintikka, J. M. E. Moravcsik, and P. Suppes (eds.), *Approaches to Natural Language.* 1973.
50. Mario Bunge (ed.), *Exact Philosophy – Problems, Tools, and Goals.* 1973.
51. Radu J. Bogdan and Ilkka Niiniluoto (eds.), *Logic, Language, and Probability.* 1973.
52. Glenn Pearce and Patrick Maynard (eds.), *Conceptual Change.* 1973.
53. Ilkka Niiniluoto and Raimo Tuomela, *Theoretical Concepts and Hypothetico-Inductive Inference.* 1973.
54. Roland Fraissé, *Course of Mathematical Logic* – Volume 1: *Relation and Logical Formula.* 1973.
55. Adolf Grünbaum, *Philosophical Problems of Space and Time.* (Second, enlarged edition.) Boston Studies in the Philosophy of Science, Volume XII. 1973.
56. Patrick Suppes (ed.), *Space, Time, and Geometry.* 1973.
57. Hans Kelsen, *Essays in Legal and Moral Philosophy* (selected and introduced by Ota Weinberger). 1973.
58. R. J. Seeger and Robert S. Cohen (eds.), *Philosophical Foundations of Science.* Boston Studies in the Philosophy of Science, Volume XI. 1974.
59. Robert S. Cohen and Marx W. Wartofsky (eds.), *Logical and Epistemological Studies in Contemporary Physics.* Boston Studies in the Philosophy of Science, Volume XIII. 1973.
60. Robert S. Cohen and Marx W. Wartofsky (eds.), *Methodological and Historical Essays in the Natural and Social Sciences. Proceedings of the Boston Colloquium for the Philosophy of Science 1969-1972.* Boston Studies in the Philosophy of Science, Volume XIV. 1974.
61. Robert S. Cohen, J. J. Stachel, and Marx W. Wartofsky (eds.), *For Dirk Struik. Scientific, Historical and Political Essays in Honor of Dirk J. Struik.* Boston Studies in the Philosophy of Science, Volume XV. 1974.
62. Kazimierz Ajdukiewicz, *Pragmatic Logic* (transl. from the Polish by Olgierd Wojtasiewicz). 1974.
63. Sören Stenlund (ed.), *Logical Theory and Semantic Analysis. Essays Dedicated to Stig Kanger on His Fiftieth Birthday.* 1974.
64. Kenneth F. Schaffner and Robert S. Cohen (eds.), *Proceedings of the 1972 Biennial Meeting, Philosophy of Science Association.* Boston Studies in the Philosophy of Science, Volume XX. 1974.
65. Henry E. Kyburg, Jr., *The Logical Foundations of Statistical Inference.* 1974.
66. Marjorie Grene, *The Understanding of Nature. Essays in the Philosophy of Biology.* Boston Studies in the Philosophy of Science, Volume XXIII. 1974.
67. Jan M. Broekman, *Structuralism: Moscow, Prague, Paris.* 1974.
68. Norman Geschwind, *Selected Papers on Language and the Brain.* Boston Studies in the Philosophy of Science, Volume XVI. 1974.
69. Roland Fraissé, *Course of Mathematical Logic* – Volume 2: *Model Theory.* 1974.
70. Andrzej Grzegorczyk, *An Outline of Mathematical Logic. Fundamental Results and Notions Explained with All Details.* 1974.
71. Franz von Kutschera, *Philosophy of Language.* 1975.
72. Juha Manninen and Raimo Tuomela (eds.), *Essays on Explanation and Understanding. Studies in the Foundations of Humanities and Social Sciences.* 1976.

73. Jaakko Hintikka (ed.), *Rudolf Carnap, Logical Empiricist. Materials and Perspectives.* 1975.
74. Milic Capek (ed.), *The Concepts of Space and Time. Their Structure and Their Development.* Boston Studies in the Philosophy of Science, Volume XXII. 1976.
75. Jaakko Hintikka and Unto Remes, *The Method of Analysis. Its Geometrical Origin and Its General Significance.* Boston Studies in the Philosophy of Science, Volume XXV. 1974.
76. John Emery Murdoch and Edith Dudley Sylla, *The Cultural Context of Medieval Learning.* Boston Studies in the Philosophy of Science, Volume XXVI. 1975.
77. Stefan Amsterdamski, *Between Experience and Metaphysics. Philosophical Problems of the Evolution of Science.* Boston Studies in the Philosophy of Science, Volume XXXV. 1975.
78. Patrick Suppes (ed.), *Logic and Probability in Quantum Mechanics.* 1976.
79. Hermann von Helmholtz: *Epistemological Writings. The Paul Hertz/Moritz Schlick Centenary Edition of 1921 with Notes and Commentary by the Editors.* (Newly translated by Malcolm F. Lowe. Edited, with an Introduction and Bibliography, by Robert S. Cohen and Yehuda Elkana.) Boston Studies in the Philosophy of Science, Volume XXXVII. 1977.
80. Joseph Agassi, *Science in Flux.* Boston Studies in the Philosophy of Science, Volume XXVIII. 1975.
81. Sandra G. Harding (ed.), *Can Theories Be Refuted? Essays on the Duhem-Quine Thesis.* 1976.
82. Stefan Nowak, *Methodology of Sociological Research. General Problems.* 1977.
83. Jean Piaget, Jean-Blaise Grize, Alina Szeminska, and Vinh Bang, *Epistemology and Psychology of Functions.* 1977.
84. Marjorie Grene and Everett Mendelsohn (eds.), *Topics in the Philosophy of Biology.* Boston Studies in the Philosophy of Science, Volume XXVII. 1976.
85. E. Fischbein, *The Intuitive Sources of Probabilistic Thinking in Children.* 1975.
86. Ernest W. Adams, *The Logic of Conditionals. An Application of Probability to Deductive Logic.* 1975.
87. Marian Przelecki and Ryszard Wójcicki (eds.), *Twenty-Five Years of Logical Methodology in Poland.* 1977.
88. J. Topolski, *The Methodology of History.* 1976.
89. A. Kasher (ed.), *Language in Focus: Foundations, Methods and Systems. Essays Dedicated to Yehoshua Bar-Hillel.* Boston Studies in the Philosophy of Science, Volume XLIII. 1976.
90. Jaakko Hintikka, *The Intentions of Intentionality and Other New Models for Modalities.* 1975.
91. Wolfgang Stegmüller, *Collected Papers on Epistemology, Philosophy of Science and History of Philosophy.* 2 Volumes. 1977.
92. Dov M. Gabbay, *Investigations in Modal and Tense Logics with Applications to Problems in Philosophy and Linguistics.* 1976.
93. Radu J. Bogdan, *Local Induction.* 1976.
94. Stefan Nowak, *Understanding and Prediction. Essays in the Methodology of Social and Behavioral Theories.* 1976.
95. Peter Mittelstaedt, *Philosophical Problems of Modern Physics.* Boston Studies in the Philosophy of Science, Volume XVIII. 1976.

96. Gerald Holton and William Blanpied (eds.), *Science and Its Public: The Changing Relationship*. Boston Studies in the Philosophy of Science, Volume XXXIII. 1976.
97. Myles Brand and Douglas Walton (eds.), *Action Theory*. 1976.
98. Paul Gochet, *Outline of a Nominalist Theory of Proposition. An Essay in the Theory of Meaning*. 1980.
99. R. S. Cohen, P. K. Feyerabend, and M. W. Wartofsky (eds.), *Essays in Memory of Imre Lakatos*. Boston Studies in the Philosophy of Science, Volume XXXIX. 1976.
100. R. S. Cohen and J. J. Stachel (eds.), *Selected Papers of Léon Rosenfeld*. Boston Studies in the Philosophy of Science, Volume XXI. 1978.
101. R. S. Cohen, C. A. Hooker, A. C. Michalos, and J. W. van Evra (eds.), *PSA 1974: Proceedings of the 1974 Biennial Meeting of the Philosophy of Science Association*. Boston Studies in the Philosophy of Science, Volume XXXII. 1976.
102. Yehuda Fried and Joseph Agassi, *Paranoia: A Study in Diagnosis*. Boston Studies in the Philosophy of Science, Volume L. 1976.
103. Marian Przelecki, Klemens Szaniawski, and Ryszard Wójcicki (eds.), *Formal Methods in the Methodology of Empirical Sciences*. 1976.
104. John M. Vickers, *Belief and Probability*. 1976.
105. Kurt H. Wolff, *Surrender and Catch: Experience and Inquiry Today*. Boston Studies in the Philosophy of Science, Volume LI. 1976.
106. Karel Kosík, *Dialectics of the Concrete*. Boston Studies in the Philosophy of Science, Volume LII. 1976.
107. Nelson Goodman, *The Structure of Appearance*. (Third edition.) Boston Studies in the Philosophy of Science, Volume LIII. 1977.
108. Jerzy Giedymin (ed.), *Kazimierz Ajdukiewicz: The Scientific World-Perspective and Other Essays, 1931-1963*. 1978.
109. Robert L. Causey, *Unity of Science*. 1977.
110. Richard E. Grandy, *Advanced Logic for Applications*. 1977.
111. Robert P. McArthur, *Tense Logic*. 1976.
112. Lars Lindahl, *Position and Change. A Study in Law and Logic*. 1977.
113. Raimo Tuomela, *Dispositions*. 1978.
114 Herbert A. Simon, *Models of Discovery and Other Topics in the Methods of Science*. Boston Studies in the Philosophy of Science, Volume LIV. 1977.
115. Roger D. Rosenkrantz, *Inference, Method and Decision*. 1977.
116. Raimo Tuomela, *Human Action and Its Explanation. A Study on the Philosophical Foundations of Psychology*. 1977.
117. Morris Lazerowitz, *The Language of Philosophy. Freud and Wittgenstein*. Boston Studies in the Philosophy of Science, Volume LV. 1977.
118. Stanisław Leśniewski, *Collected Works* (ed. by S. J. Surma, J. T. J. Srzednicki, and D. I. Barnett, with an annotated bibliography by V. Frederick Rickey). 1980. (Forthcoming.)
119. Jerzy Pelc, *Semiotics in Poland, 1894-1969*. 1978.
120. Ingmar Pörn, *Action Theory and Social Science. Some Formal Models*. 1977.
121. Joseph Margolis, *Persons and Minds. The Prospects of Nonreductive Materialism*. Boston Studies in the Philosophy of Science, Volume LVII. 1977.
122. Jaakko Hintikka, Ilkka Niiniluoto, and Esa Saarinen (eds.), *Essays on Mathematical and Philosophical Logic*. 1978.
123. Theo A. F. Kuipers, *Studies in Inductive Probability and Rational Expectation*. 1978.

124. Esa Saarinen, Risto Hilpinen, Ilkka Niiniluoto, and Merrill Provence Hintikka (eds.), *Essays in Honour of Jaakko Hintikka on the Occasion of His Fiftieth Birthday*. 1978.
125 Gerard Radnitzky and Gunnar Andersson (eds.), *Progress and Rationality in Science*. Boston Studies in the Philosophy of Science, Volume LVIII. 1978.
126. Peter Mittelstaedt, *Quantum Logic*. 1978.
127. Kenneth A. Bowen, *Model Theory for Modal Logic. Kripke Models for Modal Predicate Calculi*. 1978.
128. Howard Alexander Bursen, *Dismantling the Memory Machine. A Philosophical Investigation of Machine Theories of Memory*. 1978.
129. Marx W. Wartofsky, *Models: Representation and the Scientific Understanding*. Boston Studies in the Philosophy of Science, Volume XLVIII. 1979.
130. Don Ihde, *Technics and Praxis. A Philosophy of Technology*. Boston Studies in the Philosophy of Science, Volume XXIV. 1978.
131. Jerzy J. Wiatr (ed.), *Polish Essays in the Methodology of the Social Sciences*. Boston Studies in the Philosophy of Science, Volume XXIX. 1979.
132. Wesley C. Salmon (ed.), *Hans Reichenbach: Logical Empiricist*. 1979.
133. Peter Bieri, Rolf-P. Horstmann, and Lorenz Krüger (eds.), *Transcendental Arguments in Science. Essays in Epistemology*. 1979.
134. Mihailo Marković and Gajo Petrović (eds.), *Praxis. Yugoslav Essays in the Philosophy and Methodology of the Social Sciences*. Boston Studies in the Philosophy of Science, Volume XXXVI. 1979.
135. Ryszard Wójcicki, *Topics in the Formal Methodology of Empirical Sciences*. 1979.
136. Gerard Radnitzky and Gunnar Andersson (eds.), *The Structure and Development of Science*. Boston Studies in the Philosophy of Science, Volume LIX. 1979.
137. Judson Chambers Webb, *Mechanism, Mentalism, and Metamathematics. An Essay on Finitism*. 1980.
138. D. F. Gustafson and B. L. Tapscott (eds.), *Body, Mind, and Method. Essays in Honor of Virgil C. Aldrich*. 1979.
139. Leszek Nowak, *The Structure of Idealization. Towards a Systematic Interpretation of the Marxian Idea of Science*. 1979.
140. Chaim Perelman, *The New Rhetoric and the Humanities. Essays on Rhetoric and Its Applications*. 1979.
141. Wlodzimierz Rabinowicz, *Universalizability. A Study in Morals and Metaphysics*. 1979.
142. Chaim Perelman, *Justice, Law, and Argument. Essays on Moral and Legal Reasoning*. 1980.
143. S. Kanger and S. Öhman (eds.), *Philosophy and Grammar. Papers on the Occasion of the Quincentennial of Uppsala University, Sweden*. 1980.
144. Tadeusz Pawlowski, *Concept Formation in the Humanities and the Social Sciences*. 1980.
145. Jaakko Hintikka, David Gruender, and Evandro Agazzi (eds.), *Theory Change, Ancient Axiomatics, and Galileo's Methodology. Proceedings of the 1978 Pisa Conference on the History and Philosophy of Science*. 1980. (Forthcoming.)
146. Jaakko Hintikka, David Gruender, and Evandro Agazzi (eds.), *Probabilistic Thinking, Thermodynamics, and the Interaction of the History and Philosophy of Science. Proceedings of the 1978 Pisa Conference on the History and Philosophy of Science*. 1980. (Forthcoming.)

147. Uwe Mönnich, *Aspects of Philosophical Logic.* 1980. (Forthcoming.)
148. Dov M. Gabbay, *Semantical Investigations in Heyting's Intuitionistic Logic.* 1981. (Forthcoming.)
149. Evandro Agazzi, *Modern Logic – A Survey. Historical, Philosophical, and Mathematical Aspects of Modern Logic and its Applications.* 1980.
150. A. F. Parker-Rhodes, *The Theory of Indistinguishables. A Search for Explanatory Principles below the Level of Physics.* 1981. (Forthcoming.)